Introduction to Hospitality Management

John R. Walker, D. B. A., FMP

Marshall Professor and Director
Hotel, Restaurant, and Tourism Management
Alliant International University
San Diego, California

PEARSON
Prentice Hall

Upper Saddle River, New Jersey 07458

Library of Congress Cataloging-in-Publication Data
Walker, John R. 1944–
    Introduction to hospitality management/ John Walker.
        p. cm.
    Includes index.
    ISBN 0-13-111293-7
    1. Hospitality industry—Management. I. Title.

TX911.3.M27W3515 2004
647.94'068—dc21   2002035598

Publisher: *Stephen Helba*
Executive Editor: *Vernon R. Anthony*
Associate Editor: *Marion Gottlieb*
Editorial Assistant: *Ann Brunner*
Managing Editor: *Mary Carnis*
Production Management: *Linda Zuk, WordCrafters Editorial Services, Inc.*
Production Liaison: *Adele M. Kupchik*
Director of Manufacturing and Production: *Bruce Johnson*
Manufacturing Manager: *Ilene Sanford*
Manufacturing Buyer: *Cathleen Petersen*
Creative Director: *Cheryl Asherman*
Senior Design Coordinator: *Miguel Ortiz*
Formatting: *Carlisle Communications, Inc.*
Marketing Manager: *Ryan DeGrote*
Printer/Binder: *Von Hoffman*
Copyeditor: *Lorretta Palagi*
Proofreader: *Kerry Stinson*
Cover Design: *Wanda España*
Cover Image: *SuperStock, Inc.*
Cover Printer: *Phoenix Color Corp.*

Pearson Education Ltd.
Pearson Education Australia Pty. Limited
Pearson Education Singapore Pte. Ltd.
Pearson Education North Asia Ltd.
Pearson Education Canada Ltd.
Pearson Educación de Mexico, S.A. de C.V.
Pearson Education--Japan
Pearson Education Malaysia, Pte. Ltd.

10 9 8 7 6 5 4 3 2 1
ISBN 0-13-111293-7

To Josielyn and J.J.,
my love and inspiration

Contents

Access this book's Companion Website at: http://www.prenhall.com/walker

CHAPTER 2

Tourism 39

CHAPTER 3

The Hotel Business: Development and Classification   95

CHAPTER 4

Hotel and Rooms Division Operation   151

CHAPTER 5

Hotel Operations: Food and Beverage Division   203

CHAPTER 6

The Culinary Arts and Restaurant Business: Development and Classification   241

CHAPTER 7

Restaurant Operations   297

CHAPTER 8

Managed Services 337

xii   *Contents*

CHAPTER 9

Beverages   371

WINES   372
   Light Beverage Wines   372
   Sparkling Wines   372
   Fortified Wines   374
   Aromatic Wines   374
   The History of Wine   374
   The Making of Wine   375
   Matching Wine with Food   376
   Major Wine-Growing Regions of Europe and North America   378
BEER   381
   The Brewing Process   382
SPIRITS   382
   Whiskys   384
   White Spirits   386
   Other Spirits   388
   Cocktails   389
NONALCOHOLIC BEVERAGES   390
   Nonalcoholic Beer   390
   Coffee   390
   Tea   392
   Carbonated Soft Drinks   392
   Juices   393
   Bottled Water   393
BARS AND BEVERAGE MANAGEMENT   394
   Bar Setup   394
   Inventory Control   395
   Personnel Procedures   396
   Restaurant and Hotel Bars   396
   Night Clubs   397
   Microbreweries   397
   Sports Bars   400
   Coffee Shops   400
LIQUOR LIABILITY AND THE LAW   401
TRENDS IN THE BEVERAGE INDUSTRY   403
CASE STUDIES   403
CAREER INFORMATION   405
SUMMARY   406
KEY WORDS AND CONCEPTS   406
REVIEW QUESTIONS   406
INTERNET EXERCISES   407
APPLY YOUR KNOWLEDGE   407

CHAPTER 10

Recreation and Leisure 409

CHAPTER 11

The Gaming Entertainment Industry 437

CHAPTER 12

Meetings, Conventions, and Expositions   469

CHAPTER 13

Marketing, Human Resources, and Culture   505

CHAPTER 14

Leadership and Management 541

CHAPTER 15

Planning   569

CHAPTER 16

Organizing   597

CHAPTER 17

Communication and Decision Making   623

CHAPTER 18

Motivation   657

CHAPTER 19

Control   681

CHAPTER 20

Hospitality Industry Technology   709

Preface

Hospitality management is an exciting professional discipline offering numerous career opportunities. *Introduction to Hospitality Management* is a comprehensive tour of the fascinating and challenging fields of the hospitality industry: travel and tourism, lodging, foodservice, meetings, conventions and expositions, leisure and recreation.

Introduction to Hospitality Management has been written in response to requests from educators who wanted the addition of chapters on hospitality management. The new management and hospitality information technology chapters (Chapters 14 through 20) focus on what hospitality managers actually do and the most important challenges facing industry leaders today and tomorrow. The topics include leadership and management, planning, organizing, communicating and decision making, motivating, controlling, and hospitality information technology. **Post 9-11** security focus boxes, written by experts in this field, present the most up-to-date information pertinent to security in the hospitality industry.

This text is designed for the hospitality management professionals of tomorrow. By involving readers in each step of this exciting journey, *Introduction to Hospitality Management* invites students to share the unique enthusiasm surrounding the hospitality industry. Each chapter has been vetted by industry professionals and includes several hands-on examples, which help students understand the how-to aspects of the hospitality industry.

The features of *Introduction to Hospitality* include:

✓ *Chapter objectives* that help the reader focus on the main points discussed in the chapter
✓ *Bold key words and concepts* that help the reader internalize the various topics presented in the chapter
✓ *Contributing authors* who bring their expertise to each chapter
✓ *Personal Profiles* of industry practitioners that describe the careers of a number of hospitality industry leaders, including Valerie Ferguson, past chair of the American Hotel & Motel Association and regional vice president of Loews Hotels; August Escoffier; Rich Melman; Chef Paul Prudhomme; Norman Brinker; Ruth Fertel; Reg Washington; Robert Mondavi; and Steve Wynn

✓ *Day in the Life Of* features that describe the daily activities of several hospitality professionals, from chefs to cruise directors to guest services managers and convention center sales managers. Each explains the key functions of their job

✓ *Corporate Profiles* that give an overview of leading corporations of excellence including Hyatt Hotels, Marriott International, Outback Steakhouse, Red Lobster, T.G.I. Friday's, Disney, Las Vegas Convention & Visitors Authority, ARAMARK, Starbucks Coffee Company, Four Seasons Regent Hotels, Canadian Pacific Hotels, Club Med, and Cendant Hotels

✓ *Career Information* boxes that give a description of career opportunities along with a listing of related web sites

✓ *Check Your Knowledge* in-text features that encourage students to ask questions relevant to the material covered every few pages

✓ *Industry experts sidebars*

✓ Thorough identification and analysis of trends, issues, and challenges that will have a significant impact on hospitality in the future

✓ Scope of coverage and the international perspective on present and future industry issues

✓ Presentation and description of numerous career opportunities in hospitality

✓ *Summaries* that correspond to the chapter learning objectives

✓ *SCANS* (Secretary's Commission on Achieving Necessary Skills) related critical thinking review questions that review important aspects of the text. They differ from the Check Your Knowledge and Apply Your Knowledge questions

✓ *Case studies* that challenge students to address real-world situations and recommend appropriate action

✓ *Internet exercises* that invite students to "surf the Net" to answer specific, relevant hospitality questions

✓ *Apply Your Knowledge* questions that offer students the chance to apply their knowledge of hospitality industry topics

✓ A *glossary* that explains the meaning of special words throughout the text

The extensive supplement package includes the following:

✓ An *Instructors Manual*

✓ A *computerized test bank* of class-tested multiple-choice questions that may be modified to suit individual faculty needs

✓ A *PowerPoint presentation*

✓ A *free two-hour video* featuring corporations of excellence

✓ A *Student Study Guide*

✓ A *Companion Website* with web-based activities for each chapter reinforcing material and offering self-tests and other materials, located at http://www.prenhall.com/walker.

This wide variety of learning tools provides a fundamental learning aid to students and encourages their active participation in the course.

Please go online to Prentice Hall.com or call your local representative, contact information for whom may also be found on the Prentice Hall Website, http://www.prenhall.com.

Features of the Chapters

Chapter 1

Welcome to the wonderful world of hospitality. This chapter, "Introduction," provides an overview of hospitality industry characteristics; corporate philosophy; mission, goals and objectives/strategies; service, TQM and companies that strive for excellence.

Chapter 2

"Tourism" outlines the scope of tourism and identifies the major influences on the increase in tourism, the various travel modes, and the key organizations and the role they play from a local to a global perspective.

Chapter 3

"The Hotel Business: Development and Classification" illustrates the various forms of hotel development, the different types of hotels, their classification and ways to cater to the business and leisure travel markets.

Chapter 4

"Hotel and Rooms Division Operation" provides a hands-on perspective that details the rooms division department functions and activities. A complete overview of the guest cycle from reservations to checkout is included. The chapter also outlines the duties and responsibilities of key executives and department heads.

Chapter 5

"Hotel Operations: Food and Beverage Division" details the food and beverage departments and illustrates the duties and responsibilities of the key food and beverage executives.

Chapter 6

"The Restaurant Business: Culinary Arts, Development and Classification" discusses culinary arts and traces the history and development of the restaurant business. Restaurant development from operating philosophy and mission statements to market, concepts, location, ambiance, menu planning, and classification are discussed.

Chapter 7

"Restaurant Operations" focuses on the operations of a restaurant. The chapter discusses forecasting, purchasing, receiving, storage/issuing, food production and service. Budgeting, controllable expenses, restaurant accounting, operating ratios, and controls are also discussed.

Chapter 8

"Managed Services" outlines the different foodservice segments and describes the factors that distinguish managed services. Characteristics and trends in airline, military, elementary and secondary schools, colleges and universities, health care, business and industry foodservice are illustrated.

Chapter 9

"Beverages" presents the various types of wines and wine making, beer and the brewing process, spirits, nonalcoholic beverages, bars, beverage management, and liquor liability and the law.

Chapter 10

"Recreation and Leisure" introduces recreation, leisure and wellness as essential to our cultural, moral, and spiritual well-being. Government-sponsored recreation, national parks, and public recreation agencies are illustrated together with commercial recreation/theme parks and clubs. Noncommercial recreation in the form of voluntary organizations, campus, armed forces, employee recreation, and recreation for special populations is discussed.

Chapter 11

"The Gaming Entertainment Industry" reviews the history of gaming entertainment and examines the size and scope of the industry. The key players are identified and exciting entertainment projects are discussed together with careers and the relationship of the gaming industry to hotels, food and beverage, casino, and retail operations.

Chapter 12

"Meetings, Conventions, and Expositions" introduces readers to the different types of meetings, conventions, and expositions. Meeting planners, convention and visitor's bureaus, event management, and specialized services are also covered in detail.

Chapter 13

"Marketing and Human Resources" presents the elements of marketing, sales and human resources that are common to all segments of the hospitality industry.

Chapter 14

"Leadership and Management" offers an overview of the characteristics and attributes of leaders and compares different leadership styles. Hospitality leaders such as Herb Kelleher, Chairman of Southwest Airlines; Ray Kroc, founder of McDonalds; Bill Fisher, former president and CEO of the American Hotel and Lodging Association, and currently Darden Chair at the University of Central Florida; Isadore Sharp, Chairman of Four Seasons Hotels and Resorts; Van E. Eure, President of The Angus Barn Restaurant, offer their insights into successful leadership. Carlson Companies is featured and profiled as a corporation of excellence. The functions of management are detailed, and the distinction between leadership and management is made. What managers do is also covered and the three levels of management are introduced. Ethics and ethical managerial behavior are discussed.

Chapter 15

"Planning" describes the importance of planning, discusses the merits of the different types of plans, and identities the seven steps in operational planning. Strategic planning and strategic management are discussed; and strengths, weaknesses, opportunities and threats (SWOT) analysis is introduced. The process of setting goals and objectives is explained. Operational planning is detailed in seven steps. Benchmarking and policies and procedures are reviewed. Budgets and goal setting are illustrated.

Chapter 16

"Organizing" presents the purpose of organizing, how organizing is achieved, and organizational structure. Organizational design and teamwork are introduced. Numerous industry examples help explain the concepts.

Chapter 17

"Communication and Decision Making" defines and explains communication, with hospitality industry examples that introduce interpersonal and organizational communications. Factors that may impede the communication process are cited and barriers to effective interpersonal communication are discussed. Formal and informal communications are discussed and the decision making process is outlined. Rational and intuitive decision making is reviewed, along with programmed and nonprogrammed decisions. Decision-making conditions and styles are also discussed.

Chapter 18

"Motivation" introduces the motivational process together with goals and relevant theories and their applications to hospitality. Suggestions and industry examples help explain the concepts of motivation. The challenges that hospitality managers face today in motivating a diverse workforce are discussed.

Chapter 19

"Control" details the management function that closes the loop by providing necessary information to management for decision-making purposes. Setting standards, measuring performance against standards, and taking action to correct deviations are discussed. Feedforward, concurrent, and feedback control are explained in a hospitality management context. The ten characteristics of effective control systems are introduced, and contemporary issues in control and budgeting as a form of control are discussed.

Chapter 20

"Hospitality Industry Technology" (HIT) provides an overview of the various hospitality information technology systems available and identifies their characteristics. HIT applications for hotels, restaurants, and other hospitality organizations are discussed. Specific programs such as property management systems are featured, and the importance of and relationship to guest satisfaction and HIT is explained.

John R. Walker
San Diego, California

Acknowledgments

Thanks to the many students and professors, especially those who have made valuable contributions to this edition—and to the industry professionals who contributed to this text.

I am particularly grateful to Hank Christen and Paul Maniscalco for the security sidebars. Their contribution focuses on the all-important topic of disaster management.

Hank Christen, MPA, EMT, is Director of Emergency Response Operations for Unconventional Concepts Inc. (Mary Esther, Florida). He is responsible for consulting services in the fields of emergency response and counter-terrorism for Department of Defense agencies, federal agencies, and local government public safety agencies. Previously he was a Battalion Chief for the Atlanta Fire Department and was Director of Emergency Services for Okaloosa County, Florida. He served as Unit Commander for the Gulf Coast Disaster Medical Assistance Team (DMAT) and has responded to twelve national-level disasters, including the 2001 World Trade Center attack.

Mr. Christen was a member of the Department of Defense, Defense Science Board (Transitional Threats, 1997), and U.S. Army Interagency Board for Medical Logistics. He is currently a member of the Executive Session on Domestic Preparedness, John F. Kennedy School of Government, Harvard University.

Paul M. Maniscalco is an Adjunct Assistant Professor at The George Washington University, Deputy Chief/Paramedic (ret.) with the City of New York, and a Past President of the National Association of Emergency Medical Technicians. He is also an appointee of the United States Congressionally mandated National Panel to Assess Domestic Preparedness (Gilmore Commission) and has been appointed to the Harvard University, John F. Kennedy School of Government, and Department of Justice Executive Session on Domestic Preparedness, a three-year panel examining the issues of responding to acts of terrorism.

Thanks go to all my CHRIE colleagues, many of whom encouraged me to undertake this project and made valuable suggestions. I would also like to thank the following contributing authors, who graciously allowed their material and expertise to be included in this edition: Charlie Adams, Kathleen

Doeller, Claudia Green, Robert Kok, Peter LaMacchia, Brian Miller, James Reid, Andrea Sigler, Karen Smith, Dave Tucker, and Mike Zema.

The following reviewers made valuable suggestions regarding the organization and content: Jane Boyland, Johnson & Wales University, Providence, RI; John M. Courtney, Johnson County Community College; Eva Smith, Spartanburg Technical College; Muzzo Uysal, Virginia Polytechnic Institute and State University; and William H. Weber, Johnson & Wales University, Charleston, SC.

This book would not have been possible without the extraordinary help of Yasmeen Hossain; Simone Trafford; Yolanda Rucker; Bart Bartlett, Ph.D., Pennsylvania State University; Karl Titz, Ph.D., Conrad N. Hilton College, University of Houston; Denny Bhatka; Alfred Lewis, D.B.A. Alliant International University; Jay Schrock, Ph.D., University of South Florida; Ken Crocker, Ph.D., Bowling Green State University; Ed Rothenberg; Esther Lee, Evans Hotels; Tim Mulligan; Roger Huldi; Jody Nicholas; Mark Testa, Ph.D., San Diego State University; MICROS Systems, Inc.; and Sodexho.

About the Author

Dr. John R. Walker is the Marshall Professor and director of the Hotel, Restaurant and Tourism Management Program at the Alliant International University in San Diego, California. John's fifteen years of industry experience includes management training at the Savoy Hotel London. This was followed by terms as food and beverage manager, assistant rooms division manager, catering manager, and general manager with Grand Metropolitan Hotels, Selsdon Park Hotel, Rank Hotels, Inter-Continental Hotels, and the Coral Reef Resort, Barbados, West Indies.

For the past twenty years he has taught at two- and four-year schools in Canada and the United States. In addition to being a hospitality management consultant and text author, he has been published in *The Cornell Hotel Restaurant Administration Quarterly* and *The Hospitality Educators Journal*. He is the author of *Introduction to Hospitality*, published by Prentice Hall.

John is a past president of the Pacific Chapter of the Council on Hotel, Restaurant, and Institutional Education (CHRIE). He is a certified hotel administrator and a certified Foodservice Management Professional (FMP). He is married to Josielyn Teres, and they are expecting twins in June.

Photo Credits

Chapter 1 p. 2: Courtesy of Getty Images, Inc.
Chapter 2 p. 38: Courtesy of Getty Images, Inc.; p. 45, bottom: Courtesy of The Bettmann Archive
Chapter 3 p. 94: © 2000 (Hugh Sitton)/Stone; p. 119: Courtesy of Banff Springs Hotel; p. 130: Courtesy of Forte Hotels; pp. 131–132: Courtesy of Marriott
Chapter 4 p. 150: Courtesy of Getty Images, Inc.; p. 152: Courtesy of Ritz-Carlton Hotel Company; p. 155: Courtesy of The Bettman Archive; p. 167: Courtesy of Hyatt Hotels and Resorts; p. 170: Courtesy of Clarion Hotel Bayview; p. 184: Courtesy of Fairmont Hotels and Resorts
Chapter 5 p. 202: © 2000 (Stewart Cohen)/Stone; p. 220: Courtesy of Starwood Hotels & Resorts Worldwide, Inc.
Chapter 6 p. 240: © 2000 (Stewart Cohen)/Stone; p. 243: Courtesy of UPI/The Bettmann Archive; p. 256: Courtesy of Lettuce Entertain You Enterprises, Inc.; p. 257: Courtesy of Steinkamp/Ballogg, Chicago; p. 268: © Gayle Gleason, 1990, Tavern on the Green
Chapter 7 p. 296: Courtesy of Getty Images, Inc.; p. 322: Courtesy of T.G.I. Friday's
Chapter 8 p. 336: Courtesy of Sodexho
Chapter 9 p. 370: © 2000 (Victoria Pearson)/Stone; p. 381: Courtesy of The Napa Valley Wineries Association; p. 379: Courtesy of Robert Mondavi Winery; p. 391: Courtesy of Bernini's
Chapter 10 p. 408: Courtesy of Getty Images, Inc.; p. 412: Courtesy of Reuters/Bettmann
Chapter 11 p. 436: Courtesy of Getty Images, Inc.; p. 439: Courtesy of New York, New York Hotel; p. 450: Courtesy of Mirage Resorts Incorporated
Chapter 12 p. 482: Courtesy of Carol Wallace; p. 487: Courtesy of Jacob K. Javits Convention Center
Chapter 13 p. 504: Courtesy of Getty Images/EyeWire; p. 530: Courtesy of Marriott International
Chapter 14 p. 540: Courtesy of Getty Images, EyeWire; p. 544: Courtesy of UPI/Bettmann
Chapter 15 p. 568: Courtesy of Getty Images, Inc.
Chapter 16 p. 596: Courtesy of Getty Images, Inc.
Chapter 17 p. 622: Courtesy of Getty Images, EyeWire; p. 627, top: Courtesy of Jack Phadungtin; p. 627, bottom: Courtesy of Yolanda Rucker; p. 629: Courtesy of Valentina Glasenoff
Chapter 18 p. 656: Courtesy of Getty Images, EyeWire
Chapter 19 p. 680: Courtesy of Getty Images, EyeWire
Chapter 20 p. 708: Courtesy of MICROS Systems, Inc.

Introduction to Hospitality Management

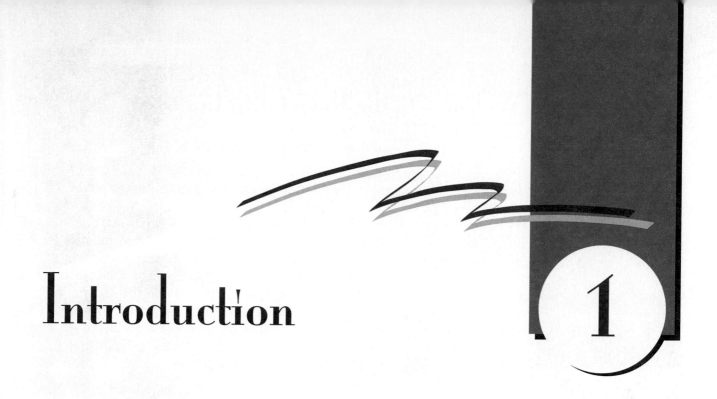

Introduction

After reading and studying this chapter, you should be able to:

✔ Name the characteristics of the hospitality industry.

✔ Explain corporate philosophy as we enter the twenty-first century.

✔ Discuss why service has become such an important facet of the hospitality industry.

✔ Understand how internships, mentoring, and job shadowing aid those who choose the hospitality industry as a career path.

✔ Write a resume.

✔ Prepare for a job interview.

Welcome to the Hospitality Industry

Mike Hurst, former owner of the famous 15th St. Fisheries Restaurant in Fort Lauderdale, Florida, and former president of the National Restaurant Association (Courtesy Mike Hurst.)

Welcome, future industry leaders to the world of **hospitality.** As Mike Hurst, former president of the National Restaurant Association says, "We're glad you're here!"

This text should form the basis of your personal library of hospitality books. It will prove to be a valuable resource, not only for career advice, but also for all those term papers required in several of your subsequent courses.

This text will give you the benefit of several years of industry and teaching experience. Several colleagues, both great professors and industry experts, will be giving you the benefit of their experience in the form of contributions to various sections of the chapters. Their insightful career suggestions are based on years of experience and knowledge. To each of them I am especially grateful. So, as Joyce Evans, a former student said let's "enjoy the journey as much as the destination."

The Pineapple Tradition

The pineapple has enjoyed a rich and romantic heritage as a symbol of welcome, friendship, and hospitality. Pineapples were brought back from West Indies by early European explorers during the seventeenth century. From that time on, the pineapple was cultivated in Europe and became the favored fruit to serve to royalty and the elite. The pineapple was later introduced into North America and became a part of North American hospitality also. Pineapples were displayed at the doors or on gate posts giving public notice to friends and acquaintances. . . .

"The ship is in! Come join us. Food and drink for all!"

Since its introduction, the pineapple has been internationally recognized as a symbol of hospitality and a sign of friendliness, warmth, cheer, graciousness, and conviviality.

The **National Restaurant Association (NRA)** forecasts a need for thousands of supervisors and managers for the hospitality and tourism industry. OK, so you're wondering if there's room in this dynamic industry for you? You bet! There's room for everyone. The best advice is to consider what you love to do and get some experience in that area—to see if you really like it—because our industry has some unique characteristics. For starters, we are in the business of giving service. When Kurt Wachtveilt, 30-year veteran general manager of the Oriental Hotel in Bangkok, Thailand—considered by many to be one of the best hotels in the world—is asked "What is the secret of being the best?," he replies, "Service, service, service!"

Hospitality and Tourism

The hospitality and **tourism** industry is the largest and fastest growing industry in the world. One of the most exciting aspects of this industry is that it is made up of so many different professions. James Reid, a professor at New York City Technical College contributed his thoughts to this section through personal correspondence with me in June 2000.

The World Travel and Tourism Council estimate that travel and tourism as a global economy are directly and indirectly responsible for 11 percent of gross domestic product, 200 million jobs, 8 percent of total employment, and 5.5 million new jobs per year until 2010.[1]

As diverse as the hospitality industry is, there are some powerful and common dynamics, which include the delivery of services and products and the customer/guest impressions of them. Whether an employee is in direct contact with a guest or customer ("**front-of-the-house**") or performing duties behind the scenes ("**back-of-the-house**") the profound and most challenging reality of working in this industry is that hospitality employees have the ability to affect the human experience by creating powerful impressions—even brief "moments of truth"—which may even last a lifetime.

In the tourism and travel industries, imagine all of the reasons why people leave their homes temporarily (whether alone or with others) to go to other places near and far. In tourism, think of the many people who provide services to travelers and have the responsibility of representing their communities and creating experiences that, when delivered successfully, are pleasurable and memorable. These are the people who welcome, inform, comfort, and care for tourists and who are collectively a part of a process that can positively affect human lives and well-being.

People travel for many reasons. A trip away from home might be for vacation, work, to attend a conference, or maybe even to visit a college campus, just to name a few. Regardless of the reason, under the umbrella of travel and tourism, many professions are necessary to meet the needs and wants of people who are away from home (Figure 1–1).

The hotel business provides job opportunities to many associates who help make reservations, greet, assist, and serve guests in hospitality operations of varied sizes and in locations all over the world. Examples include a husband-and-wife team that operates their own bed-and-breakfast (B&B) in upstate Vermont. This couple provides the ideal weekend retreat for avid skiers during frosty February making them want to return year after year. Another example would be

---

[1]Internet: http://www.wttc.org.

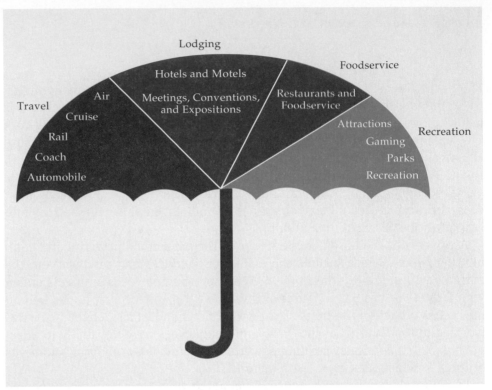

Figure 1–1   *Scope of the Hospitality and Tourism Industry*

the hundreds of guests necessary to keep the 5,505-room MGM Grand in full swing 365 days a year! Room attendants, engineers, front desk agents, food servers, and managers are just a few of the positions that are vital to creating experiences for visitors who come to Las Vegas from across the globe.

The restaurant business is also a vital piece of the travel and tourism umbrella for many reasons. People go to restaurants to fulfill diverse needs and wants. Eating is a biological need that restaurants serve; however restaurants—and the people who work in them—fulfill numerous other human desires, such as the need for socialization and to be entertained.

Commander's Palace restaurant in the French Quarter of New Orleans may be the perfect location for a certain group of friends to celebrate a twenty-first birthday. The individual guest who turned twenty-one may remember this fête for a lifetime because the service and food quality were excellent and added value to the experiences for all of the celebrants. For this kind of collective and powerful impression to be made, many key players are needed to operate and support the service delivery system. The several front-of-the-house staff members, such as the food servers, bartenders, greeters, managers, and bus attendants, and the back-of-the-house employees, such as the chefs, dishwashers, food purchaser, and stewards (to name a few), had to coordinate a diversity of activities and responsibilities to create this dynamic, successful, and, for the restaurant ownership, profitable event.

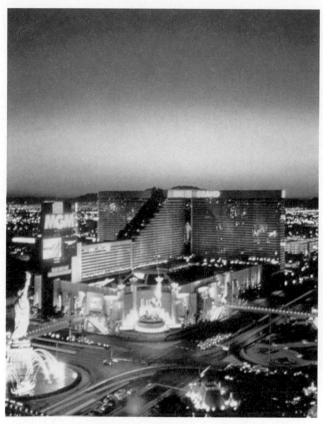

MGM Grand (Courtesy Ms. Shelley Mansholt.)

In managed services, foodservices are provided for airlines, military facilities, schools, colleges and universities, health care operations, and business and industry. These foodservice operations have the dual challenge of meeting the needs and wants of the guests and the client (i.e., the institution itself). The employees who are part of these enterprises have responsibilities very much like those of other restaurant operations. The quality of food products delivered in an airline, for example, may be the key to winning customers back in the future and creating positive word of mouth advertising that attracts new customers as well.

Since recorded history, beverages have provided a biological need that has expanded the beverage menu far beyond water alone! Whether it is the cool iced tea garnished with lemon and mint served poolside at a Riviera resort, or the champagne toast offered at a fiftieth wedding anniversary party in Boston, beverages have played a major role in satisfying humans and adding to the many celebrations of life.

As with food products, the creation and delivery of beverage products are vital components of the hospitality industry. The creation of and delivery systems for beverage products involve many people that consumers rarely see. These key players include the farmer in Napa Valley who tends to his vineyard every day of the year, the coffee bean harvester in Columbia, the Sake server

Commander's Palace (Courtesy Commander's Palace.)

in Tokyo, or the individuals crating the oranges in Florida. These individuals behind the scenes have diverse and crucial responsibilities so that the consumer, whether in a resort, office, hospital, college, or roadside snack bar, have the quality of products when they need and want them.

Check Your Knowledge

1. What is the contribution of hospitality, travel, and tourism to the global economy?

Characteristics of the Hospitality Industry

Hospitality businesses are open 365 days a year and twenty-four hours a day. No, we don't have to work all of them but we do tend to work longer hours than some other industries. Those on their way to senior positions in the hospitality industry and many others, for that matter, often work ten to twelve hours per day. Evenings and weekends are included in the workweek—so we have to accept that we may be working when others are enjoying free time. The hospitality industry depends heavily on **shift work.** Early in your career, depending on the department, you would be likely to work one of four shifts. Supervisors and managers often begin at 8 A.M. and work until 6 or 8 P.M. Basically, there are four shifts, beginning with the morning shift, so you may be getting up as early as 6 A.M. to get to the shift starting at 7 A.M. The mid-shift is normally from 10 A.M. to 7 P.M.; the evening shift starts at 3 P.M. and goes on until 11:30 P.M.; and finally there is the **graveyard shift** which begins at 11 P.M. and lasts until 7:30 A.M. Well, success does not come easily.

One essential difference between the hospitality business and other business sectors is that we produce **guest satisfaction**—an ephemeral product or, as they say in the services literature, an **intangible.** The guest cannot "test drive" a night's stay, "kick the tires" prior to boarding a shuttle, or "squeeze the steak" before dining. Our product is for the guest's use only, not for possession. Even more unique, in order for us to produce this product we must get the guest's input. Imagine GE building a refrigerator while the customer is in the factory participating in the actual construction of the product—it's ridiculous! Yet we do it every single day, numerous times per day, and in a uniquely different way each time. The literature refers to this as the **inseparability** of production and consumption of the service product and inherent heterogeneity of the product due to each guest's unique demands.

The other unique dimension of our industry is the **perishability** of our product. For example, we have 1,400 rooms in inventory, that is, 1,400 rooms available to sell, but we sell only 1,200 rooms. What we do with the 200 unsold rooms nights? Nothing—we have permanently lost 200 room nights and their revenue.

Norman Brinker

As Norman Brinker, Chairman of the board of Brinker International and visionary inspirational leader of the restaurant industry, says, the key is to "Find out what you love to do and you'll never work a day in your life. . . . Make work like play and play like hell!"

(Courtesy Norman Brinker.)

Check Your Knowledge

1. List and describe the four shifts in the hospitality industry.
2. What is the famous quote from Norman Brinker?

Each year the NRA invites the best and brightest students from universities and colleges to participate in the annual restaurant show in Chicago. The highlight of the show is the "Salute to Excellence" day where students and faculty attend forums, workshops, and a gala award banquet with industry leaders. The event is sponsored by Coca-Cola and several other corporations involved in the industry.

During the day students are invited to write their dreams on a large panel, which is later displayed for all to enjoy reading. Here are a few of the previous year's hopes and dreams:

✔ To help all people learn and grow (Jason P.)

✔ To be the best I can. (NMC)

✔ To establish a chain of jazz cafes in six years and go public in ten years. (Richard)

✔ Successfully please my customers. (J. Calicendo)

✔ To be happy and to make others happy too.

✔ To put smiles on all faces.

✔ To be one of the most creative chefs—I would like to be happy with everything I create.

✔ To make a difference in the lives of people through food! (Mitz Dardony)

✔ To be successful professionally, socially, and financially. (Marcy W.)

✔ To preserve our natural resources by operating a restaurant called "Green." (Kimberley Mauren)

✔ Anything I do I like to do it in such a way that I can always be meaningful to people. (Christian Ellis-Schmidt)

✔ To reach the top because I know there is a lot of space up there. (P.W., Lexington College)

✔ To use the knowledge that I've gained throughout my career and pass it on to others in hopes of touching their lives in a positive way! To smile and to make smiles. (Armey P. DaCalo)

✔ I want to be prosperous in my desire to achieve more than $. Happiness and peace are the keys to life. (D. McKinney)

✔ To teach and be as good as those who have taught me. (Thomas)

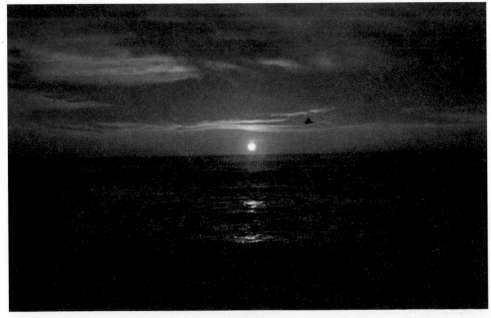

Where are you going? (Courtesy John R. Walker.)

So what are your dreams and goals? Take a moment to think about your personal dreams and goals. Keep them in mind and look back on them often. Be prepared to amend them as you develop your career.

_____

_____

_____

_____

_____

_____

Corporate Philosophy

Current **corporate philosophy** has changed from one of managers' planning, organizing, implementing, and measuring to that of managers' counseling associates, giving them resources, and helping them to think for themselves. The outcome is a more participative management style, which results in associate **empowerment,** increased productivity, and guest and employee satisfaction. Corporate philosophy has strong links to quality leadership and the **total quality management (TQM)** process. (TQM is discussed in a later section.)

Corporate philosophy embraces the values of the organization, including ethics, morals, fairness, and equality. The new paradigm in corporate American hospitality is the shift in emphasis from the production aspect of our business to the focus on guest-related services. The philosophy of "Whatever it takes" is winning over "It's not my job." Innovation and creativity are winning over "That's the way we've always done it." Successful organizations are those that are able to impart corporate philosophies to employees and guests alike—Disney Corporation, as discussed later, is a good example of a corporation that has a permeating corporate philosophy.

Service Philosophy Is a Way of Life

J. W. (Bill) Marriott, Jr., chairman of the board of directors of Marriott International Corporation, wrote in the foreword of Karl Albrecht's best-selling book "At America's Service" that Marriott's philosophy comes from core values that can be traced back over seventy years to the *personal* core values of J. Willard Marriott, who wove them into the fabric of the company and then passed them on to his son, Bill Marriott, Jr.

The values originate from deep inside the people themselves—authentic, bone deep, passionately held. Marriott's core values include the belief that people are number one ("Take care of Marriott people and they will take care of

J. W. (Bill) Marriott, Jr., chairman of the board of directors of Marriott International Corporation (Courtesy Marriott International.)

Mission Statement

The Ritz-Carlton, Laguna Niguel, will be recognized internationally as the leading five-star, five-diamond resort in North America. We will be unique in combining the genuine warmth and vitality of southern California with the traditional setting found in the finest hotels in Europe.

Every guest will feel that he or she is our most important guest. They will find us easy to do business with, and will be impressed by our uncompromising, consistent service and our ability to anticipate and fulfill even their unexpressed wishes. They will appreciate our creative, sophisticated, world-class cuisine and services. Our versatile entertainment will enhance our elegant, relaxing atmosphere. In addition, our guests will enjoy the unparalleled beauty of our location along with the museum-quality art collection.

Our employees will be proud of their association with the hotel and will be an integral part of our success. They will see the Ritz-Carlton as the best hotel to work in, a place where they can grow personally and professionally. Our staff will remain committed to continuously improving and refining our facilities and service.

The owners and the corporate office will be proud of the hotel, and will have confidence in us. They will see us as a source of qualified managers for new hotels. The owners and corporate office will be committed to helping us refine the facility's quality and improve its profitability, in partnership with the executive committee.

The community will also be proud of the hotel, and will see it as a cooperative, involved business resident of the county.

Marriott guests"), a commitment to continuous improvement and overcoming adversity, and a good old-fashioned dedication to hard work and having fun while doing it.

Marriott's core purpose—to make people away from home feel that they are among friends and are really appreciated—serves as a fixed point of reference of guidance and inspiration.[2]

Corporate Culture

Corporate culture is the overall style or feel of a company. A company's culture governs how people relate to one another and their jobs. It can be summed up with the phrase "This is how we do things around here." The casual image of the Chart House restaurant chain is a definite part of their corporate culture. However, don't be fooled—their managers may appear casual, but they are very professional. Each of the major corporations has a culture, some more pronounced than others. It is a good idea to align yourself with a corporation that blends with your own personal culture, values, and style.

Mission Statement

A **mission statement** is a short statement of the central purposes, strategies, and values of a company. Essentially, a corporation's mission statement should answer the question "What business are we in?" A good mission statement will go beyond the obvious and include the corporation's purpose, values and strategies.

Another hotel's mission statement is very simple: "To WOW the guests."

Check Your Knowledge

1. What is the purpose of a mission statement?

[2]This section draws on Jim Collins, "Foreword," in *The Spirit to Serve,* J. W. Marriott, Jr., and Kathi Ann Brown. New York: Harper Business, 1997, p. xiii.

Goal

A **goal** is a broad statement of what a company or department wishes to accomplish. For example, a hotel may have the goal of being the industry leader in the **average daily rate (ADR).**

Objective

An **objective** is a quantification of the goals in measurable terms. In a hotel, for instance, one of the objectives might be to increase occupancy from 80 to 85 percent. Another might be to achieve an average daily rate (ADR) of $128 by December 2002. Objectives can be written for each department on a variety of topics from alcohol awareness training to reduction of employee turnover. Today, most corporations involve their employees in goal setting. This not only ties in with total quality management, but also encourages employees to buy into the process and increases the likelihood that goals may even be exceeded.

Strategy/Tactics

Strategy/tactics are the actions that are needed to accomplish the goal. Using the hotel occupancy example, the strategy will state how the goal will be met. The strategy identifies the specific actions necessary to produce the desired result. In order for the hotel to increase the occupancy from 80 to 85 percent, specific actions to be taken might include the following:

> Conduct a travel agent sales blitz in key feeder cities.
> Host ten travel agent familiarization (FAM) tours.
> Send direct mail to a number of American Express, Visa, MasterCard, and Discovery card holders, and so on.

Once the corporate philosophy, culture, mission, goals, objectives, and strategies are finalized, the management functions will have guidance and direction to help steer the organization to success.

The Focus on Service

So with so much focus on service, why is it so inconsistent today? Giving good service is a very difficult task; our educational system does not seem to teach service. Few businesses give enough priority to education and training in service. We suffer from an overreliance on technology. Service providers are often not motivated to give good service. An example would be that, when checking a guest into the hotel, the front desk associate may greet the guest, but then look down at the computer for the remainder of the service encounter, even when asking for the guest's name. Or consider the reservations associate who says nothing when asked for a specific type of guest room because he is waiting for the computer to indicate availability.

In his best-selling book *At America's Service,* Karl Albrecht lists the "Seven Deadly Sins of Service" as:

1. Apathy
2. Brush-off
3. Coldness
4. Condensation
5. Robotics
6. Rule book
7. Runaround

Money magazine carried an article entitled "The Six Rudest Restaurants in America."[3] It detailed a number of characteristically negative experiences guests had with restaurants noted more for their high ordeals than their hors d'oeuvres. These included some of the swankiest of the swank. The author, Michael Williams, identified the most common insults to guests:

1. Grossly overbooked reservations
2. Holding better tables for favorite guests
3. Maître d's who could suddenly conjure up a table for a heavy tip
4. Treating guests with attitudes bordering on arrogance

Success in Service

What needs to happen to achieve success in service? Given that approximately 70 percent of the American and Canadian economies and an increasing percentage of other countries are engaged in service industries, it is critical to offer guests exceptional service, but what is exceptional service? Service is defined in *Webster's New World Dictionary* as "the act or means of serving." To serve is to "provide goods and services for" and "be of assistance to."

With thousands of guest encounters or "moments of truth" each day, it is critical to incorporate service excellence through each hospitality organization. Some corporations adopt the expression "If you're not serving the guest, you had better be serving someone who is." This is the essence of teamwork, someone in the back of the house is serving someone in the front of the house, who is serving the guest.

A customer is anyone who receives or benefits from the output of someone's work. The external customer is the customer that most people think of in the traditional sense. The satisfaction of external customers ultimately measures a company's success since they are the people who are willing to pay for its

[3]Michael Williams, "The Six Rudest Restaurants in America," *Money,* vol. 16, no. 10, October 1987, p. 116.

Personal Profile: Luis Barrios

General Manager, Catamaran Resort Hotel
Chairman of California Hotel/Motel Associations, Education Committee

Luis Barrios has come a long way in his career. He graduated from the hotel school at Miami-Dade Community College, from the Marketing and the General Managers program at Cornell University, and later from the Leadership and Guest Services program at the University of Disney. He was also at the Universidad Javeriana, Bogota, Columbia, in the economics program. His career began as a food and beverage controller, and then he was in sales with the Hilton Corporation at the Waldorf Astoria in New York in 1969. He became a director of sales for Hilton International Hotels in St. Thomas, Virgin Islands. He later went back to being a food and beverage controller at the Statler Hilton.

(Courtesy Luis Barrios.)

In 1974, Luis became food and beverage controller and assistant director of food and beverage in the New York Sheraton. Two years later, he became director of food and beverage at the Omni Shoreham in Washington, D.C.

Between 1976 and 1994, he served at the Omni Hotels. He was first a food and beverage director and then assistant general manager at Ambassador East in Chicago, and at Omni Biltmore Plaza in Providence. Then, he became general manager at the Massachusetts and Virginia Omni properties as well as the Mission Inn in Riverside, Omni San Diego, in San Diego and the Omni Northstar Hotel in Minneapolis.

While he was the general manager of the Catamaran Resort Hotel in San Diego, he was also general manager for the Lodge at Torrey Pines in La Jolla for two years.

For his great work in California, Luis was awarded the 1993 San Diego Hotel Person of the Year Gold Key Award. He is also president of the San Diego Hotel/Motel Association. He is a member of the board of directors for the California Hotel/Motel Association, chair of the Education Committee for the California Hotel/Motel Association, and a member of the Marketing Committee, San Diego Convention & Visitors Bureau.

Mr. Barrios had this to say to potential hospitality industry professionals:

Welcome to the exciting world of hospitality! Ours is a business that is fun, exciting and creative. It is a field that embraces many professions in order to achieve our objective.

Our business is a well-organized discipline, one that offers you the unique opportunity to exercise your professional expertise. Whether your expertise is in accounting, marketing, human resources, or engineering you will enjoy the experience of dealing with people from all over the world, people with different backgrounds, customs, and expectations.

Working in the hotel industry is to experience the same operational challenges and opportunities as shared by individuals that manage a community: water and energy conservation, understanding transportation, communications and garbage disposal, all the while being required to be graceful hosts, wine connoisseurs, and psychologists.

On the other hand, we must approach our daily tasks with the determination to create unique experiences for both those who work with us and our guests who are the essence of our industry. It is then imperative to understand the needs of all our customers (internal and external). We must then respond to them with a positive attitude, efficient service, and a quality product if we are to succeed in creating wonderful memories.

services. The internal customers are the people inside any company who receive or benefit from the output of work done by others in the company.

For success in service we need to:

1. Focus on the guest.
2. Understand the role of the guest-contact employee.
3. Weave a service culture into education and training systems.
4. Emphasize "high-touch" instead of just "high-tech."
5. Thrive on change.

As hospitality professionals we need to recognize situations and act to relieve them or avoid them. Well, imagine how an associate can win points by showing empathy, that is, putting herself in someone else's shoes, in the following situation: A party of eight people arrives at a restaurant: Mom, Dad, and the kids, who are running all over the place. Mom and Dad just had a huge fight in the mini van. Obviously the associate would want to welcome the party to the restaurant and find a way to seat them as quickly as possible, then give the kids something to play with and munch on until the food comes. Also, offer Mom and Dad a margarita, a glass of wine or other cocktail, and so on.

Another key objective in the service equation is to create guest loyalty. We not only need to keep guests happy during their stay, but also to keep them returning—with their friends, we hope! It costs several times more to attract new guests than to retain existing ones. Imagine how much more profit a hospitality business would make if it could retain just 10 percent more of its guests as loyal guests? Losing a guest equates to losing much more than one sale— the potential can be loss of a lifetime guest. Consider a $20 restaurant lunch for two people. If the guests return twice a month over several years—say, ten—the amount quickly becomes huge ($7,200). If they bring their friends, that amount will be even higher.

OK, so now please write down your worst service experience. . .

_____

_____

_____

_____

_____

_____

And your most positive service experience. . .

_____

_____

_____

_____

We know that service is a complex yet critical component of the hospitality industry. Albrecht and Zemke, in their book *Service America,* suggest two basic kinds of service: "Help me!" and "Fix it."[4] "Help me!" refers to guests' regular and special needs, such as "Help me find the function room" or "Help me to get a reservation at the best restaurant in town." "Fix it" refers to services such as "Please fix my toilet, it won't flush" or "Please fix the TV so we can watch the World Series."

Moments of Truth

"Moments of truth" is a phrase credited to Jan Carlson, who, on becoming president of Scandinavian Airline System (SAS) when it was ranked at the bottom of the European airline market, realized that he had to spend a lot of time on the front line coaching SAS associates in how to handle those guest encounters or, as he called them, moments of truth. As a result of his efforts, SAS was soon ranked at the top of the European airlines for service. Service commitment is a total organizational approach that makes a quality of service as perceived by the customer, the number one driving force for the operation of the business.[5]

Every hospitality organization has thousands of moments of truth every day. This leads to tremendous challenges in maintaining the expected levels of service. Let's look at just some of the "moments of truth" in a restaurant dining experience[6]:

1. Guest calls the restaurant for a table reservation.
2. Guest tries to find the restaurant.
3. Guest parks.
4. Guest is welcomed.
5. Guest is informed that the table is not ready.
6. Guest either waits or goes to the lounge for a cocktail.
7. Guest tries to attract the bartender's attention for a cocktail because there are no seats available.
8. Guest is called over a loudspeaker or paged.
9. Guest is seated at the table.
10. Server takes order.
11. Server brings beverages or food.
12. Server clears food or beverages.
13. Server brings check.
14. Guest pays for meal.
15. Guest departs restaurant.

From your own experiences you can imagine just how many moments of truth there are in a restaurant dining experience.

[4]Karl Albrecht and Ron Zemke, *Service America!* Homewood, IL: Dow Jones-Irwin, 1985, pp. 2–18.

[5]Karl Albrecht, *At America's Service.* New York: Warner Books, 1992, p. 13.

[6]Ibid, p. 27.

Check Your Knowledge

1. Why is service so important?
2. What is a moment of truth?

Ways to Improve Service

To help improve service in the hospitality industry the Educational Foundation of the National Restaurant Association, one of the hospitality industry's leading associations, developed a number of great programs that will enhance your professional development. Further information may be obtained from the NRA's web site (**http://www.restaurant.org**).

Among the various programs and courses is one on Foodservice Leadership. Effective leaders are those who make things happen because they have developed the knowledge, skills, and attitude required to get the most out of people in their operation. To be an effective leader you must be able to:

✔ Apply your own particular brand of leadership to the operation.
✔ Manage change effectively.
✔ Foster teamwork.
✔ Solicit input from employees, and involve them in planning and decision making.
✔ Motivate employees with challenges and goals.
✔ Make sure you deliver on all promises you make.

Traits of **leadership** include:

✔ Integrity
✔ Honesty
✔ Trustworthiness
✔ Confidence
✔ Creativity
✔ Flexibility/adaptability
✔ Good communication skills
✔ Willingness to teach and share power
✔ Ability to motivate others

Characteristics of all leaders include these:

✔ Strong sense of purpose
✔ Persistence
✔ Self-knowledge
✔ Always seeks new learning experiences
✔ Gets pleasure, even joy, out of work
✔ Socially responsible
✔ Takes risks, likes to experiment
✔ Establishes relationships based on trust and respect

✔ Sees mistakes as opportunities
✔ Seeks to serve the needs of others.

Leadership involves change; in fact, change is the one thing we can be sure of in the coming years. Our guests are constantly changing, so is technology, product availability, and, of course, our competition. To cope with this constant change the NRA's group suggests that (1) all change is likely to meet with some resistance, and (2) when implementing change, do the following:

1. State the purpose of the change.
2. Involve all employees in the process.
3. Monitor, update, and follow up.

One of the ways in which leaders involve employees in the process is through total quality management (TQM) and empowerment.

Service and Total Quality Management

The increasingly open and fiercely competitive marketplace is exerting enormous pressure on service industries to deliver superior service. Inspired by rising guest expectations and competitive necessity, many hospitality companies have jumped on the service quality bandwagon.

The Malcolm Baldrige National Quality Award is the highest level of national recognition for quality that a U.S. company can receive. The award promotes an understanding of quality excellence, greater awareness of quality as a critical competitive element and the sharing of quality information and strategies.

The Ritz-Carlton Hotel Company, winner of the 1993 and 1999 Malcolm Baldrige National Quality Award, was founded on principles of groundbreaking levels of customer service. The essence of this philosophy was refined into a set of core values collectively called the Gold Standards. The credo is printed on a small laminated card that all employees must memorize or carry on their person at all times when on duty. The card lists the three steps of service:

1. A warm and sincere greeting . . . use the guest name, if and when possible
2. Anticipation and compliance with guests' needs
3. Fond farewell, give them a warm good-bye and use their names if and when possible.

The quality movement began at the turn of the century as a means of ensuring consistency among the parts produced in the different plants of a single company so that they could be used interchangeably. In the area of service, TQM is a participatory process that empowers all levels of employees to work in

The Employee Promise

At the Ritz-Carlton, our Ladies and Gentlemen are the most important resource in our service commitment to our guests.

By applying the principles of trust, honesty, respect, integrity, and commitment, we nurture and maximize talent to the benefit of each individual and the company.

The Ritz-Carlton fosters a work environment where diversity is valued, quality of life is enhanced, individual aspirations are fulfilled, and the Ritz-Carlton mystique is strengthened.

The Ritz-Carlton Basics

1. The credo is the principal belief of our company.
2. Our motto is: "We are ladies and gentlemen serving ladies and gentlemen." Practice teamwork and lateral service to create a positive work environment.
3. The three steps of service shall be practiced by all employees.
4. All employees will successfully complete training certification to ensure they understand how to perform to the Ritz-Carlton standards in their positions.
5. Employees will understand their work areas and hotel goals as established in each strategic plan.
6. All employees will know the needs of their internal and external customers (guests and employees) so that we may deliver the products and services they expect. Use guest preference pads to record specific needs.
7. Each employee will continuously identify defects throughout the hotel.
8. Any employee who receives a customer complaint owns the complaint.
9. Instant guest pacification will be ensured by all. React quickly to correct the problem immediately. Follow up with a telephone call within twenty minutes to verify the problem has been resolved to the customer's satisfaction. Do everything you possibly can to never lose a guest.
10. Guest incident action forms are used to record and communicate every incident of guest dissatisfaction. Every employee is empowered to resolve the problem and to prevent a repeat occurrence.
11. Uncompromising levels of cleanliness are the responsibility of every employee.
12. Smile—we are on stage. Always maintain positive eye contact. Use the proper vocabulary with our guests. (Use words like *good morning, certainly, I'll be happy to,* and *my pleasure.*)
13. Be an ambassador of your hotel in and outside of the workplace. Always talk positively. No negative comments.
14. Escort guests rather than pointing out directions to another area of the hotel.
15. Be knowledgeable of hotel information (hours of operation, etc.) to answer guest inquiries. Always recommend the hotel's retail and food and beverage outlets prior to outside facilities.
16. Use proper telephone etiquette. Answer within three rings and with a smile. When necessary, ask the caller, "May I place you on hold?" Do not screen calls. Eliminate call transfers when possible.
17. Uniforms are to be immaculate; wear proper and safe footwear (clean and polished), and your correct name tag. Take pride and care in your personal appearance (adhering to all grooming standards).
18. Ensure all employees know their roles during emergency situations and are aware of fire and life safety response processes.
19. Notify your supervisor immediately of hazards, injuries, equipment, or assistance that you need. Practice energy conservation and proper maintenance and repair of hotel property and equipment.
20. Protecting the assets of a Ritz-Carlton hotel is the responsibility of every employee.

groups to establish guest service expectations and determine the best way to meet or exceed those expectations. Notice that the term *guest* is preferred over the term *customer.* The inference here is that if we treat customers like guests, we are more likely to exceed their expectations. One successful hotelier has insisted for a long time that all employees treat guests as they would like to be treated themselves.

TQM is a continuous process that works best when managers are also good leaders. A successful company will employ leader-managers who create a stimulating work environment in which guests and employees (sometimes called internal guests; one employee serves another employee who in turn serves a guest) become an integral part of the mission by participating in goal and objective setting.

Installing TQM is exciting because once everyone becomes involved there is no stopping the creative ways employees will find to solve guest-related problems and improve service. Other benefits include cost reductions and increased guest and employee satisfaction, leading ultimately to increased profits.

Top executives and line managers are responsible for the success of the TQM process; when they commit to ownership of the process, it will be successful. Focused commitment is the foundation of a quality service initiative, and leadership is the critical component in promoting commitment. Achieving TQM is a top-down, bottom-up process that must have the active commitment and participation of all employees from the top executives down to the bottom of the corporate ladder. The expression "If you are not serving the guest, then you had better be serving someone who is" still holds true today.

The difference between TQM and quality control (QC) is that QC focuses on error detection, whereas TQM focuses on error prevention. Quality control is generally based on industrial systems and, because of this, tends to be product oriented rather than service oriented. To the guest, services are experiential; they are felt, lived through, and sensed. The moment of truth is the actual guest contact.

The game of business has changed. Leaders empower employees who welcome change. Empowerment is a feeling of partnership in which employees feel responsible for their jobs, and have a stake in the organization's success. Empowered employees tend to do the following:

✔ Speak out about their problems and concerns.
✔ Take responsibility for their actions.
✔ Consider themselves a network of professionals.
✔ Have the authority to make their own decisions when serving guests.

To empower employees, managers must do the following:

1. Take risks.
2. Delegate.
3. Foster a learning environment.

Corporate Profile: The Ritz–Carlton Hotel Company

A Commitment to Excellence and Quality Service Worldwide

The Ritz-Carlton Hotel Company was officially organized in the summer of 1983, although the Ritz-Carlton's history and tradition long precede that date. Indeed this tradition has entered our language: "to be ritzy" or "putting on the Ritz" denotes doing something with class. With the purchase of The Ritz-Carlton, Boston, and the acquisition of the exclusive rights to use the name came a rich heritage. Built in 1927, The Ritz-Carlton, Boston, has nurtured a tradition of excellence rooted in the philosophy of the celebrated hotelier, Cesar Ritz. The landmark property is the only Ritz-Carlton of that era to operate continuously since opening.

Beginning with one hotel in 1983, the company now operates thirty-one hotels worldwide (twenty-one city hotels and ten resorts) in the United States, Hong Kong, Australia, Mexico, South Korea, and Spain. Expansion in Asia includes the opening of hotels in Singapore and Osaka, Japan.

The Ritz-Carlton Hotel Company, with headquarters in Atlanta, Georgia, has built its reputation on reliable service and commitment to quality. The Ritz-Carlton mission is to provide the finest personal service and facilities, instill well-being, and fulfill even the unexpressed wishes and needs of guests. Under the charismatic leadership and insistence on high standards of Horst Schulze, president and chief operating officer of Ritz-Carlton, the company was awarded the prestigious Malcolm Baldrige National Quality Award in 1993 and again in 1999. The Ritz-Carlton is the only hospitality organization to have ever won this coveted honor for quality management, given by the U.S. Department of Commerce.

Horst Schulze, founding president and CEO of Ritz-Carlton Hotels

Quality planning begins with Schulze, whose commitment to excellence is apparent in the many innovations and changes he has initiated over the years. Perhaps the most significant is the launching of a comprehensive quality management program. Hallmarks of the program include participatory executive leadership, thorough information gathering coordinated planning and execution, and a trained workforce that is empowered "to move heaven and earth" to satisfy customers. Committed employees rank as the most essential element. All are schooled in the company's Gold Standards, which include a credo, motto, three steps of service, and twenty Ritz-Carlton basics. Each employee is expected to understand and adhere to these standards, which describe processes for solving problems that guests may have as well as detailed grooming, housekeeping, and safety and efficiency standards. "We are Ladies and Gentlemen serving Ladies and Gentlemen" is the motto of all Ritz-Carlton hotels, exemplifying anticipatory service provided by all staff members.

To provide such service, the employee training process is the finest in the industry. To underscore the importance of maintaining quality service as the organization grows, Mr. Schulze, himself conducts the employee orientation at each new hotel. The two-day orientation, however, is just the beginning. Employee indoctrination at The Ritz-Carlton Hotel Company includes 100 additional hours of on-the-job training, daily inspections for appearance, periodic performance reviews, and, again, an unrelenting emphasis on quality. The Ritz-Carlton aims to convince employees that they are important members of an elite team always looking for ways to improve. The company also rewards exceptional performance with things like fully paid vacations. Much of the responsibility for ensuring high-quality guest services and accommodations rests with the staff. A significant example of the responsibility given to employees is the fact that each Ritz-Carlton staff member is empowered to make a decision that could cost the hotel up to $2,000 to help guests with their problems. Mr. Schulze insists that it is not the amount of money that is important, but rather the emphasis on the corporate environment that encourages employees to make decisions and speak up. "They need to feel part of the organization and really work for the organization," Schulze says.

The company's philosophy ultimately results in high standards properties. All Ritz-Carlton hotels offer twenty-four-hour room service, twice-daily maid service, complimentary shoeshines, terrycloth robes in all guest rooms, a floor reserved for nonsmokers, and in-house fitness facilities. Other special features include The Ritz-Carlton Club, a private lounge offering complimentary food and beverages throughout the day and the services of a special concierge, as well as dining rooms that represent culinary excellence and top value. A highly trained concierge staff stands by to respond to additional guest needs.

The Ritz-Carlton Hotel Company also maintains a sophisticated guest recognition program designed to determine and fulfill the needs of repeat visitors by tracking their individual requests and preferences. A guest who visits The Ritz-Carlton, Atlanta, can expect the same individualized service at any Ritz-Carlton, from New York to Sidney, Australia.

Each property is designed to be a comfortable haven for travelers and a social center for the community. The architecture and artwork are carefully selected to complement the hotel's environment. "We go to great lengths to capture the spirit of a hotel and its locale," says Mr. Schulze. "This creates a subtle balance and celebrates a gracious, relaxed lifestyle. The Ritz-Carlton is warm, relaxed yet refined; a most comfortable home away from home."

Check Your Knowledge

1. List five attributes, traits, and characteristics of a leader.
2. What is a Malcolm Baldrige National Quality Award?

4. Share information and encourage self-expression.
5. Involve employees in defining their own vision.
6. Be thorough and patient with employees.

The Disney Approach to Guest Service

The Disney mission statement is simple: "We create Happiness." Disney is regarded as one of the excellent corporations throughout the text. The following discussion, adapted from a presentation given by Susan Wilkie to the PAC-CHRIE conference in April 1998, outlines their approach to guest service.

When conceiving the idea to build Disneyland, Walt Disney established a simple philosophical approach to his theme park business, based on the tenants of quality, service, and show. The design, layout, characters, and the magic of Disneyland grew out of Walt's successful experience in the film industry. With Disneyland he saw an opportunity to create a whole new form of entertainment—

Gretsky's Secret

When asked the secret of his phenomenal success as the greatest ice hockey player of all time, Wayne Gretsky said, "Everyone goes to where the puck is. Me—I go to where the puck is going." The message is: Keep your eye on the future!

I Am Your Guest

We can all find inspiration from these anonymous words about people who make our business possible:

- *I am your guest*—Satisfy my needs, add personal attention and a friendly touch, and I will become a "walking advertisement" for your products and services. Ignore my needs, show carelessness, inattention, and poor manners, and I will cease to exist as far as you are concerned.

- *I am sophisticated*—Much more so than I was a few years ago. My needs are more complex. It is more important to me that you appreciate my business; when I buy your products and services I'm saying you are the best.

- *I am a perfectionist*—When I am dissatisfied, "take heed." The source of my discontent lies in something you or your products have failed to do. Find that source and eliminate it or you will lose my business and that of my friends as well. For when I criticize your products or services, I will talk to anyone who will listen.

- *I have other choices*—Other businesses continually offer "more for my money." You must prove to me again and again that I have made a wise choice in selecting you and your company above all others.

a three-dimensional live show. He wanted Disneyland to be a dynamic, ever-changing experience.

To reinforce the service concept, Disney has guests, not customers, and cast members, not employees. These terms set the expectations for how guests will be served and cared for while at the park or resort. This commitment to service means:

- ✔ Disney clearly understands their product and the meaning of their brand.
- ✔ They look at the business from the guests' perspective.
- ✔ They consider it their personal responsibility to create an exceptional experience for every individual who enters their gates.

Michael Eisner, chairman and CEO, said, "our inventory goes home at night." Disney's ability to create a special brand of magic requires the talents of thousands of people fulfilling many different roles. But the heart of it is the frontline cast members. So, what is it that makes the service at Disney so great? The key elements of Disneyland guest services include:

- ✔ Hiring, developing, and retaining the right people
- ✔ Understanding their product and the meaning of the brand
- ✔ Communicating the traditions and standards of service to all cast members
- ✔ Training leaders to be service coaches
- ✔ Measuring guest satisfaction
- ✔ Recognizing and rewarding performance

Disney has used profile modeling but say it all comes down to a few simple things:

- ✔ Interpersonal/relationship building skills
- ✔ Communication
- ✔ Friendliness

Disney uses a team approach to interviewing called "peer interviews." In one interview there may be three candidates and one interviewer. The candidates may include a housewife returning to the workforce, a teacher looking for summer work, a retiree looking for a little extra income, or a teenager looking for a first job. All three candidates are interviewed in the same session. The interviewer is looking for how they individually answer questions, but also how well they interact with each other—a good indicator of their future on-stage treatment of guests.

The most successful technique used during the forty-five minutes is to *smile.* The interviewer smiles at the people being interviewed for forty-five minutes to see if they *return the smiles.* If they don't, it doesn't matter how well they interview—they won't get the job.

On the first day at work, every new Disney cast member participates in a one-day orientation program at the Disney University—"Welcome to Show Business." The main goal of this experience is to learn the Disney approach to helpful, caring, and friendly guest service.

How does this translate into action? When a guest stops a street sweeper to ask where to pick up a parade schedule and the sweeper not only answers the question, but recites the parade times from memory . . . suggests the best viewing spots on the parade route . . . offers advice on where to get a quick meal before parade time . . . *and* ends the interaction with a pleasant smile and warm send-off, well, people are impressed. It also makes the sweepers feel their jobs are interesting and important—which they are!

Opening Disneyland

Disneyland opened on July 17, 1955, to the predictions that it would be a failure. And in truth, everything that could go wrong did:

- Plumbers went on strike.
- Tickets were duplicated.
- Attractions broke down.
- There was a gas leak in Fantasyland.
- The asphalt on Main Street didn't harden in time, so in the heat of July, horses' hooves and women's high heels stuck in the street.

As Walt once said, "You may not realize it when it happens, but a kick in the teeth might be good for you." Walt had his fair share of challenges, one of which was obtaining financing to develop Disneyland—he had to deal with more than 300 banks.

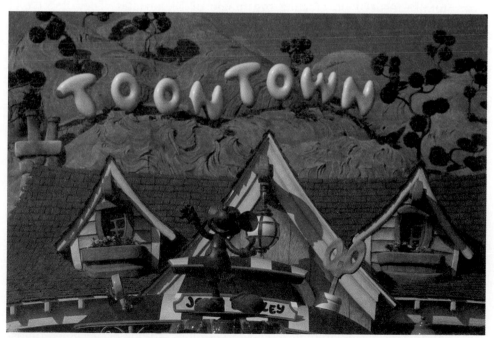

Toon Town at Disneyland
(Courtesy California Division of Tourism.)

The Show is why people go to Disneyland. Each land tells its own unique story through its theme and attention to detail and the cast members each play a role in the Show. The most integral component of the training is the traditions and standards of guest service. The first of these is called the "Personal Touch." The cast members are encouraged to use their own unique style and personality to provide a personal interaction with each guest. One of the primary ways Disney accomplishes this is through name tags. Everyone, regardless of position, goes by his or her first name. This tradition was started by Walt and continues today. It allows cast members to interact on a more personal level with guests. It also assists internally, by creating an informal environment that facilitates the flow of open communication and breaks down some of the traditional barriers.

So what is the Disney service model?

It begins with a Smile. This is the universal language of hospitality and service. Guests recognize and appreciate the cast members' warmth and sincerity.

Make Eye contact and use body language. This means stance, approach, and gestures. For instance, cast members are trained to use "open" gestures for directions—not pointed fingers—because open palms are friendlier and less directive.

Respect and welcome all guests. This means being friendly, helpful, and going out of the way to *exceed* guests' expectations.

Value the magic. This means that when they're on stage, cast members are totally focused on creating the magic of Disneyland. They don't talk about personal problems, world affairs, and they don't mention that you can find Mickey in more than one place. . . .

Initiate guest contact. Cast members are reminded to actively initiate guest contact. Disney calls this being "aggressively friendly." It's not enough to be responsive when approached. Cast members are encouraged to take the first step with guests. They have lots of little tricks for doing this, such as noticing a guest's name on a hat and then using the name in conversation, or getting down on bended knees to ask a child a question.

Creative service solutions. For example, one of the Disneyland Hotel cast members recently became aware of a little boy who had come from the Midwest with his parents to enjoy the park and then left early because he was ill. The cast member approached the supervisor with an idea to send the child chicken soup, a character plush toy, and a get-well card from Mickey. The supervisor loved the idea and all cast members are now allowed to set up these arrangements in similar situations without a supervisor's approval.

End with a "thank you." The phrases cast members use are important in creating a service environment. They do not have a book of "accepted phrases," rather through training and coaching, cast members are encouraged to use their own personality and style to welcome and approach guests, answer questions, anticipate their needs, thank them, and express with sincerity their desire to make the guest's experience exceptional.

Taken individually, these might sound pretty basic. But, taken together, they help define and reinforce the Disney culture. Once initial cast member training is completed, these concepts must be applied and continually reinforced by leaders who possess strong coaching skills. Disney uses a model called the "Five Steps of Leadership" to lead the cast member performance.

Each step in the leadership model is equally important in meeting service and business goals. Each leader must:

1. Provide clear expectations and standards.
2. Communicate those expectations through demonstration, information, and examples.
3. Hold cast members accountable for their feedback.
4. Coach through honest and direct feedback.
5. Recognize, reward, and celebrate success.

To supplement and reward the leadership team, Disney provides technical training to every new manager and assistant manager. In addition, the management team also participates in an acculturation process at the Disney University to learn the culture, values, and the leadership philosophy necessary to be successful in the Disney environment.

Disney measures the systems and reward process by distributing 1,000 surveys to guests as they leave Disneyland and 100 surveys to guests who stayed at each of the Disney hotels. The guests are asked to take the surveys home and mail them back to Disney. In return their names are entered for a drawing for a family weekend package at the park and hotel.

Feedback from the surveys has been helpful in improving the guest experience. For example, as a result of the surveys, the entertainment division realized that the opportunity to interact with a character was a key driver to guest satisfaction. So the entertainment team designed a brochure called "The Characters Today," which is distributed at the main entrance daily. This brochure allows guests to maximize their opportunity to see the characters. This initiative has already raised guest satisfaction by ten percentage points.

Cast members are also empowered to make changes to improve service. These measures are supplemented by financial controls and "mystery shops" that allow Disney to focus resources on increasing guest satisfaction.

The reward system does not consist of just the "hard" reward system we commonly think of, such as bonuses and incentive plans, important though they are. Recognition is not a "one size fits all" system. Disney has found that noncash recognition is as powerful, if not more powerful a recognition tool in many situations. Some examples are:

✔ Disney recognizes milestones of years of service. They use pins and statues and have a formal dinner for cast members and guests to reinforce and celebrate the value of their experience and expertise at serving Disney's guests.

✔ Throughout the year, Disney hosts special social and recreational events that involve the cast members and their families in the product.

✔ Disney invites cast members and their families to family film festivals featuring new Disney releases to ensure they are knowledgeable about the latest Disney products.

✔ Michael Eisner and the Disneyland management team host the Family Christmas Party after hours in the park. This allows cast members to enjoy shopping, dining, and riding the attractions. Management dresses in costumes and runs the facilities.

Internships, Mentorships, and Job Shadowing

Internships, either paid or unpaid, offer an opportunity to learn about a particular company and to show the employer that you would make a great permanent employee. Most two- and four-year programs have an internship requirement of supervised practical training which might begin at the front desk, in reservations or communications, or as housekeeping or bell staff in the Rooms Division. In the Food & Beverage Division the likely beginning positions are server or banquet associate in a house person's position or in the stewarding department, the kitchen, or stores. (These positions will be explained in more detail throughout the text.) An internship will also help you to better relate to the concepts and materials presented in the classroom. Here are some tips for interns:

1. Don't be afraid to talk with people. Don't be intimidated because you are a student. People are sometimes too busy to roll out the red carpet, so you have to make the first move to talk with coworkers and supervisors.
2. Ask for things to do. Don't wait to be told what to do. Solving problems and taking initiative are the best ways to stand out from the crowd.
3. Learn all you can about the industry. Talk with people in different departments as well as clients and vendors.
4. Read everything you can get your hands on. You won't find everything you need to know in the training manual. Reading contracts, letters, memos, press releases, and trade publications help you become informed on all elements of the business.
5. Don't gripe about the grunt work. There is always something more to learn. How long you do grunt work depends on what you make of it. Everything has a purpose, so learn how the small tasks fit into the big picture.
6. Act like a student! Look for every opportunity to learn!
7. Hitch your wagon to a star. Learn from the people who are the superstar performers and most respected individuals in the department.
8. Get in the information loop. Decisions aren't always made in a conference room.

9. Ask to attend meetings and events. You will learn how things really get done.
10. Don't burn any bridges. You never know when you will see someone late in your career or when you will need a reference.

A **mentor** is a guide through life, someone who can show you the ropes along the way. A mentor can help you avoid some basic career mistakes by offering advice or by simply listening to you talk through a problem to its solution.

Remember to thank your mentor with a personal handwritten note from time to time. If you do not have a mentor at present then now is a good time to get one. Ask someone you respect to be your mentor or ask more than one person. For instance, some people have one mentor for school and one for industry.

Job shadowing is often the first experience related to work or a career that many of us experience. The purpose of job shadowing is to gain familiarity with a particular job or jobs. Today, several high schools and colleges arrange with industry to organize "Groundhog Day" in February when thousands of students look toward the hospitality industry for a day's experience of job shadowing. Suggestions for a successful job shadow:

1. Learn about the company before you arrive.
2. Set a goal for what you want to accomplish.
3. Dress professionally.
4. Show true interest in the environment.
5. Ask questions.
6. Make the most of limited time.
7. Network.
8. Be an active participant.
9. Follow safety and security procedures.
10. Follow up with a "thank you" to your host.

Don't forget to have fun! And remember while you're interning or job shadowing that somebody has to be general manager, department head, supervisor, and so on.

Internships

An internship gives you a chance to try out the company and the position. It is a good idea to do at least one internship as an hourly paid employee, then continue on as a regular part-time employee during the school year, and work full time during the summer, preferably going through the various departments for a couple of years then doing a management internship. The management internship will offer a chance to experience aspects of supervision that are essential for future success.

Career Paths and Résumé Writing

Creating your own career path can be both an exciting and a daunting task. Often, we do not know exactly where we want to be in five or ten years. The best advice is to follow your interests. Do what you love to do and success will soon come. Often we assess our own character and personality to determine a suitable path.

Some opt for the accounting and financial and control side of the business; others, perhaps with more outgoing personalities, vie for sales and marketing; others prefer operations, which could be either in back or in front of the house.

Résumés

It is a good idea to build your résumé with work experience. The experience will also help you relate your academic course work to the real world. Most colleges have a system of faculty advisors, many of whom have industry contacts that may be helpful in taking the first step along a career path.

Corporate recruiters have to distinguish your résumé from among hundreds they receive each year. Here are some tips from a selection of recruiters that should help you to succeed in your career.[7]

Are you conscientious? Make sure your résumé is letter perfect. Have your résumé proofread by several industry practitioners as well as professors and friends.

A good résumé includes the following information:
- ✔ Heading with your name, address and telephone number
- ✔ Career objective
- ✔ Career experience
- ✔ Other accomplishments such as scholarships, awards, honors, teams, volunteer work, and so on
- ✔ Education
- ✔ References, including telephone numbers

A suggested format for a résumé is shown in Figure 1–2.

Perfecting a résumé requires careful thought. It is a good idea to show it to several people who know you and some who are used to reviewing résumés. It is natural to be slightly unsure of the right words to use. One suggestion is to consider your accomplishments. You may have worked on the school prom committee or as a volunteer for a worthy organization. Everyone has done something that can embellish the résumé—remember that you have to stand out from your peers or competition.

Consider a young woman who was a star on the track team in high school. She was not going to put that on her résumé because she did not think it was important. But, when asked what she did to become an accomplished athlete, she replied that she had to train (long hours of practice require dedication); when asked what it took to win, she said determination. These same qualities are the same as what it takes to be successful in business.

Cover Letters

Every time you mail a résumé, you should also send a cover letter to introduce yourself and explain why you are sending your résumé. Because this is your

---

[7]Jeff B. Speck, "The Inside Scoop: What Corporate Business Recruiters Really Look for When Reviewing Hundreds of Resumes," *National Business Employment Weekly* (*College Edition*), vol. 6, no. 3, Fall 1989, p. 28.

Figure 1–2 *Sample Résumé Format*

first contact with the company you are approaching, you need to make a good impression. A business-like letter has your name, address, and telephone number at the top right-hand corner of the page. The letter should begin with "Dear Ms. or Mr. _____:" and might continue "I am pleased to apply for the position of _____ at the XYZ company. I will be available for summer work experience on May 28, 2000. Your company was recommended to me by _____ who worked with you last year. Enclosed is a copy of my résumé in which you will notice (here is where you mention some skills or relevant experience that qualifies you for the position)."

The final paragraph should restate your keen interest in the position and end by requesting an interview. The appropriate closing is "Yours sincerely," followed by your name, leaving room for your signature.

Are you qualified? Recruiters typically look to three things to judge a student's job qualifications: academic record, work experience, and extracurricular activities.

Academic Record

A recruiter can easily discard résumés of students with a cumulative GPA below a B. Jeff Speck suggests that omitting a mediocre GPA from your résumé is not the best solution, simply because most students willingly include their averages.[8] If you have a low overall GPA, one solution might be to list your GPA in the major if that is significantly higher.

If you have good grades, were on the dean's list, graduated with honors, and so on, put this on your résumé. Academic distinction is one sure way of gaining the attention of a recruiter.

Work Experience

Your record should prove that you have accomplished something every summer and possibly while going to school. Obviously, experience in the same or a similar capacity is desirable. An internship or co-op work experience is an additional asset. Include other work experiences that you have had because they all add up—even jobs such as hostessing can suggest that you have obtained some good interpersonal experience. Being a busperson or a quick service food employee may not sound very exciting, but it is where most of us began. Each of the beginning level positions gives us exposure to a workplace environment and allows us to gain experience.

Extracurricular Activities

Achieving recognition as an Eagle Scout or in activities like student leadership always improves your chances for employment. If you excelled in sports or club activities use this information on your résumé to show commitment and dedication. Volunteer work is an excellent way to look good on a résumé, especially if you organize an event that contributes to an organization. A résumé, in itself, will not secure you employment, but it can open the doors to an interview.

Check Your Knowledge

1. What are the reasons for Disney's service success?
2. Which do you think are the most important tips on internships, mentors, and job shadowing?
3. What path will your career follow?

---

[8]Ibid, p. 28.

Job Interviews

No matter how many interviews we do, most people still get butterflies in the stomach when faced with another one. These feelings are natural because we are on edge about a face-to-face meeting that could have a major impact on our career and lives. An interview is like sitting next to someone on an airplane flight—it takes us about twenty seconds to determine if we really want to talk to the person sitting next to us or read a magazine.

How to Interview

Mona Melanson, a staffing consultant with Bank of America, has wisely suggested a ten-step approach to polish your interviewing skills.[9]

1. Ask yourself how well you fit the jobs for which you're interviewing. You are going to be grilled about your skills, education, motivation, accomplishments, strengths, and weaknesses. The interviewer is asking himself or herself, "Why should I hire you for this job?"

2. A good way to begin is to match your skills and qualifications to those required for that position. You could gather data from a variety of sources, in categories such as education and training, extracurricular activities, summer/part-time jobs, and volunteer/community service. In these categories, jot down feedback from your professors, employers, and other people with whom you have interacted. Remember that in management training interviews, recruiters want to see leadership and initiative capabilities.

3. Once you have completed your list, you will probably be surprised at how many items there are. Next, highlight five or six items that correspond to some of the job qualifications specified. Then prepare a brief talk about those so you can use them during an interview.

4. Do your homework on the company. Do research in the library, call the company's public relations office, and ask your career office for the names of former students now working for the corporation in which you are interested. Find out about the corporation's philosophy, mission, goals, objectives, and culture. Become knowledgeable about the size, organization structure, and future plans of the corporation.

5. Be ready to ask questions of the interviewer. Ideally, these should be work-related questions; wait until later to discuss salary (have patience; nothing disturbs an interviewer more than someone who wants to discuss money up front). The appropriate time to inquire about the compensation

[9]The section draws on Mona Melanson, "Beat the Butterflies: A Ten-Step Approach to Polish Your Interview Skills," *National Employment Weekly (College Edition),* vol. 6, no. 3, Fall 1989, p. 31.

and benefit package is generally toward the end of the interview—if the interviewer has not already mentioned it.

6. Stage a number of dress rehearsals with someone else—a roommate, a friend, a career counselor, or a professor. Give your interviewer a list of questions that you think you might be asked. Record or—even better—video your interviews. Remember, some taboos include the following:
   - Shaking hands like a wet fish
   - Mumbling, fidgeting
   - Going off on tangents
   - Appearing unnecessarily tense
   - Using slang or malapropisms
   - Speaking too softly or too loudly
   - Avoiding eye contact

   Body language is important during interviews. Some experts suggest adopting a posture similar to that of the interviewer. Remain composed, relaxed, and confident, and demonstrate visible interest.

7. Dress in a business-like manner. A man should wear a business suit, dress shoes, a pressed white shirt, or a reasonably conservative shirt—and no earrings. A woman should wear a business suit, blouse, hose, and shoes, with conservative jewelry and makeup. For both men and women, the first impression is extremely important. Image is everything!

8. Arrive early; if possible, go to the location once before the interview to be certain you know where it is. Remember that a smile and a firm handshake make a good impression. Once the interview has begun, listen to the questions carefully, because interviewers often complain that students do not answer questions correctly. One tip is to rephrase part of each question you are asked at the beginning of your answer. This technique also gives you more time to formulate your responses. Remember to stress your strengths. For example, offer statements such as "I have been told by one of my professors that I express myself well both in writing and orally" or "I work well under pressure" or "I have a positive attitude."

9. At the close of the interview, thank the interviewer for the opportunity to discuss your qualifications. Before shaking hands, it is fully acceptable to ask the interviewer about when you might expect to hear about a decision.

10. Write a thank-you note to the interviewer, reinforcing the reasons why you feel you could perform well on that job.

Here are some suggestions for questions to ask the interviewer:
   ✔ What are the duties and responsibilities of this position?
   ✔ Please describe the training program.
   ✔ How would you characterize the management philosophy at your company?
   ✔ If I join your company, what will my career path likely be?
   ✔ Given my education and background, how would you estimate my chances for advancement?

Career Information

The hospitality industry offers careers that are often fast-paced, exciting, and very rewarding. Many different and stimulating types of work fall into this category, requiring varying skill levels and amounts of responsibility. It is a field that offers rapid advancement to those individuals with commitment and dedication.

The hospitality field is not for people seeking a regular five-day forty-hour workweek with weekends off. Hospitality professionals get paid to work when other people are enjoying themselves. Restaurants are often open seven days a week and hotels operate twenty-four hours a day 365 days a year. As a manager you can expect to work varying hours ranging from fifty to sixty-five hours per week. The days and times you will be expected to work will vary, along with your days off.

If you choose to become a hospitality manager it is important that you work in the field of hospitality while attending college! A part-time job and/or internship can help you find out what you want to do. By the time you are a junior you should be working at least twenty to thirty hours per week while going to school. It is also important to develop the foundation skills needed to be a hospitality manager. Learning the basic skills associated with your area of hospitality are invaluable when you become a manager. Effective restaurant managers possess a working knowledge of the various job functions, which include cooking, scheduling, purchasing, waiting tables, expediting, washing dishes, and in many cases bartending.

An important tool for tracking your progress in developing basic skills is a résumé. Writing a résumé and keeping it current forces you to examine your strengths and weaknesses in your chosen area of hospitality. It also will cause you to ask hard questions about what you really want to do with your career. Having a current résumé also allows you to take advantage of opportunities that may present themselves unexpectedly, such as scholarships, internships, or a better employment offer.

Upon graduation from college, experience needs to reflect desire! Selling yourself in an interview is difficult if not impossible unless you have relevant experience. Recruiters' ultimate fear is employee turnover. Hiring an individual and then having that person quit in a few months is an expensive proposition for companies. Employers are extremely reluctant to hire a person who does not have relevant experience.

America has become a service-oriented economy and people are traveling and dining out more than ever. The demand for hospitality managers has never been better. Careers offer entry-level salaries of $30,000 to $40,000 per year for college graduates. Companies are also realizing that to keep their managers they have to address quality-of-life issues. Many companies now limit the number hours managers work and give them two days off per week. The old stories of managers working endless hours and never having time off are gone. If you ever find yourself in such a situation it is probably time to look for another employer. Such an environment will ruin your personal relationships and eventually cause you to "burn out" and leave the industry.

A successful career doesn't just happen. It requires planning, effort, ability, and education. If you take the time to find out which hospitality career is for you and develop your foundation skills while going to college you will find that you are entering a field that has no substitutes.

Related Web Sites

http://www.hcareers.com—resource for hospitality careers
http://www.chrie.org—Council of Hotel, Restaurant & Institutional Educators web site
http://www.internshipsprograms.com—internship site

Courtesy of Charlie Adams.

✔ Does your company offer promotional opportunities by region, nationally, or internationally?

Do not ask how much salary the position offers until either you have been offered a position or until you are well into the final stages of the interview.

Here are some questions an interviewer might ask:

✔ What are your future career plans?

✔ When are you available and what are your available hours?
✔ What is your (hotel, restaurant, or tourism) work experience?
✔ What are/were your duties and responsibilities?
✔ How well do you think you succeeded in meeting your duties and responsibilities?
✔ What are your goals and ambitions?
✔ Where do you see yourself three/five years from now?
✔ What did you like most and least about your job?
✔ Describe how you would prepare an item of the menu.
✔ Why should I hire you?
✔ What qualifications do you have that make you think you will be successful in the hospitality industry?

Overall, remember that good judgment comes from experience, and experience comes from bad judgment, and success is not what you are, it is what you have overcome to be what you are.

Summary

1. The hospitality and tourism industry is the largest and fastest growing industry in the world.
2. Now is a great time to be considering a career in the hospitality and tourism field because thousands of supervising managers are needed for this dynamic industry.
3. Common dynamics include delivery of services and the guest impressions of them.
4. Hospitality businesses are open 365 days a year and twenty-four hours a day and are likely to require shift work.
5. One essential difference between the hospitality business and other businesses is that in hospitality, we are selling an intangible and perishable product.
6. Corporate philosophy is changing from managers planning, organizing, implementing, and so on, to that of managers counseling associates, giving them resources, and helping them to think for themselves.
7. Corporate philosophy embraces the values of the organization including ethics, morals, fairness, and equal-

ity. The philosophy of "Do whatever it takes" is critical for success.
8. Corporate culture refers to the overall style or feel of the company or how people relate to one another and their jobs.
9. A mission statement is a statement of central purposes, strategies, and values of the company. It should answer "What business are we in?"
10. A goal is a specific target to be met; objectives or tactics are the actions needed to accomplish the goal.
11. Total quality management has helped improve service to guests by empowering employees to give service that exceeds guest expectations.
12. Internships, mentorships, and job shadowing provide an opportunity to learn about the industry and companies and to show a potential employer that you would make a great employee.

Key Words and Concepts

Average daily rate (ADR)	Empowerment	Guest satisfaction	Internships
Back-of-the-house	Front-of-the-house	Hospitality	Job shadowing
Corporate culture	Goal	Inseparability	Leadership
Corporate philosophy	Graveyard shift	Intangible	Mentor

Mission statement	Objective	Strategy/tactics	Tourism
National Restaurant	Perishability	Total quality management	
Association (NRA)	Shift work	(TQM)	

Review Questions

1. Why is service so critical in the hospitality and tourism industry?
2. Describe and give an example of the following:
   Mission statement
   Goal

Objective
Moment of truth

3. What is the Disney service model?
4. Describe why Ritz-Carlton won the Malcolm Baldrige award.

Internet Exercises

1. Organization:
   Web site:
   Summary:
   (a) Find the latest statistics or figures for the global hospitality & tourism economy.

2. Organization:
   Web site
   Summary:
   (a) What is it about Ritz-Carlton that makes it such a great hotel chain?

3. Organization:
   Web site:
   (a) Compare and contrast Disneyland's and Walt Disney World's web sites.

World Travel and Tourism Council
http://www.wttc.org
The World Travel and Tourism Council (WTTC) is the global business leaders' forum for travel and tourism. It includes all sectors of industry, including accommodation, catering, entertainment, recreation, transportation, and other travel-related services. Its central goal is to work with governments so they can realize the full potential economic impact of the world's largest generator of wealth and jobs—travel and tourism.

Ritz-Carlton Hotels
http://www.ritzcarlton.com
The Ritz-Carlton is renowned for its elegance, sumptuous surroundings, and legendary service. With thirty-five hotels worldwide, a majority of them award winning, the Ritz-Carlton reflects 100 years of tradition.

Disneyland and Walt Disney World
http://disney.go.com and **http://www.disney.com**

Apply Your Knowledge

1. Write your personal career goals.
2. Write a résumé for yourself.

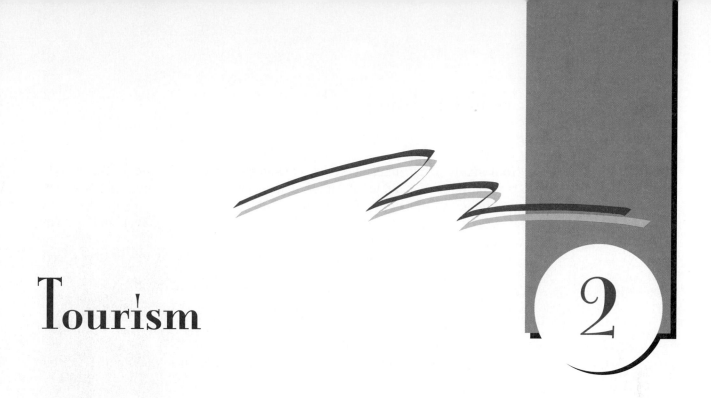

Tourism

After reading and studying this chapter, you should be able to:

✔ Define tourism.
✔ Trace the five ages (or periods) of tourism.
✔ Describe the evolution of the major modes of travel.
✔ Outline the important international and domestic tourism organizations.
✔ Describe the economic impact of tourism.
✔ Identify promoters of tourism.
✔ List reasons why people travel.
✔ Describe the sociocultural impact of tourism.
✔ Describe ecotourism.

What Is Tourism?

Tourism is a dynamic, evolving, consumer-driven force and is the world's largest industry if all of its interrelated components are placed under one umbrella, travel, lodging, foodservice, and recreation.

The World Travel and Tourism Council declares the travel and tourism industry to have the following characteristics:

✔ A twenty-four-hour-a-day, seven-day-a-week, fifty-two-week-a-year economic driver

✔ Accounted for 10.6 percent of world GDP

✔ Employer of 200 million people or 7.8 percent of the global workforce

✔ Travel and tourism will support the creation of more than 5.5 million jobs per year during the 2000s

✔ Spending on tourism in the U.S. was $82 billion in 2000 and $72.3 billion in 2001

✔ Leading producer of tax revenues

Given the declining manufacturing and agricultural industries, and in many countries the consequent rise in unemployment, it is to the service industries that world leaders should turn for real strategic employment gains.

Tourism, as mentioned, the world's largest industry, offers the greatest global employment prospects. This trend is caused by the following factors:

1. The opening of borders
2. An increase in disposable income and vacations
3. Cheaper and more exclusive flights
4. An increase in the number of people with more time and money
5. More people with the urge to travel

According to the World Travel and Tourism Council—the industry's business leaders' forum—tourism and travel generates, directly and indirectly, 10.6 percent of global gross domestic product (GDP), investment, and employment. It is forecast to grow strongly at 40 to 50 percent in real terms during the next ten years. This means a growth of nearly 10.8 million jobs in the United States by 2010.

The futurist, John Naisbit, says that the global economy of the twenty-first century will be driven by three superservice industries: telecommunications, information technology, and travel and tourism.[1]

The fact that tourism is expected to grow so rapidly presents both tremendous opportunities and challenges. The good news is the variety of exciting career prospects for today's hospitality and tourism graduates. Tourism, although a mature industry, is a young profession. Careful management of tourism and travel will be necessary to avoid repercussions and negativism toward the "pesky"

---

[1]Richard Kelley, "To Create Jobs, Sumitears Should Take a Breath of Rocky Mountain Air and Promote Tourism," http://www.wttc.org, July 20, 1997.

tourist—which is already happening to some extent in Europe, where the sheer number of tourists overwhelms attractions and facilities.

There is an interdependency between the various segments of tourism, travel, lodging, foodservice, and recreation. Hotel guests need to travel in order to reach the hotel. They eat in nearby restaurants and visit attractions. Each segment is, to an extent, dependent on another for business.

Definition of Tourism

The word *tourism* did not appear in the English language until the early nineteenth century. The word *tour* was more closely associated with the idea of a voyage or perhaps a theatrical tour than with the idea of an individual "traveling for pleasure purposes, which is the accepted use of the word today."[2] The World Tourism Organization's definition of tourism is "Tourism comprises the activities of persons traveling to and staying in places outside their usual environment for not more than one consecutive year for leisure, business, and other purposes."[3]

A **tourist,** by United Nations (U.N.) definition, is a person who stays for more than one night and less than a year. Business and convention travel is included in this definition.

For many developing nations, tourism represents a relatively high percentage of gross national product and an easy way of gaining a balance of trade with other nations.

Tourism means different things to different people. For example, a hotelier might say that tourism is wonderful because it brings guests who fill rooms and restaurants. However, a government official might define it as the economic benefit of more money coming into the country, state, or city. To simplify tourism, it is sometimes categorized in terms of the following factors:

　　Geography: International, regional, national, state, provincial, country, city

Grenelle Foster

"Ask Mr. Foster," the oldest U.S. travel agency, began in 1888 when Ward Grenelle Foster opened a "travel information office" in St. Augustine, Florida. When the town's residents or travelers had queries concerning directions or visitors' information, they were directed not to the local Seven Eleven, but instead to W. G. Foster's gift shop, where they could "ask Mr. Foster." Foster later adopted this phrase as the name for his small business.

In the 1890s, "Ask Mr. Foster" expanded to all three coasts of the Sunshine State and later to New York and other metropolitan centers. The offices were usually conspicuously located in large buildings, such as hotels and department stores, with heavy foot traffic. The company provided free information and reservations. Their brochure promised to "plan your trip, secure your ticket, make your reservations for hotels, steamers, autos, schools, and railroads—anywhere in the world."

Despite its immense success, Foster decided to sell the business in 1928. It then changed hands several times before it was bought in 1979 by the Carlson Companies, the hospitality conglomerate based in Minneapolis, Minnesota. In 1988, the company had more than 750 offices in forty-six states, and its total sales exceeded that of American Express travel agency sales.[4]

[4]Donald E. Lundberg, *Tourist Business*, New York: Van Nostrand Reinhold, 1990 p. 9.

---

[2]A. J. Butkarat and S. Meddlik, *Tourism: Past, Present and Future.* London: Heinemann, 1974, p. 3.

[3]Rosa Songel, "Statistics and Economic Measurement of Tourism," World Tourism Organization. http://www.world-tourism.org/omt/wtich.htm

> *Ownership:* Government, quasi-government, private
> *Function:*   Regulators, suppliers, marketers, developers, consultants, researchers, educators, publishers, professional associations, trade organizations, consumer organizations
> *Industry:*   Transportation (air, bus, rail, auto, cruise), travel agents, tour wholesalers, lodging, attractions, recreation
> *Motive:*   Profit or nonprofit[5]

Industry practitioners use these categories to identify and interact with the various industry sectors and organizations involved with tourism.

The Five Ages of Tourism

The historical development of tourism has been divided up into five distinct ages (or periods),[6] four of which parallel the advent of new means of transportation.

> Pre–Industrial Revolution (prior to 1840)
> The railway age
> The automobile age
> The jet aircraft age
> The cruise ship age

Pre–Industrial Revolution

As early as 300 B.C., ancient Egyptians sailed up and down the Nile River, carrying huge rocks with which to build pyramids as tombs for their leaders.[7] The Phoenicians were among the first real travelers in any modern sense. In both the Mediterranean basin and the Orient, travel was motivated by trade. However, trade was not the only motivation for travel in these times; commerce and the search for more plentiful food supplies also stimulated travel.[8]

The Roman Empire provided safe passage for travelers via a vast road system that stretched from Egypt to Britain. Wealthy Romans traveled to Egypt and Greece, to baths, shrines, and seaside resorts.[9] The Romans were as curious as modern-day tourists. They visited the attractions of their time, trekking to Greek temples and to places where Alexander the Great slept, Socrates lived, Ajax committed suicide, and Achilles was buried. The Romans also traveled to

---

[5]Robert McIntosh and Charles R. Goeldner, *Tourism Principles, Practices, Philosophies,* 6th ed. New York: John Wiley and Sons, 1990, pp. 11–13.

[6]McIntosh and Goeldner, op. cit.

[7]Edward J. Mayo and Lance P. Jarvis, *The Psychology of Leisure Travel: Effective Marketing and Selling of Travel Services.* Boston: CBI Publishing Company, 1981, p. 5.

[8]Donald E. Lundberg, *The Tourist Business,* 6th ed. New York: Van Nostrand Reinhold, 1990, p. 16.

[9]Ibid.

Egypt to visit the Pyramids, the Sphinx, and the Valley of the Kings—just as today's tourists do.[10] The excavated ruins of the Roman town Pompeii, which was buried by an eruption of Mt. Vesuvius, yielded several restaurants, taverns, and inns that tourists visit even today.

Medieval travel was mostly confined to religious travel, particularly pilgrimages to various shrines: Moslems to Mecca and Christians to Jerusalem and Rome. The Crusades began in 1095 and lasted for the next 200 years, stimulating a cultural exchange that was, in part, responsible for the Renaissance.

Across Europe, travel and trade flourished. With the increase in living standards came a heightened awareness of cultural pursuits. Later, aristocrats undertook Grand Tours of Europe, stopping at major cities for weeks or months at a time. It was considered a necessary part of "rounding out" a young lady's or gentleman's education. Fortunately, travel now has become possible for almost everyone.

The Railway Age

Railroads played a major role in the development of the United States, Canada, and several other countries. The pioneering spirit carried by the railroads opened up the great American West. Prior to the advent of rail travel, tourists had to journey by horse and carriage. By comparison, the railway was more efficient, less costly, and more comfortable. Resort communities came within the reach of a larger segment of the population in North America and Europe. The railroads brought changes in the lodging industry, as taverns along the turnpikes gave way to hotels near the railway stations.

The first railroad was built in the United States in 1830, but only twenty-three miles of rail were laid by the end of that year. In contrast, by 1860, there were 30,626 miles of track. In 1869, rail journey across America was made possible by the transcontinental connection, which enabled the journey to be completed in six days.[11] Before that, such a journey took several months by wagon or several weeks by clipper ships rounding Cape Horn, South America.

To ensure passenger comfort, railroads had excellent dining cars and sleeping berths. Railroads continued to extend their lines into the twentieth century until the Great Depression of the 1930s and World War II. These events began a decline in railroad usage that was accelerated by the invention of the automobile. The freedom of the open road gave automobile travel a competitive advantage over train travel.

To prevent a complete collapse of the passenger rail system, the U.S. government created AMTRAK in 1971. AMTRAK is a semipublic organization that initiated operations on May 1, 1971, serving more than 500 stations over forty-five states. Eight of the fifteen members of its board are selected by the president of the United States, three by the railroads, and four by preferred private

[10]Ibid.

[11]Jan Van Harssel, *Tourism: An Exploration*, 3rd ed. Englewood Cliffs, NJ: Prentice Hall, 1994.

AMTRAK train
(Courtesy AMTRAK.)

stockholders.[12] AMTRAK is subsidized by the U.S. Congress, in amounts ranging from $500 million to $800 million per year. Last year it was $762 million; this subsidy represents between 35 and 50 percent of its total revenue.[13] AMTRAK has eliminated many unprofitable lines and improved overall efficiency and service quality.

However, many passengers opt for the speed and sometimes price advantages of the airlines. To counter this, AMTRAK offers special prices on regional or transcontinental travel. Tour packages are also popular, particularly with retired people who prefer relaxing and watching the ever-changing scenery to driving.

Although rail travel has declined in the United States, railroads in Europe and Asia play far more important roles in passenger and freight transportation. Railroads are more cost effective and a more efficient means of transportation in densely populated areas. Europeans have developed trains that can travel up to 250 miles per hour. The French Trés Grande Vitesse (TGV, very high speed) runs between Paris and Marseilles in three hours. The channel tunnel (Chunnel) links England with France and enables both trains and automobiles to travel the twenty-three miles of the English Channel.

In Japan, the bullet train can go up to 250 miles per hour. Not all trains go quite that fast, but the ride is remarkably smooth—a beverage glass can rest on a table and not spill. As with the United States, the Japanese and European rail systems are heavily subsidized by their respective governments. However, without such subsidies, the roads and the air would be more congested.

Many Americans visiting Europe take advantage of the Eurailpass. The Eurailpass, which must be purchased from travel agents outside of Europe, allows visitors to travel throughout Europe, with the exception of the United Kingdom. Visitors can get on and off the train at hundreds of cities and enjoy the local attractions.

[12]Paul R. Dittmer and Gerald G. Griffen, *The Dimensions of the Hospitality Industry: An Introduction.* New York: Van Nostrand Reinhold, 1993, p. 359.

[13]Michael Milligan, *Travel Weekly,* October 14, 2002, p. 44.

Bullet train (Courtesy Japan Tourist Bureau.)

Automobile Travel

Automobiles evolved from steam engines in the late 1800s, when Karl Benz and Gottlieb Daimler built a factory for internal combustion engines, which is now Mercedes Benz.[14]

In 1891, the production of automobiles began in large numbers. Before long, Henry Ford produced his first vehicle and invented the techniques for making automobiles on an assembly line. By 1914, Henry Ford was producing one Model-T Ford every twenty-four seconds.[15] The assembly-line production continues today with the additional help of robots.

Model-T Ford

[14]Dittmer and Griffen, op. cit., p. 352.
[15]Ibid.

The United States has about 150 million registered autos. The country with the next largest amount is Japan, which has about 33 million registered vehicles.

The call of the great open road and the increased financial ability of more families to purchase automobiles led to a tremendous growth in travel and tourism. Motels and restaurants sprang up along the highways. The automobile made more places accessible to more people.

Air Travel

The Wright brothers, who enjoyed the hobby of gliding, decided to fit an engine to one of their gliders with movable fins and wingtip controls. To find an engine light enough, they had to build their own. In 1903, they tested their thirteen-horsepower engine. On the first run it lifted the craft in the air for twelve seconds and covered a distance of 120 feet.[16]

In 1909 an airplane crossed the English Channel, and by 1919 scheduled passenger service began between London and Paris. Realizing that others were about to attempt to cross the Atlantic, Charles Lindbergh persuaded a group of investors in St. Louis to fund construction of a new airplane in San Diego. The "Spirit of St. Louis" was built in sixty days. With 450 gallons of gasoline on board (the tanks even blocked forward visibility), Lindbergh made the first solo crossing of the Atlantic Ocean in 1927. This history-making twenty-eight-hour flight was a major turning point in aviation history. This monumental achievement was a catalyst for massive investment in the airline industry.

The first scheduled air service in the United States began in 1915 between San Diego and Los Angeles. Later, in 1930, the Douglas Company in California introduced the DC-2, which could carry fourteen passengers and fly at a speed of 213 miles per hour. The most renowned airplane, the DC-3, came into service in 1936. To this day, well over 2,000 of them are still flying.[17]

In 1944, an international conference was held in Chicago to establish international air routes and services. American and European delegates disagreed about how much to restrict competition—the Americans pushed for unrestricted competition.

However, seventy airlines from forty nations ratified an important agreement of transportation rates and created the International Air Transportation Association (IATA). The IATA is the major trade association of the world's airlines. Through international agreements on financial, legal, technical, and traffic matters, the worldwide system of air travel became possible.[18]

American and European representatives met again in Bermuda in 1946 to work out a compromise. The **Bermuda agreement,** by which countries exchanged benefits, was to later become a model for bilateral negotiations. The "six freedoms of the air" agreed upon in Bermuda were as follows:

[16]Van Harssel, op. cit., p. 27.

[17]Ibid.

[18]Ibid.

Spirit of St. Louis

✔ The right to fly across another nation's territory
✔ The right to land in another country for noncommercial purposes
✔ The right to disembark passengers and cargo from the carrier's home country in a foreign country
✔ The right to pick up passengers and cargo destined for the carrier's home country from a foreign country
✔ The right to transport passengers and cargo from one foreign country to another foreign country
✔ The right of an airplane to carry traffic from a foreign country to the home nation of that airline and beyond to another foreign country

In 1954, the first Boeing 707 came into service. By 1958, Pan American Airways inaugurated transatlantic flights from New York to Paris. A Boeing 707 could carry 111 passengers over a range of about 6,000 miles at a cruising speed of 600 miles per hour. Also in 1958, McDonnell-Douglas introduced the DC-8, which boasted a similarly impressive performance.

Other aircraft were introduced to handle the medium- and short-range routes. The Boeing 727 was introduced in 1964. It became the workhorse of the U.S. domestic market, carrying 145 passengers at a cruising speed of 600 miles per hour. In 1968, the Boeing 737 established itself as the short-range challenger to the McDonnell-Douglas DC-9. The Boeing 747, introduced in 1970, was the first of the wide-body aircraft. It could transport 400 to 500 passengers at a cruising speed of 600 miles per hour over distances of about 7,000 miles.

A consortium of European countries developed the Airbus. The Airbus A 340 is designed for the long-distance market, and the Airbus A 320 is for the short-distance market.

The **Concorde** was the first supersonic aircraft, developed at a cost of $3 billion by the British and French governments. The Concorde has a cruising speed of 1,336 miles per hour, vastly reducing the time needed to fly from London to New York. A 747 flight leaving at 11 A.M. London time will land at 1:40 P.M. New York time. On a Concorde, a flight leaving at 11:00 A.M. London time would land at 9:50 A.M., New York time. Air France operated the Concorde from Paris, Dakar, and Rio de Janeiro. British Airways (BA) operated Concordes between

Boeing, 707, 727, 737 (Courtesy Boeing Corporation.)

Boeing 747 (Courtesy Boeing Corporation.)   *Concorde* (Courtesy British Airways.)

London and Bahrain and from London to Washington, D.C., or New York. However, due to a crash outside Paris in August 2000, British Airways grounded its Concorde fleet after learning that the supersonic plane's airworthiness certification will be revoked due to safety concerns over the Concorde's tires.

Air transportation has further reduced the cost per mile of travel, enabling millions of people to become tourists. As a result, hotels, restaurants, and attractions have grown to keep pace with demand. The speed of air transportation enables vacationers to take intercontinental trips. Europe and Asia are only hours away as are all the cities of North and Latin America.

The Airline Deregulation Act of 1978

Air transportation changed dramatically in 1978. Deregulation transferred the responsibility for airline activity to the Federal Aviation Administration (FAA) and the Department of Transportation (DOT). The purpose of the **Airline Deregulation Act** was to allow free-market competition whereby airlines could decide their own fare structures and rates. Deregulation resulted in retrenchment of major air carriers, new airlines, lower airfares, and "megacarriers."[19]

The effects of deregulation were to force several noncompetitive airlines out of business. Pan Am, once the flag bearer of international aviation, lost money

[19]Dittmer and Griffen, op. cit., p. 365.

and went out of business because it became bloated with too many layers of bureaucracy and too large a payroll. Simply because they had been in business longer, many of the pilots and cabin crew at Pan Am were more highly paid than their competitors. Over the years, costs such as fuel also escalated.

Not only did airlines go out of business, but some were also absorbed by other airlines. For example, Texas Air bought Eastern Airlines, Continental, People's Express, Frontier, and New York Air. They are operated by Continental Airlines.

In the late 1980s, most of the major airlines were in an expansion mode. They incurred heavy debt, spending money on new planes and terminals. This debt service made major airlines vulnerable to price wars, with resultant operational losses.

Over the past few years, with the exception of Southwest, major U.S. airlines have lost billions of dollars. One reason is competition from international airlines, several of which are subsidized by their national governments.

Since September 11, 2001, and the downturn in the economy, business travelers continue to spend less, and airlines' pension and security costs are on the rise. The major airlines are laying off employees, delaying delivery of new jets, and closing some reservations and maintenance centers in efforts to reduce costs. United Airlines recently entered into Chapter 11 bankruptcy protection.[20] Adding to these problems is the sentiment expressed by some that many airline employees are already overpaid and taxpayers' money should not be used to prop up inept airlines.[21] What do you think?

USAir's strategic partnership with British Airways is an example of internationalism that benefits airlines that must compete in a global marketplace. For an airline like USAir to expand into the global market, such a strategic alliance makes sense. Thomas Lagow, USAir's executive vice president of marketing, says that the issue is simple: USAir answers to shareholders, employees, and passengers—if they're happy, that's all that matters.[22]

Alliances of this nature will allow airlines access to each other's feeder markets and to resources that will enable them to flourish in what will ultimately be a worldwide deregulation. A feeder market is a market that provides the source—in this case, passengers for the particular destination.

Ultimately, any major European airline without a strategic alliance in the United States will only limit its own horizons and lose market share.

Several major U.S. carriers such as Northwest have been close to bankruptcy for some time. However, they have negotiated salary cuts of up to 15 percent in return for employee representation on the board and 3.5 percent of the company's stock. American Airlines has also worked out a similar cost-reduction

[20]*San Diego Union-Tribune,* October 19, 2002, p. B1.

[21]Stewart Toy and Andrea Rothman, "Air France: Is This the Right Flight Plan?" *Business Week,* August 2, 1993, p. 48.

[22]Michele McDonald, "USAir's Lagow: BA Link's Strategic Partnership," *Travel Weekly,* August 30, 1993, p. 10.

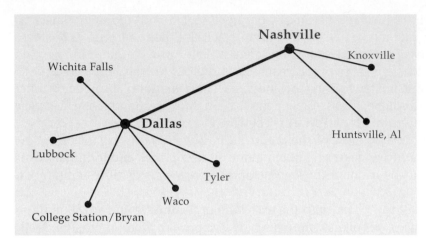

Figure 2–1 *The Hub-and-Spoke System*

package with its employees.[23] At United Airlines, labor gave $3.4 billion in concessions over five years for up to 25 percent of the company's stock, plus significant control over major decisions.[24] In May 2000, United Airlines announced it would purchase USAir, a move that was not keenly accepted by its employees.

Southwest operates more efficiently than the competition despite the fact that its workforce is unionized. Southwest gets more flight time from its pilots than American—672 hours a year versus 371, and racks up 60 percent more passenger miles per flight attendant. These efficiencies have resulted in annual profits for twenty-seven consecutive years as a result of Southwest's dedication to a low-cost, high-customer-satisfaction strategy.

Carriers such as Southwest and Jet Blue with lower operating costs and consequently lower fares, have forced larger companies to retreat. This has had a positive impact on the efficiency of the airline industry.

To reduce losses brought about by deregulation, major carriers eliminated unprofitable routes, often those serving smaller cities. New airlines began operating shuttle services between the smaller cities and nearest larger or hub city. This created the hub-and-spoke system (see Figure 2–1).

The Hub–and–Spoke System

In order to remain efficient and cost effective, major U.S. airlines have adopted a hub-and-spoke system. The **hub-and-spoke system** enables passengers to travel from one smaller city to another smaller city via a hub or even two hubs. Similarly, passengers may originate their travel from a small city and use the hub to reach connecting flights to destinations throughout the world.

The hub-and-spoke system has two main benefits: (1) Airlines can service more cities at a lower cost, and (2) airlines can maximize passenger loads from small cities, thereby saving fuel.

[23]Kevin Kelly and Aaron Bernstein, "Labor Deals That Offer a Break from Us vs. Them," *Business Week*, August 2, 1993, p. 30.

[24]Ibid.

Cruise Ships

More than 200 cruise lines offer a variety of wonderful vacations, from the "Love Boat" to freighters that carry only a few passengers. Travelers associate a certain romance with cruising to exotic locations and being pampered all day.

Being on a cruise ship is like being on a floating resort. Accommodations range from luxurious suites to cabins that are even smaller than most hotel rooms. Attractions and distractions range from early morning workouts to fabulous meals, with nightlife consisting of dancing, cabarets, and possibly gambling. Day life might involve relaxation, visits to the beauty parlor, organized games, or simply reclining in a deck chair by the pool reading a novel. Nonstop entertainment includes language lessons, charm classes, port-of-call briefings, cooking, dances, bridge, table tennis, shuffleboard, and more.

For example, the Crown Princess is a "super Love Boat" weighing in at 70,000 tons and costing $200 million. This ship is longer than two football fields and capable of carrying up to 1,596 passengers. The Crown Princess was designed by Italian architect Reizo Piano. Its exterior resembles the head of a dolphin, and it features the "Dome," a 13,000-square-foot entertainment complex forward on the top deck. The Dome boasts a casino with blackjack, craps, roulette tables, and masses of slot machines as well as a dance floor, bar, and lounge with wrap-around windows.

Radisson Hotels International entered the $4.6 billion cruise business with a dramatic catamaran—a twin-hulled ship designed to prevent most of the pitching and rolling that causes seasickness. The new ship, the *Radisson Diamond,* can carry up to 354 passengers. With rates at about $600 per day, this ship is at the top end of the cruise market.

The cruise market has increased more dramatically in recent years and has rebounded from the September 11 catastrophe. In 2002, it is estimated that 7.4 million Americans will be cruising. Rates vary from a starting point of $85 per person per day on Carnival Cruise Lines to $600 on the *Radisson Diamond.* Rates typically are quoted per diem (per day) and are cruise-only figures, based on double occupancy.

Love Boat (Courtesy Princess Cruise Lines.)

Radisson Diamond (Courtesy Carlson Corporation.)

Some 215 ships are providing lake and river, but mostly ocean-going cruises. The spectacular new ships with the multideck atriums and razzle-dazzle entertainment cater to the market with median income of $51,500 a year.

Carnival Cruise Lines is the most successful, financially—netting about 20 percent of sales. It targets adults between the ages of twenty-five and fifty-four, and expects to attract close to 2 million passengers with its spectacular atriums, and round-the-clock activities. Its largest income, other than the fare itself, is from beverage service. Casino income is also high and its casinos are the largest afloat. Carnival hopes that passengers will enjoy buying drinks and putting quarters, or preferably dollars, into the shipboard slot machines. They also hope their passengers will not mind their small cabins, since the activities on the ship occupy all of their waking hours and much of the night.

No two ships are alike. Each has its own personality and character. The nationality of the ship's officers and staff contributes greatly to the ship's ambiance. For example, the ships under the Holland America flag have Dutch officers and Indonesian/Filipino crew, and those belonging to the Epirotiki flag have Greek officers and crew.

Casual ships cater to young couples, singles, and families with children. At the other end of the spectrum, ships that appeal to the upscale crowd draw a mature clientele that prefers a more sedate atmosphere, low-key entertainment, and dressing for dinner.

In 2002 alone, about 7.4 million passengers vacationed on a ship. Many passengers are remarkably loyal to their particular vessel; as many as half of the passengers on a cruise may be repeat guests.

See Figure 2–2 for examples of cruise lingo.

Most cruise ships sail under foreign flags because they were built abroad for the following reasons[25]:

1. U.S. labor costs for ships, officers, and crew, in addition to maritime unions, are too high to compete in the world market.
2. U.S. ships are not permitted to operate casino-type gambling.
3. Many foreign shipyards are government subsidized to keep workers employed, thereby lowering construction costs.

[25]Lundberg, op. cit., p. 102.

A Day in the Life of Jeff Martin
Cruise Director, Royal Caribbean International

Voyager of the Seas, the largest and most innovative cruise ship ever built, was introduced by Royal Caribbean International on November 21, 1999. It weighs 142,000 gross tons and has a total guest capacity of 3,700 with 1,200 crew members. *Voyager of the Seas* is truly a revolution in the cruising industry. A virtual city in itself, she features the world's first floating ice skating rink, a rock climbing wall, an inline skating track, and the largest and most technically advanced theater afloat. There is a four-story Royal Promenade shopping and entertainment boulevard spanning the length of the ship that acts as a hub for the ship's vast array of activities and entertainment. Cruise director Jeff Martin joined Royal Caribbean International as cruise staff in 1982. As a cruise director for the past twelve years (and with twenty years of experience in the field of entertainment) he was instrumental in implementing the unique entertainment and activities program aboard with a support staff of 130 people. What follows is an account of a day in the life of the cruise director of the largest ship in the world.

(Courtesy Royal Caribbean International.)

Monday—First Day at Sea

7:30–8:30 A.M.   Yesterday we embarked 3,650 guests in Miami and headed for our first port of call, Labadee, our own private island on the coast of Hispaniola. Before most of the guests are up for the day, I plan and submit our daily activities schedule for the rest of the voyage to our hotel director for his approval. All of the cruise staff management team has submitted their reports after our staff meeting at embarkation yesterday. Scheduling of the twelve activities staff for the week is handled by the assistant cruise director, who also submits the payroll and overtime hours for my approval. Our social hostess says that three couples were married in the wedding chapel yesterday and they are included in the 108 couples that have chosen to spend their honeymoon with us. A special party will be held later on in the week to celebrate this happy occasion. The youth activities manager reports that there are over 600 children aboard ranging in age from three to seventeen. The youth activities manager and her team of thirteen are responsible for providing age-appropriate activities for our junior cruisers. We offer a special deck and pool area/arcade for children in addition to our extensive youth facilities, which include a teen disco.

Fourteen hundred international guests are aboard and they consist of sixty different nationalities. The international host (who speaks five languages) provides translations of our daily program and acts as the cruise director's liaison for all of our international guests. Daily announcements and publications are translated in the most predominant languages. For this voyage, those happen to be Spanish and Portuguese.

A large part of our business is group and incentive business. The group coordinator appropriates lounges and facilities for these special group events under the auspices of the cruise director. This week we have twenty-five groups comprised of 800 people. There will be seminars, group meetings, presentations, and cocktail parties. We have a state-of-the-art conference center/executive board room/screening room in addition to a large convention facility named "Studio B," which doubles as the ice rink. A retractable floor over the ice rink makes this a great space for large conventions. The shore excursion manager reports that tour sales are good for this voyage among the fifty land-based excursions that we offer. All of this information is consolidated into a report to the hotel director that is submitted on a daily basis.

8:45–9:30 A.M.   Hotel director's meeting. All of the division heads in the Hotel Department meet to discuss the daily operation of this floating hotel. Today's agenda includes a monthly safety meeting. Each division head presents his or her monthly report on safety and environmental protection. Hospitality and the safety of our guests and crew are our top priorities. Following this meeting is an introduction of the senior officers by the captain to the new crew members who are just beginning their forty hours of training.

9:45 A.M.   The start of my public duties. I give a daily announcement and rundown of all the activities and entertainment happenings around the ship.

continued

10:00 A.M.   Morning walkaround. Time to kick off the first session of Jackpot Bingo for the week. On my way through the promenade, I encounter our interactive performers hamming it up with our guests. This is a troupe of four highly skilled performers. (Some of them are former Ringling Brothers' clowns.) They play different characters throughout the voyage and add quite a lot to the guest experience. I also stop by the Royal Caribbean Online Internet center, which is quite busy. We also offer an in-stateroom hook-up of personal computers for unlimited Internet access (for a fee.) The business services manager is in charge of offering these services as well as booking future cruises for our traveling guests. (We have a weekly average of 40 percent repeat guests.)

10:30 A.M.   The Studio B ice rink is busy with guests skating at our first All Skate session. There are several sessions throughout the day. The ice skating cast (ten individuals) are responsible for running the sessions as well as skating in our Ice Show. The show is featured four times throughout the voyage and even has a competition segment that is judged by five audience members. The team consists of an international cast of skaters some of whom are former national amateur champions in their native countries (and a few former Olympic team members).

11:00 A.M.   Time to change out of my day uniform into a business suit and put on stage makeup for the taping of our onboard talk and information show, "Voyager Live." I produce this segment from our state-of-the-art television studio on board. We have four video programmers and an interactive television technician. Interactive TV allows our guests to order room service, excursions, and movies with the click of a button in the privacy of their staterooms.

On today's show, I have the pleasure of interviewing the Osmonds. Royal Caribbean International is one of the few cruise lines that offers a celebrity entertainment program. There is an extensive shoreside entertainment network responsible for the booking of our acts as well as our in-house production shows. In conjunction with the production manager, I make sure that the entertainers are well taken care of once they come on board. Luckily, the Osmonds are as nice in person as they appear on stage. In the past, I have encountered a few difficult and challenging celebrity entertainers. Also featured on today's show are two members of the ice skating cast and our port and shopping guide, the person who dispenses shopping tips for the islands. Several commercials for our onboard services are interspersed between segments. I am one of the main sources for revenue promotion on board. The television programming is a great asset in a small floating city of this size. Thirty-seven channels offer safe-ty information, music, shopping tips, CNBC, CNN, ESPN, and free movies in several languages.

Noon   Lunch with the staff in the Officers and Staff Dining Room.

1:00 P.M.   Change out of the business suit into shorts and a Polo shirt to emcee the Belly Flop Competition at 1:30 poolside. Always a "big" event among our guests. Quite a few laughs. This is followed by horse racing, cruising style. We pick six jockeys who move six wooden horses by a roll of the dice. The betting is fierce as the guests cheer their favorite horses on. I become the track announcer for three races and horse auctioneer. Today we auction off the six horses for our Voyager Derby later in the week. The horses go to the highest bidder and then the "owners" run them in a race later on in the week for all the money. The six horses go for $2,100. A nice pot for one lucky winner.

2:30 P.M.   I stop by the Sports Court to check out the action. The sports court is full of families enjoying our Family Hour activities with the youth staff. Four sports and fitness supervisors run the sports program. We offer a nine-hole miniature golf course, golf driving simulator, full-court basketball/volleyball, inline skating, Ping Pong, and a rock climbing wall that rises up the smokestack 200 feet above sea level—the best view in the Caribbean. By the end of the day, 125 people will have climbed the wall.

3:00–4:30 P.M.   POWER NAP TIME. The day will not end until about 12:30 A.M. Being "on stage" and available practically twenty-four hours a day can take its toll. This nap will carry me through until the end of the evening.

4:45 P.M.   Time to change into white tie and tails for the Captain's Champagne Reception held on the Royal Promenade deck. The social hostess will introduce the captain to our guests if they desire to have a photograph taken with him. After a big fanfare at 5:45, I introduce the captain on the bridge overlooking the 800 guests gathered in their formalwear. The captain gives his welcome speech, introduces the senior officers and then we send the main seating guests into the dining room for their formal dinner.

6:00 P.M.   Back to the office to catch up on e-mail and general administrative business. It is also time to work on budget and revenue forecasting for the upcoming year.

7:45 P.M.   Off to the Royal Promenade deck to mingle with the second seating guests at the second Champagne Reception. The captain repeats his speech for these guests and then we send them off to their dinner at 8:30.

8:30 P.M. Meet in the Champagne Bar with the hotel director before dinner. Tonight we will entertain guests who are on their fiftieth cruise and also a representative from an insurance company who is thinking of booking 700 guests on a future cruise with us.

9:00 P.M. On my way to the dining room, I introduce our production show in the La Scala Theater for the main seating guests. The three-tiered theater has a capacity of 1,350 guests. It features state-of-the-art production facilities that include fly space, video support, Surround Sound, movable scenery, hydraulics, pyrotechnics, and an orchestra pit. Tonight's show is a collection of Broadway hits entitled "Broadway's Rhythm and Rhyme." The cast consists of fourteen singers and dancers and a ten-piece orchestra as well as full technical support. A production manager is in charge of six stage staff, a rigger, and sound and light technicians. The show will last an hour. (Just enough time for me to get through my entrée before I have to come back and close the show off at 10:00 P.M.)

10:45 P.M. After dessert, I introduce the show for second seating guests and watch the show for quality control.

11:45 P.M. After the show finishes, I do a final walk around the lounges on the ship with my assistant. Karaoke has just finished in one of the secondary lounges and we have music playing everywhere. We have thirty-five musicians comprising several bands featuring all varieties of music (classical guitar, string quartet, jazz ensemble, piano bar, Calypso, Latin, Top 40). The disco is lively with singles' night tonight and there are a few couples enjoying light jazz in the Jazz Club.

12:30 A.M. A full day. Definitely a far cry from Julie, on the "Love Boat"! Time for bed as I have to be on the gangway at 8:00 A.M. to welcome our guests to Labadee.

In addition, cruise ships sail under foreign flags (called "flags of convenience") because registering these ships in countries such as Panama, the Bahamas, and Liberia means fewer and more lax regulations and little or no taxation.

Employment opportunities for Americans are mainly confined to sales, marketing, and other U.S. shore-based activities, such as reservations and supplies.

Aft:	Toward the rear or stern of the ship
Beam:	Ship's width at the widest point
Bridge:	Part of the ship where the navigation is done
Bulkhead:	Shipboard name for wall or partition
Cabin:	Name given to a passenger's room
Captain:	Master of the ship; the captain is the final authority and has total responsibility for every aspect of the ship's safety and operations
Companion way:	Flight of stairs
Cruise director:	Individual who plans and directs all shipboard entertainment, including passenger activities, shows, shore excursions
Forward:	Toward the bow or front of ship
Galley:	Seagoing word for kitchen
Gangway:	Ship's boarding ramp
Knot:	Nautical speed (about 1-1/16 of a land mile per hour)
Port side:	Left-hand side of the ship as you face forward
Starboard side:	Right-hand side of the ship as you face forward
Stern:	Aft or rear of the ship
Tonnage:	A customary measure of a ship's size
Wake:	Waves behind a ship

Figure 2–2 *Cruise Lingo*

The maître d' on the Love Boat was explaining the dining room staff's duties beginning with breakfast at 6 A.M., followed by lunch and dinner. A student asked, "When does the second shift come on?" The maître d' laughed and said, "There is no second shift." Needless to say, that student's interest declined, especially when he realized the crew would be at sea for months at a time.

Table 2–1 shows the number of passengers taking a cruise lasting more than two days according to the Cruise Lines Association (CLA).

On board, certain positions such as cruise director and purser, are sometimes occupied by Americans.

Segmenting the Cruise Market

There are marked differences between the segments of the cruise industry.

Mass Market: Generally people with incomes in the $30,000 to $60,000 range, interested in an average cost per person of between $85 and $175 per day, depending on the location and size of the cabin.

Middle Market: Generally people with incomes in the $60,000 to $80,000 range, interested in an average cost per person of $175 to $350 per day. These ships are capable of accommodating 750 to 1,000 passengers. The middle market ships are stylish and comfortable with each vessel having its own personality that caters to a variety of different guests. Among the cruise lines in the middle market are Princess Cruises, Norwegian Cruise Lines, Royal Caribbean, Holland America Lines, Windstar Cruises, Cunard Lines, and Celebrity Cruises.

Luxury Market: Generally people with incomes higher than $80,000, interested in an average cost per person of more than $350 per day. In this market, the ships tend to be smaller, averaging about 700 passengers, with superior appointments and service. What constitutes a luxury cruise is partly a matter of individual judgment, partly a matter of advertising and public relations. The ships that received the top accolades from travel industry writers and others who assign such ranks, cater only to the top 2 percent of North American income groups. Currently, the ships considered to be in the very top category are *Sea Goddess I, Sea Goddess II, Seabourn Spirit, Seabourn Legend, Seabourn Pride, Crystal Harmony, Crystal Hanseatic, Radisson Diamond, Silver Wind,* and *Song of Flower.*

Carnival Triumph Lido Deck
(Courtesy Carnival Cruise Lines.)

Table 2–1 Passengers Taking a Cruise Longer Than Two Days

Year	Passengers
1970	500,000
1980	1.4 million
1990	3.6 million
2000	5.4 million
2010	7.2 million

Source: Personal communication The Cruise Line Industry Association, January 2001.

These six-star vessels have sophisticated cuisine, excellent service, far-reaching and imaginative itineraries, and highly satisfying overall cruise experiences.

The rising demand for new cruise operators and recent mergers have sparked the travel industry. Larger ships with resort-like design, numerous activities, and amenities such as "virtual golf," pizzerias, and caviar bars have changed with time.

Years ago, when the last of the great transatlantic liners took to the sea, no one could have predicted that ships of today's size and luxury would exist. However, today's cruise liners are growing at a rapid pace, with thirty-four new vessels scheduled to be built between 1999 and 2003.

Significant growth opportunities still exist for the industry. With only about 10 percent of the cruise market tapped, and with an estimated market potential of billions, the cruise industry can be assured of a bright future.

Check Your Knowledge

1. In your own words, define the term *tourism.*
2. What impact did the different ages of tourism have on today's tourism?
3. *Research:* Which city in the United States is the biggest hub city for air travel? Approximately how many flights does this city have a day?
4. Explain the significance of the Airline Deregulation Act of 1978.

Tourism Organizations

Governments are involved in tourism decisions because tourism involves travel across international boundaries. Governments regulate the entrance and exit of foreign nationals. They become involved in the decisions surrounding national parks, heritage, preservation, and environmental protection, as well as cultural and social aspects of tourism. Tourism is to some extent an international ambassador, fostering goodwill and closer intercultural understanding among the peoples of the world.

International Organizations

Looking first at the macro picture, the **World Tourism Organization (WTO)** is the most widely recognized organization in tourism today.[27] The WTO is the

---

[27]McIntosh and Goeldner, op. cit., p. 43.

only organization that represents all national and official tourism interests among its allied members.

The **International Air Transportation Association (IATA)** is the global organization that regulates almost all international airlines. The purpose of IATA is to facilitate the movement of people and goods via a network of routes. In addition to tickets, IATA regulations standardize waybills and baggage checks and coordinate and unify handling and accounting procedures to permit rapid interline bookings and connections. The IATA also maintains stability of fares and rates.

International Civil Aviation Organization (ICAO) is comprised of more than eighty governments. ICAO coordinates the development of all aspects of civil aviation, specifically with regard to the formulation of international standards and practices.

Each of several international development organizations shares a common purpose that includes tourism development. The better known organizations include the following:

> The World Bank (WB), which lends substantial sums of money for tourism development. Most of this money is awarded in the form of low-interest loans to developing countries.
>
> The International Bank for Reconstruction and Development, which is similar to the World Bank.
>
> United Nations Development Program (UNDP), which assists countries with a variety of development projects, including tourism
>
> **Organization for Economic Cooperation and Development (OECD),** which was established by an international convention signed in Paris in 1960. The purpose of the OECD is to do the following:
> 1. Achieve the highest sustainable economic growth and employment, and a rising standard of living in member countries while maintaining financial stability—thus contributing to the development of the world economy
> 2. Contribute to sound economic expansion in member as well as nonmember countries through economic development
> 3. Contribute to the expansion of world trade on a multilateral, nondiscriminating basis, in accordance with international obligations
>
> The OCED's tourism committee studies various aspects of tourism, including tourism problems, and makes recommendations to governments. The committee also works on standard definitions and methods of data collection, which are published in an annual report entitled "Tourism Policy and International Tourism in OECD Member Countries."

Other banks and organizations with similar interests include the Asian Development Bank, Overseas Private Investment Corporation, Inter-American Development Bank, and Agency for International Development.

The **Pacific Area Travel Association (PATA)** represents thirty-four countries in the Pacific and Asia that have united behind a common goal: excellence in travel and tourism growth. PATA's accomplishments include shaping the future of travel in the Asia/Pacific region; it has had a remarkable record of success with research, development, education, and marketing.

Domestic Organizations

The United States Travel and Tourism Administration (USTTA) is the main government agency in the United States responsible for the promotion of tourism. USTTA was established in 1981 by the National Tourism Policy Act. The mission of USTTA is to develop travel to the United States from other countries, expand growth of the U.S. travel industry, and encourage foreign exchange earnings. USTTA is responsible to the Secretary of Commerce, whose job it is to coordinate the various governmental policies, issues, and programs that affect tourism development.

The Travel Industry of America (TIA) is the national association that speaks for the common interests and concerns of all components of the U.S. travel industry. Its mission is to benefit the whole U.S. travel industry by unifying its goals, coordinating private sector efforts to encourage and promote travel to and within the United States, monitoring government policies that affect travel and tourism, and supporting research and analysis in areas vital to the industry. Established in 1941, TIA's membership represents more than 2,000 travel-related businesses, associations, and local, regional, and state travel promotion agencies of the nation's 6.02-million-employee travel industry.

State Offices of Tourism

The next level of organizations concerned with tourism is the state office of tourism. State offices of tourism are charged by their legislative bodies with the orderly growth and development of tourism within the state. They promote information programs, advertising, publicity, and research in terms of their relationship to the recreation and tourism attractions in the state.

City-Level Offices of Tourism

Cities have also realized the importance of the "new money" that tourism brings. Many cities have established **convention and visitors bureaus** (CVBs) whose main function is to attract and retain visitors to the city. The convention and visitors bureaus comprise representatives of the city's attractions, restaurants, hotels and motels, and transportation. These bureaus are largely funded by the transient occupancy tax (TOT) that is charged to hotel guests. In most cities, the TOT ranges from 8 to 18 percent. The balance of funding comes from membership dues and promotional activities.

The Economic Impact of Tourism

The World Travel and Tourism Council, a Brussels-based organization, commissioned a study[28] from the Wharton Economic Forecasting Association. Their report suggested that the total demand for travel and tourism will be $2,571 billion by 2010, or more than 10 percent of the world's gross national product (GNP). Tourism, says the study, grows about twice as fast as world GNP. Of the industry's total world spending, about 31 percent takes place in the European Community and 30 percent on the North American continent.

International arrivals, according to the WTO, were 693 million in 2001. It is estimated that they will reach 1 billion in 2010 and 1.6 billion by 2020—more than triple the 475 million people who traveled abroad in 1992.

In 2001, an estimated 45.5 million overseas residents visited the United States, down by 10.6 percent from the previous year—a result of terrorist attacks on the economy. Nearly every state publishes its own tourism economic impact study. New York, for example, estimates its tourism revenue to be $38.5 billion; Florida, about $51.7 billion; Texas, $33; and California, just over $53 billion. Tourism is Hawaii's biggest industry with revenues of $23 billion.

The National Travel and Tourism Awareness Council's annual "The Tourism Work for America Report"[29] indicates that travel and tourism is one of the nation's leading sectors. Statistics include the following:

- ✔ International travelers spend about $72.3 billion on travel-related expenses (e.g., lodging, food, and entertainment) in the United States annually.
- ✔ 20.8 million people are directly employed in the industry, making travel and tourism the nation's second largest employer, after health services.
- ✔ Travel generates about $95.6 billion a year in tax receipts.
- ✔ Spending by international visitors within the United States is about $21 billion more than is travel-related spending by Americans outside the United States.
- ✔ Nearly 46 million international travelers visit the United States each year.

Travel and tourism supports about 200 million jobs worldwide. This represents about 7.8 percent of the global workforce, according to the World Travel and Tourism Council (WTTC). By employing approximately one out of every ten workers, travel and tourism is the world's largest employer and is the largest industry. The estimates are that in the year 2012, there will be 249 million jobs accounting for 8.6 percent of total employment, which is 1 in every 11.7 jobs.

---

[28]http://www.wttc.org/economic_research/kystats.htm
[29]Ibid.

Rank		International Tourism Receipts (US$ billion)		Change (%)	Market share (%)
		2000	**2001***	**2001*/2000**	**2001***
1	United States	82.0	72.3	−11.9	15.6
2	Spain	31.5	32.9	4.5	7.1
3	France	30.7	29.6	−3.7	6.4
4	Italy	27.5	25.9	−5.7	5.6
5	China	16.2	17.8	9.7	3.8
6	Germany	17.9	17.2	−3.7	3.7
7	United Kingdom	19.5	15.9	−18.8	3.4
8	Austria	10.0	12.0	19.7	2.6
9	Canada	10.7	–		
10	Greece	9.2	–		
11	Turkey	7.6	8.9	17.0	1.9
12	Mexico	8.3	8.4	1.3	1.8
13	Hong Kong (China)	7.9	8.2	4.5	1.8
14	Australia	8.0	7.6	−4.8	1.6
15	Switzerland	7.5	7.6	1.6	1.6

Table 2–2　World's Top 15 Tourism Earners

*Data as collected by WTO June 2002.

Source: World Tourism Organization (WTO)©.

The Multiplier Effect

Tourists produce secondary impacts beyond their original expenditures. When a tourist spends money to travel, to stay in a hotel, or to eat in a restaurant, that money is recycled by those businesses to purchase more goods, thereby generating further use of the money. In addition, employees of businesses who serve tourists spend a higher proportion of their money locally on various goods and services. This chain reaction continues until there is a leakage, meaning that money is used to purchase something from outside the area. Figure 2–3 illustrates the **multiplier effect.**

"Most developed economies have a multiplier effect between 1.5 and 2.0."[30] This means that the original money spent is used again in the community between 1.5 and 2.0 times.

Tour Operators

The National Tour Association estimates that nearly 500,000 tours are conducted annually by 1,636 U.S. **tour operators**. These tours carry 21.2 million

---

[30]http://www.world-tourism.org/market_research/facts@figures/menus.htm

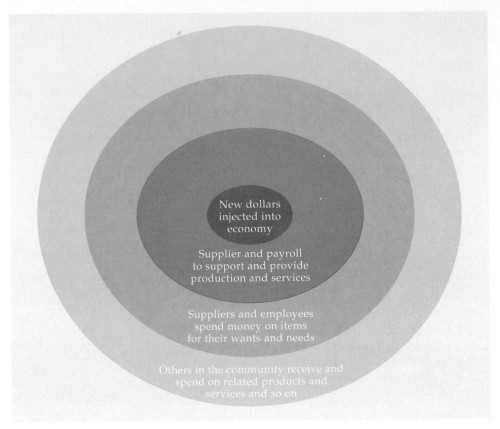

Figure 2–3   *The Multiplier Effect*

passengers, who spend an average of $168.46 per passenger per day on both one-day and multiday tours.

Promoters of Tourism

Travel Agencies

A **travel agent** is a middleperson who acts as a travel counselor and sells on behalf of airlines, cruise lines, rail and bus transportation, hotels, and auto rental companies. Agents may sell individual parts of the overall system or several elements, such as air and cruise tickets. The agent acts as a broker, bringing together the client (buyer) and the supplier (seller). An agent has quick access to schedules, fares, and advice for clients about various destinations.

The first U.S. travel agents emerged in the 1880s, selling steamship and rail tickets and some arranged tours. "Ask Mr. Foster," the oldest U.S. travel agency, got its name because a Mr. Foster opened a travel information office in St. Augustine, Florida, as explained earlier in the chapter. Eventually, offices opened in various parts of Florida and spread to New York and other major U.S. cities.

The American Society of Travel Agents (ASTA) is the world's largest travel trade association, with over 24,000 members in more than 165 countries. Total airline sales processed by travel agencies reached $6,383,226,000 for July 2000. The Airlines Reporting Corporation (ARC) reports that travel agency's weekly sales are about $38,989. According to *Travel Weekly Magazine,* the top fifty travel agencies in terms of sales generated (approximately $25 billion in revenue) represent 30 percent of total agency sales.

Agents use computer reservation systems (CRS) to access availability and make bookings. In the United States, the main vendors are Sabre, Apollo, Worldspan, System One, and Galileo. Sabre owns a 70 percent share of Travelocity, the online site. And Cendant Corporation owns Galileo, which forms the hub of Cendant's travel-related business of hotels, car rental, and vacation ownership. Worldspan is jointly owned by Delta, Northwest, and American airlines. Worldspan manages 50 percent of all online bookings worldwide.[31]

According to the ASTA, a travel agent is more than a ticket seller. Agents serve their clients in the following ways:

✔ Arranging transportation by air, sea, rail, bus, car rental, etc.
✔ Preparing individual itineraries, personally escorted tours, group tours, and prepared package tours
✔ Arranging for hotel, motel, and resort accommodations; meals; sightseeing tours; transfers of passengers and luggage between terminals and hotels; and special features such as tickets for music festivals, the theater, etc.
✔ Handling and advising on many details involved with travel, such as insurance, travelers checks, foreign currency exchange, documentary requirements, and immunizations and other inoculations.
✔ Using professional know-how and experience (e.g., schedules of air, train, and bus connections, rates of hotels, quality of accommodations, etc.).
✔ Arranging reservations for special-interest activities, such as group tours, conventions, business travel, gourmet tours, sporting trips, etc.[32]

Approximately 47,000 travel agencies are currently operating in the United States. The average agency has between four and seven full-time employees. The average starting salaries are $18,000. The average salary for an agent with three to five years service is $26,000. Agents with ten plus years average $30,000. Managers make an average of $38,000. Twenty-one percent of agents

---

[31]http://www.worldspan.com/home.asp?fpageID = 5
[32]Courtesy of the American Society of Travel Agents.

receive commissions ranging between 6 and 11 percent of their sales. The average sales volume per agency is as follows:[33]

- ✔ 33 percent of agencies have sales of less than $1 million.
- ✔ 6 percent of agencies have sales between $1 and $3 million.
- ✔ 27 percent of agencies have sales between $2 and $5 million.
- ✔ 14 percent of agencies have sales of more than $5 million.

Agencies make their money on commissions. They usually make 10 percent on air travel within the United States and about 11 percent on international travel. Commission on hotel accommodations ranges from 10 to 15 percent and commission on cruise packages ranges from 11 to 14 percent.

Commission Caps

In 1995, the airlines imposed a **commission cap** of $50 for a domestic round-trip flight (it has since been reduced to $20) and 5–8 percent for an international booking. This restriction forced several agencies to close. During the first quarter of 1996, 505 full-service agency locations shut down—a 59 percent jump from the previous year.[34] Other agencies were forced to increase the scope of services offered. Now, cruise line officials are also looking at travel agent commission rates, which they feel are too high. Rick Sasso, Celebrity's president, observes that if bookings start to become a normal practice on the Internet, a client might still pick up the booking at a travel agency. Cruise lines could tell an Internet broker that they have booked and that they may go to any travel agent to pick up the document. In that case, the level of commission would probably be about five percent, approximately half the normal commission. Airlines are also selling direct to customers over the Internet and further eroding travel agents' commissions.

Travel Corporations

There are a number of large and successful travel corporations—the largest being American Express Travel Services. American Express (AMEX) is a corporation that has a travel services division with locations worldwide. Each location is licensed and bonded with the International Air Transportation Association (IATA), which provides travel services and tickets through the corporation. The travel services division provides other services including foreign currencies, AMEX traveler's checks in different currencies, and gift checks. Currently, the travel services division is trying to promote foreign currencies to increase revenues.

The majority of American Express Travel Services' revenues is generated in business travel through corporate accounts. The airlines give the travel agency an override to portion with the corporate client. The business contract is individually set up, based on annual travel expenses. For example, if IBM's annual

---

[33]Personal conversation with Jay Sullivan, September 14, 2002.

[34]ARTA Home Page, April 26, 1996.

Thomas Cook and Son

People with knowledge about travel have been arranging trips for others for centuries, but Thomas Cook is credited with being the first professional travel agent.

A wood-turner by trade, Cook was a deeply religious person and a temperance enthusiast. In 1841, he chartered a train to carry 540 people to a temperance convention. Cook arranged the round-trip from Leicester to Loughborough, a distance of twenty-two miles, at a shilling per person. Although Cook made no profit for himself, he did realize the potential in arranging travel for other people. From the outset, he saw that the travel business was more than a business—it was an opportunity for education and enlightenment.

In 1845, Cook became a full-time excursion organizer. Reasoning that the five percent commission he received from Midland Countries Railroad was not enough to maintain a solvent business, he became a tour operator and, later, a retailer of tours as well. Dedicated to making tours as convenient and interesting as possible, Cook printed a "handbook of the trip" for an 1845 tour from Leicester to Liverpool. Soon after, he produced coupons that could be used to cover hotel expenses. In 1846, Cook took 350 people by steamer and train on a tour of Scotland, using a touring guide, the first of its kind, prepared especially for the trip. By 1851, Cook's clientele had grown to over 165,000 people. It was that year that Cook made plans to visit London for the first World Exhibition at the Crystal Palace.

After Cook moved his offices to London, he began conjuring up all sorts of imaginative trips. Soon he was arranging "grand circular tours of Europe" with itineraries that included four different countries. He helped popularize Switzerland as a touring center by taking a group through the country in 1863. Soon after the American Civil War, Cook's son, John M. Cook, Jr., traveled with a group to the United States and visited New York, Washington D.C., and a handful of Civil War battlefields.

In 1872, Cook achieved another first—an around-the-world trip that took the ten-member group 222 days to complete. Today, the same trip could be taken over a weekend.

Throughout the latter half of the nineteenth century, "The Cook's Tour" included an escorted group expedition, most often conducted by Thomas or one of his sons. After Cook became blind, members of his family took over the business, however, Cook stayed on as manager of the firm. He arranged a trip into Yellowstone Park soon after it opened. In 1875, preparations were finalized for Cook tours to visit Norway, and, then, in collaboration with the P and O Steamship Line, they traveled to India. In the 1890s, the Cooks ran pioneering trips across Europe to Asia via the Trans-Siberian Railroad.

Cook's company was successful partly because he made travel convenient and relatively simple. Another reason was Thomas Cook's enthusiasm for travel as an enlightening venture, not just for the upper class, but for anyone who could afford his much lower prices. In essence, Cook can be credited with making world travel possible for the middle class.

The Cook family was well aware of the elasticity of demand for travel. If the cost was reduced, more people would travel. The more people traveled by a particular mode of transportation, the more likely it was that the cost of transportation could be reduced. For example, by chartering whole trains and steamers and by booking large blocks of rooms, Cook was able to reduce travel expenses considerably. The cost of operating a train, steamship, or airplane that is 100 percent full is only a little more than that of operating one that is 25 percent full, and the cost per seat at 100 percent capacity is substantially less.

The Cooks also pioneered the travel conglomerate (one company engaging in a number of enterprises) long before the term was ever used. Before 1875, the firm had acquired the exclusive right to

continued

carry the mail, as well as special travelers and government officials, between the cities of Assiont and Assonan on the Nile.

Upon Thomas Cook's death in 1893, ownership and management of the firm passed to his three sons. The business, by that time, had grown to include three divisions: tourists, banking, and shipping. Later, in 1931, Thomas Cook and Sons merged with the Wagon Lit Company, operators of the sleeping car and express trains in Europe. Still, the Cooks continued to do everything possible to make the trip easy for the traveler. Cook's agents often met planes with a car, waiting at the entrance to customs to whisk travelers directly to a reception or anywhere else they wanted to go. The all-inclusive price for a tour made it easier for people to plan vacations and to budget their time and money.

Following World War II, the British government acquired the principal interest in the Thomas Cook and Son Company but later sold it in 1972 for $858.5 million. Today, the Trust Houses Forte, the largest hospitality company in Britain, and the Automobile Association of Britain are part of the owning consortium. The company now has more than 625 offices and 10,000 employees around the world and is composed of five relatively independent divisions. Considered to be the largest of its kind, the company today has manifold interests other than the sale of travel.

We have seen that until the nineteenth century, discretionary travel was limited to a very small percentage of people. This changed dramatically as the Industrial Revolution gave millions of people in North America and Europe some discretionary income. More important, trains and airlines made travel comparatively cheap and convenient. In response to travel demand, entrepreneurs such as Thomas Cook, and later, travel expediters, helped promote and make travel arrangements easier.

travel expenses are $1 million, the airline will give AMEX a 1.4 percent override commission to split with IBM. AMEX chooses their airline vendors according to who gives the largest override percentage and whose negotiated rates are most appealing. The same policy applies to other vendors in the industry, such as cruise lines. Every travel agent, whether in-house or off-premise, receives a commission from a vendor, based on their annual sales volume. Usually this commission varies, but the standard is 8 to 10 percent of the sale.

Travel managers for AMEX function as national account managers. Their pay is based on their grade level, region, and market. Their salary also depends on who they service. A small, local clientele generates a lower salary and a broader service center provides a higher salary. Depending on whether they are on- or off-site, a travel manager's salary for AMEX is between $50,000 and $90,000 for corporate clients. The salary range for general public leisure travel is between $35,000 and $60,000. Each travel manager is hired internally and their pay is based mostly on seniority.[35]

American Express Travel on the Internet searches for the best ticket price, or the most convenient flights in the same reservations systems used by thou-

[35]Phone interview with an employee of Harvey Golub, President, American Express Travel Services, January 5, 2001.

sands of travel agents. In a snap, users can check out the price or search for other options, then book their own reservations on-line. Users can view descriptions of packages to sunny, snow-filled, cultural, or just plain fun destinations, along with full-color photos and a list of amenities. These packages may not be booked on-line. A toll-free number is listed at the site, or consumers may visit an American Express Travel office. Visitors to the site currently have three options: They can book airline tickets, they can view vacation offers, and they can look up the most convenient American Express Travel office. In addition, card members may take advantage of special travel, retail, restaurant, and entertainment offers and shop for a variety of merchandise on another Internet site called ExpressNet.

Corporate Travel Manager

A **corporate travel manager** is a type of entrepreneur working within the framework of a large corporation. For example, Mitsubishi Electronics, in Cypress, California, was spending about $4 million for travel and entertainment. In addition, twenty-nine field offices operated independently across the United States, Canada, and Mexico. The total expenditure for travel and entertainment was $11 million. Enter John Fazio, recruited by Mitsubishi to improve efficiency and reduce costs. Fazio invited interested agencies to submit proposals based on Mitsubishi's travel needs. The fifteen initial proposals were narrowed to eight; finally two were asked to submit their best and last offers. These offers were evaluated based on Mitsubishi's criteria: technological capabilities, locations, and ability to give personal service.[36]

An interesting trend in corporate travel is agentless booking via electronic mail (e-mail). Travel is initiated at the keyboard, not at the switchboard. Increasingly, technologically savvy corporations are making travel bookings via e-mail. A forerunner in this process is Wal-Mart Stores. Seeking to increase booking efficiency and trim costs, Wal-Mart requested that World Wide develop a system, now known as Quality Agent, to meet their goals. Quality Agent is a Windows-based front end to the reservation system that processes reservations without human intervention. Currently, larger travel agencies are developing similar e-mail programs for their clients.[37]

Travel and Tour Wholesalers

Tour wholesalers consolidate the services of airline, cruise line, and bus line with ground service suppliers into a tour that is sold through a sales channel to the public.[38] Tour wholesaling came into prominence in the 1960s because airlines had vacant seats—which, like hotel rooms, are perishable. Airlines

[36]Based on Stephen Arrendell, "Getting It Together," *Travel Weekly*, May 31, 1993.

[37]Rick Fairlie, "It's in the Mail," op. cit.

[38]Personal conversation with Jay R. Schrock, October 28, 2002.

naturally wanted to sell as many seats as possible and found that they could sell blocks of seats to wholesalers close to departure dates. These tickets were for specific destinations around which tour wholesalers built a tour. Wholesalers then sold their tours directly through retail agents.

The tour wholesale business is concentrated with about one hundred independent tour wholesalers; however, ten major companies account for about 30 percent of the industry's business. Tour wholesalers offer a wide range of tours at various prices to many destinations. This segment of the industry is characterized by three key types of wholesalers:

1. An independent tour wholesaler
2. An airline working in close cooperation with a tour wholesaler
3. A retail travel agent who packages tours for his or her clients

In addition, incentive travel houses and various travel clubs round out the tour wholesale business.[39]

Certified Travel Counselor (CTC)

Leading experts in the travel industry worked together to form an Institute of Certified Travel Agents (ICTA). The ICTA offers specialized professional studies for those seeking higher proficiency in the travel industry. The professional designation of CTC is awarded to individuals who have successfully passed examinations and who have five years full-time experience in a travel agency or in the marketing and promotion of travel.[40]

National Offices of Tourism (NOT)

National offices of tourism seek to improve the economy of the country they represent by increasing the number of visitors and consequently their spending in the country. Connected to this function is the responsibility to oversee and ensure that hotels, transport systems, tour operators, and tour guides maintain high standards in the care and consideration of the tourist.[41] The main activities of NOTs are as follows:

✔ Publicizing the country
✔ Assisting and advising certain types of travelers
✔ Creating demand for certain destinations
✔ Supplying information
✔ Ensuring that the destination is up to expectations
✔ Advertising[42]

[39]This section draws on McIntosh and Goeldner, op cit., pp. 100–103.

[40]http://www.icta.com/aboutict.htm.

[41]John R. Walker. *Tourism,* San Diego: Tourism Publications, 2003, p. 43.

[42]Ibid. p. 64.

Personal Profile: Patti Roscoe

Patricia L. Roscoe, chairperson of Patti Roscoe and Associates (PRA) and Roscoe/Coltrell Inc. (RCI), landed in California in 1966, charmed by the beautiful San Diego sun compared to the cold winters in Buffalo, New York, her hometown. She was a young, brilliant middle manager who was to face the challenges of a time period when women were expected to become either nurses or teachers. She became involved with the hotel industry, working for a large private resort hotel, the Vacation Village. Those were the years to be remembered. She gained a very thorough knowledge of Southern California tourism, as well as of the inherent mechanisms of the industry. With the unforgettable help and guidance of her manager, she began to lay the foundations of her future career as a very successful leader in the field. The outstanding skills that she learned are, in fact, the very basis of her many accomplishments.

The list of her awards and honors is astounding: She earned the prestigious CITE distinction (Certified Incentive Travel Executive), she was named San Diego Woman of Accomplishment in 1983, and in February, 1990, Ms. Roscoe was honored as San Diego's 1989 Allied Member of the Year during the tourism industry Gold Key Awards. In 1990, she was given the Wonder Woman Award by the U.S. Small Business Administration for her outstanding achievements in the field. In 1993, the San Diego Convention and Visitors Bureau conferred on her the prestigious RCA Lubach Award for her contributions to the industry.

She is also extremely involved in civic and tourism organizations, including the Rotary Club, the American Lung Association of San Diego and Imperial Counties, and the San Diego Convention and Visitors Bureau.

The key to her success perhaps lies in her remarkable skills of interacting with people. It is the human resources, in fact, that represent the major strength of PRA. Its employees are experienced, dedicated, and service oriented. But what makes them so efficient is their dedication to working together as a team. Patti Roscoe guides, inspires, and motivates these teams. She is a self-admitted "softy," a creative and emotional leader who enjoys training her employees and following their growth step by step, to eventually give them the power of initiative they deserve, as a tool to encourage their creativity and originality. She constantly seeks to balance the concept of teamwork with the individual goals and private lives of her employees. It is through the achievement of such a balance that a profitable, healthy community is preserved. PRA is a bit more than a community, however: It is a family, and just like a mother, Patti's formula is discipline and love. At the same time, Patti's leading efforts are aimed at training her employees to "think outside of the box," and "keep one's view as broad as possible," which is the only way to rise above the commonplace, the rhetorical, and the trivial, to escape provincialism, and thus become unique individuals.

That's how the magic is done. PRA excels in creating "something that becomes exclusively yours—that has never been done before." PRA is decentralized into service teams to foster an entrepreneurial environment in which initiative and creativity can be boosted to the fullest. Therefore, PRA staff design personalized, unique events to give their customers an unforgettable time.

Since its opening in 1981, PRA has become one of the most successful destination management companies in the country, providing personal, caring service characterized by flexibility and creativity.

Destination Management Companies (DMCs)

A **destination management company** is a service organization within the visitor industry that offers a host of programs and services to meet clients' needs. Initially, a destination management sales manager concentrates on selling the destination to meeting planners and performance improvement companies (incentive houses).

The needs of such groups may be as simple as an airport pick-up or as involved as an international sales convention with theme parties. DMCs work closely with hotels; sometimes DMCs book rooms, and other times hotels request the DMC's know-how on organizing theme parties.

Patricia Roscoe, chairperson of Patti Roscoe and Associates (PRA), says that meeting planners often have a choice of several destinations and might ask, "Why should I pick your destination?" The answer is that a DMC does everything, including airport greetings, transportation to the hotel, VIP check-in, theme parties, sponsoring programs, organizing competitive sports events, and so on, depending on budget.

Sales managers associated with DMCs obtain leads, which are potential clients, from the following sources:
- ✔ Hotels
- ✔ Trade shows
- ✔ Convention and visitors bureaus
- ✔ Cold calls
- ✔ Incentive houses
- ✔ Meeting planners

Each sales manager has a staff or team that would include the following:
- ✔ Special events manager, who will have expertise in sound, lighting, staging, and so on
- ✔ Accounts manager, who is an assistant to the sales manager
- ✔ Operations manager, who coordinates everything, especially on-site arrangements, to ensure that what is sold actually happens.

For example, Patti Roscoe's destination management company organized meetings, accommodations, meals, beverages, and theme parties for 2,000 Ford Motor Company dealers in nine groups over three days.

Roscoe also works closely with incentive houses, such as Carlson Marketing or Meritz Travel. These incentive houses approach a company and offer to evaluate and set up incentive plans for the sales team, including whatever it takes to motivate them. Once approved, Carlson contacts a destination management company and asks for a program.

In conclusion, thousands of companies and associations hold meetings and conventions all over the country. Many of these organizations use the services of professional meeting planners, who in turn seek out suitable destinations for the meetings and conventions.

Why People Travel

There are many reasons why people travel, however they fall under two main headings: travel for pleasure and travel for business. Research indicates that when consumers are asked what they associate most with success and accomplishment, the number one response is travel for pleasure.

Marbella Beach Resort,
Marbella, Spain

Among the reasons people travel for pleasure are the following:
- ✔ Visiting friends and relatives
- ✔ Health
- ✔ Enlightenment, education
- ✔ Beauty, nature, and national parks
- ✔ Religion
- ✔ Indulgence
- ✔ Sports
- ✔ Festivals
- ✔ Shopping
- ✔ Fun of the trip
- ✔ Gaming
- ✔ Adventure
- ✔ Heritage
- ✔ Ecotourism
- ✔ Attractions

Pleasure Travel

Seventy-five percent of domestic travel is for pleasure (leisure, recreation, holidays, and visiting friends and relatives—VFR). Approximately 670 million person-trips are taken for pleasure, according to the United States Travel Data Center's (USTDC) national travel survey. Nearly half of all the pleasure travelers visited friends and relatives.

The motivation for **pleasure travel** can be compared to Maslow's hierarchy of human needs. Maslow suggests that people have five sets of basic needs:

1. *Physiological needs:* food, water, oxygen, sex, etc.
2. *Safety needs:* security, stability, order, protection
3. *Love needs:* affection, identification, belonging (family and friends)

4. *Esteem needs:* self-respect, prestige, success, achievement
5. *Self-actualization needs:* self-fulfillment[43]

Some people in their late teens and early twenties may be sun, sand, and sea travelers—the spring break variety. Others may be more interested in the cultural and sporting activities associated with travel—or even the educational aspects.

McIntosh and Goeldner suggest that basic travel motivations can be divided into four categories:

1. *Physical motivator:* physical rest, sporting, and beach activities; healthful and relaxing entertainment
2. *Cultural motivator:* the desire for knowledge of other countries—music, art, folklore, dances, paintings, and religion
3. *Interpersonal motivator:* the desire to meet new people; to visit friends or relatives; to escape from the routine, the family, or the neighbor; or to make new friends
4. *Status and prestige motivator:* the desire for recognition, attention, appreciation, and a good reputation[44]

When surveyed, people tend to list the following reasons for travel:
✔ To experience new and different surroundings
✔ To experience other cultures
✔ To rest and relax
✔ To visit friends and family
✔ To view, or participate, in sporting/recreational activities

Travel is likely to increase in the coming years, which will have a significant impact on tourism. Some of the reasons for the anticipated increases are as follows:
✔ *Longer life span.* The average person in the United States now has a life expectancy of about seventy-five years. In fact, in just a few years, some baby boomers will be taking early retirement.
✔ *Flexible working hours.* Today, many people work four, ten-hour days and have longer weekends. Of course, many others—especially in the hospitality and tourism industries—work on weekends and have leisure time during the week.
✔ *Early retirement.* Increasingly, people are being given the opportunity to retire at age fifty-five. This early retirement is generally granted to employees with thirty years of service to their company or government agency.
✔ *Greater ease of travel.* Today, it is easier to travel on holidays and weekends, for both business and leisure purposes. Each mode of travel affords increasing opportunities to take advantage of the additional leisure time.
✔ *Tendency to take shorter, more frequent trips.* People now tend to take shorter, but more frequent, minivacations rather than taking all of their

---

[43]Abraham Maslow, "A Theory of Human Motivations," *Psychological Review*, vol. 50, 1943, pp. 370–396.

[44]McIntosh and Goeldner, op. cit., p. 131.

vacation time at once. Europeans generally take much longer vacations than North Americans. For them, four weeks is the normal vacation benefit of new employees, and six weeks is typical after a few years.

✔ *Increase in the standard of living.* More people in many developing countries have increased their income and wish to travel. China, with its newfound enterprise zones is producing hundreds of thousands of entrepreneurs who will soon be traveling to foreign countries. Millions of East European residents of the former Soviet Block countries now have the capability and the right to travel. And finally, an additional 300 million people will soon have passports.

Stanley Plog, a respected social scientist, has suggested that travelers can be separated into two extremes: (1) psychocentrics, who prefer familiar travel destinations, and (2) allocentrics, who prefer new and different destinations.

Most travelers fall into a large bell-shaped curve between these two extremes. Figure 2–4 illustrates the types of destinations that psychocentrics and allocentrics are likely to visit. Psychocentrics, as the figure illustrates, prefer to travel to well-known destinations that have been visited by millions before. These destinations tend to be constant and predictable. Allocentric personalities tend to be more adventurous, curious, energetic, and outgoing; they will usually be attracted to novel destinations like the South Pacific, Asia, and Africa. Generally, twice as many people are inclined to be allocentric. This has an effect on small-scale tourist areas. First visited by allocentrics, the area (be

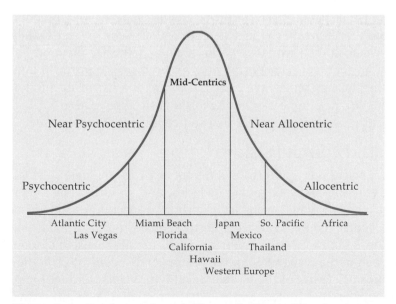

Figure 2–4 *Psychocentric and Allocentric Types of Destinations*
(Adapted from Stanley Plog, "Why Destination Areas Rise and Fall in Popularity," a paper presented to the Southern California Chapter of the Travel Research Association, October 10, 1972, as cited in Edward Mayo and Lance Jarvis, The Psychology of Leisure Travel, Boston: CBI Publishing Company, 1981, p. 118.)

it a village, town, or resort) then becomes more popular and is forced into becoming more commercialized. Waikiki Beach on Oahu is an example of this—as few as thirty years ago, there were no high-rise hotels there.

Motivations for Travel

Over the course of history, the motivations for most travel have been fairly obvious: religion, conventions, economic gain, war, escape, migration. It would seem that motives for what is left—travel for pleasure—would be straightforward and plainly understandable. This, however, is not the case. Unfortunately, little research has been undertaken to reveal the reasons why people travel and vacation. Because research and an established motivation theory are lacking, the comments included here are necessarily impressionistic and are made principally to stimulate investigation.

Some surprising findings show up in consumer research. A study asked consumers which of twenty-two items they associated with success and accomplishment. The leading choice was "travel for pleasure." As psychologist Abraham Maslow theorized, at the very top of the hierarchy of human needs seem to be those for self-actualization. This desire reflects the fundamental need to develop one's own potential, to gain esthetic stimulation, to create or build one's own personality and character. Certainly there are tremendous variations in what individuals need at the self-actualization level. Millions of people prefer not to travel or vacation because they are more comfortable in their present circumstances. They may be afraid to leave those circumstances, or to take the chance of being injured or victimized while traveling or visiting a strange destination. Other people seem to thrive on the change brought about by travel. Some need the letdown of a quiet vacation; others seek the same pitch of excitement that exists in their workday world. If we hypothesize the need for change, for diversion, for new scenery, for new experiences, then travel and vacationing take their place somewhere near the top of the list of means for meeting these needs. In fact, some psychotherapists posit a basic need for fun and freedom. Pleasure travel is certainly a rich source for fulfilling this need.

Different Places for Different People

Obviously, travelers select destinations for different reasons—climate, history or culture, sports, entertainment, shopping facilities, and so forth. The major appeal of England for Americans seems to be history and culture. American Express surveyed people going to several destinations—Florida, California, Mexico, Hawaii, the Bahamas, Jamaica, Puerto Rico, the Virgin Islands, and Barbados. Almost half of the respondents were professionals, generally middle-aged, and well educated. Many of them were wealthy travelers who took frequent vacations outside the United States. These respondents ranked the appeals of travel in descending order of importance:
- ✔ Scenic beauty
- ✔ Pleasant attitudes of local people
- ✔ Suitable accommodations
- ✔ Rest and relaxation

✔ Airfare cost
✔ Historical and cultural interests
✔ Cuisine
✔ Water sports
✔ Entertainment (e.g., nightlife)
✔ Shopping facilities
✔ Sports (golfing and tennis)

Four basic considerations emerged as factors influencing travel: entertainment, purchase opportunities, climate for comfort, and cost. Even within a group, of course, different factors apply. One individual may select a destination primarily because of opportunities for challenging golf and tennis, another because of the friendly local people, and another because the place offers rest and relaxation. Most of the group would, however, be influenced by air fare costs.

Expectation and Reality

Professors Karen Smith and Claudia Green of New York and Pace Universities comment: With the growth in international tourism, challenges have emerged for the traveler as well as the destination location.[45] Travelers often have culturally based expectations for the travel experience that may or may not be met by international travel. Current research is focusing on the impact of the traveler's culture on the expectations for service as well as ways to assess customer expectations and evaluate customer satisfaction. Service providers in destination locations are making efforts to meet the needs of diverse populations of travelers.

Satisfaction, or dissatisfaction, with the travel experience, of course, depends on how it is viewed by the traveler. A glorious sunset and majestic mountain may be seen as a great bore if an individual is highly gregarious and alone on the trip. The best service in a restaurant with the finest food and decor is meaningless if the person is dyspeptic at the moment. One traveler loves the rain, another despises it. Mountains are one person's delight, heights make another person dizzy. The anthropologist revels in the remote village, the city dweller finds the same place dull. So much depends on what the person expects of the experience and how he or she actually experiences it.

Travel is an experience, not a tangible object. It results in psychic reward or punishment. It creates pleasant anticipation or aversion, excitement and challenge, or fatigue and disappointment. The anticipation, the experience, and the memory occur in the mind, leaving no tangible evidence as to why travel was undertaken and why the same trip is experienced in so many different ways by different people. Travel literature and films often falsify reality or are shot so selectively that the actual environment is not recognizable by the visitor. The phony shot that makes the pool look longer than it is, the colors that never exist in nature, the lavish buffet that was rigged especially for the photograph,

[45]Karen Smith, New York University and Claudia Green, Pace University.

the glorious sunset that occurs once a year—all of this creates expectations that cannot be realized, and leads to disappointment.

Push/Pull Model

An interesting way of modeling travel motivations is to divide them into factors that pull, that is, attractions, and those that push, that is, personal needs. Arlin Epperson, a travel consultant, proposes the push/pull model. He lists push factors as the intangible desires that are generated from within the person. Examples include those shown in Figure 2–4.

Disney World attracts those motivated by a pull factor. A relaxing week on a Caribbean beach is probably inspired by a push factor. Much travel is likely motivated to some degree by both push and pull factors. For example, a vacation in an isolated mountain cabin would allow for escape, self-discovery, and rest, while at the same time providing scenic beauty.

Business Travel

Twenty-five to thirty percent of all airline travel is undertaken by business travelers. An airline study shows that the business–leisure mix varies widely according to destination area. More than 90 percent of the travel between the United States and the Caribbean is for pleasure. The figure for U.S. mainland to Hawaii pleasure travel is more than 80 percent; for United States–trans-Atlantic flights, about 70 percent; and for United States to Latin America flights, also 70 percent. Pleasure is the predominant reason for slightly more than 60 percent of passengers' flying between the United States and the Asia-Pacific area.

About 60 to 70 percent of the guests who check into Sheraton Hotels around the world are traveling for business reasons. Much **business travel** is hard work, whether it is travel in one's own automobile, or in the luxury of a first-class seat aboard an airline. A good portion of business travel is, however, mixed with pleasure.

It is difficult to say whether as much as half of his or her time may be spent gambling or gamboling. The trip to Europe may involve contacting potential customers, but it also may allow for sight-seeing or for an evening at the Folies Bergere.

Business travel accounts for approximately 20 percent of all travel in the United States and is a $170 billion industry. Counted as business travelers are those who travel for business purposes such as meetings; all kinds of sales, including corporate, regional, product, etc.; conventions; trade shows and expositions; and combinations of more than one. In the United States, meetings and conventions alone attract millions of people annually. Sometimes the distinction between business and leisure travel becomes blurred. If a convention attendee in Atlanta decides to stay on for a few days after the conference, are they to be considered a "business" or "leisure" traveler? Business travelers, when compared to leisure travelers, tend to be younger, spend more money, travel further, and travel in smaller groups, but they do not stay as long.

Business travel has increased in recent years due to the growth of convention centers in a number of cities. Similarly, business travelers have given a boost to hotels, restaurants, and auto rental companies. A hotel located near a major convention center often runs a higher occupancy and average daily rate (ADR) than other types of hotels. Business trips to meetings generally last from one to three days. Business travel to attend conventions and trade shows ranges from about five to eight days. For most companies, the third largest controllable expense is business travel and entertainment.

The typical business traveler still resembles the traveling salesperson of old. He or she is thirty-nine years old, married, has a median household income of $40,000 to $50,000, and holds a professional or management job. One in five employed Americans takes at least one overnight business trip each year. Female business travelers, of which there are approximately 16 million, comprise about 29 percent of all U.S. business travelers, and are on the increase. This has prompted hotel operators to take note of the needs and concerns of women business travelers.

Business travel, long the mainstay of airlines and hotels, will likely gradually decline as a percentage of all travel, which includes leisure travel. Leisure travel is forecast to increase due to a favorable economic climate, which in turn produces increased discretionary income. Many people now have more leisure time and higher levels of education, and the cost of travel has remained constant, or dropped, compared to inflation and other costs combined. These factors indicate a bright future for the travel industry.

An analysis of business travel costs by the *Wall Street Journal* tracks travel prices with the weekly Dow Jones Travel Index, which looks at average business and leisure fares on twenty major routes, as well as the cost of hotel rooms and car rentals. An annual increase in travel costs of four percent is significant for a group who spends upwards of $130 billion a year in travel. Bob Litchman, head of corporate travel at Bay Networks in Santa Clara, California, says a four percent increase would add $600,000 to his domestic travel budget. Business travelers pay most of the increases, economists say, because they are the passengers who really contribute to an airline's earnings. The major domestic airlines receive thirty-three cents per passenger per mile for full-fare tickets—more than twice what they get for discounted tickets. In other words, airlines sometimes lose money on their leisure travelers and make money with their business travelers.

An increasing number of business travelers are able to make their own travel arrangements on-line. For example, in the middle of a client meeting Suzie Aust, a meeting consultant, realizes that she has forgotten to book the next day's flight. She pulls out her laptop, gets on-line, and books the flight. Corporate America is worried about travelers like Suzie because they are often able to skirt corporate policies when making their own reservations. Some companies use a product from Microsoft and American Express. Code-named Rome, the product will allow companies to control their own travelers by insisting that employees buy their own tickets through American Express. Needless

*Execustay by Marriott
Corporate Apartment*

to say, American and United Airlines are each rolling out similar products. Ed Gilligan, president of corporate services for American Express, estimates that American companies lose $15 billion a year due to deviations from corporate policy. And the portion of that sum lost to on-line reservation systems is "ramping up quickly," he says. About 1.8 million business travelers are wired, according to Addison Schonland, director of aviation, travel, and marketing for CIC Research, in San Diego. The Eastman Group, a Newport Beach, California, management consulting and travel software group, predicts that by 2006, 99 percent of all airline travel will be ticketless.

Hotels are, for many business travelers, supposed to be a home away from home. However, in some cases, they are more like the office away from the office. For hotels that are aiming to please their business travelers, they must not overlook the homier touches such as feather pillows and old-fashioned innkeeping virtues: cleanliness, comfort, safety, attentive service, and peace and quiet.

Trends in Business Travel

Businesses are trimming perks for their employees, and more business travelers are spending weekends on the road and more nights in economy hotels, according to an American Express survey. The survey indicates the following:

- ✔ More companies require employees to take the lowest reasonable airfare available. That means more employees are flying in and out of less-convenient airports, and they are taking connecting, instead of nonstop, flights.
- ✔ Thirty-seven percent make employees stay over a Saturday night when it will reduce the airfare.

✔ Seventy-seven percent impose a size limit on rental cars, up from 70 percent.

✔ Fourteen percent regularly make employees stay in economy hotels such as Hampton Inn or Courtyard by Marriott.

There will be an increase in **ticketless travel** and rental car navigation systems.

For frequent flyers, American Airlines has introduced frequent-flyer mileage for home mortgages—a mile is earned for every dollar of interest paid. This is in addition to one mile for every dollar spent on long-distance calls placed with MCI and one mile for every dollar charged on the Citibank Visa Card. Experts agree that almost all of the new mileage promotions will come from nonflying activities.

The number of female business travelers will increase, and airlines, hotels, restaurants, car rental agencies, and associated businesses will need to pay increasing attention in order to exceed their expectations.

Check Your Knowledge

1. What is TOT? What is the TOT in your city of residency?
2. Brainstorm on the services offered by AMEX.

Social and Cultural Impact of Tourism

From a social and cultural perspective, tourism can leave both positive and negative impacts on communities. Undoubtedly, tourism has made significant contributions to international understanding. World tourism organizations recognize that tourism is a means of enhancing international understanding, peace, prosperity, and universal respect for, and observance of, human rights and fundamental freedom for all without distinction as to race, sex, language, or religion. Tourism can be a very interesting sociocultural phenomenon. Seeing how others live is an interest of many tourists, and the exchange of sociocultural values and activities is rewarding.

Providing that the number of tourists is manageable and that they respect the host community's sociocultural norms and values, tourism provides an opportunity for a number of social interactions. A London pub or a New York café are examples of good places for social interaction. Similarly, depending on the reason for the tourist visit, myriad opportunities are available to interact both socially and culturally. Even a visit to another part of the United States would be both socially and culturally stimulating. For example, New Orleans has a very diverse social and cultural heritage. Over the years, the city has been occupied by Spanish, French, British, and Americans. The food, music, dance, and social norms are unique to the area.

The competitiveness of international destinations is based on such attributes as service quality as well as value for the price, safety, security, entertainment, weather, infrastructure, and natural environment.[46] Political stability is also important in determining the desirability of a destination for international tourism. Imagine the feelings of an employee in a developing country who earns perhaps $5 per day when he or she sees wealthy tourists flaunting money, jewelry, and a lifestyle not obtainable. Another example might be nude or scantily clad tourists sunbathing in a Moslem country. Critics argue that, at best, tourism dilutes the culture of a country by imposing the culture of the mass tourism market. Most of the food prepared in the Western-style hotels is American or European, with perhaps the addition of an Americanized local dish.

Most resorts offer little opportunity for meaningful social interaction between the tourist and the host community. Developers build the hotel (which can cause disruptions as well as create opportunities); likely as not, an international hotel company will manage the hotel, which may mean that the top positions are filled by non-natives, leaving only the lower positions to the locals.

Proponents of the sociocultural benefits of tourism are able to point out that tourism is a clean and green industry, that some hotels are built with great concern for the environment and use local craftspeople, designers, and materials in order to harmonize with the locals. Tourism brings new revenue to the area; it also creates and maintains higher levels of employment than if there were no tourism. In some countries, a hotel may be restricted as to the number of foreigners it employs and the length of their contracts. This allows for the promotion of the local employees to higher positions. Tourism may act as a catalyst for the development of the community because taxes help the government provide other services such as schools, hospitals, and so on. In addition, tourists often enjoy the cultural exchanges they have at all levels in the community. The excursions, shopping, dancing, and so on serve to embellish the tourists' experiences.

Tourism is not likely to have a significant sociocultural impact in developed countries, where the economy is active and well diversified.[47] The most noticeable change in established value patterns and behavior occurs when tourism is a major contributor to the gross national product.

In some developing countries tourism is a major contributor to the GNP. However, tourism may contribute to the generation gap between the young,

[46]Ibid. Personal correspondence Karen Smith and Claudia Green June 28, 2000.

[47]Van Harssel, op. cit., p. 190.

who are quick to adapt to the ways of the tourists, and the older people, who hold more traditional values.

Efforts to preserve the cultural heritage of a community may be further eroded when tourist "junk" is imported and offered for sale to tourists. In every society, people have opposing points of view about tourism development and cultural heritage preservation. The important thing to remember is to strike a balance between what is appropriate for a destination in terms of the number of tourists and the type of tourists that the community is capable of sustaining.

An example of how tourism can have a negative impact is shown in the center of Paris, in the once-beautiful park known as the Bois de Bologna, which now looks more like a refugee camp. Tourists have been allowed to take over with a massive campsite that includes dilapidated trailers, laundry hanging on makeshift clotheslines, and pets along for the vacation. This is a real shanty town in the heart of one of the world's most beautiful cities.

Further examples of tourism pollution include the famous beaches in the south of France. The Cote d'Azure for years has been a popular haunt of the rich and famous. Cities like Nice, St. Tropez, and Juez le Pain became celebrity hangouts once they were discovered in the 1950s and 1960s. Now at the height of the season, public beaches are wall-to-wall people. Private beaches will rent a parasol and a six-foot by four-foot plot for the day for approximately $40.

The effects of too many tourists have necessitated that the famous Cathedral of Notre Dame restrict the number of visitors to 400 per day, down from several thousand. The sheer number of visitors was causing serious problems for the building.

Similarly, the prehistoric cave paintings at Lascoux in southwest France were closed in 1964 to prevent further deterioration of the paintings. Human breath, which gives off CO_2, is harmful to paint. Now, its replica, Lascoux II, which was built to allow visitors a chance to experience the caves, is in trouble for the same reason.

Beach Scenes Cote d'Azure (Used with permission of the French Government Tourist Office.)

Corporate Profile: Club Med

In 1950, a Belgian diamond cutter and water polo champion conceived the first Club Med village, funded with army surplus tax money, on the little Spanish island of Majorca. The goal of that first resort was to unite people from diverse backgrounds, encourage them to share a good time, and offer them a unique escape from the stress and the tension of the everyday events of post-World War II Europe. The first adventurous vacationers to experience that new environment were mostly young couples or singles, living together in a beautiful natural setting, enjoying the atmosphere of camaraderie and no worries, playing sports, or just simply relaxing on a warm soft beach.

The following decade was a particularly profitable one, because of the overall social climate that characterized the 1960s. The young generation, generally speaking, was wrapped up in a whirl of ideals, such as peace, communion, and the sharing of feelings and experiences, all in the framework of a return to nature. The so-called flowerchild phenomenon saw the young long for a return to primitive purity, innocence, and freedom of expression. It is not surprising, then, that Club Med's clientele rose by 500 percent in that decade. In fact, the features that characterized the resorts made them just the right environment to meet the needs of this target market. Club Med began its expansion throughout the Mediterranean coastlines and islands, including Greece and Italy. Centers began to spring up on the coasts of Africa and the Middle East. Today Club Med—short for Mediterranean—has more than one hundred resorts and vacation villages around the world, hosted by twenty-eight countries in the Mediterranean as well as in the Caribbean, Africa, Mexico, the Bahamas, South Pacific, South America, Asia, and the United States. The little village in Majorca blossomed into a colorful, joyful, sunny, colossal empire: Club Med is the world's largest vacation village organization and the ninth largest hotel chain, with 93,000 beds and 20,000 employees. More than 9 million guests have come to the villages since 1950.

Today's philosophy doesn't differ much from the original one. Club Med intends to provide a spectacular nat-

A Club Med Resort

ural setting in which its guests can enjoy life and its amenities, away from the troubles and the worries of the everyday frantic rat race. The theme on the printed advertisements points straight to this: "Club Med: Life as it should be." Sports, various entertaining activities, good food, real concern for guests' needs, and a carefree lifestyle worked wonders. Imagine all of these amenities in the context of white sand beaches and a clear blue sea that seems to stretch out indefinitely to meet a virtually cloudless sky at the horizon.

Club Med's original formula was copied by several other organizations in the travel and tourism industry. The increased competition caused Club Med to revise its management strategies and develop a different product in order to gain and hold market share. Changes in the industry were accompanied by social changes. As the years went by, the baby boomers of the 1960s and 1970s grew up, got married, and began to travel with their families. The target market thus changed again, and the necessity to change along with the market was promptly acknowledged.

The policy Club Med's managers embraced was one of differentiation and flexibility. Through assiduous market research, studies, and surveys, Club Med identified the continuously changing needs and characteristics of both the market and the clientele. On the basis of their results, they were able to take effective action to keep up with such evolution. Marketing strategies therefore were re-elaborated, and the product Club Med offers was repackaged according to the demands of the industry, while still remaining faithful to the original philosophy. The image of Club Med was also reconsidered in order to determine the most appropriate one at all times.

Other significant changes included an entrance into the cruise business—Club Med I is a luxurious cruise ship that offers the excitement of yachting (thanks to a retractable platform that allows activities such as waterskiing, diving, etc.) together with the comforts of the cruise. Activities within the village were also improved and upgraded, following the guests' requests for more in-depth sports teaching, more amenities in the rooms, specialized restaurants, more security, and communication tools.

The clientele target was also widened: Club Med now attempts to attract customers other than the original youth/couples. As a consequence, the individual villages were updated by specializing in a particular area. Although all clubs offer the same basic services, some focus mainly on sports, some on tours and excursions, some on convention and meeting facilities, some on entertainment, and so on. Customers now range from sports enthusiasts to families (mini-clubs and baby-clubs were recently established), honeymooners, and corporate clients. The new trend at the moment is that of finding ways to attract the older clientele.

Club Med also has had another innovative idea: Wild Card, which offers a bargain rate to vacationers who don't mind gambling on which village they visit. Wild Card confirms participants on a one-week vacation at one of Club Med's Villages in the Bahamas, Caribbean, or Mexico for $999 per person, double occupancy; this is a savings of up to $500 over the weekly standard rate. Included is the price of the airfare from specified gateway cities.

Wild Card presents a win-win situation. Club Med wins because it can utilize vacant space on air charters and accommodations; guests win because they get a great vacation at a bargain price. As a result, about 75 percent of Wild Card bookings are from first-time guests. This means a great deal of new business is being generated in addition to Club Med's 50 percent repeat business rates—one of the highest in the resort industry.[1]

To cope with the changes and implementations in the global structure of the villages, human resources staff (GOs—gentle organizers, etc.) also have been selected and trained more thoroughly. GOs come from all over the world; they must have some foreign language proficiency (to keep up with an extremely cosmopolitan clientele), skills in sports or entertainment, and, most of all, be extremely enthusiastic and very people oriented. In fact, the spirit of the village depends almost entirely on the creative ideas and contact generated by the staff.

Overall, Club Med has shown a very remarkable ability to reinvent itself according to the continuous evolution of the market and society. The genuine commitment to excellence that has been demonstrated should help Club Med retain its status as the ultimate destination resort organization.

---

[1]Joel Sleed, *"Club Med Tells Its Customers Where to Go,"* San Diego Union-Tribune, February 4, 1993, p. D4.

Just imagine what will happen when another 300 million people become tourists by virtue of increasing standards of living and more people obtaining passports. Currently only about 15 percent of the U.S. population has passports. The population of Eastern Europe and the nouveau riche of the Pacific Rim countries will substantially add to the potential number of tourists.

Ecotourism

Within the past few years, the tourism industry has witnessed a phenomenon that continues to take tourists and industry leaders alike by storm. **Ecotourism,** often dubbed "adventure tourism," "responsible tourism," or "**sustainable tourism,**" has become the fastest growing segment within the world's largest industry. For tourists, it is the latest trend. For ecologists, scientists, and students, it is a lifelong dream. And for the tourism industry leaders, it is a potentially prosperous business. But amidst the awe of what ecotourism can provide,

*The Prehistoric Cave
Paintings at Lascoux*
(Used with permission of
the French Government
Tourist Office.)

there has been much confusion and controversy as to what ecotourism actually is and whether it actually works.

Although the term may be new—it has only been in existence for about a decade—the concept has been alive for much longer. There is no true definition of what ecotourism really is, perhaps because it is difficult to describe and because there have been many distinct interpretations of the concept. Whether it is called ecotourism, adventure tourism, or nature travel, the definitions contain elements and concepts that are associated with what is known as sustainable development.[48] It is believed that tourism—ecotourism in particular—is a key tool in achieving sustainable development, which is "to meet the needs of the present without compromising the ability of the future generations to meet their own needs."[49] One of the most widely accepted descriptions is that of The Ecotourism Society, an organization based in the United States, in which ecotourism is described as "responsible travel to natural areas that conserves the environment and sustains the well-being of the local people."[50]

In the early 1970s, people in several remote areas of the world saw that tourism could be important, however they did not want to destroy the exotic environment that surrounded them. One such place was Cancun, Mexico. At the time, Cancun was a prime beach location, but the number of tourists was not very high. Unlike today, there were more natives than visitors. Developers recognized the potential Cancun had and "drew up a master plan that placed priority on environmental protection."[51] Unfortunately, Mexico began to experience political and economic instability. The recession caused the government and business leaders to scramble to find a way to bring money into the economy—

[48]Internet: David T. Schaller, "Indigenous Ecotourism and Sustainable Development: The Case Study of Rio Blanco, Ecuador," http://www.geog.umn.edu/~ shaller/Section2RioBlanco.html.

[49]Internet: Paul Samson, "The Concept of Sustainable Development," Green Cross International, July 1995. http://greencross.unige.ch/greencross/digiforum/concept.html.

[50]"Tourism's Green Machine," Glenn Hasek. *Hotel and Motel Management*, vol. 209, no. 17, October 3, 1994, pp. 25–26.

[51]"Ecotourism: A Dream Diluted," Mary Farquharson. *Business Mexico*, vol. 2, no. 6, June 1992, pp. 8–11.

Tourists visit Kenya to view giraffes such as these—one example of ecotourism

specifically, U.S. dollars. Tourism in Mexico was, then, one of the few industries in the country that showed signs of growth. Instead of having environmentally friendly attractions, however, as Cancun was meant to have, it was sacrificed in order to make room for large-scale development.[52]

As a result, the natives were moved off their homeland and pushed onto the side of a mountain. They live in what looks like cardboard shacks and do not have running water or a sewage system. The area beaches are becoming cluttered with travelers and garbage and the reef that is found off of the coastline has been damaged by ships coming into the wharf. Water treatment is insufficient and it is practically impossible to meet the growing capacity requirements.[53] Mass tourism has proven to be destructive.

As similar stories become known to the world, ecologists, together with tourism leaders, realize how important it is to preserve the environment so that generations to come can continue to enjoy earth's natural beauty. Because of this, most ecotourism destinations can be found in areas with vast natural surroundings and plentiful flora and fauna. Places like deserts, tropical rainforests, coral reefs, and ice glaciers are prime locations. Also important in ecotourism is the presence of a culture that is unique to the visitor. The focus of ecotourism is to provide tourists with new knowledge about a certain natural area and the culture that is found within, along with a little bit of adventure. As for the natives, ecotourism is to help improve the local economy and conservation efforts. All parties are to gain a new appreciation for nature and people.

Thus far, ecotourism projects tend to be developed on a small scale. It is much easier to control such sites, particularly because of limits that are normally set upon the community, the local tourism business, and the tourists. Limitations may include strict control of the amount of water and electricity being used, tougher recycling measures, regulating park and market hours, and more importantly, limiting the number of visitors to a certain location at one

[52]Ibid.
[53]Ibid.

time, and limiting the size of the business. Another reason ecotourism projects are kept small is to allow more "in depth" tours and educational opportunities.

Generally speaking, most of the more popular ecotourism destinations are located in underdeveloped and developing countries. As vacationers are becoming more adventurous and are visiting remote, exotic places, inclusively, they are participating in activities that, hopefully, impact nature, host communities, and themselves, in a positive manner. However, because of the growing interests of travelers, many developed countries are following the trend. It is apparent from Yellowstone National Park in the United States to the Mayan Ruins of Tikal in Guatemala; from the Amazon River in Brazil to the vast Safari lands of Kenya; from the snow-capped Himalayas in Nepal to the sultry jungles of Thailand; and from the Great Barrier Reef in Australia to the massive ice glaciers in Antarctica. There is no doubt that this is an attractive trend in many parts of the world.

Some of the more successful examples of ecotourism can be found in Central America, the Caribbean, Africa (particularly in Kenya), and Nepal. For instance, "Mundo Maya" is a unique project in that it is a joint endeavor comprising of the countries in which the Maya civilization was, and still is, found. These countries include Belize, El Salvador, Guatemala, Honduras, and the five Mexican states of Quintana Roo, Yucatán, Campeche, Tabasco, and Chiapas. "The area's countless tourist attractions reflect the geographical diversity of the Maya World and its rich, cultural heritage, both ancient and modern. . . ."[54] Tourists can climb the massive, stone pyramids; sit in one of the housing rooms; hike through the jungles; watch for exotic birds, howling monkeys, and other animals; and, in some places, see the coral reefs in the Caribbean coastline. What is especially appealing about Mundo Maya is that the traveler can visit one area or country at a time or take a package that includes every country and major attraction.[55]

Another prosperous site is the U.S. Virgin Islands. Here, developer Stanley Selengut designed an "ecoresort" with the idea that ecotourism does not have to be as big as traditional tourism. Specifically, ecotourism should be more conscious of the damage it causes, or may cause, in an area that is virtually virgin and very fragile. Maho Bay Camps is a series of "luxury" tent/cottages scattered strategically about the island. The camps are not luxurious, but they are sufficiently equipped to accommodate guests, and include communal bathrooms. For the more upscale-minded, Selengut opened a second resort, with private bathrooms, called Harmony, which is made almost entirely from recycled products.

Africa's tourism industry, especially ecotourism, is growing tremendously. The most popular activity is a Safari tour, in which visitors can see, up close, wildlife like elephants, gazelles, lions, buffaloes, cheetahs, and many others. Kenya is an important destination for safaris. Also popular in Africa are the rich rain forests of Rwanda and Zaire, home to several endangered primates, like

---

[54] Internet: "The Mundo Maya Project," http://www.yucatan.com.mx/mayas/ingles/fsl5.html.
[55] Ibid.

the mountain gorillas. These animals, and the area, gained much recognition when Dian Fossey lived in the jungles to study the gorillas.[56]

Thousands of miles away, ecotourism is becoming popular in Southeast Asia, where places like Malaysia, Thailand, and the Philippines are developing tourism programs based on environmental conservation and protection. As with other regions of the world that are covered by dense rain forests, Southeast Asia is home to a vast variety of wild flora and fauna. River boat rides and visiting small villages that dot the islands are also quite popular.

As a result of the concerns about and interests in ecotourism, many conferences have been held to inform the general population and, particularly, the tourism professionals and ecologists about the advantages and disadvantages of ecotourism. Conferences also provide advice and suggestions for running a successful ecotourism attraction. The 1992 Earth Summit, presented by the United Nations in Rio de Janeiro, Brazil, focused on the environment and development in general with tourism being the key to accomplishing sustainable development throughout the world. The Earth Summit also produced **Agenda 21,** which addresses issues pertaining to the environment and sustainable development and is intended to prepare the world to successfully meet the challenges in the coming century.

The World Conference on Sustainable Tourism, held in Spain in 1995, dealt specifically with tourism and resulted in the Charter of Sustainable Tourism. It recognized "the objective of developing a tourism [industry] that meets economic expectations and environmental requirements, and respects not only the social and physical structure of the location, but also the local population".[57] It also emphasizes that "environmentally and culturally vulnerable spaces, both now and in the future, should be given special priority . . . for sustainable tourism development".[58] Sustainable tourism, especially ecotourism, can be a main source of worldwide promotion of sustainable development geared toward tourists and communities in all countries.

Check Your Knowledge

Mini project: Put together, what you would consider your perfect vacation. Your information should include, but not be limited to, information about location, air travel (arrival and departure city), ground transportation, tourist attractions, weather, expense report, and currency exchange.

---

[56]Internet: "Ecotourism: Paradise Gained, or Paradise Lost?" Panos, 1995, Panos. http://www.oneworld.org/panos/panos_eco2.html.

[57]Ibid.

[58]Ibid.

Trends in Tourism and Travel

- ✔ Ecotourism, sustainable tourism, and heritage tourism will continue to grow in importance.
- ✔ Globally, the number of tourist arrivals will continue to increase by about 8 percent per year, topping 1 billion by 2010.
- ✔ Governments will increasingly recognize the importance of tourism not only as an economic force, but also as a social-cultural force of increasing significance.
- ✔ More bilateral treaties are being signed, which will make it easier for tourists to obtain visas to visit other countries.
- ✔ The promotion and development of tourism is moving from the public sector (government) to the private sector (involved industry segments).
- ✔ Internet bookings will increase.
- ✔ Franchising of travel agencies and home-based travel agents will increase.
- ✔ Technology will continue to advance allowing even more information to be available more quickly to more places around the world.
- ✔ Marketing partnerships and corporate alliances will continue to increase.
- ✔ Employment prospects will continue to improve.
- ✔ Ticketless air travel will become commonplace.
- ✔ Travel and tourism bookings via the Internet is increasing rapidly.

Case Study

Airline Commission Caps

Travel agents have begun legal action and public campaigns to combat several airlines' decisions to lower commissions for writing tickets, and have warned of higher ticket costs if other airlines follow. Most U.S. airlines have lowered the commission rate on tickets for domestic flights to a $20 cap for a round-trip fare. International commissions also fell and vary from airline to airline.

As consumers begin to balk at rising ticket prices and Wall Street presses for continued earnings growth, airlines must cut costs by turning to their second largest expense, the $12 billion spent annually for costs such as travel agent commissions. It has become clear that airlines can do nothing about fuel prices and can do very little, if anything, about labor costs. The only area that airline management has any power over is the area of distinction expenses.

American Express Corporate Services Agencies, which books mostly business travelers, warned that if other airlines follow suit, some travel agencies will go out of business. That would send more businesses to airlines' reservation agents, who do not offer the lowest available fares from all carriers, or could result in travel agents passing costs along to consumers.

The American Society of Travel Agents, which represent 24,000 agents, and The Association of Retail Travel Agents, a trade group that represents 4,000 travel agents, have announced they will seek U.S. congressional approval to allow small, "business-sized" travel agents to bargain collectively with the major airlines and to steer customers to "friendly" airlines when negotiating fails. The associations believe that the cut in commissions in less than three years is a slap in the face.

After the introduction of the initial cap of $25 for one-way domestic tickets and $50 for round-trip tickets, many agents complained caps would eliminate jobs and reduce earnings. A class action lawsuit followed on behalf of 33,000 travel agents, alleging price fixing. Some travel agents also steered customers away from other airlines such as Delta in retaliation.

In September 1996, American, Delta, Northwest, and United agreed to pay $72 million in cash to settle the lawsuit.

Discussion Questions

1. If you owned a travel agency, what would your reaction to the reduced commission cap be?
2. What options would you consider?

This case is based on Cliff Edwards, "Travel Agents Assail Commission Cuts." Associated Press, San Diego Union-Tribune, September 23, 1997, p. 2.

Case Study

Developing the San Diego Waterfront

San Diego, California, has a diversified economic base with tourism as an important component of the economy. The city hosts about 18 million tourists who spent some $6 billion, and tourism is steadily expanding each year. Most tourists are domestic, although a fair number of foreigners also visit the city. The attractions for tourists in San Diego are the mild Mediterranean-type climate; attractive natural setting; beaches developed with resort and park facilities; and major attractions including Sea World, the world-famous San Diego Zoo and Wild Animal Park, interesting and well-preserved historic areas, and picturesque shopping districts.

continued

A variety of resort and urban hotels have been developed, the most notable being the historic Hotel del Coronado. The policy of government, which is supported by most residents, is for the continued but controlled development of tourism as a major source of income and employment.

A major focal point for tourism development is the downtown area located next to the waterfront of San Diego Bay. As a result of concerted planning efforts and substantial investment during the past several years, the San Diego downtown is undergoing new development and redevelopment. Changes include a recently completed convention center; the preservation and renovation of numerous shops and restaurants in the historical Gaslamp Quarter; the development of a maritime museum on the waterfront of historic ships; the Seaport Village shopping and restaurant complex and related park, also located on the waterfront; and others. New urban residential complexes are also developing. In response to the revitalization of downtown, several new high-rise hotels have been developed and some historic hotels have been renovated to provide good quality tourist facilities. Many conferences and conventions are now being attracted to the downtown and this area, with its interesting features, has become an important center for tourism for both business conferences and holiday tourists.

San Diego recognizes the importance of its waterfront and the views it affords as a major attraction for both residents and tourists. If properly conserved and carefully developed, waterfronts give an urban area a unique character. However, in the case of San Diego, and some other cities, the economic pressure to develop prime waterfront sites can lead to cutting off public access to the waterfront, thereby preempting waterfront areas from public use and blocking views of the water from inland downtown buildings. In San Diego, the new convention center already stretches along a considerable length of the waterfront and plans are to expand it further along this area. New high-rise hotels near the convention center are blocking waterfront access and views of the bay, and more hotels have been proposed for this area. Expansion is planned for the popular Seaport Village, however this complex is low rise and does not greatly impinge on views. It is designed to provide pedestrian access along the waterfront. Other projects are being considered for development on the waterfront. Thus, there is the dilemma of the waterfront area, the most significant natural feature of the downtown environment, not being effectively integrated into development patterns because of economic development pressures. At the same time, many persons recognize the need to preserve public access, use of the waterfront, and views of the bay. The problem relates particularly to the need for careful land-use planning with utmost consideration given to social and economic implications.

Discussion Questions

1. Why is it considered so desirable to develop public and private amenity features on the waterfront and preserve public access to the waterfront and water views in urban areas? From the residents' standpoint? From the standpoint of developing successful tourism?

2. What approach can San Diego take in properly developing its downtown waterfront area both to achieve economic development objectives and to preserve access to and along the waterfront and views of the adjacent bay?

3. If the choice of development of a particular waterfront site lies between developing the site for a high-rise hotel, for which there is proven market demand, or a waterfront public park for use by both residents and tourists, which do you think is the best use of the site? What approaches could be applied to achieve both objectives?

This case is courtesy of Edward Inskeep, a tourism consultant and author with the WTO.

Career Information

Tourism

Travel and tourism offer careers that provide information, transportation, accommodations, goods, and other services to travelers. Tourism is established almost everywhere in the world and is the world's largest employer. If restaurant or hotel management-specific career options do not appeal to you, then you may want to consider a career in travel and tourism.

The best advice about the tourism career path is to be proactive during your college years. More than likely you will have to open your own doors to your first career position in tourism. It is important to start early in your college experience and learn as much about the industry as possible through trade publications, magazines, travel, seminars, course work, volunteer work at convention and visitors bureaus, shadowing at travel agencies, going on tours, and membership in professional organizations. It is beneficial to work in the travel and tourism industry while you are going to school. An internship can provide you with opportunities you may not be able to find on your own.

The travel and tourism business is changing because of the Internet. Many people can access information now that they once had to rely on travel agents and tour guides to provide. However, there will always be a market of individuals who are willing to pay someone else to provide these services.

Travel can serve as an important step toward global understanding, cultural appreciation and tolerance. "To travel is to live" according to the Danish writer Hans Christian Anderson. Clearly the travel industry can provide the opportunity for personal travel, professional accomplishment, and a rewarding career.

Related Web Sites

http://www.lee-county.com/leeisland/tcap/careerlist. htm#uvw—employment possibilities associated with tourism
http://www.traveljobs.com/—travel jobs
http://www.prit.bc.ca/—advice and jobs in tourism
http://www.travelcareernetwork.com/—careers in the travel industry
http://www.vonl.com/chips/sltt.htm—books on tourism
http://www.crewunlimited.com/—cruise line placement
http://www.traveling.com/—industry information and employment
http://www.priceline.com/—service that lets people make their own travel arrangements

Courtesy of Charlie Adams.

Summary

1. Tourism can be defined as the idea of attracting, accommodating, and pleasing groups or individuals traveling for pleasure or business. It is categorized by geography, ownership, function, industry, and travel motive.

2. The development of tourism started before the Industrial Revolution and continued parallel with the improvement of means of transportation: railway, automobile, aircraft, and cruise ships.

3. Tourism involves international interaction and, therefore, government regulation. Several organizations, such as the World Tourism Organization, are responsible for environmental protection, tourism development, immigration, and cultural and social aspects of tourism.

4. Tourism is the world's largest industry and employer. It affects other industry sectors, such as public transportation, foodservice, lodging, entertainment, and recreation. In addition, tourism produces secondary impacts on businesses that are affected indirectly, which is known as the multiplier effect.

5. Travel agencies, tour operators, travel managers, wholesalers, national offices of tourism, and destination management companies serve as middlepersons between a country and its visitors.

6. Physical needs, the desire to experience other cultures, and an interest in meeting new people are some of the motives people have when they travel. Because of flexible work hours, early retirement, and the easy accessibility of traveling, tourism is constantly growing.

7. From a social and cultural perspective, tourism can further international understanding and economically improve a poor country. However, it can also disturb a culture by confronting it with mass tourism, causing the destruction of natural sites. A trend in avoiding tourism pollution is ecotourism.

8. Business travel has increased in recent years due to the growth of convention centers in several cities. As a result, business travelers have given a boost to hotels, restaurants, and auto rental companies. The number of female business travelers is rising as well.

Key Words and Concepts

Agenda 21
Airline Deregulation Act of 1978
Bermuda agreement
Business travel
Commission Caps
Concorde
Conventions and visitors bureaus
Corporate travel manager
Destination management companies
Economic impact of tourism
Ecotourism
Hub-and-spoke system
International Air Transportation Association (IATA)
International Development Organization
Multiplier effect
National offices of tourism
Organization for Economic Cooperation and Development (OECD)
Pacific Area Travel Association (PATA)
Pleasure travel
Segmenting the cruise market
Sustainable tourism
Ticketless travel
Tour operators
Tour wholesalers
Tourism
Tourism promotion organizations
Tourist
Travel agents
World Tourism Organization (WTO)

Review Questions

1. Give a broad definition of tourism and explain why people are motivated to travel.

2. Describe the importance of Benz, Ford, and Lindbergh in the development of tourism.

3. Explain the differences in the development of the European and U.S. railway systems.
4. Give a brief explanation of the economic impact of tourism. Name two organizations that control or further the economic impact of tourism.

5. Choose a career in the tourism business and give a brief overview of what your responsibilities would be.
6. Discuss the positive and negative impacts that tourism can have on a country in consideration of tourism pollution and ecotourism.

Internet Exercises

1. Organization:
   Web site:
   Summary:
   (a) How much was spent on international tourism in 1999?
   (b) What does the *Tourism: 2020 Vision* predict?

2. Organization:
   Web site:
   Summary:
   (a) What were effects of the Airline Deregulation Act of 1978?
   (b) What indirect benefits does the airline industry offer the public?

World Tourism Organization
http://world-tourism.org/
The WTO is the only intergovernmental organization that serves in the field of travel and tourism and is a global forum for tourism policy and issues. It has about 138 member countries and territories. Its mission is to promote and develop tourism as a significant means of fostering international peace and understanding, economic development, and international trade.
Air Transport Association
http://www.air-transport.org/
The ATA is the first and only trade organization for the principal U.S. airlines. Its purpose is to support and assist its members by promoting the air transport industry and its operations, safety, cost effectiveness, and technological advancement. It has promoted the interest of the commercial airline industry for more than sixty years and now is a key player in the global transportation market.

Apply Your Knowledge

1. Analyze your family and friends' recent or upcoming travel plans and compare them to the examples in the text for reasons why people travel.

2. Suggest some ecotourism activities for your community.
3. How would you promote or improve tourism in your community?

The Hotel Business: Development and Classification

After reading and studying this chapter, you should be able to:

✔ Describe briefly the development of the U.S. lodging industry.

✔ Define the following terms: *hotel franchising, partnerships, leasing, syndicates,* and *management contracts.*

✔ Discuss financial aspects of hotel development.

✔ Classify hotels by type, location, and price.

✔ Explain vertical integration.

✔ Name some prestigious and unusual hotels.

✔ Describe the effects of a global economy on the hotel industry.

Hotel Development and Ownership

Hotels in North America began as inns or taverns, which were vastly different from today's full-service hotels. It is interesting to trace this development over the years, especially from a financial viewpoint.

The industry, as we know it today with a number of high-profile companies, is vastly different from even a generation ago. The taverns in Boston were called "the candles of liberty" by Patrick Henry. In fact, the Green Dragon and the Bunch of Grapes were meeting places for the Sons of Liberty during the American Revolution. The Boston Tea Party was planned in the Green Dragon.[1]

Taverns soon sprang up in all the colonies and became a focal point of the community. They flourished, not only in the major cities, but also along the communication routes known as turnpikes. Later, canals also became a part of the growing transportation system. Naturally, then as now, people on the move required food, beverages, and accommodations.

The first hotel to open in the United States was the 70-room City Hotel on Broadway, New York City, in 1794. This was followed by others, notably the 170-room Tremont House, which opened in Boston in 1829. The Tremont was the first hotel to have bellpersons, front desk employees, locks on guest room doors, and free soap for guests.

Perhaps because there was no royalty in the New World, hotels emerged as people palaces. Each new hotel featured a new architectural design, and displayed grand lobbies, ballrooms, superior plumbing, or some other guest convenience—such as elevators, which were first installed in New York's Fifth Avenue Hotel in 1859. Electricity was first used by the Hotel Everett on Park Row in New York.[2]

Transportation changed the nature of the hotel industry. First it was rail travel that prompted hotels to develop as the popular resorts and frontiers opened. From the Hotel del Coronado, near San Diego, California, to the five-star Breakers Resort in Palm Beach, Florida, and the famous Greenbriar Resort in West Virginia, railroads and hotels complemented one another in providing the traveling public with remarkable experiences. In Canada, the Canadian Pacific (CP) railroad enabled passengers to view the spectacular Rocky Mountains. To this day, CP operates the largest chain of Canadian hotels.

The first motel was opened by California architect Arthur Hineman in 1925, in San Luis Obispo, California. This location is about 200 miles north of Los Angeles—a long day's drive in those days. Hineman designed the motel so guests could drive right up to the doors of their rooms or to an adjacent garage. The forty one-story bungalows were grouped around a courtyard. It cost

---

[1]This section draws on Donald E. Lundberg, *The Hotel and Restaurant Business,* 4th ed. New York: Van Nostrand Reinhold, 1984, p. 24.

[2]Daniel J. Boorstin, *The Americans: The National Experience.* New York: Vintage Books, 1965, p. 139.

The Motel Inn, San Luis Obispo, California

$80,000 to build in its ornate Spanish-mission style, with a three-tiered tower, white pillars, and tree-fringed courtyard—unusually luxurious for the 1920s.

During the Depression of the 1930s, many hotel owners defaulted on their mortgages. As a result, banks and institutions soured on the idea of mortgage loans for hotels. For this reason, few downtown hotels were built after World War II, even in the 1950s and early 1960s. Hilton, the preeminent emerging chain at the time, acquired and rebuilt older hotels, like the Stevens in Chicago (now the Chicago Hilton and Towers) and the Plaza in New York City.[3]

The automobile created a wave of hotel and motel construction in the 1940s, 1950s, and 1960s. As Americans began to explore the open road, hotels and motels developed to cater to their accommodation needs. Likewise, air transportation was a catalyst for the development and redevelopment of city hotels and destination resorts. In 1958, the Boeing 707 enabled faster transcontinental and trans-Atlantic flights. Business and leisure travel took off in what was to become the largest worldwide industry.

The vibrant economy of the 1950s meant that there was more disposable income for travel and tourism. With the advent of rail, automobile (car and bus), and air transportation, society became more mobile. This mobility began to transform the industry from small, wholly owned, and independently operated properties to the concepts of development by franchising, partnership, leasing, and management contracts.

Additional reasons for U.S. travel after World War II included the huge number of marriages of returning GIs, the baby boom, a housing shortage, particularly in

[3]Charles A. Bell, "Agreements with Chains-Hotels Companies," *The Cornell Hotel and Restaurant Administration Quarterly*, **34,** 1, February 1993, pp. 27–33.

the East, and the fact that jobs were available out West. For these reasons, families began to move about and that movement necessitated travel by both new families and older relatives in order to see each other. Cars, tires, and gas were no longer rationed; good, toll-free interstate roads were built; and the economy improved. World War II veterans went to college on the GI Bill and with more education, money, and knowledge of other countries, along with a relatively peaceful world, they had a greater desire and capability to travel beyond the United States. Some of them, now senior citizens, are returning to the World War II battle sites today.

When businesses and services moved to the suburbs, so did the hotels and motels chains. Now, with the resurgence of people moving back into revitalized cities, with cultural, tourist, and business centers, and with the desirability of trendy, refurbished old homes, apartments, and lofts, more downtown hotels will be revitalized or built. As of 2000, there were plans to build sixteen new hotels in New York City.[4]

Hotel development is linked to the broader economy and the real estate maxim of "Highest and Best Use," that is, which investment will yield the greatest return? If a person or corporation has money to invest, where would it yield the best return? Some could be put in the stock or bond market and some in the property market, but is it best to invest in office buildings, shopping malls, or hotels? Obviously, there are many aspects to consider.

In an Arthur Anderson investor study,[5] many of the organizations said that they were continuing to invest in hotels over other forms of real estate, because hotels are still available for less than replacement costs.

Franchising

Franchising in the hospitality industry is a concept that allows a company to expand more rapidly by using other people's money than if it had to acquire its own financing. The company or franchisor grants certain rights, for example, to use its trademark, signs, proven operating systems, operating procedures and possibly reservations system, marketing know-how, purchasing discounts, and so on for a fee. In return, the franchisee agrees by signing the franchise contract to operate the restaurant, hotel, and so on in accordance with the guidelines set by the franchisor. Franchising is a way of doing business that benefits both the franchisor—who wants to expand the business rapidly—and the franchisee—who has financial backing but lacks specific expertise and recognition. Some corporations franchise by individual outlets and others franchise by territory.

Franchising began in the hotel industry in 1907, when the Ritz Development Company franchised the Ritz-Carlton name in New York City.[6] Howard Johnson began franchising his hotels in 1927. This allowed for rapid expansion, first on

[4]David Gotzmer, personal correspondence, June 2000.

[5]Jeffrey C. Summers, "Available Capital and Strong Industry Economics Fuel Vibrant Market for US Hotel Investors' Acquisitions," *Real Estate Finance Journal,* **12,** 3, Winter 1997, pp. 91–95.

[6]Lundberg, op. cit., p. 121.

the East Coast and later in the Midwest and finally in the mid-1960s into California. Today, there are more than 900 restaurants in the chain.

Holiday Inns (now Holiday Corporation, the largest lodging enterprise in the world) also grew by the strategy of franchising. In 1952, Kemons Wilson, a developer, had a disappointing experience while on a family vacation when he had to pay for an extra room for his children. Therefore, Wilson decided to build a moderately priced family-style hotel. Each room was comfortably sized and had two double beds; this enabled children to stay for free in their parents' rooms. In the 1950s and early 1960s, as the economy grew, Holiday Inns grew in size and popularity. Holiday Inns added restaurants, meeting rooms, and recreational facilities. They upgraded the furnishings and fixtures in the bedrooms and almost completely abandoned the original concept of being a moderately priced lodging operation.

Franchised Hotels

North America is host to more than 180 hotel brand extensions and franchised hotel brands. Franchising remains a mostly North American activity, with limited opportunities in international markets. This is because what was once plentiful—the capital needed to drive hotel franchising—is now less accessible. Brand strategies for franchisers in the new millennium seem to be influenced mostly by mergers and a peaking market. Despite the constant progress, one area remains tense, and that is the relationship between hotel companies and franchisees. Tensions exist for varying reasons including fees, services, reservations inspections and maintenance of standards.

One of the key factors in the successful development of Holiday Corporation was that they were one of the first companies to enter the **midprice range** of the market. These inns or motor hotels were often located away from the expensive downtown sites, near important freeway intersections and the more reasonably priced suburbs. Another reason for their success was the value they offered: comfort at a reasonable price, avoiding the expensive trimmings of luxury hotels.

About this time, a new group of budget motels emerged. Motel 6 (so named because the original cost of a room was $6 a night) in California slowly spread across the country, as did Days Inn and others. Cecil B. Day was in the construction business and found Holiday Inns too expensive when traveling on vacation with his family. He bought cheap land and constructed buildings of no more than two stories to keep the costs down. These hotels and motels were primarily for commercial travelers and vacationing families, were located close to major highways, and were built to provide low-cost lodging without frills. Some of these buildings were modular constructions. Entire rooms were built elsewhere, transported to the site, and placed side by side.

It was not until the 1960s that Hilton and Sheraton began to franchise their names. Franchising was the primary growth and development strategy of hotels and motels during the 1960s, 1970s, and 1980s. However, franchising presents two major challenges for the franchisor: maintenance of quality standards and avoidance of financial failure on the part of the franchisee.

It is difficult for the franchise company to state in writing all of the contingencies that will ensure that quality standards are met. Recent franchise agreements are more specific in terms of the exterior maintenance and guest service levels. Franchise fees vary according to the agreements worked out between

Franchising Trends

Factors propelling franchise growth include these:

- Fresh looks (curb appeal)
- Location—near highways, airports, and suburbs
- Expansion in smaller cities throughout the United States
- New markets—located in proximity to golf courses and other attractions
- Foreign expansion—a move to increase brand awareness

the franchisor and the franchisee; however, an average agreement is based on 3 or 4 percent of room revenue.

The world's largest franchisor of hotels, with 6,624 hotels, is Cendant of Parsippany, New Jersey. Choice Hotels International, ranked second with 4,545 franchised hotels, is a subsidiary of the Blackstone Group, New York. Six Continents is now the third largest franchisor with 2,600 hotels. Table 3–1 shows franchise hotels among the top ten corporate chains.

Franchising provides both benefits and drawbacks to the franchisee and franchisor. The benefits to the franchisee are as follows:

✔ A set of plans and specifications from which to build
✔ National advertising
✔ Centralized reservation system
✔ Participation in volume discounts for purchasing furnishings, fixtures, and equipment
✔ Listing in the franchisor's directory
✔ Low fee percentage charged by credit card companies

The drawbacks to the franchisee are as follows:

✔ High fees—both to join and ongoing
✔ Central reservations generally producing between 17 and 26 percent of reservations
✔ Franchisees must conform to the franchisor's agreement
✔ Franchisees must maintain all standards set by the franchisor

Table 3–1   Franchised Hotels Among the Top Ten Corporate Chains

Company	No. of Guest Rooms	Hotels Franchised	Total Hotels
Cendant Corp.	552,528	5,200	6,624
Choice Hotels International	361,674	4,545	4,545
Six Continents Hotels	486,321	3,200	3,312
Hilton Hotels Corp.	308,426	1,482	2,037
Marriott International		1,321	2,463
Carlson Hospitality Worldwide	120,297	726	813
Accor	N/A	757	3,654
U.S. Franchise Systems	N/A	500	500
Société du Louvre	N/A	409	933
Starwood Hotels & Resorts Worldwide		313	745

Source: Hotel and Motel Management, HotelMotel.com, September 16, 2002, and Hotels, July 2002.

The benefits to the franchise company are as follows:
- ✔ Increased market share/recognition
- ✔ Up-front fees

The drawbacks to the franchise company are as follows:
- ✔ The need to be very careful in the selection of franchisees
- ✔ Difficulty in maintaining control of standards

Franchising continues to be a popular form of expansion both in North America and the rest of the world.

Corporate Profile: Cendant Corporation

In its first year, 1990, Cendant Corporation (formerly Hospitality Franchise Systems, Inc.) was a company consisting of middle-of-the-market hotel chains Ramada and Howard Johnson. Now Cendant is an empire consisting of a loose confederation of businesses and brands in related services, including hotels, rental cars, real estate, mortgages, and vacation ownership/timeshares. Cendant is a global provider of real estate and travel services, the world's largest franchisor of residential real estate brokerage offices, and the global leader in corporate employee relocation. Cendant is also the largest franchisor of hotels and rental cars, the leading provider of vacation timeshare exchanges, and the second largest vehicle management company worldwide.

Included under Cendant's management are Days Inn, Howard Johnson, Ramada, Knights Inn, Super 8, Travelodge, Villager Lodge, Wingate Inn, Century 21, ERA (Electronic Realty Associates), Coldwell Banker, Avis Rent-a-Car, and PHH Corp. Combined, these businesses account for approximately half a million hotel rooms in the United States, Canada, Latin America, and Europe, and more than 11,500 franchised real estate offices with more than 190,000 brokers in the United States, Mexico, Canada, Puerto Rico, Europe, Africa, and the Asia-Pacific region. Under the leadership of Henry R. Silverman, founder, chairman, and chief executive officer of Cendant, company stock has increased nearly 1,400 percent since its initial offering.

Cendant's acquisition policies have been extremely successful, largely because of Silverman's talent and intuition in locating companies "that are either being poorly managed or overstaffed, and then upgrading the

(Courtesy of Cendant)

management and closing divisions and laying off employees."[1] As a result of the uninterrupted acquisitions, the company's revenue, net income, and profitability have steadily increased for eighteen consecutive quarters. Revenue in the first quarter of 1997 increased 88 percent to $527 million from $280 million for the first quarter of 1996. Net income increased 111 percent to $91 million from $43 million in the same quarter.[2]

Although clearly in the consumer services industry, its clients include other businesses and corporations—not individual consumers. As a franchisor, the company licenses the owners and operators of independent businesses to use Cendant's brand names, without taking on big business risks and expenses. Cendant does not operate hotels or real estate brokerage offices, but instead, provides coordination and services that allow franchisees to retain local control of their activities. At the same time, they benefit from the economies of scale of widely promoted brand names and well-established standards of service, national and regional direct marketing, co-marketing programs, and volume purchasing discounts. All Cendant brands share "extensive market research, use well-developed technology, such as proprietary reservation systems and, in the case of lodging, a room inventory tracking system, which is extremely technology intensive and eliminates waste."[3] By monitoring quality control and extensively promoting the brand names, Cendant offers its independent franchise owners franchise fees that are relatively low compared to the increased profitability they gain.

Through franchising, Cendant limits its own risks and is able to keep overhead costs low. Chief Financial

continued

Officer Michael P. Monaco says Cendant "limits the volatility in the business as best as we can because fees come from revenue, not the franchisee's profitability.[4] CEO Henry Silverman concurs: "Increases or decreases in rate of occupancy have very little impact on us. Our biggest outcome driver is more units—unit growth."[5] A further advantage of being a franchiser of such dimension is that the company is even more protected from the cyclical nature of the economy than are other franchise ventures. In times of prosperity, independent owners are favored, however, that is not the case during a recession. Silverman adds that "cash flow of [owners-operators] will be more volatile than ours. The franchiser's cash flow is relatively more stable and will go up slightly each year with inflation, slightly each year with occupancy and/or royalties, and significantly if you continue growing units."[6]

The critical mass created by all the businesses working together makes Cendant more valuable as a whole than as the sum of its parts, gives it outstanding purchasing power and market control, and makes it extremely effective in selling to a wide audience. Although the individual businesses may, at first glance, seem desperate, all the various acquisitions undergone by the company are part of a carefully designed strategy. "What we try to do," CEO Silverman says, "is assemble different brands that have huge internal synergy."[7] "Synergy" is a key word for Cendant. It is the magic formula that creates mutual benefits within companies in an industry segment and cross-fertilizes businesses across industries.

Diversification is a common practice in the hotel industry. Marriott, for example, combines hotel properties, foodservices, timeshare, and senior living products. However, no other hotel company has had such rapid growth and expansion. But diversification was a necessity as well as a strategic choice. It was precisely Cendant's quick expansion as a hotel franchise company that created the need to diversify in order to sustain that growth rate. The businesses the company decided to acquire were carefully selected according to Silverman's view of the peculiar demographics of the North American market. The wave of baby boomers consists of 76 million people who are approaching fifty years of age, and this trend will continue for about ten to twelve more years. In Silverman's view, this clientele consumes primarily two things: travel and residential real estate. In light of this trend, Cendant's diversification from the hotel market turned to real estate, mortgage companies, and timeshare operators.

Cendant's future leaves skeptics in doubt. Will Cendant be able to sustain and continue this enormous growth? All signs are in favor of it. Again looking at demographics, Silverman anticipates that a possibility for the future may be entering the assisted-living business (a combination of a hotel and a nursing home), which does not have, at this point, enough critical mass to invest in. But, as Silverman stated, "It probably will require some national marketing at some point."[8]

---

[1] Toni Giovanetti, "HFS, Once Confined to Hotels, Now Encompasses a Global Business Matrix," *Hotel Business*, **6,** 9, May 7–20, 1997, p. 26.

[2] HFS Incorporated, News Release, May 1, 1997.

[3] Todd Pitock, "The Artful Acquirer," *Journal of Business Strategy*, **18,** 2, March/April 1997, p. 19.

[4] Ibid.

[5] Philip Hayward, "Silverman on Silverman," *Lodging*, May 1997, p. 49.

[6] Ibid.

[7] John Greenwald, "HFS Stands for Growth," Time, March 17, 1997, p. 41.

[8] Hayward, op. cit., p. 50.

Is There a Franchise in Your Future?
Courtesy of Robert Kok

Many of you may not realize the pervasiveness of franchised operations in the United States. Predictions are that more than 50 percent of all retail sales in the United States (including restaurants) will soon be transacted through franchised units. Further, franchises are available not only in the hotel, restaurant, travel, and recreation industries, but also in a large variety of other businesses that might interest you. These businesses include automotive tires and parts, retailing of all kinds, mail and copy services, janitorial and decorating services, personnel agencies, and so on. Today, many franchises can be operated from home by those interested in lifestyle changes.

If you end up working for a hospitality-related organization after graduation, chances are that your career will be influenced by franchising. You may work directly for a franchisor (the company that sells a franchised concept to an entrepreneur), whether on the corporate staff (e.g., training, franchise consulting) or in an operations position in a franchisor-owned unit. Many franchisors own their own units in order to test new operational or marketing ideas and to demonstrate the viability of the business to potential franchisees (the entrepreneurs who buy the franchised unit).

Alternatively, you may work for a franchisee (the entrepreneurs who buy a franchised unit). Some franchisees are small businesses, owning only one or a few units. Other franchises are large corporations themselves, owning hundreds of units doing hundreds of millions of dollars in sales every year. For instance, RTM, Inc., owns and operates over 600 Arby's restaurants. Additionally, it owns and franchises two midsized chicken restaurants, Lee's Famous Recipe Chicken and Mrs. Winner's Chicken & Biscuits. Working for a company as large as RTM would be similar to working for a large franchisor.

A third way that franchising may involve you is through ownership. Rather than starting your own independent business after college, many of you may want to consider buying a franchise. Several advantages can result. First, by working with a larger company you get the benefits of its experience in running the business that you have chosen to enter. Many of the mistakes that a new entrepreneur may make have already been overcome by your franchisor. The company might provide cash flow. The company might also provide other support services at little or no cost, such as marketing and advertising, site selection, construction plans, assistance with financing, and so on. All of this assistance leads to a second key reason for buying a franchise—reducing your risk of failure. Franchising is probably less risky than starting your own business from scratch.

A key question to be answered before you buy a franchise is whether you are better suited to being a franchisee or an independent entrepreneur. Consider the following factors that many franchisors seek. Are you strongly motivated to succeed and do you have a past history of business success, even if it is in a different business? Do you have a significant sum of money as well as access to credit? Are you willing to accept the franchisor's values, philosophy, and ways of doing business, as well as its technical assistance? Do you have the full support of your immediate family as you develop your business? Are you willing to devote substantially all of your working time to the business?

Franchising does have some disadvantages, as noted by many former franchisees. Your expectations of success may not be met. Perhaps the business did not have the potential that you expected, or perhaps you were not willing to invest the time needed. In a few cases, an overzealous or dishonest franchisor representative has misled franchisees.

As a franchisee, your freedom is somewhat restricted. You must operate within the constraints set out by your franchise agreement and the operational standards manual. Although there may be some room for you to express your creativity and innovation, it is generally limited. This may mean that, over time, the work might become monotonous and unchallenging, yet you have a long-term commitment to the company due to the franchise agreement that you signed. Your failure to consistently follow the franchisor's methods for running the business could result in the termination of your contract and your forced removal from the business.

Finally, the franchisor itself may not be performing well, thereby hurting your local business. Also, they may allow other franchisees to open units so near to your operation that your business is adversely affected.

Buying a franchise can be a very rewarding business experience in many ways. But like any other business venture it requires research and a full discussion with family, friends, and business advisors, such as your accountant and attorney. You should carefully weigh whether or not you are psychologically suited to be a franchisee. Perhaps you perform more effectively in a corporate structure as an employee. Perhaps you are better suited to starting your own business from scratch. A careful analysis can help you make an informed decision.

Partnership

Another interesting mode of developmental financing was used by Travelodge: a **partnership.** Under this plan, a husband and wife who wanted to enter the motel business invested one-half the cost of the motel. The couple received a salary for managing the property, and profits from the operations were divided 50-50 between the company and the couple.[7] Travelodge, now a part of HFS, began and expanded utilizing the partnership arrangement.

Leasing

Leasing became popular in the 1950s and 1960s; it still exists, but to a lesser extent. The **leasing arrangement** allows both the individual and the chain to enter the market or expand within it. A hotel is leased for a percentage of gross sales, generally 20 to 50 percent.[8] For example, U.S. international hotel expansion began with the lease of the Hotel Caribe Hilton in San Juan, Puerto Rico. The government of Puerto Rico wanted to encourage tourism by having a brand name hotel with management expertise. The government leased the hotel to Hilton in return for two-thirds of the gross operating profit plus marketing expenses.[9]

Several developing countries have adopted the lease concept. In Cuba, all went well until Castro took over after the Cuban Revolution. The Havana Hilton's occupancy dropped to 14 percent, which resulted in a loss. The lessons learned from this led to the management contract, which involved less

---

[7]Lundberg, op. cit., p. 48.

[8]Ibid., p. 83.

[9]Ibid., p. 44.

risk for hotel corporations. Profit-sharing lease agreements became management contracts. A base fee of 5 percent of gross revenues was introduced, plus an incentive fee of 10 percent of the gross operating profit.

In some locations, like Western Europe, the lease was to the hotel corporation's advantage. In London, the Hilton had a twenty-five-year-lease, and rent was fixed at 8 percent of the original cost with little provision for increase. As a result, Hilton took out almost 75 percent of the gross operating cost.[10]

Leasing may make a comeback with the lack of capital in the current marketplace. Hotel brokers have been looking for new ways to deal with underfinanced properties. Krieger and Snyder of Scottsdale, Arizona, have developed a new type of leasing. Leasing gives the benefits of ownership without the initial capital outlay. The hotel operator or lessee manages the hotel with a lease based on gross guest room revenues. The operator is responsible for insurance, hiring and firing, food and beverage, and the marketing of the hotel. In return, the operator gets a major part of every dollar of room revenue that comes into the hotel and the major part of every increase in revenue.[11]

Syndicates

Syndicates were and still are a popular form of hotel financing. A syndicate involves a group of investors who may (or may not) be friends or acquaintances of the eventual hotel operator. The group arrangement usually allows for a larger investment and a larger property, and naturally allows for the risk to be spread among the syndicate members.

Management Contracts

Management contracts have been responsible for the hotel industry's rapid boom since the 1970s. They became popular among hotel corporations because little or no up-front financing or equity was involved. Even if the hotel corporation was involved in the construction of the hotel, ownership generally reverted to a large insurance company. This was the case with the La Jolla, California, Marriott Hotel. Marriott Corporation built the hotel for about $34 million, then sold it to Paine Webber, a major investment banking firm, for about $52 million on completion. Not a bad return on investment!

The management contract usually allows for the hotel company to manage the property for a period of five, ten, or twenty years. For this, the company receives as a management fee, often a percentage of gross and/or net operating profit, usually about 2 to 4.5 percent of gross revenues. Lower fees in the 2 percent range are more prevalent today, with an increase in the incentive fee based on profitability. Some contracts begin at 2 percent for the first year,

[10]This section draws on Bell, op. cit., pp. 27–33.

[11]Steve Bergsman, "Arizona Company Applies Leasing to Lodging Deals," *Hotel and Motel Management*, **206,** 16, September 23, 1991, pp. 2, 29.

2.5 the second, and 3.5 the third and for the remainder of the contract.[12] Increased competition among management companies has decreased the management contract fees in the past few years. In recent years, hotel companies increasingly have opted for management contracts because considerably less capital is tied up in managing as compared with owning properties. This has allowed for a more rapid expansion of both the U.S. and international markets.

Hotel management companies often form a partnership of convenience with developers and owners who generally do not have the desire or ability to operate the hotel. The management company provides operational expertise, marketing, and sales clout, often in the form of a centralized reservation system (CRS).

Some companies manage a portfolio of properties on a cluster, regional, or national basis. The largest twenty-five management companies are listed in Table 3–2. Most of these companies manage hotels in the same classifications. This enables them to focus their efforts on managing properties of a similar nature rather than properties in different classifications.

In the early 1990s, because of plummeting real estate values, the high cost of debt service (mortgage payments) and the economic downturn, hotel-operating results and cash flows fell drastically. Recent contracts have called for an increase in the equity commitment on the part of the management company. Between 1988 and 1992, there was an increase from about 25 percent to about 42 percent in chain operators' equity contributions.[13] In addition, owners increased their operational decision-making options—something seldom done previously.

Table 3–2 Top Ten Management Companies[a]		
Company	Hotels Managed	Total Hotels
Marriott International	798	2,398
Accor	511	3,654
Extended Stay America	431	431
Tharaldson Enterprises	341	341
Société du Louvre	327	993
Six Continents Hotels & Resorts	314	3,274
Westmont Hospitality Group Inc.	287	287
Starwood Hotels & Resorts/		
Starwood Hotels & Resorts WW	222	743
Hilton Hotels Corp.	210	1,986
Prime Hospitality Group	199	234

[a]The rankings include a mixture of independent owner/operators, branded operators, and third-party management companies. The rankings are based on the actual number of hotels they manage, not just affiliate with.

Source: "Hotels' 325: Corporate 300," *Hotels*, July 2002, p. 44.

[12]James Eyster, "The Revolution in Domestic Hotel Management Contracts," *The Cornell Hotel and Restaurant Administration Quarterly*, **34,** 1, February 1993, p. 19.

[13]Ibid.

The strongest trend in contract negotiations is the expansion of the variety of contract provisions. For example, some owners may need or want equity participation. However, they may be unwilling to share control with an equity partner.[14] Generally, a compromise is worked out. Hotel owners focus on management companies with the following characteristics[15]:

✔ Experience and reliability
✔ Excellence in reporting
✔ Communication and human resources
✔ Successful strategies for improved profitability
✔ Proven ability to meet rigorous operator performance standards

With international expansion, a hotel company entering the market might actively seek a local partner or owner to work within a form of joint venture.

Today, hotel management companies exist in an extremely competitive environment. They have discovered that the hotel business, like most others, has changed and they are adapting accordingly. Today's hotel owners are demanding better bottom-line results and reduced fees. Management companies are seeking sustainability and a bigger share of the business.

The management industry itself is consolidating and institutional owners know they can require management companies, particularly the bigger, more capitalized ones, to actually make contributions to the property—up to 10 or 20 percent investments.[16]

Check Your Knowledge

1. What main factor changed the nature of the hotel industry? What impact does it have today?
2. In your own words, define the following terms: *franchising, partnership, leasing, syndicates,* and *management contracts.*

Financial Management and Profits

The hotel industry is characterized by a high degree of risk, which primarily is the result of two factors: the cyclical nature of demand and the high degree

---

[14]The International Hotel Association, Paris, "The Management Game: How to Keep One Step Ahead," *Hotels,* **27,** 6, May 1993, p. 65.

[15]Heather A. Sanders and Leo M. Renaghan, "Southeast Asia: A New Model for Hotel Development," *The Cornell Hotel and Restaurant Administration Quarterly,* **33,** 5, October 1992, pp. 16–23.

[16]Mike Sheridan, "The Rules Have Changed and It's a Whole New Ball Game," *Hotel Management,* **38,** 7, July 1996, pp. 52–58.

of capital investment.[17] A greater proportion of profit from hotels comes from the manipulation of real estate rather than from the sale of lodging, food, and beverages.

People construct hotels for a variety of reasons: pride of ownership or ego, profit from building, profit from promoting and financing, or profit from appreciation in value of the property. The great increase in value of the Hilton and Sheraton companies has not come from operating profits but from buying, selling, and tax advantage, and in appreciation of value of the hotels with time. Financial management is the name of the game, and the game is complex.

Perhaps the most amazing corporate development was that accomplished in just twenty-six years by Ernest Henderson. His financial skill, keen analysis, and shrewdness, combined with energy and hard work, catapulted the Sheraton Corporation from very modest beginnings to 154 hotels at his death in 1967. How was this financial success achieved? It was not with Disney's magic wand! Henderson was a capitalist and an opportunist. He bought and sold hotels whenever and wherever a deal could be worked out. The incentives and depreciation won out over ego and sentiment.

Leveraged money was used whenever possible. For example, if the Sheraton Corporation was interested in buying a hotel that had a $100,000 income each year, the corporation might be willing to buy at eight times the income ($800,000). Henderson would borrow half of the $800,000 from a bank or insurance company at 6 percent interest. If the owner would agree to take a second mortgage of $500,000, Sheraton could take over the property for a cash outlay of only $100,000, or a down payment of 12.5 percent.[18]

Creative Financing

The 1970s and 1980s were a difficult time for hotel expansion. Some hotels were planned for questionable markets as companies tried to stretch their abilities to manage fast growth. This situation was brought about by several factors[19]:

- ✔ A period of inflation-fueled expansion from 1976 to 1978, following on the heels of the **recession** and real estate bust of the mid-1970s
- ✔ A transitional period of stagnation from 1979 to mid-1981, characterized by economic stagnation and rapidly increasing **inflation**
- ✔ The recession of 1989 to 1993, which was characterized by further decreases in productivity, a decreasing rate of inflation, and above-average interest rates

These factors forced lenders to be more active in the financial decision-making process regarding hotel development. Cash-flow decisions became more impor-

[17]Arbel Avner and Paul Grier, "The Risk Structure of the Hotel Industry," *The Cornell Hotel and Restaurant Administration Quarterly*, **28**, 3, November 1987, p. 26.

[18]This section draws on Lundberg, op. cit., p. 76.

[19]James J. Eyster, "Creative Financing in the Lodging Industry, Cornell University," *The Hotel and Restaurant Administration Quarterly*, **23**, 4, February 1983, pp. 29–37.

tant, and lenders kept a watchful eye on developers who, until the early 1980s, were generally left to provide an "adequate," unaided return.

The early 1980s were years of extremely high **interest rates.** It was this critical factor that caused alarm bells to ring because projects were unable to meet the internal rate-of-return standards demanded by the lender as a condition of credit. Consequently, many projects were suspended; others were financed with short-term floating-rate loans.

Another result of the downturn in the economy and overbuilding of first-class properties in most United States cities was a softening of the real estate market. These factors led to what has now become known as **creative financing** or **portfolio financing.**

Portfolio financing occurs when a number of properties are cross-collateralized and cross-defaulted in a securitized format. This offers both investors and lenders a win–win situation, with greater overall protection against risk than would otherwise be possible with a single property.

By spreading the portfolio pool among more than one location or market (e.g., resort, city center, convention, or resort properties in a variety of locations), the effect of an **economic downturn** on a particular property will be buffered by other properties. However, care must be exercised when setting up such an arrangement to ensure that if one property were in default of a loan payment, the lender could not automatically foreclose on all the other properties. This creative form of financing will often be able to access funds at a lower rate of interest, one of the critical factors in the success of a hotel venture.

However, in a publicly traded corporation, the chief executive officer's (CEO's) and chief financial officer's (CFO's) primary mission is to maximize the price of the organization's common stock. To do this, the CEO must constantly assess the two key determinants of share price: risk and return. All major hotel financial decisions must be viewed in terms of expected risk, expected return, and their combined impact on share price. These expected values are often difficult to measure; the process requires considerable judgment as well as factual knowledge. In some states, public funds have been used to finance hotel developments. The Westin Hotel in Providence, Rhode Island, is a good example. It was built with state funds as part of the convention center project.

Real Estate Investment Trust (REIT)

Real estate investment trusts (REITs) have existed since the 1960s. In those early days, they were mostly mortgage holders. But in the 1980s, they began to own property outright, often focusing on specific sectors like hotels, office buildings, apartments, malls, and nursing homes. Today, about 300 REITs, with a combined market value of $70 billion, are publicly traded. Investors like them because they do not pay corporate income tax and instead are required to distribute at least 95 percent of net income to shareholders. In addition, because they trade as stocks, they are much easier to get into or out

Personal Profile: Conrad Hilton and Hilton Hotels Corporation

Conrad Hilton "King of Innkeepers" and Master of Hotel Finance

Hilton's success was attributed to two main strategies: (1) hiring the best managers and letting them have total autonomy, and (2) being a cautious bargainer who, in later years, was careful not to overfinance. Conrad Hilton had begun a successful career in the banking business before he embarked on what was to become one of the most successful hotel careers ever.

In 1919, while on bank business in Cisco, Texas, he bought the Mobley Hotel with an investment of $5,000. Hilton rented rooms to oil industry prospectors and construction workers. Because of high demand for accommodations and very little supply, Hilton often rented a room to three or four strangers. On some occasions, he even rented out his own room and slept in a lobby chair.

Because Hilton knew the banking business well and had maintained contacts who would lend him money for down payments on properties, he quickly expanded to seven area hotels. Hilton's strategy was to borrow as much money as possible in order to expand as rapidly as possible. This worked well until the Great Depression of the early 1930s. Hilton was unable to meet the payments on his properties and lost several in bankruptcy proceedings.[1]

Hilton, like many great leaders, had the determination to bounce back. To reduce costs, he borrowed money against his life insurance and even worked on the side for another hotel company.

Hilton's business and financial acumen is legendary. *The New York Times* described Conrad Hilton as "a master of finance and a cautious bargainer who was careful not to overfinance" and had "a flawless sense of timing."[2]

Hilton was the first person to notice vast lobbies with people sitting in comfortable chairs not spending any money. So he added the lobby bar as a convenient meeting place and leased out space for gift shops and newsstands. Most of the additional revenue from these operations went directly to the bottom line. The following shows a chronology of Conrad Hilton's and Hilton Corporation's highlights:

1919—Hilton bought the Mobley Hotel.
1925—The first Hilton hotel was built in Dallas, Texas.
1938—Hilton purchased the lease on the Sir Francis Drake Hotel in San Francisco, California. This was the first Hilton outside Texas.

(Courtesy of Hilton Hotels Corporation)

1942—The Town House in Los Angeles became Hilton's headquarters. The Roosevelt and the Plaza in New York became Hilton's first East Coast ventures.

1949—Conrad Hilton bought the lease of the Waldorf Astoria in New York and made it successful because he and his organization knew how to run it. Hilton opened the first Hilton International in San Juan, Puerto Rico.

1954—The Statler Hotel Company was bought for $111 million. At this time, this was the largest transaction in the history of the hotel industry.

1960—Conrad Hilton was made chairman of the board of Hilton Hotels Corporation.

1967—Hilton International was acquired by Trans World Airlines.

1971—The Las Vegas Hilton and the Flamingo Hilton marked Hilton's entry into the gaming market.

1977—Ownership of the building and land for the Waldorf Astoria in New York was purchased for a mere $35 million.

1979—Conrad Hilton died at the age of ninety-two. Baron Hilton, Conrad's son, became chairman of the board of directors.

1982—With the addition of 391 rooms, the Las Vegas Hilton became the largest hotel in the world, with 3,174 guest rooms and an extensive gaming area.

1983—Construction began on the Conrad International Hotel and Jupiters Casino on the Gold Coast of Queensland, Australia, the company's first property under Conrad International.

1984—The 1,600-room Anaheim Hilton and Towers opened adjacent to the Anaheim Convention Center in California.

1988—Completion of the renovations at the Hilton Hawaiian Village and the San Francisco Hilton and Towers marked the culmination of Hilton's $1.2 billion restoration and expansion program of its American hotels from coast to coast.

1989—The first Hilton suites property opened in Anaheim, California. The first Crest Hill by Hilton opened in Illinois.

1991—Hilton purchased and announced a massive nine-month renovation of the O'Hare Hilton in Chicago. Hilton established Hilton Grand Vacation Company, a nationwide system of vacation ownership resorts.

1992—Hilton assumes management of the Pointe Resorts in Phoenix, Arizona. Hilton acquires the 2,000-room Bally's Casino Resort in Reno, Nevada.

1993—Hilton Hotels and Hilton Grand Vacations Company commit millions to develop a new generation of "Vacation Ownership" resorts. The first will adjoin the Flamingo Hilton in Las Vegas.

Hilton and its partners, Caesars World, Inc., and Circus Circus Enterprises, Inc., are selected to develop and manage the Casino Windsor in Canada. The alliance marks the first time three world-class gaming companies joined together to offer casino gaming in a major jurisdiction.

1994—Hilton celebrates seventy-five years of innovation, marking the diamond anniversary of company founder Conrad N. Hilton's first hotel purchase, The Mobley.

The Queen of New Orleans riverboat casino, now the Flamingo Casino New Orleans, opened to the public, becoming the first such facility to begin operations on the Mississippi River in New Orleans.

1995—Zip-In Check-In® registration program is launched at more than 220 U.S. Hilton Hotels. Hilton Honors members with guaranteed reservations can now check into a Hilton hotel in thirty seconds or less.

Hilton Hotels' Internet Travel Center opens its site on the World Wide Web. Computer users throughout the world can now make direct reservations and find out about the company programs, special offers, and other information for more than 240 U.S. Hilton and Conrad International hotels worldwide.

Hilton Inns captures fourth consecutive first place ranking as the top midpriced hotel company in the annual *Business Travel News* survey.

1996—Stephen F. Bollenbach is named president and chief executive officer of Hilton Hotels Corporation. Formerly of the Walt Disney Company, this represents the first time in Hilton's history that the CEO position is held by someone whose last name is not Hilton.

Hilton Hotels Corporation becomes the world's largest casino gaming company after the signing of a merger agreement with Bally Entertainment Corporation. The final transaction was approved by both companies' boards of directors, the companies' shareholders, and gaming regulators of several states.

Hilton Hotels Corporation and British company Ladbroke Group PLC (current owners of the Hilton name outside the United States) form a strategic alliance that reunites the famous Hilton brand worldwide for the first time in thirty-two years.

1997—Hilton Hotels Corporation bids for ITT Sheraton.[3]

1998—Hilton Hotels Corporation plans to buy Promus Hotel Corporation for $2.7 billion and announces a new management structure.

1999—Awarded Best International Hotel Programme by readers of *Inside Flyer Magazine*.

2000—Hilton Group announced plans to relaunch its seventy-nine-unit U.K. hotels division by spending over $160 million upgrading its United Kingdom and Ireland hotels in 2000.

Hilton's expansion has dramatically increased reward earnings options for its members, presenting them with more than 2,000 participating hotels and resorts for earnings and redemption worldwide and a fourfold increase in the number of participating properties. The new brands—Double Tree Hotels, Embassy Suites, Hampton Inn & Suites, and Homewood Suites by Hilton—became a part of Hilton Hotels Corporation. Hilton also acquired Promos Hotel Corporation, a leader in managing and franchising highly regarded hotel brands.[4]

Hilton Hotels Corporation and Hilton International, a subsidiary of Hilton Group PLC, have created a worldwide alliance to market Hilton, the world's best-known hotel brand. Collectively offering more than 2,000 hotels in over fifty countries worldwide, both companies are recognized as leaders in the hospitality industry.

---

[1] Paul R. Dittmer and Gerald G. Griffen, *The Dimensions of the Hospitality Industry*: An Introduction. New York: Van Nostrand Reinhold, 1993, pp. 91–92.

[2] Joan Cook, "Conrad Hilton, Founder of Hotel Chain, Dies at 92," *The New York Times*, January 5, 1979, sec. 11, p. 5.

[3] Hilton Hotels' Internet Travel Center, Hilton Press Releases, http://www.hilton.com.

[4] Canada NewsWire Ltd., March 7, 2000, Financial News section.

of than limited partnerships or the direct ownership of properties. In the hotel industry, REITs are clearly where the action is.

The two leading REIT corporations are Patriot American Hospitality and Starwood Lodging Trust. Patriot American Hospitality has acquired Wyndham Hotels, which has become its operating company and given it a well-regarded brand name. Starwood Lodging Trust acquired Westin Hotels and Resorts for $1.4 billion, and outbid Hilton for ITT Sheraton. Patriot and Starwood are the only REITs allowed to both manage and own properties.

Financing Package

The process of determining the required return involves the calculation of the appropriate level of return to compensate the firm for the risk undertaken. Financing for a hotel that is conducive to success requires that the needs and objectives of the developer, operator, and lender or investor be understood and dealt with realistically. The arrangements made depend on the state of the money market; the results of feasibility and market studies; and the strength, credit rating, and reputation of the corporations involved. Generally speaking, about 60 to 80 percent of the total budget required to bring a hotel into being can be raised by debt financing.

Keep in mind that the financing of a hotel is only a part of the total package, albeit an important part. The extent to which the property will be successful will be dependent on the quality of management. The following points may help lay the groundwork for favorable financing:

- ✔ Affiliation with a quality franchisor or referral group
- ✔ Identification with a national chain through a management contract
- ✔ A lease arrangement with a strong, well-recognized hotel operator
- ✔ Identification with a national chain by way of a joint-venture agreement
- ✔ Conventional **first mortgage loans**—the most common real estate financing, even for hotels
- ✔ Lenders, including insurance companies, commercial banks, investment banks, savings banks, institutional investors, pension funds, syndicates, partnerships, and families

In recent years, hotel financing in North America has experienced an influx of overseas capital; that has been both a blessing and a blight—depending on which type of financial package is agreed to.

One of the dangers of a foreign currency loan is that **currency fluctuations** may cause an increase or decrease in the amount of the loan repayment. Fortunately, there are safeguards, including having the loan negotiated in U.S. dollars and repaid in U.S. dollars, thereby avoiding any currency fluctuations on the part of the borrower.

Viable hotel development opportunities do exist, but developers and franchisors must be creative in locating funding. Having been caught short in the 1980 and 1990s, lenders are now basing loans on more conservative occupancy and rate projections.[20]

---

[20]Personal conversation with Luis Barrios, July 7, 2002.

Cheek Your Knowledge

1. Give reasons why you would like to build, manage, and own your own hotel. According to the book, what are the reasons people build, manage, and own hotel properties?

Classification of Hotels

According to the American Hotel and Motel Association, the U.S. lodging industry consists of 46,000 hotels and motels, with a total of 3.3 million rooms. The gross volume of business generated from these rooms is $93.1 billion.

Unlike many other countries, the United States has no formal government classification of hotels. However, the American Automobile Association (AAA) classifies hotels by diamond award, and the Mobile Travel Guide offers a five-star award.

The AAA has been inspecting and rating the nation's hotels since 1977. Less than 2 percent of the 41,000 properties inspected annually throughout the United States, Canada, and Mexico earned the five-diamond award, which is the association's highest award for excellence. In 2000, the five-diamond award was bestowed on fifty-eight lodgings in the United States, Canada and Mexico. Twelve of the properties received both the five-diamond and the five-star awards.

AAA uses descriptive criteria to evaluate the hotels that they rate annually in the United States, Canada, Mexico, and the Caribbean (see Figure 3–1).

- ✔ One-diamond properties have simple roadside appeal and the basic lodging needs.
- ✔ Two-diamond properties have average roadside appeal, with some landscaping and a noticeable enhancement in interior decor.
- ✔ Three diamonds carry a degree of sophistication through higher service and comfort.
- ✔ Four diamonds have excellent roadside appeal and service levels that give guests what they need before they even ask for it.
- ✔ Five-diamond properties have the highest service levels, sophistication, and offerings.

Josette Constantine, manager of AAA inspections, said one word to describe the five-diamond properties is "Wow!"

Even the one-diamond properties provide a valuable listing, Constantine said. One diamond doesn't represent low quality by any means. Almost 40 percent of lodging facilities are not approved for inspection at all because

	◈	◈◈	◈◈◈	◈◈◈◈	◈◈◈◈◈
General	Simple roadside appeal Limited landscaping	Average roadside appeal Some landscaping	Very good roadside appeal Attractive landscaping	Excellent roadside appeal Professionally planned landscaping	Outstanding roadside appeal Professional landscaping with a variety of foliage and stunning architecture
Lobby	Adequate size with registration, front desk, limited seating and budget art, if any	Medium size with registration, front desk, limited seating, carpeted floors, budget art and some plants	Spacious with front desk, carpeted seating area arranged in conversation groupings, good-quality framed art, live plants, luggage carts and bellstation	Spacious or consistent with historical attributes; registration and front desk above average with solid wood or marble; ample seating area with conversation groupings and upscale appointments including tile, carpet or wood floors; impressive lighting fixtures; upscale framed art and art objects; abundant live plants; background music; separate check-in/-out; bellstation	Comfortably spacious or consistent with historical attributes; registration and front desk above average; ample seating with conversation groupings and upscale appointments; impressive lighting fixtures; variety of fine art; abundant plants and fresh floral arrangements; background music; separate check-in/-out; bellstation that may be part of concierge area; concierge desk
Guestrooms	May not reflect current industry standards	Generally reflect current industry standards	Reflect current industry standards	Reflect current industry standards and provide upscale appearance	Reflect current standards and provide luxury appearance
Service	Basic attentive service	More attentive service	Upgraded service levels	High service levels and hospitality	Guests are pampered by flawless service executed by professional staff

Figure 3–1 *Summary of AAA Diamond-Rating Guidelines.* (Courtesy of Hotel and Motel Management.)

they don't meet the minimum standards of cleanliness, comfort, safety, and maintenance.[21]

Hotels may be classified according to location, price, and type of services offered. This allows guests to make a selection on these as well as personal criteria. A list of hotel classifications follows:

> City center—luxury, first-class, midscale, economy, suites
> Resort—luxury, midscale, economy suites, condominium, time-share, convention
> Airport—luxury, midscale, economy, suites
> Freeway—midscale, economy suites
> Casino—luxury, midscale, economy
> Full service
> Convention
> Economy
> Extended stay
> Bed & breakfast

Alternatively, the hotel industry may be segmented according to price. Figure 3–2 gives an example of a national or major regional brand-name hotel chain in each segment, and Figure 3–3 shows another type of rating guide.

Ellsworth Milton Statler (1863–1928)

Ellsworth Milton Statler is considered by many to be the premier hotelman of all time. He brought a high standard of comfort and convenience to the middle-class traveler at an affordable price. His life story is that of a man overcoming adversity. At age fifteen, with only two years of experience as a bellboy at a leading hotel in Wheeling, West Virginia, Statler became head bellman. Noting the oversized profits gained from the hotel's billiard room and railroad ticket concession, he persuaded the owner to lease him the concessions. A studious promoter, he billed special billiard exhibition games and brought in crowds. Soon he had launched a bowling alley, then a restaurant—*The Pie House*—which was the best in town. By 1894, at the age of thirty-one, Statler was making $10,000 a year and was ready for new fields to conquer.

Buffalo, New York, was the setting for his next venture, one that almost proved to be his undoing. Statler opened a restaurant in the basement of the Ellicott Square Building—a new office building promoted as the "largest in the world." Statler found, however, that Buffalo was an eat-at-home town, and despite an efficient operation, his creditors closed in. With incredible imagination and energy, Statler changed the eating habits of Buffalo's downtown businesspeople. He advertised "All you can eat for twenty-five cents," and in three short years the tide had turned. Statler was in the black and ready for bigger and better things.

---

[21]Julie Miller, "AH&MA Initiates Formal Alliance with AAA," *Hotel and Motel Management,* **212,** 11, June 16, 1997, p. 15.

Budget $29–$39	Economy $40–$60	Midprice $60–$100	Up Scale $100–200	Luxury $140–$450	All-Suites $65–$150
	Holiday Inn Express	Holiday Inn	Holiday Inn	Crown Plaza	
	Fairfield Inn	Courtyard Inn Residence Inn	Marriott	Marriott Marquis Ritz-Carlton	Marriott Suites
		Days Inn	Omni	Renaissance	
		Radisson Inn	Radisson		Radisson Suites
	Ramada Limited	Ramada Inn	Ramada	Ramada	Ramada Suites
	Sheraton Inn	Sheraton Inn Four Points	Sheraton	Sheraton Grande	Sheraton Suites
			Hyatt	Hyatt Regency Hyatt Park	Hyatt Suites
Sleep Inns	Comfort Inn	Quality Inn	Clarion Hotels		Quality Suites Comfort Suites
		Hilton Inn	Hilton	Hilton Towers	Hilton Suites
		Doubletree Club	Doubletree		Doubletree Suites
Thrift Lodge	Travelodge Hotels	Travelodge Hotels	Forte Hotels	Forte Hotels	
			Westin	Westin	
Sixpence Inn	La Quinta				
E-Z-8	Red Roof Inn				
	Best Western				
	Hampton Inn				Embassy Suites

Figure 3–2 *Hotels by Price Segment*

He opened a 2,257-room hotel, the Inside-Inn, which was described as the biggest exhibit at the World's Fair in St. Louis. In 1908, Statler opened a 300-room, 300-bathroom hotel in Buffalo, where his genius was seen in many details. Back-to-back rooms used common shafts for plumbing. Every guest room had ice water on tap, a towel hook beside each bathroom, a telephone, and a full-sized closet with its own light. From then on, the Statler story was one of incredible success.

In 1912, Statler built the Cleveland Statler, a property that could handle large business groups, and instituted the policy of "a free newspaper every morning." The kitchens were designed to provide an unhindered traffic flow of food and personnel. The dining rooms were located close to the kitchen instead of on a lower floor, and guest rooms were decorated with variety but always with related colors. Other Statler innovations included posted room rates, attached bed-headboard reading lamps, radios at no extra charge, and a liberal quantity of towels and writing supplies in all rooms.

One Star ★ (Economy)	Typically smaller hotels managed by the proprietor. The hotel is often two to four stories high and usually has a more personal atmosphere. It's usually located near affordable attractions, major intersections and convenient to public transportation. Furnishings and facilities are clean but basic. Most will not have a restaurant on site but are usually within walking distance to some good low-priced dining. Public access, past certain hours, may be restricted. Typical national chain: Econolodge, Motel 6.
Two Star ★★ (Moderate)	Usually denotes independent and name brand hotel chains with a reputation for offering consistent quality amenities. The hotel is usually small to medium sized and conveniently located to moderately priced attractions. The facilities typically include telephones and TVs in the bedroom. Some hotels offer limited restaurant service; however, room service and bellhop service are usually not provided. Typical national chain: Days Inn, LaQuinta Inn.
Three Star ★★★ (First Class)	Typically these hotels offer spacious accommodations that include well-appointed rooms and decorated lobbies. Bellhop service is usually not available. They are often located near major expressways or business areas, convenient to shopping and moderate to high-priced attractions. The hotels usually feature medium-sized restaurants that typically offer service breakfast through dinner. Room service availability may vary. Valet parking, fitness centers, and pools are often provided. Typical national chain: Holiday Inn, Hilton.
Four Star ★★★★ (Superior)	Mostly large, formal hotels with reception areas, front desk service, and bellhop service. The hotels are most often located near other hotels of the same caliber and are usually found near shopping, dining, and other major attractions. The level of service is well above average and the rooms are well lit and well furnished. Restaurant dining is usually available and may include more than one choice. Some properties will offer continental breakfast and/or happy hour delicacies. Room service is usually available during most hours. Valet parking and/or garage service is also usually available. Concierge services, fitness centers, and one or more pools are often provided. Typical national chains: Hyatt, Marriott.
Five Star ★★★★★ (Deluxe)	These are hotels that offer only the highest level of accommodations and services. The properties offer a high degree of personal service. Although most five-star hotels are large properties, sometimes the small independent (non-chain) property offers an elegant intimacy that cannot be achieved in the larger setting. The hotel locations can vary from the very exclusive locations of a suburban area to the heart of downtown. The hotel lobbies are sumptuous, the rooms complete with stylish furnishing and quality linens. The amenities often include VCRs, CD stereos, garden tubs, or Jacuzzis, in-room video library, heated pools and more. The hotels feature up to three restaurants all with exquisite menus. Room service is usually available twenty-four hours a day. Fitness centers and valet and/or garage parking are typically available. A concierge is also available to assist you. Typical national chains: Ritz Carlton, Four Seasons.

Figure 3–3 *Hotel Rating Guide* (Adapted from The City Travel Guide—Hotel Rating System.)

"EM," as Statler signed himself, was a dynamo of energy, and no detail of construction or operation was too small for his attention. The Statler Foundation today has assets of many millions.

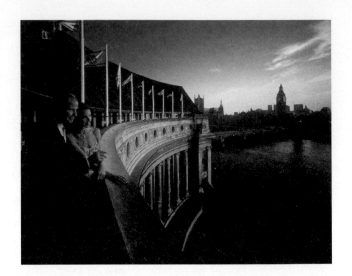

London Marriott Hotel, County Hall, a City Center Hotel. (Courtesy Marriott International.)

City Center Hotels

City center hotels, by virtue of their location, meet the needs of the traveling public for business or leisure reasons. These hotels could be luxury, midscale, business, suites, economy, or residential. They offer a range of accommodations and services. Luxury hotels might offer the ultimate in decor, butler service, concierge and special concierge floors, secretarial services, computers, fax machines, beauty salons, health spas, twenty-four-hour room service, swimming pools, tennis courts, valet service, ticket office, airline office, car rental, and doctor/nurse on duty or on call. Generally, they offer a signature restaurant, coffee shop, or an equivalent name restaurant; a lounge; a name bar; meeting and convention rooms; a ballroom; and possibly a fancy night spot.

City center hotels were constructed in waves; stimulated by government regulations, investors developed hotels when the climate was right. For example, tax incentives for urban renewal projects created favorable economic conditions in the 1960s. This led to the construction of new downtown hotels in many cities. Another boom time for hotel development was the 1980s. Together with convention centers and office buildings, hotels have been one of the catalysts in inner-city revitalization. The Copley Center in Boston and the Peachtree Plaza in Atlanta are examples of this.

The St. Regis Hotel in New York is another good example of a city center luxury hotel. An example of a midscale hotel in New York is the Ramada Hotel; an economy hotel is the Days Inn; and a suites property is the Embassy Suites.

Resort Hotels

Resort hotels came of age with the advent of rail travel. Increasingly, city dwellers and others had the urge to vacation in locations they found appealing. Traveling to these often more-exotic locations became a part of the plea-

Banff Springs Hotel

sure experience. In the late 1800s, luxury resort hotels were developed to accommodate the clientele that the railways brought.

Such hotels include the famous Greenbrier at White Sulphur Springs, West Virginia, The Hotel del Coronado in Coronado (near San Diego), California, and the Homestead at Hot Springs, Virginia. In Canada, the Banff Springs Hotel and Chateau Lake Louise drew the rich and famous of the day to their picturesque locations in the Canadian Rocky Mountains.

The leisure and pleasure travelers of those days were drawn by resorts, beaches, or spectacular mountain scenery. At first, many of these grand resorts were seasonal. However, as automobile and air travel made even the remote resorts more accessible and an increasing number of people could afford to visit, many resorts became year-round properties.

Resort communities sprang up in the sunshine belt from Palm Springs to Palm Beach. Some resorts focused on major sporting activities such as skiing, golf, or fishing; others offered family vacations. Further improvements in both air and automobile travel brought exotic locations within the reach of the population. Europe, the Caribbean, and Mexico became more accessible. As the years passed, some of the resorts suffered because the public's vacation plans changed.

The traditional family month-long resort vacation gave way to shorter, more frequent getaways of four to seven days. The regular resort visitors became older; in general, the younger guests preferred the mobility of the automobile and the more informal atmosphere provided by the newer and more informal resorts.

To survive, the resort hotels became more astute in marketing to different types of guests. For example, some resorts allow no children in the high season because they would interfere with the quiet ambiance for guests who do not want the noise of children. Other resort hotels go out of their way to encourage families; Camp Hyatt is a prominent example. Hyatt hotels have organized a program consisting of a variety of activities for children, thereby giving the parents an opportunity to either enjoy some free time on their own or join their children in some fun activities. Many resort hotels began to attract conventions, conferences, and meetings. This enabled them to maintain or increase occupancy, particularly during the low and shoulder seasons.

Guests go to resorts for leisure and recreation. They want a good climate—summer or winter—in which they can relax or engage in recreational activities. Due to the remoteness of many resorts, guests are a kind of "captured clientele," who may be on the property for days at a time. This presents resort managers with some unique operating challenges. Another operating challenge concerns seasonality—some resorts either do not operate year-round or have periods of very low occupancy. Both present challenges in attracting, training, and retaining competent staff.

Many guests travel considerable distances to resorts. Consequently, they tend to stay longer than at transient hotels. This presents a challenge to the food and beverage manager to provide quality menus that are varied and are presented and served in an attractive, attentive manner. To achieve this, resorts often use a cyclical menu that repeats itself every fourteen to twenty-one days. Also, they provide a wide variety and number of dishes to stimulate interest. Menus are now more health conscious—lighter and low in saturated fats, cholesterol, salt, and calories.

The food needs to be presented in a variety of different ways. Buffets are popular because they give guests the opportunity to make choices from a display of foods. Barbecues, display cooking, poolside, specialty restaurants, and reciprocal dining arrangements with nearby hotels give guests more options.

With increased global competition, not only from other resorts but also from cruise lines, resort managers are challenged to both attract guests and to turn those guests into repeat business, which traditionally has been the foundation of the resorts viability.

To increase occupancies, resorts have diversified their marketing mix to include conventions, business meetings, sales meetings, incentive groups, sporting events, additional sporting and recreational facilities, spas, adventure tourism, ecotourism, and so on.

Because guests are cocooned in the resort—they expect to be pampered. This requires an attentive, well-trained staff and that is a challenge in some remote areas and in developing countries.

There are a number of benefits to operating resorts. The guests are much more relaxed in comparison to those at transient hotels, and the resorts are located in scenically beautiful areas. This frequently enables staff to enjoy a better quality of life than do their transient hotel counterparts. Returning guests tend to treat associates like friends. This adds to the overall party-like atmosphere, which is prevalent at many of the established resorts.

Vacation Ownership

The Growth of an Industry

From its beginnings in the French Alps in the late 1960s, vacation ownership has become the fastest growing segment of the U.S. travel and tourism industry, increasing in popularity at the rate of nearly 16 percent each year since 1993.

Vacation ownership is the politically correct way of saying timeshare. Essentially, vacation ownership means a person purchases the use of a unit

Personal Profile: Valerie Ferguson

Past Chair of the American Hotel & Motel Association and Regional Vice President of Loews Hotels

To most "making it big" seems like a regular statement and a task easily achieved. To Valerie Ferguson, well, it comes with a lot of work, dedication, and heart. She speaks often about seizing opportunities and adding self-interest into what you do for your career.

For this African-American female, life wasn't always easy. As the managing director of Loews Philadelphia Hotel and regional vice president of Loews Hotels, she has a lot to say about what got her where she is now.

One of her most important role models was her father, Sam Ferguson. She says, "My father and I had a great relationship in which he supported me, but in which he never put any images in front of me about what I should shoot for." Sam was a chairman of the Life Sciences Department at a small California school that Valerie attended as a little girl.

For college, Valerie applied to the University of San Francisco, where she earned a degree in government. Eventually realizing that law wasn't where her heart was, she decided to move out to Atlanta where she got a job as a nighttime desk clerk at the Hyatt Regency. She fell in love with the hotel industry and saw it as a challenge. Soon enough though, she realized that the challenges she was really facing were issues of race and gender. She explains, "I was raw in my approach to the business world, but I soon came to realize that it takes more than working hard. To succeed, a person must be able to proclaim his or her goals."

She calls her career in hospitality "the opportunity of a lifetime." She believes that lodging is a vital force in the national economy. She goes around visiting key industries and attending association events to encourage hoteliers to seek out young men and women who represent the new and upcoming generation of hoteliers. She urges hoteliers to strive to create a diverse workforce that reflects the real-world marketplace.

Her success comes from being out there and connecting with people and society. Valerie is past chair of the American Hotel & Motel Association (AH&MA) board and still serves on the Diversity Committee. She is also past chair of the Atlanta Hotel Council Program; she is a

(Courtesy Valerie Ferguson.)

corporate partner with Clark Atlanta University's Kennedy Center Head Start Program and a member of the advisory councils for Georgia State University, Morehouse College, and Bethune-Cookman College. She is a member of business, civic, and educational endeavors such as the Atlanta Convention & Visitors Bureau, the Philadelphia Convention & Visitors Bureau, and a board member of the Georgia Hospitality & Travel Association (GH&TA). She is also past associate director of the National Restaurant Association. She is a director on the boards of the Pennsylvania Travel Council, Philadelphia Workforce Investment, Communities in Schools, and the Educational Institute.

Valerie was nominated general manager of the year for the Hyatt Hotels Corporation in 1991 and 1993. Through the years, she has managed positions for the Hyatt Regency Atlanta, the Lodge in Chicago, the Hyatt Regency Flint, Michigan, and the Hyatt Atlanta Airport Hotel. Her outstanding work and devotion to the hospitality and lodging industry has not gone unrewarded. In 1990, she was named one of the Top 100 Black Women in Corporate America by *Ebony* magazine.

She received the 1991 Atlanta Business League Pioneer Award and in 1993 was awarded the Network of Executive Women in Hospitality's Woman of the Year award. In 1994, she was named one of the Top 100 Black Women of Influence by the Atlanta Business League Pioneer. In that same year, she was awarded the Turner Broadcasting Trumpet Award, which saluted achievement by African-Americans. She was named the Georgia GH&TA 1997 Lodging Leader of the Year. She was also named one of the 100 Most Influential Women in Travel in 1996, 1997, and 1998 by *Travel Agent* magazine. Her most recent honorary awards for her work in the lodging industry were the 1998 NAACP Southeast Region Trailblazer Award for Business, the Martin Luther King, Jr. Drum Major for Justice Award from Coretta Scott King and the Women of the Southern Christian Leadership Conference (SCLC). She was also honored with an honorary doctorate in foodservice, presented by the North American Association of Food Equipment Manufacturers.

continued

After twenty-three years of working with the Ritz-Carlton Hotel Company and the Hyatt Hotels, Valerie left to pursue being a regional vice president for Loews Hotels and managing director for the Loews Philadelphia Hotel. She had been general manager at The Ritz-Carlton, Atlanta, in 1995 and then also as a general manager at the Hyatt Regency Atlanta. Regional Vice President Bill Rhodes says, "her drive to grow and learn" was what impressed him most about Valerie. He continues, "She is obsessed with continuing her education in the industry and is not intimidated by any situation or any opportunity. She has a lot of self-confidence and jumps in with both feet, providing a tremendous amount of leadership." She worked her way up from being director of rooms, to rooms executive, to assistant director of housekeeping and front office manager. Ed Rabin, executive vice president of Hyatt and an early Ferguson mentor says, "From the get-go she demonstrated an ability and willingness to understand and learn the business and win over guests, colleagues, and peers in the process."

When Loews was just being opened, Valerie was thrilled by the excitement that came with the adventure of being with a company yet still to grow. President and CEO of Loews Jonathan Tisch became a close friend of Valerie's as they served together on the board of the AH&MA. In 1994, Valerie ran for a seat on AH&MA's executive committee and eventually succeeded Tisch as chair. She was the first African-American and second woman to serve as AH&MA chair.

She comments on the hospitality industry, "The hospitality industry is one of the last vestiges of the American dream, where you can enter from very humble beginnings and end up a success."

The great relationship she has with people has been a great contribution to her well-deserved success. Valerie Ferguson relates well with her employees and always wants to be the person to help them aim high in their careers and achieve their goals. Ed Rubin remarks, "She has remarkable empathy for all people in all walks of life, and that is the main reason for her success." She believes in promoting diversity in the workplace and marketplace and will go to great lengths to do so. She is involved in issues involving legislation and regulation, making use of her degree in government from the University of San Francisco. She supports local initiatives by hotel associations against occupancy taxes that hurt business.

Ferguson has come a long way in her career. She is proud of what she is doing and doesn't believe that she has stopped climbing the ladder of success. She is fighting to make other women and minority members realize that there is a whole world of opportunities out there and they should set their goals high. She believes that equality of opportunity "should not come as the result of a mandate for the federal government or as the result of pressure from groups outside this industry. The impetus for change must come from within the hearts and souls of each of us."

Sources: Lodging, 23, 5, January 1998; www.loews hotels.com; www.ahma.com/about/officers/ferguson. htm; www.findarticles.com/cf_0_/mv0VOU/ 1998_ July_30/50216477/pl/article.jhtml; www.hotel-online. com/Neo/SpecialReports1998/Nov98_Ferguson.html.

similar to a condominium for blocks of times, usually in weeks. Henry Silverman of Cendant, which owns the Indianapolis, Indiana-based Resort Condominiums International (RCI), says that a timeshare is really a two-bedroom suite that is owned, rather than a hotel room that is rented for a transient night. A vacation club, on the other hand, is a "travel-and-use" product. Consumers do not buy a fixed-week, unit-size, season, resort, or number of days to vacation each year. Instead, they purchase points that represent currency, which is used to access the club's vacation benefits. An important advantage to this is the product's flexibility, especially when tied to a point system. A vacation club is not involved with real-estate ownership in any way, so the point system ties in well with the hotel marketing programs, such as those that reward frequent flyers.[22]

[22]Mike Malley, "Timeshare Synergies," *Hotel and Motel Management,* **212,** 5, March 17, 1997, p. 18.

*Horizons by Marriott
Vacation Club, Orlando*
(Courtesy Marriott
International.)

The World Tourism Organization has called timeshares one of the fastest growing sectors of the travel and tourism industry. Hospitality companies are adding brand power to the concept with corporations like Marriott Vacation Club International, the Walt Disney Company, Hilton Hotels, Hyatt Hotels, Promus' Embassy Suites, Inter-Continental and even Four Seasons participating in an industry that has grown rapidly in recent years. Still, only about 3.0 percent of all U.S. households own vacation ownership. RCI estimates that the figure could rise to 10 percent within the next decade for households with incomes of more than $50,000. No wonder hotel companies have found this to be a lucrative business.

RCI, the largest vacation ownership exchange (that allows members to exchange vacations with other locations), has more than 2.8 million member families living in 200 countries. Three thousand seven-hundred participating resorts and members can exchange vacation intervals for vacations at any participating resort.[23] Vacation ownership is popular at U.S. resorts from Key West in Florida to Kona in Hawaii and from New York City and Las Vegas to Colorado ski resorts.

Today, more than 2.8 million households own vacation intervals at more than 3,700 resorts located in ninety-plus countries. Vacationers around the world are turning to vacation ownership resorts as their preferred travel destination, with timeshare owners hailing from 200 countries. North America remains the global leader with nearly half of all the participating resorts and more than 2 million owners. Europe is second with approximately 22 percent of owners worldwide and more than 1,000 resorts. Timeshare resorts are found around the globe in popular vacation areas near beaches, rivers, lakes, and mountains, and even in major cities.

By locking in the purchase price of accommodations, vacation ownership helps ensure future vacations at today's prices at luxurious resorts with amenities, service, and ambiance that rival any of the world's top-rated vacation destinations. Through vacation exchange programs, timeshare owners can travel

[23]http:/RCI.com, October 27, 2002.

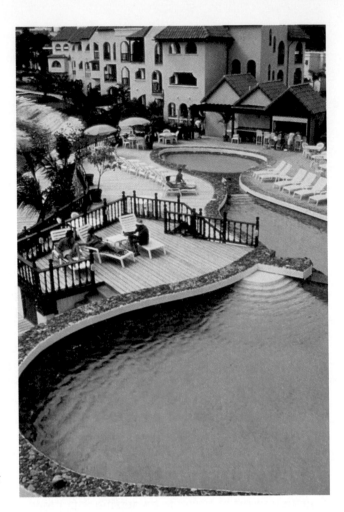

Divi Carina Bay Resort
(Courtesy of RCI.)

to other popular destinations around the world. With unparalleled flexibility and fully equipped condominiums that offer the best in holiday luxury, vacation ownership puts consumers in the driver's seat, allowing them to plan and enjoy vacations that suit their lifestyle.

Timeshare resort developers today include many of the world's leading hoteliers, publicly held corporations, and independent companies. Properties that combine vacation ownership resorts with hotels, adventure resorts, and gaming resorts are among the emerging timeshare trends. The reasons for purchasing most frequently cited by current timeshare owners are the high standards of quality accommodations and service at the resorts where they own and exchange, the flexibility offered through the vacation exchange opportunities, and the cost effectiveness of vacation ownership. Nearly one-third of vacation owners purchase additional intervals after experiencing ownership. This trend is even stronger among long-time owners: more than 40 percent of those who have owned for eight years or longer have purchased additional intervals within the timeshare.

What Is Vacation Ownership?

Vacation ownership offers consumers the opportunity to purchase fully furnished vacation accommodations in a variety of forms, such as weekly intervals or points in points-based systems, for a percentage of the cost of full ownership. For a one-time purchase price and payment of a yearly maintenance fee, purchasers own their vacation either in perpetuity or for a predetermined number of years. Owners share both the use and the costs of upkeep of their unit and the common grounds of the resort property. Vacation ownership purchases are typically financed through consumer loans of five to ten years' duration, with terms dependent on the purchase price and the amount of the buyer's down payment. The average cost of a vacation ownership is about $12,500.

Each condominium, or unit, of a vacation ownership resort is divided into intervals, either by the week or by points equivalent, which are sold separately. The condominiums are priced according to a variety of factors, including size of the unit, resort amenities, location, and season. With timeshare, owning your vacation is considered a major benefit. Once a majority or other preset percentage is sold to vacation owners, the management of the resort is usually turned over to a Resort Property Owners Association (POA), or Homeowners Association (HOA). The vacation owners then elect officers and take control of expenses, upkeep, and the future of their resort property, including the selection of a management company.

What Are Yearly Maintenance Fees?

Yearly maintenance fees are paid each year to a HOA for the maintenance of the resort. Just like taking care of a home, resort maintenance fees help maintain the quality and future value of the resort property. In a vacation ownership resort, maintenance costs are shared by all owners. They pay for on-site management, unit upkeep and refurbishing, utilities, and maintenance of the resort's common areas and amenities, such as pools, tennis courts, and golf courses. Just like residential condominium owners, they determine the fees through their HOA board of directors. The amount of the yearly maintenance fee typically depends on the size, location, and amenities of the resort. Maintenance fees are assessed and paid annually by each vacation owner.

Today, there are several types of timeshare programs from which to choose, enabling consumers to purchase the type of vacation ownership that best matches their lifestyle. Timesharing, or vacation ownership, describes a method of use and ownership. It denotes exclusive use of accommodations for a particular number of days each year. Usually sold by the week, it is also called interval or vacation interval. The purchase of a timeshare interval can take various legal forms. Under a fixed-unit, fixed-week deeded agreement, the purchaser receives a deed allowing the use of a specific condominium at a particular time every year forever, just like buying a house. Benefits may include the tax advantages of ownership, plus a voice in the management of the resort. Under this agreement, the owner may rent, sell, exchange, or bequeath the vacation interval.

Under a right-to-use plan, ownership of the resort remains with the developer. The purchaser reserves the right to use one or more resort accommodations for a specified number of years, ranging generally from ten to fifty years, after which all use rights return to the developer. These plans come in a variety of forms, most commonly as club membership. Vacation intervals are sold as either fixed or floating time. With fixed time, the unit, or unit type, is purchased for a specific week during the year. That week is reserved for the owner every year, subject to cancellation if the vacation owner does not plan to use it in the given year.

Floating time refers to the use of vacation accommodations usually within a certain season of the year, often within a three- to four-month period, such as spring or summer. The owner must reserve his or her desired vacation time in advance, with reservation confirmation typically provided on a first-come, first-served basis. The purchaser may also receive a deed under a floating-time arrangement. According to a recent national study, approximately 70 percent of timeshare condominiums in the United States are sold as floating time. Some price differences are based on demand within each season.

Vacation clubs, or point-based programs, provide the flexible use of accommodations in multiple resort locations. With these products, club members purchase points that represent either a travel and use membership or a deeded real estate product. These points are then used like currency to purchase the various size accommodations, during a certain season, for a set number of days at a participating resort. The number of points needed to access the resort accommodations will vary by the members' demand for unit size, season, resort location, and amenities. A vacation club may have a specific term of ownership or be deeded in perpetuity.

Fractional ownership enables consumers to purchase a larger share of a vacation ownership unit, usually from five to twenty-six weeks. This type of ownership is popular in ski, beach, and island resort areas.

"Lockoff" or "lockout" units allow vacation owners to occupy a portion of the unit and offer the remaining space for rental or exchange. These units typically consist of two bedrooms and two baths, or three bedrooms and three baths.

Split weeks are popular with consumers who prefer shorter vacations. The owner may split use of the interval into two separate visits to the resort, such as one three-night and one four-night stay at two different times of the year. Reservations are usually granted on a first-come, first-served basis and are based on availability.

Biennial ownership, or alternate-year ownership, allows for resort property ownership every other year and costs less than annual ownership at comparable resorts.

The Advantages of Vacation Ownership

Unlike a hotel room or rental cottage that requires payment for each use of rates that usually increase each year, ownership at a timeshare property enables vacationers to enjoy a resort, year after year, for the duration of their ownership for only a one-time purchase price and the payment of yearly maintenance fees.

Timeshare ownership offers vacationers an opportunity to save on the escalating costs of vacation accommodations over the long term, while enjoying all the comforts of home in a resort setting.

Truly a home away from home, vacation ownership provides the space and flexibility to meet the needs of any size family or group. While most vacation ownership condominiums have two bedrooms and two baths, unit sizes range from studios to three, or more, bedrooms. Unlike hotel rooms, there are no charges for additional guests. Also unlike hotels, most units include a fully equipped kitchen with dining area, washer and dryer, stereo, VCRs, and more.

Timeshare resort amenities rival those of other top-rated resort properties and may include swimming pools, tennis, Jacuzzi, golf, bicycles, and exercise facilities. Others feature boating, ski lifts, restaurants, and equestrian facilities. Most timeshare resorts offer a full schedule of on-site or nearby sporting, recreational, and social activities for adults and children. The resorts are staffed with well-trained hospitality professionals, with many resorts offering concierge services for assistance in visiting area attractions.

> ### Early "Hotels"
>
> Increased travel and trade made some form of overnight accommodations an absolute necessity. Because travel was slow and journeys long and arduous, many travelers depended solely on the hospitality of private citizens.
>
> In the Greek and Roman empires, inns and taverns sprang up everywhere. The Romans constructed elaborate and well-appointed inns on all the main roads. Marco Polo later proclaimed these inns as "fit for a king." They were located about twenty-five miles apart to provide fresh houses for officials and couriers of the Roman government and could only be used with special government documents granting permission. These documents became revered status symbols and were subject to numerous thefts and forgeries. By the time Marco Polo traveled to the Far East, there were 10,000 inns.

Travel the World Through Exchange Vacations

Vacation ownership offers unparalleled flexibility and the opportunity for affordable worldwide travel through vacation ownership exchange. Through the international vacation exchange networks, owners can trade their timeshare intervals for vacation time at comparable resorts around the world. Most resorts are affiliated with an exchange company that administers the exchange service for its members. Typically, the exchange company will directly solicit annual membership. Owners individually elect to become members of the affiliated exchange company. To exchange, the owner places his or her interval into the exchange company's pool of resorts and weeks available for exchange and, in turn, chooses an available resort and week from that pool. The exchange company charges an exchange fee, in addition to an annual membership fee, to complete an exchange. Exchange companies and resorts frequently offer their members the additional benefit of saving or banking vacation time in a reserve program for use in a different year.

Airport Hotels

Many **airport hotels** enjoy a high occupancy because of the large number of travelers arriving and departing from major airports. The guest mix in airport hotels consists of business, group, and leisure travelers. Passengers with early or late flights may stay over at the airport hotel, while others rest while waiting for connecting flights.

Airport hotels are generally in the 200- to 600-room size and are full service. To care for the needs of guests who may still feel as if they are in different time zones, room service and restaurant hours may be extended, even offered twenty-four hours. More moderately priced hotels have vending machines.

As competition at airport hotels intensified, some added meeting space to cater to businesspeople who want to fly in, meet, and fly out. Here, the airport hotel has the advantage of saving the guests from having to go downtown. Almost all airport hotels provide courtesy van transportation to and from the airport.

Convenient locations, economical prices, easy and less costly transportation costs to and from the airport are some reasons why airport hotels are becoming intelligent choices for business travelers. Airport hotels can mean a bargain for groups, especially considering that the transportation to the hotel and back from the airport is usually free or is very inexpensive, says Brian Booth, director of sales and marketing at the Dallas Hyatt Regency Airport Hotel. One of the most conveniently located hotels in the country is the Miami International Airport Hotel, which is located within the airport itself.

Freeway Hotels and Motels

Freeway hotels and motels came into prominence in the 1950s and 1960s. As Americans took to the open road, they needed a convenient place to stay that was reasonably priced with few frills. Guests could simply drive up, park outside the office, register, rent a room, and park outside of the room. Over the years, more facilities were added: lounges, restaurants, pools, soft drink machines, game rooms, and satellite TV.

Motels are often clustered near freeway off-ramps on the outskirts of towns and cities. Today, some are made of modular construction and have as few as eleven employees per hundred rooms. These savings in land, construction, and operating costs are passed on to the guest in the form of lower rates.

Casino Hotels

The **casino hotel** industry is now coming into the financial mainstream, to the point that, as a significant segment of the entertainment industry, it is reshaping the U.S. economy. The entertainment and recreation sector has become a very important engine for U.S. economic growth, providing a boost to consumer spending, thus creating tremendous prosperity for the industry. The fastest growing sector of the entertainment field is gaming, which is discussed in Chapter 11.

Casino hotels are leaning toward making their hotels into "family friendly" hotels. The gaming business is strictly for adults, however, these hotels realize that making their hotels family friendly will attract more families to spend a day or two in their hotels. Circus Circus in Las Vegas pioneered the concept more than a decade ago. Various other casino hotels are following suit. They

Venetian Hotel, Las Vegas Gaming Floor (Courtesy The Venetian.)

have baby-sitters available at any time of the day, children's attractions ranging from parks to circuses and museums, and kids menus in restaurants. For
adults, in addition to gaming, a multinational cuisine for dining, health spas
for relaxation, dance clubs, and dazzling shows are available.

Casino hotels are now marketing themselves as business hotels. They
include in their rooms work space, a fax, a copier, and computer data ports.
Other amenities include a full-service business center, travel bureau, and room
service. Larger casino hotels also attract conventions, which represent a lucrative business.

Convention Hotels

Convention hotels provide facilities and meet the needs of groups attending
and holding conventions. Apart from this segment of the market, convention
hotels also attract seasonal leisure travelers. Typically these hotels exceed 500
guest rooms with larger public areas to accommodate hundreds of people at
any given time. Convention hotels have many banquet areas within and
around the hotel complex. These hotels have a high percentage of double occupancies and rooms have double queen-sized beds. Convention hotels may also
offer a concierge floor to cater to individual guest needs. Round-the-clock room
service, an in-house laundry, a business center, a travel desk, and an airport
shuttle service are other amenities found in convention hotels.

Full-Service Hotels

Another way to classify hotels is by the degree of service offered: full-service, economy, extended-stay, and all-suite hotels. **Full-service hotels** offer a wide range of facilities, services, and amenities, including many that were mentioned under the luxury hotel category: multiple food and beverage outlets including bars, lounges, and restaurants; both formal and casual dining; and meeting, convention, and catering services. Business features might include a business center, secretarial services, fax, in-room computer hook-ups, and so on.

Most of the major North American cities have hotel chain representation such as Doubletree, Four Seasons, Hilton, Holiday Inn, Hyatt, Marriott, Omni, Ramada, Radisson, Ritz-Carlton, Loew's, Le Meridian, Sheraton, and Westin. Some of these chains are positioning themselves as basic full-service properties. An example of this strategy is Marriott's Courtyard hotels, which have small lobbies and very limited food and beverage offerings. The resulting savings are passed on to the guests in the form of more competitive rates. Thus, the full-service market may also be subdivided into upscale and midpriced hotels.

Economy/Budget Hotels

An **economy or budget hotel** offers clean, reasonably sized and furnished rooms without the frills of full-service hotels. Chains like Travelodge, Motel 6, Days Inn, and La Quinta became popular by focusing on selling beds, but not meals or meetings. This enabled them to offer rates at about 30 percent lower than the midpriced hotels. Economy properties, which represent about 15 percent of total hotel rooms, have experienced tremendous growth.

More recent entrants to this market sector are Promus' Hampton Inns, Marriott's Fairfield, and Choice's Comfort Inns. These properties do not have restaurants or offer substantial food and beverages, but they do offer guests a continental breakfast in the lobby.

Morena Valley
Travelodge #982

Fairfield Inn

Another example of a relatively new budget concept is Microtel. In 1989, despite a credit crunch and a weak economy, a group of entrepreneurs developed a budget concept called Microtel. Success criteria were developed; The group wanted an economy hotel product, the downside risk had to be limited, and the product would have to demonstrate a competitive advantage over other national budget chains. The result of several months of careful planning and construction was the ninety-nine-room Microtel in Rochester, New York, at a total cost of $2,798,000 or $28,263 per room. The land cost $266,000; construction, interest, taxes, furniture, and equipment cost $2,164,000. The room rates began at $29, and the occupancy was 89.4 percent in the first year. The franchise was sold a year later for a 117 percent return on investment (ROI).[24] This is a remarkable success story that illustrates that entrepreneurs can thrive even in a weak economy.

After enjoying a wave of growth for most of the 1990s, the economy hotel segment may be close to the saturation point. There are about 20,000 properties in this segment with many markets. The economic law of supply and demand rules; if an area has too many similar properties, then price wars usually break out as they try to attract guests. Some will attempt to differentiate themselves and stress value rather than discounting. This adds to the fascination of the business.

Extended-Stay Hotels

Other hotels cater to guests who stay for an extended period. They will, of course, take guests for a shorter time when space is available. However, the majority of guests are long term. Guests take advantage of a reduction in the rates based on the length of their stay. The mix of guests is mainly business and professional/technical, or relocating families.

---

[24]This section draws on George R. Justus, "Microtel: How 'Simple' Translates into Success," *The Cornell Hotel and Restaurant Administration Quarterly*, **32,** 4, December 1991, pp. 50–54.

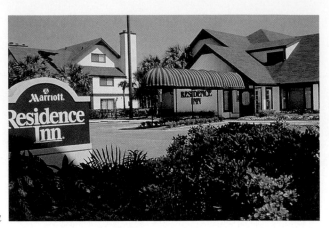

Residence Inn

Residence Inns and Homewood Suites are market leaders in this segment of the lodging industry. These properties offer full kitchen facilities and shopping services or a convenience store on the premises. Complimentary continental breakfast and evening cocktails are served in the lobby. Some properties offer a business center and recreational facilities.

All-Suite, Extended-Stay Hotels

All-suite extended-stay hotels typically offer approximately 25 percent more space for the same amount of money as the regular hotel in the same price range. The additional space is usually in the form of a lounge and possibly a kitchenette area.

Embassy Suites, owned and operated by the Promus Corporation; Residence Inns, Fairfield Suites, and Town-Place Suites, all by Marriott; Extended Stay America; Homewood Suites; and Guest Quarters are the market leaders in the all-suites, extended-stay segment of the lodging industry. Several of the major hotel chains have all-suite, extended-stay subsidiaries, including Radisson, Choice Hotels (which dominate the economy all-suite segment with Comfort and Quality Suites), ITT Sheraton Suites, Hilton Suites, Homegate Studios, and Suites by Wyndham Hotels. These properties provide a closer-to-home feeling for guests who may be relocating or attending seminars, or are on work-related projects that necessitate a stay of greater than about five days.

There are now almost 1,500 extended-stay properties. Many of these properties have business centers and offer services like grocery shopping and laundry/dry cleaning. The designers of extended-stay properties realize that guests prefer a home-like atmosphere. Accordingly, many properties are built to encourage a community feeling, which allows guests to informally interact.

Bed and Breakfast Inns

Bed and breakfast inns, or B&Bs as they are familiarly known, offer an alternative lodging experience to the normal hotel or motel. According to *Travel Assist*

Magazine, B&B is a concept that began in Europe and started as overnight lodging in a private home. A true B&B is an accommodation with the owner, who lives on the premises or nearby, providing a clean, attractive accommodation and breakfast, usually a memorable one. The host also offers to help the guest with directions, restaurants, and suggestions for local entertainment or sightseeing.

There are many different styles of B&Bs with prices ranging from about $30 to $300 or more per night. B&Bs may be quaint cottages with white picket fences leading to gingerbread houses, tiny and homey, with two or three rooms available. On the other hand, some are sprawling, ranch-style homes in the Rockies; multistoried town homes in large cities; farms; adobe villas; log cabins; lighthouses; and many stately mansions. The variety is part of the thrill, romance, and charm of the B&B experience.[25]

There are an estimated 25,000 bed and breakfast places in the United States alone. Bed and breakfast inns have flourished for many reasons. Business travelers are growing weary of the complexities of the check-in/check-out processes at some commercial hotels. With the escalation of transient rates at hotels, an opportunity has been created to serve a more price-sensitive segment of travelers. Also, many leisure travelers are looking for accommodation somewhere between a large, formal hotel and staying with friends. The B&Bs offer a home-like atmosphere. They are aptly called "A Home Away from Home." Community breakfasts with other lodgers and hosts enhance this feeling. Each B&B is as unique as its owner. Décor varies according to the region of location and the unique taste of its owner. The owner of the bed and breakfast often provides all the necessary labor, but some employ full- or part-time labor.

Hotel Integration

Vertical Integration

Vertical integration is a trend that began a few years ago. Lodging companies realized that guests' accommodation needs were not just at one level; rather, they seemed to vary by price and facilities/amenities. Almost all major lodging companies now have properties in each segment of the market. An example to illustrate this point is given in Figure 3–4.

Luxury—Clarion
Midscale—Quality Inn, Quality Suites
Budget—Comfort Inn, Friendship Inns, Rodeway Inn
Economy—Sleep Inn

Figure 3–4 *Vertical Integration of Choice Hotels*

[25]This section draws on Janet Star, "What Is a Bed and Breakfast Inn?" *Travel Assist Magazine,* March 2000, p. 14.

A Day in the Life of Sylvie Balenger
Executive Housekeeper, Four Seasons Resort

Once I punch in at 7:45 A.M. I find out what our occupancy was the previous night. We dropped in the count by ten rooms but two people called in sick. We are short one room attendant. The office coordinator tries to call in someone who is off, but no luck. We call in our afternoon room attendants a few hours early—great, they can do it. We're covered for the day.

I hold our daily morning briefing with the 30 room attendants in the housekeeping office. We need to be aware of a group request to remove our doorknob breakfast menus from our guest rooms since the meeting planners want to ensure that all of their attendees go to breakfast at the scheduled planned event in the ballroom. We cover other events in the hotel and go over the focus of the day in the cleaning of our guest rooms. Today it's dusting our lampshades. We finish up with stretching exercises for five minutes.

(Courtesy Sylvie Balenger.)

A room attendant gets an emergency phone call and has to go home. She has to drop seven rooms. We pull the lobby attendant, who has been cross-trained to clean rooms, to do the seven rooms. We ask the male lobby attendant to cover the lobby attendant's section in the lobby.

Time to attend the morning operations meeting at 8:30 A.M. with all the other operational managers. We go over the VIPs, occupancy figures for the night before and the rest of the week, any glitches with guests the previous day, and assign the follow-up. The managers bring up any operational challenges they expect for that day. The guest services manager expects a valet crunch with 200 cars arriving at the same time for a luncheon. All managers with a pager will be notified when to show up and help park cars. The banquet manager expects a tight turn in the ballroom mid-afternoon with only thirty minutes to convert it into a meeting space. Again, anticipate another crunch.

Hold another morning briefing with the supervisors and house attendants at 8:45 A.M. and go over the same notes on our grease board as we had with room atten-

dants. One of the house attendants is complaining of a sore back. He says he did it here a couple of days ago and failed to report it. I fill out a supervisor's injury report and send the house attendant to security. He is sent from there to the clinic.

I review the daily payroll for the department, which takes about thirty minutes. I received a call from a guest wanting to know who did their room last night because she forgot to turn down the sofa bed. I apologized to the guest and sent someone to the room to service it right away and we put a notation in the computer about their sofa bed request. I follow up with the turndown attendant and the P.M. shift manager to determine why this mistake occurred. The notes were made on the attendant's paper about the request. A note is placed in her file after a discussion with her. A flag is put in the computer about the mistake and I send a note of apology and an amenity. We follow up each day to ensure the mistake does not occur again during their stay.

It's 10:00 A.M. and time for the department head meeting, then lunch for fifteen minutes. I get paged to rush a suite for a VIP arrival. The president of our company is checking in and I need to inspect that suite before he arrives. The valet crunch has been called and I help park cars for twenty minutes.

I get a page informing me that our supply of toilet paper and tissues has arrived. I send a house attendant to pick it up. One case is damaged and I inform purchasing to return it and arrange for another case to be sent later. We are out of laundry bags and gloves. I found out our purchase order was delayed due to a missing signature. I find the person to sign it ASAP and purchasing rushes the order. It'll be here tomorrow.

It's early afternoon and we get a crunch at the uniform counter because all of the banquet staff for that turn in the ballroom are here to get ready for the event. I help out for twenty minutes. Then, the ironer/folder breaks down. The rolls do not go back down and we are unable to process linens. The engineer says it'll be down indefinitely. We are sold out that night and we have a big banquet. We arrange for some of our items to go out to a commercial laundry and arrange for transportation. We ask people to work overtime to take care of all the terry so that when our ironer is up we can concentrate on shift laundry. The manager will pick up the items by U-Haul to accommodate the ten bins of linen being sent out.

The crunch for the ballroom turn has been called. Help set up chairs for the afternoon meeting. I have my manager's briefing in my office for thirty minutes. We discuss our Employee of the Month nominees. We consider three room attendants, an office coordinator, and one house attendant nominated by their peers. We checked their files and they are all eligible for consideration. We are also planning on how to have a smooth turn on Sunday. We have the whole house checking out and we'll be full that night. The incoming group wants to have all their arrivals in their rooms by 3:00 P.M. We decide to ask for additional management help in stripping rooms starting at 8:00 A.M. since the departure manifest indicates that our guests checking out have flights in San Diego starting at 6:00 A.M. and we will have half of our departures out by 9:00 A.M. We schedule extra people to make beds and inspect rooms. We have the laundry staff gear up with all the linen by Saturday night and make sure our linen closets are fully stocked. We ensure engineering

has extra staff to take care of deficiencies as soon as a call is made. We ensure room service has enough private bar attendants to restock the rooms before we release them. We cannot afford to have a guest waiting for the private bar to be restocked on a day like Sunday.

The morning staff is on its way down and I bid them goodnight and thank them for a great day. I'm available for anyone who has questions and concerns about schedules, vacation requests, pay in advance requests, concerns about their supervisor that day, problems with rooms such as maintenance requests, missing supplies, and so on.

The house attendants and supervisors come down at 5:00 P.M. There was an argument between a house attendant and a supervisor. I need to be the mediator in my office and this takes about thirty minutes to resolve.

It's 5:30 P.M. and my turndown staff is ready to start. I am present at their briefing and we do exercises. A turndown attendant wants to talk to me. She wants to come to the A.M. shift and work full time instead of part time. I have an opening and explain to her we will need to find a replacement for her first and then move her down to the morning shift.

I do one more final check of my e-mails and go home around 6:00 P.M.

Check Your Knowledge

1. What characteristics do the following hotel segments encompass?
    a. City center hotels
    b. Resort hotels
    c. Airport hotels
    d. Freeway hotels and motels
    e. Full-service hotels
    f. Economy/budget hotels
    g. Extended-stay hotels
    h. Bed and breakfast inns

Marketing Consortium (Referral Organizations)

Marketing consortiums or **referral associations** offer similar benefits to properties as franchises, albeit at a lower cost. Hotels and motels with a referral association share a centralized reservation system and a common image, logo or advertising slogan. In addition, referrals may offer group buying discounts to members, as well as management training and continuing education programs. Each independent hotel refers guests to each of the other member hotels. Hotels and motels pay an initial fee to join a referral association. Size and appearance standards are less stringent than a franchise agreement; hence guests may find more variation between the facilities than with a franchise member.

Preferred Hotels Association, also known as Preferred Hotels and Resorts Worldwide, is a consortium of 105 independent, luxury hotels and resorts united to compete with the marketing power of chain operations. It promotes the individuality, high standards, hospitality, and luxury of member hotels. It also provides marketing support services and a reservation center.

Preferred Hotels Association has begun preparing for future trends in the industry. The consortium expects to increase its membership with the reemergence of independent hotels resulting from the advent of affordable technologies. A new, quality-driven advertising campaign is being developed while the group became one of the first to establish an Internet site. The association is using Guest Information Network's Net Software to develop a client database. The database is intended to help the association develop custom-tailored service packages by recording information about clients' preferences and purchasing patterns.

With the decrease in airline commissions, referral organizations, especially those at the luxury end of the market, are well placed to offer incentives to agents to book their clients with the referral group's hotels. An example would be awarding trips to the property for every ten rooms booked. Another would be for the referral hotels to offer, for instance, a 20 percent commission during slow periods. Three luxury Boston-area preferred properties—the Boston Harbor Hotel, the Bostonian Hotel, and the Charles Hotel in Cambridge, Massachusetts—joined in promoting a St. Patrick's Day weekend package. Preferred Hotels in Texas—the Mansion on Turtle Creek and Hotel Crescent Court in Dallas, La Mansion Del Rio South in San Antonio, and the Washington Hotel in Fort Worth—launched a major, year-long promotion, which includes a tie-in with major retail, credit card, and airline partners.

In addition to regional marketing programs, the referral associations that handle reservations for members have joined Galileo International's Inside Availability Service. This gives agents access to actual rates and room availability that is not always available on the standard CRS databases.

Leading Hotels of the World (LHW) was set up in 1928 as Luxury Hotels of Europe and Egypt by thirty-eight hotels, including the London Savoy; the Hotel Royal in Evian, France; and the Hotel Negresco in Nice, France, who were interested in improving their marketing. The organization worked by having hotels advise their guests to use the establishments of fellow members. It then opened a New York office to make direct contact with wealthy American and Canadian travelers wishing to visit Europe or Egypt.

LHW, which is controlled by its European members, acts as an important marketing machine for its members, especially now, with offices around the world providing reservations, sales, and promotional services. All the hotels and offices are connected by a central computer reservation system called ResStar. The number of reservations members receive from Leading Hotel members varies from place to place, but with more than 100 hotels waiting to join, it must be beneficial.

Like LHW, Small Luxury Hotels of the World (SLH) is another marketing consortium in which seventy-nine independently owned and managed hotels and resorts are members. For more than thirty-five years, it has sought to market and sell its membership to the travel industry and to provide an interhotel networking system for all members. Each hotel is assessed and regularly checked to ensure that it maintains the very highest standards.

Best, Biggest, and Most Unusual Hotels and Chains

So which is the best hotel in the world? The answer may depend on whether you watch the "Lifestyles of the Rich and Famous" or read polls taken by a business investment or travel magazine. According to the article "The World's Best Hotels," written for the *Institutional Investor*, the Oriental Hotel in Bangkok, Thailand, was for several years rated number one in the world by a poll of 100 bankers from around the world. The Oriental was followed by the Regent of Hong Kong, Vier Jahrenzeiten of Hamburg, The Mandarin Oriental of Hong Kong, and the Connaught of London. By 1992, that list had changed, with the Regent Hong Kong and the Bel-Air of Los Angeles being number one and two, respectively. Singapore's Shangri-La was third, bringing the total of Asian hotels in the top ten to six.[26] The largest hotel in the world was the 5,505-room MGM Grand in Las Vegas. This, however, has been surpassed by the new Venetian Hotel also in Las Vegas with an approximate 6,172 rooms, which opened in 1999. Table 3–3 shows the twenty-five largest hotel chains in the world.[27]

[26]Lois Madison Reamy, *Institutional Investor,* **26,** 10, September 1992, pp. 106–112.
[27]Sally Wolchuk, "World's Largest Hotels," *Hotels,* July 1999, p. 50.

Table 3–3   The 15 Largest Hotel Chains

	Company Headquarters	Rooms 2001	Rooms 2000	Hotels 2001	Hotels 2000	Rank 2000	Rank 2001
1	**Cendant Corp.** Parsippany, NJ, USA	553,771	541,313	6,624	6,455	1	1
2	**Six Continents Hotels** London, England	511,072	490,531	3,274	3,096	2	2
3	**Marriott International** Washington, DC, USA	435,983	390,469	2,398	2,099	3	3
4	**Accor** Evry, France	415,774	389,437	3,654	3,488	4	4
5	**Choice Hotels International** Silver Spring, MD, USA	362,549	350,351	4,545	4,392	5	5
6	**Hilton Hotels Corp.** Beverly Hills, CA, USA	327,487	317,823	1,986	1,895	6	6
7	**Best Western International** Phoenix, AZ, USA	306,851	307,737	4,052	4,065	7	7
8	**Starwood Hotels & Resorts Worldwide** White Plains, NY, USA	224,467	227,042	743	738	8	8
9	**Carlson Hospitality Worldwide** Minneapolis, MN, USA	135,066	129,234	788	716	9	9
10	**Hilton Group plc** Watford Herts, England	92,778	64,647	384	223	10	12
11	**Hyatt Hotels Corp./Hyatt International** Chicago, IL, USA	88,442	86,711	204	201	11	10
12	**Sol Melia SA** Palma de Mallorca, Spain	85,987	82,656	350	338	12	11
13	**TUI Group** Hannover, Germany	70,293	49,801	278	204	13	17
14	**Société de Louvre** Paris, France	69,049	53,083	933	868	14	15
15	**Wyndham International** Dallas, TX, USA	57,211	62,262	224	242	15	13

Source: Company websites.

The Best Hotel Chains

The Ritz-Carlton and the Canadian-owned and -operated Four Seasons are generally rated the highest quality chain hotels. In 1993 and again in 1999, Ritz-Carlton hotels were awarded the Malcolm Baldrige National Quality Award. Congress created this award in 1987 to promote and recognize quality achievements in U.S. businesses. Named after the late secretary of commerce Malcolm Baldrige, an early proponent of total quality management (TQM), the award is regarded as the ultimate prize among those U.S. companies that pride themselves on the quality of their products and services.[28] Ritz-Carlton has long been recognized as one of the best luxury hotel chains in the industry, however, then-President and Chief Operating Officer (COO) Horst Schulze wanted more. "We asked ourselves how we could become even better than we were," says Schulze. "The hardest thing for me to do was overcome my ego and admit that I really didn't know how to take the company beyond where it was. Once we did that, the job became easier."

The Ritz-Carlton approach to quality centers on a number of basic but complex principles, many drawn from traditional TQM theory. It is discussed in Chapter 14.

The Most Unusual Hotels

Among the world's most unusual hotels are ones like The Treetops Hotel in one of Kenya's wild animal parks—literally in the treetops. It was at this hotel in 1952 that Queen Elizabeth II learned that she had become queen of England. The uniqueness of the hotel is that it is built on the tops of trees overlooking a wild animal watering hole in the park.

Another magnificent spectacle is the Ice Hotel, situated on the shores of the Torne River in the old village of Jukkasjäsvi in Swedish Lapland. The Ice Hotel is built from scratch on an annual basis with a completely new design, new suites, new departments, even the "Absolute Ice Bar," a bar carved in ice with ice glasses and ice plates. The Ice Hotel can accommodate over 100 guests with each room having its own distinct style. The hotel also has an Ice Chapel, an ice art exhibition hall, and, believe it or not, a cinema. It is no wonder that it was one of the most popular places to be for the turn-of-the-century "Millennium Party" on New Year's Eve 1999.

Australia boasts an underwater hotel at the Great Barrier Reef, where guests have wonderful subterranean views from their rooms.

Japan has several unusual hotels. One is a cocoonlike hotel, called Capsule Hotel, in which guests do not have a room as such. Instead, they have a space of about seven feet by four feet. In this space is a bed and a television—which

---

[28]This section draws on Edward Watkins, "How Ritz-Carlton Won the Baldrige Award," *Lodging Hospitality*, **48,** 11, November 1992, p. 22.

Capsule Hotel

you almost have to operate with your toes! Such hotels are popular with people who get caught up in the obligatory late night drinking with the boss and with visiting professors who find them the only affordable place to stay in expensive Tokyo.

Japan also has love hotels, which are hotels used by couples for a few hours because they have insufficient privacy at home.

The highest hotel in the world, in terms of altitude, is nestled in the Himalayan mountain range at an altitude of 13,000 feet. Weather permitting, there is a marvelous view of Mount Everest. As many as 80 percent of the guests suffer from nausea, headaches, or sleeplessness caused by the altitude. No wonder the hottest-selling item on the room-service menu is oxygen—at $1 a minute.[29]

International Perspective

We are all part of a huge global economy that is splintered into massive trading blocks, such as the European Economic Community (EEC) and the North American Free Trade Agreement (NAFTA) among Canada, the United States, and Mexico, and comprising a total population of 350 million consumers.

The EU, with a population of 320 million people in fifteen nations, is an economic union that has removed national restrictions not only on trade but also on the movement of capital and labor. The synergy developed between these fifteen member nations is beneficial to all and is a form of self-perpetuating development.[30] As travel, tourism, commerce, and industry have increased within the EEC and beyond, so has the need for hotel accommodations.

---

[29]Jeannie Realston, "Inn of Thin Air," *American Way*, October 15, 1992.

[30]Belgium, Denmark, France, Germany, Great Britain, Greece, Ireland, Italy, Luxembourg, Portugal, Spain, the Netherlands.

Personal Profile: Isadore Sharp

Chairman, President, and Founder, Four Seasons Regent Hotels

Isadore Sharp, a first-generation Canadian, is the chairman, president, and founder of Four Seasons Regent Hotels. From one motel on Toronto's Jarvis Street in the early 1960s has grown the world's largest luxury hotel chain—a multi-million-dollar global hotel empire. Four Seasons Regent's success is largely a reflection of the drive, determination, and personal taste and style of Isadore Sharp.

Four Seasons was built slowly, deal by deal. From the first little motel that Sharp literally helped construct, to the complex Asian agreement in which Four Seasons acquired Regent Hotels International Inc., the growth of this company is largely the result of one man's vision. Isadore Sharp (called Issy by friends and family) has created a company that friends and foes alike agree is a model for how Canadian companies can compete globally in an increasingly interconnected world economy.

Currently, the Four Seasons manages and owns forty-one hotels around the world and continues to move ahead with more hotel plans in different countries. Isadore Sharp's success is all the more remarkable because he did not inherit vast wealth, and did not rise through the ranks of a major corporation with ready access to international money markets. He is a self-made man, consistent, who has control of his spirit. He believes in excellent quality for both his hotels and his company. Sharp clearly loves his business and credits the Four Seasons Regent team with the successes of the company.

(Courtesy Four Seasons Regent Hotels.)

NAFTA will likely be a similar catalyst for hotel development in response to increased trade and tourism among the three countries involved. But Argentina, Brazil, Chile, and Venezuela may also join an expanded NAFTA, which would become known as the Americas Trading Block.

It is easy to understand the international development of hotels given the increase in international tourism trade and commerce. The growth in tourism in Pacific Rim countries is expected to continue at the same rate as in recent years. Several resorts are planned in Indonesia, Malaysia, Thailand, Mexico, and Vietnam. Further international hotel development opportunities exist in Eastern Europe, Russia, and the other republics of the former Soviet Union, where some companies have changed their growth strategy from building new hotels to acquiring existing properties.

In Asia, Hong Kong's growth has been encouraged by booming economies throughout Asia and the kind of tax system for which supply-siders hunger. Before sovereignty over Hong Kong reverted back to China, the Hong Kong government levied a flat 16.5 percent corporate tax, a 15 percent individual income tax, and no tax on capital gains or dividends. Several hotel corporations have their headquarters in Hong Kong. Among them are Mandarin Oriental, Peninsula, and Shangri-La, all world-renowned for their five-star status. They are based in Hong Kong because of low corporate taxation and the ability to bring in senior expatriate executives with minimum bureaucratic difficulty.[31]

In developing countries, once political stability has been sustained, hotel development quickly follows as part of an overall economic and social progression. An example of this would be the former Eastern European countries and former Soviet republics, who for the past few years have offered development opportunities for hotel corporations.

U.S.–International Hotel Development

The future of the lodging industry involves **globalization.** Companies cannot grow unless they venture beyond the United States. International hotel development took off with the advent of the Boeing 707 in the late 1950s and the 747 in the early 1970s. With the boom in international business and tourism came the need for larger international hotel chains. American hotel chains and their management techniques were in demand by many developing countries who wanted premium-name hotels. Several hotel chains were owned by or in partnership with airlines; some still are.

In 1948, the U.S. government, casting about for ways to improve the economy of Latin American countries, asked several hotel companies if they would be willing to build properties in these countries.[32] As a Pan Am subsidiary, Inter-Continental had properties in Venezuela, Brazil, Uruguay, Chile, Colombia, Mexico, Curacao, Cuba, and the Dominican Republic. By 1981, Inter-Continental had eighty-one hotels in about fifty countries. Subsequently, Pan Am sold the Inter-Continental hotel chain to the Saison Japanese Corporation, who later sold it to Grand Metropolitan. Pan Am, after a long decline from its peak, declared bankruptcy and ceased operations in 1992.

Conrad Hilton was another pioneer in U.S. international hotel development. In 1948, he secured the contract to operate the Caribe Hilton in San Juan, Puerto Rico. Hilton won this contract over other U.S. hotel chains primarily because he was the only one to respond with a letter written in Spanish. By 1974, Hilton International was operating sixty-one hotels (23,263 rooms) in thirty-nine countries outside the continental United States.[33] In 1964, Hilton International Company became a separate company from Hilton U.S.; in 1967, it was bought by TWA. Hilton International is now owned by Britain's Ladbroke Group Plc.

Sheraton Hotel Corporation, a part of Cendant, now has 130,528 rooms and 413 hotels in seventy countries. It is second only to Group Accor of France,

[31]Personal conversation with Lim Chen, September 4, 2002.

[32]Lundberg, op. cit., p. 44.

[33]Ibid.

which operates 279,145 rooms and 2,465 hotels in sixty-six countries under its brands of Novotel, Sofitel, Pullman, Motel 6, and Formule 1.

International Investment in U.S. Hotels

Foreign investors have bought and sold not just individual U.S. hotels but also hotel chains. Bass Plc. (UK) bought Holiday Corporation; Grand Metropolitan (UK) bought Inter-Continental Hotels (they are now a part of Six Continents Hotels, owned by BASS PLC of Britain); Group Accor (France) bought Motel 6.

During the late 1980s and very early 1990s, Japanese investors bought several U.S. hotels. According to Christopher Mead, principal of Mead Ventures, Japanese interests owned all or part of 296 U.S. hotel properties. Mead predicts that the Japanese will continue to invest; the number of U.S. properties in which they have an investment may surpass 400 by the end of the decade.[34]

One interesting statistic to note is the price paid per room. Every $1,000 paid for the purchase or construction of a room equates to $1 in room rate that must be charged to make a reasonable return on investment.

During the second half of the 1980s, Japanese investors were cash rich and in a position to purchase U.S. real estate. This situation was aided by a sharp rise in the value of the yen against the dollar. U.S. land and property was valued far below what it would have been valued in Japan and was perceived to be offered at discount prices. Eventually, however, property, including hotels, became overpriced. An example of this is the La Costa Resort and Spa in La Costa, California. This 470-room property with a golf course was purchased by Sports Shinko in 1986 for $250 million—$531,914 per room. Two interesting things happened with regard to the purchase of this hotel. First, during the few months that elapsed between the signing of the sale documents and the time when the amount was to be paid (the escrow period), the purchaser saved $43 million because of the increase in the value of the Japanese yen compared to the dollar. The second was that the hotel lost $26 million in the first year of operation under the new owner. This was partly because of a lack of "due diligence." An extensive survey of the condition of the hotel would have shown that substantial amounts of money would be necessary to maintain the hotel's condition. The investors were obviously thinking long-term by anticipating that the value of land in southern California would undoubtedly increase in the next few years. Meanwhile, they built and sold a number of high-priced condos along the edge of the golf course.

[34]M. Chase Burritt, "Japanese Investment in U.S. Hotels and Resorts," *The Cornell Hotel and Restaurant Administration Quarterly*, **32,** 3, October 1991, p. 64.

About 1990, Japanese investment in U.S. hotels peaked; others, notably Hong Kong, Taiwan, and Korea, took their place. The Cheng family of Hong Kong purchased the forty-property Stouffer hotel chain from Nestle S.A. based in Switzerland. Cheng Yu-Tung also owns controlling interest in New World Development Co. Ltd. New World is the parent company of the 124-unit Ramada International chain and of New World Hotels, which has eleven properties in Asia. The Chengs also own the Regent and Grand Hyatt hotels in Hong Kong.[35] Needless to say Mr. Cheng is a billionaire.

Trends in Hotel Development

- ✔ *Capacity control:* Refers to who will control the sale of inventories of hotel rooms, airline seats, auto rentals, and tickets to attractions. Presently, owners of these assets are in control of their sale and distribution, but increasingly control is falling into the hands of those who own and manage global reservation systems and/or negotiate for large buying groups. Factors involved in the outcome will be telecommunications, software, available satellite capacity, governmental regulations, limited capital, and the travel distribution network.
- ✔ *Safety and security:* Important aspects of safety and security are terrorism, the growing disparity between the "haves" and "have nots" in the world, diminishing financial resources, infrastructure problems, health issues, the stability of governments, and personal security.
- ✔ *Assets and capital:* The issues concerning assets and capital are rationing of private capital and rationing of funds deployed by governments.
- ✔ *Technology:* An example of the growing use of "expert systems" (a basic form of artificial intelligence) would be making standard operating procedures available on-line, twenty-four hours a day, and establishing yield management systems designed to make pricing decisions. Other examples include the smart hotel room and communications ports to make virtual office environments for business travelers; and the impact of technology on the structure of corporate offices and individual hotels.
- ✔ *New management:* The complex forces of capacity control, safety and security, capital movement, and technology issues will require a future management cadre that is able to adapt to rapid-paced change across all the traditional functions of management.
- ✔ *Globalization:* A number of U.S. and Canadian chains have developed and are continuing to develop hotels around the world. International companies are also investing in the North American hotel industry.

[35]Bill Eillette, "Cheng Family Acquires Stouffer," *Hotel and Motel Management,* **208,** 7, April 26, 1993, p. 1.

Corporate Profile: Choice Hotels International[1]

This awesome story began in 1968 when Gerald Petitt, a Dartmouth engineering and business student, was seeking summer employment with IBM. He blew the roof off the company's preemployment test scores. The test scores were brought to the attention of Robert C. Hazard, Jr., who at that time was in charge of the Coors Brewery account. This had an appeal for the ski-bum in Petitt, who was originally from Denver. Robert Hazard says that Jerry Petitt did more in one summer for IBM's efforts to design a production system for the brewery than a team of five engineers did in two years.

Robert Hazard decided then, more than twenty-five years ago, to keep this talented person. They progressed in their careers with spells at American Express, Best Western, and eventually went on to Silver Spring, Maryland, where they would take a sleepy, stagnating lodging company called Quality Inns from 300 properties to more than 5,000 hotels in thirty-six countries. Because they had

(Courtesy Choice Hotels International)

been so successful at Best Western, they were enticed to join Quality in 1980 for equity plus half-million dollar salaries.

Bob and Jerry brought to Quality a combination of engineer-builders and entrepreneur-marketers. They quickly set about changing the mausoleum management style—"where you don't get creative thinking, where you try to pit good minds against each other." Instead, you get, "What will the chairman think?" and "We can all go along with it—or look for another job."[2]

To illustrate the change of management style, Bob Hazard draws the upside-down management organization, where the bosses are the 92 million guests, 4,426 hotels worldwide. He and Jerry Petitt, of course, were on the bottom.

The strategy of changing the corporate culture, of taking advantage of emerging technological and management trends with emphasis on marketing-driven management over operations has worked for Choice hotels. The development of brand segmentation was perhaps their best move. Choice Hotels International is now an international hotel franchisor comprising eight brands: Sleep, Comfort, Quality, Clarion, Friendship, Econo Lodge, Mainstay, and Rodeway.

More recently, under President Charles Ledsinger, Choice has reorganized, creating Market Area Management teams strategically placed so that licensees can be closer to support staff. Each field staff manager has forty-five properties and helps with sales, training, quality assurance reviews, and operations consolidations.

---

[1]This draws on Philip Hazard, *The Bob and Jerry Show Lodging*, **19**, 4, December 1993, pp. 37–41.
[2]Ibid, p. 58.
[3]http://www.choicehotels.com, October 27, 2002.

✔ *Consolidation:* As the industry matures, corporations are either acquiring or merging with each other.
✔ *Diversification within segments of the lodging industry:* The economy segment now has low-, medium-, and high-end properties. The extended-stay market has a similar spread of properties as do all the other hotel classifications.

Hotel Development

If you were working in the development office of a major hotel corporation, what information would you need to obtain to consider the development of a AAA three-diamond property in a town near you?

- ✔ *Rapid growth in vacation ownership:* Vacation ownership is the fastest growing segment of the lodging industry and is likely to continue growing as the baby boomers enter their fifties and sixties.
- ✔ *An increase in the number of spas and the treatments offered:* Wellness and the road to nirvana are in increasing demand as guests seek release from the stresses of a fast-paced lifestyle.
- ✔ *Gaming:* An increasing number of hotels are coming on-line that are related to the gaming industry.

Case Study

To Flag or Not to Flag—and If So, Which Flag?

Joy and Bob Brown retired from the military in 1995. They bought a motel near a picturesque New England town. The Cozy Motel is clearly visible and easily accessible from the turnpike. It has seventy-five rooms that are in good shape, having just been refurbished, and the curbside appeal of fresh paint and attractive landscaping adds to the motel's presentation.

The motel's year-round occupancy is 58 percent, which is about 10 percentage points below the national average. The average daily rate is $38. The Cozy Motel's guests are a mix of business travelers, who are mostly from companies at the nearby business park; a few retirees traveling for pleasure; an occasional bus tour; and some sports teams.

The Browns have asked several major franchise corporations to submit their best offers. The best one indicates that the cost of a franchise application fee is $20,000, and that there is a 2 percent revenue marketing fee and a reservation fee of $4 per room booked by the Central Reservation System (CRS).

Discussion Questions

1. What would you do in the Brown's situation? Should they sign a franchise agreement or not? Make assumptions, if needed.
2. What terms and conditions of a franchise agreement would be acceptable to you, or to the Browns?
3. What additional information would you, or the Browns, need to know?

Career Information

There are a variety of career opportunities directly and indirectly related to hotel development and classification. Some examples include: Working in the corporate offices to develop hotels. This would involve a knowledge of operations plus expertise in marketing, feasibility studies (to find out if the planned hotel etc. will be profitable), finance, planning. Similarly, consulting firms like Pannel Kew Foster (PKF) have interesting positions as consultants who provide specialized services in feasibility studies, marketing expertise, human resources, accounting and finance, due diligence (a check to ensure that what is being paid for a property is reasonable—it is a check to ensure the building is structurally sound, that the air conditioning etc., is not about to cost a fortune before the buyer signs and pays for the property with problems. Working for a consulting firm usually requires a Masters degree plus operational experience and an area of specialty.

AAA and Mobile both have inspectors who check hotel standards. Inspectors are required to travel and write detailed reports on the properties they stay at.

Suppliers to the industry—the companies who manufacture or distribute and sell all the furnishings, furniture and equipment (FF&E), A visit to a trade show may be an eye-opener as to the number of suppliers to the hospitality industry.

It is a good idea to explore many career paths as possible. Ask questions about life style, career challenges and yes salaries. Map out your path to see where you want to be in 5, 10, 15 and yes 20 years from now.

Summary

1. Improved transportation has changed the nature of the hotel industry from small, independently owned inns to big hotel and motel chains, operated by using concepts such as franchising, partnership, leasing, and management contracts.

2. The cyclical nature of demand, periods of inflation and recession, and the high degree of capital investment put hotel industries at high risks and call for smart financial management.

3. The financial decisions of a hotel must be based on expected risk, expected return, and their combined impact on common stock. The success of a hotel depends on creative financing combined with quality management.

4. Drastic changes in tax laws, deregulation of the thrift industry, and a softening of regional economics are reasons for the overvaluation of hotels.

5. Hotels can be classified according to location (city center, resort, airport, freeway), according to the types of services offered (casino, convention), and according to price (luxury, midscale, budget, and economy). Hotels are rated by Mobil and AAA Awards (five-star or the five-diamond rankings).

6. Vacation ownership offers consumers the opportunity to purchase fully furnished vacation accommodations, similar to condominiums, sold in a variety of forms, such as weekly intervals or point-based systems, for only a percentage of the cost of full ownership. According to the WTO, "timeshares" is one of the fastest growing sectors of the travel and tourism industry.

7. Every part of the world offers leisure and business travelers a choice of unusual or conservative accommodations that cater to the personal ideas of vacation or business trips.

8. The future of tourism involves international expansion and foreign investment, often in combination with airlines and with the goal of improving economic conditions in developing countries. It is further influenced by increased globalization, as evidenced by such agreements as NAFTA.

Key Words and Concepts

Airport hotels
All-suite extended-stay
   hotels
Bed and Breakfast Inn
Casino hotels
City center hotels
Convention hotels
Creative financing
Currency fluctuations

Economic downturn
Economy/budget hotels
First mortgage loans
Franchising
Freeway hotels
Full-service hotels
Globalization
Inflation
Interest rates

Leasing
Leasing arrangement
Marketing consortiums
   (referral organizations)
Management contracts
Midprice range
Partnership
Portfolio financing

Real estate investment trust
   (REIT)
Recession
Resort hotels
Syndicates
Vacation ownership
Vertical integration

Review Questions

1. Describe the development of the motel. What impact did the Great Depression of the 1930s have on the development of the hotel industry?
2. What are the advantages of (a) management contracts and (b) franchising? Discuss their impacts on the development of the hotel industry.
3. In what ways has the trend in globalization affected the hotel industry?

4. Explain how hotels cater to the needs of business and leisure travelers in reference to the following concepts: (a) resorts, (b) airport hotels, and (c) vertical integration.
5. Explain what vacation ownership is. What are the different types of timeshare programs available for purchase?

Internet Exercises

1. Organization:
   Web site:
   Summary:
   (a) What are the different hotel brands that can be franchised through Hilton Hotels Corporation?
   (b) What are your views on Hilton's portfolio and franchising options?

Hilton Hotels
http://www.hilton.com
Hilton Hotels Corporation and Hilton International, a subsidiary of Hilton Group PLC, have a worldwide alliance to market Hilton. Hilton is recognized as one of the world's best-known hotel brands. Collectively Hilton offers more than 2,000 hotels in more than fifty countries—truly a major player in the hospitality industry.

Click on the "Franchise Development" icon. Now click on "All HHC Franchise Brands."

2. Organization:
   Web site:
   Summary:
   (a) What are some of the top headlines currently being reported in the industry?
   (b) Click on the "Hotels Giants" icon. Browse through The site of Corporate Rankings and Industry Leaders. List the top five hotel corporations and note how many rooms each one has.

HOTELS **Magazine**
http://www.hotelsmag.com
Hotels magazine is a publication that offers vast amounts of information on the hospitality industry with up-to-date industry news, corporate trends, and nation wide developments.

Apply Your Knowledge

1. From a career perspective, what are the advantages and disadvantages of each type of hotel?

2. If you were going into the lodging sector, which type of property would you prefer to work at and why?

Hotel and Rooms Division Operation

After reading and studying this chapter, you should be able to:

✔ Outline the duties and responsibilities of key executives and department heads.

✔ Draw an organizational chart of the rooms division of a hotel and identify the executive committee members.

✔ Describe the main functions of the rooms division, front desk, and night auditor.

✔ Describe property management systems and discuss yield management.

✔ Calculate occupancy percentages, average daily rates, and actual percentage of potential rooms revenue.

✔ Outline the importance of the reservations and guest services functions.

✔ List the complexities and challenges of the concierge, housekeeping, and security/loss prevention departments.

This chapter describes the function of a hotel and the many departments that constitute a hotel. It also helps to explain why and how the departments are interdependent in successfully running a hotel.

The Functions and Departments of a Hotel

The primary function of a hotel is to provide lodging accommodation. A large hotel is run by a general manager and an executive committee comprised of the key executives who head major departments: rooms division director, food and beverage director, marketing and sales director, human resources director, chief accountant or controller, and chief engineer or facility manager. These executives generally have a regional or corporate counterpart with whom they have a reporting relationship, although the general manager is their immediate superior.

A hotel is made up of several businesses or revenue centers and cost centers. A few thousand products and services are sold every day. Each area of specialty requires dedication and a quality commitment for each department to get little things right all the time. Furthermore, hotels need the cooperation of a large and diverse group of people to perform well. Godfrey Bler, the general manager (GM) of the elegant 800-room General Eisenhower Hotel, calls it a business of details. Another wise comment comes from Matthew Fox: "If you ignore the little stuff, it will become big stuff."[1]

Hotels are places of glamour that may be awe inspiring. Even the experienced hotel person is impressed by the refined dignity of a beautiful hotel like a Ritz-Carlton or the artistic splendor of a Hyatt. The atmosphere of a hotel is

Ritz-Carlton Interior

[1]C. Nebel Eddystone III, *Managing Hotels Effectively: Lessons from Outstanding General Managers.* New York: Van Nostrand Reinhold, 1991, p. 13.

stimulating to a hospitality student. Let us step into an imaginary hotel to feel the excitement and become a part of the rush that is similar to show business, for a hotel is live theater and the GM is the director of the cast of players.

Hotels, whether they are chain affiliated or independent properties, all exist to serve and enrich society, and at the same time make a profit for the owners. Frequently, hotels are just like pieces of property on a Monopoly board. They often make or lose more money with equity appreciation or depreciation than via operations.

Hotels have been described as people palaces. Some are certainly palatial, and others are more functional. Hotels are meant to provide all the comforts of home to those away from home. A gracious feeling of warmth and welcome is a hotel's most valuable asset. Hotels have personalities that are created by the combined chorus of effort, interest, and sincerity on the part of every member of the staff.[2]

Role of the Hotel General Manager

Hotel general managers have a lot of responsibilities. They must provide owners with a reasonable return on investment, keep guests satisfied and returning, and keep employees happy. This may seem easy, but because there are so many interpersonal transactions and because hotels are open every day, all day, the complexities of operating become challenges that the general manager must face and overcome.

Larger hotels can be more impersonal. Here, the general manager may only meet and greet a few VIPs. In the smaller property, it is easier—though no less important—for the GM to become acquainted with guests, to ensure their stay is memorable, and to secure their return. One way that experienced GMs can meet guests, even in large hotels, is to be visible in the lobby and F&B (food and beverage) outlets at peak times (check-out, lunch, check-in, and dinner time). Guests like to feel that the GM takes a personal interest in their well-being. Max Blouet, who was general manager of the famous George V Hotel in Paris for more than thirty years, was a master of this art. He was always present at the right moment to meet and greet guests. In fact, he often made such a spectacle that other guests would inquire who he was and then would want to meet him. Hoteliers always remember they are hosts.

The GM is ultimately responsible for the performance of the hotel and the employees. The GM is the leader of the hotel. As such, she or he is held accountable for the hotel's level of profitability by the corporation or owners.

[2]Theodore R. Nathan, *Hotelmanship: A Guide to Hospitality Industry Marketing and Management.* Englewood Cliffs, NJ: Institute for Business Planning, 1982, p. 16.

General managers with a democratic, situational, and participating leadership style are more likely to be successful. There are, however, times when it is necessary to be somewhat autocratic—when crisis situations arise.

To be successful, GMs need to have a broad range of personal qualities. Among those most often quoted by GMs are the following[3]:

✔ Leadership
✔ Attention to detail
✔ Follow-through—getting the job done
✔ People skills
✔ Patience
✔ Ability to delegate effectively

Not surprisingly, a survey of general managers revealed that GMs were hardworking and responsible. Each had overcome difficulties and challenges and each had made sacrifices to become successful. But each was also extremely satisfied doing what he or she was doing.[4]

A successful GM hires the best people. A former GM of Chicago's Four Seasons Hotel deliberately hired division heads who knew more about what they were hired for than he did. The GM says he sets the tone—a structure of excellence—and others try to match it. Once the structure is in place, each employee works to define the hotel commitment to excellence. People who are hired need to be accomplished at what they do, and then they have to fit into the framework of the structure and be compatible with the rest of the group.[5]

Another hotel executive, Donn Takahashi, says his management philosophy is that to achieve a first-class facility, workers must be viewed as being vital to the operation. He instituted programs designed to reduce turnover, engender loyalty, and stave off competition for workers from competing hotels. He says a key to keeping employees happy is making sure there is mutual respect among all levels of workers.[6]

Management functions are generally classified into forecasting, planning, organizing, communicating, and evaluating. Centralized companies such as Marriott give detailed general manager profiles, whereas Hyatt, a decentralized company, does not. Given that the primary purpose of the hotel is to sell rooms and ensure that guests have a wonderful stay, it has been suggested that GMs assume the director-of-sales position and spend up to 75 percent of their time directly involved with sales.[7]

---

[3]Personal conversation with Steve Pelger, General Manager, Hyatt Regency, La Jolla, CA, November 1994.

[4]Eddystone, op. cit., p. xviii.

[5]Stephen Michaelides, "Narrowing the Margins of Consistency," *Restaurant Hospitality,* **76,** 10, October 1992, p. 26.

[6]Stephen G. Michaelides, "The First Resort," *Restaurant Hospitality,* **74,** 8, August 8, 1990, pp. 162–166.

[7]Howard Feiertag, "GMs Should Assume Director-of-Sales Duties," *Hotel and Motel Management,* **208,** 2, February 1, 1993, p. 14.

General managers need to understand, empathize, and allow for the cultures of both guests and employees. For example, in the Pacific Rim, spiritual dictates are frequently believed to directly affect hoteliers' profits. At the Westin Kyoto Takaragaike Prince, hotels with floors numbered four or nine are not likely to be very popular. The pronunciation of the number four and the Japanese word for *death* sound the same, and the number nine sounds very similar to *pain* in Japanese.[8]

Often, success can be heavily influenced by the country's culture. For instance, in Southeast Asia, many hoteliers employ Fung Shui experts. Fung Shui is a centuries-old tradition that maintains that placing architectural elements in correct configurations or holding events at correct times pleases spirits. For instance, at the Hyatt Regency Singapore, doors were originally positioned at right angles to the street. A Fung Shui master recognized and told the general manager that the hotel, which was then having problems, would never be successful until the angle was changed. After the doors were repositioned, occupancies began to rise.[9]

About a year after the 850-room megaresort Westin Kauai opened, it became apparent that the "Share the Fantasy" à la Disney theme chosen by management did not fit. After careful consideration, a management-by-values system was introduced. Operating synergistically with the more traditional management by objectives, management by values extracts the moral essences of the local culture and makes them goals of the hotel. Responses from a survey that asked employees to share their values were used to help create a mission statement for the hotel. Management discontinued the Disney model and its vocabulary. Employee uniforms changed from stiff corporate style to flowing Hawaiian clothes.[10]

Cesar Ritz

Cesar Ritz was a legend in his own time; yet, like so many of the early industry leaders, he began at the bottom and worked his way up through the ranks. In his case it did not take long to reach the top because he quickly learned the secrets of success in the hotel business. His career began as an apprenticed hotel keeper at the age of fifteen. At nineteen he was managing a Parisian restaurant. Suddenly, he quit that position to become an assistant waiter at the famous Voisin restaurant. There he learned how to pander to the rich and famous. In fact, he became so adept at taking care of the guests—remembering their likes and dislikes, even their idosyncrasies—that a guest would ask for him and want to only be served by him.

Cesar Ritz

[8]Robert Selwitz, "Hoteliers Put Forth Spirited Efforts to Boost Profits," *Hotel and Motel Management,* **206,** 15, September 9, 1991, pp. 2, 76.

[9]Ibid.

[10]Kathy Seal, "Westin Kauai Values Values," *Hotel and Motel Management,* **206,** 6, April 8, 1991, pp. 2, 68, 82.

At twenty-two, he became manager of the Grand National Hotel in Lucerne, Switzerland, one of the most luxurious hotels in the world. It was not very successful at the time Ritz became manager, but with his ingenuity and panache he was able to attract the "in" crowd to complete a turnaround. After eleven seasons, he accepted a bigger challenge: the Savoy Hotel in London, which had only been open a few months and was not doing well. Cesar Ritz became manager of one of the most famous and luxurious hotels in the world at the age of thirty-eight.

Once again, his flair and ability to influence society quickly made a positive impression on the hotel. To begin with, he made the hotel a cultural center for the high society. Together with Escoffier as executive chef, he created a team that produced the finest cuisine in Europe in the most elegant of surroundings. He made evening dress compulsory and introduced orchestras to the restaurants. Cesar Ritz would spare no expense in order to create the lavish effect he sought. On one occasion he converted a riverside restaurant into a Venetian waterway, complete with small gondolas and gondoliers singing Italian love songs.[11]

Ritz considered the handling of people as the most important of all qualities for a hotelier. His imagination and sensitivity to people and their wants contributed to a new standard of hotel keeping. The Ritz name remains synonymous with refined, elegant hotels and service.[12] However, Ritz drove himself to the point of exhaustion, and at age fifty-two, he suffered a nervous breakdown.

Management Structure

Management structure differs among larger, midscale, and smaller properties. The midscale and smaller properties are less complex in their management structures than the larger ones. However, someone must be responsible for each of the key result areas that make the operation successful. For example, a small property may not have a director of human resources, but each department head will have general day-to-day operating responsibilities for the human resources function. The manager will have the ultimate responsibility for all human resources decisions. The same scenario is possible with each of the following areas: engineering and maintenance, accounting and finance, marketing and sales, food and beverage management, and so on.

---

[11]Richard A. Wentzel. "Leaders of the Hospitality Industry or Hospitality Management," *An Introduction to the Industry,* 6th ed. Dubuque, IA: Kendall/Hunt, 1991, p. 29.

[12]This section draws on Donald E. Lundberg, *The Hotel and Restaurant Business,* 4th ed. New York: Van Nostrand Reinhold, 1984, pp. 33–34.

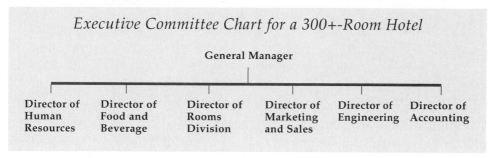

Figure 4–1 *Executive Committee Chart*

The Executive Committee

The general manager, using input from the **executive committee** (Figure 4–1), makes all the major decisions affecting the hotel. These executives, who include the **directors of human resources, food and beverage, rooms division, marketing and sales, engineering,** and **accounting,** compile the hotel's occupancy forecast together with all revenues and expenses to make up the budget. They generally meet once a week for one or two hours and might typically cover some of the following topics:

Guest satisfaction
Employee satisfaction
Total quality management
Occupancy forecasts
Sales and marketing plans
Training
Major items of expenditure
Renovations
Ownership relations
Energy conservation
Recycling
New legislation
Profitability

Some GMs rely on input from the executive committee more than others, depending on their leadership and management style. These senior executives determine the character of the property and decide on the missions, goals, and objectives of the hotel. For a chain hotel, this will be in harmony with the corporate mission.

In most hotels, the executive committee is involved with the decisions but the ultimate responsibility and authority rests with the GM. One of the major roles of the committee is communicator, both up and down the line of authority. This helps build interdepartmental cooperation.

The Departments

Rooms Division

The **rooms division manager** is responsible to the GM for the efficient and effective leadership and operation of all the rooms division departments. They include concerns such as the following:

Financial responsibility for rooms division
Employee satisfaction goals
Guest satisfaction goals
Guest services
Guest relations
Security
Gift shop

The **rooms division** consists of the following departments: front office, reservations, housekeeping, concierge, guest services, security, and communications. Figure 4–2 shows the organizational chart for a 300-plus-room hotel rooms division.

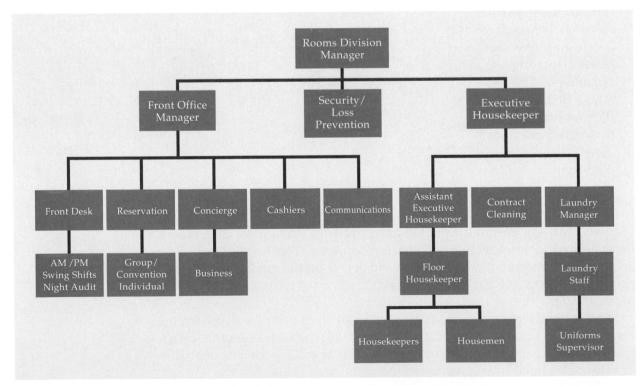

Figure 4–2   *Rooms Division Organizational Chart*

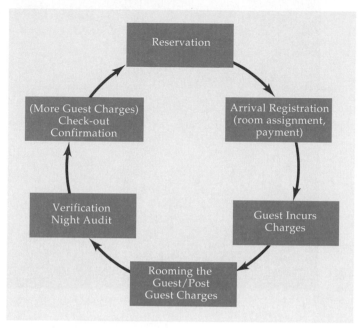

Figure 4–3 *The Guest Cycle*

The guest cycle in Figure 4–3 shows a simplified sequence of events that takes place from the moment a guest calls to make a reservation until he or she checks out.

Front Office

The **front office manager's** (FOM) main duty is to enhance guest services by constantly developing services to meet guest needs. An example of how some FOMs practice enhancing guest services is to have a guest service associate (GSA) greet guests as they arrive at the hotel, escort them to the front desk, and then personally allocate the room and take the guest and luggage to the room. This innovative way of developing guest services looks at the operation from the guest's perspective. There is no need to have separate departments for doorperson, bellperson, front desk, and so on. Each guest associate is cross-trained in all aspects of greeting and rooming the guest. This is now being done in smaller and midsized properties as well as specialty and deluxe properties. Guest service associates are responsible for the front desk, concierge, PBX, bellpersons, valet, and reservations.

During an average day in a hotel—if there is such a thing—the front office manager performs the following duties:

✔ Check night clerk report.
✔ Review previous night's occupancy.
✔ Review previous night's average rate.
✔ Look over market mix.

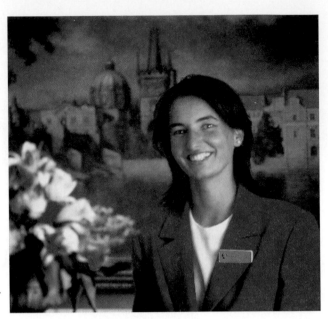

*A Front Office Manager
about to Welcome Us!*

✔ Check complimentary rooms.
✔ Verify group rooms to be picked up for next thirty days.
✔ Review arrivals and departures for the day.
✔ Review the VIP list and prepare preregistration.
✔ Arrange preregistrations for all arrivals.
✔ Attend rooms divisions and operations meeting.
✔ Review arrivals and departures for next day.
✔ Make staffing adjustments needed for arrivals and departures.
✔ Review scheduling (done weekly).
✔ Meet with lead GSAs (done daily).

In some hotels, the reservations manager and associates report to the director of sales. These positions report to the chief accountant: night auditor, night audit associates, and cashiers.

Figure 4–4 shows an organizational chart for a front office. The front office has been described as the hub or nerve center of the hotel. It is the department that makes a first impression on the guest and one that the guest relies on throughout his or her stay for information and service. Positive first impressions are critical to the successful guest experience. Many guests arrive at the hotel after long, tiring trips. They want to be met by someone with a warm smile and a genuine greeting. If a guest should have a negative experience when checking into a hotel, he or she will be on guard in encounters with each of the other departments. The position's description for a guest service agent details the work performed. Position descriptions for the three main functions of the front office are as follows:

1. To sell rooms.   The hotel departments work like a team in a relay race. Sales or reservations staff make or take the room sales up until the evening before

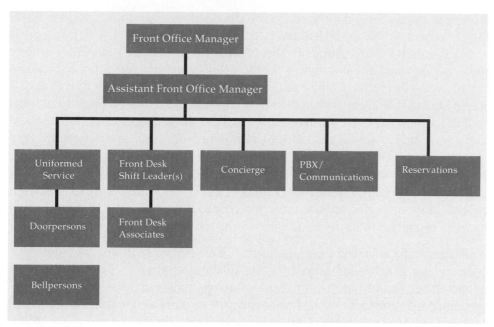

Figure 4–4 *Front Office Organizational Chart for a Larger Hotel*

the guest's arrival. At 6:00 P.M., when the reservations office closes, all the expected arrivals and available rooms are then handed over to the front desk P.M. shift. Reservations calls after 6:00 P.M. may either be taken by the front desk staff or the 1-800 number. The front desk team will try to sell out (achieve 100 percent occupancy) by selling the remaining rooms to call-in or walk-in guests—and of course the frantic calls from preferred guests who need a favor! The front desk staff must not only aim to sell all the rooms but also achieve the optimum ***average daily rate*** (ADR) for the rooms. The ADR is calculated by adding up the rate charged for each room and then dividing by the number of rooms. A simple example would be as follows:

A group booking of	100 rooms at $140 = $14,000
	10 suites at $250 = 2,500
Individual corporate bookings	250 rooms at $160 = 40,000
Special promotions	50 rooms at $125 = 6,250
Total	410 rooms $62,750
	Total room sales

$$\$62,750 / 410 = \$153 \text{ Average daily rate}$$

Optimizing the ADR is achieved by "up-selling" and yield management. Upselling occurs when the guest service agent/front desk clerk suggestively sells the features of a larger room, a higher floor, or perhaps a better view. Yield management originated in the airline industry where demand also fluctuates. Basically, a percentage of guests who book and send in a deposit in advance will be able to secure a room at a more reasonable price than someone booking a room with just three days' notice. The price will be even higher for the booking at three days' notice if demand is good.

Many other factors influence the hotel's ability to sell out. Chief among these are *demand,* the number of people needing rooms, and *supply,* the number of available rooms. A good example is the New York Hotel Convention and Trade Show. This event takes place in a city that has a high demand for hotel rooms in proportion to its inventory (number of available rooms). Because there is a fairly constant demand for rooms in New York, special events tend to increase demand to a point that forces up room rates. Another example comes from the airline industry, which always seems to raise prices at the peak travel times (Thanksgiving, Christmas, Easter, and the summer vacation times). They only give special fares when school is in session. Yield management is explained in more detail later in this chapter.

2. To maintain balanced guest accounts. This begins with advance deposits, opening the guest folio (account), and posting all charges from the various departments. Many hotels now have property management systems (PMS)[13] (property management systems are explained in more detail later in this chapter) and point-of-sale terminals (POS), which are on-line to the front office. This means that guest charges from the various outlets are directly debited to the guest's folio. Payment is either received on guest check-out, or transferred to the **city ledger** (a special account for a company that has established credit with the hotel). This means that the account will be sent and paid within a specified time period. Formerly, the allotted time was at the end of the month, followed by a thirty- or sixty-day grace period for payment to be made. However, most companies now have a goal to keep accounts receivable to a maximum of fifteen to twenty days. This helps the hotel maintain sufficient cash flow to meet its obligations to lenders for mortgage payments and employees' salaries.

A recent innovation to the PMS is in-room check-out. The system allows a guest to check his or her account via the television screen in the room. The guest operates the system via the remote control, verifying all charges and authorizing payment. The total may then be charged to a credit card with a copy sent to the guest, or (for company accounts) to his or her company. Hotels that do not have this feature as part of their PMS sometimes leave a copy of the guest's folio under the door on the last evening. This also allows the guest to check all charges before departure. The guest has the option of calling the desk to inform the cashier that the bill may be sent. Nowadays, because cash flow is so important, payment may be required on receipt of the invoice or a few days later. Credit cards have helped this process by speeding up payment to hotels.

---

[13]PMS is a system of storing and retrieving information on reservations, room availability, room rates. The system may also interface with outlets (restaurants, bars, etc.) for recording guest charges. The accounting functions may also be integrated with a main system. Some hotels may have several systems that interface with one another.

Front Desk Associate
(Courtesy John R. Walker.)

3. To offer services such as handling mail, faxes, messages, and local and hotel information. People constantly approach the front desk with questions. Front desk employees need to be knowledgeable about the various activities in the hotel. The size, layout, and staffing of the front desk will vary with the size of the hotel. A busy 800-room city center property will naturally differ from a country inn. The front desk is staffed throughout the twenty-four hours by three shifts. The hours worked by front desk employees may vary. However, generally the day shift works from 7:00 A.M. until 3:00 P.M., the swing shift runs from 3:00 P.M. until 11:30 P.M., and the graveyard shift/night auditor works from 11:00 P.M. until 7:00 A.M. On a staggered schedule, one person starts at 7:00 A.M. and ends at 3:30 P.M., and another one starts at 2:30 P.M. and goes to 11:00 P.M. This schedule provides time for a smooth handover between the shifts. These few minutes are vital because the shift leaders must exchange essential information such as how the house count is going (how many rooms left to sell), which room changes have been requested but have not been completed, which VIPs are still to arrive and any special arrangements that need to be taken care of (e.g., calling the manager on duty to escort the guests to their rooms/suites, knowing which guests have serious complaints and therefore need special attention, etc.).

These are the main duties of the early shift:

1. Check the log book and the previous night's occupancy for no-shows and send information to the accounting office for billing.
2. Conduct a house count and update the forecast (in some hotels this is done by reservations).
3. Decide on the number and mix of rooms to sell (in some hotels this is also done by reservations).
4. Preallocate VIP suites and rooms and block off group or convention rooms.
5. Handle guest check-outs including the following:
   a. Ensure all charges are on guest's folio, especially any last-minute telephone calls and breakfast. (Most medium and large hotels now have a PMS so that the moment a guest incurs charges in the restaurant, the charge will automatically be included on the guest folio. In the old

Room Status Codes

Front desk personnel commonly use the following status codes:

VR (Vacant and Ready): The room is currently unoccupied and has been cleaned and inspected. The room is available for sale.

VC (Vacant and Clean): The room is currently unoccupied and has been cleaned. Additional attention or maintenance is required. The room is not yet available for sale.

VD (Vacant and Dirty): The room is currently unoccupied, but has not yet been cleaned. The room is not available for sale.

OR (Occupied and Ready): The room is currently occupied, and daily cleaning has been completed. The room is not available for sale.

OC (Occupied and Clean): The room is currently occupied. Daily cleaning has been completed, but additional attention or maintenance is required. The room is not available for sale.

OD (Occupied and Dirty): The room is currently occupied and has not yet been cleaned. The room is not available for sale.

CO (Check-Out): The room is scheduled to be vacated on the current day. The room will become available for sale after the current guest checks out and the room has been cleaned.

OO (Out of Order): The room is undergoing redecoration, maintenance, or correction of other problems. The room is not available for sale.

DND (Do Not Disturb): The room is occupied and has not yet been cleaned, because the "Do Not Disturb" tag was displayed on the door at the scheduled time of cleaning.

V/O or O/V (Status Unclear): A personal inspection is required to determine whether the room is occupied or vacant.

Source: Dennis L. Foster, Rooms at the Inn: Front Office Operations and Administration. Columbus, OH: Macmillan/McGraw-Hill, 1992, p. 122.

days, some guests would skip off without paying for some charges incurred before check-out.)

b. Verify the accuracy of the account by going through the various charges with the guest.

c. Accept the cash or credit as payment.

d. Tactfully handle any unexpected situation (for example, when the guest says the company is paying for his or her stay and the front desk has received no instructions to that effect).

e. Send any city ledger accounts to the accounting office—generally this is done when the guest has signed the folio to approve all charges.

6. Politely and efficiently attend to guest inquiries.

7. Note important occurrences in the front office log.

8. Organize any room changes guests may request and follow up.

9. Advise housekeeping and room service of flowers/fruit for VIPs and any other amenities ordered.

10. Check issuing and control of keys.

The **desk clerk** must be able to work under pressure. Constant interruptions to the actual work of the front desk occur and employees are always on stage; therefore, it is necessary to maintain composure even during moments of apparent panic.

The evening shift duties are the following:

1. Check the log book for special items. (The log book is kept by guest contact; associates at the front office note specific and important guest requests and occurrences such as requests for room switches or baby cribs.)

2. Check on the room status, number of expected check-outs still to leave, and arrivals by double-checking registration cards and the computer in order to update the forecast of the night's occupancy. This will determine the number of rooms left to sell. Nowadays, this is all part of the capability of the PMS.

Major hotel chains offer a number of different room rates, including the following:

rack rate
corporate
association rate
government
encore
cititravel
entertainment cards
AAA
AARP (American Association of Retired Persons)
wholesale
group rates
promotional special

The rack rate is the rate that is used as a benchmark quotation of a hotel's room rate. Let us assume that the Hotel California had a rack rate of $135. Any discounted rate may be offered at a percentage deduction from the rack rate. An example would be a corporate rate of $110, an association rate of $105, and AARP rate of $95—certain restrictions may apply. Group rates may range from $95 to $125 according to how much the hotel needs the business.

Throughout the world there are three main plans on which room rates are based:

AP/American Plan—room and three meals a day
MAP/Modified American Plan—room plus two meals
EP/European Plan—room only, meals extra

Figure 4–5   *Types of Rates*

3. Handle guest check-ins. This means notifying the appropriate staff of any special requests guests may have made (e.g., nonsmoking room or a long bed for an extra tall guest).
4. Take reservations for that evening and future reservations after the reservations staff have left for the day.

Figure 4–5 shows the types of **room rates** offered by hotels.

Night Auditor

A hotel is one of the few businesses that balances its accounts at the end of each business day. Because a hotel is open twenty-four hours every day, it is difficult to stop transactions at any given moment. The **night auditor** waits until the hotel quiets down at about 1:00 A.M. and then begins the task of balancing the guests' accounts receivable. The other duties include the following:

1. Post any charges that the evening shift was not able to post.
2. Pass discrepancies to shift managers in the morning. The room and tax charges are then posted to each folio and a new balance shown.
3. Run backup reports so if the computer system fails the hotel will have up-to-date information to operate a manual system.
4. Reconcile point-of-sale and PMS to guest accounts. If this does not balance, then the auditor must do so by investigating errors or omissions. This is done

The Night Audit Process in Simple Terms

1. The night audit team runs a preliminary reconciliation report that shows the total revenue generated from room and tax, banquets and catering, food and beverage outlets, and other incidentals (phone, gift shop, etc.).
2. All errors on the report are investigated.
3. All changes are posted and balanced with the preliminary charges.
4. A comparison of charges is carried out, matching preliminary with actual charges.
5. Totals for credit card charges, rooms operations, food and beverages, and incidentals are verified.
6. The team "rolls the date"—they go forward to the next day.

by checking that every departmental charge shows up on guest folios.

5. Complete and distribute the daily report. This report details the previous day's activities and includes vital information about the performance of the hotel.
6. Determine areas of the hotel where theft could potentially occur.

The **daily report** contains some key operating ratios such as **room occupancy percentage** (ROP), which is rooms occupied divided by rooms available. Thus, if a hotel has 850 rooms and 622 are occupied, the occupancy percentage is 622 ÷ 850 = 73.17 percent. The ADR is, together with the occupancy percentage, one of the key operating ratios that indicates the hotel's performance.

Corporate Profile: Hyatt Hotels

When Nicholas Pritzker emigrated with his family from the Ukraine to the United States, he began his career by opening a small law firm. His outstanding management skills led to the expansion of the law firm, turning it into a management company. The Pritzkers gained considerable financial support, which allowed them to pursue their goals of expansion and development. These dreams came into reality with the opening of the first Hyatt Hotel, inaugurated on September 27, 1957.

Today, Hyatt Hotel Corporation is a $3.4 billion hotel management and development company; together with Hyatt International, they are among the leading chains in the hotel industry, with close to 8 percent of the market share.[1] Hyatt has earned worldwide fame as the leader in providing luxury accommodations and high-quality service, targeting especially the business traveler, but strategically differentiating its properties and services to identify and market to a very diverse clientele. This differentiation has resulted in the establishment of four basic types of hotels:

1. *The Hyatt Regency Hotels* represent the company's core product. They are usually located in business city centers and are regarded as five-star hotels.
2. *Hyatt Resorts* are vacation retreats. They are located in the world's most desirable leisure destinations, offering the "ultimate escape from everyday stresses."

3. *The Park Hyatt Hotels* are smaller, European-style, luxury hotels. They target the individual traveler who prefers the privacy, personalized service, and discreet elegance of a small European hotel.
4. *The Grand Hyatt Hotels* serve culturally rich destinations that attract leisure business as well as large-scale meetings and conventions. They reflect refinement and grandeur, and they feature state-of-the-art technology and banquet and conference facilities of world-class standard.

Hyatt Hotels Corporation has been recognized by *The Wall Street Journal* as one of the sixty-six firms around the world poised to make a difference in the industries and markets of the 1990s and beyond. As a matter of fact, the effective management that characterized the company in its early years with the Pritzker family has continued through time. Hyatt Hotels Corporation is characterized by a decentralized management approach, which gives the individual general manager a great deal of decision-making power, as well as the opportunity to stimulate personal creativity and, therefore, differentiation and innovation. The development of novel concepts and products is perhaps the key to Hyatt's outstanding success. For example, the 1967 opening of the Hyatt Regency Atlanta, Georgia, gave the company instant recognition throughout the world. Customers were likely to stare in awe at the twenty-one-story atrium lobby, the glass elevators, and the revolving roof-top restaurant. The property's innovative architecture, designed by John Portman, revolutionized the common standards of design and spacing, thus changing the course of the lodging industry. The atrium concept introduced there represented a universal challenge to hotel architects to face the new trend of grand, wide-open public spaces.

A further positive aspect of the decentralized management structure is the fact that the individual manager is able to be extremely customer-responsive by developing a thorough knowledge of the guests' needs and thereby providing personalized service—fundamental to achieving customer satisfaction. This is, in fact, the ultimate innkeeping purpose, which Hyatt attains at high levels. Perhaps the most striking result of this forecasting is, again, the introduction of innovative and diversified products and services. For business travelers, for example, Hyatt introduced the Hyatt Business Plan, which includes fax machines in every room, twenty-four-hour access to copiers and printers, and other features designed to address the needs of the targeted clientele. Hyatt has also been on the forefront in developing faster, more efficient check-in options, including a phone number, 1-800-CHECK-IN, that allows guests to check in to their hotel rooms by telephone. In addition, the needs of families have been considered as well. The company offers Camp Hyatt, the hotel industry's most extensive children's program.

The other side of Hyatt's success is the emphasis on human resources management. Employee satisfaction, in fact, is considered to be a prerequisite to external satisfaction. Hyatt devotes enormous attention to employee training and selection. What is most significant, however, is the interaction among top managers and operating employees.

Darryl Hartley-Leonard was the company's president in 1989 when he came up with the idea of "In-Touch Day." On this day, once a year, the company closes its headquarters' office and the senior management spreads out to 100 Hyatt Hotels in the United States and Canada, "spending time in the trenches"—doing the daily activities of operating employees, taking their frontline positions. Such a strategy is extremely effective: Actually performing the job enables the top executives to learn, first hand, the challenges and problems of their employees, thus understanding their daily routine and problems. The In-Touch Day concept provides tangible evidence to employees that the management is not locked into an ivory tower, but is concerned with the improvement of their jobs.

Hartley-Leonard's leadership was successful. He joined Hyatt in 1964 as a front desk clerk at a Los Angeles Hyatt hotel. After serving in a variety of management positions, he worked his way up to general manager of Hyatt Regency Atlanta (1974); two years later he became a regional vice president. But that was not it. His extraordinary abilities were further recognized and rewarded: Hartley-Leonard was named executive vice president for the corporation in 1978, president in 1986, and chairman in 1994. Currently, Jay Pritzker is the chairman of the Hyatt Hotels Corporation.

---

[1]The company owns 195 hotels and resorts worldwide: 118 in North America, Canada, and the Caribbeans, and 77 in international locations in thirty-five countries.

Night Auditor Verifying and Balancing Guest Accounts (Courtesy John R. Walker.)

The average daily rate is calculated by dividing the rooms revenue by the number of rooms sold. If the rooms revenue was $75,884 and the number of rooms sold was 662 then the ADR would be $122. See Figure 4–6 for an example of a daily report.

| **Room Occupancy Percentage (ROP):** | Rooms Occupied |
| | Total Rooms Available |

If	Total available rooms are	850
And	Total rooms occupied	622
Then:		
Occupancy Percentage:		$(622/850) \times 100 = \mathbf{73.17\%}$

| **Average Daily Rate:** | Total Rooms Revenue |
| | Total Number of Rooms Sold |

If	Rooms revenue is	$75,884
And	Total number of rooms sold is	662
Then:		
Average Daily Rate:		$\dfrac{75{,}884}{662} = \mathbf{\$114.63}$

A more recent ratio to gauge a hotel rooms division's performance is the percentage of potential rooms revenue, which is calculated by determining potential rooms revenue and dividing the actual revenue by the potential revenue.

Larger hotels may have more than one night auditor, but in smaller properties these duties may be combined with night manager, desk, or night watch-person duties.

Check Your Knowledge

1. Name the functions performed by the general manager.
2. What does an executive committee for a hotel of 300+ rooms look like?
3. What are the subdepartments that fall under the rooms division? What is each department's main function?

Clarion Hotel Bayview

| | *Daily Management Report Supplement*
January 2003 | | *Daily Report*
January 2003 | |

Occupancy%	Today	Avg or %	M–T–D Avg or %		Y–T–D Avg or %	
Rack Rooms	9	2.9%	189	3.37	189	3.37
Corporate Rooms	0	0.0%	103	1.83	103	1.83
Group Rooms	274	87.8%	2,379	42.36	2,379	42.36
Leisure Rooms	3	1.0%	395	7.03	395	7.03
Base Rooms	23	7.4%	348	6.14	345	6.14
Government Rooms	2	0.6%	32	.57	32	.57
Wholesale Rooms	1	0.3%	121	2.15	121	2.15
No-Show Rooms		0.0%	0	.00	0	.00
Comp Rooms	0	0.0%	37	.66	37	.66
Total Occ Rooms & Occ %	312	100%	3,601	64.12	3,601	64.12
Rack	$1,011	$112.33	17,207	91.04	17,207	91.04
Corporate	$0	ERR	8,478	82.31	8,478	82.31
Group	$22,510	$82.15	178,066	74.85	178,066	74.85
Leisure	$207	$69.00	24,985	63.25	24,985	63.25
Base	$805	$35.00	12,063	34.97	12,063	34.97
Govt	$141	$70.59	2,379	74.34	2,379	74.34
Wholesale	$43	$43.00	5,201	42.98	5,201	42.98
No-Show/Comp/Allowance	$0		−914	−24.69	−914	−24.69
Total Rev & Avg Rate	$24,717	$79.22	247,466	68.72	247,466	68.72

Hotel Revenue

Rooms	$24,717		247,466	77.46	247,466	77.46
Food	$1,400		37,983	11.89	37,983	11.89
Beverage	$539		9,679	3.03	9,679	3.03
Telephone	$547		5,849	1.83	5,849	1.83
Parking	$854		11,103	3.48	11,103	3.48
Room Svc II	$70		1,441	.45	1,441	.45
Other Revenue	$1,437		963	1.87	963	1.87
Total Revenue	$29,563		319,484	100.00	319,484	100.00

Figure 4–6 *Daily Report*

Clarion Hotel Bayview

Daily Management Report Supplement			*Daily Report*			
January 2003			*January 2003*			

Cafe 6th & K	Today	Avg or %	M–T–D	Avg or %	Y–T–D	Avg or %
Cafe Breakfast Covers	88	57.1%	1,180	47.12	1,180	47.12
Cafe Lunch Covers	43	27.9%	674	26.92	674	26.92
Cafe Dinner Covers	23	14.9%	650	25.96	650	25.96
Total Cafe Covers	154	100.0%	2,504	100.00	2,504	100.00
Cafe Breakfast	$608	$6.91	7,854	6.66	7,854	6.66
Cafe Lunch	$246	$5.72	5,847	8.67	5,847	8.67
Cafe Dinner	$227	$9.86	4,309	6.63	4,309	6.63
Gaslamp Lounge Food			2,431	3.74	2,431	3.74
Total Rev/Avg Check	$1,081	$7.02	20,440	8.16	20,440	8.16
Banquets						
Banquet Breakfast Covers	0	ERR	154	13.24	154	13.24
Banquet Lunch Covers	0	ERR	134	11.52	134	11.52
Banquet Dinner Covers	0	ERR	254	21.84	254	21.84
Banquet Coffeebreak Covers	0	ERR	621	53.40	621	53.40
Total Banquet Covers	0	ERR	1,163	100.00	1,163	100.00
Banquet Breakfast	$0	ERR	980	6.36	980	6.36
Banquet Lunch	$0	ERR	2,997	22.36	2,997	22.36
Banquet Dinner	$0	ERR	4,530	17.84	4,530	17.84
Banquet Coffeebreak	$0	ERR	1,093	1.76	1,093	1.76
Total Rev/Avg Check	$0	ERR	9,600	8.25	9,600	8.25
Room Service						
Room Service Breakfast Covers	13	40.6%	324	48.00	324	48.00
Room Service Lunch Covers	3	9.4%	53	7.85	53	7.85
Room Service Dinner Covers	16	50.0%	298	44.15	298	44.15
Total Covers	32	100.0%	675	100.00	675	100.00
Room Service Breakfast	$119	$9.13	2,665	8.22	2,665	8.22
Room Service Lunch	$29	$9.77	418	7.89	418	7.89
Room Service Dinner	$171	$10.67	2,907	9.75	2,907	9.75
Total Rev/Avg Check	$319	$9.96	5,990	8.87	5,990	8.87

Figure 4–6 *(continued)*

Property Management Systems

Property management systems have greatly enhanced a hotel's ability to accept, store, and retrieve guest reservations, guest history, requests, and billing arrangements. The reservations part of the property management system also provides the reservations associates with information on types of rooms available, features, views, and room rates. A list of expected arrivals can be easily generated. Before the advent of PMSs, it took reservation associates much longer to learn the features of each room and the various room rates, and to make up the arrivals list.

A property management system contains a set of computer software packages capable of supporting a variety of activities in front and back office areas. The four most common front office software packages are designed to assist front office employees in performing functions related to the following tasks:

✔ Reservations management
✔ Rooms management
✔ Guest account management
✔ General management[14]

The reservations management component allows the reservations department to quickly accept reservations and generate confirmations and occupancy forecasts for reservations taken by the hotel directly and by the CRS. Most chain-operated or affiliated hotels have a 1-800 number to allow guests to call, without charge, to make reservations anywhere in the United States and, in some cases, overseas. Travel agents also have direct computer access to the central reservations numbers. More than 100 PMS vendors offer various features, hardware platforms, and operating systems. The various software packages handle some or all of the following:

✔ Reservations
✔ Front desk
✔ Group billing
✔ Guest history
✔ Report writer
✔ Travel agent billing
✔ Tour operations
✔ Housekeeping
✔ Yield management
✔ Package plans
✔ Wholesaler blocks
✔ Call accounting interface
✔ In-room movie interface

---

[14]Michael L. Kasavana and Richard M. Brooks, *Managing Front Office Operations.* East Lansing, MI: The Educational Institute of the American Hotel and Motel Institute, 1991, p. 112.

✔ Point-of-sale interface
✔ Environmental control
✔ Central reservations
✔ General ledger
✔ Accounts payable
✔ Condo owner accounting
✔ Association management
✔ Long-term rentals
✔ Timeshare rentals[15]

Medium- to large-sized hotels typically have a minicomputer with front and back office (accounting, control, purchasing) applications. In addition, other hardware platforms may exist within the property, and applications may include back office, point-of-sale, and conference or catering scheduling.[16]

Smaller hotels may use a microcomputer either as a stand-alone system or with a local area network to support the applications.[17]

Marriott hotels have based their property management system on the IBM 173 RISC system/6000. The worldwide installation includes 250 hotels. The goal was to set up a single architecture with one integrated database for sales, catering, human resources, back office, accounting, and front office operations.[18]

Holiday Inn Worldwide (1,600 hotels) has invested more than $60 million installing PMSs in all of its properties. The $60 million covers leasing the Encore PMS for use in all its properties, development of the Holiday Inn Reservation Optimization system, free use of hardware and software for all hotels, and training for employees. The system integrates revenue optimization and customer tracking software to maximize income for the properties and options for the guests.[19]

The advantages of the Holiday Inn Reservation Optimization (HIRO) and Encore are that they include a two-way interface with Holidex (the Holiday Corporation's reservation system) and will automate and simplify front desk procedures. The HIRO system, according to Holiday officials, is the first automated length-of-stay optimization system to be integrated with a central reservation system. This ability to manage length of stay and room type works like this: For example, in August 1991, some 81 percent of the multiple-night requests to Holidex were turned down due to no availability. With HIRO those denials will be turned into room nights and should recover at least $100 million for Holiday Inn.[20]

---

[15]Resort Data Processing, Inc., Vail, Colorado 81657.

[16]Brian Katison, "The Politics of PMS," *Hotel and Motel Management, 207,* 11, June 22, 1992, pp. 33–35.

[17]Ibid.

[18]Maryfran Johnson, *ComputerWorld, 26,* 40, October 5, 1992, p. 6.

[19]Megan Row, "The PMS Wars: Holiday and Promos Are Chasing Each Other," *Lodging Hospitality, 48,* 6, June, 1992, p. 32.

[20]Alan Salomon, "Holiday Abuzz with HIRO/ENCORE," *Hotel and Motel Management, 207,* 7, April 27, 1992, pp. 33–34, 60.

Until 1993, there were problems with both central reservation systems and property management systems. For example, the most important information about any given property has not been readily available to those in the best position to sell it. Too often, travel agents have been unable to tell if rooms are available and at what price just by looking at the data on the terminal at their desks.[21]

The Hotel Industry Switch Company (THISCO) has created a pathway between the lodging industry's central reservation systems and those of the airlines. THISCO allows the travel agents to look into the hotel database.[22] This system, together with a software package from Anasail, has been installed in Hospitality Franchise Systems, which franchise Days Inn, Ramada, and Howard Johnson brands. Travelodge, Promus, and Choice Hotels have all customized the software for their own uses.

The ultimate goal is for hotels to have access to a global reservations network. Larry Chervenak, a well-known authority on hospitality technology, estimates that more than $3 billion has been invested by various players in the global competition to create reservation systems that will feed more business into hotels.[23]

Hotel systems generally piggyback on the airline systems. The two main airline computer systems, Sabre (American Airlines) and Apollo (jointly owned by United, USAir, Air Canada, and several European airlines), both have developed sophisticated global reservation systems designed to make it easy for the travel agent to make international hotel reservations.

Covla is an example of an international CRS system. It is a subsidiary of the Covla airline system known to U.S. travel agents as Apollo. It enables agents to book hotel reservations around the world. Companies like Ritz-Carlton, Swissotel, and Pan Pacific utilize this system. American Airlines has adopted Qik-Res, a software system developed by Qantas that runs on personal computers (PCs). These user-friendly software systems make it easier for travel agents to make hotel reservations in four easy steps: shop, look, check, and book. Curiously, a recent study suggests that business travelers, who account for almost half of current occupancy levels, are reached directly, with travel agents playing little or no role in formulating property selection.

Another survey, conducted by *Hotel and Motel Management,* shows that business travelers generally make their own hotel reservations 65.2 percent of the time. When it came to choosing a hotel, basic criteria seemed to be important. Although location and price may be the top considerations, cleanliness was rated highest by 91.1 percent of the sample. Comfortable mattresses and pillows were second, with 89.1 percent rating these as important or very important. In terms of brand loyalty, frequent travelers were more likely to specify a particular chain than nonfrequent travelers.[24] It is important to note

---

[21]Richard Burns, "Lodging," *The American Hotel and Motel Association,* March 1993, p. 19.

[22]Ibid.

[23]Ibid.

[24]Pamela A. Weaver and Ken W. McCleary, "Basics Bring 'em Back: Extras Are Appreciated, but Business Travelers Still Value Good Service and Good Management," *Hotel and Motel Management, 206,* 11, June 24, 1991, pp. 29–32, 38.

that business travelers make their own hotel reservations; consequently, the criteria for hotel selection is also important to hotel executives.

The oversupply of rooms has encouraged operators to use information technology to reduce costs and provide better service. The computerized hotel reservation system enables hotels to fill more efficiently the maximum number of rooms on any given day. Reservation programs enable the reservation clerk to provide a high level of personalized service for repeat visitors. Hotels can use yield management systems to maximize revenues by basing the selling price of a room on the expected demand for rooms on a given night.[25]

Yield Management

Yield management is a demand-forecasting technique used to maximize room revenue that the hotel industry borrowed from the airlines. It is based on the economics of supply and demand, which means that prices rise when demand is strong and drop when demand is weak. Thus, the purpose of yield management is to increase profitability. Naturally, management would like to sell every room at the highest rack rate. However, this is not reality, and rooms are sold at discounts on the rack rate. An example would be the corporate or group rate. In most hotels, only a small percentage of rooms are sold at rack rate. This is because of conventions and group rates and other promotional discounts that are necessary to stimulate demand. What yield management does is to allocate the right type of capacity to the right customer at the right price so as to maximize revenue or yield per available room.[26]

Generally the demand for room reservations follows the pattern of group bookings being made months or even years in advance of arrival and individual bookings, which mostly are made a few days before arrival. Figures 4–7 and 4–8 show the pattern of group and individual room reservations.

Group reservations are booked months, even years, in advance. Yield management will monitor reservations and, based on previous trends and current demand, determine the number and type of rooms to sell at what price to obtain the maximum revenue.

The curve in Figure 4–7 indicates the pattern of few reservations being made 120 days prior to arrival. Most of the individual room bookings are made in the last few days before arrival at the hotel. The yield management program will monitor the demand and supply and recommend the number and type of rooms to sell for any given day, and the price for which to sell each room.

---

[25]Joseph F. Durocher and Neil B. Niman, "Automated Guest Relations That Generate Hotel Reservations," *Information Strategy: The Executives Journal,* **7,** 3, Spring 1991, pp. 27–30.

[26]Shirley Kimes, "The Basics of Yield Management," *The Cornell Hotel Restaurant Administration Quarterly,* **30,** 3, November 1989, p. 14.

Figure 4–7 *Individual Room Reservations Curve* (Adapted from Sheryl E. Kimes, "The Basics of Yield Management," *The Cornell Hotel Restaurant Administration Quarterly*, November 1989.)

Figure 4–8 *Group Booking Curve*

With yield management, not only will the time before arrival be an important consideration in the pricing of guest rooms, but also the type of room to be occupied. For example, there could be a different price for a double, queen, or king room when used for single occupancy. This rate could be above the single rack rate. Similarly, double and multiple room occupancy would yield higher room rates. It works as follows:[27]

Suppose a hotel has 300 rooms and a rack rate of $150. The average number of rooms sold is 200 per night at an average rate of $125. The yield for this property would be

$$\text{Occupancy percentage} = 200 \div 300 = 66.6\%$$

The rate achievement factor is

$$\$125 \div 200 = 62.5\%$$

and the yield would be

$$0.666 \times 0.625 = 41\%$$

The application of yield management in hotels is still being refined to take into consideration factors such as multiple nights' reservations and incremental food and beverage revenue. If the guest wants to arrive on a high demand night and stay through several low demand nights, what should the charge be?

---

[27]Adapted from Michael L. Kasavana and Richard M. Brooks, *Managing Front Office Operations*, 3rd ed. East Lansing, MI: The Educational Institute of the American Hotel and Motel Association, 1990, p. 390.

Yield management has been refined with profit analysis by segment (PABS), which uses a combination of marketing information and cost analysis. It identifies average revenues generated by different market segments and then examines the contribution margin for each of the segments considering the cost of making those sales.[28]

Yield management has some disadvantages. For instance, if a businessperson attempts to make a reservation at a hotel three days before arrival and the rate quoted in order to maximize revenue is considered too high, this person may decide to select another hotel and not even consider the first hotel when making future reservations.

Revenue per available room, or **rev par,** was developed by Smith Travel Research. It is calculated by dividing room revenue by the number of rooms available. For example, if room sales are $50,000 in one day for a hotel with 400 available rooms, then the formula would be $50,000 divided by 400, or $125. Hotels use rev par to see how they are doing compared to their competitive set of hotels. Owners use rev par to gauge who they want to run their hotels.

Check Your Knowledge

1. What does PMS stand for? What functions does this system perform?
2. What is yield management? How is yield management applied in the hotel industry?

Reservations

The **reservations department** is headed by the reservations manager who, in many hotels today, is on the same level as the front office manager and reports directly to the director of rooms division or the director of sales. This emphasizes the importance of the sales aspects of reservations and encompasses yield management. Reservations is the first contact for the guest or person making the reservation for the guest. Although the contact may be by telephone, a distinct impression of the hotel is registered with the guest. This calls for exceptional telephone manners and telemarketing skills. Because some guests may be shopping for the best value, it is essential to sell the hotel by emphasizing its advantages over the competition.

---

[28]William J. Quain, "Analyzing Sales-Mix Profitability," *The Cornell Hotel and Restaurant Administration Quarterly, 33,* 2, April 1992, pp. 56–62.

Central Reservations Office (Courtesy John R. Walker.)   *Hotel Reservations Agent* (Courtesy John R. Walker.)

The reservation department generally works from 8:00 A.M. to 6:00 P.M. Depending on the size of the hotel, several people may be employed in this important department. The desired outcome of the reservations department is to exceed guest expectations when they make reservations. This is achieved by selling all of the hotel rooms for the maximum possible dollars and avoiding possible guest resentment of being overcharged. Reservations originate from a variety of sources:

1. Telephone to the same property
   a. Fax
   b. Letter
   c. Cable
2. Corporate/1-800 numbers
3. Travel agents
4. The Internet
5. Meeting planners (may be number one in a convention hotel)
6. Tour operators (may be number one in resort areas)
7. Referral from another company property
8. Airport telephone
9. Walk in

Clearly, reservations are of tremendous importance to the hotel because of the potential and actual revenue realized. Many hotel chains have a 1-800 number that a prospective guest may call without charge to make a reservation at any of the company properties in the United States and internationally. The corporate **central reservations system** allows operators to access the inventory of room availability of each hotel in the chain. Once a reservation has been made, it is immediately deducted from the inventory of rooms for the duration of the guest stay. The central reservations system interfaces with the hotel's inventory and simultaneously allows reservations to be made by the individual hotel reservations personnel. A number of important details need to be recorded when taking reservations.

Communications (Courtesy John R. Walker.)

Confirmed reservations are reservations made with sufficient time for a confirmation slip to be returned to the client by mail or fax. Confirmation is generated by the computer printer and indicates confirmation number, dates of arrival and departure, type of room booked, number of guests, number of beds, type of bed, and any special requests. The guest may bring the confirmation slip to the hotel to verify the booking.

Guaranteed reservations are given when the person making the reservation wishes to ensure that the reservation will be held. This is arranged at the time the reservation is made and generally applies in situations when the guest is expected to arrive late. The hotel takes the credit card number, which guarantees payment of the room, of the person being billed. The hotel agrees to hold the room for late arrival. The importance of guaranteed reservations is that the guest will more likely cancel beforehand if unable to show up, which gives more accurate inventory room count and minimizes no-shows.

Another form of guaranteed reservations is advance deposit/advance payment. In certain situations—for example, during a holiday—in order to protect itself against having empty rooms (no-shows), the hotel requires that a deposit of either one night or the whole stay be paid in advance of the guest's arrival. This is done by obtaining the guest's credit card number, which may be charged automatically for the first night's accommodation. This discourages no-shows. Corporations that use the hotel frequently may guarantee all of their bookings so as to avoid any problems in the event a guest arrives late, remembering that in cities where the demand is heavy, hotels release any nonguaranteed or nonpaid reservations at 4:00 P.M. or 6:00 P.M. on the evening of the guest's expected arrival.

Communications CBX or PBX

The communications **CBX** or **PBX** includes in-house communications; guest communications, such as pagers and radios; voice mail; faxes; messages; and emergency center. Guests often have their first contact with the hotel by telephone. This underlines the importance of prompt and courteous attention to all calls, because first impressions last.

The communications department is a vital part of the smooth running of the hotel. It is also a profit center because hotels generally add a 50 percent charge to all long-distance calls placed from guest rooms. Local calls cost about $0.75 to $1.25, plus tax.

Communications operates twenty-four hours a day, in much the same way as the front office does, having three shifts. It is essential that this department be staffed with people who are trained to be calm under pressure and who follow emergency procedures.

Guest Services/Uniformed Services

Because first impressions are very important to the guest, the guest service or uniformed staff has a special responsibility. The **guest service department** or **uniformed staff** is headed by a guest services manager who may also happen to be the bell captain. The staff consists of door attendants and bellpersons and the concierge—although in some hotels the concierge reports directly to the front office manager.

Door attendants are the hotel's unofficial greeters. Dressed in impressive uniforms, they greet guests at the hotel front door, assist in opening/closing automobile doors, removing luggage from the trunk, hailing taxis, keeping the hotel entrance clear of vehicles, and giving guests information about the hotel and the local area in a courteous and friendly way. People in this position generally receive many gratuities (tips); in fact, years ago, the position was handed down from

MI Associates Committed to Providing Very Best Experience for Guests (Courtesy Marriott International.)

A Day in the Life of Ryan Adams
Guest Services Manager, Hotel del Coronado, San Diego, California

From what I gather there is supposed to be some sort of magical formula for how everything works out. You should have some plan with some kind of divine guidance; if you are spiritual, then you are on your way. However, I cannot rightly say that this has become known to me. I was lucky enough to develop a plan and have made some rather good decisions to get where I am.

I have been in the industry now for eleven years and I am always amazed at the magnetic draw this industry has on you. I always tell people, "It's not the job that is so hard, that is rudimentary; it is people that really make the challenge worth undertaking." I wake up at 5:30 A.M. every morning and prepare myself mentally before I go to work on how I am going to tackle the day.

My automatic coffee maker wakes me up and I establish my bearings as I proceed to take my shower and then turn on ESPN to catch sport highlights. I pour myself a cup of coffee and sit on the couch trying to figure out what I missed and memorize scores from the previous night's game. I then switch over to CNN to catch up on politics and headline news just in case there actually might be something of interest to my isolated world.

Picking out my suit for the day reflects my mood so I always take time to select the right color and style. I will choose blue if I feel like communicating well or brown if I am feeling emotional and warm hearted. If I am working a night shift I usually wear black with a red tie or some other kind of tie. I am a big tie fan. I believe ties are like the eyes of someone. They are the windows to the soul and express our mood or persona. I try to think of what I have to accomplish for the day as far as meetings or just pure operational work.

I usually role into work at about 7 A.M. so I can see the graveyard bellman for a half hour and then the morning valet and cashiers. You learn a lot from the night crew. They see a lot of the nonsense that happens over the midnight hour. I touch base with the front desk and the concierge to see if they have any challenges starting off the day. I then retreat to my office.

(Courtesy John R. Walker.)

As I get into my office it never fails that I have at least five voice mails and ten e-mails. I listen to my voice mails and print my e-mails and look at my calendar in Microsoft Outlook to see what meetings I have dedicated my time to. I then make a list of what I need to respond to and work on the pile of papers on my desk. I usually have a pile of papers from the night before as I get a lot of mail. I look at my fourteen-day forecast to see what events or groups we have in house and touch base with my bell phone receptionist who usually has good insight into the day's events.

My responsibilities are to oversee the functions of the bellman, elevator operators, doorman, valet runners, kiosk cashiers, mass transportation, parking control, and the concierge. I have two assistant guest services managers that come in at 11 A.M. and 2:30 P.M. to cover the other shifts. I also have a parking operations supervisor and a cashier supervisor. We hold a weekly meeting so I can share the vision of the company and my own. After all, I am not just a manager; I am a leader who has to take people somewhere where they would not have gone otherwise.

I spend most of my day in meetings. On Tuesdays I attend operations meetings. Our managing director and general manager speak to us about financial position and goals for the quarter. They also bring up special highlights or events. We hear from sales and convention management regarding groups and then catering for events. Room reservations personnel update us on their budget and how many rooms are going to be occupied for the next two weeks and then compare that to the forecasted level of occupancy. We then hear from accounting facilities, recreation, retail, guest services, and signature services. It is a very informative meeting and it also gives you a good read on the mood of upper management.

I try to spend as much face time with my associates as possible, getting feedback and safety suggestions and to let them vent frustrations as I try to win them over to the big picture. I spend a little time "shmoozing" clients who have porterages and deliveries to ensure my team is doing their best to impress. I attend their preconvention

Hotel del Coronado (Courtesy Hotel del Coronado, San Diego, California.)

meetings to discover what the clients are about. We identify their needs and fulfill them with the kind of guest service that leaves their jaws dropped.

The funny thing about modern technology is how dependent you become on it. Gone are the days of the good ol' boy network when all you had to do was ask. Now you have to set up a meeting in Microsoft Outlook, send e-mails, fill out tons of paperwork, and constantly check your voice mails and e-mails. The company has made it a little easier by supplying me with a Nextel phone, or "the leash" as we call it. This phone has walkie-talkie capability and allows the executive team to communicate on a network.

I know what you're thinking: Sounds tedious and problematic. Well it is. The challenge of making it all come together is what is so appealing to me. I usually get so involved that I forget to eat lunch, unless one of my teammates pulls me away for a bite and engages me in some endless banter about work. I stock my office refrigerator with candy bars and various beverages because I usually don't make the time to eat; it just gets too busy.

My days typically end about 5 P.M. or 6 P.M. I have by then passed on all information the night crews will need and delegated responsibilities to the two assistant guest services managers. I still have a big stack of papers to go through and file for tomorrow. I hop on my bicycle, ride by security to check in my keys, and then I am off to go home and see my lovely wife. This is the day in a life of a guest services manager.

father to son or sold for several thousand dollars. Rumor has it that this is one of the most lucrative positions in the hotel, even more than the general manager's.

The bellperson's main function is to escort guests and transport luggage to their rooms. Bellpersons also need to be knowledgeable about the local area and all facets of the hotel and its services. Because they have so much guest contact, they need a pleasant, outgoing personality. The bellperson explains the services of the hotel and points out the features of the room (lighting, TV, air conditioning, telephone, wake-up calls, laundry and valet service, room service and restaurants, and the pool and health spa).

Concierge (Courtesy John R. Walker.)

Concierge

The **concierge** is a uniformed employee of the hotel who has her or his own separate desk in the lobby or on special concierge floors. The concierge is a separate department from the front office room clerks and cashiers.

Until 1936, a concierge was not an employee of the hotel but an independent entrepreneur who purchased a position from the hotel and paid the salaries, if any, of his or her uniformed subordinates.[29]

Today's concierge, as one historically minded concierge put it, has come to embody the core of a hotel's efforts to serve guests in a day when the inn is so large that the innkeeper can no longer personally attend to each guest.[30] Luxury hotels in most cities have concierges. New York's Plaza Hotel has 800 rooms and a battery of ten concierges who serve under the direction of Thomas P. Wolfe. The concierge assists guests with a broad range of services such as the following:

- ✔ Tickets to the hottest shows in town, even for the very evening on the day they are requested. Naturally, the guest pays up to about $150 per ticket.
- ✔ A table at a restaurant that has no reservations available.
- ✔ Advice on local restaurants, activities, attractions, amenities, and facilities
- ✔ Airline tickets and reconfirmation of flights
- ✔ VIP's messages and special requests, such as shopping

Less frequent requests:

- ✔ Organize a wedding on two days' notice
- ✔ Arrange for a member of the concierge department to go to a consulate or embassy for visas to be stamped in guests' passports
- ✔ Handle business affairs

What will a concierge do for a guest? Almost anything, *Conde' Nast Traveler* learned from concierges at hotels around the world. Among the more unusual requests were the following:

---

[29]McDowell Bryson and Adele Ziminski, *The Concierge: Key to Hospitality.* New York: John Wiley and Sons, 1992, p. 3.

[30]Betsy Wade, *The New York Times,* February 21, 1993.

1. Some Japanese tourists staying at the Palace Hotel in Madrid decided to bring bullfighting home. Their concierge found bulls for sale, negotiated the bulls' purchase, and had them shipped to Tokyo.
2. After watching a guest pace the lobby, the concierge of a London hotel, now operating the desk at the Dorchester, asked the pacer if he could help. The guest was to be married within the hour, but his best man had been detained. Because he was dressed up anyway, the concierge volunteered to substitute.
3. A guest at the Hotel Plaza Athenee in Paris wanted to prevent her pet from mingling with dogs from the wrong side of the boulevard while walking. Madame requested that the concierge buy a house in a decent neighborhood so that her pampered pooch might stroll in its garden unsullied. Although the dog continued to reside at the hotel, Madame's chauffeur shuttled him to the empty house for his daily constitutional.

Concierges serve to elevate a property's marketable value and its image. They provide the special touch services that distinguish a "top property." To make sure they can cater to a guest's precise needs, concierges should make sure that they know precisely what the guest is looking for budget-wise, as well as any other parameters. Concierges must be very attentive and must anticipate guest needs when possible. In this age of highly competitive top-tier properties and well-informed guests, only knowledgeable concierge staff can provide the services to make a guest's stay memorable. As more properties try to demonstrate enhanced value, a concierge amenity takes on added significance.

The concierge needs not only a detailed knowledge of the hotel and its services, but also of the city and even international details. Many concierges speak several languages; most important of all, they must want to help people and have a pleasant, outgoing personality. At the Westin St. Francis in San Francisco, a special three-employee department has been created to refine Japanese amenities. This Japanese guest service combines the functions of concierge, front desk, and tour-briefing. Given that one-third of all visitors to San Francisco are international travelers and that most Japanese visitors do not speak English, this progressive approach to guest satisfaction is receiving positive feedback.[31]

The concierges' organization, which promotes high professional and ethical standards, is the UPPGH (Union Professionelle des Portiers des Grand Hotels), more commonly called the *Clefs d'Or* because of the crossed goldkey insignia concierges usually wear on the lapels of their uniforms. The Clefs d'Or has about 4,000 members in twenty-four countries, with approximately 150 U.S. members.[32]

✔ Also in 1998, Canadian Pacific Hotels acquired Princess Hotels, International, with seven luxury resorts in Arizona, Mexico, Bermuda, and Barbados, including the Scottsdale Princess (home of the PGA

---

[31]Leslee Jaquette, "St. Francis Caters to Japanese with Guest-Services Program," *Hotel and Motel Management, 207,* 13, July 27, 1992, pp. 6, 29.

[32]Bryson and Ziminski, op. cit., p. 194.

Corporate Profile: Fairmont Hotels & Resorts

Fairmont Hotels & Resorts is the largest luxury hotel company in North America, with a distinctive collection and a worldwide reputation for excellence. Their diverse portfolio includes historic icons, elegant resorts, and modern city-center properties. From the beaches of Hawaii and Bermuda to the heart of New York City, all of the hotels offer a superior guest experience that is uniquely "Fairmont."

Hotels under the Fairmont banner offer guests an extraordinary place that is created by combining unique architecture and structure, expressive decor and artistry, and magnificent features all in one great location. Add great service to these features and the result is an extraordinary experience that makes the memory of Fairmont Hotels & Resorts a long and lasting one.

Most of Fairmont's hotels were among the first buildings to be erected in young cities across North America. Few hotels can boast that their communities literally grew up around them. Today, modern city-center properties have been added to the collection, with core locations that allow guests to join the hustle and bustle of the city, take part in the action of the business district, and enjoy the lights and sounds of street life. The Fairmont collection includes such fine properties as The Fairmont Miramar Hotel Santa Monica, and The Fairmont San Francisco, a city landmark that is steeped in history.

The resorts are situated in some of the most breathtaking and pristine areas in the world, and travelers from across the globe associate Fairmont with the most inviting beaches, challenging golf courses, and exhilarating ski slopes.

Fairmont guarantees consistency throughout their collection of hotels and resorts by adhering strictly to company-wide standards. Central purchasing ensures that the same high-quality amenities are available to all guests wherever they visit. Features such as the Fairmont President's Club recognition program, the Fairmont Gold "hotel within a hotel," and the Business Centers cater to the needs of discriminating travelers. All of these amenities and more make every Fairmont hotel an extraordinary place, and each guest's stay an extraordinary experience.

History

Headquartered in Toronto, Canada, Fairmont is the largest luxury hotel management company in North America, offering guests luxurious accommodations in the most sought-after destinations. In October of 1999, Canadian Pacific Hotels & Resorts acquired Fairmont Hotels; bringing together two companies with over a century of rich history and exemplary hospitality. And from this grand union, Fairmont Hotels & Resorts, a new key player within the luxury hotel segment, was born.

The Fairmont Legacy

The original Fairmont Hotel was the vision of San Francisco natives Tessie and Virginia Fair. In 1907, after a one-year delay due to damage from the San Francisco earthquake, The Fairmont opened its doors for the first time. Benjamin H. Swig bought The Fairmont in 1945 and began building an exemplary portfolio of hotels, later purchasing the Grunewald (now The Fairmont New Orleans) and the renowned Plaza in New York. He chose the Fairmont name to represent his esteemed collection, honoring his first purchase and the company's flagship hotel, San Francisco's The Fairmont. Fairmont Hotels grew to seven properties in the United States and became a social hub for the rich and famous.

Fairmont Hotels & Resorts

Featuring hotels that have played an integral role in the development of cities and communities, Fairmont Hotels & Resorts are often deemed attractions in themselves. The Plaza in New York, The Fairmont San Francisco, The Fairmont Banff Springs, and Fairmont Le Château Frontenac are but four famous members of the Fairmont Hotels & Resorts collection. And while Fairmont Hotels & Resorts is a new name in the hospitality industry, its values lie in the long-standing principle of its founding companies: providing exceptional service in distinctive surroundings. Building on over a century of experience with one of the largest collections of distinctive hotels in the world and employees who strive to exceed expectations on all occasions, Fairmont Hotels & Resorts is poised to become a dominant player in the hotel industry.

The Environmental Program

Originally launched in 1990 as a grassroots quest to reduce the impact of hotel operations on the environment in which we live and work, the Fairmont Hotels & Resorts Green Partnership Program is now considered by many, including *National Geographic Traveler,* to be the most comprehensive environmental program in the North American hotel industry.

Fairmont Hotels & Resorts supports green thinking because the environment is not just out there—it is the air we breathe; the water we drink; and the places we live, work, and play! For a more corporate view of the environmental program, visit the corporate Website at *www.fairmont.com/environment.*

Guests at Fairmont Hotels & Resorts expect to have their heart captured. Satisfying the guests is important, and the policy extends to our colleagues as well. Because of its outstanding performance in the areas of recruitment, training, advancement, and performance management, Fairmont Hotels & Resorts is one of North Americas top rated companies to work for.

Tour's Phoenix Open and an annual event on the IBM/ATP men's professional tennis tour).

✔ In 1999, Canadian Pacific Hotels announced the intention to join with The Fairmont Hotels to create new hotel management company to be called Fairmont Hotels and Resorts, featuring a collection of luxury hotels across North America, Mexico, and the Caribbean. The existing Canadian Pacific Hotels portfolio, including the recently acquired Princess Hotels, will be combined with seven landmark Fairmont Hotels located in U.S. gateway cities, including such famous properties as The Plaza in New York and The Fairmont in San Francisco.

Housekeeping

The largest department in terms of the number of people employed is **housekeeping.** Up to 50 percent of the hotel employees may work in this department. The person in charge is the executive housekeeper or director of services. Her or his duties and responsibilities call for exceptional leadership, organization, motivation, and commitment to maintaining high standards. The logistics of servicing large numbers of rooms on a daily basis can be challenging.

The importance of the housekeeping department is underlined by guest surveys that consistently rank cleanliness of rooms number one.

The following are the ten rules for effective housekeeping leadership:

1. Utilize people power effectively. Spread responsibilities and tasks to get work done properly and on time.
2. Devise easy methods of reporting work that has to be done. Encourage feedback from all associates and continuous communication with the associates.
3. Develop standard procedures for routine activities. Help associates to develop consistent work habits.

4. Install **inventory controls.** Control costs for supplies and equipment.
5. Motivate housekeeping associates. Keep high morale, motivation, and understanding.
6. Accept challenges presented by guests and management. Remain unflappable in the face of any request.
7. Involve associates in planning. Encourage associates to use imagination to make the job easier and quicker without changing standards.
8. Increase educational level of staff. Support training, encouragement, and educational classes.
9. Set recruitment programs to develop management trainees. Give trainees opportunities to advance.
10. Cooperate and coordinate with other departments, such as front office, engineering and maintenance, and laundry.

The four major areas of responsibilities for the executive housekeeper are as follows:

1. Leadership of people, equipment, and supplies
2. Cleanliness and servicing the guest rooms and public areas
3. Operating the department according to financial guidelines prescribed by the general manager
4. Keeping records

An example of an executive housekeeper's day might be as follows:

7:45 A.M. Walk the lobby and property with the night cleaners and supervisors
Check the housekeeping log book
Check the forecast house count for number of check-outs
Check daily activity reports, stayovers, check-ins, and VIPs to ensure appropriate standards
Attend housekeepers' meeting
Meet challenges
Train new employees in the procedures
Meet with senior housekeepers/department managers
Conduct productivity checks
Check budget
Approve purchase orders
Check inventories
Conduct room inspections
Review maintenance checks
Interview potential employees

6:00 P.M. Attend to human resource activities, counseling, and employee development

Executive Housekeeper
(Courtesy John R. Walker.)

Perhaps the biggest challenge of an executive housekeeper is the leadership of all the employees in the department. Further, these employees are often of different nationalities. Depending on the size of the hotel, the executive housekeeper

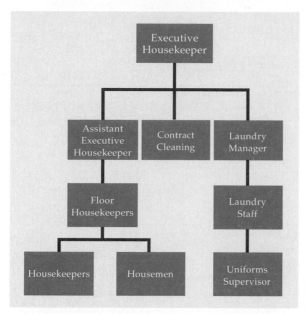

Figure 4–9
Housekeeping Personnel

is assisted by an assistant executive housekeeper and one or more housekeeping supervisors, who in turn supervise a number of room attendants or housekeeping associates (see Figure 4–9). The assistant executive housekeeper manages the housekeeping office. The first important daily task of this position is to break out the hotel into sections for allocation to the room attendants' schedules.

The rooms of the hotel are listed on the floor master. If the room is vacant, nothing is written next to the room number. If the guest is expected to check out, then SC will be written next to the room number. A stayover will have SS, on hold is AH, out of order is OO, and VIPs are highlighted in colors according to the amenities required.

If 258 rooms are occupied and 10 of these are suites (which count as two rooms), then the total number of rooms to be allocated to room attendants is 268 (minus any no-shows). The remaining total is then divided by 17, the number of rooms that each attendant is expected to make up.

Total number of rooms occupied	258
Add 10 for the suites	10
Total number of rooms and suites occupied	268
Less any no-shows	3
	265

Divide 265 by 17 (the number of rooms each attendant services) =
16 (the number of attendants required for that day)

Figure 4–10 shows a daily attendant's schedule. To reduce payroll costs and encourage room attendants to become "stars," a number of hotel corporations have empowered the best attendants to check their own rooms. This has

Housekeepers Guest Room Self–Inspection Rating

Inspection Codes:

P – POLISH	R – REPLACE	E – WORK ORDER	S – SOAP SCUM	SM – SMEAR
SA – STAIN	H – HAIR	D – DIRT	DU – DUST	M – MISSING

PART I – GUEST ROOM		S		U	COMMENTS
Entry, door, frame, threshold, latch			1		
Unusual odor OR smoke smell			3		
CLOSET, doors, louvers–containing			1		
Hangers, 8 suits, 4 skirts, 2 bags w/ invoices			2		
Two (2) robes, with info card			2		
Extra TP & FACIAL			1		
One (1) luggage rack			1		
Current rate card			1		
VALET	Shoe Horn & Mitt		2		
DRESSER	LAMP/ SHADE/ BULB		2		
	ICE BUCKET, LID, TRAY		2		
	TWO(2) WINE GLASSES		2		
	Room Service MENU		2		
MINIBAR	TOP, FRONT, 2 Wine glasses/ price list		1		
SAFE	KEY IN SAFE, SIGN		5		
CHECK BEHIND DRESSER			2		
DRAWERS	BIBLE AND BUDDHIST BOOK		1		
	PHONE BOOKS, ATT DIRECTORY		1		
TELEVISION	ON & OFF, CH 19 BEHIND		1		
COFFEE TABLE	REMOTE CONTROL/TEST 1		2		
	T.V. LISTINGS/BOOK MARK		1		
	GLASS TOP/LA JOLLA BOOK		1		
CARPET	VACUUM, SPOTS?		2		
SOFA	UNDER CUSHION/ BEHIND		2		
3 W LAMP	BULB, SHADE & CORD		1		
WINDOWS	GLASS, DOOR, LATCH – C BAR?		2		
CURTAINS	Pull – check seams		1		
PATIO	2 CHAIRS, TABLE & DECK		3		
DESK	2 CHAIRS, TOP, BASE & LAMP/SHADE		5		
	GREEN COMPENDIUM		3		
	Waste paper can		1		
BED	Tight, Pillows, bedspread		5		
	Check Under/SHEETS, PILLOWS		3		
HVAC	Control, setting, vent		1		
SIDE TABLES	Lamps & shade		2		
	Telephone, MESSAGE LIGHT		1		
	Clock Radio CORRECT TIME?		1		
MIRRORS	LARGE MIRROR OVER DRESSER		1		
PICTURES	ROOM ART WORK		1		
WALLS	Marks, stains, etc.		3		

Figure 4–10 *Daily Attendant's Schedule*

Housekeepers Guest Room Self–Inspection Rating

Inspection Codes:

| P – POLISH | R – REPLACE | E – WORK ORDER | S – SOAP SCUM | SM – SMEAR |
| SA – STAIN | H – HAIR | D – DIRT | DU – DUST | M – MISSING |

PART II – BATHROOM		S			U		COMMENTS
BATH TUB/SHOWER							
	GROUT/TILE & EDGE			2			
	ANTISLIP GRIDS			2			
	SIDE WALLS			1			
	SHOWER HEAD			1			
	WALL SOAP DISH			1			
	CONTROL LEVER			1			
	FAUCET			1			
	CLOTHESLINE			1			
	SHOWER ROD, HOOKS			1			
	SHOWER CURTAIN/ LINER			2			
VANITY	TOP, SIDE & EDGE			1			
	SINK, TWO FAUCETS			3			
	3 GLASSES, COASTERS			2			
	WHITE SOAP DISH			1			
	FACIAL TISSUE & BOX			1			
AMENITY BASKET							
	1 SHAMPOO			1			
	1 CONDITIONER			1			
	1 MOISTURIZER			1			
	2 BOXED SOAP			1			
	1 SHOWER CAP			1			
MIRROR	LARGE & COSMETIC			2			
WALLS, CEILING, & VENT				2			
TOILET	TOP, SEAT, BASE & LIP			2			
OTHER	TOILET PAPER, fold			1			
	SCALE AND TRASH CAN			2			
	FLOOR, SWEPT AND MOPPED			3			
	TELEPHONE			1			
BATH LINENS, racks							
	THREE (3) WASH CLOTHS			1			
	THREE (3) HAND TOWELS			1			
	THREE(3) BATH TOWELS			1			
	ONE (1) BATH MAT			1			
	ONE (1) BATH RUG			1			
LIGHT SWITCH				1			
DOOR	FULL LENGTH MIRROR			1			
	HANDLE/LOCK			1			
	THRESHOLD			1			
	PAINTED SURFACE			1			

Figure 4–10 *(continued)*

Housekeeping Associate
Making Up a Room
(Courtesy John R. Walker.)

reduced the need for supervisors. Notice in Figure 4–10 how the points are weighted for various items. This is the result of focus groups of hotel guests who explained the important things to them about a room. The items with the highest points were the ones that most concerned the guests.

The assistant executive housekeeper or administrative assistant will assist the executive housekeeper with a number of the duties and will be the anchorperson in the housekeeping office. This is the central headquarters for all housekeeping operations. The following are some examples from the Hilton La Jolla, Torrey Pines, California:

1. All housekeeping associates report here.
2. Section assignments are given.
3. All housekeeping telephone calls are received here.
4. All check-out and in-order rooms are processed here.
5. All guest rooms that are not cleaned by a specified time are reported.
6. All household supplies are issued.
7. Commercial laundry, counting linen, and checking linen may be handled here.
8. Table linen may be issued here.
9. All uniforms and costumes may be issued here.
10. Working records are kept.
11. All housekeeping pass keys are kept and controlled.

Guest room supplies on housekeeping associates' carts are replaced during the night shift. It is suggested that the items given away to the customer are placed on the lower shelf of the cart to discourage guests from collecting souvenirs. Taking calls and relaying information about the rooms is a vital part of the communications necessary for the smooth operation of this busy department.

The evening assistant housekeeper or housekeeper supervisor will take over the office and allocate the turndown sections to the evening. Each attendant has an allocation of sixty-three rooms to turndown and a turndown summary report to complete. The attendants also report back to the housekeeping office any discrepancies, which are in turn forwarded and communicated to the front office. The housekeeping associates clean and service between fifteen and twenty rooms per day depending on the individual hotel characteristics.

Servicing a room takes longer in some older hotels than it does in some of the newer properties. Also, service time depends on the number of check-out rooms versus stayovers because servicing check-outs takes longer. Housekeeping associates begin their day at 8:00 A.M., reporting to the executive or assistant executive housekeeper. They are assigned a block of rooms and given room keys, for which they must sign and then return before going off duty.

The role of the executive housekeeper may vary slightly between the corporate chain and the independent hotel. An example is the purchasing of furnishings and equipment. A large independent hotel relies on the knowledge and experience of the executive housekeeper to make appropriate selections, whereas the chain hotel company has a corporate purchase agent (assisted by a designer) to make many of these decisions.

The executive housekeeper is responsible for a substantial amount of record keeping. In addition to the scheduling and evaluation of employees, an inventory of all guest rooms and public area furnishings must be accurately maintained with the record of refurbishment. Most of the hotel's maintenance work orders are initiated by the housekeepers who report the maintenance work order. Many hotels now have a computer link-up between housekeeping and engineering and maintenance to speed the process. Guests expect their rooms to be fully functional, especially at today's prices. Housekeeping maintains a perpetual inventory of guest room amenities, cleaning supplies, and linens.

Productivity in the housekeeping department is measured by the person hours per occupied room. The labor costs per person hour for a full service hotel is $2.50, or twenty minutes of labor for every occupied room in the hotel. Another key ratio is the labor cost, which is expected to be 5.1 percent of room sales. Controllable expenses are measured per occupied rooms. These expenses include guest supplies like soap, shampoo, hand and body lotion, sewing kits, and stationery. Although this will vary according to the type of hotel, the cost should be about $2.00 per room. Cleaning supplies should be approximately $.50 and linen costs $.95, including the purchase and laundering of all linen. These budgeted costs are sometimes hard to achieve. The executive housekeeper may be doing a great job controlling costs, but if the sales department discounts rooms, the room sales figures may come in below budget. This would have the effect of increasing the costs per occupied room.

Another concern for the executive housekeeper is accident prevention. Insurance costs have skyrocketed in recent years, and employers are struggling to increase both employee and guest safety. It is necessary for accidents to be carefully investigated. Some employees have been known to have an accident at home but go to work and report it as a work-related injury in order to be covered by workers' compensation. To safeguard themselves to some extent, hotels keep sweep logs of the public areas; in the event that a guest slips and falls, the hotel can show that it does genuinely take preventative measures to protect its guests.

The U.S. Senate Bill 198, known as the **Employee Right to Know,** has heightened awareness of the storage, handling, and use of dangerous chemicals. Information about the chemicals must be made available to all employees. Great care and extensive training is required to avoid dangerous accidents.

The executive housekeeper must also maximize loss prevention. Strict policies and procedures are necessary to prevent losses from guest rooms. Some hotels require housekeeping associates to sign a form stating that they understand they may not let any guest into any room. Such action would result in immediate termination of employment. Although this may seem drastic, it is the only way to avoid some hotel thefts.

Laundry

Increasingly, hotels are operating their own laundries. This subdepartment generally reports to the executive housekeeper. The modern laundry operates computerized washing/drying machines and large presses. Dry cleaning for both guests and employees is a service that may also come under the laundry department.

Some hotels, especially the smaller and older ones, contract out the laundry service. This is because it is costly to alter an existing hotel to provide space for laundry. Even space itself costs money because the space might be otherwise used for revenue-producing purposes, such as meetings, functions, and so on. In addition, by contracting out, the hotel does not have to own its own linen. It may rent linen and be charged for each piece used. However, operators frequently complain that they receive inferior linen and inconsistent service. Another alternative is for the hotel to purchase its own linen and have it laundered by contract. In either case, the executive housekeeper must ensure that strict control is maintained over linen. Table 4–1 lists some advantages for both types of systems.

Linen Management System

The Chicago Hilton and Towers has installed a semicustomized linen-management and inventory control system that is expected to save the 1,620-room property between $70,000 and $100,000 annually. The system reduces labor costs by eliminating the need to manually sort linen from the different properties that are served. In addition, because the system provides a perpetual inventory, needs can be anticipated better and overtime costs by housekeeping staff can be minimized.

A Houseperson Who Transports Dirty/Clean Linen to and from the Laundry

Table 4–1   In-House Laundry Service Versus Contract Laundry Service
Advantages of an In-House Laundry Twenty-four hour anytime laundry service available for guests Smaller par-stock of linen can be maintained Full control over quality of laundered linen **Advantages of Contract Laundry Service** No maintenance costs for equipment No labor costs Fixed projected expenses toward contract Lower labor costs because no exclusive laundry staff is required No trained staff required Lower training costs Lower overhead cost of energy and water

Much of the heavy work in the housekeeping department is conducted by housepersons. They clean public areas using heavy floor polishers for marble or tile floors, vacuum the corridors on the guest room floors, do carpet shampooing and moving of furniture, and, on occasion, take the linen from the linen room to the floors. The houseperson may also assist the housekeepers with spring cleaning and the turning of mattresses.

Check Your Knowledge

1. What is a PBX or CBX?
2. What constitutes uniformed services? What is the role played by each staff member of uniformed service?
3. Name the characteristics an executive housekeeper should possess.

Security/Loss Prevention

Providing guest protection and loss prevention is essential for any lodging establishment regardless of size. Violent crime is a growing problem and protecting guests from bodily harm has been defined by the courts as a reasonable expectation from hotels. The security division is responsible for maintaining security alarm systems and implementing procedures aimed at protecting the personal property of guests and employees and the hotel itself.

Casino Security

At the Mirage resort hotel in Las Vegas, security concerns are heightened by the cash-intensive casino operation. The Polaroid ID-2000 Plus computer-based electronic security management system plays a central role in supporting the Mirage's integrated security environment. The system combines advanced database computers and electronic-imaging technologies. This improves efficiency and helps minimize transaction discrepancies.

Juli Koentopp, "The Mirage Concerning Hotel Security," Security Management, **36,** 12, December 1992, pp. 54–60.

A comprehensive security plan must include the following elements:

Security Officers
✔ Make regular rounds of the hotel premises including guest floors, corridors, public and private function rooms, parking areas, and offices.
✔ Duties involve observing suspicious behavior and taking appropriate action, investigating incidents, and cooperating with local law enforcement agencies.

Equipment
✔ Two-way radios between security staff are common.
✔ Closed-circuit television cameras are used in out-of-the-way corridors and doorways, as well as in food, liquor, and storage areas.
✔ Smoke detectors and fire alarms, which increase the safety of the guests, are a requirement in every part of the hotel by law.
✔ Electronic key cards offer superior room security. Key cards typically do not list the name of the hotel or the room number. So if lost or stolen, the key is not easily traceable. In addition, most key card systems record every entry in and out of the room on the computer for any further reference.

Safety Procedures
✔ Front desk agents help maintain security by not allowing guests to reenter their rooms once they have checked out. This prevents any loss of hotel property by guests.
✔ Security officers should be able to gain access to guest rooms, store rooms, and offices at all times.
✔ Security staff develop **catastrophe plans** to ensure staff and guest safety and to minimize direct and indirect costs from disaster. The catastrophe plan reviews insurance policies, analyzes physical facilities, and evaluates possible disaster scenarios, including whether they have a high or low probability of occurring. Possible disaster scenarios may include fires, bomb threats, earthquakes, floods, hurricanes, and blizzards. The well-prepared hotel will develop formal policies to deal with any possible scenario and will train employees to implement chosen procedures should they become necessary.

Identification Procedures
✔ Identification cards with photographs should be issued to all employees.
✔ Name tags for employees who are likely to have contact with guests not only project a friendly image for the property, but are also useful for security reasons.

Trends in Hotel and Rooms Division Operations

✔ *Diversity of workforce:* All the pundits are projecting a substantial increase in the number of women and minorities who will not only be taking hourly paid positions, but also supervising and management positions as well.

✔ *Increase in use of technology:* Reservations are being made by individuals via the Internet. Travel agents are able to make reservations at more properties. There is increasing simplification of the various property management systems and their interface with POS systems. In the guest room, the demand for high-speed Internet access, category 5 cables, and in some cases equipment itself is anticipated.

✔ *Continued quest for increases in productivity:* As pressure mounts from owners and management companies, hotel managers are looking for innovative ways to increase productivity and to measure productivity by sales per employee.

✔ *Increasing use of yield management to increase profit by effective pricing of room inventory.*

✔ *Greening of hotels and guest rooms:* This includes an increase in recycling and the use of environmentally friendly products, amenities, and biodegradable detergents.

✔ *Security:* The survey by the International Hotel Association indicated that guests continue to be concerned about personal security. Hotels are constantly working to improve guest security. For example, one hotel has instituted a women-only floor with concierge and security.

✔ *Diversity of the guest:* More women travelers are occupying hotel rooms. This is particularly due to an increase in business travel.

✔ *Compliance with the ADA:* As a result of the Americans with Disabilities Act (ADA), all hotels must modify existing facilities and incorporate design features into new constructions that make areas accessible to persons with disabilities. All hotels are expected to have at least 4 percent of their parking space designated as "handicapped." These spaces must be wide enough for wheelchairs to be unloaded from a van. Guest rooms must be fitted with equipment that can be manipulated by persons with disabilities. Restrooms must be wide enough to accommodate wheelchairs. Ramps should be equipped with handrails, and meeting rooms must be equipped with special listening systems for those with hearing impairments.

Case Study

Checking Out a Guest

A guest walked up to the front desk agent in an upscale hotel, ready to check out. As she would normally do when checking out a guest, the agent asked the guest what his room number was. The guest was in a hurry and showed his anxiety by responding, "I stay in a hundred hotel rooms and you expect me to remember my room number?"

The agent then asked for the guest's name, to which he responded, "My name is Mr. Johnstein." After thanking him, the agent began to look for the guest's last name, but the name was not listed in the computer. Because the man had a heavy accent and the agent assumed that she had misunderstood him, she politely asked the guest to spell his last name. He answered, "What? Are you an idiot? The person who checked me in last night had no problem checking me in." Again, the agent looked on the computer to find the guest.

The guest, becoming even more frustrated, said, "I have a plane to catch and it is ridiculous that it has to take this long to check me out. I also need to fax these papers off, but I need to have them photocopied first." The agent responded, "There is a business center at the end of the counter that will fax and photocopy what you need." The guest replied, "If I wanted your opinion, I would have asked you for it. Haven't you ever heard of customer service? Isn't this a five-star hotel? With your bad attitude, you should be working in a three-star hotel. I can't believe they let you work here at the front desk. Haven't you found my name yet?"

The agent, who was beginning to get upset, asked the guest again to spell out his full name. The guest only replied, "Here are my papers I want faxed if you are capable of faxing them." The agent reached to take the papers, and the guest shouted, "Don't grab them from my hand! You have a bad attitude, and if I had more time, I would talk to someone about getting you removed from your position to a hotel where they don't require such a level of customer service." The agent was very upset, but kept herself calm in order to prevent the guest from getting angrier.

The agent continued to provide service to the guest, sending the faxes and making the photocopies he had requested. Upon her return, the agent again asked the guest to repeat his last name, since he had failed to spell it out. The guest replied by spelling out his name, "J-o-h-n-s-t-o-n-e." The agent was finally able to find his name on the computer and checked him out, while he continued to verbally attack her. The agent finished by telling the guest to have a nice flight.

Discussion Questions

1. Is it appropriate to have the manager finish the check-out? Or, should the front desk agent just take the heat?
2. Would you have handled the situation in the same manner?
3. What would you have done differently?

Case Study

Overbooked: The Housekeeping Perspective

It is no secret that in all hotels, the director of housekeeping must be able to react quickly and efficiently to any unexpected circumstances that arise. Stephen Rodondi, executive house-keeper at the Regency in La Jolla, California, usually starts his workday at 8:00 A.M. with a department meeting. These morning meetings help him, and the employees, to visualize their goals for the day. On this particularly busy day, Rodondi arrives at work and is told that three housekeepers have called in sick. This is a serious challenge for the hotel because it is overbooked and has all of its 400 rooms to service.

Discussion Question

1. What should Stephen do to maintain standards and ensure that all the guest rooms are serviced?

Courtesy of Stephen Rodondi, Executive Housekeeper, Hyatt Regency, La Jolla, CA.

Case Study

Overbooked: The Front Office Perspective

Overbooking is an accepted hotel and airline practice. Many question the practice from various standpoints including ethical and moral. Industry executives argue that there is nothing more perishable than a vacant room. If it is not used, there is no chance to regain lost revenue. Hotels need to protect themselves because potential guests frequently make reservations at more than one hotel or are delayed and, therefore, do not show up.

The percentage of "no-shows" varies by hotel and location, but is often around 5 percent. In a 400-room hotel, that is twenty rooms, or an average loss of approximately $2,600 per night. Considering these figures, it is not surprising that hotels try to protect themselves by overbooking.

Hotels look carefully at bookings: Who they are for, what rates they are paying, when they were made, whether they are for regular guests or from a major account (a corporation who uses the hotel frequently), etc.

Jill Reynolds, the front office manager at the Regency La Jolla, had known for some time that the 400-room hotel would be overbooked for this one night in

continued

October. She prepared to talk with the front desk associates as they came on duty at 7:30 in the morning, knowing it would be a challenge to sell out without "walking" guests. Seldom does a hotel sell out before having to walk a few guests.

The hotel's policy and procedure on walking guests enables the front desk associates to call nearby hotels of a similar category to find out if they have rooms available to sell. If it is necessary to walk a guest, the associate explains to the guest that, regrettably, no rooms are available due to fewer departures than expected. The associate must explain that suitable accommodations have been reserved at a nearby hotel and that the hotel will pay for the room and transportation to and from the hotel. Normally guests are understanding, especially when they realize that they are receiving a free room and free transportation.

On this particular day, the house count indicated that the hotel was overbooked by thirty rooms. Three or four nearby, comparable hotels had rooms available to sell in the morning. Besides walking guests, Jill considered other options, in particular "splitting" the fifteen suites with connecting parlors. If the guests in the suites do not need the parlor, it is then possible to gain a few more "rooms" to sell separately, however roll-away beds must be placed in the rooms. Fortunately, eight parlors were available to sell.

Discussion Question

1. If you were in the same situation, what would you do?

Career Information

Hotel and Rooms Division Operation

Hotel management is probably the most popular career choice among hospitality educational program graduating seniors. The reason for hotel management's popularity is tied to the elegant image of hotels and the prestige associated with being a general manager or vice president of a major lodging chain. Managing a hotel is a complex balancing act that involves keeping employees, customers, and owners satisfied while overseeing a myriad of departments, including reservations, front desk, housekeeping, maintenance, accounting, food and beverage, security, concierge, and sales.

Becoming a GM means that a person needs to understand all of the various functions of a hotel and how their interrelationship makes up the lodging environment. The first step down this career path is getting a job in a hotel while you are in college. Once you become proficient in one area, volunteer to work in another. A solid foundation of broad-based experience in the hotel will be priceless when you start your lodging career. Some excellent areas to consider are the front desk, night audit, food and beverage, and maintenance. Another challenging but very important place to gain experience is in housekeeping. It has been said that if you can manage the housekeeping department, the rest of lodging management is easy. An internship with a large hotel chain property can also be a powerful learning experience. There is simply no substitute for being part of a team that operates a lodging property with several hundred rooms.

You may hear about graduates being offered "direct placement" or "manager in training" (MIT) positions.

(There are several name variations for these programs.) Direct placement means that you will be offered a specific position at a property on graduation. An MIT program exposes you to several areas of the hotel over a period of time and then you are given an assignment based on your performance during training. Neither one is better than the other from a career standpoint.

Another important consideration of a lodging career is your wardrobe. Hotels are places where people are judged based on their appearance and a conservative, professional image is a key to success. Clothes are the tools of the lodging professional's trade and they are not inexpensive. Begin investing in clothes while you are in school. Buy what you can afford but buy items of quality. Stay away from trendy or flashy clothes that will quickly be out of fashion.

When you take a position you can expect to work from fifty to sixty hours per week. The times you work may vary. You can expect to have a starting salary of between $30,000 and $34,000. Some hotel chains will assist with moving expenses and may even offer a one-time signing bonus. However, try not to focus too much on money, instead try to find a company that you feel comfortable with and will allow you opportunities for advancement.

Related Web Sites

http://www.hoteljobs.com/—Careers in lodging
http://www.hyatt.com/—Hyatt Hotels
http://www.marriott.com/—Marriott International

Courtesy of Charlie Adams.

Summary

1. A big hotel is run by a general manager and an executive committee, which is represented by the key executives of all the major departments, such as rooms division, food and beverage, marketing, sales, and human resources.

2. The general manager represents the hotel and is responsible for its profitability and performance. Because of increased job consolidation, he or she also is expected to attract business and to empathize with the cultures of both guests and employees.

3. The rooms division department consists of front office, reservations, housekeeping, concierge, guest services, and communications.

4. The front desk, as the center of the hotel, sells rooms and maintains balanced guest accounts, which are completed daily by the night auditor. The front desk constantly must meet guests' needs by offering services such as mailing, faxing, and messages.

5. The property management system, centralized reservations, and yield management have enabled a hotel to work more efficiently and to increase profitability and guest satisfaction.

6. The communications department, room service, and guest services (such as door attendants, bellpersons, and the concierge) are vital parts of the personality of a hotel.

7. Housekeeping is the largest department of the hotel. The executive housekeeper is in charge of inventory, cleaning, employees, and accident and loss prevention. The laundry may be cleaned directly in the hotel or by a hired laundry service.

8. The electric room key and closed-circuit television cameras are basic measures provided to protect the guests and their property.

Key Words and Concepts

Accounting director	Employee Right to Know	Human resources director	Rev par
Average daily rate (ADR)	Engineering director	Inventory control	Room occupancy
Catastrophe plans	Executive committee	Management structure	percentage
CBX or PBX	Food and beverage director	Marketing and sales	Room rates
Central reservations system	Front office manager	director	Rooms division manager
City ledger	Guaranteed reservations	Night auditor	Security/loss prevention
Concierge	Guest service department	Productivity	Yield management
Confirmed reservations	(uniformed services)	Property management	
Daily report	Hotel general manager	Systems	
Desk clerk	Housekeeping	Reservations department	

Review Questions

1. Briefly define the purpose of a hotel. Why is it important to empathize with the culture of guests?
2. List the main responsibilities of the front office manager.
3. Explain the terms *sell out, American plan,* and *rack rate.*
4. What are the advantages and disadvantages of yield management?
5. Why is the concierge an essential part of the personality of a hotel?
6. Explain the importance of accident and loss prevention. What security measures are taken in order to protect guests and their property?

Internet Exercises

1. Organization:
   Web site:
   Summary:
   (a) What is Hyatt's management training program?
   (b) What requisites must applicants meet in order to qualify for Hyatt's management training program?

Hyatt Hotel Corporation
http://www.hyatt.com
Hyatt Hotel Corporation is a multi-billion-dollar hotel management and development company. Together with Hyatt International, the company has close to 10 percent of the hotel industry market share. Hyatt is recognized for its decentralized management approach, in which general managers are given a great deal of the management decision-making process.

Click on the "Careers" icon and take a look at the Management Training Program that Hyatt has to offer.

2. Organization:
   Web site:
   Summary:
   (a) What different jobs are being offered under
       Job Search" and which one, if any, interests you?
   (b) Post your resume on-line.

Hotel Jobs
http://www.hoteljobs.com
Hoteljobs.com is a web site that offers information to recruiters, employers, and jobseekers in the hospitality industry.

Apply Your Knowledge

1. If you were on the executive committee of a hotel, what kinds of things would you be doing to ensure the success of the hotel?

2. Your hotel has 275 rooms. Last night 198 were occupied. What was the occupancy percentage?

Hotel Operations: Food and Beverage Division

5

After reading and studying this chapter, you should be able to:

✔ Describe the duties and responsibilities of a food and beverage director and other key department heads.

✔ Describe a typical food and beverage director's day.

✔ State the functions and responsibilities of the food and beverage departments.

✔ Perform computations using key food and beverage operating ratios.

Food and Beverage Management

In the hospitality industry, the food and beverage division is led by the **director of food and beverage.** She or he reports to the general manager and is responsible for the efficient and effective operation of the following departments:

✔ Kitchen/Catering/Banquet
✔ Restaurants/Room Service/Minibars
✔ Lounges/Bars/Stewarding

Figure 5–1 illustrates a food and beverage organization chart.

The position description for a director of food and beverage is both a job description and a specification of the requirements an individual needs to do the job. Figure 5–2 shows the duties and the average amount of time spent on each one.

In recent years, the skills needed by a food and beverage director have grown enormously, as shown by the following list of responsibilities:

✔ Exceeding guests' expectations in food and beverage offerings and service
✔ Leadership
✔ Identifying trends
✔ Finding and keeping outstanding employees
✔ Training
✔ Motivation
✔ Budgeting

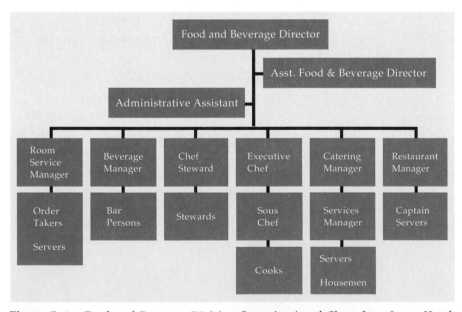

Figure 5–1 *Food and Beverage Division Organizational Chart for a Large Hotel*

POSITION TITLE: *Director of Food and Beverage: Food and Beverage*

REPORTS TO: *General Manager*

PURPOSE

Directs and organizes the activities of the food and beverage department to maintain high standards of food and beverage quality, service, and merchandising to maximize profits

EXAMPLES OF DUTIES

Average %
of time

10% Plan and direct planning and administration of the food and beverage department to meet the daily needs of the operation

10% Clearly describe, assign, and delegate responsibility and authority for the operation of the various food and beverage subdepartments, for example, room service, restaurants, banquets, kitchens, steward, and so on

10% Develop, implement, and monitor schedules for the operation of all restaurants and bars to achieve a profitable result

10% Participate with the chef and restaurant managers in the creation of attractive menus designed to attract a predetermined customer market

10% Implement effective control of food, beverage, and labor costs among all subdepartments

10% Assist area managers in establishing and achieving predetermined profit objectives and desired standards of quality for food, service, cleanliness, merchandising, and promotion

10% Regularly review and evaluate the degree of customer acceptance of the restaurant and banquet service to recommend to management new operating and marketing policies whenever declining or constant sales imply (1) dissatisfaction by the customers, (2) material change in the make-up of the customer market, or (3) change in the competitive environment

10% Develop (with the aid of subdepartment heads) the operating tools necessary and incidental to modern management principles, for example, budgeting, forecasting, purchase specifications, recipes, portion specifications, menu abstracts, food production control, job descriptions, and so on

10% Continually evaluate the performance and encourage improvement of personnel in the food and beverage department. Planning and administering a training and development program within the department will provide well-trained employees at all levels and permit advancement for those persons qualified and interested in that career development.

Other

Regular attendance in conformance with standards established by management. Employees with irregular attendance will be subject to disciplinary action, up to and including termination of employment.

Due to the cyclical nature of the hospitality industry, employees may be required to work varying schedules to accommodate business needs.

On employment, all employees are required to fully comply with rules and regulations for the safe and efficient operation of facilities. Employees who violate rules and regulations will be subject to disciplinary action, up to and including termination of employment.

Supportive Functions

In addition to performance of the essential functions, employee may be required to perform a combination of the following supportive functions, with the percentage of time performance of each function to be determined solely by the supervisor:

Participate in manager-on-duty coverage program, requiring weekend stayover, constant monitoring, and trouble-shooting problems

Operate word processing program in computer

Perform any general cleaning tasks using standard cleaning products to adhere to health standards

SPECIFIC JOB KNOWLEDGE, SKILLS, AND ABILITIES

The employee must possess the following knowledge, skills, and abilities and be able to explain and demonstrate that he or she can perform the essential functions of the job, with or without reasonable accommodation, using some other combination of skills and abilities:

Considerable skill in complex mathematical calculations without error

Ability to effectively deal with internal and external customers, some of whom will require high levels of patience, information, and the ability to resolve conflicts

Ability to move throughout all food and beverage areas and hospitality suites and continually perform essential job functions

Ability to read, listen, and communicate effectively in English, both verbally and in writing

Ability to access and accurately input information using a moderately complex computer system

Hearing, smelling, tasting, and visual ability to observe and distinguish product quality and detect signs of emergency situations

QUALIFICATION STANDARDS

Education: College degree in related field required. Culinary skills and service background required

Experience: Extensive experience in restaurant, bar, banquet, stewarding, kitchen, sales, catering, and management required

License or certification: No special licenses required

Grooming: All employees must maintain a neat, clean, and well-groomed appearance (specific standards available)

Other: Additional language ability preferred

Courtesy Hilton Hotels.

Figure 5–2 *Job Description of Food and Beverage Director*

✔ Cost control

✔ Finding profit from all outlets

✔ Having a detailed working knowledge of the front-of-the-house operations

These challenges are set against a background of stagnant or declining occupancies and the consequent drop in room sales. Therefore, greater emphasis has been placed on making food and beverage sales profitable. Traditionally, only about 20 percent of the hotel's operating profit comes from the food and beverage divisions. In contrast, an acceptable profit margin from a hotel's food and beverage division is generally considered to be 25 to 30 percent. This figure can vary according to the type of hotel. For example, according to Pannell Kerr Forster, an industry consulting firm, all-suite properties achieve a 7 percent food and beverage profit (probably because of the complimentary meals and drinks being offered to guests).

A typical food and beverage director's day might include the following:

8:30 A.M. Check messages and read logs from outlets and security. Tour outlets, especially the family restaurant (a quick inspection).

Check breakfast buffet, reservations, and shift manager.

Check daily specials.

Check room service.

Check breakfast service and staffing.

Visit executive chef and purchasing director.

Visit executive steward's office to ensure that all equipment is ready.

Visit banquet service office to check on daily events and coffee break sequence.

10:00 A.M. Work on current projects: new summer menu, pool outlet opening, conversion of a current restaurant with a new concept, remodeling of ballroom foyer, installation of new walk-in freezer, analysis of current profit-and-loss (P&L) statements. Plan weekly food and beverage department meetings.

11:45 A.M. Visit kitchen to observe lunch service and check the "12:00 line," including banquets.

Confer with executive chef.

Check restaurants and banquet luncheon service.

Have working lunch in employee cafeteria with executive chef, director of purchasing, or director of catering.

1:30 P.M. Visit human resources to discuss current incidents.

2:30 P.M. Check messages and return calls. Telemarket to attract catering and convention business.

Conduct hotel daily menu meeting.

3:00 P.M. Go to special projects/meetings.

Tour cocktail lounges.

Check for staffing.

Review any current promotions.

Check entertainment lineup.

Food and Beverage Director and Executive Chef Discuss Operations (Courtesy John R. Walker.)

6:00 P.M. Check special food and beverage requests/requirements of any VIPs staying at the hotel.

Tour kitchen.

Review and taste.

8:00 P.M. Review dinner specials.

Check the restaurant and lounges.

A food and beverage director's typical day starts at 8:00 A.M. and ends at 8:00 P.M., unless early or very late events are scheduled, in which case the working day is even longer. Usually, the food and beverage director works Monday through Saturday. If there are special events on Sunday, then she or he works on Sunday and takes Monday off. In a typical week, Saturdays are used to catch up on reading or specific projects.

The director of food and beverage eats in his or her restaurants at least twice a week for dinner and at least once a week for breakfast and lunch. Bars are generally visited with clients, at least twice per week. The director sees salespersons regularly, because they are good sources of information about what is going on in the industry and they can introduce leads for business. The director attends staff meetings, food and beverage meetings, executive committee meetings, interdepartmental meetings, credit meetings, and P&L statement meetings.

Food and Beverage Planning

Typically, the monthly forecast for a food and beverage department is prepared between the twelfth and the fifteenth of every month; a budget and forecast for the upcoming years is prepared between July and September. Every January, a planning meeting takes place with all the food and beverage department heads, and the year's special events are planned. These events include Easter, Mother's

Director of Food and Beverage Go-getters may rise to this position more quickly. It depends on the individual's capability, industry expansion, opportunities, and the labor market.	9 to 15 years
Assistant Food and Beverage Manager	3 to 5 years
Department Manager Kitchen Restaurant, room service, stewarding, or cost control	3 to 5 years
Department Experience Kitchens, restaurants, lounges, purchasing, cost control, stewarding, room service, and catering	3 to 5 years

Figure 5–3 *Career Ladder to Director of Food and Beverage*

Day, St. Valentine's Day, St. Patrick's Day, the summer program, Halloween, Thanksgiving, Christmas, New Year's Eve, New Year's Day, and so on.[1]

Food and beverage planning tasks typically include the following:

- ✔ Staffing of the department
- ✔ Controlling costs
- ✔ Liaisons with the executive chef about menus, food quality, and quantity
- ✔ Guest feedback analysis
- ✔ Regular competition analysis
- ✔ Liaisons with the purchase manager for inventory control

In addition, the food and beverage department should be sensitive to environmental issues and must work in line with the hotel's broader goals concerning the environment. Solid waste disposal plans should be well thought-out because the costs of conventional waste disposal are rising. Food and beverage department personnel should also recognize issues and trends facing the food service industry today. They must recognize consumer concerns about health and nutrition and include these concerns as part of the challenge of planning their operation.

To become a food and beverage director takes several years of experience and dedication. One of the best routes is to gain work experience or participate in an internship in several food and beverage departments while attending college. This experience should include full-time, practical kitchen work for at least one to two years followed by varying periods of a few months in purchasing, stores, cost control, stewarding,[2] and room service. Additionally, a year spent in each of the following work situations is helpful: restaurants, catering, and bars. After these departmental experiences, a person would likely serve as a department manager, preferably in a different hotel from the one in which the departmental experience was gained. This prevents the awkwardness of being manager of a department in which the person was once an employee and also offers the employee the opportunity to learn different things at different properties. Figure 5–3 shows a career ladder for a food and beverage director.

[1]Personal conversation with Evan Julian, director of food and beverage, San Diego Hilton, May 1993.

[2]Stewarding is responsible for back-of-the-house areas such as dishwashing, issuing and inventory of china, glassware, and cutlery. Stewarding duties include maintaining cleanliness in all areas.

Personal Profile: George Goldhoff

Director of Food and Beverage, Bellagio, Las Vegas, Nevada

Being hired as the pot washer for the Old Homestead Country Kitchen at the early age of fifteen hardly seemed to herald the beginnings of an auspicious career in the hospitality industry. But to George Goldhoff, with his high energy and natural leadership skills, he had found the perfect environment in which to excel. The sense of family and camaraderie between the staff members and the interaction with guests, mixed with the intensity of performance and deadlines, have never lost their appeal. Excellence in service would become his lifelong pursuit.

Fast forward twenty years later; as director of food and beverage at Bellagio of MGM/Mirage, Inc., in Las Vegas, George is responsible for the quality assurance, personnel development, and financial performance of seventeen restaurants and ten bars, comprised of 3,000 employees and over $200 million in revenues. His responsibilities may have increased since his pot washer days, but the core message in his service training remains intact: sincerity toward the guest and anticipation of their needs. His approach to service is simple: Greet all guests with a smile, make sure they are comfortable, offer them something to eat and drink. These service basics, simple instructions given to him as a five-year-old by his parents, have stayed with him. Playing host at one of his parents' dinner parties he learned early on the power of a sincere smile and the rewarding experience of pleasing others. Little did he or his parents intuit that one day his child's play would evolve into a rewarding career in hospitality.

As one of the original members of the opening team for the Bellagio, George drew from his extensive and varied food and beverage background to make the Bellagio's opening a success. In 1983 George graduated from Schenectady County Community College as a dean's list student and recipient of an athletic scholarship award. He continued on to the University of Massachusetts where he earned his B.S. degree in hotel, restaurant and travel administration. His acceptance to these two institutions, after having dropped out of high school, instilled in George the self-confidence in his abilities and the technical skills necessary to achieve his goals. For a young man without a high school diploma who was often characterized as wild and rebellious, it was a revelation, an awakening to his potentials and the realization that he could accomplish great things. His introduction to corporate culture was as an assistant front office manager and Hyatt corporate trainee in Savannah, Georgia.

Upon completion of his training, he moved to beautiful Tahoe in 1988, where he was able to combine his love for restaurants and sports. An all-around athlete, adhering to the work hard, play hard principle, he pursued speed skiing competitions at the highest levels. He stayed on as general manager of Rosie's Café for two and a half years. However, growing tired of the small town confines of Tahoe City and with the singular challenges of Rosie's Café becoming undemanding, George acted on a friend's advice, contacted a mutual friend, and took a job on a 750-foot merchant ship. For the next six months George sailed around the world cooking breakfast, lunch, and dinner for a crew of twelve, while visiting ports in Gibraltar, Malta, Egypt, the United Arab Emirates, Kuwait, and Saudi Arabia. In 1990, aspiring to be a major player not just in skiing, but in the restaurant arena as well, he sought grander, more sophisticated restaurants to manage.

(Courtesy George Goldhoff.)

George's ambitions led him to the Plaza Hotel in New York, where he started as an assistant beverage director. George immersed himself in his new position with his usual high-voltage energy and infectious enthusiasm, earning him nicknames such as the Golden Boy and Mr. Hollywood. It did not take long for George to be recognized for his positive attitude and management abilities. Within six months, he was promoted to manager of the stately Oak Room, the youngest manager in the restaurant's ninety-year history. In 1991, within a two-year period, he was promoted to managing four of the Plaza Hotel's five à la carte restaurants.

Holding to his personal belief that "You are the company you keep," he has always endeavored to associate with the highest quality restaurateurs and organizations. In 1993, he realized one of his dreams—the opportunity to work with the legendary Joe Baum—managing the famous Rainbow Room in Rockefeller Center. His commitment to service, the evident pride in his work, and his high standard of ethics earned George praise from Joe Baum as being his best maître d' ever. Such a high

continued

compliment could have gone to his head. However, George is not one to sit back and take it easy. Instead, he set even higher standards and focused his energies on new goals. He quotes his old boss and industry idol Joe Baum as saying "Values and standards are those you make for yourself. You don't have to be as good as the other guy. You have to be better—a lot better."

Against the advice of well-meaning family and peers, he left the Rainbow Room in 1997 to enroll in the MBA program at Columbia University. This was no easy decision, considering George was happily married at this point, with one child and another on the way. However, he has never been afraid to take risks, nor been one to fear taking on new challenges. In fact, his adventurous and go-getter nature revels in change. With the same self-confidence, resourcefulness, and ability to focus on multiple tasks, not surprisingly, he took first place in Columbia's Business Plan competition and was the recipient of the prestigious Eugene Lang Entrepreneurial Initiative Fund. Armed with his MBA degree and newly acquired business skills, he was ready for his next adventure.

Even before he had graduated, he was tapped by Stephen Rushmore, founder and president of Hospitality Valuation Services, to work with him as a consultant and valuation analyst. Here he was afforded the opportunity to incorporate his academic learning, fresh ideas, and extensive hotel background. He created the 1996 Hotel Valuation Index, which was later published in the *Cornell Quarterly*. Ever the entrepreneur, he left HVS in 1997 to establish his own venture, The Irish Coast, Inc., creating and implementing the Guinness Irish pub concept. He jumped into the task of perfecting the Irish pub ambience of warmth, comfort, and congeniality, the heart of hospitality. Hence, it was only a matter of time before he would find himself in Las Vegas, the "Hospitality Capital of the World." In 1998 he signed aboard with Mirage Resorts, Inc., to open the ultimate luxury resort and casino, Bellagio.

For George, it's all about service. Excellence in customer satisfaction and a genuine concern for his staff and coworkers have been his guiding principles.

Characterized by colleagues as a dreamer, he has the rare ability to communicate his vision and to motivate and inspire others into executing that vision, making it a reality. The ability to instill in those around him the desire to strive beyond and stretch past their comfort zones is just one of his leadership characteristics. His motivational secret is to "constantly remind the staff that their job is precious, even if they've been doing it year after year." He maintains that the key to service is to "know one's job and to remember that a little kindness goes a long way to making people happy. A guest always knows if someone doesn't care."

In addition to starting up and overseeing the entire food and beverage operations for the hotel, he was chosen to represent Mirage Resorts in Focus Las Vegas, a leadership development program of the Las Vegas Chamber of Commerce. Making a difference in others' lives has always been one of the appealing factors about being in the hospitality field. He has always felt personally rewarded when he can give back to others, such as promoting a new busperson, building up someone else's self-esteem, watching them gain confidence in themselves and take pride in their work. He concedes he did not reach his position on his own, but with the assistance of many caring mentors. Always mindful and appreciative of those who have helped him throughout his career, he enjoys helping others discover their own potential. He considers human relations to be one of his strengths and regards staff development to be one of his greatest priorities as a leader. Empowering your frontline employees is essential to maintaining a restaurant's competitive edge. "Give them the tools and let them do the job."

George sets great expectations for himself and those around him and is not afraid of hard work. In fact, he works with a passion. The long hours and the intensity do not faze him. His adaptability toward different situations, his ability to relate to a variety of personalities and temperaments, and his keen sense of humor serve him well both in front and back of the house. With his winning smile and straightforward demeanor, he sets his sights on a promising future and the many adventures ahead.

Kitchen

A hotel kitchen is under the charge of the **executive chef;** this person, in turn, is responsible to the director of food and beverage for the efficient and effective operation of kitchen food production. The desired outcome is to exceed guests' expectations in the quality and quantity of food, its presentation, taste, and portion size, and to ensure that hot food is served hot and cold food is served cold. The executive chef operates the kitchen in accordance with company policy and strives to achieve desired financial results.

Some executive chefs are becoming **kitchen managers;** they even serve as food and beverage directors in midsized and smaller hotels. This trend toward "right-sizing," observed in other industries, euphemistically refers to restructuring organizations to retain the most essential employees. Usually, this means cutting labor costs by consolidating job functions. For example, Michael Hammer is executive chef and food and beverage director at the 440-room Hilton La Jolla–Torrey Pines, California. Mike is typical of the new breed of executive chefs: His philosophy is to train his sous chefs—*sous* being a French word meaning "under"—to make many of the operating decisions. He delegates ordering, hiring, and firing decisions; sous chefs are the ones most in control of the group's production and the people who work on their teams. By delegating more of the operating decisions, he is developing the chefs de partie (or stations chefs) and empowering them to make their own decisions. As he puts it, "No decision is wrong—but in case it is unwise, we may talk about it later."

Mike spends time maintaining morale, a vital part of a manager's position. The kitchen staff is under a great deal of pressure and frequently works against the clock. Careful cooperation and coordination is the key to success. He explains that he does not want his associates to "play the tuba"—he wants them to conduct the orchestra. He does not hold food and beverage department meetings; instead he meets with groups of employees frequently and problems are handled as they occur. Controls are maintained with the help of software that costs their standard recipes, establishes **perpetual inventories,**[3] and calculates potential food cost per outlet. Today, executive chefs and food and beverage directors look past food cost to the actual profit contribution of an item. For example, if a pasta dish costs $3.25 and sells for $12.95, the contribution margin is $9.70.

Controlling costs is an essential part of food and beverage operations and because labor costs represent the most significant variable costs, staffing becomes an important factor in the day-to-day running of the food and beverage locations. Labor cost benchmarks are measured by covers-per-person-hour. For example, in stewarding, it should take no more than one person per hour to clean 37.1 covers. Mike and his team of outlet managers face interesting challenges, such as staffing for the peaks and valleys of guest needs at breakfast. Many guests want breakfast during the peak time of 7:00 to 8:30 A.M., requiring organization to get the right people in the right place at the right time to ensure that meals are prepared properly and served in a timely manner.

---

[3]A perpetual inventory establishes a minimum inventory level at which time an order is automatically placed, avoiding shortages.

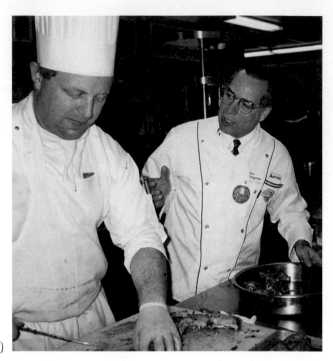

Executive Chef
(Courtesy John R. Walker.)

At the Hilton, La Jolla–Torrey Pines, Executive Chef Hammer's day goes something like the following:

1. Arrive at 6:00 to 7:00 A.M. and walk through the food and beverage department with the night cleaners.
2. Check to make sure the compactor is working and the area is clean.
3. Check that all employees are on duty.
4. Ask people what kind of challenges they will face today.
5. Sample as many dishes as possible, checking for taste, consistency, feel, smell, and overall quality.
6. Check walk-ins.
7. Recheck once or twice a day to see where department stands production-wise—this eliminates overtime.
8. Approve schedules for food and beverage outlet.
9. Keep a daily update of food and beverage revenues and costs.
10. Forecast the next day's, week's, and month's business based on updated information.
11. Check on final numbers for catering functions.

Financial results are generally expressed in ratios, such as **food cost percentage**—the cost of food divided by the amount of food sales. In its simplest form, an example would be the sale of a hamburger for $1.00. If the cost of the food was $0.30 then the food cost percentage would be 30 percent, which is about average for many hotels. The average might be reduced to 27 percent in hotels that do a lot of catering. As discussed later in this section, in

Breakfast Service

Marriott Properties Utilize Standard Operating Procedures SOP to Ensure They Consistently Meet Customer Expectations (Courtesy Marriott International.)

determining the food and beverage department's profit and loss, executive chefs and food and beverage directors must consider not only the food cost percentage but also the **contribution margin** of menu items. Another important cost ratio for the kitchen is labor cost. The **labor cost percentage** may vary depending on the amount of convenience foods purchased versus those made from scratch (raw ingredients). In a kitchen, this may be expressed as a **percentage of food sales**. For example, if food sales total $1,000 and labor costs total $250, then labor costs may be expressed as a percentage of food sales by the following formula:

$$\frac{\text{Labor cost}}{\text{Food sales}} \quad \text{therefore} \quad \frac{\$250}{\$1,000} = 25\% \text{ labor cost}$$

An executive chef has one or more **sous chefs.** Because so much of the executive chef's time is spent on administration, sous chefs are often responsible for the day-to-day running of each shift. Depending on size, a kitchen may have several sous chefs: one or more for days, one for evenings, and another for banquets.

Under the sous chefs is the **chef tournant.** This person rotates through the various stations to relieve the station chef heads, also known as **chefs de partie**. These stations are organized according to production tasks, based on the classic "brigade" introduced by Escoffier. The **brigade** includes the following:

> Sauce chef, who prepares sauces, stews, sautes, hot hors d'oeuvres
> Roast chef, who roasts, broils, grills, and braises meats

English	French	Pronunciation
Sauce chef	Saucier	sau*see*ay
Fish chef	Poissonier	pwa*so*ay
Roast chef	Rotisseur	ro*tee*sur
Relief chef	Tournant	tour*nant
Vegetable chef	Entremetier	aun*tre*me*tee*ay
Pastry chef	Patissier	pa*tis*see*ay
Pantry chef	Garde manger	gard*mon*zhay

Figure 5–4 *Chefs de Partie*

Corporate Profile: Four Seasons Regent Hotels

In 1960, Isadore Sharp opened the first Four Seasons Hotel on Jarvis Street in downtown Toronto, Canada. Today, Four Seasons Hotels and Resorts is currently the world's largest operator of medium-sized, luxury hotels, managing thirty-nine hotels in sixteen countries, under the brand names Four Seasons and Regent. Some properties, however, do not carry the brand names, such as the Ritz-Carlton in Chicago and the Pierre in New York.

By retaining absolute control of the company throughout its history, Isadore Sharp has been able to create and maintain a well-defined culture of consistently providing quality and refinement. "Sharp is a perfectionist, and the reputation of the company has grown out of his personality."[1] Sharp has established a "zero defects" culture, in which class is obtained with simplicity, and excellence is clearly distinguished from extravagance. Taste, elegance, and style are defining features of all Four Seasons properties. Their standards of impeccable service are deeply rooted and upheld by all employees and are tailored to appeal to the luxury segment of the business and leisure travel markets.

Isadore Sharp's understanding of what modern travelers want from a hotel has positioned Four Seasons as the first choice of many business travelers. They can expect their check-in to be fast and efficient, the rooms to be luxurious, the laundry to be back on time, and the food to be very good. Genuinely caring about the needs of the guests has led to the introduction of many innovative services that have made Four Seasons a benchmark for quality and service. For example, the company was the first to introduce in-room amenities and company-wide concierge services.

Quality in every aspect of the business translates into excellent food and beverage. Each of the restaurants in

all of the Four Seasons properties was designed to lead the local fine-dining market and to demolish the stereotype of the mediocre, overpriced hotel restaurant.[2] Sharp recalls that when his first hotels were opened, the industry generally considered hotel restaurants a guaranteed loss, thus, the idea was to offer the bare minimum.

However, Sharp was a novice in the hotel industry. "We didn't know the rules. Nobody told us that you couldn't make money in a hotel restaurant, so we went out and did it."[3] Four Seasons successfully challenged the hotel food stigma. Its restaurants serve imaginative and attractive dishes that suit the tastes of both the local guests and the international clientele.

Once again, meeting the guests' needs was accomplished in 1984 with the introduction of alternative cuisine—stylish and flavorful items prepared with an eye on proper nutrition—designed for the frequent business traveler who spends many nights in hotel rooms and would appreciate lighter menu options.

Alternative cuisine was conceived by diet and nutrition expert Jeanne Jones, one of the country's leading authors and consultants on the gourmet approach to good nutrition, who then passed the concept on to Four Seasons chefs. Alternative cuisine is a method of preparation that creates nutritionally balanced dishes with reduced levels of cholesterol and sodium, without sacrificing quality, originality, taste, or presentation. The principles of alternative cuisine are achieved by:

✔ *reducing fats,* using low-fat content ingredients and avoiding high-fat dairy products, oils, mayonnaise, and so on

✔ *reducing sodium* by reducing salt, high-sodium foods such as olives, pickles, and Parma ham, and by avoiding any unnatural flavoring

✔ *reducing cholesterol* by carefully limiting animal meats, avoiding organ meats, skin of poultry, egg yolks, and so on

Instead, Four Seasons chefs emphasize the use of foods containing animal protein (fish, poultry, and selected meats such as veal, flank steaks, game), complex carbohydrates (vegetables, salads, starch), simple carbohydrates (fruits), and fiber (whole grain breads, rice, pasta, cereal). The lower levels of salt used in alternative cuisine are compensated for by using herbs and reduction to give dishes full aroma and taste. The protein-rich items (meats, fish) are often in smaller quantities to reduce the calorie count and are offered with plenty of vegetables.[4] The results are pleasing to the health-conscious traveler. A typical two-course alternative cuisine lunch can have as few as 500 calories. A three-course dinner can count as little as 650.

Another culinary innovation at Four Seasons-Regent properties is the Home Cooking Program introduced in 1996. The company's chefs recognized that business travelers, who are often forced to eat in restaurants while on the road, are almost exclusively exposed to gourmet menu items and would appreciate the chance to choose simpler, "home cooking" dishes. Some of the menu offerings introduced include chicken noodle soup, chicken pot pie, bread pudding, meatloaf and mashed potatoes, and deep-dish apple pie. The program has been very successful so far. At the Four Seasons Hotel Toronto, for example, 60 percent of all room service orders include selections from their "Home Style Classics" menu. The recipes are very often the chefs' own—passed down to them by their grandmothers. At the Four Seasons Hotel Seattle, Executive Chef Sear has introduced recipes that were taught to him by his 101-year-old grandmother, including herb potatoes, pot roast, and steamed batter puddings. Some of Grandmother Sear's recipes date back to World War II, and her cookbook is one of Chef Sear's most prized possessions, to which he often refers.

Tony Ruppe, executive chef at the Four Seasons Hotel Houston, talks about the fundamentals of cooking as he learned them in his grandparents' kitchen in Oklahoma, recalling "the flavor of things, the freshness of vegetables and fruits. Real simple cooking with lots of tender loving care."[5]

These food and beverage innovations have contributed to Four Seasons-Regent Hotel restaurants ranking among the top restaurants in their respective cities. They reflect the company's single-minded commitment to quality and guest satisfaction in all aspects of the hotel experience.

Four Seasons Corporate Profile

The Four Seasons has recently won these awards:

1. In 2000, *Fortune* magazine ranked the Four Seasons "one of the best companies to work for in America." They came in forty-eighth.
2. In 2000, Four Seasons was awarded top honors in the AAA Diamond Awards.
3. Five different Four Seasons Hotels out of twenty-five hotels received the Mobile Five-Star Award for 2000.
4. *Gourmet* magazine's third annual readers survey of "America's Top Tables" had a total of nine Four Season's restaurants rated in the top twenty listings of their respective cities.

These are just some of the innovations that Four Seasons has put in place:

1. Standard housekeeping services are performed twice a day at all Four Seasons properties.
2. Room service is available twenty-four hours a day.
3. Bathrooms have phones.
4. They were the first hotels in North America to provide complementary newspapers.
5. Private concierge services are available regardless of whether one is a guest of the property or not.

---

[1] Corby Kummer, "A Man for Four Seasons," *Connoisseur*, February 1990.
[2] James Scarpa, "Rich Harvest," *Restaurant Business*, September 1, 1989.
[3] Ibid.
[4] This section adapted from Four Seasons-Regent Hotels and Resorts News, "Alternative Cuisine."
[5] This section adapted from Four Seasons-Regent Hotel and Resorts News, "Four Seasons Regent Offers Guests a Taste of Home with Its New Home Cooking Program," December 1996.

Personal Profile: Jim Gemignani, Executive Chef

Jim Gemignani is executive chef at the 1,500-room Marriott Hotel in San Francisco. Chef Jim, as his associates call him, is responsible for the quality of food, guest, and associate satisfaction and for financial satisfaction in terms of results. With more than 200 associates in eight departments, Chef Jim has an interesting challenge. He makes time to be innovative by researching food trends and comparative shopping. Currently, American cuisine is in, as are free-standing restaurants in hotels. An ongoing part of American cuisine is the healthy food that Chef Jim says has not yet found a niche.

(Courtesy John R. Walker.)

Hotels are building identity into their restaurants by branding or creating their own brand name. Marriott, for example, has Pizza Hut pizzas on the room service menu. Marriott hotels have created their own tiers of restaurants. JW's is the formal restaurant, Tuscany's is a Northern Italian-themed restaurant, the American Grill has replaced the old coffee shop, and Kimoko is a Japanese restaurant. As a company, Marriott decided to go nation-wide with the first three of these concepts. This has simplified menus and improved food quality and presentation, and yet regional specials allow for individual creativity on the part of the chef.

When asked about his personal philosophy, Chef Jim says that in this day and age, one needs to embrace change and build teams; the guest is an important part of the team. Chef Jim's biggest challenge is keeping guests and associates happy. He is also director of food service outlets, which now gives him a front-of-the-house perspective. Among his greatest accomplishments are seeing his associates develop—twenty are now executive chefs—retaining 96 percent of his opening team, and being voted Chef of the Year by the San Francisco Chef's Association.

Chef Jim's advice: "It's tough not to have a formal education, but remember that you need a combination of 'hands on' and formal training. If you're going to be a leader, you must start at the bottom and work your way up; otherwise, you will become a superior and not know how to relate to your associates."

Medieval Dinner Rules

Medieval hosts, who naturally knew nothing of germs and sanitation, forks or fingerbowls, set forth their own rules for public suppers, few of which would seem out of place today.

1. Meals should be served in due time: not too early, not too late.
2. Meals should be served in a conveyable place: large, pleasant, and secure.
3. He who maketh the feast should be of the heart and glad cheer.
4. Meals should consist of many diverse messes so that who like not of one may taste another.
5. There should be diverse wines and drinks.

Fish chef, who cooks fish dishes

Soup chef, who prepares all soups

Cold larder/pantry chef, who prepares all cold foods: salads, cold hors d'oeuvres, buffet food, and dressings

Banquet chef, who is responsible for all banquet food

Pastry chef, who prepares all hot and cold dessert items

Vegetable chef, who prepares vegetables (this person may be the fry cook and soup cook in some smaller kitchens)

(Soup, cold larder, banquets, pastry, and vegetable chefs' positions may be combined in smaller kitchens.)

Hotel Restaurants

A hotel may have several restaurants or no restaurant at all; the number and type of restaurants varies as well. A major chain hotel generally has two restaurants: a signature or upscale formal restaurant and a casual coffee-shop type of restaurant. These restaurants cater to both hotel guests and to the general public. In recent years, because of increased guest expectations, hotels have placed greater emphasis on food and beverage preparation and service. As a result, there is an increasing need for professionalism on the part of hotel personnel.

Hotel restaurants are run by restaurant managers in much the same way as other restaurants. **Restaurant managers** are generally responsible for the following:

✔ Exceeding guest service expectations
✔ Hiring, training, and developing employees
✔ Setting and maintaining quality standards
✔ Marketing
✔ Room service, minibars, or the cocktail lounge
✔ Presenting annual, monthly, and weekly forecasts and budgets to the food and beverage director

Some restaurant managers work on an incentive plan with quarterly performance bonuses. Hotel restaurants present the manager with some interesting challenges because hotel guests are not always predictable. Sometimes they will use the hotel restaurants, and other times they will dine out. If they dine in or out to an extent beyond the forecasted number of guests, problems can arise. Too many guests for the restaurants results in delays and poor service.

Hotel Restaurant Lunch Restaurant Veranda, Four Seasons, Milano

Hotel Restaurant Dinner Gardens Restaurant, Four Seasons Los Angeles at Beverly Hills

Too few guests means that employees are underutilized, which can increase labor costs unless employees are sent home early. Fortunately, over time, a restaurant manager keeps a diary of the number of guests served by the restaurant on the same night the previous week, month, and year.

The number (house count) and type of hotel guest (e.g., the number of conference attendees who may have separate dining arrangements) should also be considered in estimating the number of expected restaurant guests for any meal. This figure is known as the **capture rate,** which when coupled with historic and banquet activity and hotel occupancy, will be the restaurant's basis for forecasting the number of expected guests.

Most hotels find it difficult to coax hotel guests into the restaurants. However, many continuously try to convert food service from a necessary amenity to a profit center. The Royal Sonesta in New Orleans offers restaurant coupons worth $5 to its guests and guests of nearby hotels. Another successful strategy, adopted by the Plaza Athenee in New York, is to show guests the restaurants and explain the cuisine before they go to their rooms. This has prompted most guests to dine in the restaurant during their stay. At the Sheraton Boston Hotel and Towers, the restaurants self-promote by having cooking demonstrations in the lobby: The "onsite" chefs offer free samples to hotel guests.[4]

Progressive hotels, such as the Kimco Hotel, in San Francisco, ensure that the hotel restaurants look like free-standing restaurants with separate entrances. They also charge the restaurants rent and make them responsible for their own profit and loss statements.[5]

Compared with other restaurants, some hotel restaurants offer greater degrees of service sophistication. This necessitates additional food preparation and service skills and training. Compared to free-standing/independent restaurants, it is more difficult for hotel restaurants to operate at a profit. They usually are open from early morning until late at night and are frequently under-patronized by hotel guests who tend to prefer to eat outside of the hotel at independent restaurants.

Bars

Hotel bars allow guests to relax while sipping on a cocktail after a hectic day. This opportunity to socialize for business or pleasure is advantageous for both guests and the hotel. Because the profit percentage on all beverages is higher than on food items, bars are an important revenue source for the food and beverage departments. The cycle of beverages from ordering, receiving, storing,

---

[4]Robert Selwitz, "Keeping Guests as Diners: Hotels Use a Variety of Efforts to Fill In-House Restaurants," *Hotel and Motel Management,* June 10, 1991, pp. 59–60.

[5]John Jesitus, "Hotels Take Various Approaches in Effort to Spice up Food-and-Beverage Profits," *Hotel and Motel Management,* September 7, 1992, pp. 47–48.

issuing, bar stocking, serving, and guest billing is complex, but, unlike restaurant meals, a beverage can be held over if not sold. An example of a world-famous hotel bar is The King Cole Bar in the St. Regis Hotel in New York City. This bar has been a favored New York "watering hole" of the rich and famous for many years. The talking point of the bar is a painted mural of Old King Cole, the nursery rhyme character.

Bars are run by **bar managers.** The responsibilities of a bar manager include:

✔ Supervising the ordering process and storage of wines,
✔ Preparing a wine list
✔ Overseeing the staff
✔ Maintaining cost control
✔ Assisting guests with their wine selection
✔ Proper service of wine
✔ Knowledge of beers and liquors and their service

Bar efficiency is measured by the **pour/cost percentage.** Pour cost is obtained by dividing the cost of depleted inventory by sales over a period of time. The more frequently the pour cost is calculated, the greater the control over the bar.[6]

Food and beverage directors expect a pour cost of between 16 and 24 percent. Generally, operations with lower pour costs have more sophisticated control systems and a higher volume catering operation. An example of this would be an automatic system that dispenses the exact amount of beverage requested via a pouring gun, which is fed by a tube from a beverage store. These systems are expensive, but they save money for volume operations by being less prone to pilferage, overpouring, or other tricks of the trade. Their greatest savings comes in the form of reduced labor costs; fewer bartenders are needed to make the same amount of drinks. However, the barperson may still hand pour premium brands for show.

Hotel bars are susceptible to the same problems as other bars. The director of food and beverage must set strict policy and procedure guidelines and see to it that they are followed. In today's litigious society, the onus is on the operator to install and ensure **responsible alcoholic beverage service.** If a guest becomes intoxicated and is involved in an accident, the server of the beverage, the barperson, and the manager may all be liable.

Another risk bars encounter is **pilferage.** Employees have been known to steal or tamper with liquor; they could, for example, dilute it with water or colored liquids, sell the additional liquor, and pocket the money. There are several other ways to defraud a bar. One of the better known ways is to overcharge guests for beverages. Another is to underpour, which gives guests less for their money. Some bartenders overpour measures in order to receive larger tips. The best way to prevent these occurrences is to have a good control system, which should include **shoppers**—people who are paid to use the bar like regular guests, except they are closely watching the operation.

[6]Robert Plotkin, "Beverages: Stop Pouring Profits Down the Drain," *Restaurant Hospitality,* February 1992, pp. 136–145.

Old King Cole Bar,
The St. Regis Hotel

In a large hotel there are several kinds of bars:

Lobby bar: This convenient meeting place was popularized when Conrad Hilton wanted to generate revenue out of his vast hotel lobby. Lobby bars, when well managed, are a good source of income.

Restaurant bar: Traditionally, this bar is away from the hubbub of the lobby and offers a holding area for the hotel's signature restaurant.

Service bar: In some of the very large hotels, restaurants and room service have a separate backstage bar. Otherwise, both the restaurant and room service are serviced by one of the regular beverage outlets, such as the restaurant bar.

Catering and banquet bar: This bar is used specifically to service all the catering and banquet needs of the hotel. These bars can stretch any operator to the limit. Frequently, several cash bars must be set up at a variety of locations; if cash wines are involved with dinner, it becomes a race to get the wine to the guest before the meal, preferably before the appetizer. Because of the difficulties involved in servicing a large number of guests, most hotels encourage inclusive wine and beverage functions in which the guests pay a little more for tickets that include a predetermined amount of beverage service. Banquet bars require careful inventory control. The bottles should be checked immediately after the function, and, if the bar is very busy, the bar manager should pull the money just before the bar closes. The breakdown of function bars should be done on the spot if possible to help prevent pilferage.

The banquet bar needs to stock not only large quantities of the popular wines, spirits, and beers but also a selection of premium spirits and after-dinner liqueurs. These are used in the ballroom and private dining rooms in particular.

Pool bars: Pool bars are popular at resort hotels where guests can enjoy a variety of exotic cocktails poolside. Resort hotels that cater to conventions often put on theme parties one night of the convention to allow delegates to kick back. Popular themes that are catered around the pool might be a Hawaiian luau, a Caribbean reggae night, Mexican fiesta, or country and western events. Left to the imagination, one could conceive of a number of theme events.

Minibars: Minibars are small, refrigerated bars in guest rooms. They offer the convenience of having beverages available at all times. For security, they have a separate key, which may be either included in the room key envelope at check-in or withheld according to the guest's preference. Minibars are typically checked and replenished on a daily basis. Charges for items used are automatically added to the guest folio.

Night clubs: Some hotels offer guests evening entertainment and dancing. Whether formal or informal, these food and beverage outlets offer a full beverage service. Live entertainment is very expensive. Many hotels are switching to operations with a DJ or where the bar itself is the entertainment (e.g., sports bar). Directors of food and beverage are now negotiating more with live bands, offering them a base pay (below union scale) and a percentage of a cover charge.

Sports bars: Sports bars have become popular in hotels. Almost everyone identifies with a sporting theme, which makes for a relaxed atmosphere that complements contemporary lifestyles. Many sports bars have a variety of games such as pool, football, bar basketball, and so on, which, together with satellite-televised sporting events, contribute to the atmosphere.

Different types of bars produce revenue according to their location in the hotel and the kind of hotel itself. Nightclubs, sports bars, and the banqueting department see bulk consumption of alcoholic beverages; and restaurant bars usually see more alcohol consumption than minibars and lounge bars.

Check Your Knowledge

1. What departments does the food and beverage director oversee?
2. What are the responsibilities of a food and beverage director on a day-to-day basis?
3. Explain how the pour/cost percentage is used in a bar to measure efficiency.

Stewarding Department

The **chief steward** is responsible to the director of food and beverage for the following functions:

- ✔ Cleanliness of the back of the house (all the areas of the backstage that hotel guests do not see)
- ✔ Maintaining clean glassware, china, and cutlery for the food and beverage outlets
- ✔ Maintaining strict inventory control and monthly stock check
- ✔ Maintenance of dishwashing machines
- ✔ Inventory of chemical stock
- ✔ Sanitation of kitchen, banquet isles, storerooms, walk-ins/freezers, and all equipment
- ✔ Pest control and coordination with exterminating company
- ✔ Forecasting labor and cleaning supplies

In some hotels the steward's department is responsible for keeping the kitchen(s) clean. This is generally done at night to prevent disruption of the food production operation. A more limited cleaning is done in the afternoon between the lunch and dinner services. The chief steward's job can be an enormous and thankless task. In hotels this involves cleaning up for several hundred people three times a day. Just trying to keep track of everything can be a headache. Some hotels have different patterns of glasses, china, and cutlery for each outlet. The casual dining room frequently has an informal theme, catering and banqueting a more formal one, and the signature restaurant, very formal place settings. It is difficult to ensure all of the pieces are returned to the correct places. It is also difficult to prevent both guests and employees from taking souvenirs. Strict inventory control and constant vigilance help keep pilferage to a minimum.

A Chief Steward Checking the Silver Inventory (Courtesy John R. Walker.)

Catering Department

Throughout the world's cultural and social evolution, numerous references have been made to the breaking of bread together. Feasts or banquets are one way to show one's hospitality. Frequently, hosts attempted to outdo one another with the extravagance of their feasts. Today, occasions for celebrations, banquets, and catering include the following:

- ✔ State banquets, when countries' leaders honor visiting royalty and heads of state
- ✔ National days
- ✔ Embassy receptions and banquets
- ✔ Business and association conventions and banquets
- ✔ Gala charity balls
- ✔ Company dinner dances
- ✔ Weddings

Catering has a broader scope than banquets. **Banquets** refers to groups of people who eat together at one time and in one place. **Catering** includes a variety of occasions when people may eat at varying times. However, the terms are often used interchangeably.

For example, catering departments in large, city-center hotels may service the following events in just one day:

- ✔ A Fortune 500 company's annual shareholders meeting
- ✔ An international loan-signing ceremony
- ✔ A fashion show
- ✔ A convention
- ✔ Several sales and board meetings
- ✔ Private luncheons and dinner parties
- ✔ A wedding or two

Catering Office and Director
(Courtesy John R. Walker.)

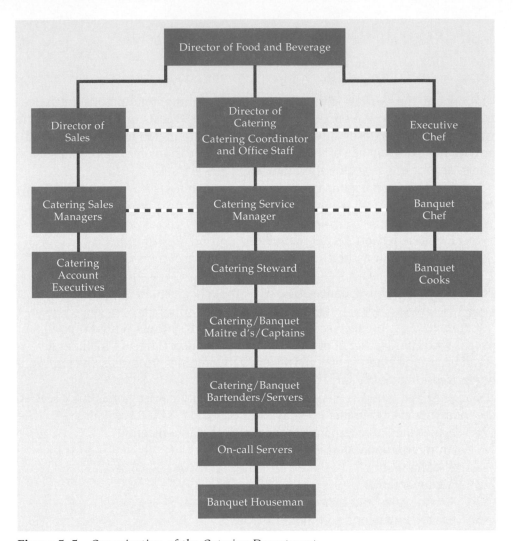

Figure 5–5 *Organization of the Catering Department*

Naturally each of these requires different and special treatment. Hotels in smaller cities may cater the local chamber of commerce meeting, a high school prom, a local company party, a regional sales meeting, a professional workshop, and a small exhibition.

Catering may be subdivided into on-premise and off-premise. In off-premise catering, the event is catered away from the hotel. The food may be prepared either in the hotel or at the event. The organization chart in Figure 5–5 shows how the catering department is organized. The dotted lines show cooperative reporting relationships and continuous lines show a direct reporting relationship. For example, the banquet chef reports directly to the executive chef but must cooperate with the director of catering and the catering service manager.

The **director of catering** is responsible to the food and beverage director for selling and servicing, catering, banquets, meetings, and exhibitions in a way that exceeds guests' expectations and produces reasonable profit. The director of catering has a close working relationship with the rooms division manager because the catering department often brings conventions, which require rooms, to the hotel. There is also a close working relationship with the executive chef. The chef plans the banqueting menus but the catering manager must ensure that they are suitable for the clientele and practical from a service point of view. Sometimes they work together in developing a selection of menus that will meet all the requirements, including cost and price.

The director of catering must be able to do the following:

1. Sell conventions, banquets, and functions.
2. Lead a team of employees.
3. Together with input from team members, make up departmental goals and objectives.
4. Set individual and department sales and cost budgets.
5. Set service standards.
6. Ensure that the catering department is properly maintained.
7. Be extremely creative and knowledgeable about food, wine, and service.
8. Be very well versed in the likes, dislikes, and dietary restrictions of various ethnic groups, especially Jewish, Middle Eastern, and European.

Position Profile

The director of catering is required to have a variety of skills and abilities as shown in the following:

Technical
- ✔ A thorough knowledge of food and beverage management including food preparation and service
- ✔ Ability to sell conventions, functions, and banquets
- ✔ Ability to produce a profit
- ✔ Ability to develop individual and department sales and cost budgets

Leadership
- ✔ Lead a team of employees.
- ✔ Set departmental mission, goals, and objectives.
- ✔ Train the department members in all facets of operations.
- ✔ Set service standards.
- ✔ Ensure that the catering department is properly maintained.

The catering department is extremely complex and demanding; the tempo is fast and the challenge to be innovative is always present. The director of catering in a large city hotel should, over the years, build up a client list and an intimate knowledge of the trade shows, exhibitions, various companies, groups, associations, and SMERF organizations (social, military, education, religious, and fraternal market). This knowledge and these contacts are essential to the director of catering's success, as is the selection of the team members.

The main sales function of the department is conducted by the director of catering (DOC) and catering sales managers (CSMs). Their jobs are to optimize guest satisfaction and revenue by selling the most lucrative functions and exceeding guests' food and beverage and service expectations.

The DOC and catering sales managers obtain business leads from a variety of sources, including the following:

Hotel's director of sales: She or he is a good source of event bookings because she or he is selling rooms, and catering is often required by meetings and conventions.

General managers: These are good sources of leads because they are very involved in the community.

Corporate office sales department: If, for example, a convention were held on the East Coast one year at a Marriott hotel and by tradition the association goes to the West Coast the following year, the Marriott hotel in the chosen city will contact the client or meeting planner. Some organizations have a selection of cities and hotels bid for major conventions. This ensures a competitive rate quote for accommodations and services.

Convention and visitors bureau: Here is another good source of leads because its main purpose is to seek out potential groups and organizations to visit that city. To be fair to all the hotels, they publish a list of clients and brief details of their requirements, which the hotel catering sales department may follow up on.

Reading the event board of competitive hotels: The event board is generally located in the lobby of the hotel and is frequently read by the competition. The CSM then calls the organizer of the event to solicit the business the next time.

Rollovers: Some organizations, especially local ones, prefer to stay in the same location. If this represents good business for the hotel, then the DOC and GM try to persuade the decision makers to use the same hotel again.

Cold calls: During periods of relative quiet, CSMs call potential clients to inquire if they are planning any events in the next few months. The point is to entice the client to view the hotel and the catering facilities. It is amazing how much information is freely given over the telephone.

Figure 5–6 shows the steps involved in booking a function. The most frequent catering events in hotels are the following:

- ✔ Meetings
- ✔ Conventions
- ✔ Dinners
- ✔ Luncheons
- ✔ Weddings

For meetings, a variety of room setups are available, depending on a client's needs. The most frequently selected meeting room setups are as follows:

Theater style: Rows of chairs are placed with a center group of chairs and two aisles. Figure 5–7 shows a theater-style setup with equipment centered on an audiovisual platform. Sometimes multimedia presentations, requiring more space for reverse image projections, reduce the room's seating capacity.

Enquiry: Incoming calls
  From prospective clients
  Director of marketing and sales
  Corporate sales office
  Cold calls by catering sales manager to seek prospective clients
Check for space available in the "bible"* or the computer program.
Confirm availability and suggest menus and beverages. Invite clients to view hotel
  when it is set up for a similar function.
Catering prepares a contract and creates a proposal and a pro-forma invoice for
  client. This enables client to budget for all costs with no surprise.
Catering manager makes any modifications and sends client a contract detailing
  events, menus, beverages, and costs.
Client confirms room booking, menus, and beverages by returning the signed contract.

---

*The bible is the function book in which a permanent record is maintained of each function
room's availability, tentative booking, or guaranteed booking.

Figure 5–6 *Booking a Function*

Classroom style: As the name suggests, tables, usually slim 18-inch ones,
are used because meeting participants need space to take notes.
Classroom-style setup usually takes about three times as much space as
theater style, and takes more time and labor to set up and break down.
Figure 5–8 shows a classroom-style setup.

Horseshoe style: This type of meeting setup (Figure 5–9) is frequently
used when interaction is sought among the delegates, such as training
sessions and workshops. The presenter or trainer stands at the open end
of the horseshoe with a black or white board, flip chart, overhead projector, and video monitor and projector.

Dinner style: Dinners are generally catered at round tables of eight or ten
persons for large parties and on boardroom-style tables for smaller numbers. Of course, there are variations of this setup (see Figure 5–10).

Figure 5–7 *Theater-
Style Seating*

Figure 5–8 *Classroom-Style
Seating*

Figure 5–9 *Horseshoe-Style
Seating*

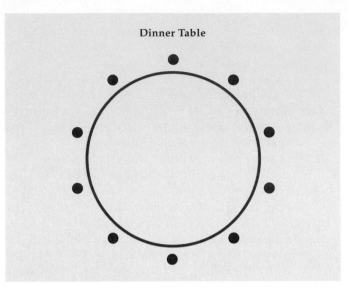

Figure 5–10   *Dinner-Style Seating*

Catering Event Order

A **catering event order (CEO),** which may also be called a **banquet event order (BEO),** is prepared/completed for each function to inform not only the client but also the hotel personnel about essential information (what needs to happen and when) to ensure a successful event.

The CEO is prepared based on correspondence with the client and notes taken during the property visits. Figure 5–11 shows a CEO and lists the room's layout and decor, times of arrival, if there are any VIPs and what special attention is required for them, i.e., reception, bar times, types of beverages and service, cash or credit bar, time of meal service, the menu, wines, and service details. The catering manager or director confirms the details with the client. Usually, two copies are sent, one for the client to sign and return and one for the client to keep.

An accompanying letter thanks the client for selecting the hotel and explains the importance of the function to the hotel. The letter also mentions the guaranteed-number policy. This is the number of guests the hotel will prepare to serve, and will charge accordingly. The guaranteed number is given about seven days prior to the event. This safeguards the hotel from preparing for 350 people and having only 200 show up. The client, naturally, does not want to pay for an extra 150 people—hence the importance of a close working relationship with the client. Contracts for larger functions call for the client to notify the hotel of any changes to the anticipated number of guests in increments of ten or twenty.

Experienced catering directors ensure that there will be no surprises for either the function organizer or the hotel. This is done by calling to check on

SHERATON GRANDE TORREY PINES
BANQUET EVENT ORDER

POST AS:	U.S.I.U. WELCOME BREAKFAST	CHERI WALTER
EVENT NAME:	MEETING	
GROUP:	UNITED STATES INTERNATIONAL UNIVERSITY	
ADDRESS:	10455 POMERADO ROAD	**BILLING:**
	SAN DIEGO, CA 92131	
PHONE:	(619) 635-4627	DIRECT BILL
FAX:	(619) 635-4528	
GROUP CONTACT:	Dr. John Walker	**Amount Received:**
ON-SITE-CONTACT:	same	

DAY	DATE	TIME	FUNCTION	ROOM	EXP	GTE	SET	RENT
Wed	January 25, 1995	7:30 AM – 12:00 PM	Meeting	Palm Garden	50			250.00

BAR SET UP:

N/A

MENU:

7:30 AM CONTINENTAL BREAKFAST

Freshly Squeezed Orange Juice, Grapefruit Juice and
    Tomato Juice
Assortment of Bagels, Muffins, and Mini Brioche
Cream Cheese, Butter, and Preserves
Display of Sliced Seasonal Fruits
Individual Fruit Yogurt
Coffee, Tea, and Decaffeinated Coffee

PRICE:_____

11:00 AM BREAK

Refresh Beverages as needed

WINE:

FLORAL:

MUSIC:

AUDIO VISUAL:
–OVERHEAD PROJECTOR/SCREEN
–FLIPCHART/MARKERS
–VCR/MONITORS

PARKING:

HOSTING PARKING, PLEASE PROVIDE VOUCHERS

LINEN:
HOUSE

SETUP:
–CLASSROOM-STYLE SEATING
–HEAD TABLE FOR 2 PEOPLE
–APPROPRIATE COFFEE BREAK SETUP
–(1) 6' TABLE FOR REGISTRATION AT ENTRANCE
    WITH 2 CHAIRS, 1 WASTEBASKET

All food and beverage prices are subject to an 18% service charge and 7% state tax. Guarantee figures, cancellations, changes must be given 72 hours prior or the number of guests expected will be considered the guarantee. To confirm the above arrangements, this contract must be signed and returned.

ENGAGOR SIGNATURE _____ DATE _____

BEO # 003069

Figure 5–11 *Catering Event Order* (Courtesy of Sheraton Grande Torrey Pines.)

how the function planning is going. One mistake catering directors sometimes make is accepting a final guest count without inquiring as to how that figure was determined. This emphasizes the fact that the catering director should be a consultant to the client. Depending on the function, the conversion from invitations to guests is about 50 percent. Some hotels have a policy of preparing for about 3 to 5 percent more than the anticipated or guaranteed number. Fortunately, most events have a prior history. The organization may have been at a similar hotel in the same city or across the country. In either case, the catering director or manager will be able to receive helpful information from the catering director of the hotel where the organization's function was held previously.

The director of catering holds a daily or weekly meeting with key individuals who will be responsible for upcoming events. Those in attendance should be the following:

> Director of catering
> Executive chef and/or banquet chef
> Beverage manager or catering bar manager
> Catering managers
> Catering coordinator
> Director of purchasing
> Chief steward
> Audiovisual representative

The purpose of this meeting is to avoid any problems and to be sure that all the key staff know and understand the details of the event and any special needs of the client.

Catering Coordinator

The **catering coordinator** has an exacting job in managing the office and controlling the "bible" or function diary. She or he must see that the contracts are correctly prepared and check on numerous last-minute details, such as whether or not flowers and menu cards have arrived.

Catering Services Manager

The **catering services manager (CSM)** has the enormous responsibility of delivering higher-than-expected service levels to guests. The CSM is in charge of the function from the time the client is introduced to the CSM by the director of catering or catering manager. This job is very demanding because several functions always occur simultaneously. Timing and logistics are crucial to the success of the operation. Frequently, there are only a few minutes between the end of a day meeting and the beginning of the reception for a dinner dance.

The CSM must be liked and respected by guests and at the same time be a superb organizer and supervisor. This calls for a person of outstanding character and leadership—management skills that are essential for success. The CSM has several important duties and responsibilities including the following:

✔ Directing the service of all functions

✔ Supervising the catering housepersons in setting up the room

✔ Scheduling the banquet captains and approving the staffing levels for all events

✔ Cooperating with the banquet chef to check menus and service arrangements

✔ Checking that the client is satisfied with the room setup, food, beverages, and service

✔ Checking last-minute details

✔ Making out client bills immediately after the function. Adhering to all hotel policies and procedures that pertain to the catering department. This includes responsible alcoholic beverage service and adherence to fire code regulations.

✔ Calculating and distributing the gratuity and service charges for the service personnel

✔ Coordinating the special requirements with the DOC catering manager and catering coordinator

Check Your Knowledge

1. What is the difference between banquets and catering?
2. What does SMERT stand for?
3. Where do the director of catering and the catering sales manager obtain their information?
4. What are the various styles used when setting up a meeting room? Give examples of when each style might be used.

Room Service/In-Room Dining

The term **room service** has for some time referred to all service to hotel guest rooms. Recently, some hotels have changed the name of room service to *in-room dining* to present the service as more upscale. The intention is to bring the dining experience to the room with quality food and beverage service.

A survey of members of the American Hotel and Motel Association showed that 56 percent of all properties offer room service and that 75 percent of airport properties provide room service. Generally, the larger the hotel and the higher the room rate, the more likely it is that a hotel will offer room service.

Economy and several midpriced hotels avoid the costs of operating room service by having vending machines on each floor and food items like pizza or

Butler Service
(Courtesy John R. Walker.)

Chinese food delivered by local restaurants. Conversely, some hotels prepare menus and lower price structures that do not identify the hotel as the provider of the food. As a result, the guests may have the impression that they are ordering from an "outside" operation when they are in fact ordering from room service.

The level of service and menu prices will vary from hotel to hotel. The Sheraton Grande at Torrey Pines, California, has butler service for all guest rooms without additional charge. This has become the trademark of the hotel.[7]

A few years ago, room service was thought of as a necessary evil, something that guests expected, but which did not produce profit for the hotel. Financial pressures have forced food and beverage directors to have this department also contribute to the bottom line. The room service manager has a difficult challenge running this department, which is generally in operation between sixteen and twenty-four hours a day. Tremendous effectiveness is required to make this department profitable. Nevertheless, it can be done. Some of the challenges in operating room service are as follows:

> Delivery of orders on time—this is especially important for breakfast, which is by far the most popular room service meal
> Making room service a profitable food and beverage department
> Avoiding complaints of excessive charges for room service orders

There are many other challenges in room service operation. One is forecasting demand. Room service managers analyze the front desk forecast, which gives details of the house count and guest mix—convention, group, and others for the next two weeks. The food and beverage forecast will indicate the number of covers expected for breakfast, lunch, and dinner. The convention resumés will show where the convention delegates are having their various meals. For example, the number of in-house delegates attending a convention breakfast can substantially reduce the number of room service breakfast orders. Experience enables the manager to check if a large number of guests are from

[7]Ann Spiselman, "Speed and Quality in Room Service," *Hotels, **27**,* 4, April 1993, p. 60.

different time zones, such as the West or East Coasts or overseas. These guests have a tendency to either get up much earlier or much later. This could throw room service demands off balance. Demand also fluctuates between weekdays and weekends; for example, city hotels may cater to business travelers, who tend to require service at about the same time. However, on weekends, city hotels may attract families, who will order room service at various times. Resort guests, usually couples and families, are more relaxed and less likely to require twenty-four-hour room service. At airport hotels, however, people come and go and want to eat at all times.[8]

Once the forecast has been determined, the manager can begin to plan to meet the expected demand. The challenge of planning for the room service operation includes the following:

Planning the amount of equipment that will be required. Items like room service carts, trays, and cutlery need to be considered.

Staffing schedules need to be carefully planned so as to ensure maximum efficiency. A balance needs to be struck between having people standing around and being rushed off their feet. When planning the schedule, managers check the workload on the forecasts to determine how many different types of setups will be required (e.g., how many executive bars will have to be set up and replenished with fresh garnishes and ice, how many in-room dinners are expected, and how many amenities will need to be made up and placed in guest rooms).

The room service menu requires careful planning. The challenge here is that the food must not only keep its presentation, but it must also have longevity. Room service menus are generally quite mainstream because of the wide variety of guests. Even in a five-star hotel, it is virtually impossible to take hamburgers off the menu because hamburgers are a favorite food item for children. Most dishes that room service offers are items selected from the restaurant menu, thereby avoiding too much additional preparation.

Pricing the menu calls for judgment and a balancing act between charging a realistic amount and having prices appear too high, which might discourage guests from ordering.

In a structured environment, the organizational challenge of room service management consists of *mise en place,* arranging everything in the correct place and ready for action. The system for guests' ordering is organized in two main ways: by telephone and by doorknob hangers for breakfast orders. The room service order-taker takes the order and makes out a bill, giving one copy to the kitchen and one to the servers. During quieter periods, the room service order-taker helps with setting up the trays and carts. Running an operation in which each person has set duties contributes to the efficient running of the department.

[8]Ibid.

To avoid problems with late delivery of orders, a growing number of hotels have dedicated elevators to be used only by room service during peak periods. At the 550-room Intercontinental Hotel in London, up to 350 room service breakfasts are served per day; there the elevator is a mobile continental breakfast service kitchen. At the 565–room Stouffer Riviera Chicago, director of food and beverage Bill Webb has a solution: Rapid action teams (RAT) are designated food and beverage managers and assistants who can be called on when room service orders are heavy.

Westin Hotels recently introduced Service Express, an innovation that allows a customer to address all needs (room service, housekeeping, laundry, and other services) with a single call. In addition, new properties are designed with the room service kitchen adjacent to the main kitchen so that a greater variety of items can be offered.

Hotels are also looking at **sous-vide** (airtight pouches of prepared food that can be quickly reheated). The food quality is good and the food can be prepared in advance during quiet times. Sous-vide works well for fish and almost anything except grilled dishes; it could streamline late-night service, especially at airport hotels, where a layover can mean 100 people clamoring for dinner at midnight.

Some properties, in an effort to make room service more cost effective, have introduced more vending machines on guest floors. This gives guests a wider selection of food and beverage items at a lower cost without waiting.[9]

The challenge of speedy and accurate communication is imperative to a successful room service operation. This begins with timely scheduling and ends with happy guests. In between is a constant flow of information that is communicated by the guest, the order-taker, the cook, and the server.

Another challenge is to have well-trained and competent employees in the room service department. From the tone of voice of the order-taker and the courteous manner with which the order is taken to the panache of the server for the VIP dinners, training makes the difference between ordinary service and outstanding service. With training, which includes menu tasting with wine and suggestive selling, an order-taker becomes a room service salesperson. This person is now able to suggest cocktails or wine to complement the entree, and can entice the guest with tempting desserts. The outcome of this is to increase the average guest check. Training also helps the setup and service personnel hone their skills to enable them to become productive employees who are proud of their work.

An example of the steps of service for an evening room service associate is given in Figure 5–12.

[9]This section draws on Spiselman, op. cit.

1. Make sure the table is properly set, and the order is correct before knocking on the door.
2. Knock on the door three times and immediately say "Good evening. This is room service."
3. As the guest opens the door, greet the guest appropriately. <u>Always ask if you may enter.</u>
4. On entering the room, ask the guest where she or he would like to dine this evening.
5. Present the order, and recommend other menu items.
6. Ask whether the guest would prefer the entrees to remain in the hot box if the order has salads or appetizers. If so, extinguish the sterno in the hot box and explain its use. If the guest would like you to take out the hot box, do so, but in a conservative manner. Never lift the hot box over the table and/or guest. Leave a service towel for the guest.
7. During this entire time it is important to mention that the room service server should be <u>reading</u> the customer they are servicing. Always remain courteous and friendly.
8. Ask the guest if he or she would like the wine opened and poured. Ask the same for beer, coffee/tea, soda, and so on.
9. On exiting, ask the guest to call room service for removal of tray/table, or if any further assistance is needed. <u>Thank them for using room service.</u>

Figure 5–12   *Evening Room Service*

Trends in Food and Beverage Operations

- ✔ The use of branded restaurants instead of hotels operating their own restaurants.
- ✔ Hotels opting not to offer food and beverage outlets. These are usually smaller to midsized properties that may have restaurants on the same lot nearby.
- ✔ Making restaurants and beverage outlets more casual.
- ✔ Using themes for a restaurant. For example, one major hotel chain has adopted a Northern Italian theme in all of its restaurants.
- ✔ Standardized menus for all hotel restaurants in a chain.
- ✔ Many hotels are converting one of the beverage outlets into a sports-themed bar.
- ✔ Technology is being used to enhance guest services and control costs in all areas of a hotel including guest ordering and payment, food production, refrigeration, marketing, management control, and communication.

Case Study

Ensuring Guest Satisfaction

The Sunnyvale Hotel is operated by a major hotel management corporation. To ensure guest satisfaction, 300 survey forms each containing sixty-five questions are mailed to guests each month. Normally, about seventy of the forms are returned. The hotel company categorizes the guest satisfaction scores obtained into colored zones with green being the best, then clear and yellow, and red being the worst. Scores can be compared with those of equivalent hotels.

The most recent survey indicated a significant decline for the Sea Grill Restaurant with scores in the red zone. Guests' concerns were in the following areas: hostess attentiveness, spread of service, and quality of food.

Upon investigation, the director of food and beverage also realized that the name of the restaurant, "Sea Grill," was not appropriate for the type of restaurant being operated. When asked, some guests commented that "it's a bit odd to eat breakfast in a fish place."

Discussion Question

1. What would you do, as director of food and beverage, to get the guest satisfaction scores back into the clear or green zones?

Case Study

Friday Evening at the Grand Hotel's Casual Restaurant

Karla Gomez is the supervisor at the Grand Hotel's casual restaurant. Karla's responsibilities include overseeing five servers and two bussers, seating guests, and taking reservations. One Friday evening, the restaurant was very busy—all twenty tables were occupied, there was a substantial wait-list, and there were people on standby. The service bar was almost full of guests and most of the seated guests in the dining area had finished their entrees or were just beginning their desserts. They were not leaving, however, in part because of cold, rainy weather outside. The guests did not seem to be in a rush to leave the restaurant, but several of the guests waiting for tables were complaining about the long wait.

Discussion Question

1. What can Karla do to solve the problem?

Career Information

Food and beverage (F&B) management careers within the hotel and resort segment of the hospitality industry offer an assortment of positions, from limited service properties that offer very simple food operations, to hotels and resorts that offer room service, banquet facilities, catering operations, and a variety of types of restaurants. Management positions can be as simple as a coffee shop manager or as complex as the director of food and beverage operations for a 5,000-room property.

Managing an F&B operation is similar to working in a restaurant with long hours and varied work schedules. Holidays tend to be the busiest time of the year, eliminating these as potential vacation periods for you. Lodging corporations either treat F&B outlets as a guest amenity working on a break-even premise or see them as profit centers. In either case, an F&B manager is required to balance the needs of the guest with the requirements of the employer.

Compensation is often less than similar positions in chain restaurants, but lodging properties offer excellent benefits packages, and signing bonuses are not unusual. Another incentive of working for hotel chains is reduced or free lodging at associated properties. Those interested in a career in hotel management should note that most general managers have an F&B background.

Food service at hotels and resorts can be challenging, to say the least. Flexibility, quick thinking, and the willingness to meet and exceed guest expectations are essential components of a successful F&B career.

Related Web Sites

http://www.fourseasons.com/—Four Seasons Hotels & Resorts
http://www.eldoradohotel.com/—Eldorado Hotel
http://www.vine2wine.com/—Links to a variety of web sites about wine
http://www.americanwineries.org/—site for the National Associations of American Wineries
http://wineserver.ucdavis.edu/winegrape/index.htm —Winery education information and links to other sites
http://www.realbeer.com/—Great web site for information on beer
http://hbd.org/brewery/—information and links to brewing
http://www.abgbrew.com/—Brewing school
http://www.siebelinstitute.com/—for brewing school in Chicago
http://www.republicbeverage.com/—for Republic Beverage career information and links to other sites
http://www.starbucks.com/hom.asp—for Starbucks Coffee; includes employment information

Courtesy of Charlie Adams.

Summary

1. The food and beverage department division is led by the director of food and beverage, who is responsible for the efficient operation of kitchen, catering, restaurants, bars, and room service; in addition, the director has to keep up with trends and preplan for special events.

2. A hotel kitchen is the responsibility of the executive chef, who is in charge of the quality and quantity of food, organization of the kitchen and his or her sous chefs, administrative duties, and careful calculation of financial results.

3. A hotel usually has a formal and a casual restaurant, which are either directly connected to the hotel or operated separately.

4. Bars are an important revenue source for a hotel, but they must adhere to strict guidelines to be profitable. Commensurate with its size, a hotel might have several kinds of bars, such as a lobby bar, restaurant bar, minibar, or even a night club.

5. The chief steward has the often unrewarded job of cleaning the kitchen, cutlery, plates, glasses, and backstage of the hotel and is in charge of pest control and inventory.

6. Catering is subdivided into on-premise and off-premise occasions, which may include meetings, conventions, dinners, luncheons, and weddings. According to the occasion, the type of service and room setup may vary. It involves careful planning and the interaction and cooperation of many people.

7. Room service offers the convenience of dining in the room, with quality food and beverage service, at a price acceptable to both the guest and the hotel.

Key Words and Concepts

Banquet
Banquet event order (BEO)
Brigade
Capture rate
Catering
Catering and banquet bar
Catering coordinator
Catering director
Catering event order (CEO)
Catering services manager (CSM)
Chef de partie (station chef)

Chef tournant
Chief steward
Classroom-style room setup
Contribution margin
Dinner-style room setup
Executive chef
Food and beverage director
Food cost percentage
Food sales percentage
Horseshoe-style room setup
Hotel bars
Kitchen manager

Labor cost percentage
Lobby bar
Minibar
Night clubs
Perpetual inventory
Pilferage
Pool bar
Pour/cost percentage
Responsible alcoholic beverage service
Restaurant bar
Restaurant manager

Room service
Service bar
Shopper
Sommelier
Sous chef
Sous-vide
Sports bar
Theater-style room setup

Review Questions

1. Briefly describe the challenges a food and beverage director faces on a daily basis.
2. List the measures used to determine the food and beverage department's profit and loss.
3. Explain the problems a hotel faces in making the following departments profitable: restaurants, bars, and room service.

4. Explain the importance of the catering department for a hotel and list the responsibilities of a catering sales manager.

Internet Exercises

1. Organization:
   Web site:
   Summary:
   (a) Click on the "Forums and Chat" icon. Go to the "Chef and Cooks Corner" and take a look at some of the latest articles. Bring your favorite one to the table (discuss in class).
   (b) Look at the most current articles on food safety. What are the major concerns being addressed?

Foodservice
http://www.foodservice.com
Foodservice.com is a web site that focuses on the foodservice industry. It has links to employment, industry resources, foodservice, technology innovations, and much more.

2. Organization:
   Web site:
   Summary:
   (a) Look under the "Education" icon. What does it mean to be "FMP Certified" and what are the eligibility requirements?
   (b) What are some of the upcoming events and what do they have to offer?

National Restaurant Association
http://www.restaurant.org
The National Restaurant Association is an organization devoted to representing, educating, and promoting the restaurant/hospitality industry.

Apply Your Knowledge

1. If a casual dining restaurant in a four-star hotel forecasts the need for 100 covers, how many servers, busers, hosts, and assistant managers would you schedule on that particular day? Calculate the labor cost of these associates for that day if the manager(s) work from 1:00 to 11:00 P.M. the server(s) work from 4:00 to 11:00 P.M., the buser(s) work from 4:30 to 11:30 P.M., and the host(s) work from 4:00 to 11:00 P.M. Use minimum wage of $5.75 for calculations. Use the rate of $12 per hour for the assistant manager(s) and $6.50 for hosts.

2. Kitchen labor costs are an important ratio used to determine the efficiency of the food and beverage department. The labor cost for a banquet meal is $126.45 and the revenue for the banquet is $505.80. What is the labor cost percentage?

The Culinary Arts and Restaurant Business: Development and Classification

6

After reading and studying this chapter, you should be able to:

- ✓ Describe the history and evolution of Culinary Arts.
- ✓ Know the food-safety suggestions.
- ✓ Trace the history and development of the restaurant business.
- ✓ List factors that influence restaurant concept and marketing.
- ✓ Discuss the important elements in menu planning.
- ✓ Outline the development of a restaurant chain.
- ✓ Describe the different characteristics of chain and independent restaurants.
- ✓ Identify some of the top chain and independent restaurants.
- ✓ List the classifications of restaurants.

Culinary Arts

This is an exciting time to be involved with the culinary arts and restaurants. Not only are new restaurant concepts and themes to fit a variety of tastes and budgets appearing on the scene, but the culinary arts are being developed by several creative and talented chefs. It is important to realize that in this industry, we are never far from food. So, let's take a look at the recent development of **culinary arts.**

North America gained most of its culinary legacy from France. Two main events were responsible for our culinary legacy coming from France. First was the French Revolution in 1793, which caused the best chefs of the day to lose their employment because their bosses lost their heads! Many chefs came to North America as a result, bringing with them their culinary talents. The second was Thomas Jefferson, who in 1784 spent five years as envoy to France and brought a French chef to the White House when he became president. This act stimulated interest in French cuisine and enticed U.S. tavern owners to offer better quality and more interesting food.

No mention of classical cuisine can be made without talking about the founders. Mari-Antoine Careme (1784–1833), who is credited as the founder of classical cuisine, and Auguste Escoffier, who is profiled in this chapter. After learning all aspects of cooking, Careme dedicated his career to refining and organizing culinary techniques. His many books contain the first really systematic account of cooking principles, recipes, and menu making.[1]

One of the main foundations of classical French cooking is the five **mother sauces:** béchamel, velouté, espagnole, tomato, and hollandaise. These elaborate sauces were essential accompaniments for the various dishes on the menu. Until about 1900, all menus were written in French—some still are—and regardless of whether a person was dining in a good hotel or restaurant in London or Lisbon, the intention was that the dish should be prepared in the same manner and taste similar to the French version. The travelers of the day either spoke French or had a knowledge of menu French.

Classical French cuisine was in vogue until the late 1960s, early 1970s when **nouvelle cuisine** became popular. Nouvelle cuisine is a lighter cuisine than French and is based on simpler preparations—with the aid of processors, blenders, and juicers—using more natural flavors and ingredients. Instead of thickening a sauce with a flour-based **roux**, a **puree** of vegetables would be used instead. Fresh was in, and this included herbs for flavor. Nouvelle cuisine combined classical techniques and principles with modern technology and scientific research. "Simpler quicker" quickly became more stylish with plate presentation becoming a part of the chef's art. North American cooking had arrived. The bounties of Canada and the United States provided the basis for

---

[1]Wayne Gisslen, *Professional Cooking,* 2nd ed. New York: John Wiley and Sons, 1989.

Personal Profile: Auguste Escoffier (1846–1935)

Auguste Escoffier is considered the patron saint of the professional cook. Called the "emperor of the world's kitchens," he is considered as a reference point and a role model for all chefs. His exceptional culinary career began at the age of thirteen, when he apprenticed in his uncle's restaurant. He worked until 1920, and retired to die quietly at home in Monaco in 1935. Uneducated, but a patient educator and diligent writer, he was an innovator who remained deeply loyal to the regional and bourgeois roots of French cookery. He exhibited his culinary skills in the dining rooms of the finest hotels in Europe, including the Place Vendome in Paris and the Savoy and Carlton hotels in London.

When the Prince of Wales requested something light but delicious as late dinner after a night in the casino in Monte Carlo, Auguste Escoffier responded with *poularde Derby*, a stuffed chicken served with truffles cooked in champagne, alternating with slices of butter-fried *foie gras*, its sauce basted with the juices from the chicken and truffles. Another interesting anecdote regarding the chef's originality in making sauces tells of a special dinner for the Prince of Wales and Kaiser Wilhelm. Escoffier was asked to create a special dish to honor such an occasion. Struggling with an apparent loss of creativity until the night before the event, the chef finally noticed a sack of overripe mangos, from which he created a sauce that he personally came out from the kitchen to serve. As he placed the plate on the table, he looked at the Kaiser and with a wicked smile said, "*zum Teufel*"—to the devil. Then was born sauce diabla, today a favorite classic sauce. Escoffier's insistence on sauces derived from the cooking of main ingredients was revolutionary at the time and in keeping with his famous instruction: *faites simple*—keep it simple.

In fact, in his search for simplicity, Escoffier reduced the complexity of the work of Careme, the "cook of kings and king of cooks," and aimed at the perfect balance of a few superb ingredients. In *Le Livre des Menus* (1912), Escoffier makes the analogy of a great dinner as a symphony with contrasting movements that should be appropriate to the occasion, the guests, and the season. He was meticulous in his kitchen, yet wildly imaginative in the creation of exquisite dishes. In 1903, Escoffier published *Le Guide Culinaire*, an astounding collection of more than 5,000 classic cuisine recipes and garnishes. Throughout the book, Escoffier emphasizes technique, the importance of a complete understanding of basic cookery principles, and ingredients he considers to be essential to the creation of great dishes.

Escoffier's refinement of Careme's *grand cuisine* has been so radical as to credit him with the development of a new cuisine referred to as *cuisine classique*. His principles have been reinstated by successive generations, most emphatically by the *novelle cuisine* brigade. Francois Fusero, *chef de cuisine* at the Hotel Hermitage, Monte Carlo, regards Escoffier as his role model, and he schools his chefs in Escoffier's style: No detail is left to chance.

regional cuisine to flourish nationally. **Infusion**—the blending of flavors and techniques from two cuisines—became popular. New England and Italian or Californian and Asian can be blended. For example, a Japanese recipe might be blended with a Mexican one to create a new hybrid recipe.

Many great chefs have influenced our recent culinary development. Among them are Julia Childs, whose television shows did much to take the mystique out of French cooking and encourage a generation of homemakers to elevate their cooking techniques and skills; Martha Stewart; and more recently Emeril "Bam" Lagasse and Bobby Flay, who have popularized cooking via the Food Network on TV.

The culinary schools have done an excellent job of producing a new generation of chefs who are making significant contributions to the evolving culinary

Chef Emeril Lagasse outside his New Orleans Fish House restaurant at the MGM Grand, Las Vegas. (Courtesy MGM Grand.)

Charlie Trotter, One of America's Finest Restaurant Chef-Owners and King of Infusion (Courtesy Chef Charlie Trotter.)

Continuing Education

"It's not a career—it's a lifestyle! Regardless of your level of responsibility, continuing education should be an integral part of your career strategy."—Lawrence Gilpatric, CEC, CCE.

arts, including chefs like Alice Waters, who at Chez Panice, her restaurant in Berkeley, California, is credited with the birth of California cuisine. Waters uses only fresh produce brought from local farmers. Paul Prudhomme is another contemporary chef who has energized many aspiring chefs with his passion for basic cooking, especially cajun style.

Charlie Trotter, chef-owner of Charlie Trotter's in Chicago, is considered by many to be America's finest chef-owner and king of infusion, who said in one of his books:[2]

> After love there is only cuisine! It's all about excellence, or at least working towards excellence. Early on in your approach to cooking—or in running a restaurant—you have to determine whether or not you are willing to commit fully and completely to the idea of *the pursuit of excellence.* I have always looked at it this way: if you strive for perfection—an all out assault on total perfection—at the very least you will hit a high level of excellence, and then you might be able to sleep at night. To accomplish something truly significant, excellence has to become a life plan.

Chef Trotter brings his knowledge and exposure together into a coherent view on what the modern fine dining experience could be. He says "I thought the blend of European refinement regarding the pleasures of the table, American ingenuity and energy in operating a small enterprise, Japanese minimalism and poetic elegance in effecting a sensibility, and a modern approach to incorporating health and dietary concerns would encompass a spectrum of elements through which I could express myself fully. Several years later, I find I am even more devoted than ever to this approach."[3]

Dr. Paul G. Van Landingham, offers these insights: The term "culinarian" has taken on new meaning as we enter the twenty-first century. In the past, to be successful in the field of culinary arts, one would only have to be a good cook. Today, to meet the challenges of the industry, it is essential for the modern chefs to be well educated and highly diversified. Keeping current with food trends is not enough. Chefs today must be "change agents." Chefs also must be familiar with the world of science and technology. Great changes will have to be made in training of the chef of the future.

Culinary Practices
Courtesy of Mike Zema

As we begin the new millennium, we see culinary education setting the pace for dining exploration. As you prepare for a career in the hospitality industry, you will find it imperative that you develop a strong culinary foundation. Within the structure of this you will need to develop skills that include

[2]Charlie Trotter, *Charlie Trotter.* Berkeley, CA: Ten Speed Press, 1994, p. 11.
[3]Ibid, p. 12.

Personal Profile: Chef Paul Prudhomme

Very rarely do we find such a fine cook who takes pride and joy in what he does and does it so perfectly. Meet Paul Prudhomme, best known as Chef Paul. His widely known special-blend herbs, cookbooks, and recipes have made him one of the most loved cooks of all time. What started as "just assisting" his mom in the kitchen has become a career for Chef Paul.

Chef Paul was born and reared on a farm near Opelousas in Louisiana's Acadiana country. He was the youngest of thirteen children. When the youngest girl left home, there was no one left to help his mom cook for the family. Paul, then only seven, would assist his mom and this is when he learned about using only the freshest ingredients while cooking. He knew at this time that he wanted to make preparing food his life's work. After completing school, his curiosity about life and cultural customs led him to leave Louisiana while in his early twenties and travel across the United States to experience every culinary environment possible. He worked as a cook in all kinds of restaurants and learned a lot about ingredients and styles of cooking in different parts of the country. He recalls, "Sometimes, when I thought the food was too bland, I'd sneak in a few dried herbs and spices. When customers complimented the dishes from my station, I'd try to remember exactly what I'd used, but that was hard, so I began keeping little notes on good mixes in my pockets. Sometimes, though, I'd get caught and this didn't make me popular with the head chefs."

(Courtesy Magic Seasoning Blends.)

In July 1979, Chef Paul and his late wife, K. Hinrichs Prudhomme, opened K-Paul's Louisiana Kitchen in New Orleans. This French Quarter restaurant attracted world travelers and continues to excite diners today. His blackened redfish and blackened steak attracted people to his kitchen. K-Paul's catering division satisfies palates in New Orleans and around the country.

In response to all of this, Chef Paul decided to reveal his seasoning secrets. He created his own line of all-natural herbs and spices. Chef Paul Prudhomme's Magic Seasoning Blends are distributed all around the United States and in over thirty countries around the world. Other cooking blends offered are his own seasoned and smoked meats (andouille and tasso) and pizza and pasta, which are available through mail order.

When someone appears on TV as a guest over and over again, we know that person has "hit it big." Chef Paul has been featured often on the three major television networks' prime time programs and has made guest appearances on NBC's *Today Show,* ABC's *Good Morning America,* CBS' *This Morning, Larry King Live,* and many others. But what has made Chef Paul famous is his best-selling cookbooks. He has also made several cooking videos, one of which made it to the top of the Billboard charts for fifty-three consecutive weeks. He has been featured in several articles in magazines such as *Life, Time, Newsweek, Bon Appetit,* and *Metropolitan Home.* Chef Paul has made appearances and given lectures and seminars all over Europe and the Orient. He serves as a consultant to Team USA of the American Culinary Federation and participates actively at conventions, seminars, and food trade shows as a guest lecturer and in support of his seasoning blends. As for cooking for the famous, Chef Paul has cooked for heads of state as well as members of the U.S. Congress.

He spends a lot of time at universities giving educational seminars to students in all walks of life as well as charity work and benefits. He was the first chef to participate in the Robert Mondavi "Great Chefs of America" television series. He was one of the twelve chefs chosen from around the world to participate in the celebration of Jerusalem's 3,000-year anniversary, at which each chef created a Kosher dish that was served at the King David's Feast in March 1996.

His great cooking skills and sweet success made Chef Paul the first American-born chef to receive the coveted Merite Agricole of the French Republic. In 1986, the American Culinary Federation honored him as "Culinarian of the Year."

Paul Prudhomme is always eager to learn. He still has the drive to travel, experiment, and make personal appearances and develop new recipes. He still uses only the earth's finest harvests, as did his mother. He has propelled the distinctive cuisine of his native Louisiana into the international spotlight and continues to push the limits by creating exciting, new American and international dishes.

Sources: This section was compiled from Chef Paul Prudhomme's biography from the *http://www.foodlocker.com/chefpaulprud.html* and *http://magicseasoning.com/meet.html* web sites.

cooking, strong employability traits, people skills, menu development, nutrition, sanitation/safety, accounting, and computer skills.

Before you can become a successful chef, you have to be a good cook. To be a good cook, you have to understand the basic techniques and principles of cooking. The art of cooking has not changed in thousands of years. And although the concept of cooking has not changed, science and technology have allowed us to improve the methods of preparation. We still use fire to cook with; grilling, broiling, and simmering are still popular methods of cooking.

Let's look at each of the skill areas that are important to becoming a successful chef.

Cooking

You will need to learn all of the basic cooking methods in order to understand flavor profiles. As you look at recipes to cook, try to enhance the basic ingredient list to improve the flavor. As an example, I tell my students to always try to substitute a flavored liquid if water is called for in a recipe. It is also important to understand basic ingredient flavors so we can improve flavor. The idea behind back-to-basic cooking means to evaluate your recipe and look for flavor improvement with each item.

Employability traits are those skills that focus on attitude, passion, initiative, dedication, sense of urgency, and dependability. These traits are not always traits that can be taught, but a good chef can demonstrate them by example. Most of the employers that contact me with job opportunities for students consider these skills to be more important than technical skills. The belief is that if you have strong employability traits, your technical skills will be strong.

One of the most important things I've learned about our industry is that *you can't do it alone.* Each person in your operation has to work together in order for you to be successful. The most important ingredient in managing people is to *respect them.*

Many words can be used to describe a manager (coach, supervisor, boss, mentor), but whatever term is used, you have to be in the game in order to be effective. Managing a kitchen is like coaching a football team—everyone must work together in order to be effective. The difference between a football team and a kitchen is that chefs/managers cannot supervise from the sidelines; we have to be in the game. One of my favorite examples of excellent people management skills is that of the general manager of a hotel who had the warewashing team report directly to him. When asked why, he indicated that they are the people who know what is being thrown in the garbage, they are the people who know what the customers are not eating, and they are the people most responsible for the sanitation and safety within an operation. There are many components to managing people—training, evaluating, nurturing, delegating, and so on—but the most important is respect.

Menu Development

To keep customers returning, we have to continuously improve our menus. Serve a solid variety of items that reflect different cooking methods and flavor profiles. Customers want to see the chef's input on the menu. Chefs are the authority on cooking and our customers will select items that we recommend. One of the buzz words in our industry today is eatertainment and we can provide that by making ourselves visible to the customer. One of the fun things about menu development is the opportunity to play with food. Experimenting with different types and flavors of foods keeps cooking exciting.

Most people will agree that the public is concerned about nutrition. This is true for most of our customers except when it comes to dining out. I like to use the term "dietary schizophrenia" to describe the dining public. Most of our customers are concerned about their nutritional level when they are at home, but when they go out to eat, they want to splurge. Some examples to support my belief include the increase in dessert sales today, up 35 percent since 1998, beef sales have increased significantly, and fast food is a way of life.

The chef's responsibility regarding nutrition is to prepare food by minimizing fat and sodium intake. Some people believe that this can't be done without losing flavor. Others totally disagree. Here are some examples of how this can be done:

- ✓ Use herbs and spices to replace salt.
- ✓ Use cooking methods that will maximize flavor and minimize fat, for example, broiling, grilling, and roasting.
- ✓ Use technologies such as processing, juicing, and reduction to enhance flavors and naturally thicken ingredients.
- ✓ Prepare vegetables and starches al dente (firm to the bite) to maximize flavor, texture, presentation, and nutritional value.
- ✓ Use flavored liquids when applicable in recipes.

Sanitation/Safety

As the number of meals consumed away from home increases, so does the food-safety risk. According to figures from the National Restaurant Association, between 6 and 12 million cases of foodborne illness occur each year, as well as between 500 and 9,000 American deaths resulting from foodborne illness. With that many lives at risk, the consumer is depending on us to minimize the risk factors. Most of us have experienced some type of foodborne illness and assumed that we had the stomach flu. What you experienced is food poisoning. Our industry needs to be on the cutting edge in training and implementing practices and procedure in food safety.

Recently I participated in writing an article for *Equipment Solutions* magazine's Safety Zone entitled "A Recipe for Safe Food." In this article we gave ingredients for a successful, safe food program. Some key food-safety suggestions and reminders follow:

Step 1. *Wash hands often.* The major cause of foodborne illness is from cross-contamination. By washing your hands often, you can minimize the transfer of harmful microorganisms from one food to another food or to a food-contact surface. I suggest foodservice personnel take the same professional attitude as the medical profession: Washing your hands often can save a life.

Step 2. *Keep it clean.* Be sure your cooking environment (equipment, small-wares, storage areas, and preparation areas) is clean and sanitized.

Step 3. *Avoid the danger zone.* Keeping food out of the danger zone is imperative. From the time product is delivered through service to the guest, food must be kept out of the 41°F to 140°F range to keep harmful microorganisms from growing.

Step 4. *Train and educate.* One excellent way to enhance food-safety knowledge is with the Educational Foundation's Serv-Safe@ Serving Safe Food Program, which provides training specific to the job responsibilities of foodservice managers and employees. I recommend that anyone who handles food—whether a professional or not—be trained in food safety.

Step 5. *Have the right attitude.* I believe it is important for foodservice staff to change their attitudes about food safety. I compare a chef's job to that of a doctor. We prepare food that is digested and can literally kill someone if not prepared properly. If we accept that responsibility and look at our job like the professionals in the medical field do, we might see a significant decrease in foodborne illness.

Step 6. *Know your equipment.* Maximize equipment integrity and productivity by reviewing the manufacturer's handbook that is provided with each piece of equipment. If the recommended maintenance suggestions and cleaning/sanitizing schedule are followed, you will minimize sanitation risks. Purchasing equipment that has built-in temperature and time-monitoring capabilities and using hotel pans no more than two and a half inches deep when holding and presenting food will maintain temperature controls and provide guests with better quality food.

Step 7. *Be HACCP friendly.* Make sure that the purveyors you do business with have a Hazard Analysis of Critical Control Points (HACCP) program in place and that delivery drivers are certified in food safety. Always check for proper temperatures, dates, and the conditions of food containers when receiving product. Work with the local health department to establish an HACCP program.

Step 8. *Use your health department.* Establish a good relationship with your local health department. This department can provide the latest information and tips on food safety, supply you with posters and support materials on temperature controls and personal hygiene, and offer suggestions on suppliers that carry food-safety monitoring systems. When your local health inspector comes in for an inspection, have one or two of your employees go around with the inspector. Use the health department's inspection form as one of your training tools. Review and highlight critical areas with your staff. Ask your inspector to come in and speak with your staff about sanitation issues.

Step 9. *Provide Your Staff with the Tools to Be Successful.* Be sure to provide your staff with the tools to implement a food-safety program in your kitchen: thermometers, test strips, cleaning supplies, disposable gloves, serving utensils, required smallwares for preparation, cleaning chemicals, and information/direction to succeed.

Step 10. *Stay informed.* Read industry publications that discuss food safety and participate in continuing education programs offered by the ACF (American Culinary Federation), NRAEF (National Restaurant Association Educational Foundation), AHMA (American Hotel Motel Association), and NAFEM (National Association of Foodservice Equipment Manufacturers). I would encourage most foodservice operations to join the Food Safety Council.

Accounting

As the level of responsibility of chefs increases, accountability for food and labor costs is a required skill for which chefs must be trained. Food and labor costs are the two largest expenses for foodservice operations. It is the chef's responsibility to select the best purveyor/supplier, negotiate the best price, insist on top quality, and expect good service. Once we receive the product, our job is to maintain the product integrity and produce the maximum yield.

As the cost of labor increases, we also need to know how to utilize our staff. Developing job descriptions, suggesting skill levels that are needed for each station, writing standardized recipes with complete descriptions for preparation, plate service, product substitution, and clean-up, scheduling, and strong people skills are all necessary to being a good chef. These skills are as important as your cooking skills.

Computer Training

It's a given that computer training is necessary in every industry. In the field of culinary arts, this is no exception. As a chef, the computer has allowed us to quickly complete a variety of paperwork tasks that prior to computers we would spend hours completing. The computer has provided us with the opportunity to maintain hundreds of recipes on one little disk, increase and decrease recipes at the touch of a button, cost out recipes with some simple math input, maintain inventory control, tabulate food costs, determine product needs, provide nutritional information on recipes, help in employee scheduling, and minimize the number of hours required for menu evaluations. It is very important for you to enhance your computer skills and implement them in the kitchen.

Food Trends and Practices for the New Millennium

As the level of professionalism rises for the chef of the twenty-first century, chefs will need a strong culinary foundation with a structure that includes multi-culture cooking skills and strong employability traits, such as passion, dependability, cooperation, and initiative. Additional management skills include strong supervisory training, sense of urgency, accounting, sanitation/safety, nutritional awareness, and marketing/merchandising.

The term "back-to-basic cooking" has been redefined to mean taking classical cooking methods and infusing modern technology and science to create healthy and flavorful dishes. Some examples of this include:

- ✓ Thickening soups and sauces by processing and using the food item's natural starches instead of traditional thickening methods
- ✓ Redefining the basic mother sauces to omit the béchamel and egg base sauces and add or replace with coulis, salsas, or chutneys
- ✓ Pursuing more cultural culinary infusion to develop bold and aggressive flavors
- ✓ Experimenting with sweet and hot flavors
- ✓ Taking advantage of the shrinking globe and disappearing of national borders to bring new ideas and flavors to restaurants
- ✓ Evaluating recipes and substituting ingredients for better flavor; that is, flavored liquid instead of water, infused oils and vinegars instead of non-flavored oils and vinegars
- ✓ Using natural thickening agents and processing and reduction instead of traditional thickening methods such as rouxs
- ✓ Substituting herbs and spices for salt
- ✓ Returning to one-pot cooking to capture flavors

This is truly an exciting time to enter the hospitality industry and particularly the culinary arts. Today, being a chef is considered a real profession that offers a variety of opportunities in every segment of the hospitality industry and anywhere in the world.

Restaurant Development

Restaurants play an important role in society. Dining out in restaurants fulfills an important sociological need. People need not only nourishment, but also the social interaction that takes place in a restaurant setting. Restaurants are one of the few places where we use all of our senses to enjoy the experience. Our taste, sight, smell, hearing, and touch are all employed to savor the food, service, and atmosphere of the restaurant.

The successful operation of a restaurant is dependent on a number of factors. From the restaurant's operating philosophy to controls, and all the factors in between, it is not easy to succeed in operating restaurants. This section covers many of the factors that are necessary ingredients in the successful operation of a restaurant.

Operating Philosophy

At the heart of an enterprise is the philosophy of the owner or operator. The philosophy represents the way the company does business. It is an expression of the ethics, morals, and values by which the company operates.

Mission, Goals, and Objectives

Many companies have formal mission statements that explain their reason for being in business. Red Lobster's mission statement (Figure 6-1) is a good example of a restaurant's mission.

Restaurant Market

The market is composed of those guests who will patronize the restaurant. A prospective restaurant owner will analyze the market to determine whether sufficient demand exists in a particular market niche, such as Italian or Southern cuisines. A **niche** is a marketing term used to describe a specific share or slot of a certain market. A good indication of the size of the market can be ascertained by taking a radius of from one to five miles around the restaurant. The distance will vary according to the type and location of the restaurant. In Manhattan, it may only be a few blocks, whereas in rural West Virginia it may

Red Lobster's mission is to provide every guest with a dining experience that exceeds expectations and ensures their return.

We serve a variety of attractive, excellent tasting food in a comfortable, inviting atmosphere.

We offer a wide range of competitive prices that provide exceptional value.

Our service is professional, knowledgeable, and friendly.

We are committed to the success of the individual, their quality of life, and to providing opportunities for recognition and professional growth and development.

We are an industry leader in providing growth and returns to our shareholders.

We are America's favorite seafood restaurant and a top choice for full-service dining.

Figure 6–1 *Mission Statement of Red Lobster Restaurants*

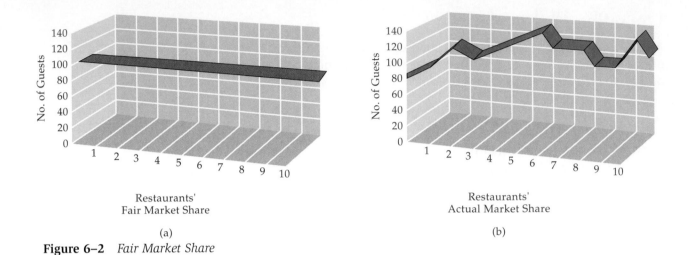

(a)   (b)

Figure 6–2   *Fair Market Share*

be a few miles. The area that falls within the radius is called the **catchment area.** The demographics of the population within the catchment area is analyzed to reveal age, number of people in various age brackets, sex, ethnicity, religion, income levels, and so on. This information is usually available from the chamber of commerce or data at the local library or real estate offices.

One yardstick used to determine the potential viability of a restaurant is to divide the number of restaurants in the catchment area by the total population. The average number of people per restaurant in the United States is about 500. Perhaps this kind of saturation is one of the reasons for the high failure rate of restaurants. Obviously, each area is different; one location may have several Italian restaurants but no Southern restaurant. Therefore, a Southern restaurant would be unique in the market and, if properly positioned, may have a competitive advantage. If someone in the catchment area wanted to eat Italian food, he or she would have to choose among the various Italian restaurants. In marketing terms, the number of potential guests for the Italian restaurants would be divided by the number of Italian restaurants to determine **fair market share** (the average number of guests that would, if all other things were equal, eat at any one of the Italian restaurants). Figure 6–2a shows 1,000 potential guests. If they all decided to eat Italian in the fair market share scenario, each restaurant would receive 100 guests. In reality, we know this does not happen—for various reasons, one restaurant becomes more popular. The number of guests that this and the other restaurants receive then is called the **actual market share.** Figure 6–2b shows an example of the actual market share that similar restaurants might receive.

Restaurant Concept

Successful restaurant concepts are created with guests in mind. All too frequently someone thinks it would be a good idea to open up a particular kind of restaurant, only to find there are insufficient guests to make it viable.

For the winners, creating and operating a restaurant business is fun—lots of people coming and going, new faces, old friends. Restaurants provide a social gathering place where employees, guests, and management can get their adrenaline flowing in positive ways. The restaurant business is exciting and challenging; with the right location, food, atmosphere, and service it is possible to attract the market and make a good return on investment.

There are several examples of restaurant concepts that have endured over the past few decades. Applebee's, Chart House, Hard Rock Cafe, Olive Garden, Red Lobster, and TGI Friday's are some of the better known U.S. chain restaurant concepts. Naturally, there are more regional and independent concepts.

The challenge is to create a restaurant concept and bring it into being, a concept that fits a definite market, a concept better suited to its market than that presented by competing restaurants.[4] Every restaurant represents a concept and projects a total impression or an image. The image appeals to a certain market—casual, formal, children, adults, ethnic, and so on. The concept should fit the location and reach out to its target market. A restaurant's concept, location, menu, and decor should intertwine.[5]

In restaurant lingo, professionals sometimes describe restaurants by the net operating percentage that the restaurant makes. TGI Friday's restaurants, for example, are usually described as 20 percent restaurants. A local restaurant may be only a 10 percent restaurant.

In order for the operation of a restaurant to be successful, the following factors need to be addressed:
- ✓ Mission
- ✓ Goals
- ✓ Objectives
- ✓ Market
- ✓ Concept
- ✓ Location
- ✓ Menu planning
- ✓ Ambiance
- ✓ Lease
- ✓ Other occupational costs

The odds in favor of becoming a big restaurant winner are not good. Approximately 540,000 commercial restaurants do business in the United States. Each year, thousands of new ones open and thousands more close, and even more change ownership for cents on the dollar. The restaurant business is relatively easy to enter, but it is deceptively difficult to succeed in it.[6]

The restaurant concept is undoubtedly one of the major components of any successful operation. Some restaurants are looking for a concept; some concepts are searching for a restaurant.

[4]John R. Walker and Donald E. Lundberg, *The Restaurant from Concept to Operation*, 3rd ed. New York: John Wiley and Sons, 2001, p. 5.

[5]Ibid.

[6]Ibid.

Corporate Profile: The Steak 'n' Shake Story

Gus Belt started Steak 'n' Shake in February of 1934. Because of the high-quality food served on glass and china at reasonable prices by friendly servers, Gus had to make changes to accommodate the ever-increasing demand. His first move was to purchase a chain of restaurants in Central Illinois called Goal Post and convert them to Steak 'n' Shakes. He then added curb service because every restaurant had a never-ending line to occupy one of the coveted seats.

The reason Steak 'n' Shake remains successful today is the authenticity of the experience and the quality of the food. The steakburger is made of the finest ground

evolve to accommodate the needs of today's consumers. In 1990 Steak 'n' Shake began to grow again. Currently there are over 400 restaurants operating in 19 states, with over 55 franchised restaurants.

Careers at Steak 'n' Shake

The company seeks bright, hand-working, hospitality-oriented leaders who can grow with the company. Throughout its history, Steak 'n' Shake has succeeded by meeting and exceeding guests' expectations. A career with Steak 'n' Shake is built upon the tradition and sta-

steak and, through the art of grilling on a very hot grill, turned into a burger beyond comparison. The shake at Steak 'n' Shake is a creamy, real-milk, hand-dipped milkshake that endures as the best milkshake on the planet. Gus Belt used to put the Multi-Mixers shake machines in the windows of his restaurant to encourage cars driving by to stop for a milkshake.

Gus Belt sold his first franchise in the late 1930s. St. Louis, Indianapolis, Northern Illinois, Daytona Beach, and Hot Springs, Arkansas soon followed. The Belt family sold Steak 'n' Shake in 1969. The company turned over twice during the 1970s. By 1981 the company had grown to over 130 units.

In 1981, E.W. Kelley and Associates purchased the company. Mr. Kelley remains Chairman of the Board to this day. Because of his marketing acumen, Mr. Kelley is considered the modern-day founder of Steak 'n' Shake. He reinvented the original concept: he understood that people today want the same things people wanted in 1934. He also realized that a successful brand must

bility of over 65 successful years in the industry, and upon the opportunity for accelerated personal growth and development. A proven promote-from-within policy provides advancement opportunities to individuals seeking a meaningful career.

Financial Success

Over the past five years, the company's revenues have more than doubled, and net earnings have nearly quadrupled. The company's stock is traded on the New York Stock Exchange under the symbol SNS (formerly COP). For two consecutive years, the company was included in *Forbes* magazine's listing of the 200 best small companies in America. Additionally, the "Midyear Investment Report 1998" in the August issue of *Money* magazine included the company in the list of the top 50 stocks of the bull market. The value of a $1,000 investment made on August 1, 1982, had grown to $73,206 on June 30, 1998, reflecting a 31% annualized return.

In New York, Restaurant Associates owns and operates Rockefeller Plaza's American Festival Cafe, SeaGrill, and Savories. The Associates' latest concept is Cucina & Co., located in the Pan Am Building in New York City. Restaurant Associates plans to create an 11,000-square-foot Grand Grill multiconcept restaurant. The theme depicts the great Pan Am Clipper terminals reminiscent of the roaring twenties, with a Grand Cafe featuring a Parisian brasserie concept adjacent to the restaurant.

The Associates also have in the works a scaled-down version of Panevino, a Tuscan farmhouse concept. When asked what trends and opportunities are emerging in the industry, Restaurant Associate Nick Valenti says, "In urban locations, I'm thinking about high-quality takeout and elements of self-service in a concept. In both urban and suburban areas, it might be time to redefine the coffee shop. Stick with traditional fare but upgrade the ingredients considerably. For instance, club sandwiches should be served with fresh turkey, ripe tomatoes, and bread toasted to order."[7]

Restaurant Location

The restaurant concept must fit the location, and the location must fit the concept (see Figure 6–3). The location should appeal to the target market (expected guests). Other things being equal, prime locations cost more, so operators must either charge more for their menu items or drive sufficient volume to keep the rent/lease costs to between 5 and 8 percent of sales.

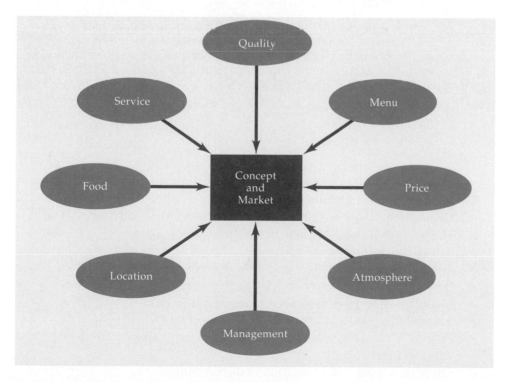

Figure 6–3 *Concept and Market (Reprinted with permission from John R. Walker and Donald E. Lundberg,* The Restaurant from Concept to Operation, 3rd ed. *New York: John Wiley and Sons, 2001, p. 62.)*

[7]This section draws on Jeff Weinstein and Brenda McCarthy, "Concept Creators," *Restaurants and Institutions,* **103,** 15, June 15, 1993, pp. 34–59.

Personal Profile: Richard Melman

Chairman of the Board, CEO, and Founder, Lettuce Entertain You Enterprises, Inc.

Richard Melman is Founder, Chairman, and CEO of Lettuce Entertain You Enterprises, Inc., a Chicago-based corporation that owns and licenses nearly 75 restaurants nationwide and in Japan.

The restaurant business has been Melman's life work, beginning with his early days in a family-owned restaurant, and later as a teenager working in fast-food eateries and a soda fountain, and selling restaurant supplies. After realizing that he wasn't cut out to be a college student and failing to convince his father that he should be made a partner in the family business, Melman met Jerry A. Orzoff, a man who immediately and unconditionally believed in Melman's ability to create and run restaurants. In 1971, the two opened R.J. Grunts, a hip burger joint that soon became one of the hottest restaurants in Chicago. Here, Melman and Orzoff presented food differently and with a sense of humor, creating the youthful and fun restaurant that was a forerunner in the trend toward dining out as entertainment that swept this country in the early '70s.

Melman and Orzoff continued to develop restaurant concepts together until Orzoff's death in 1981. Through his relationship with Orzoff, Melman formulated a philosophy based on the importance of partners, of sharing responsibilities and profits with them, and of developing and growing together. Today Melman has more than 40 working partners, most of whom have come up through the organization.

To operate so many restaurants well, Lettuce has needed to hire, train, and develop people, and then keep them happy and focused on excellence. Melman's guiding philosophy is that he is not interested in being the biggest or the best known—only in being the best he can be. He places enormous value on the more than 5,000 people who work for Lettuce Entertain You Enterprises and feels tremendous responsibility for their continued success.

Key location criteria include the following:

✓ Demographics—How many people are there in the catchment area?
✓ The average income of the catchment area population
✓ Growth or decline of the area
✓ Zoning, drainage, sewage, and utilities
✓ Convenience—How easy is it for people to get to the restaurant?
✓ Visibility—Can passersby see the restaurant?
✓ Accessibility—How accessible is the restaurant?
✓ Parking—Is parking required? If so, how many spaces are needed and what will it cost?
✓ Curbside appeal—How inviting is the restaurant?
✓ Location—How desirable is the neighborhood?

Papagus

Over the years, Melman has stayed close to the guests by using focus groups and frequent diner programs. The group's training programs are rated among the best in the business, and Melman's management style is clearly influenced by team sports. He says, "There are many similarities between running a restaurant and a team sport. However, it's not a good idea to have ten all-stars; everybody can't bat first. You need people with similar goals—people who want to win and play hard."

Melman's personal life revolves around his family. He and his wife Martha have been married for twenty-six years and have three children.

---

[1]Marilyn Alva, "Does He Still Have It?" *Restaurant Business*, **93,** 4. March 1, 1994, pp. 104-111.

Several popular types of restaurant locations include the following:
- ✓ Stand-alone restaurants
- ✓ Cluster or restaurant row
- ✓ Shopping mall
- ✓ Shopping mall—free standing
- ✓ Downtown
- ✓ Suburban

Restaurant Ambiance

The **atmosphere** that a restaurant creates has both immediate conscious and subconscious effects on guests. The immediate conscious effect is how guests react to the **ambiance** on entering the restaurant—or even more importantly as an element in the decision-making process used in selecting a restaurant. Is it noisy? Are the tables too close? The subconscious is affected by mood, lighting, furnishings, and music; these play an important role in leaving a subtle impression on guests.

Restaurant guests are placing a greater emphasis on atmospherics (the design used to create a special atmosphere). Back in the 1970s, the majority of restaurants were quite plain. Today, atmospherics are built with the restaurant concept, which has an immediate sensory impact on customers.[8]

Perhaps the most noticeable atmospheric restaurants are those with a theme. The theme will use color, sound, lighting, decor, texture, and visual stimulation to create special effects for patrons. The chain restaurants with the highest rating in atmosphere are Planet Hollywood, Hard Rock Cafe, and Chart House.

Check Your Knowledge

1. Imagine you are starting your own restaurant. In the process, you realize you need a mission statement. Write a mission statement for your new restaurant.
2. Define the following terms and briefly describe the role they play:
   a. Market
   b. Concept
   c. Ambiance

Menu Planning

The menu may be the most important ingredient in a restaurant's success. A restaurant's menu must agree with the concept; the concept must be based on what the guest in the target market expects; and the menu must exceed those expectations. The type of menu will depend on the kind of restaurant being operated.

There are six main types of menus:

À la carte menus offer items that are individually priced.

Table d'hôte menus offer a selection of one or more items for each course at a fixed price. This type of menu is used more frequently in hotels and in Europe. The advantage is the perception guests have of receiving good value.

---

[8]Robert C. Lewis and Richard E. Chambers, *Marketing Leadership in Hospitality: Foundations and Practices.* New York: Van Nostrand Reinhold, 1990, pp. 339–340.

Du jour menus list the items "of the day."

Tourist menus are used to attract tourists' attention. They frequently stress value and food that is acceptable to the tourists.

California menus are so named because, in some California restaurants, guests may order any item on the menu at any time of the day.

Cyclical menus repeat themselves over a period of time.

A menu generally consists of perhaps six to eight appetizers, two to four soups, a few salads—both as appetizers and entrees—eight to sixteen entrees, and about four to six desserts.

The many considerations in menu planning attest to the complexity of the restaurant business. Considerations include the following[9]:

✓ Needs and desires of guests
✓ Capabilities of cooks
✓ Equipment capacity and layout
✓ Consistency and availability of menu ingredients
✓ Price and pricing strategy (cost and profitability)
✓ Nutritional value
✓ Accuracy in menu
✓ Menu analysis (contribution margin)
✓ Menu design
✓ Menu engineering
✓ Chain menus

Needs and Desires of Guests

In planning a menu, the needs and desires of the guests are what is important—not what the owner, chef, or manager thinks. If it is determined that there is a niche in the market for a particular kind of restaurant, then the menu must harmonize with the theme of the restaurant.

The Olive Garden restaurants are a good example of a national chain that has developed rapidly during the past few years. The concept has been positioned and defined as middle of the road with a broad-based appeal. During the concept development phase, several focus groups were asked their opinions on topics from dishes to decor. The result has been extremely successful.

Several other restaurants have become successful by focusing on the needs and desires of the guest. Among them are Hard Rock Cafe, TGI Friday's, Red Lobster, Applebee's, and so on.

Capabilities of Cooks

The capabilities of the cooks must also harmonize with the menu and concept. An appropriate level of expertise must be employed to match the peak demands and culinary expertise expected by the guests. The length and complexity of the

[9]Walker and Lundberg, op. cit., p. 180.

menu and the number of guests to be served are both factors in determining the extent of the cooks' capabilities.

The equipment capacity and layout will have an impact on the menu and the efficiency with which the cooks can produce the food. Some restaurants have several fried or cold items on the appetizer menu simply to avoid use of the stoves and ovens, which will be needed for the entrees. A similar situation occurs with desserts; by avoiding the use of the equipment needed for the entrees, cooks find it easier to produce the volume of meals required during peak periods.

One of the best examples of effective utilization of menu and equipment is Chinese restaurants. At the beginning of many Chinese restaurant menus, there are combination dinners. The combination dinners include several courses for a fixed price. Operators of Chinese restaurants explain that about 60 to 70 percent of guests order those combinations. This helps the cooks because they can prepare for the orders and the food is produced quickly, which pleases the guests. It would create havoc if everyone ordered à la carte items because the kitchen and the cooks could not handle the volume in this way.

Equipment Capacity and Layout

All restaurant menus should be developed with regard to the capacity and layout of the equipment. Anyone who has worked in a busy kitchen on a Friday or Saturday night and been "slammed" will realize that part of the problem may have been too ambitious a menu (too many items requiring extensive preparation and the use of too much equipment).

If the restaurant is already in existence, it may be costly to alter the kitchen. Operators generally find it easier to alter the menu to fit the equipment. The important thing is to match the menu with the equipment and production scheduling. A menu can be created to use some equipment for appetizers; for this one reason, the appetizer selections on the menu often include one or two cold cuts, possibly a couple of salads, but mostly some deep fried items or soups. This keeps the stove and grill areas free for the entrees. The desserts, if they are not brought in, are mostly made in advance and served cold or heated in the microwave.

Other considerations include the following:
- ✓ The projected volume of sales for each menu item.
- ✓ Is the menu fixed or does it change with the seasons?
- ✓ Menu size. Large menus may call for a greater variety of equipment.
- ✓ Speed of service desired. Fast service may call for equipment of larger capacity.
- ✓ Nutritional awareness.[10]

---

[10]Walker and Lundberg, op. cit., p. 181.

Most chefs are sufficiently adaptable to be able to prepare quality meals with the equipment provided. Some may prepare a more detailed *mise en place,*[11] and others will go further to partially cook items so that they can be furnished to order. Of course, there is always the old standby—the daily special—that can take the pressure off the production line.

Consistency and Availability of Menu Ingredients

In the United States, most ingredients are available year-round. However, at certain times of the year, some items become more expensive. This is because they are out of season—in economic terms, the demand exceeds the supply so the price goes up. An example of this would be if a storm in the Gulf of Mexico disrupts the supply of fresh fish and shellfish and causes an increase in price. To offset this kind of situation, some operators print their menus daily. Others may purchase a quantity of frozen items when the prices are low.

Price and Pricing Strategy

The target market and concept will, to a large extent, determine the menu price ranges. An example might be a neighborhood restaurant where the appetizers are priced from $3.25 to $6.95 and entrees are in the $6.95 to $11.95 price range. The selling price of each item must be acceptable to the market and profitable to the restaurateur. Factors that go into this decision include the following:
  ✓ What is the competition charging for a similar item?
  ✓ What is the item's food cost?
  ✓ What is the cost of labor that goes into the item?
  ✓ What other costs must be covered?
  ✓ What profit is expected by the operator?
  ✓ What is the contribution margin of the item?[12]

Figure 6–4 illustrates the factors that influence a restaurant's menu prices. There are two main ways to price menus. A comparative approach analyzes the price ranges of the competition and determines the price range for appetizers, entrees, and desserts. The second method is to cost the individual dish item on the menu and multiply it by the ratio amount necessary to achieve the desired food cost percentage. For example, to achieve a 30 percent food cost for an item priced at $6.95 on the menu, the food cost would have to be $2.09. Beverage items are priced the same way. This method will result in the same expected food cost percentage for each item. It would be great if we lived in such a perfect world. The problem is that if some items were priced out according to a 30 percent food cost they might appear to be overpriced according to customers' perceptions. For example, some of the more expensive meat and fish would price out at $18 to $21 when the restaurant would prefer to keep entree

---

[11]French for *everything in place.* It means all the preparation that goes into cooking before the actual cooking starts.
[12]Walker and Lundberg, op. cit., p. 187.

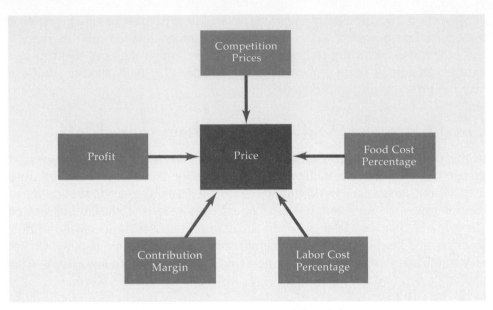

Figure 6–4 *Factors That Influence a Restaurant's Menu Prices*

prices under $15. To balance this, restaurants lower the margin on the more expensive meat and fish items—as long as there are only one or two of them—and raise the price on some of the other items, such as soup, salad, chicken, and pasta. This approach is called the **weighted average,** whereby the factors of food cost percentage, contribution margin, and sales volume are weighted.

Nutritional Value

A more health-conscious customer has prompted most restaurant operators to make changes not only to the menu selections but also to the preparation methods. Restaurant operators are using more chicken, fish, seafood, and pasta items on the menus today compared with a few years ago. Beef is more lean than ever before. All of these items are being prepared in more healthful ways such as broiling, poaching, braising, casseroling, or rotisserieing instead of frying.

Increasingly, restaurants are publishing the nutritional value of their food. McDonald's has taken a leadership role in this. Other restaurants are utilizing a heart-healthy symbol to signify that the menu item is suitable for guests with concerns about heart-healthy eating. Many restaurants are changing the oil used from the saturated fat, which is high in cholesterol, to 100 percent vegetable oil or canola oil, which is cholesterol free.

Accuracy in Menu

Laws prohibit misrepresentation of items being sold. In the case of restaurants, the so-called truth-in-menu laws refer to the fact that descriptions on the menu must be accurate. Prime beef must be prime cut, not some other grade, fresh vegetables must be fresh, not frozen, and Maine lobster had better actually come from Maine. Some restaurants have received sizable fines for violations of accuracy in menu.

Menu Analysis

One of the earliest approaches to menu analysis was developed by Jack Miller. He called the best-selling items *winners;* they not only sold more but were also at a lower food cost percentage. In 1982, Michael Kasavana and Donald Smith developed menu engineering, in which the best items are called *stars*—those that have the highest contribution margin and the highest sales. Later, David Pavesic suggested that a combination of three variables—**food cost percentage** (percentage of the selling price of an item that must be spent to purchase the raw ingredients), **contribution margin,** and **sales volume**—should be used.

Another key variable in menu analysis is labor costs. A menu item may take several hours to prepare, and it may be difficult to precisely calculate the time a cook spends in preparation of the dish. Operators add the total food and labor costs together to determine prime cost, which should not exceed about 60 to 65 percent of sales. The remaining 35 to 40 percent is for overhead and profit.

Menu Engineering

Menu engineering is a sophisticated approach to setting menu prices and controlling costs. It operates on the principle that the food cost percentage of each menu item is not as important as the total contribution margin of the menu as a whole. Usually this means that the food cost percentage of a menu item could be larger than desired, yet, the total contribution margin of the menu will increase. Through menu engineering, menu items that should be repositioned, dropped, repriced, or simply left alone can be identified.

Menu Design and Layout

Basic menus can be recited by the server. Casual menus are sometimes written on a chalk or similar type board. Quick-service menus are often illuminated above the order counter. More formal menus are generally single page, or folded with three or more pages. Some describe the restaurant and type of food offered; most have beverage suggestions and a wine selection. The more upscale American-Continental restaurants have a separate wine list.

Some menus are more distinctive than others, with pictures of the items or at least enticing descriptions of the food. Research indicates that there is a focal point at the center of the right hand page; this is the spot in which to place the star or signature item.[13]

Like a brochure for the hotel, a menu is a sales tool and motivational device. A menu's design can affect what guests order and how much they spend. The paper, colors, and artwork all play an important role in influencing guest decisions and help to establish a restaurant's image and ambiance.

[13]Walker and Lundberg, op. cit., p. 203.

Chain Menus

Chain menus are essentially menus that are used by chain restaurants. These menus are changing with surprising speed and creativity—and the key word is flavor. Items such as Tandoor Chicken Sandwich, lobster pot pie, TexMex egg rolls, and BLT salad have been added to the menu by one major chain. Planet Hollywood added Cajun egg rolls, the Spaghetti Warehouse added garlic cheese toast, Marie Callender's added parmesan sprinkled mushrooms, and the House of Blues added calamari with curry dipping sauce. Joe Marans, vice president of culinary development, says that with the growing popularity of ethnic food, he believes that people now expect "deep flavor." So his best-selling New Orleans BBQ shrimp are seasoned with cracked black pepper and a proprietary Louisiana spice, then pan-seared and finished with blackened voodoo beer and homemade Worcestershire sauce.

In the sandwich segment, the speed and convenience of wraps has boosted sales. A wrap is a large, usually gourmet-flavored, flour tortilla with a wide choice of fillings. A restaurant business magazine survey listed the following samplers:

Baker's Square—spicy chicken pita
Chevy's—Texas BBQ wrap
Shari's—spicy turkey burger
Pizzeria Uno—buffalo turkey roll-up
Mozzarella's—black-bean vegetarian burger

Salad items include the Cheesecake Factory's Tuna Salad San Tropez, while Dave and Buster's has added a chicken fajita salad. In the entree section, traditional fare is making room for specialty items, however comfort foods remain popular. Outback Steakhouse, for example, has added the outback rack, a 14-oz. rack of lamb served with Australian cabernet sauce. This was done to retain customers' interest.

Check Your Knowledge

1. Define the main menu types:
   a. À la Carte
   b. Table d'hôte
   c. Du jour
   d. Tourist menus
   e. California menus
   f. Cyclical menus
2. What are the factors that need to be looked at when considering the price of a menu item?

Classifications of Restaurants

There is no single definition of the various classifications of restaurants, perhaps because it is an evolving business. Most experts would agree, however, that there are two main categories: **independent restaurants** and **chain restaurants.** Other categories include designations as full-service restaurants, casual restaurants, and quick-service restaurants. Some restaurants may even fall into more than one category, for instance a restaurant can be both ethnic and quick service, such as Taco Bell.

The National Restaurant Association's figures indicate that Americans are spending an increasing number of food dollars away from home in various foodservice operations. Americans eat out about 200 times a year, or about 4 times a week. More than 50 percent of all consumers visit a restaurant on their birthday,[14] thereby making it the most popular day for eating out. Mother's Day and Valentine's Day are the second and third most popular days, respectively. The most popular meal eaten away from home is lunch, which brings in approximately 50 percent of fast-food restaurant sales. Figure 6–5 illustrates the foodservice industry sales by segments: full-service, quick-service, institutional, and other.

Restaurants can be broadly classified under individually owned restaurants and those restaurants that are part of a chain. Individual restaurants (also called indies) are typically owned by one or more owners, usually involved in the day-to-day operation of the business. Even if the owners have more than one store, each functions independently. These restaurants are not affiliated

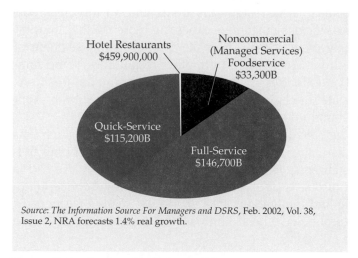

Source: *The Information Source For Managers and DSRS*, Feb. 2002, Vol. 38, Issue 2, NRA forecasts 1.4% real growth.

Figure 6–5 *Foodservice Industry Sales*

---

[14]Rocco M. Angelo and Andrew N. Vladimir, *Hospitality Today: An Introduction.* East Lansing, MI: The Educational Institute of the American Hotel and Motel Association, 1991, p. 139.

with any national brand or name. They offer the owner independence, creativity, and flexibility, but are accompanied by risk.

Chain restaurants on the other hand, comprise a group of restaurants, each identical in market, concept, design, service, food, and name. Part of the marketing strategy of a chain restaurant is to remove uncertainty from the dining experience. The same menu, food quality, level of service, and atmosphere can be found in any one of the restaurants, regardless of location. These are usually owned by family teams or other entrepreneurs.

Full-Service Restaurants

Restaurant types included in this category are fine dining, casual upscale, theme, celebrity, and steak houses.

Fine Dining

A **fine dining restaurant** is one where a good selection of menu items is offered, generally at least fifteen or more different entrees cooked to order, with nearly all the food being made on the premises from scratch using raw or fresh ingredients. Full-service restaurants may be formal or casual and may be further categorized by price, decor/atmosphere, level of formality, and menu. Most fine dining restaurants may be cross-referenced into other categories, as mentioned previously. Many of these restaurants serve **haute cuisine** (pronounced *hote*), which is a French term meaning elegant dining or *high food*. Many of the fine restaurants in the United States are based on French or Northern Italian cuisine, which, together with fine Chinese cuisine, are considered by many Western connoisseurs to be the finest in the world.

Most fine dining restaurants are independently owned and operated by an entrepreneur or a partnership. These restaurants are in almost every neighborhood. Today, with value-conscious customers expecting more for their money, it is becoming increasingly more difficult to make a profit in this segment of the business because of strong competition from other restaurants. Some companies, such as Marriott and Stouffer's, who began in the restaurant business, have since sold their restaurant chains because they could not yield the profit margin that management and investors expected.

The *Nation's Restaurant News* (*NRN*) Fine Dining Hall of Fame, which was launched in 1980, now has more than 250 restaurants. Most of them are full-service, independent restaurants. These restaurants are selected by the *NRN*'s editors and included on the basis of excellence in food quality, service, innovation, and staff training and motivation. Over the years, many of America's finest independent restaurants have been honored. Among the inductees into the Hall of Fame are the following:

Berkeley, CA—Chez Panisse
Los Angeles, CA—Spago, The Grill, Campanile, Water Grill
San Francisco, CA—La Folie, Aqua, Boulevard
St. Helena, CA—Terra

Greenwich, CT—Restaurant Jean-Louis

Orlando, FL—The Citrus Club

Tampa, FL—Bern's Steak House, Columbia

Arlington Hills, IL—Le Titi de Paris

Chicago, IL—Morton's, Arun's, Les Nomades

New Orleans, LA—Brigtsen's, Bayona, Commander's Palace

Boston, MA—Anthony's Pier 4, L'Espalier, Rialto

Kansas City, MO—The American Restaurant

St. Louis, MO—Tony's

New York, NY—Lutece, The Four Seasons, Gramercy Tavern, Aquavit, La Caravelle, Lespinasse, Daniel

Durham, NC—Magnolia Grill

Cincinnati, OH—Maisonette

Philadelphia, PA—Le Bec-Fin, Fountain at the Four Seasons Hotel, Susanna Foo Chinese Cuisine

Dallas, TX—The Mansion on Turtle Creek, Zodiac, The French Room

Houston, TX—Rotisserie for Beef and Bird, Café Annie, Américas

San Antonio, TX—Restaurant Biga

Williamsburg, VA—The Trellis

Seattle, WA—Campagne, Rover's

Washington, DC—Germaine's, I Ricchi, Galileo, Kinkead's

It is interesting to notice how many of these have a French influence in their name. In the United States, there are a number of restaurant cities, including New York, Chicago, Los Angeles, New Orleans, San Francisco, Boston, Atlanta, Houston, and Denver. Each of these cities has an example of a restaurateur extraordinaire.

In recent years, fine dining has become more fun. At places like Osteria del Circo in New York, operators are looking for guests who want spectacular meals without the fuss. Marco Maccioni, son of Sirio Maccioni of the famed Le Cirque, says that the sons did not want to simply clone Le Cirque. Thus, the brothers turned to a circus theme for its ambiance. For the menu, they sought inspiration from Mama's home cooking—pizza, pasta, and comfortable, braised dishes.

Many cities have independent fine dining restaurants that pursue those who are not content with wings and deep-fried cheese. Chefs are therefore making approachable, yet provocative food; each course is expertly prepared and may be served with wine. After dinner, guests head for the smoking room to enjoy fine cigars and single-malt scotches.

The top independent restaurant in terms of sales is the Tavern on the Green in New York City, which opened in 1976. Tavern on the Green has been number one on the most financially successful list according to Restaurants and Institutions, which compiles an annual Top 10 list. It has sales of more than $26 million from 1,000 seats—including banquets with an average dinner check of $43.50—and serves 545,000 people a year. Now that's cooking!

---

[15]"R & I Top Independents," *Restaurants and Institutions*, **102**, 10, April 1992, p. 90, and updated courtesy of Tavern on the Green, September 14, 2002.

Tavern on the Green
(Courtesy Tavern on the Green.)

Other restaurants of interest are operated by celebrity chefs like Wolfgang Puck, co-owner of Spago and Chinois in Los Angeles, and Alice Waters of Chez Panisse in Berkeley, California. Both have done much to inspire a new generation of talented chefs. Alice Waters has been a role model for many female chefs and has received numerous awards and published several cookbooks, including one for children.

The level of service in fine dining restaurants is generally high, with a hostess or host to greet and seat patrons. Captains and food servers advise guests of special items and assist with the description and selection of dishes during order taking. If there is no separate sommelier (wine waiter), the captain or food server may offer a description of the wine that will complement the meal and assist with the order taking. Some upscale or luxury full-service restaurants have table-side cooking and French service from a gueridon cart.[16]

The decor of a full-service restaurant is generally compatible with the overall ambiance and theme that the restaurant is seeking to create. These elements of food, service, and decor create a memorable experience for the restaurant guest.

There is no national fine dining luxury restaurant chain, possibly due to the following factors:

- ✓ Upscale full-service restaurants are not only labor intensive, but they also require a greater degree of skill to operate. The more sophisticated operation makes for a high labor cost.
- ✓ Only a small percentage of the population can afford the high prices that these restaurants need to charge by reason of their expensive location, decor, and labor. The restaurant is likely to be located in the high-rent district and employ a highly skilled chef and kitchen and service personnel who add to the labor costs. The luxurious furnishings and appointments of the restaurant may easily cost several million dollars. It takes more than a few dinners to pay for all these costs.

---

[16]A wheelable cart that is used to add flair to table-side service. It is also used for flambé dishes.

Court of the Two Sisters. One famous restaurant in New Orleans is the Court of the Two Sisters. It has the names of prisoners from the various wars inscribed on the walls of the entrance way. (Courtesy Court of the Two Sisters.)

✓ The logistics of a national chain may prove difficult or costly to manage. Overhead costs may outweigh savings of economy of scale.

✓ Economies of scale are not as easily reaped with such a sophisticated product—a freshly prepared, high-quality meal.

✓ Consistency and quality are very difficult to maintain for such a sophisticated clientele.

✓ There is limited market appeal. This type of restaurant is more likely to succeed in major cities such as New York, Los Angeles, Boston, Chicago, New Orleans, Houston, Atlanta, and Philadelphia. There are a number of regional or greater metropolitan restaurants, each with a few locations in a city. There is an obvious benefit in both purchasing for and marketing a cluster of restaurants. In fact, most national chains have adopted the cluster concept because it increases customer awareness and builds traffic (customers).

The owner-operators of the upscale, white tablecloth restaurants have had more than their fair share of bad fortune in the past few years. First came the reduction in the tax deductibility for business entertainment from 100 percent to 80 percent, which then dropped to 50 percent. This reduced the so-called "business lunch." A general decline in the consumption of alcohol also affected the success of fine dining establishments. In October 1987 the Wall Street stock market plunged. This forced the street-smart restaurateurs to reexamine every aspect of their business.

Success stories in such changing[17] times are hard to find. However, one savvy restaurateur even managed to make a profit with sales of $1.1 million in 1990, whereas he had experienced a loss with sales of $2 million in 1987. This was achieved using the following survival tactics:

✓ Renegotiating the restaurant's lease from $24,000 to $12,000 a month

✓ Trimming payroll, starting at the top, from an annual payroll of $675,000 in May 1989 to $200,000 in May 1991—and it's still dropping

✓ Using the same menu for lunch and dinner. This streamlined the *mise en place*—for example, the saucier (sauce chef) could come in the morning

[17]Paul Fumkin, "Prunelle Thrives Despite Tough N.Y. Obstacles," *Nation's Restaurant News,* 25, 20, May 20, 1991, p. 80.

and prepare all of the sauces for the entire day. The special at lunch was always the special at dinner.

✓ Simplifying menu terminology to speed service

✓ Changing menu price structure

✓ Building up private-banquet business

✓ Controlling cost. In 1986, food cost was 32 percent of sales, and labor cost was 34 percent of sales; in 1991, food cost was 27 percent of sales, and labor cost was 20 percent of sales.

These tactics are necessary for survival in the fiercely competitive restaurant business.

The eagerly anticipated reopening of the famed New York restaurant Le Cirque 2000 gave critics plenty to rave about. Sirio Maccioni opened the original Le Cirque in the Mayfair Hotel in 1974 and employed an army of chefs who evolved into entrepreneurs. During those years, Le Cirque became a major contributor to the American appreciation of fine French dining, garnering award after award.

Le Cirque is credited with introducing Americans to dishes that would later become standard fare of upscale restaurants. Among such dishes are potato-crusted bars, crème brûlée, white truffles, and pasta primavera. Signature dishes at Le Cirque 2000 include codfish scented with Szechwan pepper, garnished with a casserole of Swiss chard and beans; cassolette of spring vegetables with chopped black truffles; and turbot grilled on a bed of dried fennel and garnished with tender vegetables. These items are offered along with classic French standards such as bouillabaisse and pot-au-feu.[18]

Casual Upscale Restaurant

One growing segment of foodservice is **casual upscale dining.** These types of restaurants offer popular food in settings that are more appealing than a casual restaurant. Dining here is usually less time consuming and less elaborate than the fine dining restaurants, however, they still employ a professional and attentive service. Most casual upscale restaurants have a unifying theme that is apparent in the design of their menu, interior decor, and often the exterior of the building. Menu specialties are highly diverse. Many restaurants have an ethnic theme. The theme serves to augment the diner's experience. Casual upscale dining restaurants can be either independently owned or part of a restaurant chain. Examples of upscale chain dining restaurants are Chili's, On the Border, and Sebastian's.

Theme Restaurants

Many **theme restaurants** are a combination of a sophisticated specialty and several other types of restaurants. They generally serve a limited menu but aim to wow the guest by the total experience. Of the many popular theme restau-

[18]Milford Prewitt, "Maccioni Says Le Cirque 2000 Remains a Work in Progress," *Nation's Restaurant News,* **31,** 25, June 23, 1997, pp. 3, 6.

Personal Profile: Sarah Stegner

Dining Room Chef, The Ritz–Carlton, Chicago

Sara Stegner, thirty-five, joined The Ritz-Carlton Chicago in 1984, on graduation from the Dumas Pere Cooking School and was immediately recognized as a major talent.

The Evanston, Illinois, native grew up in a family devoted to food. Her grandmother was a caterer "before women did those kinds of things" and her grandfather was an avid backyard vegetable gardener. The table was the center of the family and where Stegner's passion for food emerged.

Following a year studying classical guitar at Northwestern University, Stegner followed her heart and enrolled at the Dumas Pere Cooking School. She graduated with a chef's certificate one year later and was hired as an apprentice at The Ritz-Carlton Chicago, where she has remained.

In 1990, after six years of working in various culinary capacities (including a first job of cleaning fish for twelve hours a day), Stegner was promoted to chef of The Dining Room. She worked for years under the guiding hands of Fernand Gutierrez, former executive chef and director of food and beverage at The Ritz-Carlton Chicago, and current food and beverage director at Four Seasons Mexico City. Since then, Stegner has distinguished herself as one of America's most creative young chefs.

As a result of her talents, she has captured many national honors. Chef Stegner was named "Best Chef of the Midwest in 1998" by the prestigious James Beard Foundation and The Dining Room was recently named "One of the Top 5 Restaurants in Chicago in 1999" by *Gourmet* magazine and received "Four Stars" from the *Chicago Tribune*. In addition, it is ranked "Best Hotel Dining Room in Chicago in 1999" by the prestigious Zagat Chicago Restaurant Guide and was named "Best Restaurant in Chicago in 1996" by *Gourmet;* "One of the Top 13 Hotel Dining Rooms in the U.S. in 1996" by *Bon*

(Courtesy Sarah Stegner.)

Appetit; and "One of the Top 10 Hotel Restaurants in the World in 1996" by *Hotels* magazine.

Chef Stegner is recipient of the "1995 Robert Mondavi Culinary Award of Excellence" and captured the national title of "1994 Rising Star Chef of the Year in America" by the James Beard Foundation. She also holds the title of Prix Culinaire International Pierre Taittinger 1991 U.S. Winner, where she represented America in the finals in Paris and was the only female chef present at the global competition.

In recent years, Chef Stegner has enjoyed periodic training in France, under the expertise of Chef Pierre Orsi at his two-star Michelin Pierre Orsi Restaurant in Lyon, France, and with chefs Bertolli and Gerard Bessin in Paris.

She also finds time to donate her talents to charitable causes. Six years ago, she founded The Women Chefs of Chicago, comprised of the city's top female chefs who donate cuisine for numerous events throughout the city to raise money for charity. Under her direction, The Women Chefs of Chicago have helped raise over $500,000 for Chicagoland charities in the past few years.

Drawing on The Dining Room's classic elegance and French culinary tradition, Stegner marries French technique with American products, sometimes adding a playful twist. She uses the finest seasonal produce from award-winning Midwest vegetable farmers and cheesemakers and relies on infused vegetable oils and juices to maintain strong, yet light dishes.

Her contemporary cooking results in dishes such as 70th Street Farm heirloom tomatoes with petite watercress and sweet pea vine salad drizzled with olive oil and twenty-five-year-old balsamic vinegar and slow-roasted salmon with parsley-brioche crust, parsnip puree, braised leeks, and apple cream sauce.

rants, two stand out. The first highlights the nostalgia of the 1950s, as done in the T-Bird and Corvette diners. These restaurants serve all-American food such as the perennial meatloaf in a fun atmosphere that is a throwback to the seemingly more carefree 1950s. The food servers appear in short polka-dot skirts with gym shoes and bobby socks.

The second popular theme restaurant is the dinner house category; among some of the better known national and regional chains are TGI Friday's, Houlihan's, and Bennigan's. These are casual American bistro-type restaurants that combine a lively atmosphere created in part by assorted bric-a-brac to decorate the various ledges and walls. These restaurants have remained popular over the past twenty years. In a prime location, they can do extremely well.

People are attracted to theme restaurants because they offer a total experience and a social meeting place. This is achieved through decoration and atmosphere and allows the restaurant to offer a limited menu that blends with the theme. Throughout the United States and the world, there are numerous theme restaurants that stand out for one reason or another. Among them are decors featuring airplanes, railway, dining cars, rock and roll, 1960s nostalgia, and many others.

Celebrity Restaurants

Celebrity-owned restaurants have been growing in popularity. Some celebrities, such as Wolfgang Puck, came from a culinary background, while others, like Naomi Campbell, Claudia Schiffer, and Elle Macpherson (owners of the Fashion Café), did not. A number of sports celebrities also have restaurants. Among them are Michael Jordan, Dan Marino, Junior Seau, and Wayne Gretzky. Television and movie stars have also gotten into the act. Oprah Winfrey has been part owner of The Eccentric in Chicago for a number of years. Dustin Hoffman and Henry Winkler are investors in Campanile, a popular Los Angeles restaurant. Dive, in Century City (Los Angeles), is owned by Steven Spielberg; House of Blues, by Denzel Washington, Georgia, and Dan Ackroyd. Musicians Kenny Rogers and Gloria Estefan are also restaurant owners.

Celebrity restaurants generally have an extra zing to them—a winning combination of design, atmosphere, food, and perhaps the thrill of an occasional visit by the owner(s). For example, Fashion Café, in New York, invites the guest to literally step through the lens of a camera into the glamorous world of fashion. Guests are seated in the Milan, Paris, or New York rooms, where they are entertained with daily fashion shows.

Spago, one of Wolfgang Puck's Restaurants

Corporate Profile: Fashion Café

The challenge of creating the Fashion Café Collection was to combine the intellectual appreciation of fashion with visual, stimulating displays. The nature of the collection in each location was dictated by the city and country. Local and foreign cultures interpret fashion differently, including everything from popular to local high culture.

The advent of the super model has brought a new-found focus upon the industry. Entertainment influences are, and will continue to be, a key element of fashion. Media plays a vital role as a "mood meter." Through cin-

ema, television, and specialty channels such as MTV, the media allows centuries of fashion to be viewed in mere minutes. These influences provide the strongest, visual marker of what is happening in fashion today. Fashion Café combined these factors, creating a unique crossroad between everyday living and glamorous runways.

Fashion Café super model partners Claudia Schiffer, Elle Macpherson, Naomi Campbell, along with Jacqueline Nims (director of acquisitions/curator) and Tommaso Buti (president and CEO), invited their customers into the glamorous world of fashion with a series of daily fashion shows. The fashion shows allowed patrons to view the creations of some of the world's top designers, as well as those of hot, new designers.

No longer in business, the Fashion Café is an example of how some theme restaurants are more of a fad and become unfashionable when they do not offer great food, service, and value.

Steak Houses

The steak restaurant segment is quite buoyant in spite of nutritional concerns. The upscale steak dinner houses, like Morton's of Chicago, Ruth Chris's, and Houston's, continue to attract the expense account and "occasion" diners. Some restaurants are adding additional value-priced items like chicken and fish to their menus in order to attract more customers. Steak restaurant operators admit that they are not expecting to see the same customer every week, but hopefully every two or three weeks. The Chart House chain is careful to market their menu as including seafood and chicken, but steak is at the heart of the business, with 60 percent of sales from red meat.[19]

[19]"Market Share Report," *Restaurant Business,* **91,** 9, June 10, 1992, p. 156.

Corporate Profile: Outback Steakhouse

The founders of Outback Steakhouse have proven that unconventional methods can lead to profitable results. Such methods include opening solely for dinner, sacrificing dining-room seats for back-of-the-house efficiency, limiting servers to three tables each, and handing 10 percent of cash flow to the restaurants' general managers.

March 1988 saw the opening of the first Outback Steakhouse. Outback's founders, Chris Sullivan, Robert Basham, and Senior Vice-President Tim Gannon, know plenty about the philosophy "No rules, just right" because they have lived it since day one. Even the timing of their venture to launch a casual steak place came when many pundits were pronouncing red meat consumption dead in America.

The chain went public in 1990 and has since created a track record of strong earnings. In 1992, Outback posted the strongest sales growth in the casual-steakhouse sector (77.9 percent), as well as the fastest unit growth (71.8 percent). In 1993, its food cost was 39 percent of sales, versus 36 percent or less for most restaurant chains. It was evident that the three founders were piloting one of the country's hottest restaurant concepts. The trio found themselves with 230 restaurants, instead of the five they originally envisioned.

Robert Basham, cofounder, president, and chief operating officer at Outback Steakhouse, was given the Operator of the Year award at MUFSO '96 (Multi-Unit Foodservice Operators Conference). He has helped expand the chain, a pioneer in the steak house of the

1990s, to more than 600 in 2000 restaurants with some of the highest sales per unit in the industry in spite the fact that it only serves dinner.

Perhaps the strongest indication of what this company is about lies in its corporate structure, or lack thereof. Despite its rapid growth, the company has no public relations department, no human resources department, and no recruiting apparatus. In addition, the Outback Steakhouse headquarters is very different from that of a typical restaurant company. There is no lavish tower—only modest office space in an average suburban complex. Instead of settling into a conservative chair and browsing through a magazine-lined coffee table (as is the case in most reception areas), at Outback you must belly up to an actual bar, brass foot rail and all, to announce your arrival.

Also, Outback's dining experience—large, highly seasoned portions of food for moderate prices—is so in tune with today's dining experience that patrons in many of its restaurants experience hour-long dinner waits seven nights a week. The friendly service is notable, from the host who opens the door and greets guests, to the well-trained servers, who casually sit down next to patrons in the booths and explain the house specialties featured on the menu.

Using such tactics and their "No rules, just right" philosophy, they have accomplished two main goals: discipline and solid growth. Good profits and excellent marketing potentials show just how successful the business has become.

Ponderosa, with 465 units, and Bonanza, with 156 units, have sales of $773 million together and are owned and operated by Metromedia Steak House, Inc. They are both family concepts featuring counter service and food bars. These restaurants have also added items to their menu in order to broaden customer appeal. Some of these items are an expansion of the Grand Buffet to include Mexican food items like chimichangas, tamales, and make-your-own burritos, as well as barbecued ribs and chicken.

Other chains in this segment include Outback Steakhouse, which is actually the number one volume steak sales restaurant, with sales of $1.07 billion. Stewart Anderson's Black Angus, Golden Corral, Western Sizzlin', and Ryan's Family Steak Houses all have sales of more than $250 million each. In fact, chains have the biggest stake in the segment.

Casual Dining and Dinner House Restaurants

The types of restaurants that can be included in the casual dining restaurants category are as follows:

Midscale casual restaurants
Family restaurants
Ethnic restaurants
Specialty restaurants

As implied, **casual dining** is relaxed and could include restaurants from several classifications: chain or independent, ethnic, or theme. Hard Rock Cafe, TGI Friday's, The Olive Garden, Houston's, and Red Lobster are good examples of casual dining.

Houston's is a leader in the casual restaurant segment with about $5.5 million in average per unit sales in its thirty-five restaurants. The menu is limited to about forty items and focuses on American cuisine, with a $14 average per-person ticket for lunch and a cost of $25 to $35 for dinner. While encouraging local individuality in its restaurants and maintaining exceptional executive and unit general manager stability, it succeeds with no franchising and virtually no advertising.[20]

Over the past few years, the trend in **dinner house restaurants** has been toward more casual dining. This trend merely reflects the mode of society. Dinner house restaurants have become fun places to let off steam. There are a variety of restaurant chains that call themselves *dinner house restaurants*. Some of them could even fit into the theme category. Table 6–1 lists some of the better known dinner house chains.

Hard Rock Cafe

[20]Charles Bernstein, "Chains, Champions, and Contenders," *Restaurants and Institutions*, **107**, 3, February 1, 1997.

Table 6–1
Dinner House Chains Ranked by Number of U.S. Units

Rank	Chain	No. of Units[a]
1	Applebee's Neighborhood Grill & Bar	1,142
2	Chili's Grill & Bar	626
3	Red Lobster	625
4	Outback Steakhouse	574
5	Ruby Tuesday	475
6	Olive Garden	464
7	T.G.I Friday's	452
8	Lonestar Steakhouse and Saloon	265
9	Bennigan's	237
10	Hooters	234

Source: Alan J. Liddle, "Top 100 Chain and Company Rankings," *Nation's Restaurant News,* **24,** 26, June 26, 2000, p. 136.
[a]Actual results, estimates, or projections.

Many dinner house restaurants have a casual, eclectic decor that may promote a theme. Chart House, for example, is a steak and seafood chain that has a nautical theme.

Friday's is an American bistro dinner house with a full menu and a decor of bric-a-brac that contributes to the fun atmosphere. Friday's is a chain that has been in operation for nearly forty years, so the concept has stood the test of time. Friday's is featured in Chapter 7, "Restaurant Operations," as a corporation of excellence.

A recent *Restaurants and Institutions* magazine survey indicated that the following are America's favorite chains in various categories. Their respective scores, out of a possible five points, are also shown.

Friday's
(Courtesy T.G.I. Friday's.)

Burgers	1. In-N-Out Burger	3.7
	2. Wendy's	3.58
Pizza	1. Papa John's	3.57
	2. Pizza Hut	3.47
Chicken	1. Kenny Rogers Roaster	3.61
	2. Chick-fil-A	3.58
Steak houses	1. Morton's of Chicago	3.93
	2. Outback Steakhouse	3.85
Dinner houses	1. Chart House	3.93
	2. Cheesecake Factory	3.80
	3. Olive Garden	3.76
Seafood	1. Red Lobster	3.71
	2. Legal Sea Foods	3.71

One interesting finding of the survey was the difference between male and female respondents' rankings of restaurants. For instance, Chart House was the number one choice of females, whereas it was ranked number eight by men. Similarly, Morton's of Chicago was ranked number one by males, but number twenty-one by females.

Many chains are making moves toward "high-end casual"—a segment that retains the informality of casual dining, but with prices and food quality resembling that of fine dining. To take advantage of this kind of opportunity, some restaurant companies are buying other chains' concepts and refining them. In other cases, they are developing a concept in-house, with an eye toward targeting a specific price point. Brinker International trend-watcher Lane Cardwell says there is evidence that the casual dining segment is "maturing." This is also known as increased segmentation.

Whatever it is called, high-end, casual dining is potentially uncreative. According to the National Restaurant Association, food costs averaged 27 percent at full-service restaurants with a typical tab of $10 or more, versus 29 percent at full-service eateries with average checks below $10. Also, higher-margin beverage sales were 64 percent greater at more expensive restaurants. The higher checks help leverage the fixed and variable costs to yield greater profit margins, provided guests don't balk at the higher check averages. The question is how many times a week, or a month, a customer will pay $30+ per person for a meal—no matter how much value they're getting.

Chart House, one of the pioneers of this segment, decided to sell its popular lower check Islands chain in order to concentrate on the higher check core concept. They have also engaged the services of Rich Melman to help stimulate customer counts. The major success story in this segment is Outback Steakhouse, the steak chain that made a $20 average check profitable at more than 600 units nationally.

Family Restaurants

Family restaurants evolved from the coffee shop style of restaurant. In this segment, most restaurants are individually or family operated. Family restaurants are generally located in or with easy access to the suburbs. Most offer an informal setting with a simple menu and service designed to please all of the family. Some of these restaurants offer alcoholic beverages, which mostly consist of beer, wine, and perhaps a cocktail special. Usually, there is a hostess/cashier standing near the entrance to greet and seat guests while food servers take the orders and bring the plated food from the kitchen. Some family restaurants have incorporated salad and dessert bars to offer more variety and increase the average check. Table 6–2 ranks the popular family restaurant chains.

The lines separating the various restaurants and chains in the family segment are blurring as operators upscale their concepts. Flagstar Co.'s acquisition of Coco's and Carrow's family restaurant brands have created the high-end niche of family dining—somewhere between traditional coffee shops and the casual dining segment. The value-oriented operator in the family dining segment is Denny's, also owned by Flagstar. The more upscale family concepts include Perkins, Marie Callender's, and Cracker Barrel, all of which are sometimes referred to as the "relaxed" segment. These chains tend to have higher check averages than do traditional and value-oriented family chains, and compete not only with them, but also with moderately priced, casual-themed operators, such as Applebee's and TGI Friday's.

Karen Brennan, vice president of marketing for the Coco's concept, says that people's use of restaurants is very different from five years ago. Consumers are thinking in terms of "meal solutions." The operators in this segment are seeking to capitalize on two trends affecting the industry as a whole—the tenden-

Table 6–2
Family Chains Ranked by U.S. System-Wide Sales

Rank	Chain	Fiscal Year-End	Latest (in Millions)[a]
1	Denny's	Dec. 1999	$2,079.0
2	Cracker Barrell Old Country Store	July. 1999	1,162.9
3	IHOP	Dec. 1999	1,076.6
4	Shoney's	Oct. 1999	868.8
5	Perkins Restaurant and Bakery	Dec. 1999	790.4
6	Bob Evans Restaurants	April. 2000	727.3
7	Friendly's Ice Cream	Dec. 1999	670.9
8	Waffle House	Dec. 1999	620.0
9	Steak 'n Shake	Sept. 1999	423.8
10	Big Boy Restaurant and Bakery	Dec. 1999	395.0

Source: Alan J. Liddle, "Top 100 Chain and Company Rankings," *Nation's Restaurant News,* **24,** 26, June 26, 2000, p. 122.
[a]Actual results, estimates, or projections.

Applebee's

cy of families to dine out together more often and the quest among adults for higher quality, more flavorful food offerings. Cracker Barrel derives 45 percent of its restaurant sales from the dinner "daypart" (the dinner menu is served throughout most of the day), while only about 20 percent comes from breakfast. The average check is just a little more than $6, almost $1 more than Denny's. In TV advertising, Cracker Barrel promotes the dinner daypart menu items, including a shrimp platter, a roast-pork dish, and a turkey dinner.[21]

Ethnic Restaurants

The majority of **ethnic restaurants** are independently owned and operated. The owners and their families provide something different for the adventurous diner or a taste of home for those of the same ethnic background as the restaurant. The traditional ethnic restaurants sprang up to cater to the taste of the various immigrant groups—Italian, Chinese, and so on.

Perhaps the fastest growing segment of ethnic restaurants in the United States, popularity-wise, is Mexican. Mexican food has a heavy representation in the southwestern states, although, because of near-market saturation, the chains are spreading east. Taco Bell is the Mexican quick-service market leader with a 60 percent share. This *Fortune 500* company has achieved this incredible result with a value-pricing policy that has increased traffic in all units. As of 2000, there were more than 7,000 units with sales of close to $5 billion.

The next biggest chain in the Mexican food segment, in terms of sales, is Chi-Chi's. Chi-Chi's 200 units have total sales of $300 million. The third largest quick-service chain is Del Taco Inc. of Costa Mesa, California, with 300 restaurants and sales of $235 million. El Torito is fourth largest with 104 units producing $229.4 million in sales. These Mexican-food chains can offer a variety of items on a value menu, starting at 49 cents.

[21]Mark Hamstra, "When Segments Collide: Family Restaurants Blaze Casual Trails," *Nation's Restaurant News,* **31,** 9, March 3, 1997.

Personal and Corporate Profile: Norman Brinker

Chairman and CEO of Brinker International

Traveling the road to the top is a long and tedious journey. Few people in this world have been able to make it. Among the few is none other than Norman Brinker, chairman and CEO of Brinker International. Many words can be used to describe Norman: courageous, inspirational, quality minded, tough minded, and ambitious. But to really know and understand why Norman is praised so much, one must read his life story.

Norman was born in Denver, Colorado. When he was ten, he and his parents moved to New Mexico where he raised rabbits and bred cocker spaniels for pocket money. His parents taught him the real meaning of being honest and hard working. They set the foundation for his strong morals and strength, which would always be important to Norman. His father always said to him, "If you say you are going to do something, you do it. Never, never take a shortcut and never, never tell anything but the truth." His mother taught him the goodness of doing things for the community and church. With the teachings of his parents to support him, he

(Courtesy of Norman Brinker.)

decided to go to college. He attended San Diego State University (SDSU) where he served as Associated Students' president from 1956 to 1957. He graduated with honors in marketing in 1957.

Right after graduation, he started working with Jack-in-the-Box founder Robert Peterson. By 1965, he owned 20 percent of the chain. At age thirty-two, Norman thought that it was time for him to move on so he first started out with a coffee shop in Dallas. In 1966 though, he decided to introduce a new kind of dining by opening up a Steak & Ale house. This was a casual dining place with a salad bar. Although this type of business had not been successful in the past, the Steak & Ale house prospered and had other people grasping the new concept of dining. In 1971, Steak & Ale went public. It had a total of 100 restaurants in 1976 when it merged with Pillsbury Company. Norman became executive vice president and board member of Pillsbury Company. In 1982, he became president of the Pillsbury Restaurant Group, which included Burger King, Steak & Ale, Bennigan's, and Poppin' Fresh restau-

Our major cities offer a great variety of ethnic restaurants and their popularity is increasing. For example, in 1985 in San Diego, America's sixth largest city, there were no Thai restaurants. Today there are twenty-two, in addition to new Afghan and Ethiopian restaurants.

Specialty Restaurants

Specialty restaurants feature a particular kind of food that is usually theme related. Steak houses that are not upscale usually fall under this category as do seafood restaurants and brew pubs. Seafood restaurants combine a healthy, low-fat image with a popular food product. A number of chains have introduced more baked and broiled items and dropped some of the fried ones. These seafood places boast varied themes for ambiance to enhance the diner's experience in their restaurants. The seafood-franchising segment is dominated by four chains: Red Lobster, Long John Silver, Captain D's, and Landry's Seafood House. Red Lobster is widely regarded as the national chain of excellence in the seafood segment.

rants, and was the second largest restaurant organization in the world. In 1983, he invested in and became chairman of Chili's Inc., which went public and was renamed Brinker International. Brinker International has seven chains with an annual income of about $1.7 billion and employs about 70,000 people.

His great courage, strong will, and love of life are evidenced by a brief episode from his life. In 1993, Norman had a polo accident that could have left him dead or at least paralyzed. He was in a deep coma and then on a respirator for fourteen days. He awoke only to realize that he was paralyzed. The doctors predicted that it would take at least a year to see any significant recovery. Norman, though, said he'd be back home in two months—and he was. In fact, Norman was able to go home one day earlier than he had predicted. He says, "I teach philosophy. When I first came into this business people were called operators. . . . Then, about twenty years ago, I said we need to talk about managers and management. . . . Now, we've got to be leaders. . . . It means you must have vision, you're ahead of the game, you inspire people." Norman was back to work four months after his accident. Although he continued horseback riding, he gave up polo. (Always an enthusiastic horseman, Norman competed in a number of sporting events in his early days. He won a berth on the 1952 U.S. Olympic Equestrian Team and also competed in the 1954 World Championships in Budapest, Hungary, as a member of the U.S. Modern Pentathlon Team.)

For his great work in the business world, he was named Distinguished Alumnus for the SDSU College of Business Administration in 1977. *Venture* magazine, Texas A&M University, and Southern Methodist University have also named him their Entrepreneur of the Year. In 1996, he coauthored *On the Brink: The Life and Leadership of Norman Brinker* with Donald T. Phillips.

He is one of America's most successful restaurateurs and has been an entrepreneur and innovator in the restaurant industry for more than thirty years. Norman is now chairman and CEO of Brinker International. He has been a member of the Komen Board since 1982.

A person who has lived his life with such courage, dignity, and success is an inspiration to all. Having ambition, determination, and strength is just one way to travel the road to the top.

Sources: This profile draws on Robert Christie Mill, *Restaurant Management: Customers, Operations, and Employees,* Upper Saddle River, NJ: Prentice Hall, 1998, p. 71, and these web sites: *www.business.com, www.komen.org/sgk/board, www.bspage.com/1article/peo18.html, www-rohan.sdsu.edu/dept/cbaweb/NEWA/brinker.html.*

Brew pubs offer a combination of food and beer made in the operations' own microbrewery. Most casual dining specialty restaurants offer alcoholic beverages as part of their dining experience.

Quick-Service/Fast-Food

Quick-service restaurants consist of diverse operating facilities whose slogan is "quick food." The following types of operations are included under this category: drive-thrus, delivery services, and hamburger, pizza, chicken, pancakes, and sandwich shops.

The quick-service sector is the one that really drives the industry. With sales of $111 billion, it is slightly ahead of the full-service segment by dollar volume. Recently, the home-meal replacement and fast casual concepts have gained momentum. Boston Market is a leader in both sectors and has recently sped up its service and cut customers' wait time in half.

Corporate Profile: Red Lobster

In 1968, a restaurant entrepreneur took a gamble on a new seafood restaurant concept in Lakeland, Florida. He was already in his midfifties, but Bill Darden decided to roll the dice at a time when most other men his age were looking toward retirement.

The gamble paid off—more than Darden could ever have imagined. His single seafood restaurant—Red Lobster—has since grown to become the world's largest seafood casual dining operation, with over 660 restaurants in North America, in 44 U.S. States and Canada.

Darden's restaurant career began in the 1930s in a tiny southern Georgia town called Waycross. It was there that nineteen-year-old Darden operated a small lunch counter called The Green Frog, where he served as manager, night cook, waiter, and counter server.

(Courtesy of Red Lobster)

As he saved money from The Green Frog, he began to acquire other restaurants in Florida, Georgia, and South Carolina. In 1963, Darden and his partners bought an Orlando landmark, Gary's Duck Inn, a popular seafood restaurant.

It was so popular that Darden began to think about expanding the concept—creating a no-frills seafood restaurant that offered fast, efficient service. He collected several investors, hired an ad agency, and, as they say, the rest is history.

One constant in Red Lobster's thirty-five years of consistent growth and success has been change. Keeping pace with the ever-changing expectations of the dining-out public, North America's largest full-service seafood restaurant company continues to look for new ways to assure quality and value for its guests.

This year, Red Lobster served millions of pounds of seafood to more than 140 million guests, with more than 600 restaurants in the United States and more than 50 in Canada.

"We are committed to offering our guests a fresh approach to casual dining, featuring great seafood, good times, and hospitality," says Red Lobster president Edna Morris. "Our focus on quality, value and service to our guests has resulted in over thirty years of consistent growth." All Red Lobster restaurants are company-owned and -operated, offering comfortable and efficient

table service in an informal family atmosphere. Red Lobster menus feature a broad selection of shellfish and daily fresh fish entrees, in addition to beef, chicken, and seafood-steak combination platters.

The original restaurant in Lakeland, Florida, was such an immediate success that it was necessary to enlarge and remodel it within the first month of operation. Two years later, in 1970, Red Lobster's five restaurants attracted the attention of General Mills, which purchased the chain and provided the necessary resources for rapid nationwide expansion.

By the late 1970s and early 1980s, Red Lobster was 350 restaurants strong. And in 1995, after decades of success and growth, Red Lobster (along with the Olive Garden, Bahama Breeze and later Smokey Bones BBQ Sports Bar) was spun into Darden Restaurants, headed up by none other than Joe Lee.

A Commitment to Quality

An important contributor to this successful climb is an uncompromising commitment to quality. "Through our rigorous inspection systems . . . from the seafood purchased directly from the world's best commercial fisherman to the food served in the restaurant, Red Lobster assures quality in purchasing, distribution and restaurant operations," Morris says. The Red Lobster quality assurance program is recognized as a foodservice industry leader. The program includes strict purchasing standards and inspections at various critical points. Ongoing laboratory testing of products before shipment to restaurants and quality control training for managers of each restaurant assure that quality is a priority—"from sea to table."

Additionally, in the United States, voluntary seafood inspection programs administered by the United States Department of Commerce (U.S.D.C.) are a further test of quality assurance for the restaurant chain. All Red Lobster seafood carries the U.S.D.C. and/or Canadian seafood inspection approval.

"We believe our success is the result of the strength of our original seafood concept, our commitment to quality, the job our employees consistently perform daily, and a dynamic menu that meets seafood lovers' changing tastes."

Pizza Hut
(Photo Courtesy Pizza Hut.)

Quick-service or fast-food restaurants offer limited menus featuring food such as hamburgers, fries, hot dogs, chicken (in all forms), tacos, burritos, gyros, teriyaki bowls, various finger foods, and other items for the convenience of people on the go. Customers order their food at a counter under a brightly lit menu featuring color photographs of food items. Customers are even encouraged to clear their own trays, which helps reduce costs. The following are examples of the different types of quick-service/fast-food restaurants:

    Hamburger—McDonald's, Burger King, Wendy's
    Pizza—Pizza Hut, Domino's, Godfather's
    Steak—Bonanza, Ponderosa
    Seafood—Long John Silver's
    Chicken—KFC, Church's, Boston Market, Kenny Roger's, Popeye's
    Sandwich—Subway
    Mexican—Taco Bell, El Torito
    Drive-Thru-In Delivery—Domino's, Pizza Hut

Figure 6–6 shows the top 100 market shares by restaurant segment.

Quick-service restaurants have increased in popularity because of their location strategies. They are found in very convenient locations in every possible area. Their menus are limited, which makes it easy for customers to make quick decisions on what to eat. The world equates time with money these days and most people do not want to spend time trying to look through long menus to make an eating decision. These restaurants deliver fast service and usually include self-service facilities too. Such restaurants also use cheaper, processed ingredients, which allow them to have extremely low, competitive prices. Quick-service restaurants also require minimum use of both skilled and unskilled labor, which increases the profit margins.

In some of the world's major cities, where space is expensive, stand-up restaurants open where busy office workers can eat a quick meal. Also found in many major cities is "$1 Chinese Fast Food (no MSG)," where patrons select menu items and receive small portions for one dollar. This is relatively quick and easy for the kitchen staff, because they can prepare a large serving of a particular dish, put it on low heat, and portion it out as necessary. For the customers, it is fast

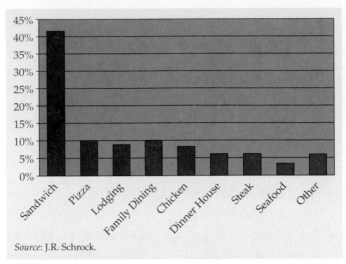

Source: J.R. Schrock.

Figure 6–6   *Approximate Market Share of Restaurant Segments*
(*Source:* J. R. Schrock*)*

and affordable because they can have a taste of three or four different dishes for a cost of $3 or $4 with rice and noodles usually included free.

In an attempt to raise flat sales figures, more quick-service restaurant (QSR) chains are using cobranding at stores and nontraditional locations, including highway plazas and shopping centers. It is hoped that the traffic-building combos will increase sales among the separate brands, such as Carl's Jr. and Green Burrito, as well as concepts like Triarc Co.'s Arby's, Zu Zu, P.T. Noodles, and T.J. Cinnamon brands.

Many QSR chains are targeting international growth, mostly in the larger cities in a variety of countries.

Drive-Thrus

Drive-thru restaurants are usually part of an existing quick-service restaurant. The concept essentially means that you can drive in, place your order, receive your food, pay for it, and drive out. You don't have to park your vehicle and go into a restaurant to eat. Drive-thrus have gained popularity in the recent past. A drive-thru establishment enjoys the advantage of low capital costs because of their small buildings and the relatively small size lot on which they fit. Their highly simplified menus also give them an operating cost advantage. Highly successful drive-thrus include McDonald's, Burger King, and Taco Bell.

Delivery Services

Delivery services are operations that deliver prepared foods to customers' homes. Delivery service also characterizes meals-on-wheels, as well as urban restaurants that deliver to a neighborhood. You call the operation to place an order after looking at restaurant menus from your home. The delivery service will process your order and deliver it to you. These services can be connected to an existing restaurant or can operate on their own. Domino's Pizza is a primary example of this kind of operation. Many restaurants followed Domino's lead and other popular delivery services in the United States now include Papa Johns and Pizza Hut.

Some delivery services function differently. They offer a limited menu from various participating neighborhood restaurants. The customer places an order with the delivery service, which in turn places the order with the restaurant, picks up the order, and delivers it to the customer.

Hamburger

The world's greatest fast-food success story is undoubtedly McDonald's. Back in the 1950s, Ray Kroc was selling soda fountains. He received an order from Mr. McDonald for two soda fountains. Ray Kroc was so interested in finding out why the McDonald brothers' restaurant needed two machines (everyone else ordered one) that he went out to the restaurant. There he saw the now-familiar golden arches and the hamburger restaurant. Ray persuaded the McDonalds to let him franchise their operation. Billions of burgers later, the reason for the success may be summarized as follows: quality, speed, cleanliness, service, and value. This has been achieved by systemizing the production process and by staying close to the original concept—keeping a limited menu, advertising heavily, being innovative with new menu items, maintaining product quality, and being consistent.

McDonald's is the giant of the entire quick-service/fast-food segment with worldwide sales of $33 billion. This total is amazing because it is more than the next three megachains combined—Burger King ($10.9 billion), KFC ($8.9 billion), and Pizza Hut ($8.2 billion).[22] McDonald's has individual product items other than the traditional burger—for example, chicken McNuggets and burritos as well as salads and fish, which all aim to broaden customer appeal.

Customer appeal has also been broadened by the introduction of breakfast and by targeting not only kids but also seniors. Innovative menu introductions have helped stimulate an increase in per-store traffic.

In recent years, because traditional markets have become saturated, McDonald's has adopted a strategy of expanding overseas. It is embarking on a rapid expansion in the world's most populous nation, China, with more than 12,000 restaurants nationwide. The reason for this expansion in China is a rapidly developing middle class with a growing appetite for Western culture and food. McDonald's is now in 119 countries and has a potential audience of 3.2 billion people. Of the company's roughly 26,000 restaurants, some 6,400 are outside of the United States.

---

[22]Kimberly D. Lowe and Erin Nicholas, "Chaos in a Crowded Market," *Restaurant and Institutions*, **107**, 17, July 15, 1997.

It is interesting to note that of the estimated $33 billion worldwide sales, about $15 billion are from outside of the United States, and about 50 percent of total profits come from outside of the United States.[23] More than two-thirds of new restaurants added by McDonald's are outside of the United States. McDonald's also seeks out nontraditional locations in the U.S. market, such as on military bases or smaller-sized units in the high-rent districts.

McDonald's is taking another step toward being the most convenient foodservice operation in the world by striking deals with gasoline companies Chevron, U.S. Petroleum Star Enterprise, and Mobil Oil Corporation to codevelop sites.

It is very difficult to obtain a McDonald's franchise in the United States because they have virtually saturated the primary markets. Carl's Jr., a California-based chain of 908 units has a franchising fee of $35,000, with a royalty fee of 4 percent and an advertising annuity of 4 percent. It often costs between $800,000 and $1 million to open a major brand fast-food restaurant. Franchises for lesser known chains are available for less money.

Each of the major hamburger restaurant chains has a unique positioning strategy to attract their target markets. Burger King hamburgers are flame broiled, and Wendy's uses fresh patties.

Fuddruckers is a restaurant chain that describes itself as the "Cadillac of Burgers." Other gourmet burger restaurants may offer larger burgers with more side dishes to choose from, and they generally have decor that would attract the nonteenage market. Some of these restaurants have beer and wine licenses. Some smaller regional chains are succeeding in gaining market share from the big-three burger chains because they provide an excellent burger at a reasonable price. In-N-Out Burger and Rally's are good examples of this. The top ten hamburger chains are listed in Table 6–3.

Table 6–3
Top Ten Quick Service Restaurant Chains

Chain	Number of Units	Countries	Sales (Billions of Dollars)
McDonald's	30,000	121	39.65
Burger King	14,450	58	11.2
KFC	11,815	102	9.7
Pizza Hut	10,200	86	7.6
Wendy's	6,175	25	8.3
Subway	17,308	74	5.17
Taco Bell	6,444	52	5
Domino's	7,046	53	3.78
Dairy Queen	5,837	56	2.79
Arby's	3,000	N/A	2.62

Source: Corporation websites, October 30, 2002.

[23]McDonald's annual report, 1997.

Ray Kroc

Of all hospitality entrepreneurs, Ray Kroc has been the most successful financially. In 1982, he was senior chairman of the board of McDonald's, an organization intent on covering the earth with hamburgers. Among the remarkable things about Kroc is that it was not until age fifty-two that he even embarked on the royal road to fame and fortune.

The original McDonald's concept was created by two brothers, Richard and Maurice, who had no interest in expanding. The McDonald brothers were content with their profitable, yet singular restaurant in San Bernardino, California. However, the golden arches impressed Kroc, as did the cleanliness and simplicity of the operation.

Kroc's organizational skills, perseverance, and incredible aptitude for marketing were his genius. His talent also extended to selecting close associates who were equally dedicated and who added financial, analytical, and managerial skills to the enterprise. Kroc remained the spark plug and master merchandiser until he died in 1984, leaving a multimillion dollar legacy.

Much of Kroc's $400 million has gone to employees, hospitals, and the Marshall Field Museum. It is distributed through Kroc's own foundation. Most importantly, Kroc developed several operational guidelines, including the concepts of "KISS"—Keep It Simple Stupid—and QSC&V—Quality, Service, Cleanliness, and Value. Kroc's "Never Be Idle a Moment" motto was also incorporated into the business.

Enterprises like McDonald's are not built without ample dedication and Ray Kroc certainly had a wealth of dedication. Today, an average McDonald's franchise can net more than $1 million annually thanks to Kroc's ingenious marketing strategies. In fact, McDonald's Corporation has become so affluent that it was named *Entrepreneur* magazine's number one franchise in 1997.

Pizza

The pizza segment continues to grow. By some estimates it is at least a $20 billion market,[24] with much of the growth fueled by the convenience of delivery. There are four main chains: Pizza Hut, Domino's, Godfather's, and Little Caesar's. Godfather's "makes pizza the way it was meant to be." They are also noted for their no wait lunch buffet and their cinnamon-streusel or cherry pie dessert pizzas. They offer a number of family combos at special prices that include drinks and a variety of pizzas and desserts. Their jumbo sampler includes four pizzas in one! Pizza Hut, with system-wide sales of $5 billion, has broken into the delivery part of the business over which, until recently, Domino's had a virtual monopoly. Little Caesar's, with 3,850 units and total sales of $1.2 billion, built a pizza empire on the perceived value of two pizzas for the price of one. Pizza Hut has now developed system-wide delivery units that also offer two pizzas at a reduced price. A Little Caesar's franchise fee is $20,000, with the cost to develop a store running between $120,000 and $160,000.

[24]Ibid.

	Table 6–4		
	Pizza Chains Ranked by Top 100 Market Share		
Rank	Chain	Fiscal Year-End	Latest[a]
1	Pizza Hut	Dec. 1999	44.03
2	Domino's Pizza	Dec. 1999	22.54
3	Papa John's Pizza	Dec. 1999	12.56
4	Little Caesar's Pizza	Dec. 1999	10.57
5	Sbarro	Dec. 1999	4.11
6	Round Table Pizza	Dec. 1999	3.35
7	Chuck E. Cheese's	Dec. 1999	2.84

Source: Alan J. Liddle, "Top 100 Chain and Company Rankings," *Nation's Restaurant News,* **24,** 26, June 26, 2000, p. 104.
[a]Actual results, estimates, or projections.

In response to the success of Pizza Hut's Stuffed Crust Pizza, Domino's highlights their Ultimate Deep Dish Pizza and their new Pesto Crust Pizza. They are currently stressing the quality of their advertising. With twelve toppings to choose from, people can have fun designing their own pizza. The new ad campaign features a puppet named "Bad Andy," who tries to disrupt the pizza-making and delivery process. Pizza chain rankings are shown in Table 6–4.

Chicken

Chicken has always been popular and is likely to remain so because it is relatively cheap to produce and it is readily available and adaptable to a variety of preparations. It also is perceived as a healthier alternative to burgers.

Kentucky Fried Chicken (KFC), with a worldwide total of more than 5,182 units and annual sales of more than 4,300 million, dominates the chicken segment. Even though KFC is a market leader, the company continues to explore new ways to get its products to consumers. More than 350 units now offer home delivery, and in many cities, KFC is teaming up with sister restaurant Taco Bell, selling products from both chains in one convenient location. KFC continues to build menu variety as it focuses on providing complete meals to families, with new products such as Tender Roast® chicken pieces, Chunky Chicken Pot Pie, and Colonel's Crispy Strips.

Church's Chicken, the 1,178-unit division of AFC Enterprises formerly America's Favorite Chicken Company, is the second largest chicken chain. It offers a simple formula consisting of a value menu featuring Southern-style chicken, spicy chicken wings, okra, corn on the cob, coleslaw, biscuits, and other items.

Under the guidance of Hala Moddelmog, president, Church's focused on becoming a low-cost provider and the fastest to market. To give customers the value they expect day in and day out, she says that it is necessary to have unit

KFC Restaurant and Rotisserie Gold, a Popular Addition to Their Menu (Photos Courtesy KFC.)

economies in order. System-wide, Church's now registers 35.8 percent in food costs and 27.9 percent labor costs.[25]

Popeye's is now the third largest chain in the chicken segment with 1,165 units. It is owned by AFC, the same parent company as Church's. Popeye's has a New Orleans-inspired "spicy chicken" chain operating more than 300 restaurants in Texas and Louisiana that is expanding into eleven markets around the country. The chain hopes to increase average-unit sales to $1 million.

There are a number of up-and-coming regional chains, such as El Pollo Loco, of Irvine, California. They focus on a marinated, flame-broiled chicken that is a unique, high-quality product. Kenny Rogers and Cluckers are also expanding rotisserie chains. Chicken chain growth is shown in Table 6–5.

Table 6–5
Chicken Chains Ranked by Growth in Number of Units

Rank	Chain	Units	Sales
1	KFC	11,815	$9.7b
2	Popeye's	1,650	1.3b
3	Chick-fil-A	1,000	1b
4	Churches	1,500	820m
5	Boston Market	650	666m

Source: Corporations websites. October 30, 2002.

[25]Ron Ruggles, "Church's: Taking Low-Cost Dining to New Heights," *Nation's Restaurant News,* **31,** 30, August 3, 1997.

Pancake

The major force in the pancake house segment is the International House of Pancakes (IHOP). Of the 900 units, almost 90 percent of them are operated as franchises by independent businesspeople. Other major companies in this segment are Country Kitchen, a division of Minneapolis-based Carlson Companies, with 253 units, and Village Inn, the 206-unit, Denver-based subsidiary of Vicorp.

Each of the pancake chains is reacting to the health-conscious customer by offering egg substitutes and a near cholesterol-free pancake. Pancake franchises cost approximately $50,000 for the franchise fee, a 4 to 5 percent annual royalty, and a 3 percent advertising fee.

Sandwich Restaurants

Indicative of America's obsession with the quick and convenient, sandwiches have achieved star status. Recently, menu debuts in the sandwich segment have outpaced all others. Classics, like melts and club sandwiches, have returned with a vengeance—but now there are also wraps.

Au Bon Pain of Boston is currently rolling out a line of eight new sourdough bagels designed to boost breakfast sales and keep regulars engaged. The bagels, which include such signature flavors as Asiago Cheese and Wild Blueberry, are also available as a sandwich option. They also introduced a line of pita-based wrap sandwiches.

A sandwich restaurant is a popular way for a young entrepreneur to enter the restaurant business. The leader in this segment is Subway, which operates 14,321 units in seventy-three countries. Cofounder Fred Deluca parlayed an initial investment of $1,000 into one of the largest and fastest-growing chains in the world. Franchise fees are $10,000 with a second store fee of $2,500. Average unit sales are about $270,000 annually, with yearly costs of about $75,000.

The Subway strategy is to invest half of the chain's advertising dollars in national advertising. Franchise owners pay 2.5 percent of sales to the marketing fund. As with other chains, Subway is attempting to widen its core eighteen- to thirty-four-year-old customer base by adding Kids Packs and Value 4-inch Round sandwiches aimed at teens and women. Sandwich restaurants stress the health value of their restaurants.

Check Your Knowledge

1. Describe the different types of restaurants and give examples of each. Highlight some of the characteristics that make up the specific restaurant types.

Corporate Profile: Au Bon Pain

In 1976, Au Bon Pain was founded as a demonstration bakery by a French oven manufacturer, Pavailler. One year later, with a keen sense for discerning the taste and trend in American culture and recognizing them as opportunities for a thriving business, Louis Kane purchased Au Bon Pain. He later merged his passion for involvement in entrepreneurial ventures with Ron Shaich's passion for strategic evolution. They became partners in 1981 creating a new company, Au Bon Pain Co., Inc. They set up a pilot facility at the company's Prudential Center location that concentrated on producing frozen dough products that could be fresh baked in each bakery cafe. Sales increased by 40 percent and the number of customers increased to 35,000 per week.

Au Bon Pain opened its first bakery cart at Logan Airport in 1982. This effort represented one of the first introductions of branded food in airports and initiated a trend that is now the dominant force in airport food service. Twelve months later, Au Bon Pain was the first in

the country to recognize the potential in expanding from a croissant and bread bakery to a French bakery cafe. The company added sandwiches and coffee to its existing line of bread and croissants. In addition, customer seats and booths were added to the stores' interiors. As a result of these internal improvements, sales climbed dramatically. A few years later, in 1986, the grilled chicken sandwich was introduced, and it soon became the number one sandwich at Au Bon Pain.

Au Bon Pain began buying back its franchised units in 1987, and four years later, it opened its one-hundredth store. In the two years that followed, it opened 100 more bakery cafes and added to the product line. Au Bon Pain International also opened franchise operations in the Philippines and Indonesia and, in 1997, added cafes in Thailand, Brazil, and Argentina.

Au Bon Pain's success lies in its philosophy—to "be able to dance." In this case, Au Bon Pain officials define "dance" as the ability to recognize the needs of their customers and to change the strategic direction of their company to meet those needs. By applying this concept, Au Bon Pain Co., Inc.'s goal is to become the dominant bakery cafe operator, both domestically and internationally. They are striving for increased customer service and, industry-defining reputation. Au Bon Pain also hopes to expand to more than 1,000 units within the next ten years through its four growth vehicles: Au Bon Pain business unit, Saint Louis Bread business unit, international and trade channels, and manufacturing service.

Trends in Restaurant Development

✓ Demographics: As the baby boomers move into middle age, a startling statistic will emerge in the early 2000's. Thirty-five to fifty-four-year-olds (the age group with the highest income) will make up almost one-third of the American population—as the forty-five to fifty-four-year-old bracket increases by an unprecedented 46 percent from 1990. Simply put, the largest demographic group will have the most money.

✓ Branding: Restaurant operators are using the power of branding, both in terms of brand name recognition from a franchising viewpoint and in the products utilized.

✓ Alternative outlets: Increased competition from convenience "c-stores" and home meal replacement outlets.

✓ Globalization: Continued transnational development.

✓ Continued diversification within the various dining segments.

✓ More twin and multiple locations.

✓ More points of service, e.g., Taco Bell at gas stations.

✓ More hypertheme restaurants.

✓ Chains vs. independents.

Career Information

Opening your own restaurant as an entrepreneur can be an exciting prospect. For the winners, the restaurant business is fun—lots of people coming and going. The business is always challenging because other restaurant owners are striving to attract your guests—but with the right location, menu, atmosphere, and management, the winners continue to attract the market. The successful restaurant offers a high return on investment. One restaurant, then two, perhaps a small chain. Retire wealthy. It happens.[1]

In addition to ownership in the restaurant business there are a number of career paths in the supply sector of the industry. Someone has to consult, plan, design, construct, and outfit each restaurant. The larger chain restaurants all have marketing, human resources, financial, and accounting positions.

For those interested in a career in the restaurant business it is a good idea to gain experience in all facets of restaurant operations. As one famous restauranteur once said to me "John first, you must know how to steal the chicken before you can stop someone else stealing the chicken." Culinary experience is a must in order to 'protect' yourself in case your chef/cook walks out. Obviously front of the house experience is a must and a good way of financing college.

[1]John R. Walker and Donald E. Lundberg. The Restaurant from *Concept To Operation* 3rd ed. John Wiley and Sons New York, 2001. p. 5.

Suggested Activity

Evaluating the Weaknesses of a Restaurant

In groups, evaluate a restaurant and write out a list of weaknesses. Use the headings outlined in the restaurant chapters. Then, for each of the weaknesses, decide on what actions you would take to exceed guest expectations.

Suggested Activity

Restaurant Concept

Create a restaurant concept and, using the headings outlined in the chapter, discuss the main elements.

Summary

1. Restaurants offer the possibility of excellent food and social interaction. In general, restaurants strive to surpass an operating philosophy that includes quality food, good value, and gracious service.
2. To succeed, a restaurant needs the right location, food, atmosphere, and service to attract a substantial market. The concept of a restaurant has to fit the market it is trying to attract.
3. The location of a restaurant has to match factors such as convenience, neighborhood, parking, visibility, and demographics. Typical types of locations are downtown, suburban, shopping mall, cluster, or stand alones.
4. The menu and pricing of a restaurant must match the market it wants to attract, the capabilities of the cooks, and the existing kitchen equipment.
5. The main categories of restaurants are fine dining and specialty independent and chain. Further distinctions can be made: quick-service, ethnic, dinner house, occasion, and casual. In general, most restaurants fall into more than one category.

Key Words and Concepts

À la carte menu	Chain restaurant	Fine dining restaurant	Puree
Actual market share	Contribution margin	Food cost percentage	Quick-service restaurant
Ambiance	Culinary arts	Haute cuisine	Roux
Atmosphere	Cyclical menu	Independent restaurant	Sales volume
California menu	Dinner house restaurant	Infusion	Specialty restaurant
Casual dining	Du jour menu	Menu planning	Table d'hôte menu
Casual upscale dining	Ethnic restaurant	Mother sauces	Theme restaurant
Catchment area	Fair market share	Niche	Tourist menu
Celebrity-owned restaurant	Family restaurant	Nouvelle cuisine	Weighted average

Review Questions

1. What is understood by the term *catchment area,* and why is it essential for the success of a restaurant to concentrate on a certain market?
2. Explain why it is important that the location of a restaurant matches its concept.
3. The menu is another very important part of a restaurant. Explain the following terms: *table d'hote, accuracy in menu,* and *equipment capacity.*
4. Describe the two main ways to price a menu.
5. Explain why there is no full-service luxury restaurant chain. List tactics used by full-service restaurant owners to increase profitability.
6. Explain why there is no single definition of the various classifications of restaurants; give examples.

Internet Exercises

1. Organization:
   Web site:
   Summary:
   (a) Although their signature food is pancakes, IHOP offers a variety of other dishes, meaning that it is not only a breakfast restaurant. What other types of restaurant can IHOP be classified as?

IHOP Restaurant
http://ihop.com/home.html
IHOP is a family restaurant that offers moderately priced, high-quality food and beverage items and table service in an attractive and comfortable atmosphere. They are best known for their award-winning pancakes, omelets, and other breakfast specialties although they operate through the day and evening hours. They have 900 restaurants open in thirty-seven states, Canada, and Japan.

2. Organization:
   Web site:
   Summary:
   (a) What kind of restaurant does the name "Olive Garden" represent?
   (b) What is the Garden Fare? How is its menu different from the design and layout of the lunch menu?

Olive Garden Restaurant
http://www.olivegarden.com/
The Olive Garden is a multi-unit chain that primarily serves exquisite Italian food. They are currently operated by Darden Restaurants, Inc., and have about 460 restaurants in the United States and Canada.

Apply Your Knowledge

1. Create your own restaurant concept including the menu and describe its workings in detail.

Restaurant Operations 7

After reading and studying this chapter, you should be able to:

✓ Apply the forecasting technique used in the chapter to measure expected volume of business.
✓ Name and describe the various types of services.
✓ Explain the important aspects of food production.
✓ Describe the key points in purchasing, receiving, storing, and issuing.
✓ Explain the difference between controllable expenses and fixed costs.
✓ Explain the components of an income statement and operating ratios.
✓ Describe the important aspects of a control system for a restaurant operation.
✓ Outline the functional areas and tasks of a foodservice/restaurant manager.

Front of the House

Restaurant operations are generally divided between what is commonly called **front of the house** and **back of the house.** The front of the house includes any-one with guest contact from the hostess to the busperson. The sample organi-zation chart in Figure 7–1 shows the differences between the front and back of the house areas.

The restaurant is run by the general manager, or restaurant manager. Depending on the size and sales volume of the restaurant, there may be more managers with special responsibilities such as kitchen manager, bar manager, and dining room manager. These managers are usually cross-trained in order to relieve each other. Figure 7–2 gives a job description for a typical assistant restaurant manager's position.

In the front of the house, restaurant operation begins with creating and maintaining what is called **curbside appeal,** or keeping the restaurant looking attractive and welcoming. Ray Kroc, of McDonald's, once spent a couple of hours in a good suit with one of his restaurant managers cleaning up the park-ing lot of one of his restaurants. Word soon got around to the other stores that management begins in the parking lot and ends in the bathrooms. Most restau-rant chains have checklists that each manager uses. In the front of the house, the parking lot, including the flower gardens, need to be maintained in good order. As guests approach the restaurant, hostesses may hold the door open and welcome them to the restaurant. At Mike Hurst's 15th Street Fisheries restaurant in Ft. Lauderdale, hostesses welcome the guests by assuring them that "we're glad you're here!"

Once inside, the **hostess,** or as TGI Friday's calls them, "smiling people greeters" (SPGs), greets guests appropriately and, if seating is available, escorts

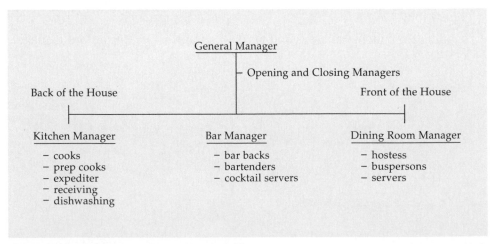

Figure 7–1 *Restaurant Organizational Chart*

POSITION TITLE: *Assistant Manager*
REPORTS TO: *Manager*

POSITION OVERVIEW:
Under the general supervision of the manager, subject to the Service Policy and Procedure Manual, assures constantly and consistently the creation of maximal guest satisfaction and dining pleasure.

RESPONSIBILITIES AND DUTIES:
A. Planning and organizing
  1. Studies past sales experience records, confers with manager, keeps alert to holidays and special events, and so on; forecasts loads and prepares work schedules for service employees in advance to meet requirements.
  2. Observes guest reactions and confers frequently with servers to determine guest satisfactions, dissatisfactions, relative popularity of menu items, and so on and reports such information with recommendations to the manager.
  3. Observes daily the condition of all physical facilities and equipment in the dining room, making recommendations to the manager for correction and improvements needed.
  4. Anticipates all material needs and supplies and assures availability of same.
  5. Inspects, plans, and assures that all personnel, facilities, and materials are in complete readiness to provide excellent service before each meal period.
  6. Anticipates employment needs, recommending to the manager plans for recruitment and selection to meet needs as they arise.
  7. Discusses menu changes with servers in advance to assure full understanding of new items.
  8. Conducts meetings of service employees at appropriate times.
  9. Defines and explains clearly for servers and buspersons their responsibilities for relationships
    ✔ with each other
    ✔ with guests
    ✔ with the hostess/host
    ✔ with the manager
    ✔ with the cashier
    ✔ with the kitchen personnel
B. Coordinating
  1. Ensures that servers are fully informed as to all menu items—how they are prepared, what they contain, number of ounces per portion.
  2. Periodically discusses and reviews with employees company objectives, and guest and personnel policies.

  3. Keeps manager informed at all times about service activities, progress, and major problems.
C. Supervising
  1. Actively participates in employment of new servers and buspersons, suggests recruitment sources, studies applications, checks references, and conducts interviews.
  2. Following an orientation outline, introduces new employees to the restaurant, restaurant policies, and fellow employees.
  3. Using a training plan, trains new employees and current employees in need of additional training.
  4. Promptly corrects any deviations from established service standards.
  5. Counsels employees on job issues and personal problems.
  6. Follows established policy in making station assignments for servers.
  7. Establishes, with approval of manager, standards of conduct, grooming, personal hygiene, and dress.
  8. Prepares, in consultation and with approval of the manager, applied standards of performance for servers and buspersons.
  9. Recommends deserving employees for promotion, and outstanding performers for special recognition and award.
  10. Strives at all times through the practice of good human relations and leadership to establish esprit de corps—teamwork, unity of effort, and individual and group pride.
  11. Remains constantly alert to the entire dining room situation—is sensitive to any deviation or problem and assists quickly and quietly in its correction, alleviating guests' complaints.
  12. Greets and seats guests cordially and courteously, to assure a sincere welcome and to express a genuine interest in their dining pleasure.
D. Controlling
  1. Controls performance, conduct, dress, hygiene, sanitation, and personal appearance of employees according to established policies, standards, and procedures.
  2. Studies all evidence of waste of time and materials, and makes recommendations for preventing further waste.
E. Other
  1. In emergency situations, may serve guests, act as cashier, or perform specifically assigned duties of the manager.
  2. Personifies graciousness and offers hospitality to guests and employees by showing "we're glad you're here" and "we're proud to serve you."

Figure 7–2 *Job Description for Assistant Restaurant Manager* them to a table. If there is a wait, the hostess will take the guests' names and ask for their table preference.

Aside from greeting the guests, one of the critical functions of the hostess is to rotate arriving guests among the sections or stations. This ensures an even and timely distribution of guests—otherwise one section may get overloaded. Guests are sometimes asked to wait a few minutes even if tables are available. This is done to help spread the kitchen's workload.

The hostesses maintain a book, or chart, showing the sections and tables so they know which tables are occupied. Hostesses escort guests to the tables, present menus, and may explain special sales promotions. Some may also remove excess covers from the table.

In some restaurants, servers are allocated a certain number of tables, which may vary depending on the size of the tables and the volume of the restaurant. Normally, five is the maximum. In other restaurants, servers rotate within their section to cover three or four tables.

The server introduces him/herself, offers a variety of beverages and/or specials, or invites guests to select from the menu. This is known as suggestive selling. The server then takes the entree orders. Often, when taking orders, the server begins at a designated point and takes the orders clockwise from that point. In this way, the server will automatically know which person is having a particular dish. When the entrees are ready, the server brings them to the table. He or she checks a few minutes later to see if everything is to the guests' liking and perhaps asks if they would like another beverage. Good servers are also encouraged, when possible, to prebus tables.

Busers and servers may clear the entree plates, while servers suggestively sell desserts by describing, recommending, or showing the desserts. Coffee and

Fraunces Tavern. The famous Fraunces Tavern was the Revolutionary headquarters of General George Washington, and was the place in which he made his famous Farewell Address. It is still operating. (Courtesy Fraunces Tavern.)

after-dinner cocktails are also offered. Suggestions for steps to take in table service include the following:

✓ Greet the guests.
✓ Introduce and suggestively sell beverages.
✓ Suggest appetizers.
✓ Take orders.
✓ Check to see that everything is to the guests' liking within two bites of the entrees.
✓ Ask if the guests would like another drink.
✓ Bring out dessert tray and suggest after-dinner drinks and coffee.

In addition to the seven steps of the table service, servers are expected to be NCO—neat, clean, and organized—and to help ensure that hot food is served hot, and cold food is served cold.

For example, during the lunch hour, servers may be scheduled to start at 11:00 A.M. The opening group of two or three people is joined by the closing group of the same number at around 11:45 P.M. If the restaurant is quiet, servers may be phased out early. When the closing group comes in, there is a quick shift meeting, or "alley rally". This provides an opportunity to review recent sales figures, discuss any promotions, and acknowledge any items that are "86'ed"—the restaurant term for a menu item that is not available. Recognition is also given to the servers during the meetings, serving as morale boosters.

Restaurant Forecasting

Most businesses, including restaurants, operate by formulating a budget that projects sales and costs for a year on a weekly and monthly basis. Financial viability is predicted on sales, and sales budgets are forecasts of expected business.

Forecasting restaurant sales has two components: guest counts or covers and the average guest check. **Guest counts** or **covers** are the number of guests patronizing the restaurant over a given time period—a week, month, or year. To forecast the number of guests for a year, the year is divided into twelve 28- and one 29-day accounting periods. The accounting periods then are broken down into four 7-day weeks. Restaurant forecasting is done by taking into consideration meal period, day of week, special holidays, and previous forecast materializations.

In terms of number of guests, Mondays usually are quiet; business gradually builds to Friday, which is often the busiest day. Friday, Saturday, and Sunday frequently provide up to 50 percent of revenue. This, however, can vary according to type of restaurant and its location.

The **average guest check** is calculated by dividing total sales by the number of guests. Most restaurants keep such figures for each meal. The number of guests forecast for each day is multiplied by the amount of the average food and beverage check for each meal to calculate the total forecast sales. Each day, actual totals are compared with the forecasts. Four weekly forecasts are combined to form one accounting period; the thirteen accounting periods, when totaled, become the annual total.

Restaurant forecasting is used not only to calculate sales projections but also for predicting staffing levels and labor cost percentages. Much depends on the accuracy of forecasting. Once sales figures are determined, all expenditures, fixed and variable, have to be deducted to calculate profit or loss.[1]

Service

More than ever, what American diners really want to order when eating out is good service. All too often, it is not on the menu. With increased competition, however, bad service may be going the way of Beef Wellington in American restaurants. Just as American cuisine came of age in the 1970s and 1980s, service is showing signs of maturing in the twenty-first century.

A new American service has emerged. A less formal—yet professional—approach is preferred by today's restaurant guests. The restaurants' commitment to service is evidenced by the fact that most have increased training for new employees. For example, at Splendido in San Francisco's Embarcadero, the amount of time new servers spend in training has increased from forty to one hundred hours.

Servers are not merely order takers; they are the salespeople of the restaurant. A server who is undereducated about the menu can seriously hurt business. One would not be likely to buy a car from a salesperson who knew nothing about the car; likewise, customers feel uneasy ordering from an unknowledgeable waiter. Getting the waitstaff familiar with the menu can be a difficult task. Karen MacNeil, a restaurant service consultant and director of the New York Professional Service School, suggests two strategies: first, start from scratch and assume all servers know nothing about food; second, make learning fun—teach no more than three menu items a day and tell stories and use images to help things stick in servers' memories. It also is a good idea for the chef to coach the servers.[2]

Suggestive Selling

Suggestive selling can be a potent weapon in the effort to increase food and beverage sales. Many restaurateurs cannot think of a better, more effective, and easier way to boost profit margins. Servers report that most guests are not offended or uncomfortable with suggestive selling techniques. In fact, customers may feel special that the server is in tune with their needs and desires. It may be that the server suggests something to the guest that he or she has never considered before. The object here is to turn servers into sellers. Guests will almost certainly be receptive to suggestions from competent servers.

[1]This section draws on Donald E. Lundberg and John R. Walker, *The Restaurant from Concept to Operation*. New York: John Wiley and Sons, 1993, pp. 86–87.

[2]This section draws on Beth Lorenzini, "Turn Servers into Menu Masters," *Restaurants and Institutions*, **103,** 6, March 1, 1993, pp. 93–100.

On a hot day, for example, servers can suggest frozen margaritas or daiquiris before going on to describe the drink specials. Likewise, servers who suggest a bottle of Mondavi fumé blanc to complement a fish dish or a Mondavi pinot noir or cabernet sauvignon to go with red meat are likely to increase their restaurant's beverage sales.

Upselling takes place when a guest orders a "well" drink like a vodka and tonic. In this case, the server asks if the guests would like a Stoli and tonic. (Stoli is short for Stolichnaya, a popular brand of vodka.)

The following are a few suggestions to change a restaurant's attitude toward suggestive selling:

1. Train servers as commissioned salespeople.
2. Provide incentives and feedback.
3. Teach servers to suggest pairings.
4. Hire the sales type.
5. Create students of food and wine.
6. Encourage servers to upsell.
7. Promote ear-grabbing phrasing.
8. Recognize the unspoken suggestions.
9. Incorporate role playing.
10. Draw the line between sell and solicit.[3]

Types of Restaurant Service

French Service

French service is generally reserved for **haute cuisine** (elegant) restaurants and complements an elegant ambiance. The food is attractively arranged on platters and presented to guests, after which the preparation of the food is completed on a gueridon table beside the guests' seats. A gueridon is a trolley-like table with a gas burner for table-side cooking. This is the most impressive and expensive form of service.

French service is conducted by an elaborate and formal staff comprised of the following:

✓ **Maître d'hotel:** Restaurant manager.
✓ **Chef de rang:** Station server in charge of service for approximately four tables. Greets guests, describes and takes menu orders, supervises service, and completes the preparation of some dishes on the gueridon and carves, slices, or debones dishes for guests.
✓ **Demi chef de rang:** Assistant station server, assists the chef de rang, takes beverage orders, and serves food.
✓ **Commis de rang:** Food server in training. Assists the demi chef de rang with serving of water, bread, and butter; serving and clearing of plates; taking orders to the kitchen; and bringing the food into the restaurant.

[3]This section draws on Pat DiDomenico, "The Power of Suggestions: Turn Servers into Sellers," *Restaurants USA*, **13,** 2, February 1993, pp. 20–23.

Personal Profile: Herman Cain

Herman Cain, president and chief executive officer of Godfather's Pizza, Inc., is a living example of leadership and management successfully combined in one person. He was born in Atlanta, Georgia, to a humble, yet rich in spirit, family. His mother's Bible was a leading light throughout his life and career, and his father's optimism and sacrifices instilled in him the values and the principles that guided him from rural poverty to the crest of corporate America.

Cain has always been seeking challenges that could satisfy his profound need for accomplishments and achievement. He graduated from Morehouse College with a degree in mathematics, and later earned a master's degree in computer science while working as a mathematician for the Navy. However, government service did not seem to offer many entrepreneurial opportunities. Cain's competitive spirit led him to seek more challenges with Coca-Cola.

In 1977, Cain began his experience in the foodservice industry, when he joined the Pillsbury Company. His exceptional abilities, both in terms of management, creativity, and, above all, hard work, were soon rewarded. Cain's career was well on its way to the top when, in only five years, at the age of thirty-four, he became vice president of corporate systems and services. Although such a position was the fulfillment of Cain's dream, as well as of his father's, Cain was not satisfied. He felt he was bound to achieve and move further beyond the limits.

After his many accomplishments with Pillsbury, he found himself hungering for new challenges and opportunities. At the age of thirty-six, Cain resigned his senior position and made a stunning move. He wanted to learn the restaurant business from the bottom up, and he accomplished this by tackling such tasks as broiling burgers at Burger King.

After only nine months, he had moved from being a trainee flipping burgers to regional vice president of the Philadelphia market. His next formidable accomplishment was the ultimate open door to today's success. He transformed his region from the worst performing area in Burger King's system to the best, which undoubtedly caught the attention of Pillsbury executives. The offer he received from Pillsbury was the ultimate challenge, one that a man with Cain's personality and skills could not refuse. His mission was to take over the presidency of a floundering pizza chain, Godfather's Pizza, and return it to profitability. Cain's dynamism, enthusiasm, and endless energy had finally found a way to be fully employed. In fact, Cain renewed Godfather's Pizza, breathing new life into a restaurant concept that had already been declared by many as terminated.

Within twelve months, the chain regained profitability. Two years later, Cain achieved corporate ownership, buying the chain from Pillsbury. Cain's success lies in a perfect combination of management and leadership skills. As a manager, he made use of his analytical abilities to diagnose the situation, make strategic plans, and develop tactics to return Godfather's Pizza to profitability. He capitalized on every opportunity.

Cain realized that Godfather's goal was not to be a direct competitor to the industry's leaders—Pizza Hut and Domino's—but that he had to place a sharp focus on what the chain could do best—produce consistent quality products and maintain high standards of service, the driving force in any restaurant concept. A newly assembled management team helped him implement effectively the strategic actions designed to return the company to prosperity.

Cain's enthusiasm and leadership skills were transmitted to all segments of the company. Cain is a tremendously inspirational figure; his voice is one of those that cannot be ignored. It demands and obtains attention. He speaks powerfully and with a convincing self-confidence. "I'm a firm believer that we are put on this earth to make a difference," Cain said.

Cain was president and CEO of the National Restaurant Association (NRA) and chairman of the board of the 520-unit Godfather's Pizza chain. Herman Cain, nicknamed "The Hermanator," made the NRA one of the most potent political powers in Washington. Outlining his vision and mission for the NRA, Cain stated three initiatives:

1. To represent the NRA as a political force in Washington.
2. To provide more education for members, primarily through the Educational Foundation of the NRA.
3. To buff the image of the restaurant industry, promoting it as more than just a provider of jobs. "It is a $320 billion gold mine of opportunity, a vehicle to achieve the American dream."[1]

Herman Cain now commutes between his Washington and Omaha offices where he focuses on keynote speaking and his product line of inspirational tapes and audio cassettes of his speaking topics.

---

[1]Patricia B. Dailey, *Restaurants and Institutions,* **107,** 14, June 1, 1992, p. 58.

French Service

Russian Service

With **Russian service** the food is cooked in the kitchen, cut, placed onto a serving dish, and beautifully garnished. The dish then is presented to the guests and served individually by lifting the food onto the guest's plate with a serving spoon and fork. Russian service can be used at a banquet or a dinner party, where the servers may wear white gloves.

American Service

American service consists of simplified Russian service techniques. The food is prepared and dished onto individual plates in the kitchen, carried into the

Russian Service

dining room, and served to guests. This method of service is more popular than Russian service because it is quicker and guests receive the food hot and beautifully presented by the chef.[4]

At Posterio, servers are invited to attend a one-and one-half-hour wine class in the restaurant; about three-quarters of the forty-member staff routinely benefit from this additional training. The best employees are also rewarded with monthly prizes and with semiannual and annual prizes, which range from $100 cash, a limousine ride, dinner at Posterio, or a night's lodging at the Prescott Hotel to a week in Hawaii. Servers at other San Francisco restaurants role play the various elements of service such as greeting and seating guests, suggestive selling, correct methods of service, and guest relations to ensure a positive dining experience. A good food server in a top restaurant in many cities can earn about $40,000 a year.

Good servers quickly learn to gauge the guests' satisfaction levels and to be sensitive to guests' needs; for example, they check to ensure guests have everything they need as their entree is placed before them. Even better, they anticipate guests' needs. For example, if the guest had used the entree knife to eat the appetizer, then a clean one should automatically be placed to the guest's right side. In other words, the guest should not receive the entree and then realize he or she needs another knife.

Another example of good service is when the server does not have to ask everyone at the table who is eating what. The server should either remember or do a seating plan so that the correct dishes are automatically placed in front of guests.

Danny Meyer, owner of New York City's celebrated Union Square Cafe and recipient of both the Restaurant of the Year and Outstanding Service Awards from the James Beard Foundation in 1992, gives each of the restaurant's ninety-five employees—from busperson to chef—a $600 annual allowance ($50 each a month) to eat in the restaurant and critique the experience.

At the critically acclaimed Inn at Little Washington in Washington, Virginia, servers are required to gauge the mood of every table and jot a number (one to ten) and sometimes a description ("elated, grumpy, or edgy") on each ticket. Anything below a seven requires a diagnosis. Servers and kitchen staff work together to try to elevate the number to at least a nine by the time dessert is ordered.

The Commander's Palace in New Orleans uses an elaborate system of color-coded tickets and hand signals in the dining room to ensure that everyone walks away a billboard for the restaurant. For example, when the maître'd touches the corner of his eye as he ushers guests to a table, it is a signal to the staff to take a good look, this is someone you should remember.

People are all impressed most by the use of their own names. Recognition of this kind is music to the ear and the ego. In upscale restaurants, guests' names are remembered by taking names from the reservation book and writ-

---

[4]T. Suji, *Professional Restaurant Service.* New York: John Wiley and Sons, 1992, p. 14.

ing them on the meal check. This not only impresses the host and her or his guests, it may also increase the tip considerably.[5]

Check Your Knowledge

1. What is considered the front of the house?
2. Define curbside appeal.
3. Suggest methods for remembering who ordered what on a table for a large party.
4. Name some of the responsibilities and duties of an assistant restaurant manager.
5. Briefly explain the following:
   a. French service
   b. Russian service
   c. American service

Back of the House

The back of the house is generally run by the kitchen manager and refers to all the areas that guests do not normally come in contact with. This includes purchasing, receiving, storing/issuing, food production, stewarding, budgeting, accounting, and control.

One of the most important aspects to running a successful restaurant is having a strong back-of-the-house operation, particularly in the kitchen. The kitchen is the backbone of every full-service restaurant, thus it must be well managed and organized. Some of the main considerations in efficiently operating the back of the house include staffing, scheduling, training, food cost analysis, production, management involvement, management follow-up, and employee recognition.

Food Production

Planning, organizing, and producing food of a consistently high quality is no easy task. The kitchen manager, cook, or chef begins the production process by determining the expected volume of business for the next few days. The same period's sales from the previous year will give a good indication of the expected volume and the breakdown of the number of sales of each menu

---

[5]This section draws on Tom Sietseima, "Restaurants Trying Harder to Please," *San Francisco Chronicle*, July 14, 1993, p. A-1.

item. As described earlier, ordering and receiving will have already been done for the day's production schedule.

The **kitchen manager** checks the head line cook's order, which will bring the prep (preparation) area up to the par stock of prepared items. Most of the prep work is done in the early part of the morning and afternoon. Taking advantage of slower times allows the line cooks to do the final preparation just prior to and during the actual meal service.

The **kitchen layout** is set up according to the business projected as well as the menu design. Most full-service restaurants have similar layouts and designs for their kitchens. The layout consists of the back door area, walk-ins, the freezer, dry storage, prep line, salad bar, cooking line, expediter, dessert station, and service bar area.

The **cooking line** is the most important part of the kitchen layout. It might consist of a broiler station, window station, fry station, salad station, saute station, and pizza station—just a few of the intricate parts that go into the setup of the back of the house. The size of the kitchen and its equipment are all designed according to the sales forecast for the restaurant.

The kitchen will also be set up according to what the customers prefer and order most frequently. For example, if guests eat more broiled or sauteed items, the size of the broiler and saute must be larger to cope with the demand.

Teamwork, a prerequisite for success in all areas of the hospitality and tourism industry, is especially important in the kitchen. Due to the hectic pace, pressure builds, and unless each member of the team excels, the result will be food that is delayed, not up to standard, or both.

While organization and performance standards are necessary, it is helping each other with the prepping and the cooking that makes for teamwork. "It's just like a relay race; we can't afford to drop the baton," says Amy Lu, kitchen manager of China Coast restaurant in Los Angeles. Teamwork in the back of the house is like an orchestra playing in tune, each player adding to the harmony.

Another example of organization and teamwork is TGI Friday's five rules of control for running a kitchen:

1. Order it well.
2. Receive it well.
3. Store it well.
4. Make it to the recipe.
5. Don't let it die in the window.

It is amazing to see a kitchen line being overloaded, yet everyone is gratified when the team succeeds in preparing and serving quality food on time.

Kitchen/Food Production

Staffing and Scheduling

Practicing proper staffing is absolutely crucial for the successful running of a kitchen. It is important to have enough employees on the schedule to enable

A Day in the Life of James Lorenz
Kitchen Manager, T.G.I. Friday's, Lafayette, Louisiana

7:00 A.M.: Arrive. Check the work of cleaning crew (such as clogs in burners, stoves/ovens, etc.) for total cleanliness

7:15–7:40: Set production levels for all stations (broiler/hot sauce/expediter, cold sauce, vegetable preparation, baker preparation, line preparation: saute/noodles, pantry, fry/seafood portioning)

8:00: The first cooks begin arriving; greet them and allocate production sheets with priority items circled

9:00: On a good day, the produce arrives at 9:00 A.M. Check for quality, quantity, accuracy (making sure the prices match the quotation sheet), and that the produce is stored properly

9:30–11:00: Follow up on production. The saute cook, who is last to come in, arrives. He or she is the closing person for the morning shift.
- ✓ Follow up on cleanliness, recipe adherence, production accuracy.
- ✓ Check the stations to ensure the storage of prepped items (e.g., plastic draining inserts under poultry and seafood), the shelf life of products, general cleanliness, and that what is in the station is prepared correctly (e.g., turkey diced to the right size and portioned and dated correctly).

10:45: Final check of the line and production to ensure readiness. Did everyone prepare enough?

11:00–2:30: All hands on deck. Jump on the first ticket. Pretoast buns for burgers and hold in heated drawers. Precook some chicken breasts for salads. Monitor lunch until 2:30 P.M.
- ✓ Be responsible for cleanliness.
- ✓ Determine who needs to get off the clock.
- ✓ Decide what production is left for the remainder of the day.
- ✓ Focus on changing over the line, change the food pan inserts (BBQ sauce, etc.).

2:30–3:15: Complete changeover of the line and check the stocking for the P.M. crew
- ✓ Final prep portioning.
- ✓ Check the dishwasher area and prep line for cleanliness.
- ✓ Check that the product is replaced in the store walk-in or refrigerator.
- ✓ Reorganize the produce walk-in. Check the storage of food, labels, and day dots, lids on.
- ✓ Thank the A.M. crew and send them home.

4:00–4:15: Welcome the P.M. crew
- ✓ Place produce order (as a double check, ask the P.M. crew what they might need).

5:00: Hand over to P.M. manager.

the restaurant, as a whole, to handle the volume on any given shift. Often it is better to overstaff the kitchen, rather than understaff it, for two reasons. First, it is much easier to send an employee home than it is to call someone in. Second, having extra employees on hand allows for cross-training and development, which is becoming a widely used method.

Problems can also be eliminated if a manpower plan is created, for example, to set levels for staffing needs. These levels should be adjusted according to sales trends on a monthly basis.

Also crucial to the smooth running of the kitchen is having a competent staff. This means putting the best cooks in the appropriate stations on the line, which will assist in the speed of service, the food quality, and the quality of the operations.

Training and Development

Implementing a comprehensive training program is vital in the kitchen, due to a high turnover rate. Trainers should, of course, be qualified and experienced in the kitchen. Often, the most competent chefs are used to train new hires. Such trainings are usually done on the job and may include study material. Some restaurants may even require new hires to complete a written test, evaluating the skills acquired through the training process.

Ensuring adequate training is necessary because the success of the business lies in the hands of the trainer and the trainee. If employees are properly trained when they begin their employment, little time and money will need to be spent on correcting errors. Thorough training also helps in retaining employees for longer periods of time.

Training, however, does not stop after passing a test. Developing the skills of all the employees is critical to the growth and success of the kitchen and, ultimately, the restaurant. A development program may consist of delegating duties or projects to the staff, allowing them to expand their horizons within the kitchen and the restaurant business. Such duties include projections of sales, inventory, ordering, schedule writing, and training.

This will help management get feedback on the running of the kitchen and on how well the development program works in their particular operation. Also, this allows for internal growth and promotion.

Production Procedures

Production in the kitchen is key to the success of a restaurant since it relates directly to the recipes on the menu and how much product is on hand to produce the menu. Thus, controlling the production process is crucial. To undertake such a task, **production control sheets** are created for each station, for example, broiler, saute, fry, pantry, window, prep, dish, and dessert. With the control sheets, levels are set up for each day according to sales.

The first step in creating the production sheets is to count the products on hand for each station. Once the production levels are determined, the amount of product required to reach the level for each recipe is decided. Once these calculations are completed, the sheets are handed to the cooks. It is important to make these calculations before the cooks arrive, considering the amount of prep time that is needed in order to produce before business is actually conducted. For instance, if a restaurant is open only for lunch and dinner, enough product should be on hand by 11:00 A.M. to ensure that the cooks are prepared to handle the lunch crowd.

When determining production, par levels should be changed weekly according to sales trends. This will help control and minimize waste levels. Waste is a large contributor to food cost, therefore the kitchen should determine the product levels necessary to make it through only one day. Products have a particular shelf life, and if the kitchen overproduces and does not sell the product within its shelf life, it must be thrown away. More importantly, this practice allows for the freshest product to reach the customers on a daily basis.

After the lunch rush, the kitchen checks to see how much product was sold and how much is left for the night shift. (Running out of a product is unacceptable and should not happen. If proper production procedures are followed, a restaurant will not have to "86" anything on the menu.) After all production is completed on all stations, the cooks may be checked out. It is essential to check out the cooks and hold them accountable for production levels. If they are not checked out, they will slide on their production, negatively impacting the restaurant and the customer.

The use of production sheets is critical, as well, in controlling how the cooks use the products, since production plays a key role in food cost. Every recipe has a particular "spec" (specification) to follow. When one deviates from the recipe, quality goes down, consistency is lost, and food cost goes up. That is why it is important to follow the recipe at all times.

Management Involvement

As in any business, management involvement is vital to the success of a restaurant. Management should know firsthand what is going on in the back of the house. It is also important that they be on the line, assisting the staff in the preparation of the menu and in the other operations of the kitchen, just as they should be helping when things are rushed. When management is visible to the staff, they are prone to do what they need to be doing at all times, and food quality is more apparent and consistent. Managers should constantly be walking and talking food cost, cleanliness, sanitation, and quality. This shows the staff how serious and committed they are to the successful running of the back of the house.

As management spends more time in the kitchen, more knowledge is gained, more confidence is acquired and more respect is earned. Employee–management interaction produces a sense of stability and a strong work ethic among employees, resulting in higher morale and promoting a positive working environment.

Management Follow-Up

To ensure that policies and standards are being upheld, management follow-up should happen on a continual basis. This is especially important when cooks are held accountable to specifications and production, and when other staff members are given duties to perform. Without follow-up, the restaurant may fold.

Employee Recognition

Employee recognition is an extremely important aspect of back-of-the-house management. Recognizing employees for their efforts creates a positive work environment that motivates the staff to excel and to ultimately produce consistently better quality food for the guests.

Recognition can take many different forms, from personally commending a staff person for his or her efforts to recognizing a person in a group setting. By recognizing employees, management can make an immediate impact on the quality of operations. This can be a great tool for building sales, as well as assisting in the overall success of the restaurant.

Purchasing

Purchasing for restaurants involves procuring the products and services that the restaurant needs in order to serve its guests. Restaurant operators set up purchasing systems that determine the following:

✓ Standards for each item (**product specification**)
✓ Systems that minimize effort and maximize control of theft and losses from other sources
✓ The amount of each item that should be on hand (par stock and reorder point)
✓ Who will do the buying and keep the purchasing system in motion
✓ Who will do the receiving, storage, and issuing of items[6]

It is desirable for restaurants to establish standards for each product, called *product specification.* When ordering meat, for example, the cut, weight, size, percentage of fat content, and number of days aged are all factors that are specified by the purchaser.

Establishing systems that minimize effort and maximize control of theft may be done by computer or manually. However, merely computerizing a system does not make it theft-proof. Instead, employing honest workers is a top priority because temptation is everywhere in the restaurant industry.

An efficient and effective system establishes a stock level that must be on hand at all times. This is called a **par stock.** If the stock on hand falls below a specified reorder point, the computer system automatically reorders a predetermined quantity of the item.

In identifying who will do the buying, it is most important to separate task and responsibility between the person placing the order and the person receiving the goods. This avoids possible theft. The best way to avoid losses is to have the chef prepare the order, the manager or the manager's designee place the order, and a third person responsible for the stores receive the goods together with the chef (or the chef's designee).

Commercial (for-profit) restaurant and foodservice operators who are part of a chain may have the menu items and order specifications determined at the corporate office. This saves the unit manager from having to order individually; specialists at the corporate office cannot only develop the menu but also the specifications for the ingredients to ensure consistency. Both chain and independent restaurants and foodservice operators use similar prepurchase functions (Figure 7–3):

---

[6]This section draws on Donald E. Lundberg and John R. Walker, *The Restaurant from Concept to Operation.* New York: John Wiley and Sons, 1993, p. 275.

Personal Profile: Ruth Fertel

There is no accolade or award for "the former first lady of American restaurants," but if there were, Ruth Fertel, founder of Ruth's Chris Steak House, would surely qualify for it.

Ruth's Chris Steak House is the nation's largest upscale restaurant chain with fifty-nine operations—fifty-four in the United States and Puerto Rico, and five internationally—selling more than 11,000 steaks daily and grossing more than $200 million annually. By virtue of this volume, Ruth Fertel is the country's most successful woman restauranteur today.

The Ruth's Chris's success story began on a hunch and a gamble. Born in New Orleans in 1927, Fertel earned a degree in chemistry with a minor in physics at Louisiana State University at the age of nineteen. She taught briefly at McNeese Junior College in Lake Charles, Louisiana, but left to marry and raise a family. Fourteen years later, and by then divorced, she reentered the workforce as a lab technician at Tulane Medical School. After four years, she was convinced that she could not earn enough to send her two sons to college and so, in 1965, she decided to go into business for herself. While scanning the classified section of the local newspaper, Fertel found an ad for a steak house that

(Courtesy Ruth's Chris Steak House.)

was for sale. Although she had no prior experience and limited funds, she decided to try it despite the advice of her lawyer, her banker, and her best friend to the contrary. She mortgaged her home to buy the small restaurant, which was then called Chris Steak House.

Fertel compensated for her lack of experience with plain hard work. In the first six months, she more than doubled her previous annual salary. Her restaurant soon became popular with the city's media personalities, political leaders, sports figures, and businesspeople. The name "Ruth's Chris" became synonymous with fine, quality steaks.

In 1977, at the urging of a loyal customer, Fertel granted her first franchise for a locally owned Ruth's Chris Steak House. Today, twenty-four restaurants are company owned and thirty-five are franchised.

Fertel attributed her success to the way she treated her customers and associates—as she would want to be treated—and to her basic "gut feeling" that has been responsible for successful decisions throughout the years.

The consistent quality of the meat she serves has also contributed to her success. Through the years, she stuck with the same suppliers and served nothing but the finest foods on the market.

✓ Plan menus.
✓ Determine quality and quantity needed to produce menus.
✓ Determine inventory stock levels.
✓ Identify items to purchase by subtracting stock levels from the quantity required to produce menus.
✓ Write specifications and develop market orders for purchases.

Figure 7–3 *Food Cost Control Process*

Professor Stefanelli at the University of Nevada, Las Vegas, suggests a formal and an informal method of purchasing that includes the following steps.[7]

Formal	*Informal*
Develop purchase order	Develop purchase order
Establish bid schedule	Quote price
Issue invitation to bid	Select vendor and place order
Tabulate and evaluate bids	
Award contract and issue delivery order	
Inspect/receive deliveries, inventory stores, and record transactions in inventory	Receive and inspect deliveries, store, and record transaction
Evaluate and follow up	Evaluate and follow up
Issue food supplies for food production and service	Issue food supplies for food production and service

The formal method is generally used by chain restaurant operators and the informal one by independent restaurant operators.

A **purchase order** comes as a result of the product specification. As it sounds, a purchase order is an order to purchase a certain quantity of an item at a specific price. Many restaurants develop purchase orders for items they need on a regular basis. These are then sent to suppliers for quotations, and samples are sent in for product evaluations. For example, canned items have varying amounts of liquid. Normally, it is the drained weight of the product that matters to the restaurant operator. After comparing samples from several vendors, the operator can choose the supplier that best suits the restaurant's needs.

Receiving

When placing an order, the restaurant operator specifies the day and time (for example, Friday, 10:00 A.M. to 12:00 noon) for the delivery to be made. This prevents deliveries from being made at inconvenient times.

Receiving is a point of control in the restaurant operation. The purpose of receiving is to ensure the quantity, quality, and price is exactly as ordered. The quantity and quality relate to the order specification and the standardized recipe. Depending on the restaurant and the type of food and beverage control system, some perishable items are issued directly to the kitchen, and most of the nonperishable items go into storage.

Storing/Issuing

Control of the stores is often a problem. Records must be kept of all items going into or out of the stores. If more than one person has access to the stores, it is difficult to know where to attach responsibility in case of losses.

[7]Ibid.

Items should only be issued from the stores on an authorized requisition signed by the appropriate person. One restaurateur who has been in business for many years issues stores to the kitchen on a daily basis. No inventory is kept in the production area and there is no access to the stores. To some, this may be overdoing control, but it is hard to fault the results: a good food cost percentage. All items that enter the stores should have a date stamp and be rotated using the first in–first out (FIFO) system.

First in–first out is a simple but effective system of ensuring stock rotation. This is achieved by placing the most recent purchases, in rotation, behind previous purchases. Failure to do this can result in spoilage.

Budgeting

Budgeting costs fall into two categories: fixed and variable. **Fixed costs** are constant regardless of the volume of business. Fixed costs are rent/lease payments, interest, and depreciation. **Variable costs** fluctuate with the volume of business. Variable costs include controllable expenses such as payroll, benefits, direct operating expense, music and entertainment, marketing and promotion, energy and utility, administrative, and repairs and maintenance.

Regardless of sales fluctuations, variable or controllable expenses vary in some controllable proportion to sales. For example, if a restaurant is open on a Monday it must have a host, server, cook, dishwasher, and so on. The volume of business and sales total may be $750. However, on Friday that sales total might be $2,250 with just a few more staff. The controllable costs increased only slightly in proportion to the sales, and the fixed costs did not change (see Table 7–1).

Restaurant Accounting

To operate any business efficiently and effectively, it is necessary to determine the mission, goals, and objectives. One of the most important goals in any enterprise is a fair return on investment, otherwise known as profit. In addition, accounting for the income and expenditures is a necessary part of any business enterprise. The restaurant industry has adopted a uniform system of accounts.

The **uniform system of accounts** for restaurants (USAR) outlines a standard classification and presentation of operating results. The system allows for easy comparison among restaurants because each expense item has the same schedule number.

Balance Sheet

A **balance sheet** for a restaurant, or any business, reflects how the assets and liabilities relate to the owner's equity at a particular moment in time. The balance sheet is mainly used by owners and investors to verify the financial health of the organization. Financial health may be defined in several ways, for example, liquidity, which means having a sufficient amount of cash available to pay

Table 7–1
Controllable Costs versus Fixed Costs in Terms of Sales

	Restaurant A Monday		Restaurant A Friday	
Sales				
Food	$600	75.0%	$ 1800	75.0%
Beverage	150	25.0	450	25.0
Total Sales	$750	100.0	$2,250	100.0
Cost of Sales				
Food	$198	26.0	$ 540	30.0
Beverage	37.50	25.0	112.50	25.0
Total Cost of Sales	$235.50		$ 652.50	
Gross Profit	$514.50		$1,597.50	
Controllable expenses				
Salaries and wages	$195	26.0%	$ 472.50	21.0%
Employee benefits	30	4.0	90	4.0
Direct operating expense	45	6.0	90	4.0
Music	7.50	1.0	7.50	1.0
Marketing	30	4.0	30	4.0
Energy and utility	22.50	3.0	67.50	3.0
Administrative/general	30	4.0	90	4.0
Repairs and maintenance	15	2.0	45	2.0
Total Controllable Expenses	$375.00		$ 892.50	

Rent and Other Occupation Costs
Income before interest, depreciation, and taxes
Interest
Depreciation
Total
Net income before taxes
Taxes
Net income

bills when they are due, and debt leverage, which is the percentage of a company's assets owned by outside interests (liabilities).

Restaurants are one of the few, fortunate types of businesses to operate on a cash basis for income receivables. There are no outstanding accounts receivable because all sales are in cash—even credit cards are treated as cash because of their prompt payment. Normally, restaurants invest significant funds in assets, such as equipment, furniture, and building (if they own it). The balance sheet will reflect how much of the cost of these assets has been paid for, and is thus owned by the company (owner's equity), and how much is still due to outsiders (liability). Furthermore, the balance sheet will show the extent to which the company has depreciated these assets, thus providing owners and investors with an indication of potential future costs to repair or replace existing assets.

Operating or Income Statement

From an operational perspective, the most important financial document is the operating statement. Once a sales forecast has been completed, the costs of servicing those sales are budgeted on an income statement. Table 7–2 shows an example of an income statement for a hypothetical restaurant.

Table 7–2
Sample Income Statement

	Amount	Percentage
Sales		
Food		
Beverage		
Others		
Total sales	_____	100
Cost of Sales		
Food		
Beverage		
Others		
Total cost of sales	_____	
Gross profit	_____	
Controllable Expenses		
Salaries and wages		
Employee benefits		
Direct operating expenses[a]		
Music and entertainment		
Marketing		
Energy and utility		
Administrative and general		
Repairs and maintenance		
Total controllable expenses	_____	
Rent and other occupation costs		
Income before interest, depreciation, and taxes		
Interest		
Depreciation		
Net income before taxes		
Income taxes	_____	
Net Income	_____	

[a]Telephone, insurance, legal, accounting, paper, glass, china, linens, office supplies, landscaping, cleaning supplies, etc.

The **income statement,** which is for a month or a year, begins with the food and beverage sales. From this total the cost of food and beverage is deducted; the remaining total is **gross profit.** To this amount any other income is added (e.g., cigarettes, vending machines, outside catering, and telephone income). The next heading is controllable expenses, which includes salaries, wages, employee benefits, direct operating expenses (telephone, insurance, accounting and legal fees, office supplies, paper, china, glass, cutlery, menus, landscaping, and so on), music and entertainment, marketing, energy and utility, administrative and general, repairs and maintenance. The total of this group is called total controllable expenses. Rent and other occupation costs are then deducted from the total, leaving income before interest, depreciation, and taxes. Interest and depreciation are deducted leaving a total of net income before taxes. From this amount income taxes are paid leaving the remainder as net income.

Managing the money to the bottom line requires careful scrutiny of all key results, beginning with the big ticket controllable items like labor costs, food costs, and beverages, on down to related controllables. Additionally, management may wish to compare several income statements representing operations over a number of different periods. The ideal method for comparing is to compute every component of each income statement as a percentage of its total sales. Then compare one period's percentage to another to determine if any significant trends are developing. For example, a manager could compare labor as a percent of total sales over several months, or years, to assess the impact of rising labor rates on the bottom line.

Operating Ratios

Operating ratios are industry norms that are applicable to each segment of the industry. Experienced restaurant operators rely on these operating ratios to indicate the restaurant's degree of success. Several ratios are good barometers of a restaurant's degree of success. Among the better known ratios are the following:

- ✓ Food cost percentage
- ✓ Contribution margin
- ✓ Labor cost percentage
- ✓ Prime cost
- ✓ Beverage cost percentage

Food Cost Percentage

The basic **food cost percentage,** for which the formula is cost/sales $\times$ 100 = the food cost percentage, is calculated on a daily, weekly, or monthly basis. The procedure works in the following manner:

1. An inventory is taken of all the food and the purchase price of that food. This is called the *opening inventory.*
2. The purchases are totaled for the period and added to the opening inventory.
3. The closing inventory (the inventory at the close of the week or period for which the food cost percentage is being calculated) and returns, spoilage,

complimentary meals, and transfers to other departments are also deducted from the opening inventory plus purchases.

4. This figure is the cost of goods sold. The cost of goods sold is divided by the total sales. The resulting figure is the food cost percentage.

The following example illustrates the procedure:

Food Sales	$3,000
Opening Inventory	1,000
Add Purchases	500
	1,5000
Less Spoilage and Complimentary Meals	100
Less Closing Inventory	500
Cost of Goods Sold	$900

$$\frac{\text{Food Cost (\$900)}}{\text{Sales (\$3,000)}} \times 100 = 30\% \text{ Food Cost Percentage}$$

The food cost percentage calculations become slightly more complicated when the cost of staff meals, management meals and entertaining (complimentary meals), and guest food returned are all properly calculated.

Food cost percentage has long been used as a yardstick for measuring the skill of the chef, cooks, and management to achieve a predetermined food cost percentage—usually 28 to 32 percent for a full-service restaurant and a little higher for a high-volume, fast-food restaurant.

Controlling food costs begins with cost-effective purchasing systems, a controlled storage and issuing system, and strict control of the food production and sales. The best way to visualize a food cost control system is to think of the food as money. Consider a $100 bill arriving at the back door: If the wrong people get their hands on that money, it does not reach the guest or the bottom line.

Contribution Margin

More recently, attention has focused not only on the food cost percentage but also on the contribution margin. The **contribution margin** is the amount that a menu item contributes to the gross profit, or the difference between the cost of the item and its sales price. Some menu items contribute more than others; therefore, restaurant operators focus more attention on the items that produce a higher contribution margin. It works like this:

The cost of the chicken dish is $2.00 and its selling price is $9.95, which leaves a contribution margin of $7.95. The fish, which costs a little more at $3.25 sells for $12.75 and leaves a contribution of $9.50. The pasta cost price of $1.50 and selling price of $8.95 leave a contribution margin of $7.45. Under this scenario it would be better for the restaurants to sell more fish because each plate will yield $1.55 more than if chicken were sold.

Labor Cost Percentage

Labor costs are the highest single cost factor in staffing a restaurant. Fast-food restaurants have the lowest **labor costs percentage** (about 16 to 18 percent) with family and ethnic restaurants at about 22 to 26 percent, and upscale full-service restaurants at about 30 to 35 percent.

Labor costs include salaries and wages of employees, employee benefits, and their training. Food service is a highly labor intensive industry depending on the type of restaurant. Quick-service restaurants have a lower payroll cost primarily due to their limited menu and limited service. Good managers try to manage their labor costs by accurate hiring and scheduling of staff according to the restaurant's cover turnover.

Prime Cost

Combined food and labor costs are known as **prime cost.** To allow for a reasonable return on investment, prime cost should not go above 60 to 65 percent of sales.

There are various methods of control, beginning with effective scheduling based on the expected volume of business. In reality, because of the high cost of labor, today's restaurateurs manage by the minute. Once a rush is over, the effective manager thanks employees for doing a great job and looks forward to seeing them again. This may appear to be micromanagement, but an analysis of restaurant operations does not leave any alternatives.[8]

Beverage Cost Percentage

The **beverage cost percentage** is calculated like the food cost percentage. The method used most often is to first determine the unit cost and then mark up by the required percentage to arrive at the selling price. This is rounded up or down to a convenient figure. The actual beverage cost percentage is then compared with the anticipated cost percentage; any discrepancy is investigated.

The National Restaurant Association publishes guidelines for restaurant operations. These valuable documents help provide a guide for operators to use when comparing their restaurants with other similar establishments. If the costs go above the budgeted or expected levels, then management must investigate and take corrective action.

Therefore, if we are operating a casual Italian restaurant, industry comparisons would show the following:

> Labor costs at 20 to 24 percent of sales
> Food costs at 28 to 32 percent of food sales
> Beverage costs at 18 to 24 percent of beverage sales

Lease and Controllable Expenses

Lease Costs

Successful restaurant operators will ensure that the restaurant's lease does not cost more than 5 to 8 percent of sales. Some chain restaurants will search for

---

[8]Personal conversation with Bobby Hays, general manager, Chart House Restaurant, Solana Beach, California, January 1994.

Corporate Profile: T.G.I. Friday's

In the spring of 1965, Alan Stillman, a New York perfume salesman, opened a restaurant located at First Avenue and 63rd Street. The restaurant boasted striped awnings, a blue exterior, and yellow supergraphics reading T.G.I. Friday's. Inside were wooden floors covered with sawdust, Tiffany-style lamps, bentwood chairs, red-and-white tablecloths, and a bar area complete with brass rails and stained glass.

T.G.I. Friday's was an immediate success. The restaurant on Manhattan's upper east side became the meeting place for single adults. In fact, *Newsweek* and the *Saturday Evening Post* called the opening of T.G.I. Friday's *"the dawn of the singles' age."*

In 1971, franchisee Dan Scoggin opened a T.G.I. Friday's in Dallas and in four other sites around the country. The success was instant; thus, began the company that is Friday's today.

By 1975, there were ten T.G.I. Friday's in eight states, but the great success that the company had seen was starting to diminish. Dan Scoggin began a country-wide tour to visit each restaurant; he talked with employees, managers, and customers to isolate the roots of successes and failures. This was the critical turning point for the company. The focus shifted from being just another restaurant chain to giving guests exactly what they wanted. The theories and philosophies Scoggin developed are the principles by which Friday's now does business.

T.G.I. Friday's goal was to create a comfortable, relaxing environment where guests could enjoy food and drink. Stained glass windows, wooden airplane propellers, racing sculls, and metal advertising signs comprised the elegant clutter that greeted guests when they entered a T.G.I. Friday's. Nothing was left to chance. Music, lights, air conditioning, decor, and housekeeping were all designed to keep guests comfortable. Employees were encouraged to display their own personalities and to treat customers as they would guests in their own homes.

As guests demanded more, T.G.I. Friday's provided more—soon becoming the industry leader in menu and drink selection. The menu expanded from a slate chalkboard to an award-winning collection of items representing every taste and mood.

T.G.I. Friday's also became the industry leader in innovation—creating the now-famous potato skins and popularizing fried zucchini. This was the first restaurant chain to offer stone ground whole wheat bread, avocados, bean sprouts, and Mexican appetizers across the country. As guests' tastes continued to change, T.G.I. Friday's introduced pasta dishes, brunch items, and croissant sandwiches.

America owes the popularization of frozen and ice cream drinks to T.G.I. Friday's, where smooth, alcoholic and nonalcoholic drinks were made with fresh fruit, juices, ice cream, and yogurt. These recipes were so precise that T.G.I. Friday's drink glasses were scientifically designed for the correct ratio of each ingredient. These specially designed glasses have since become popular throughout the industry.

Through the years, Friday's success has been phenomenal. More than 525 restaurants have opened in the United States and more than 200 restaurants in 58 other countries. With average gross revenues of $3.5 million per year at each location, it has the highest per unit sales volume of any national casual dining chain.

Friday's is privately owned by Carlson Companies, Inc., of Minneapolis—one of the largest privately held companies in the country. Today, Friday's has come to be known as a casual restaurant where family and friends meet for great food, fun, and conversation. Everyone looks forward to Friday's!

What does it take to be successful in the restaurant business, and what does it take to be a leader? The answers to these questions are crucial to success as a restaurant company. The essentials of success in business are as follows:

1. Treat everyone with respect for their dignity.
2. Treat all customers as if they are honored guests in your home.
3. Remember that all problems result from either poor hiring, lack of training, unclear performance expectations, or accepting less than excellence.
4. Remember that management tools are methods, not objectives.

As you can see, these are principles to guide decision making as opposed to step-by-step actions. However, I would submit that if these principles are not followed, then actions have very short-term effects. And if you do choose to follow them, they form a base on which you can easily decide which specific actions are necessary in any given situation.

The basics of leadership are as follows:

1. Hire the right people.
2. Train everyone thoroughly and completely.
3. Be sure that everyone clearly understands the performance expectations.
4. Accept only excellence.

continued

Here we are dealing with the very basics of how to provide strong, clear leadership. However, once again we are talking about only the minimum requirements, not all the qualities necessary to be a good leader. Individual success and that of the company, Friday's Inc., are predicated on understanding and following the essentials of success in business and the basics of leadership. Whether you are an hourly employee or a manager, it is critical that you manage your part of the business using these philosophies.

One of the things that makes Friday's unique is the philosophies and theories. These are principles that each employee understands to ensure everyone stays focused on the same goals. Friday's philosophies and theories were first conceived in the mid-1970s. They are used to solve existing problems and enable management to be proactive to problems experienced in the past.

The Guest Focus

At most companies, it appears that senior management runs the company. The employees consider senior management to be the most important people with whom they interact. As a result, decisions are made in an effort to please senior management, and decisions that affect people lower in the hierarchy are viewed as less important. Friday's success is dependent on inverting the typical management pyramid. Guests are the most important element in the organization; immediately following them are the employees who are closest to the guests—those people who have the greatest impact on the guests' experience. The livelihood of each employee depends on one group of people: guests. It is critical to determine what guests' needs are and fill those needs. To the extent that this objective is accomplished, the needs of each person in the pyramid will be fulfilled. Every decision at Friday's is made with guests in mind.

The "Five Easy Pieces Theory" stresses Friday's deep concern for the guests' satisfaction. Friday's will always cheerfully go out of their way to serve a quality product prepared to individual tastes. In the movie titled *Five Easy Pieces,* the star, Jack Nicholson, goes to a restaurant and orders a side order of whole wheat toast. The waitress makes it clear that they do not serve whole wheat toast. Nicholson notes on the menu that the chicken salad sandwich comes on whole wheat bread. The annoyed waitress

points to a sign in the restaurant that reads "No substitutions" and "We reserve the right to refuse service to anyone." Jack Nicholson orders a chicken salad sandwich on whole wheat toast, but tells the waitress to hold the mayo, hold the lettuce, hold the chicken salad, and just bring him the whole wheat toast. Unwisely, she asks where she should hold the chicken salad. Nicholson sarcastically responds, "Between your knees!" On that note, he leaves, a very dissatisfied guest. Friday's managers and employees are responsible for honoring any guest request within realistic possibilities. Many managers take a guest's request even further and get them exactly what they want—even if the ingredients are not in the restaurant.

The "Triangle Theory" explains the need to balance and expand upon the goals of the guest, employee, and company, and maximize the results to each. Managers make many decisions and must always consider the effect of those decisions on all three sides of the triangle—the guest, the employee, and the company. Some decisions can cause one side of the triangle to prosper (temporarily) at the expense of the other two. For example, if a company overprices its menu items, it can greatly improve the bottom line. However, guests will object to being cheated and will not return. This will ultimately result in lower staffing and will eventually kill the company. Management's responsibility is to balance the results among the three sides so all sides thrive. But this is only the first step. To grow and expand the business, decisions must be made that maximize or expand all three sides of the triangle at the same time.

These are just a few of the philosophies and theories on which Friday's is based.

Benefits

Starting compensation for managers is an individual issue, based on background and experience. In addition to a competitive base salary, Friday's also offers a bonus based on sales and/or profits to all managers.

Management staffing is designed to meet volume needs and may number four to seven per store. Management generally works a five-day work week.

Friday's offers a complete benefits program for both hourly and management personnel. Among its features are health and dental coverage (dependent coverage is also available), vision care, life insurance, paid vacations, tuition assistance, scholarships, disability coverage, credit union, education assistance program, and a 401(k) plan. At Friday's Inc., they also believe that recognizing employees for their outstanding effort is their opportunity to acknowledge and reinforce the behavior they want to encourage.

A day in the life of Chris, a Friday's General Manager

✓ Chris works a combination of open (typically 7 a.m.–6 p.m.), swing (11 a.m.–10 p.m.) and close (5 p.m.–3 a.m.) shifts, depending on the needs of the business and his goals for the week.

✓ Regardless of when Chris works, he is ultimately responsible for food safety and quality, employee staffing and training, guest satisfaction, and restaurant profitability.

✓ Chris's responsibilities are accomplished throughout the day by conducting food line checks, employee shift meetings, and guest table visits.

✓ As the General manager, Chris is expected to be a role model for all the employees and managers, and is responsible for upholding the company credo.

Expectations of the General Manager

The expectations of the general manager are different in each restaurant; however, there are certain commonalities as well. Some of these commonalities are as follows:

✓ General managers answer directly to the owner, or to regional directors for major corporations.

✓ General managers are expected to run good numbers for the periods. The numbers analyzed are food cost, labor cost, beverage cost. These areas are controlled in order to produce sufficient profit for the restaurant.

✓ General managers promote good morale and teamwork in the restaurant. Having a positive environment in the restaurant is of utmost importance. This will not only keep the employees happy, but it will also contribute to providing better service to the guests.

Duties and Responsibilities

The general manager of a restaurant is directly in charge of all of the operations in the restaurant. General man-

agers are also in charge of the floor managers, kitchen manager, and all of the remaining employees in the restaurant.

The general manager should always check on the floor managers to ensure that all policies and regulations are being met. This will keep operations running smoothly.

Another important duty is to organize and control the staffing of the restaurant. The floor managers usually write the employee schedule; however, the general manager is still directly responsible for proper staffing for the period. This will help keep labor costs to about 20 percent of sales. The general manager is also in charge of conducting employee reviews and training.

Qualifications for a General Manager

To be hired as a general manager, the following qualifications are necessary:

✓ The general manager should be very knowledgeable in the restaurant business.

✓ He or she should have previously worked all the stations in a restaurant and be very familiar with them.

✓ The general manager should be able to get along with all people, be fair with all employees, and not discriminate.

✓ Having a degree is not the most important thing in becoming a general manager. However, a degree is very useful in moving up the ladder in a company to regional manager, regional director, and so on.

Budgeted Costs in a Restaurant

Running a good pace in the restaurant is of absolute importance. Every restaurant has different numbers to make. The following numbers came from a T.G.I. Friday's-type restaurant. These numbers reflect their goals versus actual numbers run for a given week.

	GOAL	ACTUAL	VARIANCE
Food Cost	27.0	27.2	+0.2
Labor Cost	19.9	20.8	+0.9
Beverage Cost	19.0	18.2	−0.8

As can be seen, the T.G.I. Friday's did well with the beverage cost; however, the food cost and the labor cost are two areas to focus on for the upcoming week.

Making good percentages for the restaurant is the most important focus, simply because this is where the restaurant makes or does not make a profit. When the general manager runs good numbers, then he or she

continued

will receive a large bonus check for contributing to the profit of the restaurant. This is why it is so important to focus on these three key areas.

Scheduling the Restaurant

Appropriate scheduling plays a key role in the success of the restaurant. For one thing, overscheduling and under-scheduling have a direct effect on the labor cost. If there are too many employees working on a shift for the business acquired, then the labor cost will be high. In contrast, if there are not enough employees working, then the service will suffer and overtime will increase the labor cost.

Friday's values are summed up in the Carlson Credo, shown below.

The Carlson Credo

Whatever you do, do it with INTEGRITY.
Wherever you go, go as a LEADER.
Whomever you serve, serve with CARING.
Whenever you dream, dream with your ALL.
And never, ever give up.

—Curt Carlson, March 23, 1998

---

months or even years before they find the right location at the right price. Most leases are triple net, which means that the lessee must pay for all alterations, insurance, utilities, and possible commercial fees (e.g., landscaping or parking upkeep, security, etc.).

The best lease is for the longest time period with options for renewal and a sublease clause. The sublease clause is important because if the restaurant is not successful, the owner is still liable for paying the lease. With the sublease clause the owner may sublease the space to another restaurant operator or any other business.

Many leases are quoted at a dollar rate per square foot per month. Depending on the location, rates may range from $1.25 per square foot up to as much as $8.00 per square foot.

Some restaurants pay a combination of a flat amount based on the square footage and a percentage of sales. This helps protect the restaurant operator in the slower months and gives the landlord a bit extra during the good months.

Once a lease contract is signed, it is very difficult to renegotiate even a part of it. Only in dire circumstances is it possible to renegotiate lease contracts. The governing factor in determining lease rates is the marketplace. The marketplace is the supply and demand. If there is strong demand for space, then rates will increase. However, with a high vacancy rate, rates will be driven down by the owners in an effort to rent space and gain income.

Controllable Expenses

Controllable expenses are all the expenses over which management and ownership has control. They include salaries and wages (payroll) and related benefits; direct operating expenses such as music and entertainment; marketing, including sales, advertising, public relations, and promotions; heat, light, and power; administrative and general expenses; and repairs and maintenance. The total of all controllable expenses is deducted from the gross profit. Rent and other occupation costs are then deducted to arrive at the income before interest, depreciation, and taxes. Once these are deducted, the **net profit** remains.

Successful restaurant operators are constantly monitoring their controllable expenses. The largest controllable expense is payroll. Because payroll is about 24 to 28 percent of a restaurant's sales, managers constantly monitor their employees, not by the hour but by the minute. Bobby Hays, general manager of the Chart House Restaurant in Solana Beach, California, says that he feels the pulse of the restaurant and then begins to send people home. Every dollar that Bobby and managers like him can save goes directly to the bottom line and becomes profit.

The actual sales results are compared with the budgeted amounts—ideally with percentages—and variances investigated. Most chain restaurant operators monitor the key result areas of sales and labor costs on a daily basis. Food and beverage costs are also monitored closely, generally on a weekly basis.

Check Your Knowledge

1. What is the back of the house?
2. Create a recognition program that would encourage restaurant employees.
3. What is the storing/issuing process? Why is it important?
4. Briefly explain the term *contribution margin*.

Controls

Every dollar earned must be watched all the way to the bank, and every dollar spent must be analyzed to see if it is really necessary. **Control** provides information to management for operational decision-making purposes.

Industry experts describe the following losses resulting from a lack of controls:

✓ The food service industry loses approximately $20 billion a year to theft and cash mishandling.
✓ One out of every three employees will steal if given the opportunity. This includes theft of cash, merchandise, and time.
✓ Approximately 5 to 8 percent of gross sales is lost to internal theft.

✓   Thirty-five percent of all restaurants fail because of theft.
✓   Seventy-five percent of all missing inventory is from theft.
✓   Seventy-three percent of job applications are falsified.
✓   The majority of employees caught stealing have worked for an operation for an average of five to seven years.

Fred Del Marva, chairman and CEO of Food and Beverage Investigations, loss management investigators in Novato, California, offers the following advice to reduce back-of-the-house theft.[9]

✓   Conduct frequent inventories.
✓   Distribute receiving responsibilities.
✓   Establish a par stock.
✓   Refuse off-peak-hour deliveries.
✓   Use insider accounting.
✓   Designate an employee entry/exit.
✓   Discourage duffel bags/reserve the right to search bags.
✓   Oversee trash disposal.

Another industry expert has the following suggestion: "Owners and managers could take expensive marketing plans that are designed to increase sales by 25 percent and toss them out the window if they would just make a minimal effort to control theft," says Francis D'Addario, director of loss prevention for Hardee's food systems, Rocky Mount, North Carolina. Many operators are reluctant to crack down on theft because they simply do not want to play cop. Other operators just refuse to believe they are being cheated because they trust their long-time employees. Spotting theft is a job in itself. A variance of more than half a percent in food cost should be considered odd enough to check out. An unusual food cost variance can mean cash is going out the front door or food is going out the back.[10]

Most restaurants rely on point-of-sale (POS) systems. These systems, such as a server's hand-held ordering device that automatically prints up the order in the kitchen or bar, have improved service efficiency. However, there is a cost involved and restaurant operators need to carefully select point-of-sale systems that are appropriate for their restaurants.

Buying a POS system for a restaurant can be a major investment. It is imperative that managers get the most value for their dollars. *Restaurants and Institutions* magazine surveyed a panel of experts from companies that use POS systems who suggested the following guidelines:

1. Buy from a reliable vendor.
2. Decide what you need before buying.
3. Don't get carried away with technology.
4. Look for a computer company that knows restaurants.
5. Buy standard software packages.
6. Look for an adaptable piece of equipment.

[9]Personal conversation with Fred Del Marva, May 1994.

[10]This section draws on Beth Lorenzini, "The Secure Restaurant," *Restaurants and Institutions,* **102,** 25, October 21, 1992, pp. 84–102.

7. Try to use generic hardware.
8. Find a system that simultaneously runs several programs.
9. Consider quick credit card verification.
10. Insist on a twenty-four-hour hot line.
11. User-friendly systems can pay off.
12. Avoid downtime with a dual disk system.
13. Find a system that helps control labor costs.[11]

Foodservice Manager Job Analysis

The National Restaurant Association (NRA) has formulated an analysis of the foodservice manager's job by functional areas and tasks, which follows a natural sequence of functional areas from human resources to sanitation and safety.

Human Resource Management

Recruiting/Training
1. Recruit new employees by seeking referrals.
2. Recruit new employees by advertising.
3. Recruit new employees by seeking help from district manager/supervisors.
4. Interview applicants for employment.

Orientation/Training
1. Conduct on-site orientation for new employees.
2. Explain employee benefits and compensation programs.
3. Plan training programs for employees.
4. Conduct on-site training for employees.
5. Evaluate progress of employees during training.
6. Supervise on-site training of employees that is conducted by another manager, employee leader, trainer, and so on.
7. Conduct payroll signup.
8. Complete reports or other written documentation on successful completion of training by employees.

Scheduling for Shifts
1. Review employee work schedule for shift.
2. Determine staffing needs for each shift.
3. Make work assignments for dining room, kitchen staff, and maintenance person(s).
4. Make changes to employee work schedule.
5. Assign employees to work stations to optimize employee effectiveness.
6. Call in, reassign, or send home employees in reaction to sales and other needs.
7. Approve requests for schedule changes, vacation, days off, and so on.

---

[11]This section draws from Jeff Weinstein, "13 Things You Need to Know Before Buying a POS System," *Restaurants and Institutions*, **103**, 3, February 1, 1993, pp. 131–134.

Supervision and Employee Development
1. Observe employees and give immediate feedback on unsatisfactory employee performance.
2. Observe employees and give immediate feedback on satisfactory employee performance.
3. Discuss unsatisfactory performance with an employee.
4. Develop and deliver incentive for above-satisfactory performance of employees.
5. Observe employee behavior for compliance with safety and security.
6. Counsel employees on work-related problems.
7. Counsel employees on nonwork-related problems.
8. Talk with employees who have frequent absences.
9. Observe employees to ensure compliance with fair labor standards and equal opportunity guidelines.
10. Discipline employees by issuing oral and/or written warnings for poor performance.
11. Conduct employee and staff meetings.
12. Identify and develop candidates for management programs.
13. Put results of observation of employee performance in writing.
14. Develop action plans for employees to help them in their performance.
15. Authorize promotion and/or wage increases for staff.
16. Terminate employment of an employee for unsatisfactory performance.

Financial Management

Accounting
1. Authorize payment on vendor invoices.
2. Verify payroll.
3. Count cash drawers.
4. Prepare bank deposits.
5. Assist in establishment audits by management or outside auditors.
6. Balance cash at end of shift.
7. Analyze profit and loss reports for establishment.

Cost Control
1. Discuss factors that impact profitability with district manager/supervisor.
2. Check establishment figures for sales, labor costs, waste, inventory, and so on.

Administrative Management

Scheduling/Coordinating
1. Establish objectives for shift based on needs of establishment.
2. Coordinate work performed by different shifts, for example, cleanup, routine maintenance, and so on.
3. Complete special projects assigned by district manager/supervisor.
4. Complete shift readiness checklist.

Planning
1. Develop and implement action plans to meet financial goals.
2. Attend off-site workshops and training sessions.

Communication
1. Communicate with management team by reading and making entries in daily communication log.
2. Prepare written reports on cleanliness, food quality, personnel, inventory, sales, food waste, labor costs, and so on.
3. Review reports prepared by other establishment managers.
4. Review memos, reports, and letters from company headquarters/main office.
5. Inform district manager/supervisor of problems or developments that affect operation and performance of the establishment.
6. Initiate and answer correspondence with company, vendors, and so on.
7. File correspondence, reports, personnel records, and so on.

Marketing Management
1. Create and execute local establishment marketing activities.
2. Develop opportunities for the establishment to provide community services.
3. Carry out special product promotions.

Operations Management

Facility Maintenance
1. Conduct routine maintenance checks on facility and equipment.
2. Direct routine maintenance checks on facility and equipment.
3. Repair or supervise the repair of equipment.
4. Review establishment evaluations with district manager/supervisor.
5. Authorize the repair of equipment by outside contractor.
6. Recommend upgrades in facility and equipment.

Food and Beverage Operations Management
1. Direct activities for opening establishment.
2. Direct activities for closing establishment.
3. Talk with other managers at beginning and end of shift to relay information about ongoing problems and activities.
4. Count, verify, and report inventory.
5. Receive, inspect, and verify vendor deliveries.
6. Check stock levels and submit orders as necessary.
7. Talk with vendors concerning quality of product delivered.
8. Interview vendors who wish to sell products to establishment.
9. Check finished product quality and act to correct problems.
10. Work as expediter to get meals served effectively.
11. Inspect dining area, kitchen, rest rooms, food lockers, storage, and parking lot.

12. Check daily reports for indications of internal theft.
13. Instruct employees regarding the control of waste, portion sizes, and so on.
14. Prepare forecast for daily or shift food preparation.

Service

1. Receive and record table reservations.
2. Greet familiar customers by name.
3. Seat customers.
4. Talk with customers while they are dining.
5. Monitor service times and procedures in the dining area.
6. Observe customers being served in order to correct problems.
7. Ask customers about quality of service.
8. Ask customers about quality of the food product.
9. Listen to and resolve customer complaints.
10. Authorize complimentary meals or beverages.
11. Write letters in response to customer complaints.
12. Telephone customers in response to customer complaints.
13. Secure and return items left by customers.

Sanitation and Safety

1. Accompany local officials on health inspections on premise.
2. Administer first aid to employees and customers.
3. Submit accident, incident, and OSHA reports.
4. Report incidents to police.
5. Observe employee behavior and establishment conditions for compliance with safety and security procedures.

Trends in Restaurant Operations

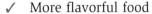

- ✓ More flavorful food
- ✓ Increased take-out meals, especially at lunch
- ✓ Food safety
- ✓ Guests becoming more sophisticated and needing more things to excite them
- ✓ More food court restaurants in malls, movie theater complexes, and colleges and universities where guests line up (similar to a cafeteria), select their food (which a server places on a tray), and pay a cashier
- ✓ Steak houses are becoming more popular
- ✓ With more restaurants in each segment, the segments are splitting into upper, middle, and lower tiers
- ✓ Twin and multirestaurant locations
- ✓ Quick-service restaurants (QSRs) in convenience stores
- ✓ Difficulty in finding good employees

Case Study

Short Staffed in the Kitchen

Sally is the general manager of one of the best restaurants in town, known as The Pub. As usual, at 6:00 P.M. on a Friday night, there is a forty-five-minute wait. The kitchen is overloaded and they are running behind in check times, the time that elapses between the kitchen getting the order and the guest receiving his or her meal. This is critical, especially if a complaint is received because a guest has waited too long for a meal to be served.

Sally is waiting for her two head line cooks to come in for the closing shift. It is now 6:15 P.M. and she receives phone calls from both of them. Unfortunately, they are both sick with the flu and are not able to come to work.

As she gets off the phone, the hostess tells Sally that a party of fifty is scheduled to arrive at 7:30 P.M. Sally is concerned, knowing that they are currently running a six-person line with only four cooks. The productivity is very high, but they are running extremely long check times. How can Sally handle the situation?

Discussion Questions

1. How would you handle the short-staffing issue?
2. What measures would you take to get the appropriate cooks in to work as soon as possible?
3. What would you do to ensure a smooth, successful transition for the party of fifty?
4. How would you manipulate your floor plan to provide great service for the party of fifty?
5. How would you immediately make an impact on the long check times?
6. What should you do to ensure that all the guests in the restaurant are happy?

Case Study

Shortage in Stock

It is Friday morning at 9:30 at The Pub. Product is scheduled to be delivered at 10:00. Sally specifically ordered an exceptional amount of food for the upcoming weekend because she is projecting it to be a busy holiday weekend. Sally receives a phone call at 10:30 from J&G groceries, stating that they cannot deliver the product until 10:00 A.M. on Saturday morning. She explains to the driver that it is crucial that she receives the product as soon as possible. He apologizes, however it is impossible to have delivery made until Saturday morning.

continued

By 1:00 P.M., they are beginning to run out of product, including absolute necessities such as steaks, chicken, fish, and produce. The guests are getting frustrated because the staff are beginning to 86 a great deal of product. In addition, if they do not begin production for the P.M. shift soon, they will be in deep trouble.

On Friday nights, The Pub does in excess of $12,000 in sales. However, if the problem is not immediately alleviated, the restaurant will lose many guests and a great amount of profits.

Discussion Questions

1. What immediate measures would you take to resolve the problem?
2. How would you produce the appropriate product as soon as possible?
3. Who should you call first, if anyone, to alleviate the problem?
4. What can you do to always have enough product on hand?
5. Is it important to have a back-up plan for a situation like this? If so, what would it be?

Career Information

Restaurant Operations

Choosing a management career in restaurant operations means you have just selected the area of hospitality that offers college graduates enormous opportunity, the highest starting salaries in the hospitality industry, and the best opportunities for advancement. Opportunities range from fast-food to five-star dining. Salaries range from $32,000 to over $40,000 for entry-level management positions. Where you will be on that continuum depends on the skills you acquired while in the restaurant industry during college and your ability to sell yourself. (The type of operation, sales volume, and location of the establishment also affect salaries.)

Higher salaries mean a more competitive environment for jobs. In the last few years, salaries have started to increase, reflecting the restaurant industry's willingness to hire experienced young talent. Recruiters refer to these graduates sometimes as grade A candidates or thoroughbreds. Recruiters want graduates who are confident in their skills and have a work record that shows a genuine interest in restaurant management.

Possessing confidence and skill is necessary to complete the management training programs and to get through your first year as a manager. Typically, restaurant managers work fifty to sixty hours a week, including weekends and holidays. It is a physically demanding job that requires being constantly on your feet and working under pressure in a fast-paced environment.

However, this kind of challenge has tremendous rewards. As a manager, you will work in an atmosphere that offers endless opportunities to delight customers and motivate employees. Few things are more gratifying than a genuinely satisfied customer or sharing in the pleasure of the restaurant crew's successfully completed shift. Restaurant operations typically pay people based strictly on performance. It is not uncommon for restaurant general managers to make six-figure incomes from restaurants that generate $5 million plus in sales.

Related Web Sites

http://www.edfound.org/—NRA educational foundation
http://www.restaurant-careers.com/—Career Bulletin Board
http://www.brinker.com/htm/006_Employment_framesource.htm—Brinker International employment opportunities
http://www.houstons.com/html/benefits.htm—Houston's Restaurants employment opportunities
http://www.darden.com/darden.html—Darden Restaurants employment opportunities
http://www.careeradviser.com/all/Restaurant_and_food_service_managers.htm—opportunity for career advice
http://www.ranw.com/books/careers.html—foodservice books on careers

Courtesy of Charlie Adams.

Summary

1. Most restaurants forecast a budget on a weekly and monthly basis that projects sales and costs for a year in consideration of guest counts and the average guest check.

2. In order to operate a restaurant, products need to be purchased, received, and properly stored.

3. Food production is determined by the expected business for the next few days. The kitchen layout is designed according to the sales forecasted.

4. Good service is very important. A distinction is made among Russian, American, and French service. In addition to taking orders, servers act as salespersons for the restaurant.

5. Budgeting costs are divided into fixed costs (such as lease or rent) and variable costs, which include controllable expenses such as salaries, entertainment, and promotion.

6. Accounting for the income and expenditures is necessary in order to gain a profit. Measures of accounting are the uniform system of accounts for restaurants, a balance sheet, and an income statement.

7. Restaurant operators rely on ratios such as food cost percentage, contribution margin, labor cost percentage, and prime cost to indicate the restaurant's degree of success.

8. The point-of-sales system is one form of control that restaurants use to protect themselves from theft.

9. The front of the house deals with the part of the restaurant having direct contact with guests. In other words, what the guests see—grounds maintenance, hosts/hostesses, dining and bar areas, bartenders, busers, etc.

10. The back of the house is generally run by the kitchen manager and refers to all areas guests normally do not come in contact with. This includes purchasing, receiving, storing/issuing, food production, stewarding, budgeting, accounting, and control.

Key Words and Concepts

American Service
Average guest check
Back of the house
Balance sheet profit
Beverage cost percentage
Budgeting costs
Chef de rang
Commis de rang
Cooking line
Contribution margin
Control

Controllable expenses
Curbside appeal
Demi chef de rang
Employee recognition
First in–first out
Fixed costs
Food cost percentage
French service
Front of the house
Gross profit
Guest counts or covers

Haute cuisine
Hostess
Income statement
Kitchen layout
Kitchen manager
Labor cost percentage
Maître d'hotel
Net profit
Operating ratios
Par stock
Prime cost

Product specification
Production control sheets
Purchase order
Purchasing
Receiving
Restaurant forecasting
Russian service
Suggestive selling
Uniform system of accounts
Variable costs

Review Questions

1. Briefly describe the two components of restaurant forecasting.
2. Explain the key points in purchasing, receiving, and storing.
3. Why is the kitchen layout an important aspect of food production?
4. Explain the purpose of suggestive selling. What characteristics make up a good server?
5. Accounting is important in order to determine the profitability of a restaurant. Briefly describe the following terms:
   a. controllable expenses
   b. uniform system of accounts
   c. prime cost

6. What is the point-of-sales system, and why is a control system important for a restaurant operation?
7. What are the differences between the back of the house and the front of the house?
8. What steps must one take in preparing production sheets?

Internet Exercises

1. Organization:
   Web site:
   Summary:
   (a) List the food-borne diseases listed on the NRA site. Find out about each disease and how the National Restaurant Association suggests you can prevent it.
   (b) What kinds of careers are available in the restaurant and hospitality industry?
   (c) What legal issues does this site advise you on if you want to start your own restaurant?
2. Organization:
   Web site:
   Summary:
   (a) What requirements must you meet in order to open a Chili's franchise? From what you have learned about the issues involved in starting your own business, how is setting up your own business different from having a franchise?
   (b) What is the "Chilihead culture"?

National Restaurant Association (NRA)
http://www.restaurant.org/
The NRA is the business association of the food industry. It consists of 400,000 members and over 170,000 restaurants. Member restaurants represent table service and quick-service operators, chains, and franchises. The NRA helps international restaurants receive the benefits of the association and gives guidance for success to nonprofit members.

Chili's Grill and Bar
http://chilis.com
Chili's is a fun and exciting place to have burgers, fajitas, margaritas, and chili. Established in 1975 in Dallas, the chain now has more than 637 restaurants in the United States and twenty other countries.

Apply Your Knowledge

In a casual Italian restaurant sales for the week of September 15 are as follows:

Food sales	$10,000
Beverage sales	2,500
Total	$12,500

1. If the food cost is 30 percent, how much did the food actually cost?
2. If the beverage cost is 25 percent of beverage sales, how much did the beverages cost?
3. If the labor cost is 28 percent, how much money does that represent and how much is left over for other costs and profit?

Managed Services

8

After reading and studying this chapter, you should be able to:

✓ Outline the different managed services segments.

✓ Describe the five factors that distinguish managed services operations from commercial ones.

✓ Explain the need for and trends in elementary and secondary school food service.

✓ Describe the complexities in college and university foodservice.

✓ Identify characteristics and trends in health care, business and industry, and leisure and recreation foodservices.

Overview

Managed services consists of all foodservice operations that are classified as not-for-profit and includes the following segments:

- ✓ Airlines
- ✓ Military
- ✓ Elementary and secondary schools
- ✓ Colleges and universities
- ✓ Health care facilities
- ✓ Business and industry
- ✓ Leisure and recreation

Several features distinguish managed services operations from **commercial food-services:**

1. In a restaurant, the challenge is to please the guest. In managed services, it is necessary to meet both the needs of the guest and the client (i.e., the institution itself).
2. In some operations, the guests are a captive clientele. These guests may be eating at the foodservice operation only once or on a daily basis.
3. Many managed operations are housed in host organizations that do not have foodservice as their primary business.
4. Most managed services operations produce food in large-quantity batches for service and consumption within fixed time periods. (For example, **batch cooking** means to produce a batch of food to serve at 11:30 A.M., another batch to serve at 12:15 P.M., and a third batch to serve at 12:45 P.M., rather than putting out all of the food for the whole lunch period at 11:30 A.M. This gives the guests who come to eat later in the serving period as good a quality meal as those who came to eat earlier.
5. The volume of business is more consistent and therefore easier to cater. Because it is easier to predict the number of meals and portion sizes, it is easier to plan, organize, produce, and serve meals; therefore, the atmosphere is less hurried than that of a restaurant. Weekends tend to be quieter than weekdays in managed services and, overall, the hours and benefits may be better than those of commercial restaurants.

Reasons for Contract Management

- Financial
- Quality of program
- Recruitment of management and staff
- Expertise in management of service departments
- Resources available: people, programs, management systems, information systems
- Labor relations and other support
- Outsourcing of administrative functions

Courtesy of Susan Pillmeier, Manager of College Relations, ARAMARK, and John Lee, Director of Staffing Services, Sodexho Marriott Services; presentation to the CHRIE conference, July 21, 2000.

Airlines

In-Flight Foodservice

It is evident that food has become a major competitive factor with the airlines. Airlines are constantly striving to be more efficient, demanding better food at the same or lower costs. Airlines may either provide meals from their own *in-flight* business or have the service provided by a contractor. In-flight food may be prepared in a factory mode at a facility close to but outside of the airport. In these cases, the food is prepared and packaged; it then is transported to the departure gates for the appropriate flights. Once the food is loaded onto the aircraft, flight attendants take over serving the food and beverages to passengers.

In-flight foodservice is a complex logistical operation: The food must be able to withstand the transport conditions and the extended hot or cold holding period from the time it is prepared until the time it is served. If a food item is to be served hot, it must be able to rethermalize well on the plate. In addition, the meal needs to look appealing, be tasty, and be able to fit with the limited space available.[1] Finally, all food and beverage items must be delivered on time and correctly to each departing aircraft.

Caterair International used to be one of the largest in-flight caterers. However, this is no longer the case with the acquisition of Dobbs International Services by Zurich-based Gate Gourmet International, a fully owned subsidiary of SAirRelations, one of the four corporate divisions of SAirGroup. The merger of the second and third largest airline caterers in the world has created the global market leader in the airline catering industry. Together, the two giants operate in twenty-seven countries on six continents from more than 140 catering facilities and produce over 250 million meals on average annually. It is estimated that sales will exceed $2 billion supported by more than 26,000 employees.

Another major player in the in-flight food service market is Sky Chefs, headquartered in Dallas, Texas. Sky Chefs was part of American Airlines, but was sold in a strategic move to reduce debt and to allow the airline to focus on its core business.

The in-flight foodservice management operators plan the menus, develop the product specifications, and arrange the purchasing contracts. They also are involved with galley, design, development of in-flight service procedures, and equipment logistics.[2]

---

[1]A. McCool, F. L. Smith, and D. L. Tucker, *Dimensions of Noncommercial Foodservice Management.* New York: Van Nostrand Reinhold, 1994, p. 278.

[2]Ibid, p. 281.

Food being Prepared, Loaded, and Served on an Aircraft (Courtesy Dobbs International, Gate Gourmet International AG)

Each airline has a representative who oversees one or more locations and checks on the quality, quantity, and delivery times of all food and beverage items. Airlines regard in-flight foodservice as an expense that needs to be controlled. The cost for the average in-flight meal is just over $6. The cost had been higher, but in order to trim costs, many airlines now offer snacks instead of meals on a number of short flights and flights that do not span main meal times. However, some domestic carriers are reducing this food cost through the sale of beverages.

Some international airlines try to stand out by offering superior food and beverages in hopes of attracting more passengers. Others reduce or eliminate foodservice as a strategic decision to support lower fares. Generally, international flights have better quality food and beverage service.

On board, each aircraft has two or three categories of service, usually coach, business, and first class. First- and business-class passengers usually receive free beverages and upgraded meal items and service. These meals may consist of items like fresh salmon or filet mignon. Figure 8–1 shows a sample in-flight menu. On international flights, the per-passenger food cost ranges from about $10.32 for Northwest Airlines to $37.10 for American Airlines.[3]

A number of smaller regional and local foodservice operators contract to a variety of airlines at hundreds of airports. Most airports have caterers or **foodservice contractors** who compete for airline contracts. With several international and U.S. airlines all using U.S. airports, each airline must decide whether to use its own foodservice (if it has one) or to contract with one of several independent operators.

[3]Ibid, p. 282.

AMERICAN FLAGSHIP SERVICE

TO START

An assortment of warm mixed Nuts
to accompany your preferred Cocktail or Beverage

APPETIZER

Basil-cured Salmon
Served with Tomato Caper Relish, Lemon and a Crouton

THE SALAD CART

A zesty Caesar Salad with Romaine Lettuce, Croutons,
Parmesan Cheese and Caesar Dressing
Anchovies are available for those who wish

ENTREES

CHATEAUBRIAND
Chateaubriand served with a fresh Herb and Cabernet Sauvignon Sauce,
offered with Mashed New Potatoes and Carrots seasoned with Thyme

GRILLED CHICKEN WITH FETTUCCINE
Breast of Chicken presented over Fettuccine tossed with Pesto,
Bacon, Tomato and enhanced by a Four Cheese Sauce

PACIFIC PRAWNS WITH THAI CURRY SAUCE
Jumbo Prawns served on a spicy Thai Curry Sauce, presented with
Jasmine Pineapple Rice and Black Bean and Mango Relish

BREAD BASKET
Sourdough and Multigrain Rolls

THE DESSERT CART

ICE CREAM SUNDAE
Häagen-Dazs Vanilla Ice Cream with a choice of Hot Fudge,
Butterscotch or seasonal Fruit Toppings and fresh Whipped Cream

FRUIT AND CHEESE
A sampler of Cheese
complemented by fresh Fruit and Crackers

PRIOR TO ARRIVAL

Pecan Chocolate Chip Cookies, freshly baked on board

Figure 8–1 *In-Flight Menu*
(Courtesy American
Airlines.)

Pizza Hut at an Airport
(Courtesy Pizza Hut.)

Airport Foodservice

Foodservice at most airports is operated by management companies like ARA-MARK Leisure Services or Host International (a division of Marriott Corporation). More recently, airports have begun to use branded concepts, whereby a Pizza Hut or other branded restaurant is located in the airport.

Military

Military foodservice is a large and important component of managed services. There are about 1.8 million soldiers, sailors, and aviators in active duty in the United States. Even with the military downsizing, foodservice sales top $6 billion per year. Base closings have prompted many military foodservice organizations to rediscuss services and concepts in order to better meet the needs of their personnel. In particular, it was noticed that the food delivery methods needed considerable adjustment. In fact, complaints by the operators focused on excessively long times for orders, delayed delivery, and poor product and inventory control. The Department of Defense thus introduced **direct vendor delivery,** which proved to be a satisfactory choice. On the whole, reports indicate excellent service and product.

Recent trends in military foodservice call for services such as officers' clubs to be contracted out to foodservice management companies. This change has reduced military costs because many of the officers' clubs lost money. The clubs now have moved the emphasis from fine dining to a more casual approach with family appeal. Many clubs are renovating their base concept even further, restyling according to theme concepts, such as sports or country-western, for example. Other cost-saving measures include menu management, such as the use of a single menu for lunch and dinner (guests seldom eat both meals at the clubs). With proper plating techniques and portion size manipulation, a single menu can be created for lunch and dinner, meaning one inventory for both meals and less stock in general. To make this technique work successfully, the menu features several choices for appetizers, entrees, and desserts.

Another trend is the testing of prepared foods that can be reheated and served without much labor. Technological advances mean that field troops do not eat out of tin cans anymore; instead, they receive their food portions in plastic-and-foil pouches called MREs, or meals ready-to-eat. Today, mobile field kitchens can be run by just two people, and bulk food supplies have been replaced by preportioned, precooked food packed in trays, which then are reheated in boiling water.

Feeding military personnel includes feeding troops and officers in clubs, dining halls, and military hospitals, as well as in the field. As both the budget and the numbers of personnel decrease, the military is downsizing by consolidating responsibilities. With fewer people to cook for, fewer cooks are required.

A model for such downsizing is the U.S. Marine Corps. Since 1986, the marines have been contracting out foodservice. With smaller numbers, they could not afford to take a marine away from training to work in the dining facilities without affecting military operations.

In addition, fast-food restaurants like McDonald's and Burger King have opened on well over 200 bases; they are now installing Express Way kiosks on more bases.[4] The fast-food restaurants on base offer further alternatives for military personnel on the move.

One problem that may arise as a result of the downsizing and contracting out of military foodservice is that it is not likely that McDonald's could set up on the front line in a combat situation. The military will still have to do their own foodservice when it comes to mobilization.

Elementary and Secondary Schools

The United States government enacted the **National School Lunch Act of 1946** in response to concern about malnourishment in military recruits.[5] The rationale was that if students received good meals, the military would have healthier recruits. In addition, such a program would make use of the surplus food that farmers produced.

Today, about 26 million children are fed breakfast or lunch—or both—each day in approximately 89,000 schools, at a cost of about $7 billion annually.

Many concerns currently face **elementary and secondary school foodservice.** One major challenge is to balance salability with good nutrition. Apart from cost and nutritional value, the broader social issue of the universal free meal arises. Proponents of the program maintain that better nourished children have a better attention span, are less likely to be absent from school, and will stay in school longer. Offering free meals to all students also removes the poor kid stigma from school lunch. Detractors from the universal program say that if we learned anything from the social programs that were implemented during the 1960s, it was that throwing money at problems is not always the best answer.

Both sides agree that there is serious concern about what young students are eating. The news about the fat and cholesterol in the popcorn served at movie theaters shocked many adults. More shocking, though, is what school children are eating, as one survey illustrates.[6] A U.S. Department of Agriculture survey found that school lunches, on average, exceeded dietary guidelines for fat by 25 percent, for saturated fat by 50 percent, and for sodium by 85 percent. Equally shocking is the percentage of children who eat one serving or less of fruits and vegetables each day (excluding french fries), as shown in Figure 8–2.

The preparation and service of school foodservice meals varies. Some schools have on-site kitchens where the food is prepared, and dining rooms

[4]James Scarpa, "Keeping the change: customers ain't dropping as many coins. Debit cards are slotted to increase sales." *Restaurant Business,* **104,** 21, September 20, 1992, p. 118.

[5]Susie Stephensen, "School Lunch: One Correct Answer? Or Multiple Choice?" *Restaurants and Institutions,* September 1, 1993, p. 114.

[6]Editors. "Soft Drinks and School Lunches." *U.S. News and World Report,* **116,** 8, May 9, 1994, p. 18.

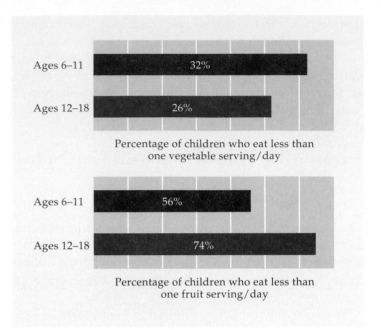

Ages 6–11   32%

Ages 12–18   26%

Percentage of children who eat less than
one vegetable serving/day

Ages 6–11   56%

Ages 12–18   74%

Percentage of children who eat less than
one fruit serving/day

Figure 8–2 *Children and the Servings of Fruit and Vegetables They Eat* (*Source:* National Cancer Institute.)

where the food is served. Many large school districts operate a **central commissary** that prepares the meals and then distributes them among the schools in that district. A third option is for schools to purchase ready-to-serve meals that require only assembly at the school.

Schools may decide to participate in the **National School Lunch Program (NSLP)** or operate on their own. In reality, most schools have little choice because participating in the program means that federal funding is provided in the amount of approximately $2.00 per meal per student.

Meeting **dietary guidelines** is also an important issue. Much work has gone into establishing the nutritional requirements for children. It is difficult to achieve a balance between healthy food and costs, taking children's eating habits into account. Under the NSLP regulations, students must eat from what is commonly known as the **type A menu.** All of the items in the type A menu must be offered to all children at every meal. The children have to select a minimum of three of the five meal components in order for the school to qualify for funding. However, USDA regulations have established limits on the amount of fat and saturated fat that can be offered. Fat should not exceed 30 percent of calories per week, and saturated fat was cut down to 10 percent of calories per week. Figure 8–3 illustrates school lunch menus and Figure 8–4 shows the school lunch menu pattern requirements.

The government-funded NSLP, which pays $4.7 billion per year for the meals given or sold at a discount to schoolchildren, is a huge potential market for fast-food chains. Chains are extremely eager to penetrate into the elementary and secondary school markets, even if it means a decrease in revenues.

WINTER ELEMENTARY LUNCH PORTION GUIDE
January 2 – April 17

DATE	MONDAY	TUESDAY	WEDNESDAY	THURSDAY	FRIDAY
Jan 2 Jan 30 Feb 27 Mar 27	1717 Bean & Cheese Burrito — 1 139 Green Beans — #16 29 Chilled Fruit Cup — #16 693 Milk — 1	648 Chicken Nuggets — 4 ea 118 Catsup — 1 tbsp 651 Celery Sticks — 1 oz 96 Ranch Dip — #40 979 WW Bread & Butter — 1 sl 40 Orange Wedges — 2 ea 693 Milk — 1	406 (Turkey) Ham w/Melted Mozzarella on Bun — 1 229 French Fries — 7/# 118 Catsup — 1 Tbsp 253 Apple Wedges — 2 ea 693 Milk — 1	188 Party Pizza — 12/sh 381 Mixed Green Salad w/ — #12 1117 Ranch Dressing — #30 1343 Golden State Cookie 693 Milk — 1	650 Cheese Quesadilla — 1 181 Spanish Rice — #12 651 Celery Sticks — 1 oz 1219 Jello w/Pears — #12 693 Milk — 1
Jan 9 Feb 6 Mar 6 Apr 13	712 Corn Dog — 1 118 Catsup — 2 Tbsp 372 Mustard — 1 Tbsp 652 Potato Rounds — 7/# 521 Carrot Sticks — 1 oz 693 Milk — 1	1802 Stuffed Potato — 1 ea 381 Mixed Green Salad w/ — #12 1117 Ranch Dressing 979 WW Bread w/Butter — 1 sl 29 Chilled Fruit Cup — #16 693 Milk — 1	812 Spaghetti w/Pork and Turkey — #8 1191 WW Dinner Roll — 32/pan 85 Creamy Coleslaw — #12 269 Chilled Peaches — #16 693 Milk — 1 *	462 Cheese Pizza — 1 92 Corn — #16 31 Gingerbread — 50/pan 693 Milk — 1	1370 Tostada Boat — 1 253 Apple Wedges — 2 ea 693 Milk — 1
Jan 16 Feb 13 Mar 13	418 Char Patty on WW Bun — 1 333 Shredded Lettuce — #16 229 French Fries — 7/# 118 Catsup — 2 Tbsp 269 Chilled Peaches — #16 693 Milk — 1	1779 Seafood Salad Sandwich — 1 746 Carrot Coins — #40 96 Ranch Dip — 80/pan 1652 Brownie — 1 693 Milk	587 Ham & Cheese Roll-up (Pork) — 1 652 Potato Rounds — 7/# 118 Catsup — 1 Tbsp 29 Chilled Fruit Cup — #16 693 Milk — 1 *	1793 Pizza Bagel — 1 ea 1273 Celery Pieces — 1 oz 96 Ranch Dip — #40 1304 Trail Mix — #12 693 Milk — 1	1717 Bean & Cheese Burrito — 1 381 Mixed Green Salad w/ — #12 1117 Ranch Dressing 40 Orange Wedges — 2 ea 693 Milk — 1
Jan 23 Feb 20 Mar 20	538 Turkey Hot Dog — 1 118 Catsup — 1 Tbsp 372 Mustard — 1 Tbsp 521 Carrot Sticks — 1 oz 273 Chilled Pineapple — #16 693 Milk — 1	691 Turkey & Gravy — #8 173 Whipped Potatoes — #8 1714 Bernies Breadsticks — 60/pan 40 Orange Wedges — 2 ea 693 Milk — 1	1805 Salisbury Steak — 1 ea 92 Niblet Corn — #16 605 Nutribun — 40/pan 1395 Kiwi Wedge — 2 ea 693 Milk — 1	686 Sausage Pizza (Pork) — 12/sh 139 Green Beans — #16 130 Cherry Jello Dessert — #12 693 Milk — 1 *	403 Grilled Cheese Sandwich — 1 652 Potato Rounds — 7/# 118 Catsup — 1 tbsp 179 Pear Wedges — 2 ea 693 Milk — 1

LUNCH   F254

HOLIDAYS: Monday, January 2 - Use Monday's menu on Tuesday, January 3
Tuesday, January 3 - Use Tuesday's menu on Wednesday, January 4
Monday, January 16 - Use Monday's menu on Wednesday, January 18: Delete #333 Shredded Lettuce
Tuesday, January 17 - Staff Development Day
Friday, February 17 - Omit Friday's menu
Monday, February 20 - Use Monday's menu on Tuesday, February 21: Delete #521 Carrot Sticks; add #183 Cowboy Beans #16

Figure 8–3 *Sample Elementary School Lunch Menu*

School Lunch Patterns
For Various Age/Grade Groups

USDA recommends, but does not require, that you adjust portions by age/grade group to better meet the food and nutritional needs of children according to their ages. If you adjust portions, Groups I-IV are minimum requirements for the age/grade groups specified. If you do not adjust portions, the Group IV portions are the portions to serve all children.

			Minimum Quantities			Recommended Quantities[2]
		Preschool		Grades K-3	Grades 4-12[1]	Grades 7-12
COMPONENTS		Ages 1-2 (Group I)	Ages 3-4 (Group II)	Ages 5-8 (Group III)	Age 9 & over (Group IV)	Ages 12 & over (Group V)
Meat or Meat Alternate	A serving of one of the following or a combination to give an equivalent quantity:					
	Lean meat, poultry, or fish (edible portion as served)	1 oz	1-1/2 oz	1-1/2 oz	2 oz	3 oz
	Cheese	1 oz	1-1/2 oz	1-1/2 oz	2 oz	3 oz
	Large egg(s)	1/2	3/4	3/4	1	1-1/2
	Cooked dry beans or peas	1/4 cup	3/8 cup	3/8 cup	1/2 cup	3/4 cup
	Peanut butter or other nut or seed butters	2 Tbsp	3 Tbsp	3 Tbsp	4 Tbsp	6 Tbsp
	Peanuts, soy nuts, tree nuts, or seeds, as listed in program guidance, meet no more than 50% of the requirement and must be combined in the meal with at least 50% of other meat or meat alternate. (1 oz of nut/seeds=1 oz of cooked lean meat, poultry, or fish.)	1/2 oz=50%	3/4 oz=50%	3/4 oz=50%	1 oz=50%	1-1/2 oz=50%
Vegetables and/or Fruits	Two or more servings of vegetables or fruits or both to total	1/2 cup	1/2 cup	1/2 cup	3/4 cup	3/4 cup
Servings of bread or Bread Alternate	A serving is: • 1 slice of whole-grain or enriched bread • A whole-grain or enriched biscuit, roll, muffin, etc. • 1/2 cup of cooked whole-grain or enriched rice, macaroni, noodles, whole-grain or enriched pasta products, or other cereal grains such as bulgur or corn grits • A combination or any of the above	5 per week	8 per week	8 per week	8 per week	10 per week
Milk	A serving of fluid milk	3/4 cup (6 fl oz)	3/4 cup (6 fl oz)	1/2 pint (8 fl oz)	1/2 pint (8 fl oz)	1/2 pint (8 fl oz)

SPECIFIC REQUIREMENTS

• Must be served in the main dish or the main dish and only one other menu item.
• Vegetable protein products, cheese alternate products, and enriched macaroni with fortified protein may be used to meet part of the meat/meat alternate requirement. Fact sheets on each of these alternate foods give detailed instructions for use.

• No more than one-half of the total requirement may be met with full-strength fruit or vegetable juice.
• Cooked dry beans or peas may be used as a meat alternate or as a vegetable but not as both in the same meal.

• At least 1/2 serving of bread or an equivalent quantity of bread alternate for Group I, and 1 serving for Groups II-V, must be served daily.
• Enriched macaroni with fortified protein may be used as a meat alternate or as a bread alternate but not as both in the same meal.
NOTE: Food Buying Guide for Child Nutrition Programs, PA-1331 (1984) provides the information for the minimum weight of a serving.

The following forms of milk must be offered:
• Whole milk
• Unflavored lowfat milk
NOTE: This requirement does not prohibit offering other milk, such as flavored milk or skim milk, along with the above.

[1]Group IV is highlighted because it is the one meal pattern which will satisfy all requirements if no portion size adjustments are made.
[2]Group V specifies recommended, not required, quantities for students 12 years and older. These students may request smaller portions, but not smaller than those specified in Group IV.

Figure 8–4 *School Lunch Menu Pattern Requirements* (U.S. Department of Agriculture, National School Lunch Program.)

"We do reduce the price of our product, and we do make less margin than in our normal operations," says Joy Wallace, national sales director/nontraditional sales for Pizza Hut. However, they believe that it is to their benefit to introduce Pizza Hut to young people very early—in other words, the aim is to build brand loyalty. As a matter of fact, in Duluth, Minnesota, James Bruner, food-service director for the city schools, was forced into offering branded pizza in several junior high and high schools. The local principals, hungry for new revenue, began offering Little Caesar's in direct competition to the cafeteria's frozen pizzas.

Taco Bell is in nearly 3,000 schools, Pizza Hut in 4,500, Subway in 650; Domino's, McDonald's, Arby's, and others are well established in the market as well.

Philadelphia schools fulfill nutritional requirements and also bring brand-name food to school: Domino's prepares pizzas to the school district's specifications at a cost that is much lower than if the school made the pizza from scratch or bought it frozen. At Broward County high schools in Florida, Pizza Hut, Domino's, or a local pizzeria (depending on students' vote) delivers pizza twice a week. Two other days a week, Subway delivers sandwiches; again, the cost is lower than making similar sandwiches at school.[7]

San Juan Capistrano high school in California has gone one step further. The high school is a franchisee of Taco Bell, KFC, and Pizza Hut. Foodservice director Bill Caldwell says that this has created a win–win situation: Students get the food they like and also gain valuable work experience in the restaurants.[8]

Despite the positives, although it is not hard to convince the children, chains need to convince the adults. Much debate has arisen as to whether chains should enter the schools or not. Many parents feel that the school environment should provide a standard example of what sound nutrition should be, and they believe that with fast food as an option, that will not be the case.

At a school lunch challenge at the American Culinary Federation (ACF) conference, chefs from around the country developed nutritious menus geared to wean children away from junk food to healthy foods. An 80-cent limit on the cost of raw ingredients was placed on the eleven finalists. Innovation and taste, as well as healthfulness, were the main criteria used to evaluate the winning entry: turkey taco salad, sausage pizza bagel, and stuffed potatoes.

Professional chefs are now working with the Department of Agriculture's Food and Consumer Services to develop healthful recipes and menus with increased appeal but without an increase in cost.[9]

[7]"Schools," *Restaurants and Institutions,* **103,** 20, August 15, 1993, p. 44.

[8]Jeff Weinstein, "Free-Flow Style Star in Kitchen Design Award," *Restaurants and Institutions,* **104,** 21, September 1, 1993, p. 120.

[9]"School Lunch Challenge: Nutritious Food," *Restaurants and Institutions,* **102,** 23, October 1, 1994, p. 29.

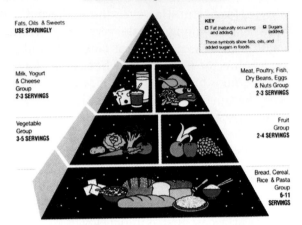

Figure 8–5   *Food Pyramid* (U.S. Department of Agriculture and U.S. Department of Health and Human Services.)

Nutrition Education Programs

Nutrition education programs are now a required part of the nation's school lunch program. As a result of this program, children are learning to improve their eating habits, which, it is hoped, will continue for the rest of their lives. To support the program, nutritional education materials are used to decorate the dining room halls and tables. Perhaps the best example of this is the food pyramid developed by the Food and Nutrition Service of the U.S. Department of Agriculture. Figure 8–5 shows this food pyramid, which shows what to eat each day for a healthy diet.

Colleges and Universities

College and university foodservice operations are complex and diverse. Among the various constituents of foodservice management are residence halls, cafeterias/student unions, faculty clubs, convenience stores, administrative catering, and outside catering.

On-campus dining is a challenge for foodservice managers because the clientele live on campus and eat most of their meals at the campus dining facility. Students, staff, and faculty may quickly become bored with the sameness of the surroundings and menu offerings. Most campus dining is cafeteria style and offers cyclical menus that rotate on a predetermined schedule.

However, a college foodservice manager does have some advantages when compared with a restaurant manager. Budgeting is made easier because the on-campus students have already paid for their meals and their numbers are easy to forecast. When the payment is guaranteed and the guest count is predictable, planning and organizing staffing levels and food quantities is relatively easy and should ensure a reasonable profit margin. For instance, the **daily rate** is the amount of money required per day from each person to pay for the foodservice. Thus, if food service expenses for one semester of ninety-eight days amount to $650,000 for an operation with 1,000 students eating, the daily rate will be

$$\frac{\$650,000 \div 98 \text{ (days)}}{1000} = \$6.63$$

College foodservice operations now offer a variety of meal plans for students. Under the old board plan, when students paid one fee for all meals each day—whether they ate them or not—the foodservice operator literally made a profit from the students who did not actually eat the meals they had paid for. More typically now, students match their payments to the number of meals eaten: Monday–Friday, breakfast, lunch, dinner; dinner only; and prepaid credit cards that allow a student to use the card at any campus outlet and have the value of the food and beverage items deducted from his or her credit balance.

Leaders of the National Associations of College Auxiliary Services (NACAS), who represent 1,200 member institutes, have noticed that on-campus services and activities are undergoing continuous change. The environment has become a critical part of policy and implementation that transcends parochial interests for those that best meet the needs of the institution and, ultimately, its students.

The driving forces of change on campuses are the advent and growth of branded concepts, privatization, campus cards, and computer use.

Leaders in the Industry

- ARAMARK—$7 billion in sales
- Compass Group
- Morrisons
- Service Master
- Sodexho Marriott Services—over $4.5 billion in sales
- Gate Gourmet
- The Wood Company

Courtesy of Susan Pillmeier, Manager of College Relations, ARAMARK, and John Lee, Director of Staffing Services, Sodexho Marriott Services; presentation to the CHRIE conference, July 21, 2000.

College Foodservice
(Courtesy ARAMARK.)

Personal Profile: Manuel Lorenzo

Manuel Lorenzo is a supervisor for Marriott Food Services and arrives at United States International University (USIU) to begin his shift at 9:00 A.M. Manuel's first duty is to check the catering board where he will find a list of scheduled catering events for the day. Manuel then plans the food preparation and starts gathering the necessary equipment.

By 10:00 A.M., Manuel goes around to all the foodservice outlets that are open during the night hours and collects money and receipts. The cash must then be immediately transported to the bank for deposit. The figures must also be entered into the company computer.

After Manuel completes handling the money, he talks with Richard Nargi the general manager of foodservices at USIU. She keeps him abreast of information for the day. This is the time any problems or concerns can be addressed. At 11:00 A.M., Manuel walks around to make sure the cafeteria is ready to serve lunch. Manuel supervises the lunch operation until it ends at 1:30. After lunch, he continues working on catering functions and makes sure everything flows and is ready for dinner.

Before leaving for the day for the day, Manuel must check to see that all catering vehicles are tanked and running properly. Then, the storerooms must be cleaned

and organized. The general manager will also have a list of projects for Manuel to complete. These tasks usually consist of maintaining sanitation standards. Last, Manuel checks staffing levels for the rest of the week and deals with basic human resource functions.

Manuel sees time management as one of the major challenges of his career. Events are constantly pending, and he has only a very limited amount of time to plan, organize, and carry out those functions. Manuel contends that the only way to be successful, in this respect, is to be highly organized. Also, Manuel says that success requires one to be a "people-person." This skill helps him deal with employees effectively and helps him understand the people he serves, so that he can serve them better.

Keeping the customer satisfied is another challenge for Manuel. University foodservice operations have the unique and difficult task of keeping long-term boarding residents happy with food quality. Manuel solves this problem by serving a wide variety of entrees, yet keeping consistent with daily staples.

Each catering event is different because of the variety in food served. With each new function, Manuel learns something about food and/or culture. Mr. Lorenzo admits that this is one of the most interesting, exciting, and rewarding aspects of his job.

Student Unions

The college student union offers a variety of managed services that caters to the needs of a diverse student body. Among the services offered are cafeteria foodservice, beverage services, branded quick-service restaurants, and take-out foodservice.

The cafeteria foodservice operation is often the "happening" place in the student union where students meet to socialize as well as to eat and drink. The cafeteria is generally open for breakfast, lunch, and dinner. Depending on the volume of business, the cafeteria may be closed during the nonmeal periods and weekends, and the cafeteria menu may or may not be the same as the residence foodservice facility. Offering a menu with a good price value is crucial to the successful operation of a campus cafeteria.

On campuses at which alcoholic beverage service is permitted, beverage services mainly focus on some form of a student pub where beer and perhaps wine and spirits may be offered. Not to be outdone, the faculty will undoubtedly have a lounge that also offers alcoholic beverages. Other beverages may be served at various outlets such as a food court or convenience store. Campus beverage service provides opportunities for foodservice operators to enhance profits.

In addition, many college campuses have welcomed branded, quick-service restaurants as a convenient way to satisfy the needs of a community on the go. Such an approach offers a win–win situation for colleges. The experience and brand recognition of chain restaurants like Pizza Hut, McDonald's, Subway, and Wendy's attract customers; the restaurants pay a fee, either to the foodservice management company or the university directly. Obviously, there is a danger that the quick-service restaurant may attract customers that the cafeteria might then lose, but competition tends to be good for all concerned.

Take-out foodservice is another convenience for the campus community. At times, students—and staff—do not want to prepare meals and are thankful for the opportunity to take meals with them. And, it is not just during examination time that students, friends, and staff have a need for the take-out option. For example, tailgate parties prior to football and basketball games or concerts and other recreational/sporting events allow entrepreneurial foodservice operators to increase revenue and profits.

The type of contract that a managed services operator signs varies depending on the size of the account. If the account is small, a fee generally is charged. With larger accounts, operators contract for a set percentage (usually about 5 percent) or a combination of a percentage and a bonus split.

Figure 8–6 shows a typical college menu for the dining hall where students usually eat on campus.

Advantages and Disadvantages of Contract Management from a Client Perspective

Advantages
- Experience in size and types of operations
- Use contracted department as a model for rest of institution
- Variety of services
- Resource and support available
- Hold contractor to a higher level of performance

Disadvantages
- Some segments perceived as institutionalized
- Potential for lost contracts

Courtesy of Susan Pillmeier, Manager of College Relations, ARAMARK, and John Lee, Director of Staffing Services, Sodexho Marriott Services; presentation to the CHRIE conference, July 21, 2000.

Responsibilities in Managed Services

A foodservice manager's responsibilities in a small or midsize operation are frequently more extensive than those of managers of the larger operations. This is because larger units have more people to whom to delegate certain functions, such as human resources. For example, following are some of the responsibilities that the foodservice manager in a small or midsize operation might have in addition to strictly foodservice responsibilities:

Employee Relations
✓ Business vs. personal needs, family problems
✓ Rewards/recognition

Personal Profile: Regynald G. Washington

General Manager, Food and Beverage, Major Entertainment Company, Orlando, Florida; and President and CEO, Washington Enterprises Inc.

For a student majoring in hotel and restaurant management, being a general manager, president, or even chief executive officer in the food industry is a goal to be achieved. For Regynald G. Washington, not only has it been a goal reached, but a dream realized. His bright smile spells success.

As a child growing up in a middle-income family in the town of Marathon in the Florida Keys, working was mandatory. At the early age of thirteen, he was introduced to the food industry. His first job consisted of waiting on and busing tables and doing other chores in the Indies Inn Resort and Yacht Club. He took this on as an exciting and new challenge.

In the 1970s, Regynald graduated from Florida International University with a degree in hotel and restaurant administration. He continued to work for Indies Inn Resort, but by this time he was running the food and beverage operation. This was the beginning of the long career road for Regynald G. Washington.

For Regynald, attitude is everything. His positive attitude toward being the best that he can be was derived

(Courtesy of Regynald Washington.)

from a phrase his parents used to repeat to him: "A chip on your shoulder earns a lack of respect from colleagues, friends, and family." His great energy and pride in his work is what makes him stand out among many other leaders in the food industry. He has a quality and people-oriented mind that keeps him focused on any task he wishes to accomplish. For Regynald, food is a world open to new ideas and discoveries. Richard Rivera, president of Red Lobster says, "When you think of attributes you'd like to see in a restaurateur, he's got them."

In the years that followed, Regynald worked for the Magic Pan Restaurant in Phoenix as a general manager. Several jobs later, he was at Concessions International,[1] an airport food and beverage, duty free, gifts, and magazine organization, in Atlanta. He was promoted to executive vice president in 1990. He worked on the business development of the Cyril E. King Airport in St. Thomas, U.S. Virgin Islands. He then formed Washington Enterprises. He developed Sylvia's Restaurant in Atlanta, which turned out to be very successful.

✓ Drug alcohol abuse/prevention
✓ Positive work environment
✓ Coaching/facilitating vs. directing

Human Resource Management
✓ Recruitment/training/evaluating
✓ Wage/salary administration
✓ Benefits administration
✓ Compliance with federal/state laws/EEO/Senate Bill 198
✓ Harassment/OSHA
✓ Disciplinary actions/terminations
✓ Unemployment/wrongful disclosure

A few years later though, a Major Entertainment company executive recruiter offered Washington an opportunity to join the new and creative food and beverage approach that the company was aiming to develop. This was the opportunity of a lifetime for Regynald. Confident and enthusiastic, Regynald took up the job offer. His talented and creative mind would be the key to the success of the new concept.

Regynald's secret to managing 2,500 employees and satisfying Epcot's customers was simply organization and care. Having organization and direction in your work eliminates stress and makes time for fun. Making sure that all the staff know what they are doing and that they are doing it well and serving guests hot food hot and cold food cold was all it took. He uses a back-to-basics formula, which requires that everything goes well, from making guests happy to proper staffing. Not only has his ambition and energy helped him climb to the top, but he also has great concern for others and wants to help his employees learn new things and move forward in their careers. He is very well focused on quality and precision on anything and everything he does. One of his number one concerns is food safety.

To make sure everything is intact and going well, Regynald and his support team perform unannounced inspections every quarter. A specific food and beverage facility is concentrated on and fully evaluated for its table turns, guest service, food quality, and training programs. Specialists act as the guests and observe and report anything that seems less than perfect. Epcot executive chefs check the kitchen food as well as the menu.

In-house sanitarians evaluate the level of sanitation at the facility. The goal of these inspections is to make sure nothing is less than perfect. Excellence is the goal for Regynald. He admires and respects the people who work with him and has ranked them as being the best food and beverage people.

Regynald also serves on the board of directors of the National Restaurant Association. The former president, Hermain Cain, has only words of admiration and praise for Regynald. He says, "Regynald is not afraid to try creative new things, and he knows what needs to be done." Regynald also works as a developer knowing all the financial procedures going on within the restaurant. He always aims to stay on top of thing.

Regynald believes that he has achieved a lot and has had many successes during his career. His career is exciting and motivating and he has the opportunity to make a difference is people's lives every single day. This is what he always wanted and now he has it. He says, "My parents really wanted me to become a lawyer, physician, or architect. They didn't believe you could reach the top and do exciting things in the restaurant industry."

Source: This profile draws on Whit Smyth, "Regynald Washington, EPCOT's Chief of Food and Beverage. "Says Pleasing Customers Is No Mickey Mouse," *Nation's Restaurant News*, **33,** 4, January 25, 1999. p. 28–30.

Financial/Budgeting
- ✓ Project budgets
- ✓ Actual vs. budget monitoring (weekly)
- ✓ Controlling food cost, labor, expenses, and so on
- ✓ Record keeping requirements/audit
- ✓ Monitoring accounts payable/receivable
- ✓ Billing/collecting
- ✓ Compliance to contracts
- ✓ Cash procedures/banking

Safety Administration
- ✓ Equipment training/orientation
- ✓ Controlling workers compensation
- ✓ Monthly inspections/audits (federal/state/OSHA requirements/Senate Bill 198)

WEEK 1

	MONDAY	TUESDAY	WEDNESDAY	THURSDAY	FRIDAY

Breakfast - Cold cereal, fruit and yogurt bar, toast, juices, milks, coffee, tea, hot chocolate and fresh fruit*

	MONDAY	TUESDAY	WEDNESDAY	THURSDAY	FRIDAY
Bakery:	Quick Coffee Cake	Assorted Danish	Cinnamon Coffee Cake	Sticky Top Roll	Banana Nut Muffins
Hot Cereal:	Oatmeal	Malt-O-Meal	Cream of Wheat	Grits	Oatmeal
Entrees:	Buttermilk Pancakes	Waffles	French Toast	Oatmeal Pancakes	Waffles w/Peaches
	Scrambled Eggs	Scrambled Eggs	Scrambled Eggs	Scrambled Eggs	Scrambled Eggs
	Sausage Gravy	Egg O'Muffin w/Bacon	Ham & Cheese	Chorizo & Eggs	Egg Burrito
	& Biscuits	Hearty Fried Potatoes	Omelette	Cottage Fries	Home Fries
	Cottage Fries	Bacon	Hash Browns	Sausage Links	

Lunch - Salad Bar, Rice & Chili Bar, Cereal, Build-Your-Own-Sandwich Bar & Fresh Fruit

	MONDAY	TUESDAY	WEDNESDAY	THURSDAY	FRIDAY
Soup:	Beef Barley	Italian Minestrone	Chicken Gumbo	Chicken Noodle	New England Clam Chowder
Entrees:	Baked Seafood & Rice	Chicken Tortilla	Fishwich	Cheesy Mushroom	BBQ Ham Sandwich
	Grilled Ham & Cheese	Casserole	Spanish Macaroni	Burger	Ground Beef &
	Potato Salad	Patty Melt	Ranch Beans	Hamburger	Potato Pie
	Wax Beans	French Fries	Italian Green Beans	Grilled Cheese	Whipped Potatoes
	Mixed Vegetables	Hominy	Braised Carrots &	Onion Rings	Italian Green Beans
		Spinachs	Celery	Carrots	Beets
Dessert:	Chocolate Pudding	Applesauce Cake	Peanut Butter	Oriental Veg. Blend	Vanilla Pudding
	Soft Serve Ice Cream	Soft Serve Ice Cream	Cookies	Coconut Cake	

Dinner - Salad Bar, Cereal, & Fresh Fruit (* Tortillas served at Breakfast & Dinner

	MONDAY	TUESDAY	WEDNESDAY	THURSDAY	FRIDAY
Soup:	Beef Barley	Italian Minestrone	Chicken Gumbo	Chicken Noodle	New England Clam Chowder
Entrees:	Oven Broiled Chicken	Beef Fajitas	Roast Turkey w/Gravy	Egg Roll Over Rice	Pizza! Pizza! Pizza!
	Grilled Liver & Onions	Fried Perch	Old Fashion Beef Stew	Grilled Pork Chop	Curly Fries
	Parsley Potatoes	Spanish Rice	Whipped Potatoes	Rice	Broccoli
	Corn	Asparagus	Corn Cobbettes	Beets	Mixed Vegetables
	Zucchini	Carrots	Brussel Sprouts	Cauliflower au Gratin	
Dessert:	Chocolate Chip	Spicy Whole	Chocolate Mayo	Peach Cobbler	Best Ever Cake
	Cookies	Wheat Bar	Cake		

Figure 8–6 *Sample College Menu* (Courtesy Marriott Foodservice Management.)

Corporate Profile: ARAMARK

In the 1950s, Dave Davidson and Bill Fishman, both in the vending business, realized that they shared the same dreams and hopes of turning vending into a service and combining it with foodservice. The two entrepreneurs joined forces to become the first truly national vending and foodservice company. Automatic Retailers of America (ARA) was born in 1959. Fishman and Davidson had the management skills, the capital, and the expertise to expand. And this they did— ARAMARK is the world's leading provider of quality managed services. It operates in all fifty states and in eleven foreign countries, offering a very diversified and broad range of services to businesses of all sizes, and to thousands of universities, hospitals, and municipal, state, and federal government facilities. Every day, they serve more than 15 million people at more than 500,000 locations worldwide.

ARAMARK's emphasis on the quality of service management was evident from the very beginning of its operations. ARAMARK entered new markets by researching the best-managed local companies, acquiring them, and persuading key managers to stay with the company.

The company's vision, in fact, states that ARAMARK is "a company where the best people want to work." Customers recommend ARAMARK to others because they constantly exceed expectations. In this case, success is measured in the growth of the company, its earnings, and its employees themselves. This is one fundamental constant in ARAMARK's early success: It grew its business by focusing on growing its management. The company's guiding principles reaffirm such a concept:

"Because we succeed through performance, we encourage the entrepreneur in each of us, and work always to improve our service.

"Because we thrive on growth, we seek new markets and new opportunities, and we innovate to get and keep new customers."

With the 1961 acquisition of Slater System, Inc., the largest foodservice business in the country, ARAMARK began the diversification process, and has continued since to amplify the portfolio of services it now offers. The focus on management skills at every level, especially the local one, gave ARAMARK an invaluable resource. In fact, with every acquisition, local managers were encouraged and rewarded for becoming multiskilled entrepreneurs. This approach to outsourcing is, put more simply, the ability of the company to take the best management skills and apply them to all the lines of business the company uses to diversify.

Among ARAMARK operations are the following:

Food, leisure, and support services. The company provides food, specialized refreshments, dietary services, and operation support to businesses, educational facilities, government, and medical institutions. ARAMARK also manages food, lodging, hospitality, and support services at national parks and other recreational facilities that serve the general public.

Health and education services. ARAMARK provides specialized management services for hospitals and medical services. It also specializes in providing early-childhood and school-age education services.

Uniform services: The company is America's largest provider of uniform services and work apparel for virtually all types of institutions.

Magazine and book services: ARAMARK is the leading wholesale distributor of magazines, newspapers, and books.

ARAMARK successfully manages the diversity of segment concepts under the guideline of one single purpose: to be the world leader in managed services. With annual revenues in excess of $5 billion, the company is among the market leaders in all of its businesses, and it is in an ideal position for further market growth. Joseph Neubauer, chairman and CEO, realizes this: "I am energized by the bright prospects for the journey ahead. . . . I can't wait to get started."

Source: Adapted courtesy of ARAMARK.

Support Staff Positions

- Sales
- Marketing
- Controller/audit
- Financial analysis
- Human resources
- Training and development
- Affirmative action/EEO compliance
- Safety administration
- Procurement/distribution
- Technical services (recipes, menus, product testing)
- Labor relations
- Legal aspects

Courtesy of Susan Pillmeier, Manager of College Relations, ARAMARK, and John Lee, Director of Staffing Services, Sodexho Marriott Services; presentation to the CHRIE conference, July 21, 2000.

Safety Budget
✓ Work on the expensive injuries

Food Production/Service
✓ Menu/recipe development
✓ Menu mix vs. competition
✓ Food waste/leftovers utilization
✓ Production records
✓ Production control
✓ Presentation/merchandising

Sanitation/FBI Prevention
✓ FBI (food-borne illness) prevention
✓ Sanitation/cleaning schedule
✓ Proper food handling/storage
✓ Daily prevention/monitoring
✓ Monthly inspection
✓ Health department compliance

Purchasing/Recruiting
✓ Ordering/receiving/storage
✓ Food and beverage specifications/quality
✓ Inventory control
✓ Vendor relation/problems

Staff Training/Development
✓ On-the-job vs. structured
✓ Safety/sanitation/food handling and so on
✓ Food preparation/presentation

A sample operating statement is shown in Figure 8–7. It shows a monthly statement for a college foodservice operation.

Managed Services Career Path

- *Assistant foodservice director:* Salary range of $28,000 to $34,000 plus benefits, which can be about 30 percent of salary and include a pension plan. If you already have experience in a variety of foodservice operations/positions, upon graduation, it is possible to gain this type of position. It is possible that you would move to a larger operation or a different type of account to broaden your experience and knowledge before moving up to the next level.
- *Foodservice director:* $35,000 to $45,000 plus benefits. It is likely that you would begin at one account and then move to a larger one after a few years.
- *General manager:* $50,000 to $55,000 plus benefits. After spending a few years at one location it is likely that you would move to another possibly larger one. For example, you may be GM of a $4 million account and go to a $10 million account.
- *District manager:* $60,000 to $65,000 plus benefits. The district manager is responsible for several accounts; other responsibilities include making proposals to gain new accounts and negotiating contracts with clients.

Check Your Knowledge

1. In your own words, define in-flight foodservice.
2. What are some of the challenges faced by in-flight foodservice operators? What can be done to solve these problems?
3. Name the foodservice operations that constitute managed services.
4. How is each foodservice operations characterized?
5. In small groups, discuss the differences between the foodservice operations, then share with the class.

DESCRIPTION		%	STUDENT UNION	%	TOTAL	%
SALES						
FOOD REGULAR	$ 951,178				951,178	
FOOD SPECIAL FUNCTIONS	40,000				40,000	
PIZZA HUT EXPRESS			$ 100,000		100,000	
BANQUET & CATERING	200,000				200,000	
CONFERENCE	160,000				160,000	
BEER			80,000		80,000	
SNACK BAR			300,000		30,000	
A LA CARTE CAFE	60,000				60,000	
** TOTAL SALES	$1,411,178		$ 480,000	100.0%	$1,891,178	100.0%
PRODUCT COST						
BAKED GOODS	$ 9,420		$ 4,700		$ 14,120	
BEVERAGE	10,000		8,000		18,000	
MILK & ICE CREAM	11,982		2,819		14,801	
GROCERIES	131,000		49,420		180,420	
FROZEN FOOD	76,045		37,221		113,266	
MEAT, SEAFOOD, EGGS & CHEESE	129,017		48,000		177,017	
PRODUCE	65,500		26,000		91,500	
MISCELLANEOUS					0	
COLD DRINK	0		0		0	
** TOTAL PRODUCT COST	$ 432,964		$ 176,160	36.7%	$ 609,124	32.2%
LABOR COST						
WAGES	$ 581,000		$ 154,000		$ 735,000	
LABOR—OTHER EMPLOYEES	101,500		545,000		156,000	
BENEFITS + PAYROLL TAXES	124,794		50,657		175,451	
MANAGEMENT BENEFITS	58,320		6,000		64,320	
WAGE ACCRUALS	0				0	
** TOTAL LABOR COST	$ 865,614		$ 265,157	55.2%	$1,130,771	59.8%
FOOD OPERATING COST-CONTROLLABLE	$ 24,000		$ 6,000		$ 30,000	
CLEANING SUPPLIES	9,000		46,000		55,000	
PAPER SUPPLIES					0	
EQUIPMENT RENTAL					0	
GUEST SUPPLIES	4,500		2,500		7,000	
PROMOTIONS	35,000		5,000		40,000	
SMALL EQUIPMENT					0	
BUSINESS DUES & MEMBERSHIP	3,000				3,000	
VEHICLE EXPENSE	3,600		700		4,300	
TELEPHONE	$ 17,000		$ 5,000		$ 22,000	

Figure 8–7 *Sample Operating Statement*

DESCRIPTION		%	STUDENT UNION	%	TOTAL	%
LAUNDRY & UNIFORMS					0	
MAINTENANCE & REPAIRS	$ 1,200		$ 200		$ 1,400	
FLOWERS	10,000		4,000		140,000	
TRAINING					0	
SPECIAL SERVICES	18,000		3,000		21,000	
MISCELLANEOUS						
** TOTAL CONTROLLABLE SUPPLIES	$ 125,300	8.9%	$ 72,400	15.1%	$ 197,700	10.5%
OPERATING COSTS-NONCONTROLLABLE						
AMORTIZATION & DEPRECIATION	$ 13,500		$ 7,000		$ 20,500	
INSURANCE	55,717		14,768		70,485	
MISCELLANEOUS EXPENSE	12,400		4,100		16,500	
ASSET RETIREMENTS					0	
RENT/COMMISSIONS	48,000		40,000		88,000	
PIZZA HUT ROYALTIES			7,000		7,000	
PIZZA HUT — LICENSING MARKETING			7,000		7,000	
TAXES, LICENSE & FEES	5,000		500		5,500	
VEHICLE — DEPRECIATION & EXPENSE	4,000				4,000	
ADMINISTRATION & SUPERVISION						
** TOTAL NONCONTROLLABLE COST	$ 138,617	9.8%	$ 80,368	16.7%	$ 218,985	11.6%
** TOTAL COST OF OPERATIONS	$1,562,495	110.7%	$ 594,085	123.8%	$2,156,580	114.0%
EXCESS OR (DEFICIT)	(151,317)	(10.7%)	(114,085%)	(23.8)	(265,402)	(14.0%)
PARTICIPATION-CONTRACTOR						
*** NET EXCESS OR (DEFICIT)						
STATISTICS						
CUSTOMER COUNT						
HOURS WORKED						
AVERAGE FOOD-SALES/CUSTOMER						

Figure 8–7 *(Continued)*

Health Care Facilities

Health care managed services operations are remarkably complex because of the necessity of meeting the diverse needs of a delicate clientele. Health care managed services are provided to hospital patients, long-term care and assisted-living residents, visitors, and employees. The service is given by tray, cafeteria, dining room, coffee shop, catering, and vending.

The challenge of health care managed services is to provide many special meal requirements to patients with very specific dietary requirements. Determining which meals need to go to which patients and ensuring that they reach their destinations employs especially challenging logistics. In addition to the patients, health care employees need to enjoy a nutritious meal in pleasant surroundings in a limited time (usually thirty minutes). Because employees typically work five days in a row, care must be taken to keep changing the area and the menu using themes and specials that maintain interest.

The main focus of hospital foodservice is the **tray line.** Once all of the requirements for special meals have been prepared by a registered dietician, the line is set up and color coded for the various diets. The line begins with the tray, a mat, cutlery, napkin, salt and pepper, and perhaps a flower. As the tray moves along the line, various menu items are added according to the color code for the particular patient's diet. Naturally, each tray is double- and triple-checked, first at the end of the tray line and then on the hospital floor. The line generally goes floor by floor at a rate of about five trays a minute; at this rate, a large hospital with 600 beds can be served within a couple of hours. This is time consuming for the employees, because three meals a day represent up to six hours of line time. Clearly, health care foodservice is very labor intensive, with labor accounting for about 55 to 66 percent of operating dollars. In an effort to keep costs down, many operators have increased the number of help-yourself food stations, buffets, salads, desserts, and topping bars.

Patient counts and lengths of stay are declining, which emphasizes the importance of finding new ways of generating revenues. According to 1994's ten largest self-operated hospitals, one of the basic service areas, the cafeteria, is generating the biggest revenue-producing opportunities.[10]

Hospital foodservice has evolved to the point where the need for new revenue sources has changed the traditional patient and nonpatient meal-service ratios at many institutions. This situation was imposed by the federal government when it narrowed the treatment-reimbursement criteria; originally 66 percent of a typical acute-care facility's foodservice budget went toward patients' meals, with the remainder allocated for feeding the employees and visitors. In the past few years, as cash sales have become more important, the 66/33 percent ratio has reversed.

Ever resourceful, managers of health care operations, like Dolly Strenko of Southwestern General Hospital in Middleburg Heights, Ohio, have created such concepts as a medical mall with a retail pharmacy; flower and gift shops; boutique; a retail bakery, with an exhibition conveyor oven; and a 112-seat restaurant deli with take-out services for adjacent medical offices and outside catering for weddings, bar mitzvahs, and other functions. Dolly has also been instrumental in elevating culinary standards, the result of hiring an executive chef who was a graduate of the Culinary Institute of America.

[10]Personal conversation with Dolly Strenko, November 1994.

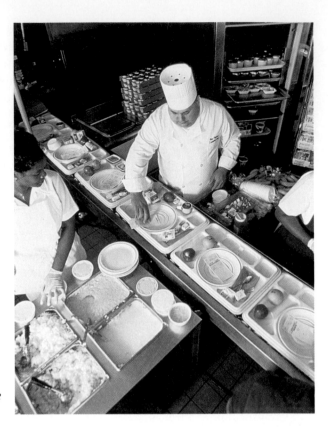

Health Care Foodservice
(Courtesy ARAMARK.)

Dolly Strenko

Experts agree that because economic pressures will increase, foodservice managers will need to use a more high-tech approach, incorporating labor-saving sous-vide and cook-chill methods. This segment of the industry, which currently is dominated by self-operated managed services, will continue to see contract specialists, such as Monson Custom management, Marriott, and ARAMARK Services, increase their market share at the expense of self-operated health care managed services. One reason for this is that the larger contract companies have the economy of scale and a more sophisticated approach to quantity purchasing, menu management, and operating systems that help to reduce food and labor costs. A skilled independent foodservice operator has the advantage of being able to introduce changes immediately without having to support layers of regional and corporate employees.

Another trend in health care managed services is the arrival of the major quick-service chains. McDonald's, Pizza Hut Express, Burger King, and Dunkin Donuts are just a few of the large companies that have joined forces with the contract managed services operators. Using branded quick-service leaders is a win–win situation for both the contract foodservice operator and the quick-service chain. As one operator put it, "The new McDonald's can be a training facility for future employees—in effect, a potential resource for our staff needs. Our union scale of $7.22 per hour could entice some 'cross-overs.' The branded image also helps the overall retail side of the foodservice operation."

The chains benefit from long-term leases at very attractive rates compared with a restaurant site. Chains assess the staff size and patient and visitor count to determine the size of unit to install. Thus far, they have found that weekday lunches and dinners are good, but the numbers on weekends are disappointing.

In contrast, several hospitals are entering the pizza-delivery business: They hook up phone and fax ordering lines, and they hire part-time employees to deliver pizzas made on the premises. This ties in with the increasing emphasis on customer service. Patients' meals now feature "comfort foods," based on the concept that the simpler the food is, the better. Hence, the resurgence of meat loaf, pot pies, meat and potatoes, and tuna salad, which contributes to customer satisfaction, and makes them feel at home and comfortable.

Business and Industry

Business and industry (B&I) managed services is one of the most dynamic segments of the managed services industry. In recent years, B&I foodservice has improved its image by becoming more colorful, with menus as interesting as commercial restaurants.

There are important terms to understand in B&I foodservice[11]:

1. **Contractors:** Companies that operate foodservice for the client on a contractual basis. Most corporations contract with managed services companies because they are in manufacturing or some other service industry. Therefore, they engage professional managed services corporations to run their employee dining facilities. Contract managed services operators have one main advantage over self-operators: They do not have to give as high a compensation and benefit package as the corporation itself.
2. **Self-operators:** Companies that operate their own foodservice operations. In some cases, this is done because it is easier to control one's own operation; for example, it is easier to make changes to comply with special nutritional or other dietary requests.
3. **Liaison personnel:** A liaison is responsible for translating corporate philosophy to the contractor and for overseeing the contractor to make certain that he or she abides by the terms of the contract.

Contractors have approximately 80 percent of the B&I market. The remaining 20 percent is self-operated, but the trend is for more foodservice operations to be contracted out. The size of the B&I sector is approximately 30,000 units. In order to adapt to corporate downsizing and relocations, the B&I segment has offered foodservice in smaller units rather than huge full-sized cafeterias.

[11]Philip S. Cooke, *in* Joan B. Bakos and Guy E. Karrick (eds.), *Dining in Corporate America: Handbook of Noncommercial Management.* Rockville, MD: Aspen Publishers, 1989, p. xvii.

Another trend is the necessity for B&I foodservice to break even or, in some cases, make a profit. An interesting twist is the emergence of multitenant buildings, the occupants of which may all use a central facility. However, in today's turbulent business environment, there is a high vacancy rate in commercial office space. This translates into fewer guests for B&I operators in multitenant office buildings. As a result, some office buildings have leased space to commercial branded restaurants.

B&I managed services operators have responded to requests from corporate employees to offer more than the standard fast-food items of pizza and hamburgers; they want healthier foods offered, such as make-your-own sandwiches, salad bars, fresh fruit stations, and ethnic foods.

Most B&I managed services operators offer a number of types of service. The type of service is determined by the resources available: money, space, time, and expertise. Usually these resources are quite limited, which means that most operations use some form of cafeteria service.

B&I foodservice may be characterized in the following ways:

1. **Full-service cafeteria** with either **straight line, scatter,** or **mobile systems**
2. **Limited-service cafeterias** offering parts of the full-service cafeteria, fast-food service, cart and mobile service, fewer dining rooms, and executive dining rooms

Business and Industry Foodservice (Courtesy ARAMARK.)

Check Your Knowledge

1. What roles other than those strictly related to foodservice does the foodservice manager perform?
2. Briefly explain some of the tasks the foodservice manager performs. What makes each task so important?

Leisure and Recreation

Courtesy of David Tucker

The leisure and recreation segment of managed services may be the most unique and the most fun part of the foodservice industry in which to work.

Leisure and recreation foodservice operations include stadiums, arenas, national parks, state parks, zoos, aquariums, and other venues where food and beverage are provided for large numbers of people. The customers are usually in a hurry, so the big challenge of the foodservice segment is to offer their product in a very short period of time. The average professional sporting event only lasts for two to three hours of actual playing time.

What makes this segment unique and fun is the opportunity to be part of a professional sporting event, a rock concert, a circus, or other event in a typical stadium or arena. There is also the choice of working in a national or state park and being part of the great outdoors, if that is to your liking. The roar of the crowd and the excitement of the event makes this a very stimulating place to work. Imagine *getting paid* to see the Super Bowl versus *paying* to see the Super Bowl.

Stadium Points of Service

Leisure and recreation facilities usually have several points of service where food and beverage are provided. In the typical stadium a vendor is yelling, "Here, get your hot dog here!" to the fans in the stands, while on the concourse other fans get their food and beverage from concession stands. These stands offer everything from hot dogs and hamburgers to local cuisine. For example, in Philadelphia the steak sandwich is popular, whereas in Baltimore, the crab cake sandwich is popular with the fans. Another place for people to get food is in a restaurant, which most stadiums have as a special area. In some cases, fans must be members of the restaurant; in other cases, fans can buy special tickets that provide them with access to this facility. These restaurants are like any other except that they provide unobstructed views of the playing area.

The other major point of service is the food and beverage offered in the premium seating areas known as superboxes, suites, and skyboxes. These premium seating areas are usually leased by corporations to entertain corporate guests and customers. In each of these areas, food and beverage service is provided for the guests. These facilities are capable of holding thirty to forty guests and usually have an area where the food is set up buffet style and a seating area where the guest can see the sporting or other event. In a large, outdoor stadium, there could be as many as sixty to seventy of these superbox type facilities.

In summary, a large stadium/arena could have vendors in the stands, concession outlets, restaurants, and superboxes all going at once and serving upwards of 60,000 to 70,000 fans. To feed all of these people takes tremendous planning and organization on the part of the foodservice department. The companies that have many of the contracts for these stadiums and arenas are ARAMARK, Fine Host, Sodexho Marriott, Compass Group, Wood Company, and Delaware North.

Other Facilities

Besides stadiums and arenas, food and beverage service is provided in several other types of facilities by the same major managed service companies that service stadiums. Most of the U.S. national parks are contracted to these companies. These parks have hotels, restaurants, snack bars, gift shops, and a myriad of other service outlets where tourists can spend their money. In addition to these parks, other venues where food and beverage is offered include zoos, aquariums, tennis tournaments like the U.S. Open in New York, and PGA golf tournaments. All of these events involve big numbers of people. For example, a PGA event, which lasts a week, including practice time and will have upwards of 25,000 spectators per day watching the pros play. These tournament events are similar to stadiums and arenas because they also include concession stands, food and beverage areas for the fans, and "corporate tents" for special catering and company guests.

Advantages and Disadvantages

A foodservice career in this segment has several advantages, which include the unique opportunity to see professional and amateur sporting events to your heart's delight, to hear the "roar of the crowd," to be in rural, scenic areas and enjoy the great outdoors, to provide a diverse set of services for the guests or fans, and to have a set work schedule.

The disadvantages of this segment include very large crowds of people to serve in a short time; a work schedule of weekends, holidays, nights; impersonal service; less creativity with food; seasonal employees; and an on-season/off-season work schedule.

Leisure and recreation foodservice is a very exciting, unique part of the hospitality industry that offers employees very different opportunities from standard hotel and restaurant jobs. With the current trend toward building new stadiums and arenas around the country, this segment offers many new career openings.

Trends in Managed Services

- ✓ College and university foodservice managers face increasing challenges. *Restaurants and Institutions* magazine asked several managers to identify some of those challenges. In general, managers mentioned trying to balance rising costs with tighter dollars. Bill Rigan, foodservice center manager at Oklahoma State University, Stillwater, pointed out two main challenges: a reduction of revenues from board-plan sales combined with increased costs such as food and utilities. He dealt with these challenges by recognizing that inasmuch as he could not change the utilities or hourly rates for employees, he would have to maximize purchasing potential. He also made optimal usage of from "scratch" cooking, convenience foods, and more efficient labor scheduling.
- ✓ Martha Willis, foodservice director at Tennessee Technological University, Cookesville, sees declining enrollment and a reduction in state funding as challenges. This translates to a cutback in services and more pressure to produce a bigger bottom line. Martha intends to achieve this by filling vacant full-time positions with part-time and student employees. The savings made by not paying full-time employee benefits can amount to 30 percent of a person's wage.
- ✓ Increased use of campus cards
- ✓ Increased use of food-to-go, for instance before sporting events
- ✓ Increase use of carts at vantage points
- ✓ Dueling demands for foodservice managers—from students who want more freshly prepared foods in convenient locations and from administrators who want more revenue from existing sources
- ✓ Twenty-four-hour foodservice
- ✓ Increased business in health care and nursing homes
- ✓ Proliferation of branded concepts in all segments of managed services, including military, school and college, business and industry, health care, and airport
- ✓ Development of home meal replacement options in each segment of the managed services sector, as a way to increase revenue
- ✓ Increasing use of fresh product

Career Information

Managed Services

Management careers in the field of managed services offer college graduates a vast array of opportunities. A tremendous advantage to this type of career is that as a manager you have more control over your time because of the structured nature of the environment. Airlines, schools, and health care foodservice, as well as college and university dining, usually work on a set schedule that is based on a menu rotation. There are no late nights unless you are supervising a catering event or special function. Within the educational environment, summers and school breaks allow managers time to get caught up on projects and or take vacations.

If you are looking for a managed services career, these areas offer a rare opportunity for a quality of life that is often not available in foodservice. One of the drawbacks to this type of career is that there is often little or no interpersonal relationships with your customers. Reduced customer contact means that there is often limited recognition and acknowledgment by patrons.

Military dining operations can offer a more restaurant or club-oriented career path. Working as a civilian for the military means competitive salaries, excellent benefits, and the opportunity to travel.

Business and industry dining is the most diverse career segment of institutional foodservice. It draws from all aspects of the industry. Hours are usually longer but still defined and there is a greater potential for bonuses and advancement.

Institutional foodservice is enjoying unprecedented growth as a multibillion dollar industry. It has expanded to include services outside the hospitality industry, such as grounds keeping, maintenance, janitorial services, and vending machine sales.

Related Web Sites

http://www.sodexhousa.com/—Sodexho
http://www.aramark.com/—ARAMARK foodservice

Courtesy of Charlie Adams.

Case Study

Chaos in the Kitchen

Jane is the foodservice director at an on-campus dining service that feeds 800 students per meal for breakfast, lunch, and dinner. Jane arrives at her office at 7:00 A.M. (half an hour before breakfast begins) only to find many problems.

After listening to her phone messages, she finds that her breakfast cashier and one of her two breakfast dishroom employees have called in sick. The cashier position is essential and the second dishroom person is necessary at 8:15 A.M. when the students leave to go to their 8:30 A.M. classes.

Shortly after listening to the messages, the executive chef tells Jane that one of their two walk-in refrigerators is not working properly, thus some of the food is above the safe temperature of 40°F.

The lead salad person later comes to her, saying that one of the three ice machines is not working. Hence, there will not be enough ice to ice down the salad bars and to use for cold beverages at lunch.

Lastly, the catering supervisor tells Jane that he has just found out that there was a misunderstanding with the bakery that supplies their upscale desserts. The desserts were requested by the president of the university for a luncheon he is having that day; however, because the employee at the bakery wrote the wrong delivery date, the desserts would not be delivered. This will cause the president to be angry.

Discussion Questions

1. How should Jane handle being short a cashier and a dishroom person at breakfast?
2. What should Jane do with the food in the defective refrigerator? Should the food that is measured to be above 40°F be saved?
3. What are Jane's options concerning the ice shortage?
4. How should Jane handle the president's function, knowing that the requested desserts have not been delivered?
5. If the special dessert cannot be purchased in time, how should the catering supervisor approach this situation when speaking with the president's office?
6. What can be done to ensure that mistakes, such as the one made by the bakery employee, do not happen again?

Case Study

Gas Leak

The kitchen at a major corporation's managed service business account includes several gas and electric stoves, ovens, broilers, steamers, BBQs, etc. On average, the kitchen serves 500 lunches. At 10:15 A.M., on a Tuesday in December, a gas leak prompts the gas company to cut off the gas supply.

Discussion Question

1. What can be done to offer the best possible lunch food and service?

Summary

1. Managed services operations include segments such as airlines, military, schools and colleges, health care facilities, and businesses.
2. Quality food has become a major competitive factor among airlines, which either provide meals from their own in-flight business or have it prepared by a contractor, such as Dobbs International or Sky Chefs.
3. Service to the military includes feeding troops and officers in clubs, dining halls, and hospitals as well as out in the field. Direct vendor delivery, menu management, prepared foods, and fast-food chains located on the base have met new trends in military foodservice.
4. Schools are either equipped with on-site kitchens and dining rooms or receive food from a central commissary. They try to balance salability with good nutrition. Today, nutrition education is a required subject in school.
5. College and university managed services operations include residence halls, cafeterias, student unions, faculty clubs, convenience stores, and catering.
6. The responsibilities of a foodservice manager are very complex. He or she is in charge of employee relations, human resource management, budgeting, safety administration, sanitation, and inventory.
7. Health care managed services operations need to provide numerous special meals to patients with very specific dietary requirements and nutritious meals in a limited time period for employees. The main areas of concern for health care managed services operations are tray lines and help-yourself food stations.
8. Business and industry managed services operations either operate with a full-service cafeteria or limited-service cafeteria. The type of service is determined by money, space, and time available.
9. Leisure and Recreation foodservice offers yet more career opportunities. L & R foodservice is often available at several points of service.

Key Words and Concepts

Batch cooking
Business and industry (B&I) managed services
Central commissary
College and university foodservice
Commercial foodservice
Contracters
Daily rate
Dietary guidelines
Direct vendor delivery
Elementary and secondary school foodservice
Foodservice contractors
Full-service cafeteria
Health care managed services
In-flight foodservice
Leisure and recreation foodservice
Liaison personnel
Limited-service cafeteria
Managed services
Military foodservice
Mobile system
National School Lunch Act of 1946
National School Lunch Program (NSLP)
Nutrition education programs
On-campus dining
Scatter system
Self-operators
Straight line system
Tray line
Type A menu

Review Questions

1. What are managed services operations?
2. List and explain features that distinguish managed services operations from commercial ones.
3. Describe the issues that schools are currently facing concerning school food service.
4. Explain the term *National School Lunch Program* (NSLP).
5. Identify recent trends in college food service management.
6. What are the pros and cons concerning fast-food chains on campus?
7. Briefly explain the complex challenges for health care managed services operations.

Internet Exercises

1. Organization:
   Web site:
   Summary:
   (a) Click on *"Careers."* Who is ARAMARK's star
       of the month? What is his or her position and
       responsibilities?
   (b) What are some of the characteristics that
       make a star of the month?
2. Organization:
   Web site:
   Summary:
   (a) What corporate services does Sodexho
       Marriott offer?
   (b) Look at the current opportunities (at
       Sodexho Marriott or ARAMARK) within
       your area.

ARAMARK
http://www.aramark.com
ARAMARK is "a global leader in managed services" according to its web site. ARAMARK is an outsourcing company that provides services ranging from everyday catering to corporate apparel.

SODEXHO SERVICES
http://www.sodexhousa.com
Like ARAMARK, Sodexho Services offers a full range of outsourcing solutions and is a leading food and facilities management services company in North America.

Apply Your Knowledge

1. From the sample operating statement (Figure 8–7), calculate the labor cost percentage by taking total sales and dividing by total labor cost × 100.
   Remember the formula: $\frac{\text{Cost}}{\text{Sales}} \times 100$.

2. Consider a retail operation at a local college where a Crilled Chicken Combo with a grilled chicken breast, fries, and a 20-oz. soda is on the menu. Cost out the ingredients by writing out everything needed for the Combo, including its service. What is your cost price? How much would you sell it for in order to make a reasonable profit?

Beverages

9

After reading and studying this chapter, you should be able to:

✓ List the various types of wine and describe the wine-making process.
✓ Suggest appropriate pairings of wine with foods.
✓ List the major wine-growing regions of the world.
✓ Distinguish the various types of beer.
✓ List the types of spirits and how they are made.
✓ Outline the history of coffee and other nonalcoholic beverages.
✓ Understand bar and beverage management.
✓ Explain a restaurant's liability in terms of serving alcoholic beverages.

Serving beverages is traditional throughout the world. According to his or her culture, a person might welcome a visitor with coffee or tea—or bourbon. Beverages are generally categorized into two main groups: alcoholic and non-alcoholic. **Alcoholic beverages** are further categorized as wines, beer, and spirits. Figure 9–1 depicts these three categories.

Wines

Wine is the fermented juice of freshly gathered ripe grapes. Wine may also be made from other sugar-containing fruits, such as blackberries, cherries, or elderberries. In this chapter, however, we will confine our discussion to grape wines. Wine may be classified first by color: red, white, or rose. Wines are further classified as light beverage wines, still, sparkling wines, fortified wines, and aromatic wines.

Light Beverage Wines

White, red, or rose table wines are 'still' light beverage wines; such 'still' table wines may come from a variety of growing regions around the world. In the United States, the premium wines are named after the grape variety, such as chardonnay and cabernet sauvignon. This proved so successful that Europeans are now also naming their wines after the grape variety and their region of origin, such as Pouilly Fuisse and Chablis.

Sparkling Wines

Champagne, sparkling white wine, and sparkling rose wine are called the **sparkling wines.** Sparkling wines sparkle because they contain carbon dioxide. The carbon dioxide may be either naturally produced or mechanically

Wine	Beer	Spirits
Still	Top fermenting	Grapes/fruit
Natural	Lager	Grains
Fortified	Bottom fermenting	Cactus
Aromatic	Ale	Sugar cane/molasses
Sparkling	Stout	
	Lager	
	Pilsner	
	Porter	

Figure 9–1 *Alcoholic Beverages*

infused into the wine. The best known sparkling wine is champagne, which has become synonymous with celebrations and happiness.

Champagne became the drink of fashion in France and England in the seventeenth century. Originating in the Champagne region of France, the wine owed its unique sparkling quality to a second fermentation—originally unintentional—in the bottle itself. This process became known as *methode champenoise.*

The Benedictine monk, Dom Perignon (1638–1715), was the cellar master for the Abbaye Hautvilliers—and an exceptional wine connoisseur. He was the first to experiment with blending different wines to achieve the so-called *cuvee* (the basis of champagne production). He also revolutionized wine by retaining the resulting carbon dioxide in the bottles. Dom Perignon's methods were refined throughout the centuries and led to the modern method used in champagne production.

Champagne may, by law, only come from the Champagne region of France. Sparkling wines from other countries have *methode champenoise* written on their labels to designate that a similar method was used to make that particular sparkling wine.

Figure 9–2 explains what the wording on champagne labels means and how to serve champagne.

Understanding the Label

The taste of the finished champagne depends ultimately on the level of sugar content, as follows:

Name	%/lt.	Taste
Extra Brut	0–1.5%	especially dry
Brut	1.5%	very dry
Extra Dry	1.2–2%	dry, semidry
Sec	2–3%	semidry, semisweet
Demi-Sec	3–5%	sweet
Doux	5+%	very sweet

Handling and Serving Champagne

Champagne should be stored horizontally at a temperature between fifty and fifty-five degrees Fahrenheit. However, it should be served at a temperature between forty-three and forty-seven degrees Fahrenheit. This is best achieved by placing the bottle in an ice bucket.

When serving champagne, there are some recommended steps to take to achieve the best results, as listed below.

1. If the bottle is presented in a champagne cooler, it should be placed upright in the cooler, with fine ice tightly packed around the bottle.
2. The bottle should be wrapped in a cloth napkin. Remove the foil or metal capsule to a point just below the wire, which holds the cork securely.
3. Hold the bottle firmly in one hand at a forty-five degree angle. Unwind and remove the wiring. With a clean napkin, wipe the neck of the bottle and around the cork.
4. With the other hand, grasp the cork so that it will not fly out. Twist the bottle and ease the cork out.
5. When the cork is out, retain the bottle at an angle for about five seconds. The gas will rush out and carry with it some of the champagne if the bottle is held upright.
6. Champagne should be served in two motions: pour until the froth almost reaches the brim of the glass. Stop and wait for the foam to subside. Then finish filling the glass to about three-quarters full.

Do's and Don'ts of Champagne

Do's: Dark, cool cellars
           Consistent temperature
           Clean champagne flutes
Don'ts: Artificial light
           Rapid chilling in the freezer
           Frosted glasses
           Cocktail glasses (this allows the bouquet to evaporate)

Figure 9–2   *Understanding Champagne Labels*

Fortified Wines

Sherries, ports, madeiras, and marsalas are **fortified wines,** meaning that they have had brandy or wine alcohol added to them. The brandy or wine alcohol imparts a unique taste and increases the alcohol content to about 20 percent. Most fortified wines are sweeter than regular wines. Each of the groups of fortified wines have several subgroups with a myriad tastes and aromas.

Aromatic Wines

Vermouths and aperitifs are aromatic wines. Aromatized wines are fortified and flavored with herbs, roots, flowers, and barks. These wines may be sweet or dry. Aromatic wines are also known as aperitifs, which generally are consumed before meals as digestive stimulants. Among the better known brands of aperitif wines are Dubonnet Red (sweet), Dubonnet White (dry), Vermouth Red (sweet), Vermouth White (dry), Byrrh (sweet), Lillet (sweet), Punt e mes (dry), St. Raphael Red (sweet), and St. Raphael White (dry).

The History of Wine

Wine has been produced for centuries. The ancient Egyptians and Babylonians recorded the fermentation process. The very first records about wine making date back about 7,000 years. The Greeks received the vine from the Egyptians, and later the Romans contributed to the popularization of wine in Europe by planting vines in the territories they conquered.

The wine produced during these times was not the cabernet or chardonnay of today. The wines of yesteryear were drunk when they were young and likely to be highly acidic and crude. To help offset these deficiencies, people added different spices and honey, which made the wine at least palatable. To this day, some Greek and German wines have flavoring added.

The making of good wine is dependent on the quality of the grape variety, type of soil, climate, preparation of vineyards, and method of wine making. Thousands of grape varieties exist, thriving in a variety of soil and climatic conditions. Different plants thrive on clay, chalky, gravelly, or sandy soil. The most important wine-making grape variety is the Vitis Vinifera, which yields cabernet sauvignon, gamay, pinot noir, pinot chardonnay, and Riesling.

Something about the fine wines also appears to inspire the muses: Where good wines are made, literature, music, poetry, cuisine, and architecture flourish. The extravagance of the architecture of the Hospice de Beaune is staggering, with ornate fretwork, gabled courtyards, and a dazzling polychrome tile roof. The medieval structure of the outside is mirrored in the inside; however, the building hides modern, twentieth-century medical devices, such as X-ray machines and operating rooms. The Hospice is enriched by a remarkable art collection, which displays distinguished pieces such as Roier van der Weyden's "Last Judgment."

The hospital is still functioning, partly because of its role in the wine world. Throughout the centuries, several Burgundian landowners have donated vineyards to the Hospice to help pay for maintaining its costs. Every autumn the wines from these vineyards—about a hundred acres of vines—are sold at a characteristic and colorful wine auction on the third Thursday in November, which determines the prices for the next year's Burgundy wines.

The Making of Wine

Wine is made in six steps: crushing, fermenting, racking, maturing, filtering, and bottling (see Figure 9–3). Grapes are harvested in the autumn, after they have been scientifically tested for maturity, acidity, and sugar concentration. The freshly harvested grapes are taken to pressing houses where the grapes are destemmed and crushed. The juice that is extracted from the grapes is called **must.**

The second step of the process is the **fermentation** of the must, a natural phenomenon caused by yeasts on the skin of the grapes. Additional yeasts also are added either environmentally or by formula. When exposed to air in the proper environment, the yeast multiplies. Yeast converts the sugar in the grapes to ethyl alcohol, until little or no sugar remains in the wine. The degree of sweetness or dryness in the wine can be controlled at the end of the fermentation process by adding alcohol, removing the yeast by filtration, or adding sulphur dioxide.

Est! Est! Est!

In Europe, during the Middle Ages, it was considered a good thing to make a pilgrimage to Rome once in a lifetime. There is a delightful story of a German bishop who liked his wine and food so much that he sent a servant to seek out the best tavern. (The tavern door was to be marked est, meaning it is.) Est *was painted on the best tavern door in the town they would reach that evening. After traveling across Germany and into northern Italy, the bishop's group came across a tavern door with* Est! Est! Est! *painted on it. Well, the bishop liked the wine and food at that tavern so much he never actually made it to Rome.*

Figure 9–3 *The Wine-Making Process*

Figure 9–4   *Wine Bottles*

Red wine gains its color during the fermentation process from the coloring pigments of the red grape skins, which are put back into the must.

After fermentation has ceased, the wine is transferred to racking containers, where it settles before being poured into oak barrels or large stainless steel containers for the maturing process. Some of the better wines are aged in oak barrels, from which they acquire additional flavor and character during the barrel aging. Throughout the aging process, red wine extracts tannin from the wood, which gives longevity to the wine. Some white wine and most red wine is barrel aged for periods ranging from months to more than two years. Other white wines that are kept in stainless steel containers are crisp, with a youthful flavor; they are bottled after a few months for immediate consumption.

After maturing, the wine is filtered to help stabilize it and remove any solid particles still in the wine. This process is called **fining.** The wine is then **clarified** by adding either egg white or bentonite, which sinks to the bottom of the vat. The wine then is bottled.

Fine **vintage** wines are best drunk at their peak, which may be a few years—or decades—away. Red wines generally take a few more years to reach their peak than do white wines. In Europe, where the climate is more variable, the good years are rated as vintage. The judgment of experts determines the relative merits of each wine-growing district and awards merit points on a scale of one to ten. The bottle shapes used are shown in Figure 9–4.

Matching Wine with Food

The combination of food and wine is one of life's great pleasures. We eat every day, so a gourmet will seek out not only exotic foods and vintage wines, but also simple food that is well prepared and accompanied by an unpretentious, but quality wine.

Over the years, traditions have developed a how-to approach to the marrying of wines and food. Generally speaking, the following traditions apply:

✓ White wine is best served with white meat (chicken, pork, or veal), shellfish, and fish.

Red Wines		
Cabernet Sauvignon	Medium Dry	Lamb, Pasta with red sauce, Red meat, Cheese
Zinfandel	Medium	Lamb, Pasta with red sauce, Red meat, Cheese
Pinot Noir	Medium	Poultry, Pork, Lamb, Red meat, Pasta with red sauce
White Wines		
Chardonnay	Medium Dry	Poultry, Pork, Seafood, Pasta with white sauce, Cheese
Sauvignon Blanc	Medium Dry	Poultry, Pork, Seafood, Pasta with white sauce, Cheese
Johannisberg Riesling	Medium Sweet	Poultry, Pork, Seafood, Pasta with white sauce, Cheese
Semillon-Chardonnay	Medium Dry	Poultry, Pork, Seafood, Pasta with white sauce, Cheese

Figure 9–5 *Matching Wine with Food*

✓ Red wine is best served with red meat (beef, lamb, duck, or game).
✓ The heavier the food, the heavier and more robust the wine should be.
✓ Champagne can be served throughout the meal.
✓ Port and red wine go well with cheese.
✓ Dessert wines best complement desserts and fresh fruits that are not highly acidic.
✓ When a dish is cooked with wine, it is best served with that wine.
✓ Regional food is best complemented by wines of the region.
✓ Wines should never accompany salads with vinegar dressings, chocolate dishes, or curries; the tastes will clash or be overpowering.
✓ Sweet wines should be served with foods that are not too sweet.

Figure 9–5 matches some of the better known varietal wines with food.

Food and wine are described by texture and flavor. Textures are the qualities in food and wine that we feel in the mouth, such as softness, smoothness, roundness, richness, thickness, thinness, creaminess, chewiness, oiliness, harshness, silkiness, coarseness, and so on. Textures correspond to sensations of touch and temperature, which can be easy to identify—for example, hot, cold, rough, smooth, thick, or thin. Regarding the marrying of food and wine, light food with light wine is always a reliable combination. Rich food with rich wine can be wonderful as long as the match is not too rich. The two most important qualities to consider when choosing the appropriate wine are richness and lightness.

Flavors are food and wine elements perceived by the olfactory nerve as fruity, minty, herbal, nutty, cheesy, smoky, flowery, earthy, and so on. A person often determines flavors by using the nose as well as the tongue. The combination of texture and flavor is what makes food and wine a pleasure to enjoy; a good match between the food and wine can make occasions even more memorable. Figure 9-6 suggests the steps to be taken in wine tasting.

Wine Tasting

Many restaurants have introduced wine tastings as special marketing events to promote the restaurant itself, or a particular type or label of wine. Wine tasting is more than just a process—it is an artful ritual. Wine offers a threefold sensory appeal: color, aroma, and taste. Wine tasting, thus, consists of three essential steps.

1. Hold the glass to the light. The color of the wine gives the first indication of the wine's body. The deeper the color, the fuller the wine will be. Generally, wines should be clear and brilliant.
2. Smell the wine. Hold the glass between the middle and the ring finger in a "cup-like" fashion and gently roll the glass. This will bring the aroma and the bouquet of the wine to the edge of the glass. The bouquet should be pleasant. This will tell much about what the taste will be.
3. Finally, taste the wine by rolling the wine around the mouth and by sucking in a little air—this helps release the complexities of the flavors.

Figure 9–6   *Wine Tasting*

Check Your Knowledge

1. How are alcoholic beverages categorized?
2. How are wines, beer and spirits categorized?
3. Describe how wine is made.

Major Wine–Growing Regions of Europe and North America

Europe

Germany, Italy, Spain, Portugal, and France are the main European wine-producing countries. Germany is noted for the outstanding Riesling wines from the Rhine and Moselle river valleys. Italy produces the world-famous Chianti. Spain makes good wine, but is best known for sherry. Portugal also makes good wine, but is better known for its port.

France is the most notable of the European countries, producing not only the finest wines but also champagne and cognac. The two most famous wine-producing areas in France are the Bordeaux and Burgundy regions. The vineyards, villages, and towns are steeped in the history of centuries devoted to the production of the finest quality wines. They represent some of the most beautiful countryside in Europe and are well worth visiting.

In France, wine is named after the village in which the wine is produced. In recent years, the name of the grape variety is also used. The name of the wine grower is also important; because the quality may vary, reputation understandably is very important. A vineyard might also include a chateau in which wine is made.

Personal Profile: Robert Mondavi

Since its founding in 1966, the Robert Mondavi Winery has established itself as one of the world's top wineries. Robert Mondavi, now in his eighties, still continues his activity as wine's foremost spokesperson, having greatly contributed to the wine industry throughout his successful life.

Robert Mondavi was born in 1913 to an Italian couple who had emigrated from the Marche region of Italy in 1910. His father, Cesare, became involved in shipping California wine grapes to fellow Italians. Extremely pleased with California, Cesare Mondavi decided to move to the Napa Valley and set up a firm that shipped fruit east. Robert Mondavi grew up among wines and vines and remained in his father's business.

Robert began by improving the family enterprise, adding to it the management, production, and marketing skills he learned at Stanford University, from which he graduated in 1936. Robert acknowledged the great business potential of the Napa Valley in the broader context of the California wine industry. What the firm needed was to be upgraded with innovations in technology, to keep up with the changes in the overall business environment.

Mondavi had an ambitious dream that was realized when the Charles Krug Winery was offered for sale in 1943. The facility was purchased, and Robert knew that the strategy for success included well-planned marketing as well as the crucial wine-making expertise that the family already had.

Mondavi understood also the importance of the introduction of innovative processes that could place the winery in a competitive position. From the 1950s to the 1960s, he performed many experiments and introduced pivotal innovations. For example, Robert popularized new styles of wine, such as the chenin blanc, which was previously known as white pinot and was not doing well in the market. Mondavi changed the fermentation, turning it into a sweeter, more delicious wine. The name was also changed, and sales increased fourfold the following year.

Similarly, he noticed that the sauvignon blanc was a slow-selling wine. He began producing it in a drier style, called it fume blanc, and turned it into an immediate success. Although the winery's operations were successful, Mondavi was still looking for a missing link to the chain. A trip to Europe, designed to study the finest wineries' techniques, convinced him to adopt a new, smaller type of barrel to age the wine, which he believed added a "wonderful dimension to the finished product."

In 1966, Robert Mondavi opened the Robert Mondavi Winery, which represented the fulfillment of the family's vision to build a facility that would allow them to produce truly world-class wines. In fact, since its establishment, the winery has led the industry, standing as an example of continuous research and innovation in wine making, as well as a "monument to persistence in the pursuit of excellence."

Throughout the years of operation, the original vision remained constant: to produce the best wines that were the perfect accompaniments to food and to provide the public with proper education about the product. As a matter of fact, the Robert Mondavi Winery sponsors several educational programs, such as seminars on viticulture, a totally comprehensive tour program in the Napa Valley wineries, and the great chefs program.

All of the family members are actively involved in the operation of the winery, united and guided by a shared determination to continue the winery's tradition of excellence.

Within the Bordeaux region, wine growing is divided into five major districts: Medoc, Graves, St. Emilion, Pomerol, and Sauternes. The wine from each of these districts has its own characteristics.

There are several other well-known wine producing regions of France, such as the Loire Valley, Alsace, and Cotes du Rhone. French people regard wine as an important part of their culture and heritage.

United States

In California, viticulture began in 1769 when Junipero Serra, a Spanish friar, began to produce wine for the missions he started. At one time the French considered California wines to be inferior. However, California is blessed with a near perfect climate and excellent vine-growing soil. In the United States, the name of the grape variety is used to name the wine, not the village or chateau used by the French. The better known varietal white wines in the United States are chardonnay, sauvignon blanc, Riesling, and chenin blanc; varietal red wines are cabernet sauvignon, pinot noir, merlot, syrah, and zinfandel.

California viticulture areas are generally divided into three regions:

1. North and central coastal region
2. Great central valley region
3. Southern California region

The north and central coastal region produces the best wines in California. A high degree of use of mechanical methods allows for efficient, large-scale production of quality wines. The two best known areas within this region are the Napa and Sonoma valleys. The wines of the Napa and Sonoma valleys resemble those of Bordeaux and Burgundy. In recent years, the wines from the Napa and Sonoma valleys have rivaled and even exceeded the French and other European wines. The chardonnays and cabernets are particularly outstanding.

The Napa and Sonoma valleys are the symbols as well as the centers of the top-quality wine industry in California. The better known wineries of California include those shown in Figure 9–7.

Wine and Health

A glass of wine may be beneficial to health. This perspective was featured in the CBS news magazine program "60 Minutes," which focused on a phenomenon called the French paradox. The French eat 30 percent more fat than Americans, smoke more, and exercise less, yet they suffer fewer heart attacks—about one-third as many as Americans. Ironically, the French drink more wine than people of any other nationality—about 75 liters per person a year. Research indicates that wine attacks platelets, which are the smallest of the blood cells and which cause the blood to clot, preventing excess bleeding. However, platelets also cling to the rough, fatty deposits on arterial walls, clogging and finally blocking arteries and causing heart attacks. Wine's flushing effect removes platelets from the artery wall. Needless to say, after the "60 Minutes" program was broadcast, sales of wine, particularly red wine, in the United States increased dramatically.

Burgundy Vineyard

Napa Valley

Several other states and Canadian provinces provide quality wines. New York, Oregon, and Washington are the other major U.S. wine-producing states. In Canada, the best wineries are in British Columbia's Okanagan Valley and southern Ontario's Niagara peninsula. Both of these regions produce excellent wines.

Wine also is produced in many other temperate parts of the world, most notably Australia, New Zealand, Chile, Argentina, and South Africa.

Beer

Beer is a brewed and fermented beverage made from malted barley and other starchy cereals, and flavored with hops. Beer is a generic term, embracing all brewed malt beverages with a low alcohol content, varying from 4 to 16 percent.[1] The term **beer** includes the following:

✓ Lager, the beverage that is normally referred to as beer, is a clear light-bodied refreshing beer.
✓ Ale is fuller bodied and more bitter than lager.
✓ Stout is a dark ale with a sweet, strong, malt flavor.
✓ Pilsner is not really a beer. The term *pilsner* means that the beer is made in the style of the famous beer brewed in Pilsen, Bohemia.

[1]H. J. Grossman, *Grossman's Guide to Wines, Spirits, and Beers.* New York: Charles Scribner's Sons, 1995, p. 293.

Napa Valley

Diamond Creek
Inglenook
Heitz
Krug
Louis Martini
Moet & Chandon
Robert Mondavi
Stag's Leap
Sterling

Sonoma Valley

Chateau St. Jean
Clos du Bois
De Loach
Dry Creek
Gundlach Bundschu
Iron Horse
Kenwood
Preston
Sebastiani

**South of
San Francisco**

Concannon
Paul Masson
Mirassou
Ridge
Calloway
Thornton

Figure 9–7 *Better Known California Wineries*

Table 9-1 Top U.S. Brewers and Importors Market Share	
U.S. Brewers	
Company	Percent of Market 1999
Anheuser-Busch	47.5
Miller	21.7
Coors	10.3
Pabst	6.3
Heineken	2.0
Labatt USA	1.7

Source: Personal correspondence Sherry Curley, Beer Maker's Insights, January 3, 2001.

The Brewing Process

Beer is brewed from water, **malt, yeast,** and **hops.** The brewing process begins with water, an important ingredient in the making of beer. The mineral content and purity of the water largely determine the quality of the final product. Water accounts for 85 to 89 percent of the finished beer.

Next, grain is added in the form of malt, which is barley that has been ground to a course grit. The grain is germinated, producing an enzyme that converts starch into fermentable sugar.

The yeast is the fermenting agent. Breweries typically have their own cultured yeasts, which, to a large extent, determine the type and taste of the beer. See Figure 9-8 for a description of the brewing process.

Mashing is the term for grinding the malt and screening out any bits of dirt. The malt then goes through a hopper into a mash tub, which is a large stainless steel or copper container. Here the water and grains are mixed and heated.

The liquid is now called **wort** and is filtered through a mash filter or lauter tub. This liquid then flows into a brewing kettle, where hops are added and the mixture is boiled for several hours. After the brewing operation, the hop wort is filtered through the hop separator or hop jack. The filtered liquid then is pumped through a wort cooler and flows into a fermenting vat where pure-culture yeast is added for fermentation.[2] The brew is aged for a few days prior to being barreled for draught beer or pasteurized for bottled or canned beer. Table 9-1 shows the major U.S. and Canadian brewers.

Spirits

A **spirit** or **liquor** is made from a liquid that has been fermented and distilled. Consequently, a spirit has a high percentage of alcohol, gauged in the United

---

[2]*Encyclopedia Americanna,* 1991, p. 452.

Figure 9–8 *The Beer-Making Process*

383

A Day in the Life of Shane Dudley
Bar Manager, Tupelo American Restaurant, San Diego, California

Shane arrives at the bar at 1:30 P.M. and for the next couple of hours he meets with wine and liquor representatives. The representatives advise Shane of any new products and give information about them. Tupelo American prides itself on being a "breaking ground" restaurant. As such, so that he can offer guests the most up-to-date product, Shane tastes the wine and spirits, and gives training sessions for the restaurant employees. Shane has assembled the best stocked bar in San Diego. This includes a great selection of single-malt scotch whiskys, single-barrel bourbons, cognacs, and vodkas. Shane checks the bar for stock to ensure that he is ready for the "Happy Hour" rush. He orders and receives stock twice a week.

(Courtesy John R. Walker.)

During the service time, Shane takes care of the regular guests, of which there are many. The barstools are all occupied and there is a buzz in the atmosphere. On busy nights, a second bartender takes care of the restaurant servers. Shane cross-trains the barbacks so they can step into a bartender's position in an emergency. At closing time, Shane does the banking and checks the restaurant before locking the doors.

The signature cocktail of the bar is the martini. Shane has brought the Martini back from the dead—he has created three hundred different martinis with fifty-five on the list at a time. No wonder three-quarters of the beverage orders are for martinis. This presents Shane with the challenge of coming up with new martini recipes.

States by its proof content. **Proof** is equal to twice the percentage of alcohol in the beverage; therefore, a spirit that is 80 proof is 40 percent alcohol. Spirits traditionally are enjoyed before or after a meal, rather than with the meal. Many spirits can be consumed straight or neat, or they may be enjoyed with water, soda water, juices, or cocktail mixes.

Fermentation of spirits takes place by the action of yeast on sugar-containing substances, such as grain or fruit. Distilled drinks are made from a fermented liquid that has been put through a distillation process (see Figure 9–9).

Whiskys

Among the better known spirits is whisky, which is a generic name for the spirit first distilled in Scotland and Ireland centuries ago. The word *whisky* comes from the Celtic word *visgebaugh* meaning *water of life*. Whisky is made from a fermented mash of grain to which malt, in the form of barley, is added. The barley contains an enzyme called diastase that converts starch to sugars. After fermentation, the liquid is distilled. Spirits naturally are white or pale in color, but raw whisky is stored in oak barrels that have been charred (burnt). This gives whisky its caramel color. The whisky is stored for a period of time, up to

Figure 9–9 *Distillation Process*

a maximum of twelve to fifteen years. However, several good whiskys reach the market after three to five years.

Most whiskys are blended to produce a flavor and quality that is characteristic of the brand. Not surprisingly, the blending process at each distillery is a closely guarded secret. There are four distinct whisky types that have gained a worldwide acknowledgment throughout the centuries: Scotch whisky, Irish whisky, bourbon whisky, and Canadian whisky.

Scotch Whisky

Scotch whisky, or Scotch, has been distilled in Scotland for centuries and has been a distinctive part of the Scots' way of life. From its origins in remote and romantic Highland glens, Scotch whisky has become a popular and international drink, its flavor appreciated throughout the world. Scotch became popular in the United States during the days of **Prohibition** (1919 to 1933) when it was smuggled into the country from Canada. It is produced like other whiskys, except that the malt is dried in special kilns that give it a smoky flavor. Only whisky made with this process can be called Scotch whisky. Some of the better-known quality blended Scotch whiskys are Chivas Regal and Johnnie Walker Black Label.[3]

[3]Michael M. Coltman, *Beverage Management*. New York: Van Nostrand Reinhold, 1989, p. 160.

Irish Whisky

Irish whisky is produced from malted, or unmalted barley, corn, rye, and other grains. The malt is not dried like the Scotch whisky, which gives Irish whisky a milder character, yet an excellent flavor. Two well-known Irish whiskys are Old Bushmill's Black Bush and Jameson's 1780.[4]

Bourbon Whisky

Liquor was introduced in America by the first settlers, who used it as a medicine. Bourbon has a peculiar history. In colonial times in New England, rum was the most popular distilled spirit. After the break with Britain, settlers of Scottish and Irish background predominated. They were mostly grain farmers and distillers, producing whisky for barter. When George Washington levied a tax on this whisky, the farmers moved south and continued their whisky production. However, the rye crop failed, so they decided to mix corn, particularly abundant in Kentucky, with the remaining rye. The result was delightful. This experiment occurred in Bourbon County; hence the name of the new product.

Bourbon whisky is produced mainly from corn; other grains are also used, but they are of secondary importance. The distillation processes are similar to those of other types of whisky. Charred barrels provide bourbon with its distinctive taste. It is curious to note that barrels can only be used once in the United States to age liquor. Aging, therefore, occurs in new barrels after each distillation process. Bourbon may be aged up to six years to improve its mellowness. Among the better known bourbon whiskys are Jack Daniels, Makers Mark, and George Dickle.

Canadian Whisky

Like bourbon, Canadian whisky is produced mainly from corn. It is characterized by a delicate flavor that nonetheless pleases the taste. Canadian whisky must be at least four years old before it can be bottled and marketed. It is distilled at 70 to 90 percent alcohol by volume. Among the better known Canadian whiskys are Seagram's and Canadian Club.

White Spirits

Gin, rum, vodka, and tequila are the most common of the spirits that are called **white spirits.** Gin, first known as Geneva, is a neutral spirit made from juniper berries. Although gin originated in Holland, it was in London that the word *Geneva* was shortened to gin, and almost anything was used to make it. Often gin was made in the bathtub in the morning and sold in hole-in-the-wall dram shops all over London at night. Obviously, the quality left a lot to

---

[4]Ibid.

Corporate Profile: The Seagram Company, Ltd.

In simpler times, consumers met around a market square to make their purchases. In our century, the process has grown infinitely more complex. The challenge for Seagram and its customers is to continue developing channels of trade for the consumer's ultimate benefit, enhancing choice convenience, and service. That is why we take time to understand our customers' business and make our technologies fit theirs . . . why we maintain the flexibility to create strategies for individual customers.[1]

The Seagram Company, Ltd., is a leading global producer and marketer of distilled spirits, wines, coolers, fruit juices, and mixers. The company operates worldwide through two major units: The Seagram Spirits and Wine Group and The Seagram Beverage Group. The Seagram Spirits and Wine Group, the company's largest operating unit, produces, markets, and distributes more than 230 brands of distilled spirits and 195 brands of wines, champagnes, ports, and sherries. Some of Seagram's best-known names, such as Chivas Regal Premium Scotch whisky, Martell cognac, and Mumm champagne, are sold throughout the world, and others are produced primarily for sale in specific markets. The company operates on a global scale: Spirits and wines are produced by the group at facilities located in twenty-two countries in North America, South America, Europe, and Australia. Regardless of this sweepingly broad scale, the sale of Seagram spirits and wines to its customers is far from a mass operation. The company focuses on cultivating individual and personalized contact with its customers, either directly or through representatives of the company. This well-organized network of "ambassadors" (wholesalers or distributors) extends Seagram's reach to the public and allows for a closer interaction between the company and its clients.

This strong focus on customers gives Seagram's a truly competitive advantage in the industry. The close interaction has been further emphasized with the adoption of an electronic data interchange (EDI) system, which provides direct, paperless exchange of order information with the customers.

In addition to this state-of-the-art technology, Seagram's business success is attributable to other remarkable factors, such as differentiation of product lines and effective exploitation of business areas that represent a future potential. The company believes that the wide range of the Spirit and Wine Group's product portfolio, and the broad diversity of its geographic markets, reduce Seagram's vulnerability to changes in the industry's environment, such as consumers' preferences, social trends, and economic conditions.

Recent emphasis of product development, in fact, has resulted in the introduction of several new brands in 1993. In the Scotch whisky category, for example, the increased portfolio of brands has allowed the company to compete at a premium level.

Just as the creation of new brands represents an investment in the company's future, the expansion into new geographies gives Seagram's a valid and broad base for future growth. In particular, the company is devoting a great deal of attention to China, which is considered to be the single most important market opportunity of the decade. Seagram has captured a significant share of this potential market by expanding its operations and increasing its presence. Infrastructures and facilities are being established and particular emphasis is placed on strengthening business relationships with its customers.

Seagram's shows a great deal of diversity in its channels of trade. The concentration on penetrating individual hotels and restaurants has proven to be particularly effective. Spirit and wine selections offered at fine hotels and restaurants set an influential standard of taste and brand perception. Seagram's brands have obtained a strong, worldwide predominance in this segment; the all-over presence of Seagram's on wine and cocktail lists greatly influences consumers' home consumption. In order to guarantee a continuity to this process, Seagram must nurture each individual relationship with future hosts over time. To this end, the company is working with major hotels and catering schools today to reach the great sommeliers and chefs of tomorrow.

[1] Courtesy of The Seagram Company, Ltd.

be desired, but the poor drank it to the point of national disaster.[5] Gin also was widely produced in the United States during Prohibition. In fact, the habit of mixing something else with it led to the creation of the cocktail. Over the years, gin became the foundation of many popular cocktails (e.g., martini, gin and tonic, gin and juice, and Tom Collins).

Rum can be light or dark in color. Light rum is distilled from the fermented juice of sugarcane, and dark rum is distilled from molasses. Rum comes mainly from the Caribbean Islands of Barbados (Mount Gay), Puerto Rico (Bacardi), and Jamaica (Myers). Rums are mostly used in mixed frozen and specialty drinks such as rum and Coke, rum punches, daiquiris, and piña coladas.

Tequila is distilled from the agave tequilana (a type of cactus), which is called *mezcal* in Mexico. Official Mexican regulations require that tequila be made in the area around the town of Tequila, because the soil contains volcanic ash, which is especially suitable for growing the blue agave cactus. Tequila may be white, silver, or golden in color. The white is shipped unaged, silver is aged up to three years, and golden is aged in oak from two to four years. Tequila is mainly used in the popular margarita cocktail or in the tequila sunrise made popular in a song by the Eagles rock group.

Vodka can be made from many sources, including barley, corn, wheat, rye, or potatoes. Because it lacks color, odor, and flavor, vodka generally is combined with juices or other mixers whose flavors will predominate.

Other Spirits

Brandy is distilled from wine in a fashion similar to that of other spirits. American brandy comes primarily from California, where it is made in column stills and aged in white-oak barrels for at least two years. The best known American brandies are made by Christian Brothers and Ernest and Julio Gallo. Their brandies are smooth and fruity with a touch of sweetness. The best brandies are served as after-dinner drinks, and ordinary brandies are used in the well for mixed drinks.

Cognac is regarded by connoisseurs as the best brandy in the world. It is only made in the Cognac region of France, where the chalky soil and humid climate combine with special distillation techniques to produce the finest brandy. Only brandy from this region may be called *cognac*. Most cognac is aged in oak casks from two to four years or more.

Because cognacs are blends of brandies of various ages, no age is allowed on the label; instead, letters signify the relative age and quality:

VSOP   = very superior old pale
VVSOP = very, very superior old pale
E   = extra or special

---

[5]C. Katsigris and M. Porter, *The Bar and Beverage Book,* 2nd ed. New York: John Wiley and Sons, 1991, p. 139.

```
F      = fine
X      = extra
VS     = very special
VO     = very old
VVO    = very, very old
XO     = extra old
```

Brandies labeled as *VSOP* must be aged at least four years. All others must be aged in wood at least five years. Five years then, is the age of the youngest cognac in a blend; usually several others of older age are added to lend taste, bouquet, and finesse. About 75 percent of the cognac shipped to Canada and the United States is produced by four companies: Courvoisier, Hennessy, Martell, and Remy Martin.

Cocktails

The first cocktails originated in England during the Victorian Era, but it wasn't until the 1920s and 1930s that cocktails became popular.

Cocktails are usually drinks made by mixing two or more ingredients (wines, liquors, fruit juices), resulting in a blend that is pleasant to the palate, with no single ingredient overpowering the others. Cocktails are mixed by stirring, shaking, or blending. The mixing technique is particularly important to achieve the perfect cocktail. Cocktails are commonly divided into two categories according to volume: short drinks (up to 3.5 ounces) and tall drinks (generally up to 8.5 ounces).

The secret of a good cocktail lies in several factors:
- ✓ The balance of the ingredients.
- ✓ The quality of the ingredients. As a general rule, cocktails should be made from a maximum of three ingredients.
- ✓ The skill of the bartender. The bartender's experience, knowledge, and inspiration are key factors in a perfect cocktail.

A good bartender should understand the effect and the "timing" of a cocktail. It is not a coincidence that many cocktails are categorized by when they are best served. There are aperitifs, digestifs, corpse-revivers, pick-me-ups, etc. Cocktails can stimulate an appetite or provide the perfect conclusion to a fine meal.

Check Your Knowledge

1. Describe the different types of beer.
2. Describe the various spirits.

Nonalcoholic Beverages

Nonalcoholic beverages are increasing in popularity. The 1990s and on into the 2000s have seen a radical shift from the free love 1960s and the singles bars of the 1970s and early 1980s. People are, in general, more cautious about the consumption of alcohol. Lifestyles have become healthier, and organizations like MADD (Mothers Against Drunk Driving) have raised the social conscience about responsible alcohol consumption. Overall consumption of alcohol has decreased in recent years, with spirits declining the most.

The healthful 1990s saw the introduction of several new beverages to the nonalcoholic list.

Nonalcoholic Beer

Guinness, Anheuser-Busch, and Miller, along with many other brewers, have developed beer products that have the same appearance as regular beer, but have a lower calorie content and approximately 95–99% of the alcohol removed, either after processing or after fermentation. The taste, therefore, is somewhat different from regular beer.

Coffee

Coffee is the drink of the present. People who used to frequent bars are patronizing coffee houses. Sales of specialty coffees exceed $4 billion. The Specialty Coffee Association of America estimates that there are more than 3,500 coffee cafes nationwide and another 3,000 espresso bars.[6]

Coffee first came from Ethiopia and Mocha, which is in the Yemen Republic. Legends say that Kaldi, a young Abyssinian goatherd, accustomed to his sleepy goats, noticed that after chewing certain berries, the goats began to prance about excitedly. He tried the berries himself, forgot his troubles, lost his heavy heart, and became the happiest person in "happy Arabia." A monk from a nearby monastery surprised Kaldi in this state, decided to try the berries too and invited the brothers to join him. They all felt more alert that night during prayers![7]

In the Middle Ages, coffee found its way to Europe via Turkey, but not without some objections. In Italy, priests appealed to Pope Clement VIII to have the use of coffee forbidden among Christians. Satan, they said, had forbidden his followers, the infidel Moslems, the use of wine because it was used in the Holy Communion and had given them instead his "hellish black brew." Apparently

---

[6]Personal conversation with Susan Davis of the Coffee Association of America June 26, 2000, *Food Arts*, **6,** 10, December 1993, p. 54.

[7]Claudia Roden, *Coffee*. Middlesex, England: Penguin Books, 1987, p. 20.

*Bernini's Coffeehouse,
La Jolla, California*

the Pope liked the drink, for his reply was, "Why, this Satan's drink is so delicious that it would be a pity to let the infidels have exclusive use of it." So his Holiness decided to baptize the drink, after which it quickly became the social beverage of Europe's middle and upper classes.[8]

In 1637, the first European coffeehouse opened in England; within thirty years, coffee houses had replaced taverns as the island's social, commercial, and political melting pots.[9] The coffee houses were nicknamed *penny universities,* where any topic could be discussed and learned for the price of a pot of coffee. The men of the period not only discussed business but actually conducted business. Banks, newspapers, and the Lloyd's of London Insurance Company began at Edward Lloyd's coffeehouse.

> ## The Infidels' Drink
>
> During the sixteenth century, travelers to Constantinople (now known as Istanbul, Turkey) enjoyed coffee there and brought it back to Europe. By the end of the sixteenth century, coffee had become noticed enough to bring about the censure of the Roman Catholic Church, which called it the wine of Islam, an infidel drink. When Pope Clement VIII tasted the drink, he is reputed to have remarked that the Satan's drink was too delicious to leave to the heathens so he made a Christian beverage of it.

Coffeehouses were also popular in Europe. In Paris, Cafe Procope, which opened in 1689 and still operates today, has been the meeting place of many a famous artist and philosopher, including Rousseau and Voltaire (who are reputed to have drunk forty cups of coffee a day).

The Dutch introduced coffee to the United States during the colonial period. Coffeehouses soon became the haunts of the revolutionary activists plotting against King George of England and his tea tax. John Adams and Paul Revere planned the Boston Tea Party and the fight for freedom at a coffeehouse. This helped established coffee as the traditional democratic drink of Americans.

Brazil produces more than 30 percent of the world's coffee, most of which goes into canned and instant coffee. Coffee connoisseurs recommend beans by name, such as arabica and robusta beans. In Indonesia, coffee is named for the

[8]Ibid.

[9]This section draws on Sara Perry, *The Complete Coffee Book.* San Francisco: Chronicle Books, 1991, p. 8.

island on which it grows; the best is from Java and is rich and spicy with a full-bodied flavor. Yemen, the country in which coffee was discovered, names its best coffee for the port of Mocha. Its fragrant, creamy brew has a rich, almost chocolatey aftertaste. Coffee beans are frequently blended by the merchants who roast them; one of the best blends, mocha java, is the result of blending these two fine coffees.

Coffee may be roasted from light to dark according to preference. Light roasts are generally used in canned and institutional roasts, and medium is the all-purpose roast most people prefer. Medium beans are medium brown in color, and their surface is dry. Although this brew may have snappy, acidic qualities, its flavor tends to be flat. Full, high, or Viennese roast is the roast preferred by specialty stores, where balance is achieved between sweetness and sharpness. Dark roasts have a fancy rich flavor, with espresso the darkest of all roasts. Its almost black beans have shiny, oily surfaces. All of the acidic qualities and specific coffee flavor are gone from espresso, but its pungent flavor is a favorite of espresso lovers.

Decaffeinating coffee removes the caffeine with either a solvent or water process. In contrast, many specialty coffees have things added. Among the better known specialty coffees are café au lait or caffe latte. In these cases, milk is steamed until it becomes frothy and is poured into the cup together with the coffee. Cappuccino is made by adding steamed hot milk to an espresso, which may then be sprinkled with powdered chocolate and cinnamon.[10]

Tea

Tea is a beverage made by steeping in boiling water the leaves of the tea plant, an evergreen shrub, or a small tree native to Asia. Tea is consumed as either a hot or cold beverage by approximately half of the world's population, yet it is second to coffee in commercial importance because most of the world's tea crop is consumed in the tea-growing regions. Tea leaves contain 1 to 3 percent caffeine. This means that weight for weight, tea leaves have more than twice as much caffeine as coffee beans. However, a cup of coffee generally has more caffeine than a cup of tea because one pound of tea leaves makes 250 to 300 cups of tea whereas one pound of coffee makes only 40 cups.

The following list shows where the different types of tea originate:

China—Oolong, Orange pekoe
India—Darjeeling, Assams, Dooars
Indonesia—Java, Sumatra

Carbonated Soft Drinks

Coca-Cola and Pepsi have long dominated the carbonated soft drink market. In the early 1970s, Diet Coke and Diet Pepsi were introduced and quickly gained

---

[10]Ibid.

in popularity. The diet colas now command about a 10-percent market share. Caffeine-free colas offer an alternative, but they have not, as yet, become as popular as diet colas.

Inasmuch as U.S. market sales tend to be flat now, companies are expanding internationally. Indeed, as much as 80 percent of Coca-Cola's profits come from international sales.[11]

Juices

Popular juice flavors include orange, cranberry, grapefruit, mango, papaya, and apple. Nonalcoholic versions of popular cocktails made with juices have been popular for years and are known as virgin cocktails.

Juice bars have established themselves as places for quick, healthy drinks. Lately, "smart drinks" that are supposed to boost energy and improve concentration have become popular. The smart drinks are made up of a blend of juices, herbs, amino acids, caffeine, and sugar, and are sold under names such as Energy Plasma Blast and IQ Booster.

Other drinks have jumped on the healthy-drink bandwagon, playing on the consumer's desire to drink something refreshing, light, and healthful. Often, these drinks are fruit flavored, giving the consumer the impression of drinking something healthier than sugar-filled sodas. Unfortunately, these drinks usually just add the flavor of the fruit and rarely have any nutritional value whatsoever.

Also, some drinks are created by mixing different fruit flavors to arrive at new, exotic flavors such as Passion-Kiwi-Strawberry and Mango-Banana Delight. Some examples of such drinks are Snapple and Tropicana Twister.

Sport enthusiasts also find drinks available in stores that professional athletes use and advertise. These specially formulated isotonic beverages help the body regain the vital fluids and minerals that are lost during heavy physical exertion. The National Football League sponsors Gatorade and encourages its use among its athletes. The appeal of being able to drink what the professionals drink is undoubtedly one of the major reasons for the success of Gatorade's sales and marketing. Other brands of isotonic beverages include Powerade and All Sport, which is sponsored by the National Collegiate Athletics Association.

Bottled Water

Bottled water was popular in Europe years ago when it was not safe to drink tap water. In North America, the increased popularity of bottled water has coincided with the trend toward healthier lifestyles.

In the 1980s, it was chic to be seen drinking Perrier (a sparkling water) or some other imported bottled water. Perrier, which comes from France, lost market share a few years ago when an employee tampered with the product. Now the market leader is Evian (a spring water), which is also French. Domestic

---

[11]Coca-Cola's 1993 annual report.

bottled water is equally as good as imported and is now available in various flavors that offer the consumer a greater selection.

Bottled waters are available as sparkling, mineral, and spring waters. Bottled water is a refreshing, clean-tasting, low-calorie beverage that will likely increase in popularity as a beverage on its own or to accompany another beverage such as wine or whisky.

Bars and Beverage Management

From an operating perspective, bar and beverage management follows much the same sequence as does food management, as shown in the following list:

✓ Forecasting
✓ Determining what to order
✓ Selecting the supplier
✓ Placing the order
✓ Receiving the order
✓ Storing
✓ Issuing
✓ Serving
✓ Accounting
✓ Controlling

Bar Setup

Whether a bar is part of a larger operation (restaurant) or is a business in its own right, the physical setup of the bar is critical to its overall effectiveness. There is a need to design the area in such a way that it is not only pleasing to the eye but is also conducive to a smooth and efficient operation. This means that bar "stations," where drinks are filled, are located in strategic spots, and that each station has everything it needs to respond to most, if not all, requests. All *well liquors* should be easily accessible, with popular call brands not too far out of reach. The brands that are less likely to be ordered (and more likely to be high priced) can be farther away from the stations. The most obvious place for the high-priced, premium brands is the back bar, a place of high visibility. Anyone sitting at the bar will be looking directly at it, thus offering the customers a chance to view the bar's choices.

As for beer coolers, their location depends on the relative importance of beer to the establishment. In many places, beer is kept in coolers under the bar or below the back bar, and sample bottles or signs are displayed for customers. However, in many places beer is their biggest seller, and they may offer numerous brands from around the world. In such places, other setups may be used, such as stand-up coolers with glass doors so that customers can easily see all the varieties available. This is also true for draft beers.

Inventory Control

A good system of internal **inventory control** accomplishes four broad objectives: It safeguards the company's assets, provides reliable accounting records, promotes operating efficiency, and encourages adherence to management policies.

Management philosophy and operating methods determine the extent and success of inventory and cash control. However, it involves more than establishing policies and procedures. Training is also important to ensure that employees treat inventory as cash and that they handle it as if it were their own money. Management's example will be followed by employees. If employees sense a lax management style, they may be tempted to steal. No control system can guarantee the prevention of theft completely. However, the better the control system, the less likely it is that there will be a loss.[12]

To operate profitably, a beverage operation manager needs to establish what the expected results will be. For example, if a bottle of gin contains twenty-five one-ounce measures, it would be reasonable to expect twenty-five times the selling price in revenue. When this is multiplied for each bottle, the total revenue can be determined and compared to the actual revenue.

One of the critical areas of bar management is the design, installation, and implementation of a system to control possible theft of the bar's beverage inventory. Theft may occur in a number of ways including giving away drinks, overpouring alcohol, mischarging for drinks, selling a call liquor at a well price, and outright stealing of bar beverages by employees. As is the case with the food operations, there is an anticipated profit margin based on the ratio of sales generated to related beverage costs. Bar management must be able to account for any discrepancies between expected and actual profit margins.

All inventory control systems require an actual physical count of the existing inventory that may be done on a weekly or monthly basis, depending on the needs of the management. This physical count is based on "units." For liquor and wine, the unit is a bottle, either .750 or 1.0 liter; for bottled beer, the unit is a case of twenty-four bottles; and for draft beer, the unit is a keg. The results of the most current physical count are then compared to the prior period's physical count to determine the actual amount of beverage inventory consumed during the period. This physical amount is translated into a cost or dollar figure by multiplying the amount consumed for each item times its respective cost per unit. The total cost for all beverages consumed is compared to the sales it generated to result in a profit margin that is compared to the expected margin.

Management should design forms that can be used to account for all types of liquor, beer, and wine available at the bar. The listing of the items should follow their actual physical setup within the bar to facilitate easy accounting of the inventory. The forms should also have columns where amounts of each

[12]Belverd E. Needles, Jr., Henry R. Anderson, James C. Caldwell, and Sherry K. Mills, *Principles of Accounting,* 6th ed. Boston: Houghton Mifflin Company, 1996, p. 318.

inventory item can be noted. A traditional way to account for the amount of liquor in a bottle is by using the "10" count, where the level of each bottle is marked by tenths, thus a half-full bottle of well vodka would be marked on the form as a ".5." Similarly, for kegs of draft beer, a breakdown of 25 percent, 50 percent, 75 percent, and 100 percent may be used to determine its physical count.

Personnel Procedures

Another key component of internal control is having procedures in place for screening and hiring bar personnel. Employees must be experienced in bartending and cocktail serving and also must be honest, since they have access to the bar's beverage inventory and its cash.

Bar managers may also implement several other procedures to control inventory and reduce the likelihood of employee theft. One popular method is the use of "spotters," who are hired to act like normal bar customers, but are actually observing the bartenders and/or cocktailers for inappropriate behavior, such as not taking money from customers or overpouring. Another method for checking bar personnel is to perform a "bank switch" in the middle of the shift. In some cases, employees steal from the company by taking money from customers without ringing it up on the register. They keep the extra money in the cash drawer until the end of the shift when they are cashing out, at which point they retrieve the stolen funds. In order to do a bank switch, the manager must "z-out" a bartender's cash register, take the cash drawer, and replace it with a new bank. The manager then counts the money in the drawer, subtracts the starting bank, and compares that figure to the one on the register's tape. If there is a significant surplus of funds, it is highly likely that the employee is stealing. If there is less than what is indicated on the tape, the employee may be honest but careless when giving change or hitting the buttons on the register. Either way, there is a potential for loss.

Restaurant and Hotel Bars

In restaurants, the bar is often used as a holding area to allow guests to enjoy a cocktail or aperitif before sitting down to dinner. This allows the restaurant to space out the guests' orders so that the kitchen can cope more effectively; it also increases beverage sales. The profit margin from beverages is higher than the food profit margin.

In some restaurants, the bar is the focal point or main feature. Guests feel drawn to having a beverage because the atmosphere and layout of the restaurant encourages them to have a drink. Beverages generally account for about 25 to 30 percent of total sales. Many restaurants used to have a higher percentage of beverage sales, but the trend toward responsible consumption of alcoholic beverages has influenced people to decrease their consumption.

Bars carry a range of each spirit, beginning with the "well" package. The well package is the least expensive pouring brand that the bar uses when guests simply ask for a "Scotch and water." The "call" package is the group of spirits that the bar offers to guests who are likely to ask for a particular name brand. For example, guests may call for Johnnie Walker Red Label. An example of a premium Scotch is Johnnie Walker Black Label, and a super premium Scotch is Chivas Regal.

A popular method of costing each of the spirits poured is calculated according to the following example:

With quantity purchasing discounts, a well-brand bottle of vodka might cost $5.00. A bottle yields twenty-five one-ounce shots, each sold for $2.50; this means that the $5.00 bottle brings in $62.50. The profit margins produced by bars may be categorized as follows:

Liquor Pouring Cost % (approx.)	12
Beer	25
Wine	38

When combined, the sales mix may have an average pouring cost of 16 to 20 percent.

Most bars operate on some form of par stock level, which means that for every spirit bottle in use, there is a minimum par stock level of one, two, or more bottles available as a backup. As soon as the stock level falls to a level below the par level, more is automatically purchased.

Night Clubs

There are several types of night clubs. In big cities, some cater to the upscale crowd that goes to clubs to see and be seen. These clubs have bars and may have live or recorded music. Some clubs feature a single type of music; other clubs feature rock 'n roll one night, soul the next, and rhythm and blues or reggae the following night. These clubs charge an entrance fee and a higher price for drinks than restaurants. However, the night club business is fickle; what is in one year may be out the next.

Microbreweries

In recent years, the advent of microbreweries and brewpubs (a combination brewery and pub or restaurant that brews its own fresh beer on-site to meet the taste of local customers) has changed the trend of homogenization that had characterized the brewing industry since the 1950s. Microbreweries are defined as craft breweries that produce up to 15,000 barrels (or 30,000 kegs) of beer a year. The North American microbrewery industry trend began in 1995, reviving the concept of small breweries serving fresh, all-malt beer. Although regional breweries, microbreweries, and brewpubs account for only a small part of the North American brewing industry in terms of total beer production (less than 3 percent), they have an extremely high growth rate.

One of the reasons for the success of microbreweries and brewpubs is the wide variety of styles and flavors of beer they produce. On one hand, this educates the public about beer styles that have been out of production for decades

Corporate Profile: Starbucks Coffee Company

Operations

Starbucks Coffee Company is the leading retailer, roaster, and brand of specialty coffee in North America. More than 5 million people visit Starbucks stores each week. In addition to its more than 2,300 retail locations, the company supplies fine dining, food-service, travel, and hotel accounts with coffee and coffee-making equipment and operates a national mail-order division.

On October 25, 1995, Starbucks Coffee International Inc., a wholly owned subsidiary of Starbucks Coffee Company, signed an agreement with SAZABY Inc., a Japanese retailer and restaurateur. This joint-venture partnership, called Starbucks Coffee Japan, Ltd., will primarily develop Starbucks retail locations in Japan. Its first Starbucks location in Tokyo opened on August 2, 1996, and an additional ten to twelve locations are planned for Tokyo metropolitan areas during the next eighteen months.

In August 1996, Starbucks Coffee International announced plans to enter two additional Pacific Rim markets. Starbucks signed an agreement forming a joint-venture partnership that will develop Starbucks retail locations in Hawaii. Coffee Partners Hawaii opened its first store in Honolulu at Kahala Mall on December 12, 1996. Approximately thirty locations will follow during the next three to four years.

The company entered Singapore, its first country in Southeast Asia, through a licensing agreement with Bonstar Pte. Ltd. The first retail location opened on December 14, 1996. Approximately ten Starbucks locations are scheduled to open in Singapore during the next twelve to fifteen months.

Locations

Starbucks currently has multiple locations in thirty states. Starbucks also operates internationally in Alberta, British Columbia, and Ontario, Canada; Tokyo; and Singapore.

In addition, Starbucks has about one-hundred licensed locations that serve customers in unique areas such as airports, university campuses, hospitals, and business dining facilities. Marriott Management Services operates most of these locations.

Starbucks and ARAMARK Corp. formed a relationship in February 1996. This arrangement includes an agreement to put licensed operations at various locations operated by ARAMARK. The first licensed location opened at the University of New Mexico in July 1996.

Specialty Sales and Marketing

Starbucks Coffee Company and U.S. Office Products announced an agreement in October 1996 to distribute Starbucks fresh roasted coffee and related products through U.S. Office Products extensive North American distributorship.

In November 1995, Starbucks announced a strategic alliance with United Airlines and is now the exclusive supplier of coffee on every United flight.

In addition, Specialty Sales and Marketing supplies coffee to the health care, business and industry, college and university, and hotel and resort segments of the food service industry; to many fine restaurants throughout North America; and to companies such as Costco, Nordstrom, Barnes & Noble, Inc., ITT/Sheraton Hotels, Westin Hotels, Star Markets, Meijer, Sodexho, Guckenheimer, and Horizon Airlines.

Product Line

Starbucks roasts more than thirty varieties of the world's finest arabica coffee beans. The company's retail locations also feature a variety of espresso beverages and locally made fresh pastries. Starbucks specialty merchandise includes Starbucks private-label espresso makers, mugs, plunger pots, grinders, storage jars, water filters, thermal carafes, and coffee makers. An extensive selection of packaged goods, including unique confections, gift baskets, and coffee-related items are available in stores, through mail order, and through a site in the Marketplace section of America Online.

In spring 1995, Starbucks introduced Frappuccino® blended beverages, a line of low-fat, creamy, iced coffee drinks. This product launch was the most successful in Starbucks history. In January 1996, the North American Coffee Partnership between Starbucks New Venture Company, a wholly owned subsidiary of Starbucks Corporation, and Pepsi Cola announced plans to market a bottled version of Frappuccino®. The product, a low-fat, creamy blend of Starbucks brewed coffee and milk, is currently being distributed on a national basis and is available in grocery stores and in many Starbucks retail locations.

A long-term joint venture between Starbucks Coffee and Breyer's Grand Ice Cream was announced on October 31, 1995. The joint venture, designed to dish up a premium line of coffee ice creams, began national distribution of five different flavors to leading grocery stores in April 1996. By July 1996, Starbucks had become the number one brand of coffee ice cream in the United States. Currently, ice cream lovers can choose from eight delectable flavors or two ice cream bars.

In March 1995, Starbucks and Capitol Records joined forces to produce Blue Note Blend, a compact disc featuring classic jazz recordings. It was played in Starbucks locations and was the first item to be sold to customers both over the counter and by mail order. The album was so successful that the company has subsequently released several other CDs, covering a wide range of tastes and moods, including Chicago blues, rhythm and blues, legendary female vocalists, an eclectic mix from the late 1960s and early 1970s, jazz, and opera.

Community Involvement

Starbucks contributes to a variety of organizations that benefit AIDS research, child welfare, environmental awareness, literacy, and the arts. The company encourages its partners (employees) to take an active role in their own neighborhoods.

To support philanthropic organizations in the communities where Starbucks operates, it established the Starbucks Foundation in 1997. The foundation, launched with an initial contribution from Howard Schultz, Starbucks chairman and CEO, of $500,000, will be supported by donations from Starbucks Coffee Company and Schultz's earnings from *Pour Your Heart into It: How Starbucks Built a Company One Cup at a Time,* a book authored by Schultz and released in September 1997.

Starbucks is the leading corporate sponsor of the international relief and development organization, CARE, with an annual corporate contribution of $100,000 in addition to a $2 contribution for every CARE coffee sampler sold.

Recognition

Starbucks has received numerous awards for quality innovation, service and giving. The following list includes a selection of the numerous awards Starbucks has won.

✓ "The Stafford Award for Corporate Leadership" in recognition of the company's sensitive reuse of older spaces within cities—*Scenic America*—May 13, 1997

✓ "Best Neighborhood Coffee Bar"—*Evening* Magazine's Best of the Northwest edition—April 21, 1997

✓ "Living and Giving Award" for significant contributions made in support of diabetes research—Juvenile Diabetes Foundation of Greater Seattle—March 22, 1997

✓ "Best Coffee"—Reader's Choice—*Northwest Palate*—January/February 1997

✓ Frappuccino® blended beverage recognized as one of "The Best New Products" of 1996—*Business Week*—January 13, 1997

✓ 1997 Consumer Enhancement and Development Award of Excellence—Coopers and Lybrand Consulting—January 1997

✓ One of the "Top 10 Growth Companies," "Top 10 Growth Chains" and "Top 10 Stock Performers" of 1996—*Nation's Restaurant News*—December 23, 1996

✓ 25th Anniversary Promotion recognized as one of the "Top Ten Promotions of 1996"—*Promo*—December 1996

✓ Bottled Frappuccino® Coffee Drink recognized as one of the "Top Ten New Products of 1996"—*Food Processing*—November 1996

✓ 1996 Most Customer-Sensitive Award for Customer Service for a chain restaurant—Knowledge Exchange—August 1996

✓ 1996 Corporate Conscience Award for International Human Rights—Council on Economic Priorities—June 4, 1996

✓ 1996 International Humanitarian Award—CARE—May 10, 1996

✓ 1996 American Business Ethics Award—American Society of Chartered Life Underwriters and Chartered Financial Consultants—March 7, 1996

✓ "Change Maker of the Year"—*Restaurants & Institutions*—December 1995

✓ One of "America's 100 Fastest Growing Companies"—*Fortune Magazine*—1992 through 1996

✓ Business Enterprise Trust Award for innovative benefits plan—December 6, 1994

La Jolla Brewing Co.

and, on the other hand, helps brewpubs and restaurants meet the individual tastes and preferences of their local clientele.

Starting a brewpub is a fairly expensive venture. Although brewing systems come in a wide range of configurations, the cost of the equipment ranges from $200,000 to $800,000. Costs are affected by factors such as annual production capacity, beer types, and packaging. The investment in microbreweries and brewpubs is well justified by the enormous potential for returns. To quote the *Wall Street Journal,* "With profit margins as high as 70%, a $250,000 microbrewery can triple the bottom line for a 200-seat restaurant and pay for itself in two years."

Microbreweries can produce a wide variety of ales, lagers, and other beers, the quality of which depends largely on the quality of the raw materials and the skill of the brewer.

Sports Bars

Sports bars have always been popular, but have become more so with the decline of disco and singles bars. They are a place people relax in the sporting atmosphere, so bar/restaurants like Trophies in San Diego or Characters at Marriott hotels have become popular "watering holes." Satellite television coverage of the top sporting events helps sports bars to draw crowds.

Coffee Shops

Another fairly recent trend in the beverage industry in the United States and Canada is the establishment of coffeehouses, or coffee shops.

Coffeehouses originally were created based on the model of Italian bars, which reflected the deeply rooted espresso tradition in Italy. The winning concept of Italian bars lies in the ambiance they create, which is suitable for conversation of a personal, social, and business nature. A talk over a cup of coffee with soft background music and maybe a pastry is a typical scenario for Italians. Much of the same concept was recreated in the United States and

CyberCafe

Canada, where there was a niche in the beverage industry that was yet to be acknowledged and filled. The original concept was modified, however, to include a much wider variety of beverages and styles of coffee to meet the tastes of their consumers, who have a tendency to prefer a greater selection of products. Consequently, the typical espresso/cappuccino offered by Italian bars has been expanded in North America to include items such as iced mocha, iced cappuccino, and so forth.

Students as well as businesspeople find coffeehouses a place to relax, discuss, socialize, and study. The success of coffee houses is reflected in the establishment of chains, such as Starbucks, as well as family-owned, independent shops.

Cyber cafes are a recent trend in the coffeehouse sector. Cyber cafes offer the use of computers, with Internet capability, for about $6 per hour. Guests can enjoy coffee, snacks, or even a meal while on-line. Reasonable rates allow regular guests to have e-mail addresses.

Check Your Knowledge

1. Describe the story of coffee.
2. What is the sequence of beverage management?
3. Discuss inventory control.

Liquor Liability and the Law

Owners, managers, bartenders, and servers may be liable under the law if they serve alcohol to minors or to persons who are intoxicated. The extent of the liability can be very severe. The legislation that governs the sale of alcoholic beverages is called **dram shop legislation.** The dram shop laws, or civil damage

Controlling Inventory

Consider this war story: The author once worked at an old hotel that had seven bars, and as an aspiring assistant manager, one of his duties was to take stock of the bars and calculate the beverage cost percentage.

Next morning, when outside auditors came to do the quarterly inventory control, they noticed that some of the bottles in the banquet bar were filled above the normal level in the neck of the bottle, but they weren't sure whether this was the normal "topping up" of the end of one bottle to the next or something else. A check of the alcoholic proof of the bottles showed that the gin and vodka had been diluted. Now the question was, who did it?

In recent weeks, the assistant managers' beverage cost percentages for each of the seven bars had shown varying results. First, one bar was up, then two weeks later, it was down. This was the case in each of the seven bars, even though the bottles all had the hotel's stamp on them and new bottles had only been issued when empty ones were returned.

In an attempt to find out what was happening, the general manager questioned each of the six assistant managers and concluded that several people were involved. He brought in a team of special investigators who took turns spending nights at strategic locations, such as behind a large sofa in the lounge that provided a good view of one bar and in an office with a peephole into another office. It was not long before one of the bell captains appeared with a fishing pole that he inserted through the wrought iron gate of the associates entrance to the historic bar. He managed to snag a bottle and bring it back through the gate. He then removed some of the spirits, diluted the bottle with a liquid, and returned it to the bar. Although the investigators were tempted to apprehend the bell captain, they decided to wait and see if anyone else was involved. Sure enough, the next night, another bar was tampered with in a similar fashion. This time, however, a senior assistant manager and a restaurant associate were involved. Again, no action was taken until the general manager could be consulted. This time, the police were called and, together, they questioned the senior assistant manager and the other two associates.

It turned out that a casino had recently opened near the hotel and several associates had lost large sums of money gambling. They had promised to repay the casino owner with spirits stolen from the hotel. The police then raided the casino and found some spirit bottles with the hotel's stamp on them. With this evidence, the casino owner, the hotel senior assistant manager, and the associates were prosecuted and convicted.

acts, were enacted in the 1850s and dictated that owners and operators of drinking establishments are liable for injuries caused by intoxicated customers.[13]

Some states have reverted back to the eighteenth-century common law, removing liability from vendors except in cases involving minors. Nonetheless, most people recognize that as a society, we are faced with major problems of underage drinking and drunk driving.

To combat underage drinking in restaurants, bars, and lounges, a major brewery distributed a booklet showing the authentic design and layout of each

[13]Gerald D. Robin, "Alcohol Service Liability: What the Courts Are Saying," *The Cornell Hotel and Restaurant Administration Quarterly,* **31,** 1 February 1991, p. 102.

state's drivers licenses. Trade associations, like the National Restaurant Association and the American Hotel and Motel Association, have, together with other major corporations, produced a number of preventive measures and programs aimed at responsible alcohol beverage service. The major thrust of these initiatives is awareness programs and mandatory training programs like **TIPS** (training for intervention procedures by servers) that promote responsible alcohol service. TIPS is sponsored by the National Restaurant Association and is a certification program that teaches participants about alcohol and its effects on people, the common signs of intoxication, and how to help customers avoid drinking too much.

Other programs include designated drivers, who only drink nonalcoholic beverages to ensure that friends return home safely. Some operators give free nonalcoholic beverages to the designated driver as a courtesy.

One positive outcome of the responsible alcohol service programs for operators is a reduction in the insurance premiums and legal fees that had skyrocketed in previous years.

Trends in the Beverage Industry

✓ The comeback of cocktails
✓ Designer bottled water
✓ Microbreweries
✓ More wine consumption
✓ Increase in coffeehouses and coffee intake

Case Study

Hiring Bar Personnel

As bar manager of a popular local night club, it is your responsibility to interview and hire all bar personnel. One of your friends asks you for a job as a bartender. Since he has experience, you decide to help him out and give him a regular shift. During the next few weeks, you notice that the overall sales for his shifts are down slightly from previous weeks with other bartenders. You suspect he may be stealing from you.

Discussion Questions

1. What are your alternatives for determining whether or not your friend is, in fact, stealing?
2. If you determine that he has been stealing, how do you handle it?

Case Study

Java Coffee House

Michelle Wong is manager of the Java Coffee House at a busy location on Union Street in San Francisco. Michelle says that there are several challenges in operating a busy coffeehouse, such as training staff to handle unusual circumstances. For example, one guest consumed a cup of coffee and ate two-thirds of a piece of cake and then said he didn't like the cake.

Another problem is suppliers who quote good prices to get her business and then, two weeks later, raise the price of some of the items.

Michelle says that the young employees she has at the Java Coffee House are her greatest challenge of all. According to Michelle, there are four kinds of employees—lazy; good, but not responsible; those who steal; and great ones who are no trouble.

Discussion Questions

1. What are some suggestions for training staff to handle unusual circumstances?
2. How do you ensure that suppliers are delivering the product at the price quoted?
3. What do you do with lazy employees?
4. What do you do with irresponsible employees?
5. How do you deal with employees who steal?

Career Information

Beverages

A career in beverage management includes everything from coffeeshops and restaurants to bars and nightclubs to wineries and breweries. Careers can involve production of the product or selling and marketing it to customers.

Winery or brewery careers are very specialized. A great way to explore this career option is to work at a winery or brewpub in your area while you are attending college. If you discover that this is what you want to do, try taking some related courses at a college or university in your area. Taking courses in viticulture and enology can help develop your knowledge about grapes and wine making in order to help you decide if this is a career path you wish to pursue. *Viticulture* is the science of growing grapes and *enology* is the science of making wine. Knowledge in these areas is becoming so important that some universities are offering specialized degrees in both areas. Brewery schools offer brewer certification programs and associate degrees in malting and brewing science or brewing technology.

Selling wine or spirits for a distributor can also be a very lucrative and interesting career. If you enjoy meeting people and like the idea of working on a commission, this may be an option you want to consider. As with any type of selling you need to be a person who is motivated, organized, and outgoing. You will also be selling a product that requires you to have very specialized knowledge. When you are hired your employer will spend time and money training you; however, it is advantageous to develop your knowledge of "adult beverages" while you are in college. Beverage management courses, seminars, and working for liquor distributors are great ways to develop this expertise.

Beverage management in nightclubs and restaurants involves late nights and sometimes long hours. Establishments can keep their bars open until well into the morning hours. Serving alcohol requires understanding hospitality law and dealing with your customers responsibly. While you are in school you should take courses in beverage management and hospitality law and also work as a barback, bartender, or part-time manager. Upon becoming a manager you will experience late nights, intoxicated people, and face the constant temptation of substance abuse. It takes self-control to work the long, irregular hours and not join your customers for a good time. If you are a disciplined person, who likes being where the action is and can handle the late hours, then this could be your type of hospitality career.

Coffee shops emerged during the 1990s and have become a separate segment of the hospitality business. Well-managed coffee bars offer a relaxed environment where customers can enjoy themselves with a good cup of coffee while reading a book or talking with friends. Coffee shops foster close relationships between customers and managers. It is not uncommon for people to visit a coffee bar several times each month. If you enjoy personal relationships and a low-stress environment, this career is worth checking out.

Related Web Sites

http://cocktails.about.com/food/cocktails/ ?once = truc& gives information on liquor

http://www.geocities.com/Paris/5289/cocktail. html—bartending and liquor

http://www.vine2wine.com/—links to a variety of web sites about wine

http://www.americanwineries.org/—National Associations of American Wineries

http://wineserver.ucdavis.edu/winegrape/index. htm—winery education information and links to other sites

http://www.realbeer.com/—great web site for information on beer

http://hbd.org/brewery/—information and links to brewing

http://www.abgbrew.com/—brewing school

http://www.siebelinstitute.com/—brewing school in Chicago

http://www.republicbeverage.com/—Republic Beverage career information and links to other sites

http://www.starbucks.com/home.asp—Starbucks Coffee employment information

Courtesy of Charlie Adams.

Summary

1. Beverages are categorized into alcoholic and nonalcoholic beverages. Alcoholic beverages are further categorized into spirits, wines, and beer.
2. Wine is the fermented juice of ripe grapes. It is classified as red, white, and rose, and we distinguish between light beverage wines, sparkling wines, and aromatic wines.
3. The six steps in making wine are crushing, fermenting, racking, maturing, filtering, and boiling. France, Germany, Italy, Spain, and Portugal are the main European wine-producing areas, and California is the main American wine-producing area.
4. Beer is a brewed and fermented beverage made from malt. Different types of beer include ale, stout, lager, and pilsner.
5. Spirits have a high percentage of alcohol and are served before or after a meal. Fermentation and distillation are parts of their processing. The most popular white spirits are rum, gin, vodka, and tequila.
6. Today people have become more health conscious about consumption of alcohol; nonalcoholic beverages such as coffee, tea, soft drinks, juices, and bottled water are increasing in popularity.
7. Beverages make up 20 to 30 percent of total sales in a restaurant, but managers are liable if they serve alcohol to minors. Programs such as designated driver and TIPS, and the serving of virgin cocktails, have increased.

Key Words and Concepts

Alcoholic beverage	Fining	Must	TIPS
Beer, malt, hops, and yeast	Fortified wines	Nonalcoholic beverage	Vintage
Champagne	Hops	Prohibition	White spirits
Clarify	Inventory control	Proof	Wine
Dram shop legislation	Malt	Sparkling wine	Wort
Fermentation	Mashing	Spirits (liquor)	Yeast

Review Questions

1. What is the difference between fortified and aromatic wines? In what combination is it suggested to serve food and wine and why?
2. Describe the brewing process of beer. What is the difference between a stout and a pilsner?
3. What are spirits? Explain the process of fermentation and distillation and the origin of Scotch whisky and brandy.
4. Why have nonalcoholic drinks increased in popularity and what difficulties do bar managers face when serving alcohol?
5. Describe the origin of coffee.
6. Describe the proper procedure for handling and serving champagne.
7. Describe the origin of cocktails. What constitutes a cocktail?
8. Describe a typical bar setup.

Internet Exercises

1. Organization:
   Web site:
   Summary:
   (a) Take a look at the detailed food and wine pairings. What can you serve with the Clos Du Bois Sonoma County Sauvignon Blanc? Compare it to what you already know about what to eat with sauvignon blanc.
   (b) The Clos Du Bois has been named Wine of the Year for nine years by *Wine & Spirits.* What is it about this wine that makes it so different from others?

2. Organization:
   Web site:
   Summary:
   (a) What are some of the services that the Institute of Technology offers its students?
   (b) List the career path options available through Siebel Institute of Technology.

Clos Du Bois
http://www.closdubois.com
Clos Du Bois is one of America's well-known and loved wineries and is premier producer of wines from Sonoma County in California. The winery was started in 1974 and since then has acquired many more vineyards and a name for itself. It now sells about a million cases of premium wine annually.

Siebel Institute of Technology
http://www.siebelinstitute.com
Siebel Institute of Technology is recognized for its training and educational programs in brewing technology.

Apply Your Knowledge

1. In groups, do a blindfold taste test with cans of Coke and Pepsi. See if your group can identify which is which and who likes Coke or Pepsi the most.
2. Complete the class survey and share the results with your classmates.
3. Demonstrate the correct way of opening and serving a bottle of non-alcoholic wine.
4. What type of wine would be recommended with the following:
   a. Pork
   b. Cheese
   c. Lamb
   d. Chocolate cake
   e. Chicken

5. Mothers Against Drunk Drivers (MADD) is a nonprofit organization working to stop drunk drivers and support victims of drunk drivers. Find out what impact MADD has had on society.

Recreation and Leisure

10

After reading and studying this chapter, you should be able to:

✓ Discuss the relationship of recreation and leisure to wellness.
✓ Explain the origins and extent of government-sponsored recreation.
✓ Distinguish between commercial and noncommercial recreation.
✓ Name and describe various types of recreational clubs.

Recreational activities include all kinds of sports, both team and individual. Baseball, softball, football, basketball, volleyball, tennis, swimming, jogging, skiing, hiking, aerobics, rock climbing, and camping are all active forms of recreation. Passive recreational activities include reading, fishing, playing and listening to music, gardening, playing computer games, and watching television or movies.

Recreation is an integral part of the nation's total social, economic, natural resource, and urban environment. It is a basic component of individual and social behavior and aspiration.[1]

Recreation, Leisure, and Wellness

As postindustrial society has become more complex, life has become more stressed. The need to develop the wholeness of the person has become increasingly important. Compared to a generation ago, the stress levels of business executives are much higher. The term *burnout*—and indeed, the word *stress*—have only become a part of our everyday vocabulary in recent years. Recreation is all about creating a balance, a harmony in life that will maintain **wellness** and wholeness.

Recreation allows people to have fun together and to form lasting relationships built on the experiences they have enjoyed together. This recreational process is called *bonding*. Bonding is hard to describe, yet the experience of increased interpersonal feeling for friends or business associates as a result of a recreational pursuit is common. These relationships result in personal growth and development.

The word *recreation* is defined in the dictionary as "the process of giving new life to something, of restoring something."[2] Recreation is synonymous with lifestyle and the development of a positive attitude. An example of this is the increased feeling of well-being experienced after a recreational activity. Some people make the mistake of trying to pursue happiness as a personal goal. It is not enough for a person to say, "I want to be happy; therefore, I will recreate." Nathaniel Hawthorne wrote in the mid-nineteenth century: "Happiness in this world, when it comes, comes incidentally. Make it the object of pursuit, and it leads us on a wild goose chase, and it is never attained. Follow some other object, and very possibly we may find that we have caught happiness without dreaming of it."[3]

Recreation is a process that seeks to establish a milieu conducive to the discovery and development of characteristics that can lead to happiness.

---

[1] Douglas M. Knudson, *Outdoor Recreation*. New York: Macmillan, 1980, p. 1.

[2] Bruno Hans Geba, *Being at Leisure, Playing at Life: A Guide to Health and Joyful Living*. La Mesa, CA: Leisure Science Systems International, 1985, p. 19.

[3] Ibid., p. 66.

Biking, Swimming, Hiking

Happiness and well-being, therefore, are incidental outcomes of recreation. Thus, happiness may be enhanced by the pursuit of recreational activities.

The setting of personal recreational goals is equally as important as any other business or personal goal. These goals might include running a mile in under six minutes or maintaining a baseball batting average above .300. The fact that a person sets and strives to achieve goals requires personal organization. This helps improve the quality-of-life.

Leisure is best described as time free from work, or discretionary time. Some recreation professionals use the words *leisure* and *recreation* interchangeably, while others define leisure as the "productive," "creative," or "contemplative" use of free time.

History shows again and again a direct link between leisure and the advancement of civilization. Hard work alone leaves no time for becoming civilized. Ironically, however, the opportunity to be at leisure is the direct result of increased technological and productivity advancements.

Government-Sponsored Recreation

Various levels of government are intertwined, yet distinct, in their parks, recreation, and leisure services. The founding fathers of America said it best when they affirmed the right to life, liberty, and the pursuit of happiness in the Declaration of Independence. The general welfare clause of the Constitution has become a legal basis for federal action affecting leisure pursuits.[4]

Government raises revenue from income taxes, sales taxes, and property taxes. Additionally, government raises special revenue from recreation-related activities such as automobile and recreational vehicles, boats, motor fuels,**transient occupancy taxes** (TOT) on hotel accommodations, state lotteries, and others.

---

[4]Janet R. MacClean, J. Peterson, and D. Martin, *Recreation and Leisure: The Changing Scene,* 4th ed. New York: John Wiley and Sons, 1985, p. 72.

New York Marathon

The monies are distributed among the various recreation- and leisure-related organizations at the federal, state/provincial, city, and town levels. Recreation and leisure activities are extremely varied, ranging from cultural pursuits like museums, arts and crafts, music, theater, and dance to sports (individual and team), outdoor recreation, amusement parks, theme parks, community centers, playgrounds, libraries, and gardens.

A number of demographic factors affect participation in recreational activities: personality, sex, age, health, cultural background, upbringing, education, environment, occupation, and social contacts.[5]

Perceptions and attitudes play a major role in determining whether or not individuals participate in recreation, and if so, how much they enjoy their experiences. People's perceptions and attitudes are products of the total environment. All of the stimuli received throughout life mold an individual's outlook and feelings. These stimuli, in turn, are controlled by the person's demographics.[6] In the end, people select recreational pursuits based on their interests and capabilities.

Recreation professionals face a number of policy and legal concepts,[7] among them the following:

- ✓ Comprehensive recreation planning
- ✓ Land classification systems
- ✓ Federal revenue sharing
- ✓ Acquisition- and development-funding programs
- ✓ Land-use planning and zoning
- ✓ State and local financing
- ✓ Off-road vehicle impacts and policy
- ✓ Use of easements for recreation

[5]Michael Chubb and Holly R. Chubb, *One Third of Our Time: An Introduction to Recreation Behavior and Resources.* New York: John Wiley and Sons, 1981, p. 191.

[6]Ibid.

[7]Knudson, op. cit., pp. 7–8.

✓ Designation of areas (such as wilderness, wild and scenic rivers, national trails, nature preserves)

✓ Differences in purposes and resources (of the numerous local, state/provincial, and federal agencies that control more than one-third of the nation's land, much of which is used for recreation)

National Parks in the United States

National Parks are the best idea we ever had. Absolutely American, absolutely democratic, they reflect us at our best rather than our worst.
—WALLACE STEGNER, 1983

The prevailing image of a **national park** is one of grand natural playgrounds, such as Yellowstone National Park; but there is much more to it than that. The United States has designated 367 national park units throughout the country, comprising a rich diversity of places and settings.

The **National Parks Service** was founded in 1916 by Congress to conserve park resources and to provide for their use by the public in order to leave them unimpaired for the enjoyment of future generations.

In addition to the better known parks such as Yellowstone and Yosemite, the Parks Service also manages many other heritage attractions, including the Freedom Trail in Boston, Independence Hall in Philadelphia, the Antietam National Battlefield in Sharpsburg, Maryland, and the U.S.S. *Arizona* Memorial at Pearl Harbor in Hawaii. The Parks Service is also charged with caring for myriad cultural artifacts, including ancient pottery, sailing vessels, colonial-period clothing, and Civil War documents.

There is nothing so American as our National Parks . . . the fundamental idea behind the parks . . . is that the country belongs to the people.
—FRANKLIN D. ROOSEVELT

The ever-expanding mandate of the Parks Service also calls for understanding and preserving the environment. It monitors the ecosystem from the Arctic tundra to coral atolls, researches the air and water quality around the nation, and participates in global studies on acid rain, climate change, and biological diversity.

The idea of preserving exceptional lands for public use as national parks arose after the Civil War when America's receding wilderness left unique national resources vulnerable to exploitation. Recent years have seen phenomenal growth in the system, with three new areas created in the last twenty years. These include new kinds of parks, such as urban recreational areas, free-flowing rivers, long-distance trails, and historic sites honoring our nation's social achievements. The system's current roster of 367 areas covers more than 80 million acres of land, with individual areas ranging in size from the 13-million-acre Wrangell-St. Elias National Park and Preserve in Alaska to the Thaddeus Kosciuszko National Memorial (a Philadelphia row house commemorating a hero of the American Revolution), which covers two one-hundredths of an acre.

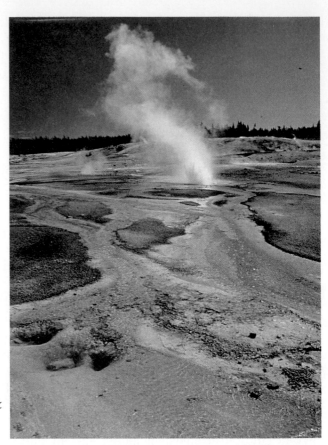

Yellowstone National Park
(Courtesy Yellowstone
National Park.)

More than 272 million visitors go to the parks each year and take advantage of the full range of services and programs. The focus once placed on preserving the scenery of the most natural parks has shifted as the system has grown and changed. Today emphasis is placed on preserving the vitality of each park's ecosystem and on the protection of unique or endangered plant and animal species.[8]

National Parks in Canada

Canada has twenty-nine large national parks and more than twenty national historical parks and sites. Banff National Park, known for the world's most beautiful mountain peaks, was the first park of the system, founded in 1885. Jasper, Kootenay, Yoho Glacier, and Mt. Revelstoke national parks, several provincial parks, and the extensive Rocky Mountain Forest Reserve combine to make an immense complex of public lands along the spine of the spectacularly scenic Rocky Mountains of Alberta and British Columbia. These parks are

[8]This section draws on information supplied by the National Parks Service.

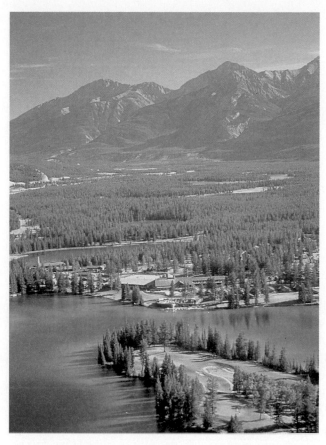

Jasper Lodge and Park

accessed by the Canadian Pacific Railway, the Trans-Canada Highway, and small aircraft.[9]

The Canadian National Parks Act states that "The parks are hereby dedicated to the people of Canada for their benefit, education, and enjoyment—and shall be maintained and made use of, so as to leave them unimpaired for the enjoyment of future generations."

The Canadian parks have highly developed tourist service islands (such as the town of Banff), well-appointed lodges and chalets, ski resorts, sports centers, and retreats, mostly natural in character. The largest of Canada's—and perhaps the world's—national parks is Wood Buffalo in Alberta and the Northwest Territories. Its 4,481,000 hectares (17,300 square miles) serve as home to the world's largest herd of bison that are roaming wild. The park is not developed for the public, but serves strictly as a wildlife preserve.

In Canada, recreation programming became a serious concern of the government after World War II. Provincial responsibility for recreation comes under several headings: outdoor activities, sports and physical recreation, arts and culture, social activities, tourism, and travel. Within each category, the government may have differing levels of responsibility: primary, in which a

[9]Knudson, op. cit., p. 261.

Public Golf Course

Public Basketball Court

department or agency is required to provide a given service; secondary, in which an agency specifically is permitted (although not required) to provide a service; and tertiary, in which an agency performs a recreation function because it is related to another primary responsibility.[10]

In the past few decades, the federal government of Canada, in response to perceived needs, has created activities themes. During the 1950s, it was physical fitness; in the 1960s, it was youth; and in the 1970s, it was cultural and multicultural expression. The 1980s and 1990s have brought a combination of previous programs, with family themes.

Public Recreation and Parks Agencies

During the early part of the nineteenth century in the United States, the parks movement expanded rapidly as a responsibility of government and voluntary organizations. By the early 1900s, fourteen cities had made provisions for supervised play facilities, and the playground movement gained momentum. Private initiative and financial support were instrumental in convincing city government to provide tax dollars to build and maintain new play areas.

About the same time, municipal parks were created in a number of cities. Boston established the first metropolitan park system in 1892. In 1898, the New England Association of Park Superintendents (predecessor of the American Institute of Park Executives) was established to bring together park superintendents and promote their professional concerns.

Increasingly, the concept that city governments should provide recreation facilities, programs, and services became widely accepted. Golf courses, swimming pools, bathing beaches, picnic areas, winter sports facilities, game fields, and playgrounds were constructed.

[10]Richard Kraus, *Recreation and Leisure in Modern Society,* 3rd ed. Glenview, IL: Scott, Foresman, 1984, pp. 159–160.

Check Your Knowledge

1. Explain the importance of taxes to government-sponsored recreation.
2. Name a few parks in the United States and in Canada. What are some characteristics that make the parks you named special?
3. Name your favorite park. Share with your classmates why it is your favorite.

Commercial Recreation

Recreation management came of age in the 1920s and 1930s, when recreation and social programs were offered as a community service. Colleges and universities began offering degree programs. Both public and private sector recreation management has grown rapidly since 1950.

Commercial recreation has been defined as "recreation for which the consumer pays and for which the supplier expects to make a profit."[11] Commercial recreation includes theme parks, attractions, and clubs.

Theme Parks

Visiting **theme parks** has always been a favorite tourist activity. Theme parks create an atmosphere of another place and time, and usually concentrate on one dominant theme around which architecture, landscaping, costumed personnel, rides, shows, foodservices, and merchandise are coordinated.[12]

Theme parks and attractions vary according to theme, which might be historical, cultural, geographical, and so on. Some parks and attractions focus on a single theme, like the marine zoological Sea World parks. Other parks and attractions focus on multiple themes, like King's Island in Ohio, a family entertainment center divided into six theme areas: International Street, October First, River-Town, Hanna-Barbera Land, Coney Mall, and Wild Animal Habitat. Another example is Great America in California, a hundred-acre family entertainment center that evokes North America's past in five themes: Home Town Square, Yukon Territory, Yankee Harbor, Country Fair, and Orleans Place.[13]

---

[11]MacLean, op. cit., p. 220.

[12]Ady Milman, "Theme Parks and Recreation," *VNR's Encyclopedia of Hospitality and Tourism.* New York: Van Nostrand Reinhold, 1993, p. 934.

[13]Other prominent theme parks and attractions are Knott's Berry Farm, Universal Studios, and Six Flags over America.

Personal and Corporate Profile: Walt Disney

A Man with a Vision and a Dream That He Was Able to Turn into Reality

To all who come to this happy place: Welcome! Disneyland is your land; here, age relives fond memories of the past, and here youth may savor the challenge and promise of the future.

Disneyland is dedicated to the hard facts that have created America, with the hope that it will be a source of joy and inspiration to all the world.

> —DISNEYLAND DEDICATION PLAQUE,
> July 17, 1955

In 1923, at the age of twenty-one, Walt Disney arrived in Los Angeles from Kansas City to start a new business. The first endeavor of Walt Disney and his brother Roy was a series of "shorts" called *Alice Comedies,* which featured a child actress playing with animated characters. Realizing that something new was needed to capture the audience, Walt Disney conjured up the concept of a mouse. In 1927, Disney began a series called *Oswald the Lucky Rabbit.* It was well received by the public, but Disney lost the rights due to a dispute with his distributor.

Mickey and Minnie Mouse first appeared in *Steamboat Willie,* which also incorporated music and sound, on November 18, 1928. Huge audiences were ecstatic about the Disney Brothers, who became overnight successes.

During the next few years, Walt and Roy made many Mickey Mouse films, which earned them enough to develop other projects, including full-length motion pictures in Technicolor. Their first film was *Snow White and the Seven Dwarfs,* which opened in 1937. The success of *Snow White* led to other hits: *Pinocchio* and *Fantasia* in 1940, *Dumbo* in 1941, *Bambi* in 1942, and *Saludos Amigos* in 1943. Disney also was successful with live-action films such as *The Reluctant Dragon, Song of the South,* and *20,000 Leagues Under the Sea.* In 1954, Disney entered the television revolution with the Disney television series; in 1955, "The Mickey Mouse Club" debuted on the ABC network.

(Courtesy Cal Tour Publications.)

Walt Disney said that Disneyland really began when his two daughters were very young. Saturday was always daddy's day, and he would take them to the merry-go-round and sit on a bench eating peanuts while they rode. Sitting there, he felt that there should be some kind of a family park where parents and children could have fun together.[1]

Walt's original dream was not easy to bring to reality. During the bleak war years, not only was much of his overseas market closed, but the steady stream of income that paid for innovation dried up. However, even during the bleak years, Walt never gave up. Instead, he was excited to learn of the public's interest in movie studios and the possibility of opening the studios to allow the public to visit the birthplace of Snow White, Pinocchio, and other Disney characters.

Disneyland had its growing pains—larger-than-expected opening day crowds, long lines at the popular rides, and a cash flow that was so tight that the cashiers had to rush the admission money to the bank in order to make payroll. Fortunately, since those early days, Disneyland and the Disney characters have become a part of not only Walt Disney, but also of the American dream.

By the early 1960s, Walt had turned most of his attention from film to real estate. Because he was upset when cheap motels and souvenir shops popped up around Disneyland, for his next venture, Walt Disney World, he bought 27,500 acres around the park. The center of Walt Disney World was to be the Experimental Prototype Community of Tomorrow (Epcot). Regrettably, Epcot and Walt Disney World were his dying dreams, as Walt Disney succumbed to cancer in 1966.

The ensuing years have given Disney phenomenal successes with Epcot, movies, a TV station, The Disney Channel, Disney stores, and Disney-MGM Studios theme park. In April 1992, EuroDisneyland, now Disneyland Paris, opened near Paris. In 1994, his Royal Highness, Prince Al Waleed

Bin Talal Bin Abdula of Saudi Arabia, purchased 25 percent of the EuroDisney Paris Resort.

Tokyo Disneyland continues to be successful; since its opening in 1983, about 140 million people have spent an average of $85 per visit (compared with $60 at Disneyland and $70 at Walt Disney World).

The Walt Disney Co. had revenues of $10.1 billion in 1994 with movies like *The Lion King,* which netted more than $1 billion.

Both Walt Disney World and Disneyland have excellent college programs that enable selected students to work during the summer months in a variety of hotel, foodservice, and related park positions. Disney has also introduced a faculty internship that allows faculty to intern in a similar variety of positions.

Walt Disney World is composed of four major theme parks: Magic Kingdom, Epcot, Disney's Animal Kingdom, and Disney-MGM Studios, with more than one hundred attractions, twenty-two resort hotels themed to faraway lands, spectacular nighttime entertainment, and vast shopping, dining, and recreation facilities that cover thousands of acres in this tropical paradise.

Walt Disney World includes twenty-five lighted tennis courts, ninety-nine holes of championship golf, marinas, swimming pools, jogging and bike trails, water skiing, and motor boating. The resort also offers a unique zoological park and bird sanctuary on Discovery Island in the middle of Bay Lake that is alive with birds, monkeys, and alligators; 226 restaurants, lounges, and food courts; a nightclub metropolis to please nearly any musical palate; a starry-eyed tribute to 1930s Hollywood; and even bass fishing. Walt Disney World is always full of new surprises: It now features the world's most unusual water adventure park, a "snow-covered" mountain with a ski-resort theme called Blizzard Beach.

Three new Disney hotels are architecturally exciting and more affordable than ever. The fun-filled Disney's All-Star Sports Resort and Disney's colorful All-Star Music Resort are categorized as value-class hotels. Disney's Wilderness Lodge is one of the park's jewels, with its impressive tall-timber atrium-lobby and rooms built around a Rocky Mountain geyser pool.

For nighttime fun, there is Planet Hollywood's newest entertainment restaurant (opened in December 1994) near Pleasure Island nightclubs. In all, the park has a cast of 37,000 hosts, hostesses, and entertainers famous for their warm smiles and commitment to making every night an especially good one for Disney guests.

There is more to enjoy than ever in ExtraTERRORestrial Alien Encounter, developed in collaboration with George Lucas, and Transportarium in New Tomorrowland. Already open are Fantasyland's

Legend of The Lion King; Epcot's INNOVENTIONS; the mind-blowing 3-D adventure, Honey, I Shrunk the Audience, in Future World; and, at the Disney-MGM Studios, the ultimate thriller, The Twilight Zone Tower of Terror™.

Magic Kingdom

The heart of Walt Disney World and its first famous theme park is the Magic Kingdom, the "happiest land on earth," where "age relives fond memories" and "youth may savor the challenge and promise of the future." It is a giant theatrical stage where guests become part of exciting Disney adventures. It is also the home of Mickey Mouse, Snow White, Peter Pan, Tom Sawyer, Davy Crockett, and the Swiss Family Robinson.

More than forty major shows and ride-through attractions, not to mention shops and unique dining facilities, fill its seven lands of imagination. Each land carries out its theme in fascinating detail—architecture, transportation, music, costumes, dining, shopping, and entertainment are designed to create a total atmosphere where guests can leave the ordinary world behind. The seven lands include the following:

Main Street, USA—Turn-of-the-century charm with horsedrawn streetcars, horseless carriages, Penny Arcade, and grand-circle tour on Walt Disney World Steam Railroad

Adventureland—Explore with Pirates of the Caribbean, wild animal Jungle Cruise, Swiss Family Treehouse, Tropical Serenade by birds, flowers, and tikis

Frontierland—Thrills on Splash Mountain and Big Thunder Mountain Railroad, musical fun in Country Bear Jamboree, Shooting Gallery, Tom Sawyer Island caves and raft rides

Liberty Square—Steamboating on the Rivers of America, mystery in the Haunted Mansion, whooping it up in Diamond Horseshoe Saloon, viewing the impressive Hall of Presidents with the addition of President Bill Clinton in a speaking role

Fantasyland—Cinderella Castle is the gateway to the new Legend of The Lion King plus Peter Pan's Flight, Snow White's Adventure, Mr. Toad's Wild Ride, Dumbo the Flying Elephant, Alice's Mad Tea Party, musical cruise with doll-like dancers in It's a Small World, Cinderella's Golden Carousel, and Skyway cable car to Tomorrowland

Mickey's Toontown Fair—Mickey's House, Grandma Duck's Farm, Mickey's Treehouse playground, and private photo session in Mickey's Dressing Room

New Tomorrowland—Sci-Fi city of the future, new frightening Alien Encounter, Transportarium time machine travels in Circle-Vision 360, new whirling Astro-Orbiter,

continued

speedy Space Mountain, new production of Carousel of Progress, Grand Prix Raceway, elevated Transit tour, new Disney Character show on Tomorrowland Stage

Epcot

Epcot is a unique, permanent, and ever-changing world's fair with two major themes: Future World and World Showcase. Highlights include Illumi-Nations, a nightly spectacle of fireworks, fountains, lasers, and classical music.

Future World shows an amazing exposition of technology for the near future for home, work, and play in INNOVENTIONS. The newest consumer products are continually added. Major pavilions exploring past, present, and future are shown in the Spaceship Earth story of communications. The Universe of Energy giant dinosaurs help explain the origin and future of energy. There are also the Wonders of Life with spectacular Body Wars, Cranium Command and other medical health subjects, the World of Motion soon-to-be test track, Journey into Imagination, The Land with spectacular agricultural research and environmental growing areas, and The Living Seas, the world's largest indoor ocean with thousands of tropical sea creatures.

Around The World Showcase Lagoon are pavilions where guests can see world-famous landmarks, and sample the native foods, entertainment, and culture of eleven nations:

Mexico—Mexico's fiesta plaza and boat trip on El Rio Del Tiempo plus San Angel Inn for authentic Mexican cuisine

Norway—Thrilling Viking boat journey and Restaurant Akershus

China—Wonders of China Circle-Vision 360 film tour from the Great Wall to the Yangtze River plus Nine Dragons Restaurant

Germany—Authentic Biergarten restaurant

Italy—St. Mark's Square street players and L'Originale Alfredo di Roma Ristorante

United States—The American Adventure's stirring historical drama

Japan—Recreating an Imperial Palace plus Teppanyaki Dining Rooms

Morocco—Morocco's palatial Restaurant Marrakesh

France—Impressions de France film tour of the French countryside, Chefs de France

United Kingdom—Shakespearean street players plus Rose & Crown Pub

Canada—Halifax to Vancouver Circle-Vision 360 tour.

Each showcase has additional snack facilities and a variety of shops featuring arts, crafts, and merchandise from each nation.

Disney-MGM Studios

With fifty major shows, shops, restaurants, ride-through adventures, and backstage tours, the Disney-MGM Studios combines real working motion picture, animation, and television studios with exciting movie attractions. The newest adventure in the Sunset Boulevard theater district is the Twilight Zone™ Tower of Terror, with a stunning thirteen-story elevator fall. The famous Chinese Theater on Hollywood Boulevard houses The Great Movie Ride.

Other major attractions include a Backstage Studio Tour of production facilities, Catastrophe Canyon, and New York Street; a tour of Walt Disney Animation Studios, Florida; exciting shows at Indiana Jones™ Epic Stunt Spectacular and Jim Henson's Muppet* Vision 3-D; plus a thrilling space flight on Star Tours.

Especially entertaining for movie and TV fans are the SuperStar Television and Monster Sound Show, where audience members take part in performances. Favorite Disney films become entertaining stage presentations in the Voyage of the Little Mermaid theater and in Beauty and the Beast, a live, twenty-five-minute musical revue at Theater of the Stars. The best restaurants include the Hollywood Brown Derby, 1950s Prime Time Cafe, Sci-Fi Dine-In Theater, Mama Melrose's Ristorante Italiano, and the Studio Commissary.

All this—and much more—is what helps make Walt Disney World the most popular destination resort in the world. Since its opening in 1971, more than 500 million guests, including kings and celebrities from around the world and all six U.S. presidents in office since the opening, have visited the parks. What causes the most comment from guests is the cleanliness, the friendliness of its cast, and the unbelievable attention to detail—a blend of showmanship and imagination that provides an endless variety of adventure and enjoyment.

Sunny beaches, exciting new adventures, a fabulous resort, and outdoor recreation facilities make a Walt Disney World excursion in Florida the ultimate dream vacation. There is a special Disney magic that frees guests from everyday cares to enjoy this unique world of fantasy, fun, thrills, and relaxation. There is something special for every age and every taste.[2]

---

[1] Randy Bright, *Disneyland: Inside Story.* New York: Abrams, 1987, p. 33.

[2] Pamela S. Weiers, "Escape to Disney's Fun and Sunshine Now," *The New York Times* Advertising supplement, February 5, 1995.

Clubs

Private clubs are places where only members gather for social, recreational, professional, or fraternal reasons. Many of today's clubs are adaptations of their predecessors, mostly from England and Scotland. For example, the North American Country Club is largely patterned after the Royal and Ancient Golf Club of St. Andrews, Scotland, founded in 1758, and recognized as the birthplace of golf.

Club management is similar in many ways to hotel management. Managers are responsible for forecasting, planning, budgeting, human resource development, food and beverage facility management, and maintenance. The main differences between club management and hotel management is that with clubs, the guests feel as if they are the owners (in many cases they are), and frequently behave as if they are the owners. Their emotional attachment is stronger than that of hotel guests who do not use hotels with the same frequency that members use clubs. Another difference is that most clubs do not offer sleeping accommodations.

Club members pay an initiation fee to belong to the club and annual membership dues thereafter. Some clubs also charge a set utilization fee, usually related to food and beverages, which is charged whether or not those services are used. There are approximately 14,000 private clubs in America,[14] including both country clubs and city clubs.

The Club Manager's Association of America (CMAA) is the professional organization to which many of the club managers of the 6,000 private country clubs belong.[15] The association aims to keep managers abreast of current practices and procedures. The professional guidelines that club managers set for themselves include the following:

- ✓ Club managers shall be judicious in their relationships with club members, aware of the need to maintain a line of professional demarcation between manager and the club membership.
- ✓ Club managers shall set an example by their demeanor and behavior that employees can use as a guide in their conduct with club members and guests.
- ✓ Club managers shall serve the community in every way possible.
- ✓ Club managers shall pursue their quest for knowledge through educational seminars and meetings that will improve their ability to manage their clubs.
- ✓ Club managers shall actively participate in local and national association meetings and activities.

[14]Richard Martin, "Tradition Gives Way to Reform," *Nation's Restaurant News,* **23,** 4, January 23, 1989, p. F-7.

[15]Personal interview with Joe Purdue, Club Managers Association of America, January 1995.

✓ Club managers shall be above reproach. There can be no half measure of integrity in their obligations to their clubs, their employees, their club members, or in their dealings with purveyors.

✓ Club managers shall be ready at all times to offer assistance to their associates, their club officials, and all others engaged in the maintenance and conduct of their club operations.

✓ Club managers shall not be deterred from compliance with the law as it applies to their clubs.[16]

Figure 10–1 is a sample job description for a club general manager, and Figure 10–2 lists the club management competencies.

Club Management Structure

The internal management structure of a club is governed by a constitution and bylaws. These establish election procedures, officer positions, a board of directors, and standing committees. Guidance and direction also are provided for each office and committee and how it will function.[17]

The members elect the officers and directors of the club. The officers represent the membership by establishing policies by which the club will operate. Many clubs and other organizations maintain continuity by having a succession of officers: from secretary to vice president, president, and board of directors. The person elected president is the person the membership feels is the most qualified person to lead the club for that year. Regardless of who is elected president, the club manager must be able to work with that person and the other officers.

The president presides at all official meetings and is a leader in policy making.[18] The vice president will, in the absence of the president, perform the presidential duties. If the club has more than one vice president, then the title *first, second, third,* and so on may be used. Alternatively, vice presidents may be assigned to chair certain functions, such as membership. Vice presidents usually chair one or more committees.

The treasurer obviously must have some financial/accounting background because an integral part of his or her duties is to give advice on financial matters such as employing external auditors, preparing budgets, and installing control systems.

The secretary records the minutes of meetings and takes care of club-related correspondence. This position can be combined with that of treasurer, in which case the position is titled *secretary-treasurer.* The secretary may also serve on or chair certain committees.

Committees play an important part in the club's activities. If the committees are effective, the operation of the club is more efficient. The term of commit-

[16]Ted E. White, *Club Operations and Management.* Boston: CBI Publishing, 1979, pp. 6–7.

[17]Ibid., p. 17.

[18]Ibid.

I. **Position:** General Manager

II. **Related Titles:** Club Manager; Club House Manager

III. **Job Summary:** Serves as chief operating officer of the club; manages all aspects of the club including its activities and the relationships between the club and its board of directors, members, guests, employees, community, government, and industry; coordinates and administers the club's policies as defined by its board of directors. Develops operating policies and procedures and directs the work of all department managers. Implements and monitors the budget, monitors the quality of the club's products and services, and ensures maximum member and guest satisfaction. Secures and protects the club's assets, including facilities and equipment

IV. **Job Tasks (Duties):**

1. Implements general policies established by the board of directors; directs their administration and execution

2. Plans, develops, and approves specific operational policies, programs, procedures, and methods in concert with general policies

3. Coordinates the development of the club's long-range and annual (business) plans

4. Develops, maintains, and administers a sound organizational plan; initiates improvements as necessary

5. Establishes a basic personnel policy; initiates and monitors policies relating to personnel actions and training and professional development programs

6. Maintains membership with the Club Managers Association of America and other professional associations. Attends conferences, workshops, and meetings to keep abreast of current information and developments in the field

7. Coordinates development of operating and capital budgets according to the budget calendar; monitors monthly and other financial statements for the club; takes effective corrective action as required

8. Coordinates and serves as ex-officio member of appropriate club committees

9. Welcomes new club members; meets and greets all club members as practical during their visits to the club

10. Provides advice and recommendations to the president and committees about construction, alterations, maintenance, materials, supplies, equipment, and services not provided in approved plans and/or budgets

11. Consistently ensures that the club is operated in accordance with all applicable local, state, and federal laws

12. Oversees the care and maintenance of all the club's physical assets and facilities

13. Coordinates the marketing and membership relations programs to promote the club's services and facilities to potential and present members

14. Ensures the highest standards for food, beverage, sports and recreation, entertainment, and other club services

15. Establishes and monitors compliance with purchasing policies and procedures

16. Reviews and initiates programs to provide members with a variety of popular events

17. Analyzes financial statements, manages cash flow, and establishes controls to safeguard funds; reviews income and costs relative to goals; takes corrective action as necessary

18. Works with subordinate department heads to schedule, supervise, and direct the work of all club employees

19. Attends meetings of the club's executive committee and board of directors

20. Participates in outside activities that are judged as appropriate and approved by the board of directors to enhance the prestige of the club; broadens the scope of the club's operation by fulfilling the public obligations of the club as a participating member of the community

V. **Reports to:** Club President and Board of Directors

VI. **Supervises:** Assistant General Manager (Club House Manager); Food and Beverage Director; Controller; Membership Director; Director of Human Resources; Director of Purchasing; Golf Professional (Director of Golf); Golf Course Superintendent; Tennis Professional; Athletic Director; Executive Secretary

Courtesy: Club Managers Association of America

Figure 10–1 *Job Description, Club Manager*

tee membership is specified, and committee meetings are conducted in accordance with Robert's Rules of Order, which are procedural guidelines on the correct way to conduct meetings. Typical committees include the following: house, membership, finance/budget, entertainment, sports, special/ad hoc, and so on.

Private Club Management
History of Private Clubs
Types of Private Clubs
Membership Types
Bylaws
Policy Formulation
Board Relations
Chief Operating Officer Concept
Committees
Club Job Descriptions
Career Development
Golf Operations Management
Golf Course Management
Tennis Operations Management
Swimming Pool Management
Yacht Facilities Management
Fitness Center Management
Locker Room Management
Other Recreational Activities

Food and Beverage Operations
Sanitation
Menu Development
Nutrition
Pricing Concepts
Ordering/Receiving/Controls/Inventory
Food and Beverage Trends
Quality Service
Creativity in Theme Functions
Design and Equipment
Food and Beverage Personnel
Wine List Development

Accounting and Finance in the Private Club
Accounting and Finance Principles
Uniform System of Accounts
Financial Analysis
Budgeting
Cash Flow Forecasting
Compensation and Benefit Administration
Financing Capital Projects
Audits
Internal Revenue Service
Computers
Business Office Organization
Long-Range Financial Planning

Human and Professional Resources
Employee Relations
Management Styles
Organizational Development
Balancing Job and Family Responsibilities
Time Management
Stress Management
Labor Issues
Leadership vs. Management

Building and Facilities Management
Preventive Maintenance
Insurance and Risk Management
Clubhouse Remodeling and Renovation

Contractors
Energy and Water Resource Management
Housekeeping
Security
Laundry
Lodging Operations

External and Governmental Influences
Legislative Influences
Regulatory Agencies
Economic Theory
Labor Law
Internal Revenue Service
Privacy
Club Law
Liquor Liability
Labor Unions

Management and Marketing
Communication Skills
Marketing Through In-House Publications
Professional Image and Dress
Effective Negotiation
Member Contact Skills
Working with the Media
Marketing Strategies in a Private Club Environment

Courtesy: Club Managers Association of America

Figure 10–2 *Club Management Competencies*

Country Clubs

A **country club** offers recreational facilities; the focus generally is on golf, but tennis and swimming are frequently included. Occasionally, other activities, such as horseback riding, pool rooms, card rooms, aerobic facilities, and other activities are also provided for the members' enjoyment.

Nearly all country clubs have one or more lounges and restaurants, and most have banquet facilities. Members and their guests enjoy these services and can be billed monthly. The banquet facilities are used for formal and informal parties, dinners, dances, weddings, and so on by members and their personal guests. Some country clubs charge what might seem to be an excessive amount for the initiation fee in order to maintain exclusivity—as much as $250,000 in some cases.

Country Club (Photo courtesy of the Club Managers Association.)

Country clubs have two or more types of membership. Full membership enables members to use all of the facilities all of the time. Social membership only allows members to use the social facilities: lounges, bars, restaurants, and so on and perhaps the pool and tennis courts. Other forms of membership can include weekday and weekend memberships.

A few years ago, country clubs were often considered to be bastions of a social elite. Although that description still may be somewhat true, today there are numerous examples of new clubs that have opened without the "stuffy" waiting list and "what's-your-pedigree?" approach to would-be members. Additionally, at the newer clubs, the cost of initiation and membership may be considerably less than at some of the more established clubs.

City Clubs

City clubs are predominantly business oriented; they vary in size, location, type of facility, and services offered. Some of the older, established clubs own their own buildings, and others lease space. Clubs exist to cater to the wants and needs of members. Clubs in the city fall into the following categories:

- ✓ Professional
- ✓ Social
- ✓ Athletic
- ✓ Dining
- ✓ University
- ✓ Military
- ✓ Yachting
- ✓ Fraternal
- ✓ Proprietary

Professional clubs, as the name implies, are clubs for people in the same profession. The National Press Club in Washington, D.C., the Lawyer's Club in New York City, and the Friars Club for actors and other theatrical people in Manhattan are good examples.

Personal Profile: Sally Burns Rambo

A Giver of the First Order

General Manager
Lakewood Country Club Dallas
Voted 1991 Club Manager of the Year

After graduating from high school at sixteen, Sally Burns Rambo began her professional career working in a bank. The actual launch in the business environment came when she began to work at the local newspaper. Her talent earned her a promotion to office manager. Working as office manager gave her an opportunity to become well known in the community. This led to her being offered a club's office manager position by the Eastern Hills Country Club members.

During the first six months that she worked at the club, two club managers were fired, so leaders of the club persuaded Sally to serve as interim manager until someone else was appointed. However, nobody else was ever appointed for that position, and Sally was the general manager of the club for the next twenty-one years.

Her talents and skills were not forgotten after her retirement. In fact, she was again persuaded to manage a club that was in serious decline. Sally recalls that she regretted taking this position for about four months, because the club was in extremely bad condition. But she accepted the challenge with enormous determination: "You've never been a quitter and you're not going to quit now," she told herself. By improving the quality of food and service, she made Lakewood a fun place to be. Members and guests enjoyed themselves and looked forward to visiting the club.

Sally has always been a risk-taker and an innovator. She introduced a novel concept in her club, which was initially not approved by some members. She decided to feature a country western band, that, in spite of warnings against the idea, proved to be a great success. Many other successes followed with some of the top names in entertainment. Sally believed that the important thing was for the club to give its members something they could take pride in. The quality of these parties helped the club regain membership. Sally is a hands-on manager who makes sure all details are attended to. She adds that "you make your money on member-sponsored parties" and "you have to get your business volume that way rather than through regular dining room business because most members will not dine at the club every day."

Key ingredients in Sally's success include her continually educating herself, and her caring enthusiasm to staffing. "Hire the right people, pay them well, let them show what they know, and they will make you look good." Sally has a staff of 102 full-time employees, serving 1,400 members, including families—up from less than 400 when she took over as manager.

Sally is a firm believer in dedication and hard work. In fact, she often works twelve hours a day and she never drinks on the job![1]

---

[1] Eldon Miller, "1991 Club Manager of the Year," *Club Management*, December 1991.

Social clubs allow members to enjoy one another's company; members represent many different professions, yet they have similar socioeconomic backgrounds. Social clubs are modeled after the famous men's social clubs in London, such as Boodle's, St. James's, and White's. At these clubs, it is considered bad form to discuss business. Therefore, conversation and social interaction focus on companionship or entertainment unrelated to business.

The oldest social club in America is thought to be the Fish House in Philadelphia, founded in 1832. To ensure that the Fish House would always be socially oriented rather than business oriented, it was formed as a men's cooking club with each member taking turns preparing meals for the membership.[19]

Other social clubs exist in several major cities. The common denominator is that they all have upscale food and beverage offerings and have club managers to manage them.

Athletic clubs give city workers and residents an opportunity to work out, swim, play squash and/or racquetball, and so on. Some of the downtown athletic clubs provide tennis courts and running tracks on the roof. Athletic clubs also have lounges, bars, and restaurants at which members may relax and interact socially. Some athletic clubs also have meeting rooms and even sleeping accommodations.

Dining clubs are generally located in large city office buildings. Memberships are often given as an inducement to tenants who lease space in the office building. These clubs are always open for lunch and occasionally for dinner.

University clubs are private clubs for alumni. With a few exceptions, they are for one university's alumni. University clubs are generally located in the high-rent district and offer a variety of facilities and attractions focusing on food and beverage service.

Military clubs cater to both NCOs (noncommissioned officers) and enlisted officers. Military clubs offer similar facilities as other clubs for recreation and entertainment, and food and beverage offerings. Military clubs are located on base and have in recent years given over their club management to civilians.

Yacht clubs provide members with moorage slips, where their boats are kept secure. In addition to moorage facilities, yacht clubs have lounge, bar, and dining facilities similar to other clubs. Yacht clubs are based on a sailing theme and attract members with various backgrounds who have sailing as one of their common interests.

Fraternal clubs include many special organizations such as the Veterans of Foreign Wars, Elks, and Shriners. These organizations foster camaraderie and often assist charitable causes. They generally are less elaborate than other clubs, but have bars and banquet rooms that can be used for various activities.

Proprietary clubs operate on a for-profit basis. They are owned by corporations or individuals; people wanting to become members purchase a membership, not a share in the club. Proprietary clubs became popular with the real estate boom in the 1970s and 1980s. As new housing developments were planned, clubs were included in several of the projects. Households paid a small initiation fee and monthly dues between $30 and $50, allowing the whole family to participate in a wide variety of recreational activities.

Clearly, the opportunities for recreation and leisure abound. The goal must be to achieve a harmony between work and leisure activities and to become truly professional in both giving and receiving these services. The next few years will see a substantial increase in the leisure and recreational industries.

[19]Stephen Birmingham, *America's Secret Aristocracy.* New York: Berkeley Books, 1990, p. 209.

Noncommercial Recreation

Noncommercial recreation includes voluntary organizations, campus, armed forces, and employee recreations as well as recreation for special populations.

Voluntary Organizations

Voluntary organizations are nongovernmental, nonprofit agencies, serving the public-at-large or selected elements with multiservice programs that often include a substantial element of recreational opportunity. The best known voluntary organizations include the Boy Scouts, Girl Scouts, YMCA, YWCA, and YM-YWHA.

In the early 1900s, YMCAs began to offer sporting facilities and programs. The Ys, though nonprofit, were pioneers in basketball, swimming, and weight training. Later, commercial health clubs also began to evolve, offering men's and women's exercise on alternating days. As the sports and fitness movement grew, clubs became oriented toward special interests. Now, clubs can be classified as follows: figure salons, health clubs, body-building gyms, tennis clubs, racquetball centers, or multipurpose clubs.[20]

A multipurpose club has more exclusive recreation programs than a health club. Leagues, tournaments, and classes are common for racquet sports, and most clubs offer several types of fitness classes. Some innovative clubs offer automatic bank tellers, stock market quote services, computer matching for tennis competition, auto detailing, laundry and dry cleaning services, and wine-cellar storage.

Club revenue comes from membership fees, user fees, guest fees, food and beverage sales, facility rental, and so on. Human resources accounts for about 66 percent of expenses at most clubs.

It is amazing to realize that in the center of a city, there may be several voluntary organizations, each serving a particular segment of the population.

[20]John C. Crossley and Lynn M. Jamieson, *Introduction to Commercial Recreation*. Champaign, IL: Sagamore Publishing, 1988, p. 248.

A Day in the Life of Luis Azucena
Recreation Director, Dolores Park, San Francisco, California

A recreation director doesn't just look over the park and make sure everything is running well; that may well be the duty of most other kinds of directors, but not a recreation director.

The park we are talking about isn't just any park, it's Dolores Park. This park is one of San Francisco's best, most romantic, and peaceful places to be. Its beautiful view, grassy hills, and shade trees make for a bucolic refuge from urban life. The park's greatest asset, no doubt, is the sublimely peaceful view of downtown. The director of all this is no other than Luis Azucena.

Luis Azucena loves what he does. He is able to do what he wants to do in his job. For a typical day, Luis works afternoons and evenings usually from about 1 P.M. to 10 P.M. Dolores Park is a large city-owned park that consists of a club house, soccer fields, tennis courts, and computer rooms. When Luis comes in, he looks through paperwork that has to be completed. He does the cleaning himself to make sure everything is tidy and neat. From 1:30 P.M. to about 3:00 P.M., Luis is involved in giving adult tennis lessons along with another director, Mr. Lou Maunaupau. Luis usually coaches about ten players. Some of them are young. After doing this, it's time for Luis's lunch break.

After lunch, at about 4:00 P.M., Luis goes to the soccer field and meets with his summer soccer league players, who are kids from the community area. He organizes this league. He helps them get their uniforms and ID cards and then they warm up. This game is recreational, so Luis strives to teach them good sportsmanship. For instance, his players end games with handshakes. In winter or when the weather isn't favorable, Luis arranges indoor games. He helps put teams together for the community.

(Courtesy of Luis Azucena.)

After all this, Luis helps kids with their homework and plays board games with them. While he does this, people from around the community come to the park to have picnics or to attend community political, recreational, or just-for-fun events. Dolores is a center of attraction for people, especially on the weekends and holidays.

Volunteers often come in to help with activities that go on in the park. This is called "workcreation." They work with the community and its kids, helping with games, activities, or even schoolwork. Luis's day comes to an end at about 10 P.M. He goes home feeling satisfied and positive about what he is doing.

Luis loves sports and fitness. He works with the school districts around the community to help kids become more involved in sports and also have time for schoolwork. He has worked at his job for several years and is very happy to be where he is now.

Richard Kraus writes that a study of the city of Toronto that examined various land uses and leisure programs in the city's core found the following organizations: a Boy's Club, a mission, the Center of the Metropolitan Association for the Retarded, a Catholic settlement house, a day care center, an Indian center, a YM-YWHA, a service center for working people, a Chinese center, a Ukrainian center, and several other organizations meeting special needs and interests. These were all in addition to public parks, recreation areas, and nineteen churches.

Campus, Armed Forces, and Employee Recreation

Campus Recreation

North America's colleges and universities provide a major setting for organized leisure and recreational programs with services involving millions of participants each year. The programs include involvement by campus recreation offices, intramural departments, student unions, residence staffs, or other sponsors. The activities have heavy components of the following types: competitive sports and games; outdoor recreation trips and events; cultural programs such as music, drama, dance, and films; and leisure-oriented activities.[21]

The various recreational activities help in maintaining good morale on campus. Some use recreational activities such as sports or orchestras or theater companies as a means of gaining alumni support. Students look for an exciting and interesting social life. For this reason, colleges and universities offer a wide range of recreational and social activities that may vary from campus to campus.

Armed Forces Recreation

It is the official policy of the Department of Defense to provide a well-rounded morale, welfare, and recreational program for the physical, social, and mental well-being of its personnel. Each of the services sponsors recreational activities under the auspices of the Morale, Welfare, and Recreation Program (MWR), which reports to the Office of the Assistant Secretary of Defense for Manpower, Reserve Affairs, and Logistics. MWR activities are provided to all military personnel and civilian employees at all installations.

MWR programs include the following types of activities:

✓ Sports, including self-directed, competitive, instructional, and spectator programs
✓ Motion pictures
✓ Service clubs and entertainment
✓ Crafts and hobbies
✓ Youth activities for children of military families
✓ Special interest groups such as aero, automotive, motorcycle, and power boat clubs, as well as hiking, skydiving, and rod and gun clubs
✓ Rest centers and recreation areas
✓ Open dining facilities
✓ Libraries

Recreation is perceived as an important part of the employee benefits package for military personnel, along with the G.I. Bill, medical services, commissaries, and exchanges.

---

[21]Kraus, op. cit., p. 213.

Employee Recreation

Business and industry have realized the importance of promoting employee efficiency. Human resource experts have found that workers who spend their free time at constructive recreational activities have less absenteeism resulting from emotional tension, illness, excessive use of alcohol, and so on. Employee recreation programs may also be an incentive for a prospective employee to join a company.

In the United States and Canada, almost all of the leading corporations have an employee recreation and wellness program. Some companies include recreation activities in their team-building and management-development programs.

Recreation for Special Populations

Recreation for special populations involves professionals and organizations who serve groups such as the mentally ill, mentally retarded, or physically challenged. In recent years, there has been increased recognition of the need to provide recreational programs for special populations. These programs, developed for each of the special population groups, use therapeutic recreation as a form of treatment.

One of the sports programs for people with disabilities that has received considerable attention in recent years is the Special Olympics, an international program of physical fitness, sports training, and athletic competition for children and adults with mental retardation. The program is unique because it accommodates competitors at all ability levels by assigning participants to competition divisions based on both age and actual performance.[22]

Today, the Special Olympics serves more than 1 million individuals in the United States and more than seventy other countries. Among the official sports are track and field events, swimming, diving, gymnastics, ice skating, basketball, volleyball, soccer, softball, floor hockey, bowling, Frisbee disk, downhill skiing, cross-country skiing, and wheelchair events. The National Parks and Recreation Association and numerous state and local agencies and societies work closely with Special Olympics in promoting programs and sponsoring competitions.[23]

Trends in Recreation and Leisure

- ✓ An increase in all fitness activities
- ✓ An increase in personal leisure time devoted to computer activities

[22]Richard Kraus and John Shank, *Therapeutic Recreation Service: Principles and Practices,* 4th ed. Dubuque, IA: Wm. C. Brown, 1983, p. 143.
[23]Ibid.

✓ A surge in travel and tourism
✓ In addition to a continuation of traditional recreation and leisure activities, special programs targeted toward at-risk youths and latch-key children are also being developed
✓ Several additional products in the commercial sector
✓ Additional learning and adventure opportunities for the elderly, such as Elderhostel

Case Study

Service Proposal for Guests

You recently joined the front desk of a nice resort hotel in New England and your hotel manager has complimented you on your guest service ability. She has asked you to develop a walking/jogging trail for the guests.

Discussion Question

1. What would be some of the key elements to consider in developing a proposal for your hotel guests?

Case Study

Overpopulation of National Parks

Our national parks are under serious threat from a number of sources including congestion resulting from overvisitation, consequent environmental degradation, and pollution.

There are too many people and too many vehicles in the most popular national parks. Many bring their city lifestyle, leaving garbage lying around, listening to loud music, and leaving the trails.

Discussion Question

1. List the recommendations you have for the park superintendents to help save the parks.

Career Information

Recreation and Leisure

The recreation and leisure areas cover a broad range of potential career paths. There are options in the parks and recreation field as well as careers to be had in club and resort management. Working in a country club may sound exciting, but it actually entails long, difficult hours spent dealing with demanding members. A recent survey of club general managers revealed that, on average, they are thirty- to forty-year-old males who work more than sixty hours per week managing a club with more than 600 members.

Many of you may wish to pursue a career in club management because you do not want to work in a hotel or restaurant. However, 81 percent of the general managers surveyed above stated that they came from a food and beverage background. Historically, many general managers have worked their way up from a dining room server at a private club, with the average having spent ten to fifteen years in the industry and more than seven years at their current club.

Regardless of what type of club you wish to work in—city, country, athletic or social—clubs fall into two categories: equity clubs, which are owned by the members, or nonequity clubs, which are owned by individuals or corporations. ClubCorp is one of the largest corporate owners of clubs and it operates more than 220 country clubs, business clubs, and golf resorts. Recent expansions in corporate ownership have made it slightly easier to enter the club management profession.

If you are serious about a career in club management, you should join a local student chapter of the Club Managers Association of America (CMAA). CMAA meetings are a great place for networking in order to gain access to a summer job or internship. Experience gained during your college tenure will provide you with the knowledge you need to begin your career in the recreation and leisure industries.

Related Web Sites

www.clubcorp.com—ClubCorp
www.cmaa.org—Club Managers Association of America
www.nps.gov—National Parks Service
www-p.afsv.af.mil—United States Air Force Services

Courtesy of Charlie Adams.

Summary

1. Recreation is free time that people use to restore, rest, and relax their minds and bodies. Recreational activities can be passive or active, an individual or a group activity.

2. Recreational activities range from cultural pursuits such as museums or theaters, to sports or outdoor recreation such as amusement parks, community centers, playgrounds, and libraries. These services involve various levels of government.

3. National parks preserve exceptional lands for public use, emphasizing the protection of their ecosystems and endangered plant and animal species and honoring historical sites. Two of the best known of the current 367 parks in the United States include Yellowstone and Yosemite national parks.

4. Today, city governments are increasingly expected to provide recreational facilities such as golf courses, swimming pools, picnic areas, and playgrounds as a community service.

5. Commercial recreation—for example, theme parks, clubs, and attractions—involves a profit for the supplier of the recreational activity.

6. Clubs are places where members gather for social, recreational, professional, or fraternal reasons. There are many different types of clubs such as country clubs or city clubs, according to the interests they represent to their members.

7. Noncommercial recreation includes governmental and nonprofit agencies, such as voluntary organizations, campus, armed forces, employee recreation, and recreation for special populations such as the physically challenged.

Key Words and Concepts

City club
Club management
Commercial recreation
Country club
Government-sponsored
recreation

Leisure
National parks
National Parks Service
Noncommercial recreation
Private clubs

Recreation
Recreation for special
populations
Recreation management
Theme parks

Transient occupancy taxes
Voluntary organizations
Wellness

Review Questions

1. Define recreation and its importance to human well-ness. What factors affect an individual's decision to participate in recreational activities?
2. Describe the origin of government-sponsored recreation in consideration of the origin and purpose of national parks.

3. Briefly describe the difference between commercial and noncommercial recreation.
4. Briefly explain the purpose of a theme park and the purpose of clubs.
5. Explain the concept of recreation for special populations.

Internet Exercises

1. Organization:
   Web site:
   Summary:
   (a) What kinds of facilities are offered by Del Mar Fairgrounds?
   (b) What does the fair do to promote the ecosystem?

2. Organization
   Web site:
   Summary:
   (a) What kinds of activities are offered at the Prestonwood Country Club?
   (b) Parents may wish to take their kids on vacations. In these situations, what might this country club offer those kids?

Del Mar Fairgrounds
www.delmarfair.com
The Del Mar Fairgrounds is an indoor and outdoor, multi-use public assembly facility with an emphasis on agri-culture, education, entertainment, and recreation in a fiscally sound and environmentally conscientious atmosphere. For more than half a century, the Del Mar Fairgrounds has been located in San Diego where it has been a great tourist attraction.

Prestonwood Country Club
http://www.prestonwoodcc.com
Prestonwood is a full-service country club that offers activities and fine food.

Apply Your Knowledge

1. Create your own personal recreation goals and make a plan to reach them.

2. Describe the features of commercial versus noncommercial recreation.

The Gaming Entertainment Industry

11

After reading and studying this chapter, you should be able to:

✓ Outline the history of the gaming entertainment industry.
✓ Describe the various activities related to gaming entertainment.
✓ Explain how gaming entertainment is converging with other aspects of the hospitality business.
✓ Discuss the controversies surrounding the gaming entertainment industry.

One of the most significant developments in the hospitality industry during the past two decades has been the astounding growth of the casino industry and its convergence with the lodging and hospitality industries. What has emerged from this development is an entirely new arena of hospitality known as the gaming entertainment industry. With its rapid expansion in North America and throughout the world, new opportunities have been created for hospitality careers. This chapter explores the gaming entertainment industry and details exciting developments yet to come in this dynamic and controversial segment of the hospitality business.

Gaming Entertainment Defined

For the purposes of this chapter, the term **gaming entertainment** refers to one subset of the gaming industry, namely, the casino industry. What used to be known as the casino business is now known as gaming entertainment. The dramatic growth of this part of the hospitality business has brought with it significant changes in how businesses in this industry operate and what they offer their guests. The changes have been so great that a new name needed to be created to accurately describe all of the amenities this industry provides.

The gaming industry includes casinos (both land-based and riverboats), card rooms, charitable games, lottery-operated games, and wagering on greyhound and horse races. The gaming industry as a whole is larger than most people can believe. Approximately five hundred billion dollars (that is right, almost a half-trillion dollars), is **wagered,** or **bet,** on games or races every year.

The total amount bet is called the **handle** in the gaming industry, and is often a misunderstood concept. When a customer places a bet in any type of gaming activity, sometimes they win and sometimes they lose. The total amount of all bets is the handle, and the net amount of spending by the customer is termed **win** by the gaming industry.

The annual industry win, some forty-eight million dollars, is much lower than industry handle, and represents actual consumer spending for gaming activities. Casinos account for about half of the U.S. gaming win, with lotteries following close behind. Lotteries and casinos together make up around 85 percent of consumer spending in the gaming industry.[1]

What is the difference between gambling and gaming? **Gambling** is playing a game of risk for the thrill of the "action" and the chance of making money. True gamblers spend a great deal of time learning and understanding a favorite game of risk and enjoying its subtle attributes, and they find an enjoyable challenge in trying to "beat the house" or win more than they lose from a casino.

---

[1]E. M. Christainsen, "The United States 1996 Gross Annual Wager," Supplement to *International Gaming and Wagering Business,* **18.** 1997.

(Courtesy of Las Vegas News Bureau.)

A gambler has little interest in anything other than the casino floor and the games it offers. It is true that the 60 million visitors who come to Las Vegas and Atlantic City and the hundreds of thousands who frequent casino operations love the green felt tables, the whirling roulette wheels, the feel of the chips, and the thrill of the game. The rows of colorful **slot machines** sounding out musical tones and flashing lights, the distant sounds of someone hitting a jackpot, and bells ringing and guests shouting creates an environment of excitement and anticipation that can only be found on the casino floor. The gaming industry has exploded from just two jurisdictions in 1976 to many. In 1997, there was some form of legal gambling in forty-eight states, including Washington, DC, Puerto Rico, and the U.S. Virgin Islands.[2]

Not long ago, the presence of a slot machine or a blackjack table was all that was needed to bring in the visitors. However, with the rapid spread of **casinos** throughout North America, this is no longer true. The competitive nature of the casino business has created a bigger, better product to meet the needs of their guests. As Steve Wynn, former Mirage Resorts CEO and now owner of the $270 million Desert Inn, puts it, now the casino floor is "a thing which people pass on their way to visit the things that really matter to them." The product that has evolved over the past decade is what is called gaming entertainment.

Gaming entertainment offers games of risk only as part of a total package of entertainment and leisure time activities. Gaming entertainment serves a customer base of "social gamblers," customers who play a game of risk as a form

[2]"The U.S. 96 Gross Annual Wager," *International Wagering Gaming and Business,* August 1997.

of entertainment and a social activity, combining gambling with many other activities during their visit. Social gamblers, by this definition, are interested in many of the amenities of the gaming entertainment operation and take part in many diverse activities during a stay.

Gaming entertainment refers to the casino gaming business and all of its aspects, including hotel operations, entertainment offerings, retail shopping, recreational activities, and other types of operations in addition to wagering on the gaming floor. The heart of gaming entertainment is what Glen Schaeffer, president of Circus Circus, has dubbed the "entertainment megastore" with thousands of rooms; dynamic, interesting, exterior architecture; nongaming attractions—that is, a building someone can design a vacation around, with 100,000 square feet or more of casino at its core. Schaeffer has said this product "is to tourism what the Pentium chip is to technology," a dynamic new tourism product that serves as a destination attraction. Gaming entertainment is the business of hospitality and entertainment with a core strength in casino gaming, also known as the global hospitality-gaming-entertainment market.

According to this definition, a gaming entertainment business always has a casino floor area that offers various games of risk and that serves as the focal point for marketing to and attracting guests. Next in importance to the guests is high-quality food and beverage operations.

Gaming entertainment is one of the last hospitality concepts to support the full-service, table-side gourmet restaurant, in addition to the lavish buffet offerings that many casino locations offer. The number of foodservice concepts is wide and diverse—from signature restaurants featuring famous chefs, to ethnic offerings, to quick-service, franchised outlets. The gaming entertainment industry offers unlimited career opportunities in restaurant management and the culinary arts that were unheard of just a decade ago.

Gaming entertainment also goes hand-in-hand with the lodging industry, because hotel rooms are part of the package. Full-service hotels are part and parcel of gaming entertainment. Rooms, food and beverage, convention services, banquet facilities, health spas, recreation, and other typical hotel amenities support gaming entertainment. Most of the largest and most complex hotels in the world are found in gaming entertainment venues, a number of which are described in detail later in this chapter.

So far we have discussed gaming entertainment as a place to gamble on the casino floor, eat and drink, have a place to sleep and relax, and maybe do some business. But gaming entertainment offers much more. The entertainment offerings range from live performances by the most famous entertainers to production shows that use the latest high-tech wizardry. Gaming entertainment encompasses theme parks and thrill rides, museums, and cultural centers. The most popular gaming entertainment destinations are designed around a central theme that includes the architecture and the operations.[3]

---

[3]V. H. Eade and R. H. Eade, *Introduction to the Casino Entertainment Industry.* Upper Saddle River, NJ: Prentice Hall, 1997.

Unlike its predecessor, the casino business, the gaming entertainment business has numerous revenue-generating activities. Gaming revenue is produced from casino win, or the money guests spend on the casino floor. The odds of any casino game favor the house, some more than others. Casino win is the cost of gambling to guests, who often win over the house in the short run, and are therefore willing to place bets and try their luck.

Nongaming revenue comes from sources that are not related to wagering on the casino floor. As the gaming entertainment concept continues to emphasize activities other than gambling, nongaming revenue is increasing in importance. Gaming revenues for Las Vegas, as a percentage of total revenues, have been declining for the past twenty years and now make up just slightly more than half of total revenues. Hotel room revenues in Las Vegas make up about 20 percent of total revenues and other nongaming revenues make up 11 percent of total revenue. This is what gaming entertainment is truly about—hospitality and entertainment based on the attraction of a casino.

What forms does gaming entertainment take? The megaresorts of Las Vegas and Atlantic City garner the most publicity as the meccas of the gaming entertainment industry. However, there are smaller properties throughout Nevada and other casino based businesses in forty-eight states and seven Canadian provinces. These casinos take the form of commercially operated businesses, both privately and publicly held. Some are land-based, meaning the casinos are housed in regular buildings. Others are riverboats that cruise up and down a river, or barges that are moored in water and do not cruise, called dockside casinos.

Casinos are also operated by Native American tribes on their reservations and tribal lands. These are land-based casinos and are often as complex as any operation in Las Vegas. Gaming entertainment is also popular on cruise ships as part of the cruise vacation product or on what are called "cruises to nowhere," where gaming and entertainment on board the ship are the main attraction.

There is strong support for gaming in the marketplace as an entertainment activity. Thirty-two percent of U.S. households gamble in casinos, an increase of 11 million households since earlier in the decade. U.S. households make 176 million visits annually to casinos. According to market research, more than 90 percent of U.S. adults say casino entertainment is acceptable for themselves or others. Sixty-two percent of U.S. adults say casino entertainment is acceptable for anyone, and 30 percent say it is acceptable for others but not themselves. Only eight percent of Americans say casino entertainment is not acceptable for anyone.[4]

The demographic makeup of the typical gaming entertainment guest has remained consistent during the past several years. In comparison to the average American, casino players tend to have higher levels of income and education and are more likely to hold white-collar jobs. The customer profile of Las

[4]Harrah's Casinos. Harrah's Survey of U.S. Casino Entertainment. Harrah's Entertainment, Inc., Memphis, TN, 1996.

(Courtesy Las Vegas
News Bureau.)

Vegas has gotten younger, and people who spend money want a total entertainment experience.

Gaming entertainment operators are becoming more retail-driven and try to bring people in with a new hotel, magic shop, exclusive restaurants, or other shops. And guests have responded to these efforts. According to the latest Las Vegas Visitor Profile Study, the average visitor to Las Vegas stays 3.7 nights, budgets $580 for gambling, and spends $58 per night on lodging, $111 on food and drink, $38 on local transportation, $63 on shopping, $27 on shows, and another $7 on sightseeing. The average bet among those who play table games is usually a little more than $12.

Knowing the customers and their preferences is becoming critical in the gaming entertainment business. For example, Harrah's Entertainment, aiming to become America's first national-brand casino, created a Total Gold players' card. Gamblers accumulate points for their computer-monitored play. The card is then used to dispense cash back to players or vouchers good for complimentary rewards at any of its thirteen U.S. casinos.

Most casino companies have similar players' clubs that operate like the airlines' frequent-flier programs. But Harrah's Entertainment Inc. became the first gaming entertainment chain to "comp," or redeem, those points system-wide. For instance, players can earn cash-value points gambling in Kansas City and then cash them in toward the price of a hotel room at Harrah's Las Vegas casino. Harrah's believes that linking the Total Gold card to a computer database of its estimated 6 million customers nationwide elevates the gaming entertainment firm to a new level of marketing sophistication.

Historical Review of Gaming Entertainment

Las Vegas—the name alone summons images of millions of neon lights, elaborate shows, outrageous performers, and bustling casinos, where millions are won and lost every night. Las Vegas is all of that, but much more. This city represents the American dream. A dusty watering hole less than seventy years ago, it has been transformed into one of the most elaborate cities in the world and one of the hottest vacation spots for the entire family. Las Vegas is second only to Walt Disney World as the favorite vacation destination in the United States.

The gaming entertainment business has its roots in Las Vegas. From the early 1940s until 1976, Las Vegas had a monopoly on the casino business, not the gaming entertainment business. Casinos had no hotel rooms, entertainment, or other amenities. The hotels that existed were just a place to sleep when a guest was not on the casino floor. This was the era when a slot machine or a blackjack table was enough to attract guests to the operation. Regulatory reforms of casino gaming, such as the development of centralized gaming control by powerful regulatory agencies, were an important development during these early years. These include the Gaming Control Board and Nevada Gaming Commission. There were strict rules established as to who and what must be licensed.

A number of state-run lotteries were established during the 1960s when states began to realize that large revenues could be gained from lottery gaming. In the mid-1970s, a federal Commission on the Review of the National Policy Toward Gambling issued a report affirming that the legalization and control of gambling activity is a matter for the jurisdiction of state governments. The legal status of gaming is not the same as other businesses. Gaming is said to be a "privileged" business. Those who conduct most common types of businesses have a "right" to do so. There is no "right" to conduct a gaming business. The states have broad authority to regulate gaming. To exercise the full extent of this power, however, the legislature must exercise it by granting broad power to regulatory authorities.

Casino gambling, seen as a desperate remedy for Atlantic City's severe economic situation at the time, was approved by a voter referendum in a statewide ballot in November 1976.[5] Following the referendum, casino gambling was legalized in the state of New Jersey by the Casino Control Act. The state looked to the casino hotel industry to invest capital, create jobs, pay taxes, and attract tourists, thus revitalizing the economy and creating a financial environment in which urban redevelopment could occur.

The act initiated a number of fees and taxes specific to the casino hotel business that would provide revenues to support regulatory costs, to fund social services for the disabled and the elderly throughout the state, and to provide investment funds for the redevelopment of Atlantic City. The Casino Control Act created the Casino Control Commission, whose purpose was not only to ensure the success and integrity of the Atlantic City casino industry, but also to carry out the objective of reversing the city's economic fortunes.

Sensing that the objectives of the Casino Control Act were being fulfilled in New Jersey, and wanting similar benefits for their state, but not wanting land-

---

[5]C. G. Braunlich, "Lessons from the Atlantic City Casino Experience," *Journal of Travel Research,* **34**, 3, pp. 46–56.

based casino gambling, Iowa legalized riverboat casinos thirteen years later. They were followed in rapid succession by Illinois, Mississippi, Louisiana, Missouri, and Indiana. With the spread of the casino industry throughout the United States and Canada, the competitive nature of the industry began to create a need for what is now known as gaming entertainment with the addition of noncasino attractions. Gaming entertainment is, therefore, a natural evolution of the casino industry.

Native American Gaming

In *California v. Cabazon Band of Mission Indians et al.* (1987), the Supreme Court decided 6–3 that once a state has legalized any form of gambling, the Native Americans in that state have the right to offer and self-regulate the same games, without government restrictions. The state of California and the county of Riverside had sought to impose local and state regulations on card and bingo clubs operated by the Cabazon and Morongo bands of Mission Indians. These court decisions were unequivocal in their recognition of the rights of tribes with regard to certain gaming activities.

Congress, which some observers say was alarmed by the prospect of tribal gaming going out of control, responded to these court decisions by passing the **Indian Gaming Regulatory Act of 1988 (IGRA).** The IGRA provides a framework by which games are conducted to protect both the tribes and the general public. For example, the IGRA outlines criteria for approval of casino management contracts entered into by tribes and establishes civil penalties for violation of its provisions. The act clearly is a compromise in that it balances the rights of sovereign tribal nations to conduct gaming activities with the rights of the federal and state governments to regulate activities within their borders.

The three objectives of the IGRA were to (a) provide a statutory basis for the operation of gaming by Native American tribes as a means of promoting tribal economic development, self-sufficiency, and strong tribal governments; (b) provide a statutory basis for the regulation of gaming by a Native American tribe adequate to shield it from organized crime and other corrupting influences; and (c) establish an independent regulatory authority the National Indian Gaming Commission (NIGC), for governing gaming activity on Native American lands.

IGRA defines three different kinds, or "classes," of Native American gaming activities: (a) Class I gaming, consisting of social games played solely for prizes of minimum value or traditional forms of Native American gaming; (b) Class II gaming, consisting of bingo, games similar to bingo, and card games explicitly authorized by the laws of the state; and (c) Class III gaming, consisting of all forms of gaming that are neither Class I nor Class II gaming, and therefore including most of what are considered casino games.

The significance of the definition of Class III gaming activity is that it defines the games that (a) must be located in a state that permits such gaming for any purpose by any person, organization, or entity and (b) are conducted in conformance with a compact that states are required to negotiate "in good faith" with the tribes.

A Day in the Life of Richard Duke
Casino Shift Manager, Las Vegas Hilton Hotel and Casino, Las Vegas, Nevada

The casino gaming industry is clearly an important provider of jobs.

I arrive at work at approximately 9:30 A.M. My first task is to update myself on the previous day's operations. This includes how much the casino won or lost, what customers are gambling at our property, and how they are doing.

Prior to the beginning of each shift (graveyard, days, or swing), we conduct a shift meeting. This meeting takes approximately twenty minutes. The casino shift manager going off duty will conduct the meeting and the incoming shift manager along with his or her pit managers will attend. In the meeting we pass on to the next shift any pertinent information relevant to the day's operations. We also discuss those customers presently gambling in our casino, their credit lines, betting limits, and activities.

After the shift meeting, I go out onto the casino floor and evaluate our current level of casino business. I discuss with my pit managers how many casino games we will need for the expected day's business. We also determine at this time whether we will need any private games for our high limit customers.

Once these accommodations are decided on, the remainder of the day consists of keeping abreast as to who is gambling in our casino, managing employees, and monitoring casino activities. I continually visit with our established customers and meet and welcome new ones. This means knowing who they are, what casino games they play, what their casino credit limit is, and how much is still available and whether they are winning or losing.

Customer problems and complaints fall within my authority as well. If they are casino customers, I pretty much handle it myself. If they are hotel guests only and they come to me with their problem, I usually team up with the hotel manager and we resolve the situation together. We spend a lot of time and exhibit concern when it comes to customer problems or complaints. We always try to find a way to say "yes" to customer requests and try to reach an equitable agreement to problems.

I also spend a lot of time each day managing and monitoring employees. Those that fall within my realm of authority are dealers, box supervisors, floor supervisors, and pit managers. Good employee relations are a big concern of mine. I feel a happy employee is the key to good customer service. This in turn makes my job easier and generates revenue for the company.

Toward the end of the day, I prepare a report as to the status of the casino. Then I conduct a shift meeting with the incoming managers.

I usually leave the property at approximately 6:30 P.M.

(Courtesy of Las Vegas News Bureau.)

While the federal gaming law precludes state taxation, the tribes in several states have made voluntary payments and also negotiated payments to state governments under certain circumstances. Often tribes give local governments voluntary payments in recognition of services the tribe receives, and some pay revenues in exchange for permission to maintain a casino gambling monopoly in a state. In Michigan, Connecticut, and Louisiana, tribes have agreed to make payments to the state as part of their comprehensive compacts for casino gambling. In almost all the states, the tribes make payments to the state for state costs incurred in the process of regulation of the casinos as provided for in the negotiated agreements.

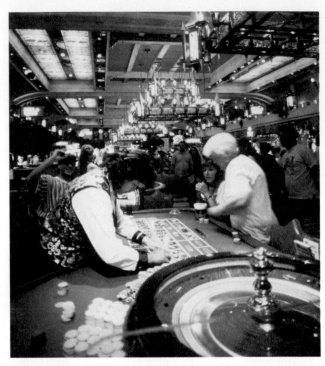

The gaming industry is clearly an important provider of jobs. (Courtesy of Las Vegas News Bureau.)

Gambling on Native American lands account for more than 11 percent of all the winnings from gambling in the United States. Approximately one dollar out of every four lost by players to casinos is lost at Native American casinos. There are 281 gaming facilities on reservation lands in thirty-two states, and Native American gaming has been the fastest growing sector of casino gaming in the United States. Additional Native American gaming is conducted by the First Nations Bands of Canada.

Check Your Knowledge

1. Define the following:
   a. Wagered
   b. Bet
   c. Handle
   d. Win
   e. Action
   f. Beat the house
   g. Social gambler
2. Briefly describe the history of the gaming industry.
3. What does the Indian Gaming Regulatory Act of 1988 consist of?

Size and Scope of Gaming Entertainment

Recently, a merging frenzy has occurred in the gaming industry. As of 2000 there were four large casino operators—Park Place Entertainment Inc., MGM Grand Inc., Harrah's Entertainment Inc., and Mandalay Resort Group. These four hold all the cards in the gaming industry, so to speak!

Why is the gaming/entertainment industry growing so quickly? Basically, because people like to wager, and historically, there has been more demand than supply for wagering opportunities. As public acceptance of legalized gaming has grown, and state and local governments have permitted gaming entertainment establishments to open, supply is beginning to meet demand.

The gaming entertainment industry pays more than 2 billion dollars per year in gambling privilege taxes to state governments. Casino development has been credited with revitalizing economies through new capital investment, job creation, new tax revenue, and increased tourism. A 1996 study of the gaming entertainment industry by the Arthur Andersen consulting firm resulted in the following comments:

> The casino gaming industry is clearly an important provider of jobs, wages and taxes to the U.S. economy. The jobs created are well paying which match the national average wage and exceed average wages of several other industries. In addition, the number of jobs created for every $1 million in reported revenues is significantly higher than several high-growth and other more mature industries analyzed for purposes of comparison in this study. Unlike many other major U.S. industries that rely on foreign labor, casino gaming hires its employees principally from within the U.S. Furthermore, the casino gaming industry creates additional jobs in a number of domestic supplier businesses. These secondary impacts further ripple through the economy, ultimately impacting all industries across the length and breadth of the country.[6]
>
> Casino gaming relies more heavily than most industries on domestic labor and domestic suppliers. Casino operations are relatively labor intensive, thus they create more direct jobs than those in other industries. For every $1 million in revenues, the casino gaming industry creates 13 direct jobs, far exceeding the numbers created by other industries such as the soft drink, cellular phone services, video cassette sales and rentals, and cable television services industries. In fact, it is the spending by casino employees, as opposed to spending by new tourists drawn to a region by a casino, that accounts for a large percentage of casino's positive impacts on overall consumer spending.[7]

---

[6]Arthur Andersen, *Economic Impacts of Casino Gaming in the United States,* Volume 1: *Macro Study.* American Gaming Association, 1996.

[7]Arthur Andersen, *Economic Impacts of Casino Gaming in the United States,* Volume 2: *Micro Study.* American Gaming Association, 1997.

Casino gaming has created more than 700,000 direct and indirect jobs with wages of approximately $21 billion. When unemployment is high and an area is in economic despair, casinos create jobs. Atlantic City created 40,000 jobs and evened out seasonality of employment in that economy.

Casino gaming companies pay an average of 12 percent of total revenues in taxes. Casino gaming companies contribute to federal, state, and local governments through gaming-related and other taxes. Direct taxes include property, federal/state income, and construction sales and use taxes, which all industries pay, and gaming taxes, which are levied only on the gaming industry at rates ranging from 6.25 to 20 percent of gaming revenues.

Although casino gaming companies pay a particularly high percent of their total revenues, federal taxes represent less than 18 percent of the total tax burden, with the remainder being paid at the state and local levels. Gaming taxes, by far the largest tax paid by the industry, are often specifically designated by state and local governments for expenditure on such things as infrastructure improvements, education, and benefits for the elderly and disabled.

The casino entertainment industry, a relatively new part of the hospitality business, has some controversial elements to it. The majority of people find a visit to a casino enjoyable and entertaining and have no objections to gaming entertainment businesses. However, others have strong objections to casino gaming based on their moral beliefs, or opinions, that there are social costs associated with gaming entertainment operations. Although the moral beliefs of others can never be questioned, the social costs of casino entertainment should be reviewed. A major concern associated with casino entertainment is the impact on crime, both organized crime and street crime.

Organized Crime and Casinos

The common assumption that casinos increase crime is partially grounded in stereotypes from the early years of the industry. There was an irrefutable connection between organized crime and several participants in the commercial casino industry during the first two decades of its existence in Nevada. However, confusion persists in the minds of many about the present structure of casino ownership and the character of casino regulation. Links to organized crime, which have some historical relevance, are not substantiated by current research. Experience has taught us that issues of political corruption and organized crime are more likely to be by-products of illegal gambling than of well-regulated legal commercial gaming. This reality, along with the corporatization of commercial gaming industries and the professionalization of regulatory bodies, has undermined the crime argument against gambling.

Casino operators have proven they can, with proper controls, manage their business with integrity. In this way, they have overcome the stigma attached to casino gaming, ensuring that their industry has become part of the hospitality/entertainment sector. Regulatory and enforcement agencies must be well funded and professionally organized to carry out complicated background investigations, regulation, and enforcement. These activities can be extremely expensive. For example, the budget for the New Jersey Division of Gaming Enforcement is more than $36 million while the budget for New Jersey's Casino Control Commission is nearly $26 million.

Since the early 1970s, the ownership of casinos in America has predominantly shifted to publicly held companies whose shares are traded on the major stock exchanges. For example, the five largest in terms of annual revenue (Park Place Entertainment, MGM Grand, Mandalay Resort Group, and Harrah's Entertainment) are all traded on the New York Stock Exchange. Of the next fourteen largest casino companies, four are traded on the NYSE, two on the AMEX, and eight on NASDAQ. As publicly traded entities, these companies are answerable to the Securities and Exchange Commission, as well as to the gaming commissions in their respective states and to local law enforcement. The largest of these companies are in the portfolios of major institutional investors such as Prudential Insurance Co., Kemper Financial Services, First Interstate Bancorp, and the Oppenheimer Group.

Casino entertainment is one of the most tightly regulated industries in the United States. Nevada employs 372 regulators at a cost of $19 million, while New Jersey employs 650 regulators at a cost of $50 million. These costs are paid for by the casino industry through regulatory fees.[8]

Organizations that supply labor and goods to the casino hotel industry have had a different history. In 1991, after lengthy investigations, Atlantic City's local chapter of the Hotel Employees and Restaurant Employees International Union was forced to accept the appointment of a federal monitor with broad disciplinary and oversight powers. Union officials found to have ties to organized crime were removed from office. In 1995, the national office of the same union was also taken over by a federal overseer.

Street Crime and Casinos

With the opening of casinos in Atlantic City in 1978, and despite a strengthened police force, the growth in the crime index of Atlantic City began to exceed that of the state as a whole. As casinos opened, crime rates began to rise. Between 1977 and 1984, total violent crimes increased by more than 116 percent. In 1977, before the first casino opened, the Atlantic City Metropolitan Statistical Area (MSA) ranked fiftieth among the nation's 257 MSAs in per capita violent and property crime. In 1981, the Atlantic City MSA was ranked first. Overall, from 1977 to 1990, the crime rate in that city rose by an incredible 230 percent. This was more than 25 times the single-digit growth rate of 9 percent reported from the remainder of the state of New Jersey and has required the city to increase its police department's budget by 300 percent. The Atlantic City experience is often cited by those who contend that casinos promote street crime.

Uniform crime statistics fail to take into account the dramatic influx of visitors to Atlantic City. Conventional crime-rate statistics are based on resident

[8]International Gaming Institute (University of Las Vegas, Nevada), *The Gaming Industry: Introduction and Perspectives.* New York: John Wiley, 1996.

populations. Atlantic City has so many visitors that its actual population is always considerably higher than what is used to compute crime rates. The consequence of using crime rate statistics based on resident populations, and not adjusted for extremely high counts of visitors, is an artificial inflation of those rates. Typically, when the number of tourists is accounted for, the crime rate in casino jurisdictions is not significantly different from other noncasino metropolitan areas that entertain a large number of tourists and other visitors.

Key Players in the Industry

Until recently the leading participants in the gaming entertainment business were Venetian, Mirage Resorts, Harrah's Entertainment, Hilton Hotels Corporation, ITT Corporation, Bellagio, and MGM Grand. Today, there are only four industry giants: Park Place, MGM, Harrah's, and Mandalay. Changes in the industry happen in the wink of an eye. They all have diverse

The Venitian and the Mirage: two popular casino resort hotels.

property portfolios and solid business practices and are well respected by Wall Street.

Mandalay Resorts operates casinos primarily in Las Vegas. The company's Mirage property is a tropical-themed casino and hotel that features a volcano erupting at regular intervals. Its Treasure Island casino and hotel has a pirate theme, highlighted by live sea battles between a pirate ship and a British frigate. Other Las Vegas casino/hotel properties include the Golden Nugget (located in downtown Las Vegas) and the Monte Carlo (50 percent owned through a joint venture with Circus Circus).

Harrah's Entertainment operates casinos in major gaming markets throughout the United States. Its casinos are located in Reno, Lake Tahoe, Las Vegas, and Laughlin, Nevada; and in Atlantic City, New Jersey. One of the most geographically diverse casino companies, it also operates riverboat and dockside casinos in Illinois, Louisiana, Missouri, and Mississippi; and Native American reservation casinos in Arizona and Washington. In all, the company operates more than 700,000 square feet of gaming space. Although Harrah's also operates nearly 6,500 hotel rooms and more than 50 restaurants, it derives nearly 80 percent of its revenues from its casinos.

The Flaming Hilton, MGM Grand, and Bellagio: three successful casino resort hotels.

Harrah's Entertainment, Inc., is the premier name in casino entertainment. The Harrah's brand was born in Reno, Nevada, in the late 1930s and has since grown to become the largest casino entertainment company in North America. Harrah's history is a rich combination of casino expertise and quality, which was launched in northern Nevada and expanded across the continent. Today, Harrah's is a $1.5 billion dollar company, publicly traded on the New York Stock Exchange. The gaming division of the former Promus Companies is now a separate, publicly traded company, with seventeen properties in nine states and one foreign country, and 23,000 employees.

Hilton owns, manages, and/or franchises more than 220 hotels around the world. Hilton, with its $3-billion purchase of Bally Entertainment, is the nation's largest gambling business. U.S. gaming operations include three casino hotels in Las Vegas, two in Atlantic City, two in Reno, and one in Laughlin; a riverboat casino in New Orleans; and interest in a Canadian casino.

Formerly a superconglomerate involved in everything from white bread to Chilean politics, ITT Corp. is focused on the hospitality, gambling, and information services industries. It owns the Sheraton chain, with more than 400 hotels, and the three Caesar's World hotel/casinos. ITT's business information services include ITT World Directories, which produces telephone directories in seven countries, and ITT Educational Services (83 percent-owned), which offers vocational and technical training. The company has agreed to be bought by the much smaller Starwood Lodging, a real estate investment trust, following a takeover battle instigated by Hilton Hotels' unsolicited offer for ITT.

ITT purchased Caesar's World Inc. in 1994, including Caesar's Palace in Las Vegas, Caesar's Tahoe, Caesar's Atlantic City and other operations, thereby merging the lodging and gaming entertainment businesses.

Circus Circus is betting its hotels and casinos will be big winners. Named for its carnival-themed Circus Circus Hotel, the company owns or operates casinos and hotels in three states. The company owns nine casino/hotels in Nevada, including the Circus Circus, Excalibur, and Luxor in Las Vegas; 50 percent stakes in three casino/hotels in Las Vegas, Reno, and Elgin, Illinois; and two casino-only operations in Las Vegas and Tunica, Mississippi. It also operates a casino for another owner in Las Vegas. The company is continuing to build gambling resorts for middle-income families and is developing a mile-long strip at the south end of the Las Vegas strip with hotels, casinos, a retail complex, and entertainment facilities.

MGM Grand prides itself on operating the world's largest hotel/casino. The MGM Grand Hotel, located on 113 acres along the Las Vegas strip, has more than 5,000 rooms and a 171,500-square-foot casino with some 3,700 slot machines, about 160 table games, some 50 shops, a theme park, and a special-events center featuring acts such as Neil Diamond and Luther Vandross. Across the strip is the 2,000-room New York-New York Hotel and Casino, MGM Grand's 50 percent joint venture with Primadonna Resorts. MGM Grand also runs a hotel/casino in northern Australia that caters to Asian gamblers. The company has agreed to develop casinos in Atlantic City, New Jersey, and South Africa. Kirk Kerkorian owns a 61.6 percent share of MGM Grand.

Personal Profile: Stephen A. Wynn

Former Chairman and CEO of Mirage Resorts, Las Vegas; Current Owner of Desert Inn

Hotels magazine selected Stephen Wynn as the ninth independent hotelier of the world for playing a major role in transforming Las Vegas from a gambling venue for adults into a multidimensional resort destination for the whole family and also for managing the Mirage, one of the world's best run megahotels.

The $750 million, 3,000-room Mirage resort casino changed the face of Las Vegas. Mirage has fine gourmet restaurants, a huge lagoon-like pool, an atrium filled with palm trees, a children's game arcade and, of course, a first-rate casino.

Wynn also operates Treasure Island, the midcasino hotel, which beckons tourists inside every night with a sign featuring a smiling pirate. Treasure Island has free street-side mock battles nightly, complete with cannon fire and a sinking ship. When the show is over, many in the crowd walk over the dock into the thirty-six-story hotel's casino, seven restaurants, and retail shops. The hotel has a pool, spa, game arcade, showrooms, convention center, and two wedding chapels—with built-in video cameras.

Steve also runs two other casino-hotels: the 2,000-room Golden Nugget in downtown Vegas and the 300-room Golden Nugget in Laughlin, Nevada. With close to 8,200 rooms, Mirage, Inc., is ranked number sixty-one among the world's largest hotel chains.

Steve has 18,000 highly motivated employees who keep guestrooms, casinos, and other attractions impeccable, according to industry analysts. The Mirage properties are exceptional, drawing a commanding share of a demanding market with an exceptionally high company-wide occupancy.

Wynn began his career in Vegas at age twenty-five with a degree in English literature from the University of Pennsylvania. In a very short time, he became an executive and part owner of the Frontier Hotel. He owned and operated a Nevada wine-importing company from 1969 to 1972. He then turned a real estate deal into a profit, which allowed him to begin a major investment in Golden Nugget in 1972. (The Golden Nugget was renamed the Mirage in 1991.)

In 1973, Wynn acquired control of the company, which, at the time, had no rooms. In 1980, he opened the $140 million Golden Nugget/Atlantic City, which he sold to Bally Corporation for $400 million in 1987. That year, Wynn started building the Mirage.

Stephen Wynn's latest adventure is the $1.4 billion, 3,500-room Bellagio, opened in 1998. Bellagio features a $35 million water show in a man-made lake, a $77 million water-themed show produced by Cirque du Soleil, and shopping provided by Armani, Tiffany, Gucci, and Channel. He also invested $60 million in art for the new Bellagio Resort because he wants to attract art lovers and other chic people who are looking for more than a prize-fight. In addition, Wynn has plans for a $500 million-plus resort in Biloxi, Mississippi, and another resort in Atlantic City, New Jersey.

Wynn is confident that both his projects and Las Vegas will continue to thrive. This can be seen through the numbers tracking the performance of Mirage Resort, Inc.

Stephen Wynn recently sold his interest in Mirage Resorts and bought the $270 Million Desert Inn.

Two other gaming entertainment companies, Boyd Gaming and Grand Casinos, Inc., are expanding rapidly into markets across the United States.

Boyd Gaming operates ten gaming and hotel facilities in four states. The company's six Las Vegas properties are The Stardust Resort and Casino, Sam's Town Hotel and Gambling Hall, the Eldorado Casino, the Joker's Wild Casino, the California Hotel and Casino, and the Fremont Hotel and Casino. Outside Nevada, Boyd operates the Sam's Town Hotel and Gambling Hall, a dockside gaming and entertainment complex in Tunica County, Mississippi; Sam's Town Casino, a Kansas City, Missouri, casino complex; and the Silver Star Hotel and Casino, a land-based gaming and entertainment facility owned by the Choctaw Indians.

Grand Casinos, Inc., is a casino entertainment company that develops, constructs, and manages land-based and dockside casinos in emerging gaming markets. Grand Casinos, Inc., has been a publicly traded company since 1991 and is listed on the New York Stock Exchange under the trading symbol GND. The company currently owns and operates the three largest casino hotel resorts in the state of Mississippi, manages two land-based casinos in Louisiana, and manages two casino hotel resorts in Minnesota.

Exciting Gaming Entertainment Projects

The Mirage megaresort on the Las Vegas strip has a volcano that erupts every few minutes and a tropical rain forest with soaring palms and sparkling waterfalls. Guests checking into the hotel face a giant aquarium where live sharks swim. The pool is a tropical paradise of waterfalls and connected lagoons. The property contains a European shopping boulevard and a wide variety of themed food and beverage operations. There is meeting and convention space for up to 5,000 attendees. The showroom is the home of the famous magic and illusions of Siegfried & Roy and their white tigers. The resort is also the home of a family of Atlantic bottlenose dolphins.

Station Casino Kansas City is one of the largest floating casino operations in the world. The 140,000-square-foot, two-barge casino is home to 3,000 slot machines and 190 table games. In addition to the casino, the facility includes twelve restaurants, eleven lounges, a 200-room hotel, a 1,400-seat special events arena, a microbrewery, an arcade, a child-care center, and an eighteen-screen

The famous aquarium behind the front desk at the Mirage in Las Vegas.

movie theater. The attractions at Station Casino are coordinated through a Victorian theme, including a cobblestone street that winds through a re-creation of Victorian-era Kansas City, complete with antiques and a hand-painted sky.

New York New York in Las Vegas is an eye-catching property with twelve hotel towers, each a replica of a Manhattan skyscraper. There is a Coney Island-style amusement area, a casino that feels like Central Park at dusk, a food court designed to simulate a Little Italy neighborhood, a 300-foot-long replica of the Brooklyn Bridge, and a 150-foot-tall model of the Statue of Liberty at the front of the resort. The property is jointly owned by MGM Grand and Primadonna Resorts.

Star Trek: The Experience attraction and outer-space themed SpaceQuest casino located in the Las Vegas Hilton is a $70 million joint venture of Hilton Corp. and the Paramount Parks Division of Viacom International Inc. The project targets baby boomers and Generation X customers interested in science fiction and space-related entertainment. The SpaceQuest, separate from the main casino, simulates a ride aboard a space station. Television screens create an illusion of space flight. Gaming equipment unique to the 20,000-square-foot SpaceQuest casino includes slot machines activated by breaking a light beam.

Wild Wild West Casino at Bally's Park Place in Atlantic City, New Jersey, is the city's first highly themed, entertainment-oriented, technologically advanced casino entertainment product. The casino has an 1880s frontier mining town, mountain scapes, model trains, animatronic characters, and colorful storefronts. There is a fifty-foot-high canyon with waterfalls, a talking gold prospector, and a wisecracking vulture perched on a twelve-foot-high cactus.

The Masquerade Village at the Rio Hotel & Casino in Las Vegas is a Tuscany village themed retail area with twenty stores and six restaurants, including a wine cellar tasting room. Its Masquerade Show in the Sky features five themed floats suspended from the ceiling that parade above the casino via an overhead track. Costumed entertainers and musicians perform from atop the floats and from other posts inside the casino during free shows throughout the day. Guests are invited to ride on the floats and participate in the shows.

Luxor Las Vegas, operated by Circus Circus, was constructed as a thirty-story pyramid and houses the world's largest atrium, measuring 29 million cubic feet. It also features a beam of light emanating from its peak that is so intense it can be seen as far away as Los Angeles, California. The 4,500 rooms are appointed in Egyptian architecture. The lobby area includes a life-sized replica of the great Temple of Ramses II and large Egyptian murals. The resort includes a museum containing reproductions of the items found in King Tutankhamen's tomb, which was discovered in 1922 by Howard Carter. The items are positioned exactly as they were found, according to records maintained by the Carter expedition. The resort also has a Theater of Time, the site of an IMAX 3D theater using the IMAX Personal Sound Environment headset, an advanced liquid crystal display technology for three-dimensional viewing.

The registration area of the Luxor Las Vegas megaresort, with its Egyptian antiquity theme. The lobby is at the base of a thirty-story pyramid with the largest atrium in the world.

Grand Casino Tunica, with the largest dockside casino between Las Vegas and Atlantic City, is located in Tunica County, Mississippi, just south of Memphis. The three-story, 140,000-square-foot gaming area is unlike any in the area. With more than 3,000 slot machines and 108 table games, guests can enjoy the atmosphere of the San Francisco Gold Rush, the New Orleans Mardi Gras, the Great American West of the 1870s, or an 1890s Mississippi riverboat town. Six restaurants, two entertainment lounges, a Kids Quest, a Grand Arcade, and a luxury hotel are located on this 2,000-acre site. There are plans to develop it into a premier destination resort.

The Monte Carlo Pub & Brewery, located in the Monte Carlo Resort & Casino in Las Vegas, is one of the largest brewpubs in the United States. Six different styles of Monte Carlo-labeled beer are regularly produced, including a light beer, an India pale ale, and an American-style, unfiltered wheat ale. The pub also features a traditional Irish stout, a rich amber ale, and a regular brewer's special. Gourmet, brick-oven pizzas and sausage platters, and a full line of salads and sandwiches are on the menu. Huge copper beer barrels and antique furnishings add to the brewpub's atmosphere. The hotel offers a meeting room and function area from which guests can get a bird's-eye view of the entire operation. The brewpub also features an outdoor patio that overlooks the lavish 21,000-square-foot Monte Carlo pool area, which includes a wave pool and an easy river ride.

Treasure Island megaresort's entrance is across a long wooden bridge that traverses the waters of Buccaneer Bay. Every ninety minutes each evening, cannon and musket fire are exchanged in a dramatic pyrotechnic battle between the pirate ship *Hispañiola* and the British frigate HMS *Britannia* in the middle of the bay. The showroom in this property is home to the world-famous performance troupe Cirque du Soleil, and features an unusual circus act with no animals but an overabundance of imagination.

Guests can observe the beer-making process at the Monte Carlo Pub and Brewery located in the Monte Carlo Resort & Casino in Las Vegas. Note the catwalk above is part of a function area used in the property for reception and cocktail parties to view the brewpub operations.

Forum Shops at Caesar's Palace draws an estimated 50,000 people a day and makes an average of $1,200 per square foot, far above the industry norm of $400. The Roman streetscape themed, half-million-square-foot retail area features the Festival Fountain Plaza, which incorporates animatronic statues of gods, such as Bacchus, Apollo, and Venus, with a fountain and light show. Another main feature is the Atlantic attraction, a fountain featuring animatronic figures that come to life during the Lost City of Atlantis laser light show that includes fire and other special effects. The backdrop for this attraction is a 50,000 gallon aquarium that can support 650 fish from 25 fish families. The Race for Atlantis ride uses a giant screen IMAX 3-D motion simulator, the first of its kind to combine IMAX's large format film making with 3-D computer animation, sound engineering, and motion simulation. The result is a multisensory experience that takes riders on an exhilarating chariot race through the legendary kingdom of Atlantis. Upscale retailers include Christian Dior, Versace, Niketown, a Virgin Megastore, and Wolfgang Puck's Spago restaurant. The FAO Schwarz store is the company's largest and features a 46-foot animatronic Trojan Horse.

The pirate battle in front of the Treasure Island megaresort. Thousands of guests to Las Vegas watch this show every ninety minutes in front of the hotel entrance.

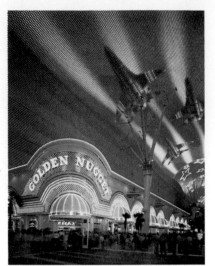

The Fremont Street Experience in the downtown area of Las Vegas consists of a four-block long pedestrian mall light and sound show, with sky parades that take place every two hours.

Fremont Street Experience consists of a four-block long pedestrian mall light and sound show with sky parades that take place every two hours. A canopy known as a space frame, which is really a giant video-quality animation screen, covers the entire area. The light shows are broadcast on 2 million-plus light bulbs from end to end that can produce 40,000 shades of color. There is virtually no image, animated or actual, that cannot be produced. The clarity and depth are close to movie quality. Digital sound accompaniments come from a 54,000-watt sound system pumped through clusters of exposed speakers, forty in each block.

Foxwoods Resort Casino, near Ledyard, Connecticut, only a several-hour drive from New York City, is one of the largest gaming entertainment operations in the world. It is owned and managed by the Mashantucket Pequot Tribal Nation. There are two full-service hotels, restaurants and lounges, retail stores, amusement rides, and a museum and research center supporting the Pequot community.

The Aladdin opened on August 17, 2000. It is a $1 billion plus hotel and casino. It has 2,567 rooms, 116,000-square-foot casino, 21 restaurants, a 500,000-square-foot mall with 135 stores, a 1,200-seat show room, a 33,000-square-foot spa, and 75,000 square feet of meeting and convention space. The Aladdin's fifty-foot genie golden lamp centerpiece and its theme, the classic Arabian tale of the thousand and one nights, appeal to all.

Borgata is a new development in Atlantic City, New Jersey. Boyd Gaming Corp. broke ground on the $1 billion Borgata, the most expensive megaresort casino in Atlantic City, which badly needs new hotel rooms. It will be Atlantic City's first megaresort and the city's first new casino since the Taj Mahal opened in 1990.

Bellagio is a megaresort that appeared on the Las Vegas strip at a cost of more than $1.5 billion dollars, which is more than the initial construction cost of Disneyworld. The 3,000-room hotel is fronted with a nine-acre lake featuring

2,200 fountains that perform a choreographed water dance several times each evening. The lobby includes an art gallery containing $150 million in fine art, including works by Picasso, Renoir, and Rembrandt. The signature showroom is home to a $70-million creation by Cirque du Soleil performed on a stage submerged in water, and a 15,000-square-foot conservatory featuring a massive flower display with classical gardens and European fountains and pools.

ITT Caesars Riverboat at Bridgeport, Indiana, is located on the Indiana side of the Ohio River, just west of Louisville, Kentucky. The vessel is 450-feet long and 104-feet wide, with more than 80,000 square feet of casino space on four decks. The casino has 3,000 slot machines and 150 table games. The site of the new riverboat megaresort is a 232-acre tract of riverfront property that includes a 500-room convention-style Sheraton hotel, upscale shopping mall, sports arena, IMAX theater, Magical Empire, attractions, and an eighteen-hole golf course. The terminal for the riverboat is 130,000 square feet and houses four restaurants and an adjacent children's theme park. To facilitate visits from Louisville across the river, the company is developing a "Caesar's Chariots" gondola system that will transport customers up and over the Ohio River in sky cars. The people mover can carry 1,000 persons per hour.

The MGM Grand, a 5,000-room megaresort in Las Vegas, is themed out as the "City of Entertainment." An area called the Studio Walk resembles a Hollywood sound stage and features a number of Hollywood landmarks, five restaurants, a food court, six retail stores, and a nightclub. The entrance to the resort is graced by a "liquid gold," six-story lion entry, fronting 80-foot entertainment walls that run multimedia and light shows continuously.

The Beau Rivage megaresort is the most magnificent resort on the Mississippi Gulf Coast and, perhaps, in the entire Southeast. This thirty-two-story, 1,780-room resort, with its stately oak-tree-lined entrance, cascading fountains, lush formal gardens, and fragrant magnolias, graces acres of white sand beach overlooking the Gulf. As the newest Mirage Resorts property, Beau Rivage features twelve distinctive restaurants, an 85,000-square-foot casino, a 1,500-seat show-

The Bellagio in Las Vegas, a 3,000-room Mediterranean themed resort named after the Italian city on Lake Como.

room, an elegantly appointed spa and salon, a shopping esplanade, and a 30,000-square-foot conference and convention center for banquets and business meetings, all under one roof.

Hilton Hotel Paris Casino Resort is a $700 million, 3,000-room operation inspired by the prominent landmarks of Paris, France, a city that draws about one-third as many visitors annually as Las Vegas. The project includes a half-sized, fifty-story replica of France's Eiffel Tower and an 85,000-square-foot casino. It has 130,000 square feet of casino space, a half-acre health spa, and a retail complex supplied by several French companies. An existing monorail that links the MGM Grand Hotel and Bally's Las Vegas (owned by Hilton) stops at a replica of a Paris Metro Station.

Las Vegas Sand's Venetian resort, casino, and convention complex is the largest megaresort ever planned. The $2 billion project includes 6,000 suites, each with 700 square feet of space, including sunken living rooms, two-line phones, and in-room fax machines. Inspired by the canals, bridges, and ancient architecture of Venice, Italy, the property includes a 1,200-foot replica of Venice's Grand Canal, which fronts 150 stores. The Venetian has two casinos of 100,000 square feet each.

The MGM Grand Detroit megaresort is an art-deco complex constructed in downtown Detroit. In addition to a spacious 100,000-square-foot gaming area with forty-foot-high ceilings, the complex includes a thirty-six-story, 800-room hotel designed to be the Midwest's premier resort hotel; a diverse array of signature restaurant and retail facilities; a state-of-the-art, five-screen movie theater; approximately 70,000 square feet of convention, ballroom, and meeting facilities; a 1,200-seat showroom theater; and a climate-controlled parking garage.

Le Jardin is Atlantic City's newest megaresort with 2,000 rooms and three acres of vaulted glass atriums. Lush horticultural gardens change with the seasons. It will be springtime 365 days a year, taking the seasonality out of the Atlantic City gaming entertainment market.

Check Your Knowledge

1. What impact does the gambling industry have on crime?
2. Briefly describe the following gaming entertainment projects:
   a. New York New York
   b. The Monte Carlo Pub & Brewery
   c. Treasure Island
   d. Forum Shops at Caesar's Palace
   e. Bellagio
   f. MGM Grand

Positions in Gaming Entertainment

Careers in the gaming entertainment industry are unlimited. Students of the industry who understand the multidisciplinary needs of the business find five initial career tracks in hotel operations, food and beverage operations, casino operations, retail, and entertainment operations.

Hotel Operations

The career opportunities in gaming entertainment hotel operations are much like the career opportunities in the full-service hotel industry, with the exception that food and beverage can be a division of its own and not part of hotel operations. The rooms and guest services departments offer the most opportunities for students of hospitality management. Because gaming entertainment properties have hotels that are much larger than nongaming hotels, department heads have a larger number of supervisors reporting to them and more responsibilities. Reservations, front desk, housekeeping, valet parking, and guest services can all be very large departments with many employees.

Food and Beverage Operations

Gaming entertainment has a foundation of high-quality food and beverage service in a wide variety of styles and concepts. Some of the best foodservice operations in the hospitality industry are found in gaming entertainment operations. There are many career opportunities in restaurant management and the culinary arts. As with hotel operations, gaming entertainment properties are typically very large and contain numerous food and beverage outlets, including a number of restaurants, hotel room service, banquets and conventions, and retail outlets. Many establishments support gourmet, high-end signature restaurants. It is not unusual to find many more executive-level management positions in both front- and back-of-the-house food and beverage operations in gaming entertainment operations than in nongaming properties.

Casino Operations

Casino operations jobs fall into five functional areas. Gaming operations staff include slot machine technicians (approximately one technician for forty machines), table-game dealers (approximately four dealers for each table game), and table-game supervisors. Casino service staff includes security, purchasing, and maintenance and facilities engineers. Marketing staff includes public relations, market research, and advertising professionals. Human resources staffs includes employee relations, compensation, staffing, and train-

Personal Profile: Stacy L. Burns

Following a Career in Gaming Entertainment

After her third year attending Purdue University's Restaurant, Hotel, Institutional, and Tourism Management program, Stacy took a summer internship with the Showboat Hotel and Casino in Atlantic City, New Jersey, in 1992. She rotated through all departments in hotel operations for the 800-room, full-service casino hotel, and developed working experience in line positions including PBX reservations, front desk, housekeeping, environmental services, linen, uniforms, and bell desk. As part of her internship, Stacy supervised shifts in PBX, housekeeping, environmental services, front desk, and valet. After her internship was completed, Stacy decided to accept full-time employment with the Showboat and assumed a position as kitchen manager in the casino's buffet operation. She supervised every aspect of food preparation and display in a 650-seat buffet room. After two years with Showboat, Stacy returned to Purdue and earned her bachelor of science degree.

Following graduation, Stacy decided to follow a career in gaming entertainment. Hired by the Sands Hotel and Casino in 1995 as assistant manager for room service and food court operations, Stacy was responsible for the day-to-day activities of a $5-million-per-year room service operation and a four-unit food court outlet. She was also part of the opening team for a state-of-the-art, Hollywood themed, 400-seat buffet operation.

In 1996, Stacy joined the opening team for the riverboat casino operations of Ameristar Casino in Council Bluffs, Iowa, as front office manager. She was responsible for the initial installation of property management hardware and software including call accounting, PBX, and all point-of-sale systems used throughout the hotel and food and beverage operations. Stacy developed standard operating procedures and hired and trained employees in a number of departments including PBX, reservations, guest services, valet, front desk, and gift shop departments.

Stacy moved to Las Vegas at the end of 1996 to take a position as guest service manager with Harrah's Entertainment Inc. flagship property on the strip in Las Vegas. She became responsible for managing front desk operations and front services, with specific attention to bell desk, valet, and limousines for the casino megaresort. Stacy had full responsibility for the redesign of new facilities in a major property renovation. She worked with architects and engineers to redesign the bell desk, baggage room, valet, Porte Cochere, and front desk areas. One of her tasks was to complete spec-out and purchase two limousines at a cost of $70,000 each.

Early in 1998, she was promoted to a hotel manager position at the Lake Tahoe Harrah's in Reno, Nevada. Stacy's career path is typical of a focused and energetic student of the industry who is willing to work hard and learn new responsibilities with each new position.

ing specialists. Finance and administration staff includes lawyers, accounts payable, audit, payroll, and income control specialists.[9]

While there was little organized dealer training as recently as a decade ago, the explosive growth of the gaming industry has increased the need for trained dealers skilled at working a variety of table games including **blackjack, craps, roulette, poker,** and **baccarat.** Now, through the use of textbooks and videotapes combined with hands-on training at a mock casino, future dealers learn the techniques and fine points of dealing at classes offered by both colleges and private schools.

[9]K. Hashimoto, S. Fried Kline, and G. G. Fenich, *Casino Management*. Dubuque, IA: Kendall/Hunt, 1995.

Retail Operations

The increased emphasis on nongaming sources of revenues in gaming entertainment business demands an expertise in all phases of retail operations, from store design and layout to product selection, merchandising, and sales control. Negotiating with concession subcontractors may also be a part of the overall retail activities. Retail operations often support the overall theme of the property and can often be a major source of revenue; however, retail management careers are often an overlooked career path in the gaming entertainment industry.

Entertainment Operations

Because of the increased competition, gaming entertainment companies are creating bigger and better production shows to turn their properties into destination attractions. Some production shows have climbed into the $30 to $40 million range and require professional entertainment staffs to produce and manage them. Gaming entertainment properties often present live entertainment of all sorts, with headline acts drawing huge audiences. For example, at the MGM Grand, there are three entertainment showcases. These include the 15,000-seat Grand Arena, used for professional boxing matches and for stars like Tina Turner; the smaller 1,700-seat theater that houses an elaborate production show called EFX; and a 700-seat theater that plays host to lesser stars like Tom Jones and Rodney Dangerfield.

As a result of this emphasis on entertainment, there exists career opportunities for those interested in stage and theater production, lighting and box office management, and talent management and booking.

Trends in the Gaming Entertainment Industry

- ✓ Gaming entertainment is depending less on casino revenue and more on room, food and beverage, retail, and entertainment revenue for its profitability and growth.
- ✓ The gaming entertainment industry and lodging industry are converging as hotel room inventory is rapidly expanding in gaming entertainment properties.
- ✓ Gaming entertainment, along with the gaming industry as a whole, will continue to be scrutinized by government and public policy makers as to the net economic and social impact of its activities.
- ✓ As the gaming entertainment industry becomes more competitive, exceptional service quality will become an increasingly important competitive advantage for success.
- ✓ The gaming entertainment industry will continue to provide management opportunities for careers in the hospitality business.

Case Study

VIP

A frequent guest of the casino makes a last-minute decision to travel to your property for a weekend stay. The guest enjoys gaming as a leisure activity and is one of the casino's better customers. When he arrives at the casino, he is usually met by a casino host and treated as a very important person due to his level of wagering at the blackjack tables. This guest is worth approximately $50,000 in casino win per year to the hotel. Due to his last-minute arrangements, however, the guest cannot notify a casino host that he is on his way to the hotel. Upon arriving, he finds a very busy registration desk. He must wait in line for twenty minutes, and when he tries to check in, he is told that the hotel is full. The front desk clerk acts impatient when the guest says that he is a frequent customer. In a fit of frustration, the would-be guest leaves the hotel and makes a mental note that all casinos have similar odds at the blackjack table and maybe another property will give him the respect he deserves.

Discussion Question

1. What systems, or procedures, could you institute to make sure this type of oversight does not happen in your property?

Case Study

Negotiating with Convention Groups

Your convention sales department receives a call from a trip director for a large convention group. The group will use many function rooms for meetings during the day and will generate a substantial amount of convention services revenue. Likewise, their food and beverage needs are quite elaborate and will be great for the food and beverage department budget. However, the group is very sensitive concerning room price and is willing to negotiate the time of week for their three-night stay.

Discussion Question

1. What are the considerations that a gaming entertainment property must take into account when determining room rates for convention groups?

Career Information

Gaming Industry

The multibillion dollar gaming entertainment industry is growing throughout the world. America will continue to see significant growth in the industry, but the extraordinary growth will occur internationally. Career opportunities will abound due to the gaming industry's growth, continuous operation, and labor-intensive nature.

Gaming entertainment offers careers in casino gambling, entertainment, foodservice, and lodging. Each area is an essential part of the gaming entertainment experience but it is important to remember that casinos still make the majority of their revenue from gambling! The other areas are designed to attract the customer and then keep them in the casino.

Management careers can be very different depending on your focus. If your interest is gaming management, it is important that you take courses in finance, law, human resources, management, and gambling. You also need to work in the gaming industry while in college, so that you can open doors for yourself through networking. Casinos still believe in promoting from within and so you will have to work your way up the corporate ladder. You also need to understand that because of the continuous operation of a casino your work schedule will vary. It is not uncommon to work several twelve-hour days straight, but the rewards for dedication and hard work can be very worthwhile. Casinos are exhilarating places where the rich and famous come to play and be entertained.

Related Web Sites

http://extranet.casinocareers.com/jobs/index.cfm —career bulletin board
http://www.casinoemployment.com/—employment bulletin board
http://www.parkplace.com/—gaming company information
http://www.mirage.com/—gaming company information
http://www.harrahs.com/—gaming company information and employment

Courtesy of Charlie Adams.

Summary

1. The casino industry has developed into a new business called gaming entertainment with the introduction of full-service hotels, retail, and entertainment offerings.
2. To operate gaming entertainment businesses, it is necessary to understand the relationship between the casino and other departments in the operation.
3. Gaming entertainment is strictly regulated by state governments, and the integrity developed over time by these regulations is necessary for the survival of the industry.
4. Nongaming revenue is increasing as a percentage of total revenue of gaming entertainment businesses.
5. Native American gaming entertainment businesses are a means for economic self-development by tribal people.

Key Words and Concepts

Baccarat	Drop entertainment	Indian Gaming Regulatory	Slot machine
Bet	Gaming entertainment	Act (IGRA)	Social gambler
Blackjack	Gambling	Poker	Wager
Casino	Handle	Roulette	Win
Craps			

Review Questions

1. Briefly describe the history of legalized gaming in the United States.
2. What defines a gaming entertainment business?
3. Explain the attraction of gaming entertainment to the destination of a tourist.

4. Why is it necessary for strict regulations to be in force on the casino floor?
5. How are hotel operations in a gaming entertainment business different from hotel operations in a nongaming environment?

Internet Exercises

1. Organization:
   Web site:
   Summary:
   (a) What are some of the gaming features that attract customers to the Las Vegas Hilton?
   (b) What does it mean to be a "Barron's club member" and what are the benefits to joining?

2. Organization:
   Web site:
   Summary:
   (a) How many gaming properties and brand names worldwide does Park Place Entertainment serve?
   (b) What are your views on the gaming industry in Nevada now that gaming is permitted on Native American reservations?

Las Vegas Hilton
http://www.lv-hilton.com
Located on the Las Vegas Strip, the Las Vegas Hilton has a lot to offer. From gaming and concerts, to hosting some of the biggest conventions, the Las Vegas Hilton will certainly keep you busy.

Park Place Entertainment
http://www.parkplace.com
Park Place Entertainment is one of the largest and most diversified gaming companies in the world. This site gives information on the company and the gaming business as a whole.

Apply Your Knowledge

1. Name the major gaming entertainment hotels in Las Vegas.

2. Give examples of nongaming revenue.

Meetings, Conventions, and Expositions

After reading and studying this chapter, you should be able to:

✓ Name the main hospitality industry associations.
✓ Describe the various types of meetings.
✓ Explain the difference between meetings, expositions, and conventions.
✓ Describe the role of a meeting planner.
✓ Explain the primary responsibilities of a convention and visitors bureau or authority.
✓ List the steps in event management.

Historical Review

People have gathered to attend meetings, conventions, and expositions since ancient times, mainly for social, sporting, political, or religious purposes. As cities became regional centers, the size and frequency of such activities increased, and various groups and associations set up regular expositions.

Associations go back many centuries to the Middle Ages and before. The guilds in Europe were created during the Middle Ages to secure proper wages and maintain work standards. Associations began in the United States at the beginning of the eighteenth century, when the Rhode Island candle makers organized themselves.

Today, according to the American Society of Association Executives (ASAE), in the United States with 23,000 members, about 6,000 associations operate at the national level, and a hundred thousand more function at the regional, state, and local levels. The association business is big business. Associations spend about $60.0 billion holding 315,000 meetings and conventions that attract approximately 32.6 million attendees (see Figure 12–1).

The hospitality and tourism industry itself consists of a number of associations, including the following:

- ✓ The American Hotel and Lodging Association
- ✓ The National Restaurant Association
- ✓ The International Association of Convention and Visitors Bureaus
- ✓ Hotel Sales and Marketing Association International
- ✓ Meeting Planners Association
- ✓ Association for Convention Operation Management
- ✓ Club Managers Association of America
- ✓ Professional Convention Management Association

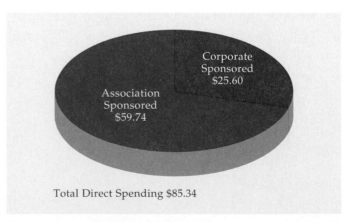

Figure 12–1 *The Conventions Market*

In reality, associations are the only independent political force for industries like hospitality, offering the following benefits:[1]

✓ Governmental/political voice
✓ Marketing avenues
✓ Education
✓ Member services
✓ Networking

Thousands of associations hold annual conventions at various locations across North America and the rest of the world. Some associations alternate their venues from east to central to west; others meet at fixed locations such as the National Restaurant Association (NRA) show in Chicago or the American Hotel and Motel Association (AH&MA) convention and show in New York.

As Figure 12–1 indicates, professional and trade associations hold 70 percent of the conventions market, which totals $75 billion a year.[2]

Types of Meetings

Meetings are conferences, workshops, seminars, or other events designed to bring people together for the purpose of exchanging information.[3] Meetings can take any one of the following forms:

Clinic: A workshop-type educational experience in which attendees learn by doing. A clinic usually involves small groups interacting with each other on an individual basis.

Forum: An assembly for the discussion of common concerns. Usually experts in a given field take opposite sides of an issue in a panel discussion, with liberal opportunity for audience participation.

Seminar: A lecture and a dialogue that allow participants to share experiences in a particular field. A seminar is guided by an expert discussion leader, and usually thirty or fewer persons participate.

Symposium: An event at which a particular subject is discussed by experts and opinions are gathered.

Workshop: A small group led by a facilitator or trainer. It generally includes exercises to enhance skills or develop knowledge in a specific topic.

Meetings are mostly organized by corporations; associations; or social, military, educational, religious, and fraternal groups (**SMERF**). The reasons for having a meeting can range from the presentation of a new sales plan to a total

---

[1]John Hogan, *Lodging*, December 1993.

[2]From Deloitte and Touche, Convention Liaison Council, as quoted in *USA Today*, April 5, 1994.

[3]Rhonda J. Montgomery and Sandra K. Strick, *Meetings, Conventions, and Expositions: An Introduction to the Industry.* New York: Van Nostrand Reinhold, 1995, p. 13.

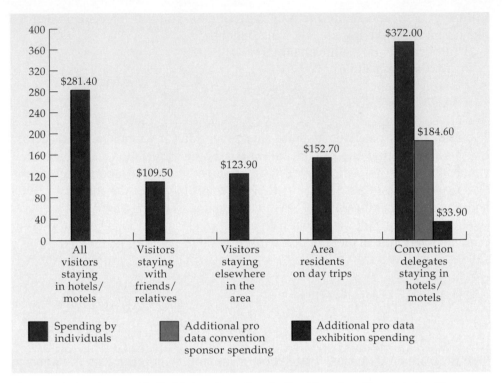

Figure 12–2 *Average Daily Visitor Spending in San Francisco* (Reprinted with permission from the San Francisco Convention Center Corporation.)

quality management workshop. The purpose of meetings is to affect behavior. For example, as a result of attending a meeting, a person should know or be able to do certain things. Some outcomes are very specific; others may be less so. For instance, if a meeting were called to brainstorm new ideas, the outcome might be less concrete than for other types of meetings. The number of people attending a meeting can vary.

Successful meetings require a great deal of careful planning and organization. In San Francisco, a major convention city, convention delegates spend approximately $400 per day,[4] almost twice that of vacation travelers. Figure 12–2 shows convention delegates' spending in San Francisco.

Meetings are set up according to the wishes of the client. The three main types of meeting setups are **theater style, classroom style,** and **boardroom style.** Theater style generally is intended for a large audience that does not need to make a lot of notes or refer to documents. This style usually consists of a raised platform and a lectern from which a presenter addresses the audience. Classroom setups are used when the meeting format is more instructional and participants need to take detailed notes or refer to documents. A workshop-type meeting often uses this format. Boardroom setups are made for small numbers of people. The meeting takes place around one block rectangular table.

---

[4]Wendy Tanaka, "Convention Attendees Spend More," *San Francisco Examiner,* August 28, 1994, p. B2. Updated February 28, 2001.

Expositions are events designed to bring together purveyors of products, equipment, and services in an environment in which they can demonstrate their products and services to a group of attendees at a convention or trade show.[5] Exhibitors are an essential component of the industry because they pay to exhibit their products to the attendees. Exhibitors interact with attendees with the intention of making sales or establishing contacts and leads for follow-up. Expositions can take up several hundred thousand square feet of space, divided into booths for individual manufacturers or their representatives. In the hospitality industry, the two largest expositions are the AH&MA's annual New York show (held in November at the Javits Center) and the NRA's Annual Exposition held every May in Chicago. Both events are well worth attending.

Conventions are generally larger meetings with some form of exposition or trade show included. A number of associations have one or more conventions per year. These conventions raise a large part of the association's budget. A typical convention follows a format like this:

✓ Welcome/registration
✓ Introduction of president
✓ President's welcome speech, opening the convention
✓ First keynote address by a featured speaker
✓ Exposition booths open (equipment manufacturers and trade suppliers)
✓ Several workshops or presentations on specific topics
✓ Luncheon
✓ More workshops and presentations
✓ Demonstrations of special topics (e.g., culinary arts for a hospitality convention)
✓ Vendors' private receptions
✓ Dinner
✓ Convention center closes

Figure 12–3 shows a convention event profile for a trade show.

NRA Show (Courtesy National Restaurant Association.)

[5]Deny G. Rutherford, *Introduction to the Conventions, Expositions, and Meeting Industry.* New York: Van Nostrand Reinhold, 1990, p. 44.

16:15:28

San Diego
Convention Center Corporation
EVENT PROFILE

Page: 1
9506059

EVENT STATISTICS

Event Name:	/6/San Diego Apartment Association Trade Show	ID:	9506059
Sales Person:	Joy Peacock	Initial Contact:	8/3/1999
Event Manager:	Trish A. Stiles	Move In Date:	6/22/2001
ConVis Contact:		Move In Day:	Thursday
Food Person:		Move In Time:	6:01 am
Event Tech.:		First Event Date:	6/23/2001
Event Attend.:		First Event Day:	Friday
Nature of Event:	LT Local Trade Show	Start Show Time:	6:01 am
Event Parameter:	60 San Diego Convention Center	End Show Time:	11:59 pm
Business Type 1:	41 Association	# of Event Days:	1
Business Type 2:	91 LOCAL	Move Out Date:	6/23/2001
Booking Status:	D Definite	Move Out Day:	Friday
Rate Schedule:	III Public Show, Meetings and Location	Out Time:	11:59 pm
Open to Public:	No	Date Confirmed:	8/3/2000
Number Sessions:	1	Attend per Sesn:	3000
Event Sold By:	F Facility (SDCCC)	Tot Room Nights:	15
Abbrev. Name:	/6/Apartment Assn	Public Release:	Yes
Est Bill Amount:	Rent - 6,060.00 Equip –	0.00 Food –	0.00
Last Changed On:	8/20/00 in: Comment Maintenance	By – Joy Peacock	

This Event has been in the facility before

CLIENT INFORMATION

Company: San Diego Apartment Assn, a non-profit Corporation
    Contact Name: Ms. Leslie Cloud, Sales and Marketing Coord.
                 1011 Camino Del Rio South, Suite 200, San Diego, CA 92108   ID: SDAA
                 Telephone Number: (619) 297-1000
                      Fax Number: (619) 294-4510
           Alternate Number: (619) 294-4510

Company: San Diego Apartment Assn, a non-profit Corporation
    Alt Contact Name: Ms. Pamela A. Trimble, Finance & Operations Director
                 1011 Camino Del Rio South, Suite 200, San Diego, 92108
                 Telephone Number: (619) 297-1000
                      Fax Number: (619) 297-4510

EVENT LOCATIONS

ROOM	MOVE IN	IN USE	ED	MOVE OUT	BS	SEAT	RATE	EST. RENT	ATTEND
A	6/22/01 6:01 am	6/23/01	1	6/23/01 11:59 pm	D	E	III	6,060.00	5000
AS	6/22/01 6:01 am	6/23/01	1	6/23/01 11:59 pm	D	E	III	0.00	10
R01	6/22/01 6:01 am	6/23/01	1	6/23/01 11:59 pm	D	T	III	0.00	450
R02	6/22/01 6:01 am	6/23/01	1	6/23/01 11:59 pm	D	T	III	0.00	350
R03	6/22/01 6:01 am	6/23/01	1	6/23/01 11:59 pm	D	T	III	0.00	280
R04	6/22/01 6:01 am	6/23/01	1	6/23/01 11:59 pm	D	T	III	0.00	280
R05	6/22/01 6:01 am	6/23/01	1	6/23/01 11:59 pm	D	T	III	0.00	460

FOOD SERVICES

ROOM	DATE	TIME	BS ATTEND	EST. COST FOOD SERVICE

There are No Food Services booked for this event

Figure 12–3   *Convention Program* (Courtesy San Diego Convention Center.)

San Diego
Convention Center Corporation
EVENT PROFILE

EVENT EQUIPMENT/SERVICES

ROOM	MOVE IN	IN USE	ED MOVE OUT	QUANTITY EQUIPMENT

There is No Equipment booked for this event

FOLLOW-UP/CHECKLIST ITEMS

FOLLOW-UP	DATE	ITEM	COMPLETED DATE	ASSIGN TO
	9/26/01	C DUE/date contracted		Vincent R. Magana
	8/22/01	c from sales	8/23/01	Sonia Michel
	8/22/01	c to licensee	8/23/01	Sonia Michel
	8/22/01	date c 1st printed	8/22/01	Sonia Michel

EVENT COMMENTS

8/3/01–JMP–This is a very strong hold for this group. CAD is pursuing a release of Hall A from Group Health and then this will be confirmed on a first option. Also holding an alternate date in April until this is released. All other rooms are clear.

200 BOOTHS – have used Carden in the past.
This is a trade show for the Apartment industry — products and services needed to keep a rental property in shape. Use Rooms 1–5 as seminar rooms. Trish has been the Event Coordinator for 2000 – 01.

8/18/01 - JMP-CAD has been able to clear Hall A on a first option for move-in on 22nd from Group Health. Made definite and requested Sonia produce a contract. NOTE TO SONIA: Contract should be signed and mailed to alternate contact Pam Trimble. Meeting logistics only will go through Leslie. Note to housekeeping: we did the cleaning for the 2001 show.

LICENSE AGREEMENT REQUEST

EVENT COMMENTS

Requested:	Saturday, 08/20/01, 2:56 pm
License #:	9506059
Sales Person:	JMP
Nature of Event:	Local Trade
Full Legal Name of Licensee:	Yes
Insurance Y/N:	Yes
Deposit Schedule:	50-50
Special Arrangements or Directions:	Contract should be signed and sent to alternate contact Pam Trimble. Leslie is responsible for meeting logistics only.
Gross Revenues F/B Revenue:	$1000 concessions
In House A/V Revenue:	$600
Security Revenue:	$200
Telecom. Revenue:	$220

(Below, identify MI/MO or event days and attendance for each event).
Other business in Center: GROUP HEALTH, definite, Hall B-1 (m/o 22nd), 3000ppl; ALCOHOLICS ANON, definite, Hall B, move-in; SECURITY EXPO, tentative, Hall C (m/i 22nd, show 23rd), 6600ppl; ENTRP. EXPO, contracted, Ballroom (m/i 23rd), 2000ppl.

Figure 12–3 *(continued)*

Conventions are not always held in convention centers; in fact, the majority are held in large hotels over a three-to five-day period. The headquarters hotel is usually the one in which most of the activity takes place. Function space is allocated for registration, the convention, expositions, meals, and so on.

Associations used to be viewed as groups that held annual meetings and conventions with speeches, entertainment, an educational program, and social events. They have changed in activity and perception.

Meetings, Incentives, Conventions, and Exhibitions

Courtesy of Karen Smith, Claudia Green, and Andrea Sigler

Meetings, incentive travel, conventions, and exhibitions (MICE) represent a segment of the tourism industry that has grown dramatically in recent years. Gone are the days when a meeting planner's activities centered around organizing a wedding or an annual corporate dinner. Meeting planners in the twenty-first century are required to have strong business and organizational skills to plan detail-driven, high-visibility events.

The MICE segment of the tourism industry can be especially lucrative. Industry statistics point to the fact that the average MICE tourist spends over twice the amount of money of other tourists.[6]

Increasingly meeting planners are under pressure to show a strong return on investment (ROI). This reflects a shift in this segment of the tourism industry to an important revenue source for organizations. Whether a meeting planner is organizing a meeting, a convention or exhibition, the primary sources of revenue are as follows:

✓ Attendee registration fees
✓ Exhibit space rentals
✓ Sponsorship fees
✓ Conference program advertising fees

The pricing strategy for organizing events varies. Considerations include whether it is a consumer event or a trade event. For example, when organizing an event in which a large public attendance is desired, it may be best to keep attendance fees low in an effort to attract the largest number of attendees. In that case, the meeting planners would attempt to attract corporate sponsors, exhibitors, or advertisers to make up the difference in revenue.

Several factors are evaluated when determining the site. Considerations include facility service level and perception; accessibility; hotel room availability; conference room availability; price; city; restaurant service and quality; personal safety; local interest and geographic location and hospitality.[7]

[6]Pierre Vitagliano, "How SITE Chose Singapore," Singapore Tourism Board, **48**, 8, August 1996, pp. 89–91.

[7]Bill Geist, "Bureau Websites 'Net' Clear Advantage in Marketing, Selling Destinations," *Convene*, **47**, 4, May 1, 1998, p. 43.

Meetings

Meetings are primarily conducted by either the corporate or nonprofit industries. Corporations in the medical, financial, and entertainment fields hold an extensive number of meetings—both for their employees and the public. Meetings are held primarily for the purposes of education, training, decision making, research, change, sales, team building, new product introduction, problem solving, strategy, or reorganization.

Meetings are often held as a marketing tool as well as a revenue source by associations, nonprofit entities, museums, performing arts organizations, and educational institutions. Estimates put association meeting expenditures collectively approaching $20 billion, while corporate expenditures are calculated to $12 billion.[8]Meetings are generally held in hotels, conference centers, universities, corporate offices, or resorts, but more and more we find meetings housed in unique venues such as historic sites. With today's executives spending anywhere from 25 to 70 percent of their days in meetings, it is no wonder that the meeting planning profession has become such a high-growth career.

Whether a meeting is held as an in-house training event for internal employees or is designed as a mega-meeting attracting high-level international delegates, the average lead time required for organizing a meeting is three to six months. An effective meeting plan begins with defining a specific meeting objective. This objective will serve as a framework for determining the various choices that need to be made in organizing a meeting. The public statement of a meeting objective may differ from the internally defined objective. For example, a nonprofit association could serve as host of a conference to provide the public with information on a specific subject. At the same time, this nonprofit entity may count on this conference as a major fund-raising source. Goals for meetings are developed by the need to:

- ✓ Increase awareness of a particular issue
- ✓ Raise money for an activity or organization
- ✓ Provide information to colleagues or clients

Increase Awareness

For associations and nonprofit entities, a frequent objective of meetings is to heighten awareness of the organization and gain public recognition and support.

Raise Money

If the goal is to raise money, most decisions regarding the meeting will be driven by that goal. Meeting planners are increasingly concerned with ROI in organizing meetings. This is true whether the planner works for a private corporation or a nonprofit organization.

---

[8]Peter Shure, "Associations: Often Misunderstood and Frequently Overlooked," *Convene*, **54**, 3, March 1, 2000.

Provide Information

In the information age, dissemination of information has become one of the major challenges in a changing, dynamic environment. Both public and private organizations are increasingly concerned with providing their employees with information on new products and services. This is a common motivation for meetings.

Incentives

Nearly half of all meeting planners are involved in organizing incentive travel.[9] The **incentive market** of MICE continues to experience rapid growth as meeting planners and travel agents organize incentive travel programs for corporate executives to reward them for reaching specific sales targets. Incentive trips generally vary from three to six days in length, and can range from a moderate trip to an extremely lavish vacation for the employee and spouse. The most popular destination for incentive trips is Europe, followed closely by the Caribbean and Hawaii.[10]

Conventions

Conventions are annual gatherings of a group of individuals, with no limit of numbers, who meet for a common interest. Conventions can vary from 75 people who meet on an annual basis to exchange information on a specific topic such as collecting antique pottery, to the more than 50,000 individuals who annually gather at the Southern Baptist Convention.

Most conventions are housed in hotels, but conventions with the largest attendance are frequently held in city convention centers. Today conventions generally include an exhibition component, although it is not mandatory that they do so.

Exhibitions

Just as meetings and conventions may be housed in a variety of types of venues, so may exhibitions. Large, state-of-the-art exhibitions are found at convention centers, but exhibition space may also be provided by large "convention" hotels as well as universities.

An exhibition may simply be a few table-top booths designed to display goods and services or an exhibition can be an elaborate, hallmark event such as the biannual Paris Air Show or Comdex. Comdex is the largest U.S. exhibition and is held annually in Las Vegas to showcase new computer products and services.

Today's exhibitions frequently include live demonstrations and seminars in addition to exhibit booths. **Convention centers** throughout the world compete to host the largest exhibitions, which can be responsible for adding several million dollars in revenue to the local economy. As a result of this intense com-

---

[9]Christina Lovio-George, "Loyalty: Relationships Boost Travel," *Business Marketing*, **80**, 5, May 2000, pp. 37–39.

[10]Ibid.

petition for housing of the most visible events, convention centers are under intense pressure to provide state-of-the-art technology, equipment, and service to exhibitors and meeting planners.

Typically, exhibitions are either **consumer shows** or **trade shows.** Consumer shows such as a Boat Show or Auto Show are open to the general public. On the other hand, a trade show such as the Gift Show is available only to people employed by retail establishments selling gift items. Attendance at trade show events requires precertification and registration to participate.

Forecast

The advent of technology and the Internet has dramatically affected the way tourism information is obtained for this business sector. Data is now available on virtually every aspect of business—from finance and investment to lifestyles and entertainment. The demand for this information has driven the increase in the numbers of meetings, conventions, and exhibitions.

While it was expected that information provided through technology would diminish the number of "live" or "face-to-face" meetings, the opposite has been the practice. In fact, the need for establishing personal contact has become more pronounced.

The nature of delivering meetings, however, has been impacted by technology in that data is now available in real time, via teleconferencing and satellite conferences. Another way that technology has influenced the delivery of meetings is from the perspective of the audience member who increasingly expects a presentation to include illuminating, visual data.

New technology continues to drive changes in the industry. Planners utilize technology as a means of producing meetings more efficiently. Many organizational tasks are routinely managed by technology such as attendee registration, marketing, travel and housing, as well as delivering program proceedings. Other changes to appear during the next two years include the planning of more international meetings, increased family attendance at meetings, heightened security measures for attendees, shorter meetings due to financial constraints, more targeted, focused meetings, and testing the loyalty of attendees.[11]

Special Events and Off-Premise Catering
Courtesy of Kathleen A. Doeller

The **special events** facet of the hospitality industry is the business of conceiving, designing, developing and producing ideas. Likewise, it is the business of details, timing, logistics, spacial mechanics, and organization. Typically, it includes teamwork and a dependence on vendor relationships. It also requires patience, flexibility, clear communication via written documents, and excellent listening and speaking skills. A sense of humor goes a long way also.

---

[11]MPI/ASAE Meetings Outlook Survey.

What is considered a special event? Special events come in many different sizes and markets:

Sporting events: golf tournaments, football tournaments, baseball tournaments, tennis tournaments, car races, balloon races

Festivals: arts and crafts and music

Corporate: incentive programs, grand openings, anniversaries, product launches

Convention: Spouse programs, incentive programs, sailing regattas, receptions and dinners, awards programs, team building

Social: birthdays, weddings, bar/bat mitzvahs, anniversaries, themed events, and just because

A special event incorporates the services of many vendors and suppliers. A special event organizer, producer, or coordinator will call on any one or several of the following services: florists, design and production houses, prop companies, transportation companies (buses and limousine, valet, or parking directors), bar catering services, rental companies, audiovisual experts, game and activity companies, entertainment agencies, printers and stationers, and temporary staffing agencies.

It is the **off-premise catering** consultant or special event consultant that conceives, develops, and expedites a vision. The vision takes on a life of its own via a theme that runs throughout the large picture of an event. The large picture includes the total ambiance: colors, fabrics and textiles, sizes and shapes (down to the type of dining chair), music and entertainment, functional and atmospheric lighting, and, of course, great food served graciously and expediently.

Catering—whether it is provided by a hotel, restaurant or off-premise caterer—is central to the success of a special event. Quality, quantity, and timing are the key ingredients to the success of the food service. All of the creativity and magnificence of an event may soon be forgotten if the execution of food service is less than excellent. Excellent catering requires a well-organized team that is able to anticipate the needs of the guests.

Know Your Client

An expert catering consultant will solicit information from the meeting planner in order to provide and satisfy the specific needs of a group. Significant information required to build a successful event includes, but is not limited to, the following:

- ✓ Group demographics: gender mix, age, profession, regional location, religious doctrine
- ✓ Conference/convention purpose
- ✓ Event date in relation to the rest of the meeting program
- ✓ Dietary preferences, restrictions, and special requests
- ✓ Meal and menu program for entire convention
- ✓ Past events held by the group

✓ Expected attendance number
✓ Event budget

All of the aforementioned are of equal importance, however, the budget carries the most weight. Knowing the budget before you go to the drawing board provides the consultant with the parameters by which you can design an event. The proposal process is now ready to begin.

The Special Event Job Market

Becoming a special event consultant or an off-premise catering/event specialist requires a delicate balance of many skills. Experience gained from several avenues will propel you to the heights of success. As with any career, an "experience ladder" must be climbed.

First, allow yourself to gain all the experience you can in the food and beverage aspect of the hospitality industry. If time and resources permit, it is highly recommended that you gain knowledge from a culinary arts program. Second, experience gained as a banquet food server in a high-volume convention or resort hotel property is invaluable. Also, paying your dues as a guest service agent at a hotel front desk or as a concierge provides you with the opportunity to hone your customer service skills. Promote yourself to a banquet manager or a CSM (convention service coordinator), which provides the opportunity to learn and perfect organizational skills—to which end is the ability to multitask and deal with hundreds of details simultaneously. After all, the business of special events is the business of managing details.

The next step is obtaining a sales position. An excellent appointment to aspire to is an executive meeting manager, sometimes called a small meeting manager, in a convention or conference hotel. Here, you are responsible for booking small room blocks (usually twenty rooms or less), making meeting room arrangements, meal plans, and audiovisual requirements. On a small scale, hundreds of details are coordinated for several groups at any one time. From this position, you may laterally move to a catering sales position within a hotel.

The catering sales position in a hotel will expose you to many different kinds of events: weddings, reunions, corporate events, holiday events, and social galas and balls. In this position, one either coordinates or has the opportunity to work with various vendors. This is where the florists, prop companies, lighting experts, entertainment agencies, rental companies, and audiovisual wizards come into play. Two to three years in this capacity grooms you for the next rung on the ladder.

Now, you can pursue several different angles: a promotion to a convention service manager within a hotel, moving into off-premise catering as a sales consultant, joining a production company, or perhaps affiliating yourself with a destination management company (DMC). Typically, without sales experience within a DMC, your first experience with them will be as an operations manager. Once proficient in this capacity, you then join the sales team.

Personal Profile: Carol C. Wallace

President and CEO, San Diego Convention Center Corporation

Carol Wallace was destined to be in charge from the time she was twelve years old. One of four children who grew up in a single-parent household, she was called upon at an early age to help out. Her mother, who finished high school only after her own children were grown, influenced her life tremendously. Often, she and her mother would sit down and talk about plans for the family's future, setting the stage for the rest of her life.

Carol adopted her mother's tough-love philosophy that "crying won't get me what I need, but hard work will." She earned a degree in English from Ohio State University in 1974. She married while in college and gave birth to two children. She would later divorce, becoming a single mother herself for several years.

Fresh out of college and eager to prove herself, she accepted a position with the Ohio Lung Association. During that time she had an opportunity to travel to Dallas, Texas, and loved the city so much that she moved there with her children. She immediately found an entry-level position with the Dallas Convention Center as an event manager. It took her less than a decade to rise through the ranks from event manager to the number two position, assistant general manager.

Just when it seemed as if she could go no further, the Denver Convention Center contacted her about a planned convention center expansion and offered her the number one position. This offer came as no surprise to those who knew Carol. By now, her reputation for being a leader and visionary was growing among industry movers and shakers.

In 1989, she moved her family to Denver and accepted the position as Executive Director of the Colorado Convention Center, then under construction. She joined the construction team, developed a management program, hired staff, and successfully opened the 960,000-square-foot facility in 1990.

Dallas and Denver proved to be the critical stepping stones that would lead Carol to her present position as President and CEO of the San Diego Convention Center Corporation. In 1991, San Diego city officials approached her with an offer to head up the San Diego Convention Center and an expansion that would double the size of the existing facility. She accepted the job and credits her successful career with her love of the industry and a willingness to take risks.

Since 1991, she has worked at the San Diego Convention Center Corporation and is responsible for a $27.7 million budget and overseeing three facilities: the world-class San Diego Convention Center, San Diego Concourse, and San Diego Civic Theater.

Under her leadership, the San Diego Convention Center opened a $216 million expansion in September 2001. The highly successful facility has twice been named one of the top three convention facilities in the world. It is also one of San Diego's most powerful engines, generating $4.5 million in economic impact, and $24.8 million in operating revenues annually.

As the Corporation's president and CEO, Carol exudes confidence as a leader and sets high expectations for herself—she's not afraid of hard work. As someone who worked her way to the top from the bottom, she enjoys working hard in an industry that she loves.

Carol is active in a variety of industry groups. She is the past president of the International Association of Assembly Managers. Recently she was selected as one of nine industry commissioners for the Accepted Practices Exchange Commission. She currently holds a board position for the International Association for Exhibition Management. Other professional affiliations include the Professional Convention Management Association, the American Society of Association Executives, and the International Convention Center Association.

Carol is the recipient of numerous awards. In October 2000, she received The Manpower Balance Award at the Women Who Mean Business Awards Dinner, making her the first woman in the convention industry to receive this recognition for her commitment to her family, community, and profession.

She serves on the board of directors for Alliant International University, San Diego and Narobi, Africa; the San Diego Hotel-Motel Association; the San Diego Convention and Visitors Bureau; the San Diego Rotary Club; and the San Diego Chamber of Commerce.

After another two years creating and selling your heart out, you will be ready for the big leagues. The palette is now yours to paint your future. How about aspiring to be the next Super Bowl halftime creator and producer? Or, perhaps creating the theme and schematics for the Olympics is in your future. Many avenues are available for exploring. Call on your marketing ideas, your business sense, your accounting skills, your aptitude for design, or your discriminating palette for creating unique entertaining and dining concepts. Continually educating yourself and discovering fresh ideas through adventurous experiences is essential to designing and selling special events. Don't forget to embark on as many internships as you can in the name of gaining knowledge and experience. Show your enthusiasm for what is different and unconventional. Know that creativity has no boundaries. Visualize the big picture and go for it!

Key Players in the Industry

The need to hold face-to-face meetings and attend conventions has grown into a multibillion dollar industry. Many major and some smaller cities have convention centers with nearby hotels and restaurants.

The major players in the convention industry are **convention and visitors bureau**(CVBs) meeting planners and their clients, the convention centers, specialized services, and exhibitions. The wheel diagram in Figure 12–4 shows the number of different people and organizations involved with meetings, conventions, and expositions.

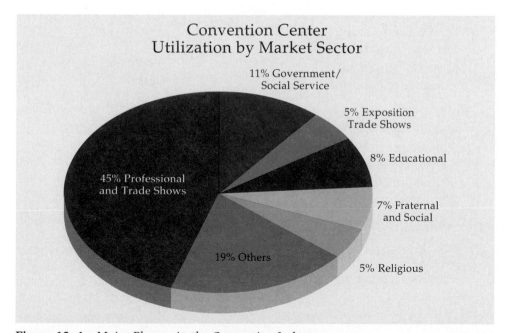

Figure 12–4   *Major Players in the Convention Industry*

Meeting Planners

Meeting planners may be independent contractors who contract out their services to both associations and corporations as the need arises or they may be full-time employees of corporations or associations. In either case, meeting planners have interesting careers. According to the International Convention Management Association (ICMA), about 212,000 full- and part-time meeting planners work in the United States.

The professional meeting planner not only makes hotel and meeting bookings but also plans the meeting down to the last minute, always remembering to check to ensure that the services contracted for have been delivered. In recent years, the technical aspects of audiovisual and simultaneous translation equipment have added to the complexity of meeting planning.

The meeting planner's role varies from meeting to meeting, but may include some or all of the following activities:[12]

Premeeting Activities

- ✓ Plan meeting agenda
- ✓ Establish meeting objectives
- ✓ Predict attendance
- ✓ Set meeting budget
- ✓ Select meeting site
- ✓ Select meeting facility
- ✓ Select hotel(s)
- ✓ Negotiate contracts
- ✓ Plan exhibition
- ✓ Prepare exhibitor correspondence and packet
- ✓ Create marketing plan
- ✓ Plan travel to and from site
- ✓ Arrange ground transportation
- ✓ Organize shipping
- ✓ Organize audiovisual needs

On-Site Activities

- ✓ Conduct pre-event briefing
- ✓ Prepare executive plan
- ✓ Move people in/out
- ✓ Troubleshoot
- ✓ Approve invoices

Postmeeting Activities

- ✓ Debrief
- ✓ Evaluate
- ✓ Provide recognition and appreciation

[12]Montgomery and Strick, op. cit., pp. 171–172.

*Meeting Planner at Site
Inspection*
(Courtesy John R. Walker.)

✓ Arrange shipping
✓ Plan for next year

The meeting planner has several critical interactions with hotels, including negotiating the room blocks and rates. Escorting clients on **site inspections** gives the hotel an opportunity to show their level of facilities and service. The most important interaction is normally with the catering/banquet/conference department associates; especially the services manager, maître d', and captains; these frontline associates can make or break a meeting. For example, meeting planners often send boxes of meeting materials to hotels expecting the hotel to automatically know which meeting they are for. On more than one occasion, they have ended up in the hotel's main storeroom, much to the consternation of the meeting planner.

Fortunately for most meeting planners, once they have taken care of a meeting one year, subsequent years typically are very similar.

Convention centers and hotels provide meeting space and accommodations as well as food and beverage facilities and service. The convention center and a hotel team from each hotel capable of handling the meeting will attempt to impress the meeting planner. The hotel sales executive will send particulars of the hotel's meeting space and a selection of banquet menus and invite the meeting planner for a site inspection. During the site inspection, the meeting planner is shown all facets of the hotel, including the meeting rooms, guest-sleeping rooms, the food and beverage outlets, and any special facility that may interest the planner or the client.

Convention and Visitors Bureaus

Convention and visitors bureaus (CVBs) are a major player in the meetings, conventions, and expositions market. The International Association of Conventions and Visitors Bureaus (IACVB) describes a CVB as a not-for-profit umbrella organization that represents an urban area that tries to solicit business- or pleasure-seeking visitors.

The convention and visitors bureau comprises a number of visitor industry organizations representing the various industry sectors:

✓ Transportation
✓ Hotels and motels
✓ Restaurants
✓ Attractions
✓ Suppliers

The bureau represents these local businesses by acting as the sales team for the city. A bureau has four primary responsibilities:

1. To encourage groups to hold meetings, conventions, and trade shows in the area it represents
2. To assist those groups with meeting preparations and to lend support throughout the meeting
3. To encourage tourists to partake of the historic, cultural, and recreational opportunities the city or area has to offer
4. To develop and promote the image of the community it represents[13]

The outcome of these four responsibilities is for the cities' tourist industry to increase revenues. Bureaus compete for business at trade shows, where interested visitor industry groups gather to do business. For example, a tour wholesaler who is promoting a tour will need to link up with hotels, restaurants, and attractions in order to package a vacation. Similarly, meeting planners are able to consider several locations and hotels by visiting a trade show. Bureaus generate leads (prospective clients) from a variety of sources. One source, associations, have national/international offices in major cities like Washington, D.C. (so that they can lobby the government), New York, Chicago, and San Francisco.

A number of bureaus have offices or representatives in these cities or a sales team who will make follow-up visits to the leads generated at trade shows. Alternatively, they will make cold calls on potential prospects such as major associations, corporations, and incentive houses. The sales manager will invite the meeting, convention, or exposition organizer to make a **familiarization (FAM) trip** to do a site inspection. The bureau assesses the needs of the client and organizes transportation, hotel accommodations, restaurants, and attractions accordingly. The bureau then lets the individual properties and other organizations make their own proposals to the client. Figure 12–5 shows the average expenditure per delegate per stay by the convention type; Figure 12–6 shows the breakdown of delegate expenditures per stay; and Figure 12–7 indicates the percentage of each item of expenditure.

---

[13]Montgomery and Strick, op. cit., p. 19.

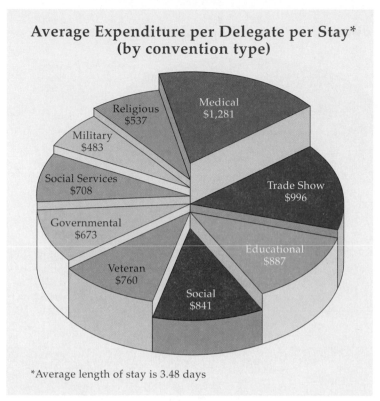

Average Expenditure per Delegate per Stay*
(by convention type)

Medical
$1,281

Religious
$537

Military
$483

Social Services
$708

Governmental
$673

Trade Show
$996

Educational
$887

Veteran
$760

Social
$841

*Average length of stay is 3.48 days

Figure 12–5 *Average Expenditure per Delegate per Stay* (Adapted from and reprinted with permission from *Hotel and Motel Management*, **209**, 3, February 22, 1994, updated February 28, 2001, p. 6. Copyright by Advanstar Communications, Inc.)

Jacob K. Javits Convention Center in New York City (Courtesy John R. Walker.)

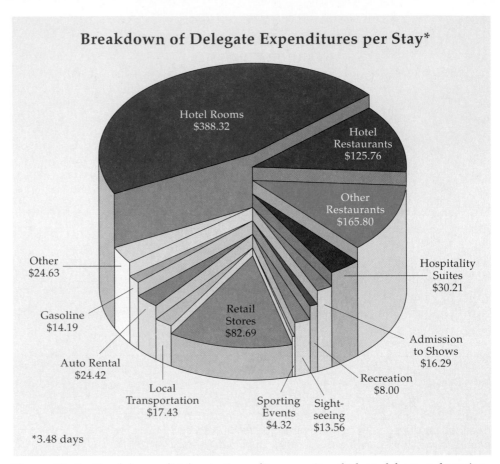

Figure 12–6 *Breakdown of Delegate Expenditure per Stay* (Adapted from and reprinted with permission from *Hotel and Motel Management*, **209**, 3, February 22, 1994, updated February 28, 2001, p. 6. Copyright by Advanstar Communications, Inc.)

Convention Centers

Convention centers are huge facilities where meetings and expositions are held. Parking, information services, business centers, and food and beverage facilities are all included in the centers.

Usually convention centers are corporations owned by county, city, or state governments and operated by a board of appointed representatives from the various groups having a vested interest in the successful operation of the center. The board appoints a president or general manager to run the center according to a predetermined mission, and goals and objectives.

Convention centers have a variety of exposition and meeting rooms to accommodate both large and small events. The centers generate revenue from the rental of space, which frequently is divided into booths (one booth is about 100 square feet). Large exhibits may take several booths' space. Additional revenue is generated by the sale of food and beverages, concession stand rentals, and vending machines. Many centers also have their own subcontractors to handle staging, construction, lighting, audiovisual, electrical, and communications.

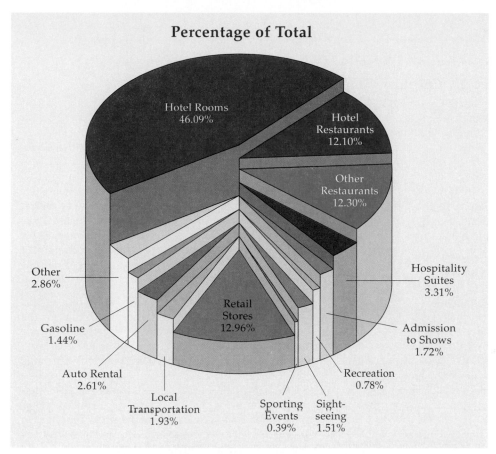

Percentage of Total

Hotel Rooms
46.09%

Hotel
Restaurants
12.10%

Other
Restaurants
12.30%

Other
2.86%

Hospitality
Suites
3.31%

Retail
Stores
12.96%

Gasoline
1.44%

Admission
to Shows
1.72%

Auto Rental
2.61%

Recreation
0.78%

Local
Transportation
1.93%

Sporting
Events
0.39%

Sight-
seeing
1.51%

Figure 12–7 *Percentage of Delegate Expenditure per Item* (Adapted from and reprinted with permission from *Hotel and Motel Management,* **209**, 3, February 22, 1994, updated February 28, 2001, p. 6. Copyright by Advanstar Communications, Inc.)

In addition to the megaconvention centers, a number of prominent centers also contribute to the local, state, and national economies. One good example is the Rhode Island Convention Center. The $82-million center, representing the second largest public works project in the state's history, is located in the heart of downtown Providence, adjacent to the 14,500-seat Providence Civic Center. The 365,000-square foot center offers a 100,000-square-foot main exhibit hall, a 20,000-square-foot ballroom, eighteen meeting rooms, and a full-service kitchen that can produce 5,000 meals per day. The exhibit hall divides into four separate halls, and the facility features its own telephone system, allowing individualized billing. A special rotunda function room at the front of the building features glass walls that offer a panoramic view of downtown Providence for receptions of up to 365 people. Extensive use of glass on the facade of the center provides ample natural light throughout the entrance and prefunction areas.

A convention center can draw millions of new dollars into the economy of the city in which it is located. Figure 12–8 shows the average center income from delegate spending at conventions, trade shows, and congresses held at

A Day in the Life of Kathleen Doeller

Director of Marketing, Culinary Concepts, San Diego, CA.

Every day is different, but much is the same. I do have routine operations and sales meetings two mornings per week at 7:30 A.M. On the other days, after returning from the gym, I meditate for thirty minutes and review my daily appointment calendar. I dress according to the day's schedule of appointments and events. Unfortunately, the San Diego freeways are jammed early, so with a jumbo mug of java in hand, I'm out the door without any delay.

On arriving in the office—whatever the time of day—I make my rounds and greet all my team members in the warehouse, the kitchen, and the office. I check in with my assistant (she starts her day at 7 A.M.) and inquire as to the status of the day's activities. I then retreat to my office, shut the door, check my voice-mail (yes, clients and employees do leave messages at all hours of the night), check my e-mail, and then review my To Do list. Another cup of coffee, and I'm ready to attack the day.

I process anywhere from one to five creative proposals per day. It takes an immense amount of brain juice to cre-atively customize themes, schemes, and details for various clients. And, in this day of technology, everybody wants it *now!* I do have an open-door policy, which sometimes gets construed as "come on in anytime." Needless to say, interruptions do occur. In addition to responding to inquiries and requests for proposals, a schedule of follow-up calls is made in an attempt to close a sale. Plus, vendor purchases and operational details are worked out on those accounts that have gone definite (i.e., the sale has closed).

As well as wearing a "sales consultant's hat," I also handle the marketing for the company I work for. Therefore, in the course of a day, I write and process press releases, write the text for our web page, schedule and coordinate trade shows, attend trade association meetings, serve on committees, participate on educational panels, counsel personnel, draw event diagrams, and meet with vendors/suppliers for walk-throughs at venue sites. Typically, in the course of a week, I meet with two or three meeting planners who are in town for site inspections.

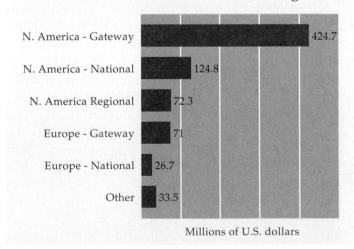

Conventions, Trade Shows, and Congresses

Category	Millions of U.S. dollars
N. America - Gateway	424.7
N. America - National	124.8
N. America Regional	72.3
Europe - Gateway	71
Europe - National	26.7
Other	33.5

Millions of U.S. dollars

Figure 12–8   *Average Convention Center Income from Delegate Spending* (Courtesy San Diego Convention Center.)

On the days that I have events, I am on the event site three to four hours before start time. I meet the rental company, the design and decor company, and florist to review diagrams and check inventories. Once the catering captain and his or her staff arrives, I pass the baton to them. I am on site until the guests arrive and food service commences. This means I am on my way to another event or headed for home around 8 or 9 P.M.

I am also the hospitality chairperson for the San Diego Meeting Planners International chapter. My committee and I have designed and implemented a buddy–mentor system for our members. Our committee meets once a month in addition to our regular monthly chapter meeting. We also communicate with each other regularly via e-mail and phone. In the course of a day, I give some kind of attention to this responsibility.

Being organized and a guru of time management allows me to also devote time and energy as an adjunct professor at the United States International University. I teach Convention Sales and Services during the fall term. Education is a passion of mine, and I believe strongly in the foundation of education as preparation for the business world. It gives me great joy to be a part of the hospitality degree program here. I appreciate the opportunity to learn about all the different countries and cultures represented by the students in my class. Just as students have homework and outside classroom projects, so does the professor! Lesson preparation, lining up guest speakers and hotel site visits, and grading papers are all done in the late evening or early mornings.

The common denominator in my life is *balance*. Balance requires an ever present state of mind, and I do actually schedule quiet time and self-time. I do my meditation in my beautiful garden, I exercise regularly, and I treat myself to dining experiences at new restaurants with friends and family. Random get-a-ways are also important to renew my spirit, mind, and body. A change of scenery is good for everyone, in my opinion. Jaunts to the cool pines in the mountains as well as experiencing cosmopolitan cities refresh all of my senses. The world has so much to offer and experience, if only I could see and do it all!

I have learned that the course a life takes is based on choices. Responsibility is always attached to a choice. Knowing that and accepting the responsibility—and the outcome of the choice—are the growing and learning steps of life. Blending responsibilities with pleasure, spirituality, family, and friends, and proceeding by keeping one's values and ethics in check will yield balance and a zest for great things in one's life. I mix and blend this recipe every day . . . knowing that it works . . . knowing that it keeps me strong . . . knowing that it is all in the course of a day.

North American gateway cities, North American national/regional cities, European gateway cities, European national cities, and other cities.

Event Management

The larger convention center events are planned years in advance. As stated earlier, the convention and visitors bureau is usually responsible for the booking of conventions more than eighteen months ahead. Obviously, both the convention and visitors bureau and the convention center marketing and sales teams work closely with each other. Once the booking becomes definite, the senior event manager assigns an event manager to work with the client throughout the sequence of pre-event, event, and postevent.

The **booking manager** is critical to the success of the event by booking the correct space and working with the organizers to help them save money by allocating only the space really needed and allowing the client to begin setting up on time. A contract is written based on the event profile. The event profile stipulates in writing all of the client's requirements and gives relevant information,

Corporate Profile: Las Vegas Convention and Visitors Authority

The Las Vegas Convention and Visitors Authority (LVCVA) is one of the top convention and visitors bureaus, charged with the following mission: "To attract to the Las Vegas area a steadily increasing number of visitors to support the hotel and motel room inventory in Clark County."[1]

During the 1994 financial year, the Las Vegas Convention and Visitors Authority hosted more than 290 conventions attended by more than 1 million delegates. The LVCVA is organized in the following way: State law establishes the number, appointment, and terms of the authority's board of directors. A twelve-member board provides guidance and establishes policies to accomplish the LVCVA mission.

Seven members are elected officials of the county, and each represents one of the incorporated cities therein; the remaining five members are nominated by the Las Vegas Chamber of Commerce and represent different segments of the industry. The board is one of the most successful public/private partnerships in the country. Under the presidency of Manuel J. Cortez, the Las Vegas Convention and Visitors Authority and its board of directors have received numerous awards, among them the following:

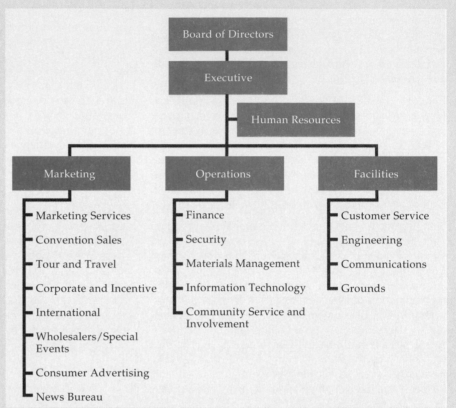

Organizational chart, Las Vegas Convention and Visitors Authority (Courtesy The Las Vegas Convention and Visitors Authority.)

World Travel Awards

✓ World's Leading Tourist and Convention Board

✓ World's Leading Conference and Convention Center

✓ World's Leading Gaming Destination

✓ Top North American Tourist and Convention Board

The Las Vegas Convention and Visitors Authority's organizational structure is shown above. The board of directors employs a president (executive) to serve as chief executive officer. Other members of the executive staff are vice president marketing, vice president operations, and vice president facilities. The marketing division's first priority is to increase the number of visitors to Las Vegas and southern Nevada. The division is composed of eight teams that specialize in various market segments to increase the number of visitors and convention attendance. The teams are also shown above.

The marketing services team is responsible for providing visitor services including research, registration, convention housing, hotel/motel reservations, and visitor information. The research team tracks the dynamics of the Las Vegas and Clark County tourism marketplace, along with the competitive gaming and tourism environment. The registration department coordinates and provides temporary help for conventions and trade shows being held in Las Vegas. The housing division receives and processes hotel and motel housing forms from convention and trade show delegates, forwarding the reservations to participating hotels daily. The reservations department operates toll-free telephone lines, transferring the calls of travel agents, tourists, conventioneers, and special event attendees to hotels and motels within a requested location and price range.

Five visitor centers operate in Jean, Boulder City, Mesquite, Laughlin, and Las Vegas seven days a week and serve more than 38,000 visitors a month. A brochure room supports the visitor centers by answering thousands of telephone calls and letters requesting a variety of information on Las Vegas including recreation, weddings, entertainment, and special events. The staff sends out posters, brochures, and other information.

The convention sales team coordinates convention sales efforts at the Authority and contributes to the success of convention sales citywide by providing sales leads to the hotels. Sales managers travel throughout the United States and the world, meeting with association meeting planners to sell the benefits of holding conventions in Las Vegas. Members of the team also attend numerous conventions and trade shows where they host or sponsor special events and functions to entice conventions and trade shows to Las Vegas.

With a market share of 88 percent of leisure travelers visiting Las Vegas, travel promotion is vital to the LVCVA. The tour and travel team is responsible for positioning Las Vegas as a complete and affordable destination, and the preeminent gaming and entertainment capital of the world. Because 39 percent of all leisure travelers use a travel agent, the tour and travel team aggressively markets Las Vegas with travel agents.

Familiarization trips for travel agents are conducted by team members to generate enthusiasm and excitement around Las Vegas bookings. Travel agent presentations are also scheduled in both primary and selected secondary airline market cities. Similar events are also scheduled for Laughlin, which also advertises a 1-800 number for tourism information.

The corporate and incentive markets are traditionally considered the high end of the travel industry. These buyers are extremely sophisticated and value-conscious, and are looking for the highest quality facilities and amenities. Corporate and incentive team members attend various trade shows throughout the United States and Canada, as well as selected cities in Europe and Asia, promoting Las Vegas as a complete, value-oriented, flexible, and accessible resort destination for corporate meetings.

With increases in visitation from almost every country, the LVCVA's international team is charged with maintaining a high profile in the international marketplace, positioning Las Vegas and southern Nevada as the preferred destination and the gateway to the West. Team members travel throughout the world from the Pacific Rim countries of Japan, Korea, and Taiwan to the European countries of Germany, Switzerland, France, and Austria, as well as Canada and South America. Team sales executives provide information, brochures, and sales material in foreign languages emphasizing Las Vegas as a world-class, full-service resort destination.

The team also serves on an air service task force through McCarran International Airport and provides a steady flow of current information to key airline executives seeking support for nonstop service to Las Vegas when considering new destinations. In November 1994, the LVCVA, in partnership with McCarran International Airport, welcomed the first regularly scheduled international nonstop flight to Las Vegas. Condor Airlines' inaugural flight from Cologne, Germany, to Las Vegas is an example of the work of the joint air service task force.

In recent years, wholesale travel has been one of the fastest growing segments of the Las Vegas tourism market. During the past three years, the wholesale market has increased more than 75 percent, and the wholesaler team positions Las Vegas as a destination without limits on the variety of packages and activities that can be arranged. To provide education on the variety of activities offered by Las Vegas, the wholesaler team plans and implements several annual familiarization tours for wholesalers.

Annual Special Events

- ✓ Las Vegas Senior Classic
- ✓ Las Vegas Invitational
- ✓ National Finals Rodeo
- ✓ Big League Weekend
- ✓ Las Vegas Bowl

continued

✓ Laughlin River Days

✓ Laughlin River Flight

✓ Laughlin Rodeo Days

In recent years, special event planners have also showed increased interest in Las Vegas and Laughlin as event destinations. Team members travel to several special event trade shows and conferences to maximize the opportunities for special events to be held in Las Vegas. The team works in cooperation with Las Vegas Events and the Laughlin Marketing Partners to aggressively pursue events that provide television exposure and draw large numbers of participants, spectators, and visitors.

Las Vegas Territory Matching Grant Funds

The Las Vegas Territory grants program provides funding for the advertising and promotion of special events in rural Clark County to attract visitors to the outlying areas. These events create a more enhanced vacation experience and provide a variety of additional activities for the Las Vegas visitor. Some examples are Boulder City Art in the Park, Henderson Industrial Days, Mesquite Arts Festival, NLV Parade of Many Cultures, and Mt. Charleston Festival in the Pines.

Travelers responded to the new advertising theme— "A World of Excitement in One Amazing Place"—and the Las Vegas tourism and convention business continues to flourish.

The advertising team is responsible for developing the general marketing strategy that provides a blueprint for the development of specific marketing initiatives, advertisements, and public relations efforts. These strategies are incorporated into each division of the marketing department.

The Las Vegas News Bureau is a part of the LVCVA. The news bureau provides information about Las Vegas and southern Nevada through direct contact with national and international freelance journalists and working members of print and broadcast media. The bureau also maintains a complete photographic collection of Las Vegas, depicting the resort and entertainment growth of the area over a period of almost fifty years.

The operations department provides administrative support services to the marketing and facilities divisions, as well as security for the entire authority.

Finance

The finance division maintains a general accounting system for the authority to ensure accountability in compliance with legal provisions and in accordance with gen-

```
                      /Finance
                      /Security
OPERATIONS — Materials Management
                      /Information Technology
                      /Community Service and Involvement
```

Activities within Operations Department

erally accepted accounting principles. Finance is composed of financial services, accounting, and payroll activities. Additional responsibilities include the preparation of the authority's annual financial report (CAFR) and the annual budget. The CAFR has received the Government Finance Officers Association (GFOA) Excellence in Financial Reporting Award a number of times in recent years.

Materials Management

Materials management supports the marketing, operations, and facilities divisions by providing for purchasing of materials, services, and goods needed to meet its goals and objectives. Materials management is responsible for the storage and distribution of various supply items through an extensive warehousing program, as well as through printing and mail distribution.

Security

The security division provides protection of authority property, equipment, employees, and convention attendees twenty-four hours a day, 365 days a year, and also oversees paid parking and fire safety functions. The team patrols both the convention center and Cashman Field properties, and is trained in first aid assistance. Several officers have been recognized by the authority board and convention organizations for providing lifesaving measures to convention attendees.

Information Technology

The information technology division (ITD) is responsible for efficiently and effectively meeting the automation and information needs of the authority. ITD sustains a staff of technically competent professionals to design, maintain, implement, and operate the systems necessary to support the goals of the authority.

Rental Waiver Program

The LVCVA successfully runs an annual rental waiver program that provides $100,000 in grant money for in-kind use of Cashman Field facilities and equipment. Dozens of legitimate, registered Nevada nonprofit groups use the facility each year, transforming Cashman Field into a virtual civic center.

The LVCVA's research division tracks trends and statistics that give an accurate picture of the tremendous growth in southern Nevada from 1984 through 1994. The LVCVA's unique structure—housing both the building management and marketing teams within the same organization—has produced significant operational efficiencies and resulted in the optimal use of facilities. The figure included here provides an indication of the LVCVA's success in marketing the destination.

Funding for the bureau comes mainly from the transient occupancy tax (TOT). This is a tax on hotel accommodations that the city charges all its visitors. The amount of the tax varies from about 10 percent to 19.25 percent. Over a year, this adds up to millions of dollars. Only a part of the TOT tax goes to the CVB; most of it goes into the city's general fund or to fund specific projects. The balance of the bureau's budget comes from members fees and promotions.

[1]The author gratefully acknowledges that this section draws on information given by the Las Vegas Convention and Visitors Authority.

Providence Convention Center (Courtesy Providence R.I. Convention Center.)

such as which company will act as decorator subcontractor to install carpets and set up the booths.

The contract requires careful preparation because it is a legal document and will guarantee certain provisions. For example, the contract may specify that the booths may only be cleaned by center personnel or that food may be prepared for samples only, not for retail. After the contract has been signed and returned by the client, the event manager will from time to time make follow-up calls until about six months before the event when arrangements such as security, business services, and catering will be finalized.

The event manager is the key contact between the center and the client. She or he will help the client by introducing approved subcontractors who are able to provide essential services. Figure 12–9 shows a job description for an event manager.

Two weeks prior to the event an event document is distributed to department heads. The **event document** contains all the detailed information that each department needs to know in order for the event to run smoothly. About ten days before the event, a WAG meeting (week at a glance) is held. The WAG meeting is one of the most important meetings at the convention center because it provides an opportunity to avoid problems—like two event groups arriving at the same time or additional security for concerts or politicians. About this same time, a preconvention or pre-expo meeting is held with expo managers and their contractors—shuttle bus managers, registration operators, exhibit floor managers, and so on.

Once the setup begins, service contractors marshall the eighteen-wheeler trucks to unload the exhibits by using radio phones to call the trucks from a nearby depot. When the exhibits are in place, the exposition opens and the public is admitted. Figure 12–10 shows an event document for the Sixth International Boat Show at the San Diego Convention Center. It gives information regarding the exact amount of space allocated, the contact person, and the schedule of events.

Specialized Services

A number of companies offer specialized services such as transportation, entertainment, audiovisual, escorts and tour guides, convention setup, and destination management.

Check Your Knowledge

1. Define the following forms of meetings:
   a. Forum
   b. Seminar
   c. Workshop
   d. Clinic
   e. Symposium
2. What is SMERF?
3. What are the functions of a meeting planner?
4. What is a FAM trip?
5. *Research:* How many meetings take place each year in the convention center nearest you?
6. What are the functions of a booking manager?

SAN DIEGO CONVENTION CENTER

EVENT MANAGER

DEFINITION

Under moderate direction from the services manager, plans, directs, and supervises assigned events and represents services manager on assigned shifts.

KEY RESPONSIBILITIES

- Plans, coordinates, and supervises all phases of the events to include set ups, move ins and outs, and the activities themselves
- Prepares and disseminates set-up information to the proper departments well in advance of the activity, and ensures complete readiness of the facilities
- Responsible for arranging for all services needed by the tenant
- Coordinates facility staffing needs with appropriate departments
- Acts as a consultant to tenants and the liaison between in-house contractors and tenants
- Preserves facility's physical plant and ensures a safe environment by reviewing tenants plans; requests and makes certain they comply with facility, state, county, and city rules and regulations
- Prepares accounting paperwork of tenant charges, approves final billings, and assists with collection of same
- Resolves complaints, including operational problems and difficulties
- Assists in conducting surveys, gathering statistical information, and working on special projects as assigned by services manager
- Conducts tours of the facilities

MINIMUM REQUIREMENTS

- Bachelor's degree in hospitality management, business, or recreational management from a fully accredited university or college, plus two (2) years of experience in coordinating major conventions and trade shows
- Combination of related education/training and additional experience may substitute for bachelor's degree
- An excellent ability to manage both fiscal and human resources
- Knowledge in public relations; oral and written communications
- Experienced with audiovisual equipment

225 Broadway, Suite 710 • San Diego, CA 92102 • (619) 239-1989
FAX (619) 239-2030
Operated by the San Diego Convention Center Corporation

Figure 12–9   *Job Description for an Event Manager* (Courtesy San Diego Convention Center.)

EVENT DOCUMENT
REVISED COPY
/6/SAN DIEGO INTERNATIONAL BOAT SHOW
Tuesday, January 2, 2001 – Tuesday, January 9, 2001

SPACE: Combined Exhibit Halls AB, Hall A - How Manager's Office, Box Office by Hall A, Hall B –
Show Manager's Office, Mezzanine Room 12, Mezzanine Room 13, Mezzanine Rooms 14 A&B, AND
Mezzanine Rooms 15 A&B

CONTACT: Mr. Jeff Hancock
National Marine Manufacturers Association, Inc.
4901 Morena Blvd.
Suite 901
San Diego, CA 92117
Telephone Number: (619) 274-9924
Fax Number: (619) 274-6760
Decorator Co.:   Greyhound Exposition Services
Sales Person: Denise Simenstad
Event Manager: Jane Krause
Event Tech.:   Sylvia A. Harrison

SCHEDULE OF EVENTS:

Monday, January 2, 1995
  5:00 am – 6:00 pm   Combined Exhibit Halls AB
Service contractor move in GES,
Andy Quintena

Tuesday, January 3, 1995
  8:00 am – 6:00 pm   Combined Exhibit Halls AB
Service contractor move in GES,
Andy Quintena

 12:00 pm – 6:00 pm   Combined Exhibit Halls AB
Exhibitor move in

Wednesday, January 4, 1995
  8:00 am – 6:00 pm   Combined Exhibit Halls AB
Exhibitor move in
Est. attendance: 300

Thursday, January 5, 1995
  8:00 am – 12:00 pm   Combined Exhibit Halls AB
Exhibitor final move in

 11:30 am – 8:30 pm   Box Office by Hall A
OPEN: Ticket prices, Adults $6, Children 12 & under $

Figure 12–10   *Event Document, International Boat Show* (Courtesy San Diego Convention Center.)

Trends in Conventions, Meetings, and Expositions

- ✓ *Globalization/international participation:* More people are going abroad to attend meetings.
- ✓ *The cloning of shows:* Some international shows do not travel very well (i.e., agricultural machinery). Thus, organizations such as Bleinheim or Reed Exposition Group lift components and create shows in other countries.
- ✓ *Competition:* Competitiveness has increased among all destinations. Convention centers will expand and new centers will come on-line.
- ✓ *Technology:* The industry needs to be more sophisticated. The need for fiber optics is present everywhere.
- ✓ Shows are growing at a rate of 5 to 10 percent per year.

Case Study

Double-Booked

The convention bureau in a large and popular convention destination has jurisdiction over the convention center. A seasoned convention sales manager, who has worked for the bureau for seven years and produces more sales than any other sales manager, has rebooked a 2,000-person group for a three-day exposition in the convention center. The exposition is to take place two years from the booking date.

The client has a fifteen-year history of holding conventions, meetings, and expositions in this convention center and has always used the bureau to contract all space and services for them. In fact, the sales manager handling the account has worked with the client for seven of the fifteen years. The bureau considers this client a "preferred customer."

The convention group meeting planner also appears in a magazine ad giving a testimony of praise for the convention bureau, this particular sales manager, and the city as a destination for conventions.

Shortly after the meeting planner rebooks this convention with the bureau, the bureau changes sales administration personnel, not once, but three times. This creates a challenge for the sales managers in terms of producing contracts, client files, and event profiles, and in the recording and distribution of information. The preferred customer who rebooked has a contract, purchase orders for vendor services, a move in and setup agenda, and an event profile, all supplied by the sales manager. The sales manager has copies of these documents as well. The two hotels where the group will be staying also have contracts for the VIP group.

continued

As is the nature of this particular bureau, other sales managers have been booking and contracting space for the same time period as the group that rebooked. In fact, the exhibit hall has been double booked, as have the break-out rooms for seminars, workshops, and food and beverage service. The groups that were contracted later are all first-time users of the facility.

This situation remains undetected until ten days prior to the groups' arrival. It is brought to the attention of the bureau and the convention center only when the sales manager distributes a memo to schedule a pre-convention meeting with the meeting planner and all convention center staff.

Due to the administrative personnel changes, necessary information was not disseminated to key departments and key personnel. The convention center was never notified that space had been contracted for the preferred customer. The preferred customer has been told about this potentially catastrophic situation. Now there is a major dilemma to rectify.

Discussion Questions

1. Ultimately, who is responsible for decision making with regard to this situation?
2. What steps should be taken to remedy this situation?
3. Are there fair and ethical procedures to follow in order to provide space for the preferred customer? If so, what are they?
4. What measures, if any, should be taken in handling the seasoned sales manager?
5. What leverage does the meeting planner have to secure this and future business with the bureau?
6. List five ramifications if the preferred customer is denied space and usage of the convention center.
7. How can this situation be avoided in the future?

Case Study

Not Enough Space

Denise is the sales manager of a large convention center. A client has requested an exhibition that would not only bring excellent revenue but is an annual event that several other convention centers would like to host.

Exhibitions typically take one or two days to set up, with three or four days of exhibition, and one day to break down. Professional organizations handle each part of the setup and breakdown.

When Denise checks the space available on the days requested for the exhibition, she notices that another exhibition is blocking a part of the space needed by her client.

Discussion Question

1. What can Denise do to get this exhibition to use the convention center without inconveniencing either exhibition too much?

Career Information

Meetings, incentive travel, conventions, and expositions (the MICE segment) offer a broad range of career paths. Successful meeting planners are detail oriented, organized people who not only plan and organize meetings but also negotiate hotel rooms and meeting space in hotels and convention centers.

Incentive travel includes aspects of organizing high-end travel, hotels, restaurants, attractions and entertainment. With big budgets this can be an exciting career for those interested in a combination of travel and hotels etc. in exotic locations.

Conventions and convention centers have several career paths from assistants to sales managers, sales managers for a special type of account (e.g., associations) or for a territory. Senior sales managers are expected to book large conventions and expositions—yes, everyone has their quota. Event managers plan and organize the function/event with the client once the contract has been signed. Salaries range from $35,000 - 70,000 for both assistants on up to sales or event managers.

Careers are also possible in the companies that services the MICE segment. Someone has to equip the convention center and ready it for an exposition. Someone has to supply all the food and beverage items and so on. Off premise catering and special events also offers careers for creative people who like to create concepts and orchestrate themes around which an event or function may be planned.

For all the career paths it is critical to gain experience in the areas of your interest. Request people you respect to be your mentor and ask questions. By showing your enthusiasm people will respond with more help and advice.

Summary

1. Conventions, meetings, and expositions serve social, political, sporting, or religious purposes. Associations offer benefits such as a political voice, education, marketing avenues, member services, and networking.
2. Meetings are events designed to bring people together for the purpose of exchanging information. Typical forms of meetings are conferences, workshops, seminars, forums, and symposiums.
3. Expositions bring together purveyors of products, equipment, and services in an environment in which they can demonstrate their products. Conventions are meetings that include some form of exposition or trade show.
4. Meeting planners contract out their services to associations and corporations. Their responsibilities include premeeting, on-site, and postmeeting activities.
5. The convention and visitors bureaus are nonprofit organizations that assess the needs of the client and organize transportation, hotel accommodations, restaurants, and attractions.
6. Convention centers are huge facilities, usually owned by the government, where meetings and expositions are held. Events at convention centers require a lot of planning ahead and careful event management. A contract based on the event profile and an event document are parts of effective management.

Key Words and Concepts

Associations	Convention center	Incentive market	Special event
Boardroom style	Convention and visitors	Meeting	Symposium
Booking manager	bureaus	Meeting planner	Theater style
Classroom style	Event document	Off-premise catering	Trade show
Clinic	Exposition	Seminar	Workshop
Consumer show	Familiarization (FAM) trip	Site inspection	
Convention	Forum	SMERF	

Review Questions

1. What are associations and what is their purpose?
2. Explain the term SMERF.
3. Describe the main types of meeting setups.
4. What are a workshop and a seminar?
5. Explain the difference between an exposition and a convention.
6. What is a convention center?
7. List the duties of CVBs.
8. Conventions require careful planning. Explain the purpose of an event profile and an event document.
9. Discuss the different promotional tools, how they relate to each other, and their relationship to the marketing mix.

Internet Exercises

1. Organization:
   Web site:
   Summary:
   (a) Choose a service or event most relevant to you, such as a graduation, wedding, or even a private party. Combine your own ideas with those from the web site and design your own event. List some of the challenges you expect to come across (like parking and staffing) for the event and discuss possible solutions.
   (b) By simply browsing through the web site, discuss the importance of networking in the meetings, conventions, and expositions industry.

All Time Favorites
http://www.alltimefavorites.com
All Time Favorites is an event planning company that specializes in putting together packages for different events such as conventions, corporate events, private parties, and weddings.

2. Organization:
   Web site:
   Summary:
Sample the legal forms section and answer the following.
   (a) What does the ADA clause stand for?
   (b) What are the requirements set by the ADA clause?
   (c) Read through the Recreation Consent Form and discuss its relevance.

M & C Online
http://www.meetings-conventions.com
This excellent web site offers in-depth information on meetings and conventions from different perspectives ranging from legal issues to unique themes and concepts.

Apply Your Knowledge

1. Make a master plan with all the steps necessary for holding a meeting/seminar on careers in hospitality management.

Marketing, Human Resources, and Culture

After reading and studying this chapter, you should be able to:

✓ Discuss the importance of environmental scanning as it relates to marketing and sales
✓ List and explain each of the steps in the marketing process
✓ Show how a competitor analysis is conducted
✓ Explain the term *product life cycle*
✓ State the difference between marketing and sales
✓ List and explain the steps in human resources management and development processes

Each segment of the hospitality industry uses the services of the marketing, sales, and human resources departments.

Marketing

Marketing and sales are critically important to the success of hospitality organizations. Without guests, there is no need for frontline employees or anyone else for that matter! Marketing is all about finding out what guests' wants and needs are and providing them at a reasonable cost and profit.

Marketing begins with a corporate philosophy and a mission, but the philosophy and mission should not just hang on an office wall. It should be practiced every day by everyone. Peter Drucker, highly respected management guru, says that the only valid definition of business purpose is to create customers. In the hospitality industry, we would quickly add "and keep them coming back." Creating a customer means finding a product or service that a number of people want or need. When Kemmons Wilson began Holiday Inns, he was successful because he fulfilled a need that many families and businesspeople had: a quality lodging experience at a value. Ray Kroc is another example of giving the American public what they wanted. Through McDonald's quick-service restaurants, he met the need for food on the run.

Alastair Morrison identifies eleven characteristics of marketing or customer orientation:[1]

1. Customer needs are the first priority.
   ✓ Answering customer needs produces more satisfied customers.
   ✓ All departments, managers, and staff share a common goal.
2. Understanding customers and their needs is a constant concern and research activity.
   ✓ Knowing customers and their needs increases the ability to satisfy these needs.
3. Marketing research is an ongoing activity that should be assigned a very high priority.
   ✓ Changes in customer needs and characteristics are identified.
   ✓ Viability of new services and products are determined.
4. Frequent reviews are made of strengths and weaknesses relative to competitors.
   ✓ Strengths are accentuated and weaknesses addressed.
5. The value of long-term planning is fully appreciated.
   ✓ Changes in customer needs are anticipated and acted on; marketing opportunities are realized.

[1]Alastair M. Morrison, *Hospitality and Travel Marketing*, Albany, NY: Delmar, 1989, p. 14.

6. Customers' perceptions of the organization are known.
   ✓ Services, products, and promotions are designed to match the customers' image.
7. Interdepartmental cooperation is valued and encouraged.
   ✓ Increased cooperation leads to better services and greater customer satisfaction.
8. Cooperation with complementary organizations is recognized as worthwhile.
   ✓ Increased cooperation generates greater customer satisfaction.
9. Change is seen as inevitable and not as being unnecessary.
   ✓ Adaptations to change are made smoothly and are not resisted.
10. The scope of business or activities is broadly set.
    ✓ Opportunities that serve customers more comprehensively, or those that tap into related fields, are capitalized on.
11. Measurement and evaluation of marketing activities is frequent.
    ✓ Effective marketing programs or tactics are repeated or enhanced; ineffective ones are dropped.
    ✓ Marketing expenditures and human resources are used effectively.

Large corporations and small independent hospitality operators both go through similar decision-making processes to seek out new market opportunities and to increase market share in existing markets.

Environmental Analysis

Before the first decisions about marketing can be made, it is advisable to gain background information on topics such as environmental analysis. **Environmental analysis** means studying the economic, social, political, and technological influences that could affect the hospitality business. Figure 13–1 illustrates the environmental scanning process.

Economic Impacts

The economy can affect hospitality corporations in a macro way (the big picture) or in a micro way (the local picture). In a macro sense, interest rates affect the cost of borrowing money, and exchange rates affect the number of tourists visiting specific destinations. Some economists suggest that the economy goes through cycles. We can all agree that the mid-1980s seemed like boom times compared to the recession of the early 1990s. As a result, people today are more value conscious, which is why the economy segment of the lodging industry has grown in recent years.

The importance of **economic analysis** should not be underestimated. The knack of being at the right place at the right time may be luck for some, but it is a carefully calculated move for others. There are many good examples of hospitality leaders who saw the environment changing and with it the wants, needs, and expectations of guests: Ray Kroc, with quick-service restaurants;

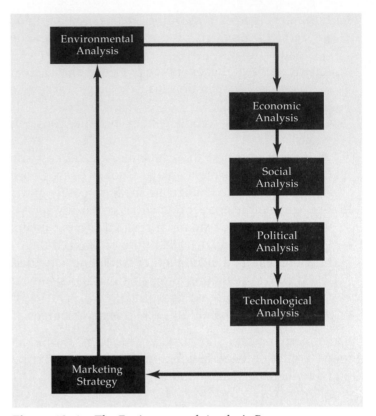

Figure 13–1 *The Environmental Analysis Process*

Richard Melman, with table dining; Robert Hazard, with hotels; and Herb Kelleher, with the airline business, were all trailblazers with one thing in common—the ability to scan the environment and be leaders in the path of progress by developing products and services that anticipated and provided for peoples' wants and needs.

To many who come across a good idea, it may seem like common sense to exploit an opportunity. Still, many corporations are struggling today because they have not done a good environmental scan.

Social Analysis

A survey of our social landscape reveals that lifestyles in the 1990s are more hectic. With more two-income families, additional stresses are placed on those families who must juggle parenting and work. Higher divorce rates have led to more single-parent families and increased female careerism. A greater emphasis on fitness and wellness has led to more of a grazing approach to eating. Foodservice trends are definitely toward healthier eating. In this and other sectors of the hospitality industry, customers have become more knowledgeable and, as a consequence, have higher expectations; these higher expectations, coupled with a quest for value, add up to ever-changing scenarios for hospitality operators.

Demographics are a part of social analysis. Demographics are a profile of society in a given area and include age, sex, household and per capita income, family size, occupation, education, religion, race/ethnicity, and national origin. Demographic information is used by marketing specialists to identify groups of people with similar characteristics and problems for which the marketers may develop a solution.

We all know that people living in the more expensive areas are more likely to go on a cruise than those in the low-income neighborhoods. Cruise lines therefore know to whom to send promotional materials and which television and radio programs are popular with the various target markets. A target market, just as it sounds, is a market that is targeted for the product or service that a company is planning to offer or already offers.

In general, consumers in the 1990s have developed a taste for instant gratification. People are taking more vacations, but shorter ones, to destinations that are closer to home. Lifestyles have become more casual; hence, the increase in casual-theme restaurants. As a nation, approximately 30 percent of our food dollar is eaten away from home.

Political Analysis

Both federal and state legislators and judiciary affect the hospitality industry in a number of ways: employment legislation, minimum wage, health care, taxes on benefit packages, the tax deduction of business meals dropping to 50 percent from 80 percent, and city-wide no-smoking ordinances. Much may also depend on the political party in control.

Technological Analysis

Since labor is the single highest cost in the hospitality business, any technology that leads to greater efficiency is worth investigating. In all sectors of the industry, technological advances are benefiting guests and businesses alike. Consider how much safer a guest feels with an electromagnetic room door opener than a key. The key was easy to duplicate, but the plastic card becomes invalid as soon as the guest checks out. In restaurants, hand-held remote ordering devices have helped speed service to guests from both the bar and kitchen. Computers are now able to store hundreds of menus and, at the push of a button, calculate the amount of ingredients for a recipe for any number of guests. Some can even make out purchase orders as well.

The benefit of environmental scanning is to focus the attention of the top management prior to formulating the next steps in the marketing process, namely, the following:
- ✓ Marketing planning
- ✓ Market assessment

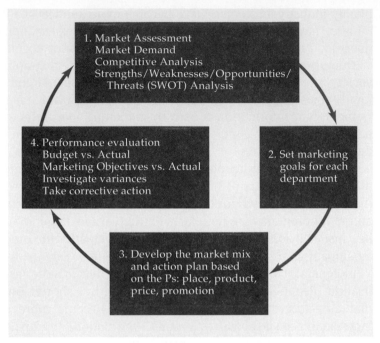

Figure 13–2   *Marketing Planning*

✓ Market demand
✓ Competitive analysis
✓ Positioning
✓ Marketing goals and objectives
✓ Marketing mix
✓ Action plan based on the Ps **(place, product, price, promotion)**
✓ Performance evaluation
✓ Budget vs. actual
✓ Investigate variance
✓ Take corrective actions

Figure 13–2 illustrates the elements of marketing planning.

Market Assessment

Market assessment simply tries to determine if there is a need for a product or service in the market and to assess its potential. This is done by examining the existing market, its size, demographics, key players, customers' wants and needs, and general conditions and trends.

Market Demand

Market demand is not always so easy to quantify. However, by doing our best to gather all available information we can guesstimate the demand for a particular product or service.

Within the hospitality industry, there is obviously considerable variation among the different components: travel and tourism, lodging, foodservice, leisure, and recreation. To assess the market for Amtrak or a discount airline, it would be necessary to consider peoples' travel habits: Who are the potential users, how many are there, and where are they located?

For a lodging company that might want to determine the number of female business travelers, information is available from organizations like the American Hotel and Motel Association or consultants and research organizations such as Pannel Kerr Forster. Some surveys have indicated that approximately 40 percent of all business travel is by females. Therefore, we can deduce that if there were 10,000 hotel rooms in a city center and if they were, on average, 70 percent occupied with a 40 percent business (versus conventions and family) mix there would be

$$10,000 \times 0.7 \times 0.4 = 2,800 \text{ women business travelers visiting that city}$$

Competitor Analysis

Analyzing the competitions' strengths and weaknesses will help us determine which strategies to use in the **marketing action plan.** All hospitality businesses have competitors. The competition may be across the street or across the country or the world. Usually in the lodging, restaurant, and foodservice sectors, the competition is close; for example, most people going to New Orleans for Mardi Gras will stay at a hotel in the city. The question is which one. Similarly, guests selecting restaurants and foodservice establishments will usually choose one within a given radius of about ten miles—give or take a few miles. Therefore, most restaurants realize that their competition is either other restaurants of a similar nature or those within a similar price range; in some cases, such as quick-service restaurants, the competition may also be convenience stores, or even take-out meals.

Competition may be farther away when it comes to destination vacation spots. A family living in St. Louis may want a winter vacation in Mexico, but may also consider the Caribbean, Hawaii, Florida, or southern California.

For the purpose of comparison with competitors, marketers make a matrix of the important elements. In each case, the elements may be selected by the marketing person, owner/operators, and top management/department heads. Figure 13–3 shows a **comparison matrix** form. The appropriate elements are listed in the left-hand column under the heading of benefit. Then, our operation is compared with others using a 1–10 or 1–100 scoring system and/or written comments.

One of the benefits of a comparison matrix is that it helps to focus attention on where our operations are better or worse compared to the competition. Obviously, some elements are beyond owner's and management's control. For example, you cannot move a hotel or restaurant over a few blocks because you don't like its current location.

The elements that are controllable are those that are given the greatest attention; service and quality of food are good examples. Another benefit of a

		Competitors					
Benefit	Our Operation	1	2	3	4	5	6

Figure 13–3 *Comparison Matrix*

comparison matrix is to identify the market segments that we and the competition are best suited to serve. An example of this is Hyatt Hotels and Resorts introducing Camp Hyatt in order to attract families at a time when their usual business guests are not using the hotels much. By targeting regular Hyatt hotel business guests, Camp Hyatt has been successful in offering a benefit and a service to a specific target market.

Positioning

Positioning means to occupy a specific place in the market and project that position to the **target market.** In the process of doing the competitive analysis of the strengths and weakness of the competition, it usually becomes apparent which position a corporation or independent hospitality business should occupy and project. Some companies are deliberately adopting the new concept of positioning in several market segments. Marriott and Choice Hotels are good examples.

Because McDonald's is so strong in the children's market, Wendy's and Burger King position themselves as more adult quick-service burger restaurants. Motel 6 operations position themselves as the least expensive national chain where guests will receive a clean comfortable room for about $26. Positioning statements help get the message across to the target market (e.g., "Did somebody say McDonald's?").

Marketing Goals and Objectives

Setting **marketing goals and objectives** gives a measure by which progress toward the goals can be monitored. Goals are set for the total enterprise and for each department. An example of a marketing goal for a hotel might be to increase weekend occupancy from 43.2 percent to 48.2 percent by a specified date. Another could be to increase the average daily rate from $76 to $80. Other goals target each market segment, such as corporate meetings and conventions, sport, leisure, and so on. Goals are set for each of the hospitality operations' units or departments. Campus foodservice managers would set sales goals for outside catering, satellite restaurants, tailgate parties, and so on.

Objectives are the how-to tactics used in order to meet or exceed the goals. Using the preceding examples, management would plan and organize specific activities that would result in a five percent increase in weekend occupancy. Objectives must be planned for each goal.

Marketing Mix

The **marketing mix** is the term used to focus on the pertinent Ps: place, product, price, promotion, partnership, packaging, programming, and people.

Place means the location, which is extremely important for hospitality businesses. The expression "In business, the three most important things are location, location, location!" stresses that importance. Hotels, motels, restaurants, tourist attractions, and destinations to a large extent either thrive or perish based on their location.

The only problem is that owners and managers must, if they have a prime location, produce the revenue to keep the mortgage or lease payments to a certain percentage of total sales. In a restaurant, for example, operators aim to keep mortgage or lease payments to about 6 to 8 percent of sales in order to allow an appropriate amount to cover other costs and produce a reasonable profit.

The *product* must suit the wants and needs of the target market. The product is positioned to meet those wants and needs as a result of the previous steps in the marketing process. Additionally, surveys and focus groups (small groups that are a representative sample of the target market) provide feedback on the extent to which the product meets their wants and needs.

A great example of ensuring that the product suits the needs of the target market was Marriott's development of Courtyard Inns, which they developed after extensive research on what their target market wanted. They constructed prototype rooms on which focus groups were invited to comment. This careful product development led to the launch of a very successful new type of lodging concept.

All products and services are at some stage in the **product life cycle,** just as humans go through the life cycle from birth/introduction, growth, maturity, and declining period. Figure 13–4 shows the stages in the product life cycle. An example of a product that was introduced a few years ago and had a very quick growth rate, an early maturity, and rapid decline was the disco. To a large extent, sports bars and coffeehouses have taken over.

Price plays an important role in purchasing decisions, as we all know from experience. Most guests are price sensitive—as the old expression says, there is no loyalty that $0.25 won't change. In other words, if the fast-food restaurant across the street offers the same product for $0.25 less, then (other things being equal) they will get the business.

Obviously, things like value are closely linked with price. People will only purchase a particular product or service if they perceive that it is a good value—hence the value-meal packs and real-meal deals. The closer price is to value, the more likely the guest will be satisfied and will return.

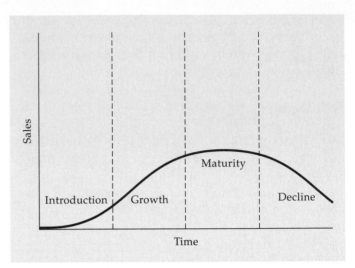

Figure 13–4 *Product Life Cycle*

In recent years, pricing in the hospitality industry has had an interesting effect on consumer behavior. In the early 1980s, hospitality enterprises increased prices and found that guests kept coming. Many businesses were liberal with **expense accounts** that enabled executives to stay in better hotels and entertain clients in expensive restaurants.

At that time these costs were all tax deductible. Then, in 1986, tax deductions of business expenses for restaurant meals were reduced to 80 percent (they subsequently were reduced to 50 percent). These measures, combined with the recession, had a profound effect on restaurants, especially upscale restaurants.

Quite naturally, business dropped off as guests who were spending money on dining traded down to the midpriced restaurants, and midpriced clientele moved into the quick-service segment. Quick-service restaurants flourished, and convenience stores and supermarkets began to put delicatessens into the stores.

Price also played a part in the surge of economy and midprice hotels and motels that have come on-line in recent years. Guests resisted paying more than what they considered to be a reasonable price for hotel accommodations. The fact that the luxury hotel market was overbuilt also helped.

Price may be determined in two main ways: the comparative approach and the cost-plus approach. The comparative approach assesses what other similar operations are charging for the same or similar service/product. The cost-plus approach means that all the costs are accounted for and a selling price is determined after an amount for profit is allocated. As you can likely already determine, both methods have advantages and disadvantages.

Promotion, which includes the techniques for communicating information about the products/services available, is the most highly visible element of the marketing mix. The most important promotional tools are advertising, personal selling, sales promotion, and public relations.

Advertising is any form of paid, nonpersonal communication used by an identified sponsor to persuade or inform certain audiences about a product.[2] For example, a restaurant advertises in a local newspaper, on the radio, or on television, to reach its target market. Other forms of advertising include magazines and billboards.

Personal selling in the hospitality industry can take the form of sales blitzes or "upselling" in restaurants, or at the front desks of hotels.

Sales promotions offer inducements to buyers. In the hospitality industry, they include free gifts, such as when a quick-service restaurant gives away a toy. Promotions may also include coupons. Most newspapers or *Penny Saver*s have restaurant coupons, and the entertainment guide may offer discount coupons for hotel rooms and even airline transportation. These sales promotions usually seek to boost sales during slow periods.

Public relations (PR) includes all communications aimed at increasing good will in the user communities. PR seeks to build a positive image of the organization and its products. Ronald McDonald Houses are a famous example of public relations. Other examples include sponsorship of local organizations and events, and providing scholarships.

Partnerships occur when two or more hospitality/tourism organizations come together, providing an overall marketing campaign. They include related marketing programs and cooperative advertising, which is when two or more companies are mentioned on the same advertisement. An example of this would be the American Airlines, Citibank, Visa Card.

Publicity is also about the organization's communication with the public. However, it is not paid for by the organization. It is free and, therefore, not controlled by the organization. This can be good or bad, as in the case of Jack in the Box and the *E. coli* bacteria outbreak. On the other hand, consideration should be taken of the goodwill created by organizations participating in charity events.

Packaging is when organizations combine two or more items or activities, such as fly-drive-hotel-attractions visits, and sell them as a group. Another very successful form of packaging is the convenient McDonald's Happy Meal concept. Although different from the previous example, it nonetheless appeals to a particular market segment.

Programming is when a company like Hyatt offers Camp Hyatt to families with children. A complete program of events is planned so that parents and children may, if they wish, do separate activities. Club Med also programs some of its locations for specific activities like snorkeling, sailing, tennis, and so forth. Some of these are for families, and some only for adults.

In the hospitality and tourism industry, *people* are an important part of the marketing mix—one airplane is much like the next, but it is the "people service" that makes the difference. Radisson Hotel's "Yes I Can" program was based on customer research and proved successful because employees really cared and wanted to make a difference.

[2]Ricky W. Griffin and Ronald J. Ebert, *Business,* 4th ed. Upper Saddle River, NJ: Prentice-Hall, p. 455.

Check Your Knowledge

1. What are the characteristics of marketing?
2. Briefly describe market demand, competitor analysis and positioning.
3. What is the marketing mix?

Performance Evaluation

Evaluating the actual operations against expected performance is ongoing and lets an organization see how well it has done compared with how well it said it would do. Providing performance feedback enables management to plan future marketing strategies. If expected and actual performance vary, then the discrepancy is examined and alternative strategies are developed. Having established the results and the reasons for any variances, the final step in the marketing process is to take the necessary corrective action to achieve the company's goals.

Sales

Sales is an important part of marketing. The difference between marketing and sales is that with marketing, the focus is on the guest. With sales the focus is on the product or service for sale.

More people have the title *sales manager* or *account executive* than *marketing director*. The sales department is responsible for making sales to guests in the target market to increase **market share.** Sales can be to new accounts or existing ones. Each sales department is organized in a way that best suits the organization. Some companies have national—even international—sales offices in addition to unit sales departments. The sales team may then be split up according to the various target markets: association, corporate, catering,

Director of Marketing and Sales Meeting

Personal Profile: Carroll R. Armstrong

President and CEO, Baltimore Convention and Visitors Bureau

Thirty years ago, Carroll R. Armstrong was well on his way to becoming a successful jazz musician when he changed careers. Since that time, his career has progressed to his present position of CEO, Baltimore Convention and Visitors Bureau. Carroll has been a force in the success in four major convention centers. A colleague describes Carroll as the number one convention center marketing professional in the country. However, his biggest challenge was opening the San Diego Convention Center.

In 1987, when Carroll arrived in San Diego, he looked at the existing convention centers. Carroll concluded that if San Diego was to be successful, the center must compete for business in several markets; in addition to the traditional convention center markets, two nontraditional convention center markets, incentive business and the corporate markets, were increasingly important. These additional market segments would help maximize the property and create additional revenue.

In the 1980s, many of the convention centers operated in an institutional mode. Because they were state or city owned, they were expected to lose money. The challenge of the San Diego Convention Center was that it could not open and operate in the same way as others did. The convention center would have to be more economically self-sufficient. The center would have to be the pump primer and operate like any other business.

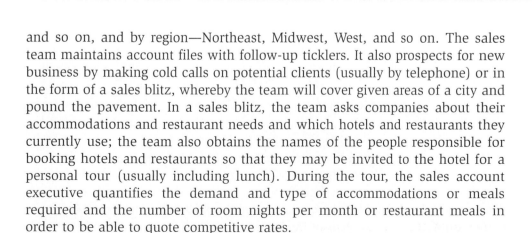

The philosophy that Carroll created was that the center would operate like a fine hotel. Whereas many other centers contract out their foodservice and consequently have mediocre reputations, the San Diego Convention Center's catering has white-glove "Escoffier" food preparation and service. Carroll realized that the me-generation wants service with style, and, if they are getting value, they will pay the few extra costs.

The strategy of differentiating the center by service has been successful because the center has won the meeting planners' choice award from *Meeting News Magazine.* This recognizes that one of the major goals of the convention center is to run the center like a first-class hotel, so that delegates can walk from the hotels to the convention center without noticing any difference. To achieve this, the center has uniformed doorpersons and concierge-like, guest-relations staff to answer questions and offer suggestions about everything from a meeting room location to city-wide entertainment. Additionally, guest-service guides stand near elevators to direct attendees to appropriate rooms taking those who spend the most.

In 1996, in recognition of his expertise and leadership Carroll was appointed president of the Baltimore Convention and Visitors Bureau.

and so on, and by region—Northeast, Midwest, West, and so on. The sales team maintains account files with follow-up ticklers. It also prospects for new business by making cold calls on potential clients (usually by telephone) or in the form of a sales blitz, whereby the team will cover given areas of a city and pound the pavement. In a sales blitz, the team asks companies about their accommodations and restaurant needs and which hotels and restaurants they currently use; the team also obtains the names of the people responsible for booking hotels and restaurants so that they may be invited to the hotel for a personal tour (usually including lunch). During the tour, the sales account executive quantifies the demand and type of accommodations or meals required and the number of room nights per month or restaurant meals in order to be able to quote competitive rates.

A Day in the Life of Denise Simenstad
National Sales Manager, San Diego Convention Center, San Diego, California

Denise Simenstad is the national sales manager at the San Diego Convention Center. Her work here starts early and usually ends when the timing is good. What she does in those hours though is good customer service and remarkable work.

Denise comes into work at about 8 A.M. When she arrives at her office, she checks her voice-mail, e-mail, and in-box messages. From then on, the day is not her own. She's working and attending to customer activity.

Her day-to-day activities keep her busy well throughout the day. Denise responds to customer inquiries. These inquiries consist of prospective customers calling her to inquire about date and space availability at the convention center, the cost of renting of meeting rooms or exhibit halls, and checking if there are other similar shows booked in the facility.

(Courtesy Denise Simenstad.)

She then usually leads a tour or, as it is better known, a "site inspection" of the facility to show customers the available physical space, including the lobby, exhibit halls, ballroom, meeting space, and outdoor space. Then she shows them the ancillary services that the convention center provides such as the audiovisual facilities, food and beverage, telecommunications, security services, business services center, and so on. All that makes for a complete tour.

Denise then prepares proposals (dates, rates, and space letter) for prospective customers. This ranges from a group of 100 people for one day to a trade show for 15,000 people to 250,000 guests for five days. She has to include a package of information concerning the floor plans, rates, regulations, and other pertinent information.

After all that, Denise answers customers' questions about the facilities available and capabilities. She fields questions on the sizes of rooms, capacities of the facilities, rates, distance between pillars on exhibit floor, floor loads, dimensions of freight doors, number of committable hotel rooms in the downtown area, number of packages available, and more.

Then comes the duty of having to issue and negotiate license agreements (contract) with outlines, dates, space and rates, insurance requirements, indemnification issues, cancellation classes, guarantees, and so on.

To start wrapping up, Denise attends meetings with other sales managers in the office to discuss business strategy concerning who is considering them for a meeting, how they can close the deal, what other managers are working on, what type of business seems to be prevalent right now, and so on. The meeting sessions continue with yet another meeting with event managers, the people responsible for the operational aspect of an event once it is contracted. In this meeting they all go over any operational concerns, and check to ensure that what sales promised is delivered. If a client is in-house, then they have a gift delivered to their hotel room (just prior to arrival) and then go on the floor to check the show and ensure that clients are satisfied with service received.

The day usually ends at about 5:30 P.M. for Denise. The day can go on even longer if a customer is in town. In this case, she makes sure that her customers are wined and dined and attended to well by entertaining them, providing breakfast, lunch, and/or dinner and basically showing them what San Diego is all about.

Each member of the sales team has a quota of dollar sales to achieve. Therefore, sales professionals guard their clients very carefully. Making a sale and influencing the guest to become a repeat guest is vital in today's competitive marketplace. About 80 percent of a hotel's and some restaurants' business comes from about 20 percent of the guests.

Human Resources Management

It is precisely because the hospitality industry offers intangible services and products that **human resources management** is so critical to the success of the organization. One hotel restaurant or tourism enterprise is often much the same as the other; what makes the difference is service and professionalism.

As we already know, the hospitality industry is the largest in the world, employing some 70 million people. No other industry has as much frontline guest contact between employees and guests—especially entry-level employees. Employment ranges from entry-level positions to specialized positions, supervisory positions, and managerial/executive positions. Human resources is all about attracting, selecting, orienting, training, developing, and evaluating the performance of an organization's most important resources, the human ones.

In addition to these activities, several other functions are part of the human resources process, including job descriptions, job specifications, advertising, payroll and benefits, grievances, and ensuring conformance to federal and state or provincial legislation.

The complexity of human resources management and development in the hospitality industry is increased by the fact that many unskilled workers are employed for entry-level positions, often with little or no training. Also, there is enormous and increasing cultural diversity within the industry. Figure 13–5 shows the human resources management and development process.

Each segment of the hospitality industry follows the human resources functions. In this section, we will examine them sequentially. The business and economic conditions of recent years necessitated what has been called reengineering, downsizing, or right-sizing.

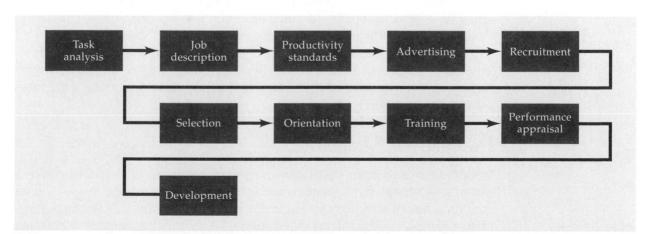

Figure 13–5 *Human Resources Management and Development Process*

Task Analysis

Because human resource or labor costs are the highest single cost of being in business, it has become necessary to examine each task of each employee to determine its outcome on the guest experience. A good example of analyzing a task from a guest's viewpoint is to start when a guest arrives at a hotel. Traditionally, one person acted as a greeter/doorperson and took the guest's luggage; that person gave the luggage to a bellperson, who in turn transported it to the front desk. After the guest had registered, it was quite possible that another bellperson transported the guest's luggage to the assigned room. This not only involved the guest interacting with three or four different individuals, but it also annoyed the guest because of the amount of tipping involved.

Ordinarily, **task analysis** and **job analysis** examine the tasks necessary to perform the job; when approved and listed, these tasks become the job description. An example is that the job description of a hotel doorperson would include greeting an arriving automobile, opening the passenger or driver door, welcoming the guests to the hotel, offering to remove the guests' luggage from the car, transporting it to the front desk (or holding it on the cart) while the guests register, and then escorting the guests and transporting the luggage to the allocated room. Some innovative hotels have cross-trained their employees to the point that the person who greets guests outside the hotel actually rooms the guests by handling the check in, allocating the room, and then escorting the guests. This means that the guests only come in contact with one or two employees. The program has been extremely well received by guests.

Job Description

A **job description** is a detailed description of the activities and outcomes expected of the person performing the job (see Figure 5–2). The job description is important because it can become a legal document. Some cases have come before the courts and administrative agencies in which employees who were dismissed have sued the former employer, claiming that they did not know or were not properly informed of the duties required.

Today, many companies have employees sign their job descriptions to avoid any confusion or misunderstandings about their job and its responsibilities. The job description specifies the knowledge, qualifications, and skills necessary to do the job successfully. Job descriptions can be used as good performance measurement tools.

Productivity Standards

With today's high labor costs, increasing employee productivity has become a major issue. **Productivity standards** may be established for each position within the organization. They are determined by measuring or timing how long it takes to do a given task. Departments then are staffed according to forecasted demand, whether restaurant covers, hotel occupancy, or attendance at a theme park.

Employee productivity is measured in dollar terms by dividing sales by labor costs. If sales totaled $46,325 and labor costs were $9,265, productivity would be measured as a factor of five. This means that for every dollar in labor costs, $5 in sales was generated. Another way of expressing employee productivity is to divide sales by the number of employees, to arrive at the sales generated per employee.

Other measures of productivity might be the number of covers served by a foodservice employee or the number of guests checked in by a front-desk agent.

Recruitment and Selection

Recruitment and **selection** are the processes of finding the most suitable employee for an available position. The process begins with announcing the vacancy; sometimes this is done first within the organization, then outside. Applications are received from a variety of sources:

✓ Internal promotion
✓ Employee referrals
✓ Applicant files
✓ Transfers within the company
✓ Advertising
✓ Colleges and universities
✓ Government-sponsored employment services

Application forms and résumés are accepted and screened by the human resources department. Many companies require applicants to come to the property and personally fill out the application form. The human resources department then reviews the application form and résumé for accuracy and to ensure that the prospective employee is legally entitled to work in the country. It is advisable to do extensive background checks, although most previous employers will, for legal reasons, generally only give the beginning and ending dates of employment. See Figure 13–6 for a description of the recruitment and selection process.

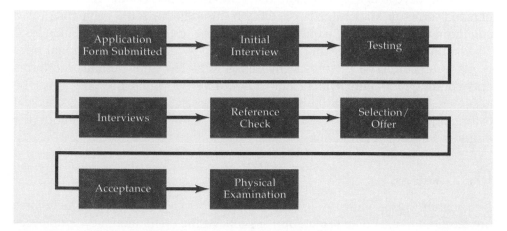

Figure 13–6 *The Recruitment and Selection Process*

*Human Resources Manager
Checking References
(Courtesy John R. Walker.)*

Applicants are invited to attend an interview with the employment manager. This is a general screening interview to determine that the applicant is suitable for employment in a general way. Employment managers look for dress, mannerisms, attentiveness, attitude, and interest; they also ask questions that encourage the applicant to answer in some detail. This necessitates asking open-ended questions such as "What did you like most and least about your last job?" Questions like this invite the applicant to open up. The two-way exchange of information allows the prospective employee to ask or learn about the job and the corporation. Assuming the applicant makes a favorable impression, she or he will be invited for a second interview with the department head. The interview with the department head will assess the candidate's ability to do the job and his or her interpersonal suitability to join the department team.

Selection means to select the most suitably qualified candidate for the available position. Providing candidates meet the minimum requirements stated in the job specification, then the best individual may be selected from the qualified applicants. Part of the selection process might involve tests (personality, aptitude, skill, psychological) to ensure that candidates possess the requisite interpersonal skills or knowledge to do the job. In addition, some companies, as a condition of employment, require new employees to take a drug-screening test.

Assuming the reference and background checks are positive, a formal offer is made in writing to the prospective employee. The offer outlines the terms and conditions of employment and has a date by which the offer must be accepted. The last step in the recruitment and selection process is a medical examination. The medical examination acts as a precaution for both the employee and the corporation.

Orientation

Either prior to beginning or during the first few days of employment, new hires are required to attend an **orientation** session. At the orientation, new employees learn details about the corporation's history and about compensation and benefits. Safety and fire prevention are also introduced as well as the property's service philosophy. Department heads and the general manager usually introduce themselves to the new employees and wish them well in their new positions.

Training

Training in many organizations is an ongoing activity that is conducted by a training department, a training manager, or by line management or specially selected individuals within each department. The first step in establishing a training program is to identify training needs and then set training objectives. Because the training must be geared toward guest expectations, training often focuses on areas where current service falls short of guest expectations.

There are five main types of employee training: apprentice, simulation, certification, on-the-job, and off-the-job. Apprentice training is given to people who are new to a particular job. The training is specially designed to teach participants the correct way to do a particular task. This often follows the "tell me, show me, let me do it" routine.

Simulation training simulates the actual workplace. For example, there are specially prepared simulation exercises for travel agents on the Sabre and Apollo airline reservation systems. Once the trainee has reached the required level of proficiency, she or he then is allowed to do real ticketing.

Certification training enables individuals to gain corporate or professional certification by attaining passing scores on practical or theoretical tests. These tests are generally job specific and are helpful in motivating employees to develop in a professional manner. The Culinary Federation of America operates a certification program, as does the National Restaurant Association and the American Hotel and Motel Association.

On-the-job training (OJT) helps maintain standards by having managers, supervisors, trainers, or fellow employees coach individuals in the most effective way to do the required work. OJT allows the trainee to quickly learn the best way to do the work based on the experience of trial and error. New hotel housekeepers may work with an experienced employee for a few days to learn the preferred way to do rooms.

Off-the-job training is done away from the workplace and is usually used for nontechnical training, such as effective communications, team-building, motivation, and leadership. These topics often are handled by outside experts. These training methods help individuals to quickly learn the job and to improve their performance in doing the work. Some interesting anonymous industry comments heard in training sessions include the following:

✓ People in the organization are a reflection of the leadership.
✓ We don't run restaurants, we manage associations.
✓ We hire cheerleaders.
✓ What do you do to get your employees to smile? SMILE! I'm lucky if they don't look as if they are in pain!!
✓ We are hiring people today that we wouldn't have let in as customers a few years ago.
✓ You can teach nice people, but you can't teach people to be nice.
✓ You achieve what you inspect, not what you expect.

Performance Appraisal

The purpose of a **performance appraisal** is to compare an employee's actual performance to preestablished standards as described in the job description. Performance appraisal has been viewed by the industry as positive as well as negative. The positive attributes of performance appraisal include giving feedback to employees, building the appraisal into a personal development plan, establishing a rationale for promotion and wage/salary increases, and helping to establish objectives for training programs.

Some of the negative aspects of performance reviews include the following:

✓ Too many appraisals expect the immediate supervisor to take sole responsibility for doing the appraisal.
✓ Managers often do a poor job of giving feedback to employees.
✓ Managers save up incidents to dump on employees at evaluation times.
✓ Managers are biased in their appraisals.
✓ Managers may be either too hard or too soft on employees.
✓ Too many employees are not aware of the performance criteria that they will be evaluated against.

Another major difficulty with most performance appraisal systems is that the judgments involved are frequently subjective, relating primarily to personality traits or observations that cannot be verified. Three common distortions in performance appraisals include the following:

✓ *Recent behavior influence.* An evaluator's judgment may be influenced by the employee's recent behavior (good or bad). It is important to guard against giving recent behavior greater emphasis in the appraisal than behavior in general.
✓ *The halo effect.* The halo effect occurs when a supervisor is overly concerned with one particular aspect of the overall job, such as punctuality. If an employee is punctual, he or she will likely receive a better evaluation than one who is occasionally late even if his or her productivity is somewhat less.
✓ *Like-me syndrome.* We all tend to like people who are similar to ourselves; naturally, there is a tendency to give a better appraisal to those employees who are most like ourselves.

There is an inherent weakness in all appraisals. Any system by which a superior rates a subordinate is likely to cause resentment in the person being rated or anxiety in the rater. The basic answer to the anxiety problem is to develop a supportive social system aimed at reducing individual anxiety and thus freeing up energies for constructive purposes. The supportive system includes help from peers and supervisors that will make the employee feel more positive toward the experience and offer a real chance for improvement.

One of the best analogies about managerial feedback to employees was given by Dr. Ken Blanchard in *The One Minute Manager,* who said that there is no such thing as an unmotivated person. An unmotivated employee may be a superstar at the local bowling alley. But imagine that, as Fred rolls the ball down the alley, a supervisor stands there and says "You only knocked down seven pins; why didn't you knock them all down?" Then, to make matters worse, the manager places a curtain in front of the pins so that Fred will not know what to aim for or how well he bowled. Finally, the supervisor removes both the curtain and the pins. When Fred is asked to bowl again, he replies, "I can't; I don't have anything to aim at!" This is analogous to the many people who work for organizations without knowing job performance expectations and the criterion for appraisal.

Performance appraisals make the link between performance standards and organizational goals. Another critical element is the link between the job analysis, job description, and appraisal form. Figure 13-7 shows the importance of the linkage among job analysis, job description, and performance appraisal.

Performance appraisals need to be fair, equal, and nondiscriminatory. Performance—not personality—needs to be judged. Although there are a variety of ways to judge employee performance, the graphic scale is the most widely used rating scale. Such scales generally have either five or seven numbers (see Figure 13-8). An alternative format is shown in Figure 13-9. The biggest advantage of the graphic rating scale is that it saves time for the person completing it, time that should be spent on other things.

Self-appraisal is a form of appraisal that lets employees evaluate their own performance. This may then become the basis of discussion with the supervisor/manager. It also complements an MBO (Management by Objective) program as it enables employees to have a say in setting their own objectives. Obviously, the supervisor/manager will also complete an appraisal form and sit down to compare notes with the employee.

Job Analysis	Describes the job and personal requirements for a particular job.
Performance Standards	States expected performance.
Performance Appraisal	Appraises the level of employee performance and compares each element to standards.

Figure 13-7   *Link among Job Analysis, Job Description, and Performance Appraisal*

Appearance

Neat and in good taste	Neat but occasionally not in good taste	Sometimes careless	Untidy	Not suitable for the job
1	2	3	4	5

Ability to Learn

Learns with exceptional rapidity	Grasps instructions readily	Average ability to learn new things	Somewhat slow in learning	Limited in new duties
1	2	3	4	5

Figure 13–8   *Graphic Rating Scales*

Accuracy

1. (   ) Rarely makes mistakes
2. (   ) Above average
3. (   ) Average
4. (   ) Below average
5. (   ) Highly inaccurate

Figure 13–9 *Performance Appraisal Checklist*

Developmental appraisal is a progressive appraisal technique, aimed at helping the employee to develop and to improve in the performance of his or her duties. A specific employee development plan will stipulate the kind of development that will help the employee to improve performance. An example of this form is shown in Figure 13–10.

The important thing to remember when considering performance appraisal and the law is that managers must run a tight ship. Appraisals must not only be fair but must also be seen to be fair. This means that when appraisals are used as a criteria for promotion (or in extreme circumstances, the release of an employee), the appraisal system must withstand careful scrutiny. It only takes one disgruntled employee to file a grievance with the Equal Employment Opportunity Commission for a substantial amount of management time and money to be spent. Even if the company were to win the case it would still lose money. Team appraisals are becoming popular because most people don't want to let the team down, so each member encourages others to excel.

MBO – DEVELOPMENTAL TYPE APPRAISAL FORM

Priority Urgency	Duties	Performance Expectations	Performance Appraisal				
			Far Below Standard	Below Standard	Meets Standard	Above Standard	Well Above Standard

EMPLOYEE DEVELOPMENT PLAN:

1. What kind of development will help improve performance?
   (_____) a. on-the-job training
   (_____) b. training course
   (_____) c. self-development
   (_____) d.

2. How will this developmental training be arranged? _____
   _____
   _____

3. How long will it take? _____
   _____
   _____

Figure 13–10 *MBO/Development Appraisal Form*

Compensation

Compensation is the term used to describe what most people call a paycheck. Actually, however, compensation is more than a paycheck; it is the total reward system, consisting of established policies and procedures to govern the compensation package. The compensation package includes wages, salaries, and benefits. The term *wages* is generally used with hourly employees, and the term *salaries* is usually used for employees who work for a set rate of pay. Compensation and benefits can amount to 25 to 39 percent of payroll, making them the highest single cost factor in the hospitality industry.

The Fair Labor Standards Act requires industries to distinguish not between management and nonmanagement, but between exempt and nonexempt employees. **Exempt employees** are those who fall under section 13 (a) (1) of the federal minimum wage law. Exempt employees are not paid overtime because they are performing managerial supervisory duties a minimum of 60 percent of their work time. **Nonexempt employees** are paid overtime for any hours worked beyond the thirty-five- or forty-hour workweek.

Appropriate levels of compensation are set once the job is evaluated for skill levels, responsibility, competencies, knowledge, and working conditions. Frequently, a range is set, with increments allowing for progression after a specified time. Jobs then are graded and priced, taking into account items such as tips or service charges.

Some companies offer bonuses or other incentives based on achieving certain results; others have instituted **employee stock ownership plans.** The idea of employee ownership of a company is not new, but it does improve commitment and performance, as does the concept of profit sharing.

Over the years, various legislative acts have been enacted that have affected hospitality human resources. The **Fair Labor Standards Act** (1938 and as amended) is a broad federal statute that covers the following:

- ✓ Federal minimum wage law
- ✓ Employee meals and meal credit
- ✓ Equal pay
- ✓ Child labor
- ✓ Overtime
- ✓ Tips, tip credits, and tip-pooling procedures
- ✓ Uniforms and uniform maintenance
- ✓ Record keeping
- ✓ Exempt versus nonexempt employees

The **Equal Pay Act** of 1963 prohibits companies from paying different salaries on the basis of sex. The **Civil Rights Act** of 1964 went further and established the **Equal Employment Opportunity Commission** (EEOC). This act makes it unlawful to discriminate with respect to hiring, compensating, working conditions, privileges, or terms of employment. In 1967, the **Age Discrimination Act** was passed, prohibiting employment discrimination against those over forty years of age.

Employee safety has become significantly more important because of the large increase in workers' compensation claims. This increase has resulted in large increases in insurance premiums. Employers have been forced to pay special attention to employee safety, including the use and handling of dangerous chemicals.

Employee assistance programs (EAPs) have been instituted at many progressive companies. Employees who have problems may request help (assistance) in confidence, without losing their jobs. The emphasis of most EAPs is on prevention and on intervening before a crisis stage is reached.

Employee Development

Employee development is a natural progression from appraisal. A development plan is made by the employee and his or her supervisor. The plan will outline the development activity and indicate when the development will take place. In well-run corporations, employee development is ongoing; it may take the form of in-house training or workshops and seminars on specific topics.

Certification is an excellent form of employee development because it validates a person's ability to do an excellent job and become more professional. Certification can be internal or external. Internal certification occurs when a company has stipulated certain criteria associated with a position (such as knowing the menu, being able to describe each item, and so on). External certification occurs when an employee takes courses toward a professional designation, such as the National Restaurant Association's Foodservice Management Professional (FMP).

Employee Retention

Employee retention is the exact opposite of employee turnover. Whether it is called retention or turnover, the subject is still a major concern for the hospitality industry, in general, and human resources directors, in particular.

It is frustrating for management to spend time and effort on employees who go through the employment process only to leave a short time later. Retention is expressed as a percentage; if a department has one hundred employees on January 1 and sixty-three stay through the year, then the retention rate is 63 percent. This means that thirty-seven people left the organization and had to be replaced. Experts estimate that the turnover of one hourly position per week costs between $150,000 and $213,000 per year.[3]

Peter Yu, president of Richfield Hotel Management, estimated that the entire industry loses $1.8 billion per year because of employee turnover. Each turnover costs Richfield about $1,400. Richfield has a 35 to 40 percent retention rate, which has improved by 10 percent since beginning an employee-maintenance program; the next goal is to achieve 50 percent retention.[4]

To reduce losses, Ritz-Carlton intensified its employee-selection process. Then the company encouraged employees' input in creating their work environment. Within a few years, the company lowered its turnover rate from 90 percent to 30 percent. Ritz-Carlton aspires to maintain a 20 percent turnover rate.[5]

[3]Timothy N. Troy, "Hospitality Associations Waging War in Minnesota," *Hotel and Motel Management,* **208,** 15, September 6, 1993, p. 6.

[4]Ibid.

[5]Ibid.

Marriott International became a public company in October 1993, when Marriott Corporation split into two separate companies. Marriott International manages lodging and service businesses. It has operations in fifty states and fifty-seven countries, with approximately 145,000 employees. It has annual sales of about $8 billion.

Host Marriott Corporation focuses on two basic businesses—real estate ownership and airport and toll-road concessions. Host Marriott has operations or properties in thirty-eight states and six countries, with approximately 23,000 employees. The company has annual sales of about $1.3 billion, with significant operating cash flow.

Marriott International, Inc.

"We are committed to being the best lodging and management services company in the world by treating employees in ways that create extraordinary customer service and shareholder value."
—Mission statement

Marriott International owns the trademarks, trade names, and reservation and franchise systems that were formerly owned by Marriott Corporation. The new company has two operating groups. Their divisions are leaders in their respective businesses and enjoy strong customer preference.

The Lodging Group is comprised of several Marriott's hotel management divisions: Marriott Hotels and Resorts, managing or franchising full-service hotels (2,000 hotels); Courtyard, the company's moderately priced lodging division (478 hotels); Residence Inns, the leader in the extended-stay segment (333 hotels); Fairfield Inn, Marriott's economy lodging division (417 hotels); TownePlace Suites, the newest moderately priced lodging product designed for the extended-stay traveler (the first opened in 1997); Ritz-Carlton, the premier hotel brand in the luxury segment (35 hotels); Renaissance Hotels and Resorts, providing upscale, full-service accommodations for business, group, and resort travelers (99 hotels); and Marriott Vacation Club International, a premier developer and operator of time-share projects (71,000 interval owners at 31 resorts). In total, the group manages or franchises over 1,200 hotels with approximately 229,000 rooms.

The service group has three principal divisions. Marriott Management Services provides food and facilities management for business, education, and health care clients, with more than 3,000 accounts. Marriott Senior Living Services manages communities offering independent and assisted living for older Americans. Marriott Distribution Services provides food and related products to the company's operations and external clients through eleven distribution centers. J. W. Marriott, Jr., is chairman, president, and chief executive officer of Marriott International.

Host Marriott Corporation

The leading operator of airport and tollroad food, beverage, and merchandise concessions, Host Marriott expanded in 1992 by acquiring the airport operations of Dobbs Houses, Inc. Host Marriott now serves approximately seventy-five airports, primarily in the United States, with some concessions in Australia, New Zealand, and Pakistan. The company also operates ninety-three food and merchandise units on fourteen U.S. tollroads and has concessions at forty-two sports and entertainment attractions. Host is a licensee of seventeen major nationally branded food and merchandise concepts.

The company owns 122 Marriott lodging properties (including two hotels now under construction) and fourteen retirement communities, located in thirty-three states and three countries that are managed under long-term agreements with Marriott International, Inc. Host Marriott or its subsidiaries act as general or limited partners in a number of Marriott lodging partnerships, and own certain parcels of land.

Host Marriott's lodging portfolio includes twenty-eight full-service hotels, among them the San Francisco Marriott and the New York Marriott Marquis; fifty-four Courtyard hotels (moderate price segment); eighteen Residence Inn properties (extended-stay segment); and thirty Fairfield Inn properties (economy segment). Richard E. Marriott is chairman of Host Marriott.

Equal Employment Opportunity

Equal employment opportunity (EEO) is the legal right of all individuals to be considered for employment and promotion on the basis of their ability and merit. The intent of this legislation is to prevent discrimination against applicants for the reasons given in the Civil Rights Act. The EEOC is the organization that individuals may turn to if they feel that they have been discriminated against. If it agrees, the commission will file charges against individuals or organizations.

Americans with Disabilities Act

The **Americans with Disabilities Act** (ADA) has two components: employment and public accommodations. The ADA prohibits discrimination against persons with disabilities and stipulates that employers must make "readily achievable" modifications to their premises and to the work practices and working conditions for the disabled. Existing facilities need not be retrofitted to provide full accessibility. However, barrier removal that is readily achievable and easily completed without significant difficulty or expense is required in all existing buildings.

Harassment

Employers are responsible for creating and maintaining a working environment that is pleasant, and for avoiding hostile, offensive, intimidating, or discriminatory conduct or statements. In other words, the workplace must be kept free from all forms of **harassment,** including those based on sex, race, religious choice, ethnic background, and age. Sexual harassment, in particular, has occurred frequently during the past few years. Although very controversial in its identification and definition, sexual harassment does include unwanted sexual advances, requests for sexual favors, and verbal or physical actions of a sexual nature. It is important to note that an offensive environment does not need to involve a request for sexual favors. An offensive environment also may be created by lewd jokes or comments, displaying explicit or sexually suggestive material, or hands-on behavior.

To handle such an issue in an appropriate manner, the management should take the following actions:

1. Establish a sexual harassment policy that defines clearly what will not be tolerated and states the penalties for violation.
2. React promptly to reports with even-handed, thorough investigation.
3. Keep all instances confidential.
4. Keep appropriate documentation and decide on the appropriate disciplinary action.

Culture

Culture is a learned behavior. Someone who lives in the United States learns from its culture a unique set of beliefs, values, attitudes, habits, customs, traditions, and other forms of behavior. Besides other cultures like African, Asian, Latino, European, and American, there are cultural variations, such as African-American, Asian-American, Hispanic-American, European-American, and French-Canadian, for example. These cultural variations are a blend of cultures.

Culture influences the way people behave, and there are many differences among the various cultures. For instance, American culture is more individualistic than the Asian or Latin cultures. Consider also the differences between the genders in these cultures. America's multicultural society gives us an opportunity to learn from one another instead of simply thinking "my way is best." It is best to be aware of and respect the culture of others and try to harmonize with it; otherwise, misunderstanding might occur.

Multicultural management recognizes cultural differences among employees that are attributable to membership in distinct ethnic groups. Multicultural management is an approach to managing the workplace that allows for differences in values arising from gender, economic level, and age, as well as ethnic group. In today's hospitality industry, it is necessary for managers—and, indeed, all employees—to have a cross-cultural awareness and an understanding of ethnic identity. Cultural barriers in hospitality workplaces do exist, therefore it is important to understand ethnic diversity, minorities, and how to train ethnic groups in order to understand the various cultural aspects in our hospitality workplace.

Cultural Barriers

Culture can be manifested in many ways, such as style of dress, language, food, gestures, manners, and so on. Although many individuals have difficulty dealing with foreign customs and language, these are relatively easy components, because they are visible and comprehensible. It is much harder to detect and to deal with values, assumptions, and perceptions.

Adjusting to another culture can be particularly frustrating if one comes from a low-context culture and has to operate in a high-context culture. A low-context culture is one in which the bulk of information, intentions, and meanings are conveyed in words and sentences; context, therefore, plays a smaller role. High-context cultures are those in which the context is of great importance and what is behind the words is as important as the words themselves.

The North American and North European cultures are low-context cultures. Information and intentions are expressed in words and sentences in the clearest possible manner. The prevailing culture in Japan is a high-context culture;

not only does what is said count, but how it is said, who said it, and when. What was not said is also significant, as are the pauses, the silences, and the tone. In high-context cultures, reading between the lines and interpreting the meaning behind the words is of utmost importance; the words themselves have different meanings and do not always convey true intentions to an outsider. For example, the Japanese rarely use the word *no;* instead, they use a host of substitutes that may not convey their true intention to the Western ear. Similarly, when Japanese use affirmative statements, they do not assign the same meaning to them as we do.

Language

Language can be another barrier to cultural understanding. Even when people use the same language, misunderstandings and misinterpretations occur. The same words and symbols have different meanings to individuals from different cultural backgrounds.

Ethnic Diversity

Ethnic diversity refers to accepting all people regardless of appearances or mannerisms. Cultural diversity enriches the workplace. America's ethnic diversity is growing. By the year 2000, the workforce consisted of Hispanics, 29 percent; African-Americans, 18 percent; and Asian-Americans, 11 percent.[6] These core groups will be the backbone of the hospitality industry. The growth projected for the Asian and Hispanic populations in the United States will, in the twenty-first century, mean that one-quarter to one-third of all workplaces will belong to racial or ethnic minority groups.[7]

Personal Cultural Barriers

We too often approach others from our own cultural perspective and expect them to be like us. We react when people respond or behave in a way that is "different." These behaviors may lead to stereotyping—always expecting certain groups to behave in certain ways. A bad experience with one person does not mean that all experiences with others from that culture will be bad. Preconceived negative attitudes about certain groups are called *prejudice.*

Ideally, the managers of tomorrow will welcome the ethnic diversity that they are bound to encounter, and they will have a personal desire to learn more about cultures and environments different from their own. But even those employers who don't see cultural pluralism as an extension of the practices of American democracy realize that they must be prepared to function effectively

---

[6]Dennis Law, "Making Diversity Work," *Restaurants and Institutions,* **104,** 2, January 15, 1994, p. 84.
[7]Ibid.

as hospitality managers in a pluralistic environment. Culture has a profound impact on the attitudes, priorities, and behavior of individuals and groups. To be able to interact with people from different cultures is vital in order to understand their values, norms, and priorities.

Hospitality managers have a responsibility to develop and recognize the realities facing the hospitality industry in the next ten to fifteen years. Ethnic and cultural diversity is a large part of that reality.

Trends in Marketing, Human Resources, and Culture

✓ Human resources directors becoming marketing oriented in order to attract and retain the best possible employees
✓ Human resources directors becoming more proactive in employment and staffing
✓ Use of the Internet for posting vacancies and e-mail for applications
✓ Use of more behavioral, structured interviews
✓ Relationship marketing, including keeping track of guests, sending birthday cards, etc.
✓ Partnering, such as a Subway store at a gas station, twin restaurant locations, or cooperative advertising (i.e., American Express and Delta Airlines)
✓ Direct marketing with databases of mailing lists
✓ Use of the Internet for communicating information and for reservations

Case Study

Cooperation

The executive housekeeper of the Lattuca Inn has repeatedly complained to you about Bernise, a long-time housekeeper at the hotel. As the human resources manager, you feel obliged to confront Bernise about ignoring her boss. Bernise says she does not like the executive housekeeper and, after speaking with her, she still refuses to cooperate.

Recently, Bernise was asked to present a voucher for her lunches. Reports have come in from the employee cafeteria showing that she still will not cooperate.

Discussion Question

1. As human resources manager, what should you do?

Case Study

Too Much of a Good Thing

Schrock's Pub and Steak House in Little Doe, Montana, is a booming success and has been for more than thirty years. Once the only establishment in Little Doe, Schrock's is now facing competition from other independent restaurant/bars and a few large, national chains along the lines of Chili's and Applebee's. Schrock and his sons, proprietors of Schrock's after purchasing the pub from Ken Crocker prior to World War II, saw the effect that the new competition was having on overall sales and revenue. They realized that while they were unable to compete on price, they could indeed compete in other areas such as menu offerings and ambiance. Through strict controls on cost, both in the kitchen and in the bar, they were able to remain competitive. Whereas in the past, a dish was prepared at the whim and attitude of the cook, to the delight of the patrons, all recipes were now standardized. Under the new kitchen controls, food cost to sales were lowered and each item's contribution margin increased. The same type of controls were instituted in the bar with similar results.

All was well with Schrock's Pub until Jay, the grandson of Jacob, returned home from the university, where he majored in hospitality/restaurant management. When the elder Schrock sat down with Jay to review the business prior to Jay's becoming assistant general manager, Jay noted that Schrock's seemed to be holding onto its usual customer base. Sales were relatively flat and overall profit, while not as good as prechain competition days, was okay. Jay noticed and pointed out to the elder Schrock that since all the new controls were put into effect, consumer complaints were increasing. The complaints centered around the portion size and lack of bite in the bar drinks. Obviously, the clientele, although loyal, were expressing some dissatisfaction when they compared the new Schrock's to the old. Further research found that customers did not think that the service was as personal as it used to be. For example, everyone knew John Reigal did not particularly like the taste of vodka, but Al the bartender was no longer able to tailor John's drinks due to the new control system. Similar stories about the lack of responsiveness of the waitstaff were forthcoming from an informal focus group.

The family then began to discuss the merits of standardization that had kept Schrock's afloat as opposed to the less conventional approach that made Schrock's a success in the early years. The discussion swirled around issues of efficiency, empowerment, control, and competitive edge.

The Schrock's have contracted you, a senior associate at Norman Hotel and Restaurants Inc., an international consulting firm, to assist in bettering Schrock's Pub.

Discussion Question

1. How would you advise them?

Case Study

The Forum Takes Wing

In August 1994, Steve Departe, former chef at the exclusive Broodmoore Country Club, and his wife Alice Cable opened The Forum, a classic European restaurant in a small suburb of a large, Midwestern city.

Given their experience, including Alice's family's having a successful chain of pizza shops, the Forum opened to great acclaim. The local newspaper's restaurant critic gave it four out of five forks. The critic especially praised the level of service, the atmosphere, and the appetizers and entrees. The food was of top quality and prepared fresh with great flair. The waitstaff was pulled from various area restaurants and country clubs and, thus, had a great deal of experience and knowledge of foodservice.

Not only did The Forum receive good press, it also enjoyed good word-of-mouth recommendations. For a town and metro area accustomed to Midwestern fare—steak, chops, ribs, chicken, and so forth—The Forum was a success.

The Forum also contained a lounge to handle the waiting crowds. In keeping with Chef Departe's vision, it had an extensive selection of premium wines for both the lounge and dining room. Also true to his vision, beer selection was limited to a few imports and only the top domestic brand. The liquor selection was not spectacular, but offered a great deal more variety than many other local restaurants and stand-alone lounges.

The dining room, especially on the weekends, was full. It was not very large, seating only eighty-five customers. Reservations were a must for Friday and Saturday, however Sunday was usually the slowest day. The weekdays were often very slow, but the rush during the weekend evened out the week. The average check per diner was about $16.50 on the weekends. This represented an average contribution margin of almost $6.00. Food cost to sales ranged from 43.1 to 47.3 percent. A separate analysis of the lounge showed a contribution margin of almost $4.00 per person and food and beverage cost to sales ratio of only 27 percent.

When Chef Departe became aware of the results, he did some research on the surrounding proprietors and friends in the industry. He concluded that his food cost to sales ratio was too high. He also noticed the abundance of sports bars in the area and their relatively low food cost to sales ratio and high contribution margins.

During the summer of 1995 and fall of 1996, Chef Departe expanded his lounge business to include a few inexpensive bar items such as chicken wings and onion rings. He also extended the selection of beers available. Chef Departe eventually gave the lounge a sports theme, taking advantage of the local baseball team being in the playoffs and the new football expansion team. He installed two large-screen televisions for the fans and ran "munchie" and dinner specials during televised events of the home team. The results astounded Chef Departe, as his lounge total sales climbed and his margin increased. By December 1996, The Forum had been redesigned and reopened as The Arena, a premier sports bar specializing in hot wings and fried mushrooms.

Much to the dismay of Chef Departe, the results did not mirror his lounge's initial success. Within a month, his total revenues were 40 percent below the previous year. His staff of trained, expert servers were let go and replaced with fewer and less well trained college students.

Discussion Questions

1. What do you think went wrong with the running of the restaurant?
2. How would you advise Chef Departe and his wife as far as changing the concept of the restaurant is concerned?
3. What marketing strategies would you use to bring in customers and keep the contribution margins high and the food cost to sales ratio low?
4. How would you handle the situation?

Career Information

Marketing, Human Resources, and Culture

Many hospitality seniors are drawn to the area of marketing and human resources as a career. Marketing in the hospitality industry is synonymous with "sales." Both of the careers involve working closely with people on an individual basis.

Sales positions for college graduates are most often found through hotel chains and country clubs. An excellent way to prepare for this position is to work in a hotel sales office or member-relations area in a country club as a part-time assistant or as an intern. Another significant opportunity would be to help open a hotel or participate in a sales blitz. Opportunities like these will give you exposure to client relations, marketing programs, revenue meetings, sales calls, special events, and public relations.

To be a successful salesperson, you have to be self-motivated, gregarious, and organized. Communicating and understanding the wants and needs of customers is the hallmark of effective salespeople. A career in marketing and sales includes a great deal of freedom and responsibility. Salespeople often work alone and are away from the property a great deal of the time. It is a job where you dress professionally, have some latitude in determining your work agenda, and meet new people every business day. Other responsibilities include scheduling your workday, setting appointments, and keeping current customers or members satisfied. Careers in sales and marketing include attractive bonuses and offer a path for promotions and professional growth that can be the focus of your entire career.

Human resources is another specialized area offering increased career opportunities and professional growth. A career can lead to becoming a vice president of human resources. Companies are paying close attention to their investment in employees and are offering a wide variety of incentives to attract and retain talented people. Today, it is not uncommon for individual lodging properties to have a human resources position. Smaller properties will hire new college graduates and split their responsibilities between human resources and another job assignment. Human resources is no longer the exclusive domain of human resource majors. Companies are expanding human resources opportunities to include hospitality majors. Part of the allure for college graduates is the typical five-day workweek, conventional hours, and working in an office setting.

Related Web Sites

http://www.hoteljobresource.com/advertised_positions. htm—hotel sales jobs

www.hsmai.org;—Hospitality Sales and Marketing Association International

www.clubcorp.com—ClubCorp

http://www.shrm.org/hrmagazine/—*Human Resources* magazine

Courtesy of Charlie Adams.

Summary

1. Marketing and human resources are specialized departments that serve other departments of the hospitality industry.
2. The main purpose of marketing is to create customers. It includes environmental, social, political, technological, and competitive analysis. Place, product, price, promotion, packaging, programming, and people make up the marketing mix of hospitality.
3. Efficient, guest-focused employees are important for the success of an industry. Applicants have to go through a recruitment and selection process, orientation, and careful training.

4. Employees are evaluated by performance appraisals. In order for an appraisal to be fair there has to be a close link between job analysis, job description, and the appraisal.
5. Every hospitality industry is required to comply with the Equal Employment Opportunity Commission, to make modifications to the workplace and its practices to accommodate workers with disabilities, and keep the workplace free of all forms of harassment.
6. As America's ethnic diversity is growing, management needs to recognize cultural differences. In this sense it is essential to avoid stereotyping and to consider differences such as language, values, and perceptions.

Key Words and Concepts

Age Discrimination Act
Americans with Disabilities Act
Civil Rights Act
Comparison matrix
Compensation
Competitor analysis
Culture
Demographics
Economic analysis
Employee assistance program
Employee development
Employee retention

Employee stock ownership plan
Environmental analysis
Equal employment opportunity
Equal Employment Opportunity Commission
Equal Pay Act
Ethnic diversity
Exempt and nonexempt employees
Expense accounts
Fair Labor Standards Act
Harassment

Human resources management
Job analysis
Job description
Market assessment
Market demand
Market share
Marketing action plan
Marketing goals and objectives
Marketing mix
Orientation
Performance appraisal

Place, product, price, promotion
Political analysis
Positioning
Productivity standards
Product life cycle
Recruitment
Selection
Social analysis
Target markets
Task analysis
Technological analysis
Training

Review Questions

1. What is meant by the term *market assessment?* In this context explain the purpose of environmental analysis.
2. Explain the purpose of competitive analysis and explain the terms *comparison matrix* and *positioning.*
3. Describe the importance of price and product and list two ways used to determine price.
4. What is the difference between marketing and sales?

5. Name and describe positive and negative effects of performance evaluation, in consideration of the like-me syndrome and halo effect.
6. What is the EEOC? and ADA?
7. Define culture and its impact on the hospitality industry in today's pluralistic environment.

Internet Exercises

1. Organization:
   Web site:
   Summary:
   (a) What can the HSMAI foundation do for you?
   (b) Take a look at the HSMAI "Think Tank." What conclusions can you draw from the current topic being addressed?
2. Organization:
   Web site:
   Summary:
   (a) Briefly discuss two of the latest news articles related to human resources and how they impact the industry.
   (b) Click on the "Student Program" icon and look at "Getting Started" in HR management. What are some of the current career options being addressed?

Hospitality Sales & Marketing Association International
http://www.hsmai.org
Hospitality Sales & Marketing Association International is an organization of international hospitality sales and marketing professionals
Click on the "Resources" icon and answer the following questions.
Society for Human Resource Management
http://www.shrm.org
The Society for Human Resource Management is one of the largest human resource associations. This web site provides in-depth information to both students and professionals around the globe.

Apply Your Knowledge

1. Describe the complexities of performance appraisal.
2. Who are exempt and non exempt employees?
3. What is culture and multicultural management?

Leadership and Management

After reading and studying this chapter, you should be able to:

- ✓ Distinguish the characteristics and practices of leaders and managers.
- ✓ Define leadership and management.
- ✓ Distinguish between transactional and transformational leadership.
- ✓ Describe the key management functions.
- ✓ Differentiate between leadership and management.
- ✓ Define ethics and apply the importance of ethical behaviors to the hospitality industry.

Leadership

Our fascination with **leadership** goes back many centuries. Lately, however, it has come into prominence in the hospitality, tourism, and other industries as they strive for perfection in the delivery of services and products in an increasingly competitive environment. Leaders can and do make a difference when measuring a company's success.

Few tasks or goals can be accomplished by one person working alone. You have probably already experienced being part of a group that had good leadership—it might have been with a school, social, sporting, church, or other group in which the leader made a difference. The reverse might also be true—you may have been in a group with ineffective leadership. Few groups can accomplish much without an individual who acts as an effective leader. The leader can and often does have a significant influence on the group and its direction.

Characteristics and Practices of Leaders

So, what are the ingredients that result in leadership excellence? If we look at the military for examples of leadership excellence, we see that leaders can be identified by certain characteristics. For example, the *U.S. Guidebook for Marines* lists the following leadership traits:

✓ Bearing	✓ Integrity
✓ Courage	✓ Judgment
✓ Decisiveness	✓ Justice
✓ Dependability	✓ Knowledge
✓ Endurance	✓ Loyalty
✓ Enthusiasm	✓ Tact
✓ Initiative	✓ Unselfishness

A Marine officer would likely choose integrity as the most important trait. Integrity has been described as doing something right even though no one may be aware of it.

In addition to the leadership traits just listed, the following identifiable practices are common to leaders:

1. *Challenge the process:* Be active, not passive; search for opportunities; experiment and take risks.
2. *Inspire a shared vision:* Create a vision; envision the future; enlist others.
3. *Enable others to act:* Do not act alone; foster collaboration; strengthen others.
4. *Model the way:* Plan, set examples; strive for small wins.
5. *Encourage the heart:* Share the passion; recognize individual contributions; celebrate accomplishments.

Definitions of Leadership

Because of the complexities of leadership, the different types of leadership, and individual perceptions of leaders, leadership has several definitions. Many definitions share commonalities, but there are also differences. In terms of hospitality leadership, the following definition is appropriate: *Leading is the process by which a person with vision is able to influence the activities and outcomes of others in a desired way.*

Leaders know what they want and why they want it—and they are able to communicate those desires to others to gain their cooperation and support. Leadership theory and practice has evolved over time to a point where current industry practitioners may be identified as transactional or transformational leaders.[1]

Transactional Leadership

Transactional leadership is viewed as a process by which a leader is able to bring about desired actions from others by using certain behaviors, rewards, or incentives. In essence, an exchange or transaction takes place between leader and follower. Figure 14–1 shows the transactional leadership model. This concept illustrates the coming together of the leader, the situation, and the followers. A hotel general manager who pressures the food and beverage director to achieve certain goals in exchange for a bonus is an example of someone practicing transactional leadership.

Transformational Leadership

Leadership involves looking for ways to bring about longer term, higher order changes in follower behavior. This brings us to transformational leadership. The term **transformational leadership** is used to describe the process of eliciting performance above and beyond normal expectations. A transformational leader is one who inspires others to reach beyond themselves and do more than they originally thought possible; this is accomplished by raising their commitment to a shared vision of the future.

Transformational leaders practice a hands-on philosophy, not in terms of performing the day-to-day tasks of subordinates, but in developing and encouraging

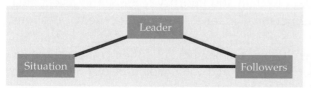

Figure 14–1 *Transactional Leadership Model*

[1] For a more detailed review of the many leadership theories, consult one of the many texts on the topic.

their followers individually. Transformational leadership involves three important factors:

1. Charisma
2. Individual consideration
3. Intellectual stimulation

Of course, it is also possible to be a charismatic transformational leader as well as a transactional leader. Although this does involve a measurable amount of effort, these leaders are guaranteed to rake in success throughout their careers.

Examples of Excellence in Leadership

Martin Luther King, Jr.

Dr. Martin Luther King, Jr., was one of the most charismatic transformational leaders in history. King dedicated his life to achieving rights for all citizens by nonviolent methods. His dream of how society could be was shared by millions of Americans. In 1964 Dr. King won the Nobel Peace Prize.

Another transformational leader was Herb Kelleher, former president, CEO, and current board member of Southwest Airlines. He was able to inspire his followers to pursue his corporate vision and reach beyond themselves to give Southwest Airlines that something extra that set it apart from its competitors.

Kelleher recognized that the company did not exist merely for the gratification of its employees; he knew that Southwest Airlines must perform and be profitable. However, he believed strongly that valuing individuals for themselves was the best way to attain exceptional performance. Passengers who have flown Southwest Airlines may have seen Herb Kelleher, because he traveled frequently and was likely to be found serving drinks, fluffing pillows, or just wandering up and down the aisle talking to passengers. The success of Southwest and the enthusiasm of its employees indicate that Herb Kelleher achieved his goal of weaving together individual and corporate interests so that all members of the Southwest family benefited. Kelleher proved that transformational behavior (visioning, valuing, articulating, inspiring, empowering, and continually communicating) could be practiced by leaders in all types of organizations and at all levels.[2]

In their fascinating book entitled *Lessons in Leadership: Perspectives for Hospitality Industry Success,* Bill Fisher, former president and CEO of the American Hotel and Motel Association and currently Darden Chair at the University of Central Florida, and Charles Bernstein, editor of *Nation's Restaurant News,* interviewed more than 100 industry leaders and asked each to respond in an up-close-and-personal manner to some excellent questions. Some of their answers follow.

"Experience is a hard teacher. It gives the test first, and then you learn the lesson." Richard P. Mayer, former chairman and CEO of Kentucky Fried Chicken

[2]Donald D. White and David A. Bednar, *Organizational Behavior: Understanding and Managing People at Work,* 2nd ed. Boston: Allyn and Bacon, 1991, p. 413.

and president of General Foods Corporation, says that the key traits and factors that he looks for in assessing talent included the following:

✔ Established personal goals
✔ The drive and ambition to attain those goals, tempered and strengthened with integrity
✔ Proven analytical and communications skills
✔ Superior interpersonal capabilities
✔ A sense of humor
✔ An awareness and appreciation of the world beyond her or his business specialty
✔ Receptivity to ideas (no matter the source)
✔ A genuine, deep commitment to the growth and profitability of the business[3]

James Irwin is president and CEO of Emco Foodservice Systems, a major food service distribution firm headquartered in Pittsburgh, Pennsylvania, and a member of the Food Service Distribution Hall of Fame. He commented that "many people are not willing to pay the price for success, yet do not realize the rewards far outweigh the costs. Many people follow a path of 'least resistance' that limits their ability to exercise their full potential." He suggested that "success is exceptional performance and achievement on a consistent basis over a period of time," and "a successful person will lead with an authority earned by integrity and not compromise ethics or morals for financial gain or position."[4]

The essence of success has as many meanings as there are people to ponder it. One concept of success is to couple one's personal and family interests, dreams, and aspirations with a business or professional career such that they complement and fortify each other. Another aspect of leadership is the ability to motivate others in a hospitality-working environment; decision making is also essential. These are discussed later in the chapter.

Isadore Sharp is the founder, chairman, and CEO of the Four Seasons Hotels and Resorts.[5] Sharp has been named Canada's outstanding CEO of the year. He was chosen from a blue-chip list of Canadian executives as the business leader who best exemplifies excellence in corporate achievement, leadership, vision, innovation, and global competitiveness. In just forty years, Sharp built his business from a single hotel on Jarvis Street in downtown Toronto to one of the world's largest luxury hotel and resort operation, with fifty-five hotels in twenty-five countries.

A Great Restaurant Industry Leader

Another great leader in the restaurant industry was Ray Kroc of McDonald's, whose actions tell the tale. Consider the following example of how Ray Kroc instilled his vision of cleanliness: On his way back to the office from an important lunch at the best place in town, Ray Kroc asked his driver to pass through several McDonald's parking lots. In one parking lot, he spotted paper littering the parking area. He went to the nearest pay phone, called the office, got the name of the store manager, and called him to offer help in picking up the trash. Both Ray Kroc, the owner of the McDonald's chain in his expensive business suit, and the young manager of the store met in the parking lot and got on their hands and knees to pick up the paper.

This anecdote has been told thousands of times within the McDonald's system to emphasize the importance of the vision of cleanliness.

[3]W. P. Fisher and C. Bernstein, *Lessons in Leadership: Perspectives for Hospitality Industry Success.* New York: Van Nostrand Reinhold, 1991, p. 44.

[4]Ibid, p. 29.

[5]Harvey Chipkin, "Portrait of a Visionary," *Lodging,* **27**, 3, Nov. 2001, p. 67.

Isadore Sharp, Founder, Chairman, and CEO, Four Seasons Hotels and Resorts
(Courtesy of Four Seasons Hotels and Resorts.)

Issy Sharp, as he is known, has the ability to conceive a vision of what is possible, the business acumen to plan for success, and the unique gift to inspire others to help carry the dream through to reality. Sharp was an architect working with his father in a two-man construction company when he chose to develop a property in Toronto into an elegant, hospitable home-away-from-home for business or leisure travelers.

Since opening the first hotel, Four Seasons has grown into a top international luxury hotel chain. Sharp credits his staff for the Four Seasons' success. Sharp also plays a key role in the community; not only is he a director of several corporations, but he also has a special affinity for activities that support cancer research because he lost a young son to the disease. He initiated the corporate sponsorship for the Terry Fox Marathon of Hope and continues to direct the annual run, which has been tagged as the largest fund-raising event in the world, having raised millions.[6]

Demands Placed on Leaders

Demands on a leader in the hospitality industry include those made by owners, the corporate office, guests, employees, regulatory agencies, and competitors (Figure 14–2). In response to many demands, the leader must balance two additional forces: how much energy to expend on getting results and how much to expend on relationships (Figure 14–3).

Applied social scientists like Peter Drucker, powerful industry leaders like Bill Marriott, and public service leaders like former New York mayor Rudolph Giuliani all seem to have common traits, among which are the following[7]:

1. High ego strength
2. Ability to think strategically

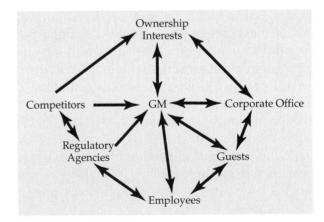

Figure 14–2 *Dynamics of Demands on General Managers in the Hospitality Industry*

---

[6]This draws on Doug Caldwell, "Isadore Sharp: Outstanding CEO of the Year," *Canadian Manager*, Spring 1993, pp. 16–17.

[7]Frances Hesselbein, "How to Be," in F. Hesselbein, M. Goldsmith, and R. Beckhard (eds.), *The Leader of the Future.* San Francisco: Jossey-Bass, 1996, p. 136.

Figure 14–3 *Amount of Energy the General Manager Needs to Spend on Getting Results and Maintaining Relationships*

3. Orientation toward the future
4. A belief in certain fundamental principles of human behavior
5. Strong connections that they do not hesitate to display
6. Political astuteness
7. Ability to use power both for efficiency and for the larger good of the organization

Leaders vary in their values, managerial styles, and priorities. Peter Drucker the renowned management scholar, author, and consultant of many years has discussed with hundreds of leaders their roles, their goals, and their performance. These discussions took place with leaders of large and small organizations, with for-profit and volunteer organizations. Interestingly, Drucker observes, "All the leaders I have encountered—both those I worked with and those I watched—realized:

1. The only definition of a leader is someone who has followers. Some people are thinkers. Some are prophets. Both roles are important and badly needed. But without followers, there can be no leaders.
2. An effective leader is not someone who is loved or admired. She or he is someone whose followers do the right things. Popularity is not leadership. Results are.
3. Leaders are highly visible. They therefore set examples.
4. Leadership is not about rank, privileges, titles, or money. It is about responsibility.[8]

Drucker adds that regardless of their enormous diversity with respect to personality, style, abilities, and interests, effective leaders all behave in much the same way:

1. They did not start out with the question "What do I want?" They started out asking *"What needs to be done?"*
2. Then they asked, *"What can and should I do to make a difference?"* This has to be something that both needs to be done and fits the leader's strengths and the way she or he is most effective.
3. They constantly asked, "What are the organization's *mission* and *goals?* What constitutes *performance* and *results* in this organization?

---

[8]This draws on Peter F. Drucker, "Foreword," in F. Hesselbein, M. Goldsmith, and R. Beckhard (eds.), *The Leader of the Future.* San Francisco: Jossey-Bass, 1996, pp. xii–xiii.

4. They were extremely tolerant of diversity in people and did not look for carbon copies of themselves. It rarely even occurred to them to ask, "Do I like or dislike this person?" But they were totally—fiendishly—intolerant when it came to a person's *performance, standards,* and *values.*

5. They were not afraid of *strength* in their associates. They gloried in it. Whether they had heard of it or not, their motto was the one Andrew Carnegie wanted to have put on his tombstone: "Here lies a man who attracted better people into his service than he was himself."

6. One way or another, they submitted themselves to the *mirror test*—that is, they made sure the person they saw in the mirror in the morning was the kind of person they wanted to be, respect, and believe in. This way they fortified themselves against the leader's greatest temptations—to do things that are popular rather than right and to do petty, mean, sleazy things.[9]

Finally, these leaders were not preachers; they were doers.

(Courtesy of Van E. Eure.)

Van E. Eure's foodservice career began when she was a teenager, waiting tables at the Angus Barn, known to loyal patrons as North Carolina's "Beefeater's Haven." Her father, Thad Eure, Jr., and his partner, Charlie Winston, established the Angus Barn in 1960. After college, Eure taught high school English and elementary school in Kenya, Africa, for five years; in 1982, she returned to the United States to join her father in the restaurant business. In 1984, she was promoted to senior dining room manager and, following the death of her father in 1988, she took over the operation of the restaurant with her mother, Alice Eure. Today, the restaurant has a seating capacity of 600 and employs 180 people.

Eure's professional and civic activities include the following: member, Knights of the Vine; member, La Chaine des Rotisseurs; board member, North Carolina Citizens of Business and Industry; board member, Public Service Company of North Carolina; board member, Theatre in the Park; member, The Fifty Group (a local networking organization of top executives); and member, The Foundation of Hope (for research and treatment of mental illness, founded by Thad Eure, Jr.). Eure has been named Master Lady by the Raleigh Chapter of Knights of the Vine and awarded the Mondavi Medal of Honor by the national La Chaine des Rotisseurs.

Leadership focuses on style and ideals, whereas management focuses on the method and process. Leadership does not produce consistency and order, as the word itself implies, it produces movement.[10]

The leadership challenge is about leading people, not merely managing them. Leadership begins where management ends, where the systems of rewards and punishments, control and scrutiny, give way to innovation, individual character, and the courage of convictions.[11]

[9]Ibid, p. ix.

[10]Ibid.

[11]James M. Kouzes and Barry Z. Posner, *The Leadership Challenge: How to Get Extraordinary Things Done in Organizations.* San Francisco: Jossey-Bass, 1987, p. xvii.

Markets, customers, technology, and competitors continually change. The active leader anticipates these changes and strategically adapts the organization to continue to prosper in the following ways:

1. Repositioning products and services to build a competitive advantage
2. Recruiting talented people to execute the new strategies
3. Establishing organizational resources that focus tightly on new stategies[12]

The most effective leaders share a number of skills, and these skills are always related to dealing with employees. The following suggestions outline an approach to becoming a hotel leader rather than just a manager:

✔ *Be decisive.* Hotel managers are confronted with dozens of decisions every day. Obviously, you should use your best judgment to resolve those decisions that come to roost at your doorstep. As a boss, make the decisions that best meet both your objectives and your ethics, and then make your decisions known.

✔ *Follow through.* Never promise what you can't deliver, and never build false hopes among your employees. Once expectations are dashed, respect for and the reputation of the boss are shot.

✔ *Select the best.* A boss, good or bad, is carried forward by the work of his or her subordinates. One key to being a good boss is to hire the people who have the best potential to do what you need them to do. Take the time and effort to screen, interview, and assess the people who have not only the skills that you require, but also the needed values.

✔ *Empower employees.* Give people the authority to interact with the customer. The more important people feel, the better they work.

✔ *Enhance career development.* Good bosses recognize that most of their people want to improve themselves. However, career development is a two-edged sword: If we take the imitative to train and develop our people properly, then the competition is likely to hire them. The only way a boss can prevent the loss of productive workers looking for career development is to provide opportunities for growth within the organization.

In recent years, the role of the hotel general manager has changed from that of being a congenial host, knowledgeable about the niceties of hotelmanship, to that of a multi-group pleaser. Guests, employees, owners, and community all need to be not just satisfied, but delighted, with the operations performance. Oh sure, the guest comes first—but you had better deliver the numbers (profit). Many general managers are so bogged down with meetings, reports, and "putting out fires" that they hardly have any time to spend with guests. One GM who makes time is Richard Riley, GM of the fabulous Shangri-La hotel Makati, Manila, Philippines. Richard extends an invitation for guests to visit with him in the hotel lobby between 5:00 and 7:00 P.M. every Thursday. As GM of a luxury Caribbean resort in Barbados, West Indies, the author personally greeted every guest to the property. Obviously there is a difference between a small resort and a large city hotel; resort guests stay for at least two, sometimes four, weeks in

---

[12]James A. Belasco, *Teaching the Elephant to Dance.* New York: Plume, 1991, p. 6.

Corporate Profile: Carlson Companies

With operations in more than 140 countries, Carlson Companies is one of the largest privately held corporations in the United States and a leader in providing hospitality management, franchising, and direct-to-consumer services.[1]

Led by Chairperson and Chief Executive Officer Marilyn Carlson, Carlson Companies continues to build on a cornerstone set by her father Curt Carlson nearly sixty-five years ago: developing long-lasting relationships with clients.

The history of Carlson Companies is one of the classic business success stories in the American free enterprise system. Starting in 1938 with merely an idea and $55 of borrowed capital, entrepreneur Curtis L. Carlson founded the Gold Bond Stamp Company in his home city of Minneapolis, Minnesota. His trading stamp concept, designed to stimulate sales and loyalty for food stores and other merchants, proved to be right for the times and swept the nation in a wave of dramatic growth.

Marilyn Carlson Nelson
(Courtesy of Carlson
Companies.)

Through the years, Carlson diversified into hotels, travel, and other related businesses. In the 1960s, Carlson and several other partners collectively bought an interest in the original Radisson Hotel in downtown Minneapolis. Eventually Carlson became sole owner of the hotel brand and expanded it around the globe. Today, there are 432 Radissons in fifty-nine countries.

To reflect the company's growing diversification, its name was changed in 1973 from the Gold Bond Stamp Company to Carlson Companies. Four hotel brands are part of Carlson Hospitality Worldwide, one of Carlson's major business groups. They are Regent International Hotels, Radisson Hotels and Resorts, Country Inns & Suites by Carlson, and Park Plaza and Park Inn hotels. In addition, Carlson hospitality brands include T.G.I. Friday's and Pick Up Stix restaurants, and Radisson Seven Seas Cruises.

Carlson Hospitality Worldwide encompasses more than 1,570 hotel, resort, restaurant, and cruise ship oper-

high season, so they need the individual attention. Since the tragedy of September 11, 2001, managers have found it even more difficult to maintain profitability. Immediately after the horrific event, occupancy slumped to single digits and was expected to take months to fully recover. American hotels were not the only ones to suffer low occupancies in the wake of the terrorist event. The tragedy made it very evident that the world's economy is interlinked. Overseas, in Europe, Asia, and elsewhere, hotel occupancies plummeted as American and Japanese tourists and businesspeople stayed home.

Hospitality Management

Managers forecast, plan, organize, make decisions, communicate, motivate, and control the efforts of a group to accomplish predetermined goals. Management also establishes the direction the organization will take. Sometimes this is done with the help of employees or outside consultants, such ations in eighty-one countries. Lodging operations include more than 810 locations in sixty-three countries. Restaurant operations include more than 753 locations in fifty-five countries, and cruise operations include six luxury ships with an additional vessel under construction.

These hospitality group brands and services, combined with sister companies Carlson Marketing Group, Carlson Wagonlit Travel, and other travel industry companies and consumer incentive programs, provide employment for more than 188,000 people around the world.

In addition to global business success, Carlson Companies is also recognized as a top employer. Both *Fortune* and *Working Mother* magazines have rated the company as one of their "100 Best Places to Work in America."

Marilyn Carlson Nelson became chief executive officer of Carlson Companies in 1998 on the retirement of her father and company founder, Curt Carlson. On his death in 1999, she succeeded him as chairman of the board.

Marilyn is a regular on *Fortune* magazine's list of the Most Powerful Women in Business, and has been selected by *Business Week* as one of the Top 25 Executives in Business. Marilyn has been ranked by *Travel Agent* magazine as the "Most Powerful Woman in Travel" annually since 1997.

In 2002, she was appointed by President George W. Bush to chair the National Women's Business Council. The council serves as an independent source of advice and counsel to the president, Congress, the U.S. Small Business Administration, and the Interagency Committee on Women's Business.

Marilyn has also served as national chair of the Travel Industry Association of America and is a member of the Council of the World Economic Forum and serves on the forum's board of governors for travel and tourism.

Among the hospitality industry-related honors she has received are the Cutting Edge Award by American Hotel & Lodging Association and the Stephen W. Brener Lodging Hospitality Silver Plate Award presented at the Annual New York University Hospitality Industry Investment Conference. She was named Hospitality Executive of the Year by the Penn State Hotel and Restaurant Society in 2000.

Marilyn graduated from Smith College with a degree in international economics and attended the Sorbonne in Paris and the Institute des Hautes Etudes Economiques Politiques in Geneva, Switzerland, studying political science and international economics.

---

[1]This section draws on Bill Carlino, "Carlson Cos," *Nation's Restaurant News*, **27**, 13, March 29, 1993, pp. 43–84.

---

as marketing research specialists. Managers obtain the necessary resources for the goals to be accomplished, and then they supervise and monitor group and individual progress toward goal accomplishment.

Managers, such as presidents and chief executive officers who are responsible for the entire company, tend to focus most of their time on strategic planning and the organization's mission. They also spend time organizing and controlling the activities of the corporation. Most top managers do not get involved in the day-to-day aspects of the operation. These duties and responsibilities fall to the middle and supervisory management. In hospitality lingo, one would not expect Bill Marriott to pull a shift behind the bar at the local Marriott hotel. Although capable, his time and expertise are used in shaping the company's future. Thus, although the head bartender and Bill Marriott may both be considered management, they require slightly different skills to be effective and efficient managers.

What Is Management?

Management is simply what managers do—forecast, plan, organize, make decisions, communicate, motivate, and control. Management is defined as *the* *process of coordinating work activities so that they are completed efficiently and effectively with and through other people.*[13] In looking at this statement, we can see that the functions of management and coordinating the work of others are ongoing. Additionally, management involves getting efficient and effective results.

Efficiency is getting the most done with the fewest number of inputs. Managers work with scarce resources: money, people, time, and equipment. You can imagine the rush in the kitchen to be ready for a meal service. But, it's not enough to just be efficient, management is also about being effective. **Effectiveness** is "doing the right thing." As an example, cooks do the right thing when they cook the food correctly according to the recipe and have it ready when needed.

Who Are Managers?

The changing nature of organizations and work has, in many hospitality organizations, blurred the lines of distinction between managers and nonmanagerial employees. Many traditional jobs now include managerial activities, especially when teams are used. For instance, team members often develop plans, make decisions, and monitor their own performance. This is the case with total quality management.

So, how do we define who managers are? A *manager* is someone who works with and through other people by coordinating their work activities in order to accomplish organizational goals.[14]

Managers are often classified into three levels: **frontline managers** are the lowest level managers; they manage the work of line employees. They may also be called supervisors. A front office supervisor, for example, takes charge of a shift and supervises the guest service agents on the shift.

Middle managers are akin to department heads; they fall between frontline managers and top management. They are responsible for short- to medium-range plans, and they establish goals and objectives to meet those goals. They manage the work of frontline managers.

Top managers are responsible for making medium- to long-range plans and for establishing goals and strategies to meet those goals. Ali Kasiki is a top-level manager. He holds the title of managing director and is involved in creating and implementing broad and comprehensive changes that affect the entire organization. Figure 14–4 shows the three levels of management plus nonmanagerial employees.

Throughout the management chapters (Chapters 14 through 20), we will be discussing management as it relates to the hospitality industry.

---

[13]Stephen P. Robbins and Mary Coulter, *Management,* 7th. ed. Upper Saddle River, NJ: Prentice Hall, 2002, p. 6.

[14]Ibid, p. 5.

| Top Managers |
| Middle Managers |
| Frontline Managers |
| Nonmanagerial Associates |

Figure 14–4 *Three Levels of Management Plus Nonmanagerial Associates*

Key Management Functions

The key management functions are *planning, organizing, decision-making, communicating, motivating,* and *controlling.* These management functions are not conducted in isolation; rather they are interdependent and frequently happen simultaneously or at least overlap. Figure 14–5 shows the key management functions leading to goal accomplishment.

Hospitality companies exist to serve some purpose and someone has to determine the purpose and the means for its achievement. That someone is management.[15] The **planning** function involves setting the company's goals and developing plans to meet or exceed those goals. Once plans are complete, **organizing** is the process of deciding what needs to be done, who will do it, how the tasks will be grouped, who reports to whom, and who makes decisions.

Decision making is a key management function. The success of all hospitality companies, whether large multinational corporations or sole proprietorships, depends on the quality of the decision making. Decision making includes determining the vision, mission, goals, and objectives of the company. Decision making also includes scheduling employees, determining what to put on the menu, and responding to guest needs. The chapter on decision making details long- and short-range decisions, centralized and decentralized decisions, programmed and nonprogrammed decisions, and the steps in the decision-making process.

Communication with and motivation of individuals and groups are required to get the job done. **Motivating** involves keeping morale high, molding corporate culture, and managing conflicts and communication.[16]

A General Manager's Survival Kit

Ali Kasiki of the Peninsula Beverly Hills, California. offers his list[1]:

- *Know* yourself, your own core competencies, and your values.
- *Hire* a seasoned management team.
- *Build* barriers of entry; that is, make yourself indispensable.
- *Be* very flexible.
- *Get* close to your guests and owners to define reality versus perception.
- *Show leadership,* from both the top and the bottom.
- *Delegate.* There is no way you can survive without delegation.
- *Appeal* to trends.
- *Trust* your instincts.
- *Take* risks and change the ground rules.
- *Being* overconfident is bad.
- *Look* successful, or people will think you're not.
- *Manage* the future—it is the best thing you can do. Bring the future to the present.

[1]Personal correspondence with Ali Kasiki, November 4, 2001.

[15]Ibid, p. 6.

[16]Gary Dessler, *A Framework for Management.* Upper Saddle River, NJ: Prentice Hall, 2002, p. 7.

Figure 14–5 *Key Management Functions Leading to Goal Accomplishment*

Controlling is the final management function that brings everything full circle. After the goals are set and the plans formulated, management then organizes, communicates, and motivates the resources required to complete the job. Controlling includes the setting of standards and comparing actual results with those standards. If significant deviations are seen, they are investigated and corrective action taken to get performance back on target. This process of monitoring, comparing, and correcting is the controlling function.

Managerial Skills

In addition to the management functions of forecasting, planning, organizing, communicating, motivating, and controlling, managers also need other major skills: conceptual, interpersonal, and technical.

Conceptual skills enable top managers to view the corporation as a complete entity and yet understand how it is split into departments to achieve specific goals. Conceptual skills allow a top manager to view the entire corporation, especially the interdependence of the various departments.

Managers need to lead, influence, communicate, supervise, coach, and evaluate employees' performances. This necessitates a high level of interpersonal human skills. The ability to build teams and work with others is a human skill that successful managers need to cultivate.

Managers need to have the technical skills required to understand and use modern techniques, methods, equipment, and procedures. These skills are more important for lower levels of management. As a manager rises through the ranks, the need for technical skills decreases and the need for conceptual skills increases.

We next need to realize the critical importance of the corporate philosophy, culture, and values, and corporation's mission, goals, and objectives. Figure 14–6 shows the degree of managerial skills required by top managers, middle managers, and supervisory managers.

The Manager's Changing Role

The manager's role is changing so fast that some, like management guru Peter Drucker, say "I'm not comfortable with the word *manager* anymore, because it

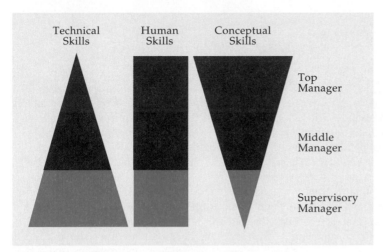

Figure 14–6 *Management Skill Areas*

implies subordinates."[17] Managers may still have subordinates but today's successful manager takes more of a team leader/coach approach.

There are, of course, other ways to "slice and dice" what managers do. For example, managers don't just plan, organize, make decisions, communicate, motivate, and control. They wear a variety of hats, including the following:

✔ *Figurehead role.* Every manager spends some time performing ceremonial duties. For example, the president of a corporation might have to greet important business guests/clients or represent the corporation by attending dinners.

✔ *Leader role.* Every manager must function as a leader, motivating and encouraging employees.[18]

✔ *Liaison role.* Managers spend a lot of time in contact with people in other departments both within the organization and externally. An example would be the sales manager liaising with the room's division director.

✔ *Spokesperson role.* The manager is often the spokesperson for the organization. For example, a manager may host a college class visit to the property.

✔ *Negotiator role.* Managers spend a lot of time negotiating. For example, the head of a company may negotiate with a union representative to establish wages and benefits for employees.

---

[17]Peter Drucker, "The Coming Age of Organization," *Harvard Business Review,* January–February 1998, p. 45. See also Fred Andrews, "The Sage of Value and Service," *New York Times,* November 17, 1999, pp. C1–C14; as cited in Dessler, *Framework for Management,* p. 6.

[18]These are based on Henry Mintzberg, "The Manager's Job: Folklore and Fact," as cited in Dessler, *Framework for Management,* p. 8.

You, Too, Are a Manager[1]

Your classmates have just voted you to be the leader-manager of the summer study-abroad trip to France. None of you know much about France or how to get there, what to do when there, and so on. Where would you start? (Resist the temptation to delegate the whole trip to a travel agent, please.)

You might start by thinking through what you need to do in terms of planning, organizing, deciding, communicating, motivating, and controlling. What sort of plans will you need? Among other things, you'll need to plan the dates your group is leaving and returning, the cities and towns you'll visit, the airline you'll take there and back, how the group will get around France, and where you'll stay when you're there. As you can imagine, plans like these are very important: You would not want to arrive at Orly Airport with a group of friends depending on you and not know what to do next.

Realizing how much work is involved—and that you cannot do it all and still maintain good grades—you get help. You divide up the work and create an organization by asking someone to check airline schedules and prices, another person to check hotel prices, and someone else the sites to see and the transportation needs. However,

the job won't get done with the group members simply working by themselves. Each person requires guidance and coordination from you: The person making the airline bookings can't confirm the bookings unless she knows what city and airport the trip will originate in. Similarly, the person making the hotel arrangements can't make any firm bookings until he knows what cities are being visited. To improve communications you could set up regular meetings with e-mail updates between meetings. Leadership and motivation could be a challenge because two of the group members do not get along well. So ensuring that everyone stays focused and positive will be a challenge.

Of course, you'll have to make sure the whole project remains "in control." If something can go wrong, it often will, and that's certainly the case when groups of people are traveling together. Everything needs to be double-checked. In other words, managing is something we do almost every day, often without even knowing it.

[1]Adapted from Gary Dessler, *A Framework for Management.* Upper Saddle River, NJ: Prentice Hall, 2002, p. 8.

These roles, together with the management functions, encompass what managers do. Remember, managers need to be many things—often in quick succession—even to the point of wearing two or more hats at once.

The twenty-first-century managers face not only a more demanding and increasingly complex world but also a more dynamic and interdependent one. The "global village" is a reality and socio-cultural traditions and values need to be understood and diversity respected and encouraged by future managers. The two most important changes going on right now are the technological advances and the internationalization of hospitality and tourism. The extent to which you as a future **leader-manager** can master these events and functions will determine your future.

The manager's role is not only internal but also external. For instance, a manager must be responsive to market needs and income generation. Managers must continually strive to be innovative by realizing efficiencies in their respective areas of responsibility through process improvement, for example, by determining how to reduce long check-in lines at airports and hotels. Some companies use innovative and creative ways to streamline the check-in procedures to make the process a more worthwhile experience for the guests. Disney, for instance, uses the creative approach of sending Mickey and the gang to entertain the guests while they stand in line.

Distinction between Leadership and Management

Leadership and management are ageless topics. Leadership has been described as a social influence process that can occur in nearly any interaction among people. Leadership has a broader scope than management, which came in vogue about 100 years ago with its more narrow focus on accomplishing organizational goals. Modern management was invented, in a sense, to help the new railroads, steel mills, and auto companies achieve what legendary entrepreneurs envisioned. Without such management, these complex enterprises tended to become chaotic in ways that threatened their very existence.[19]

Managing is the formal process in which organizational objectives are achieved through the efforts of subordinates. *Leading* is the process by which a person with vision is able to influence the behavior of others in some desired way. Although managers have power by virtue of the positions they hold, organizations seek managers who are leaders by virtue of their personalities, their experience, and so on.

The differences between management and leadership can be illustrated as follows[20]:

Manager	Leader
administers	innovates
is a copy	is an original
maintains	develops
focuses on systems and structure	focuses on people
relies on control	inspires the truth
has a short-range view	has a long-range perspective
asks how and when	asks what and why
has an eye on the bottom line	has an eye on the horizon
initiates	originates
accepts the status quo	challenges it
does things right	does the right thing

[19]John P. Kotter, *A Force for Change: How Leadership Differs from Management.* New York: Free Press, 1990, p. 97.

[20]Warren Bennis, *On Becoming a Leader.* Reading, MA: Addison-Wesley, 1994, p. 45

Check Your Knowledge

1. What are the characteristics of leaders?
2. Describe the different types of leadership.
3. What is the distinction between leadership and management?

Ethics

Ethics is a set of moral principles and values that people use to answer questions about right and wrong. Ethics can also be defined as the study of the general nature of morals and the specific moral choices to be made by the individual in his or her relationship with others.[21] Much individual interpretation of ethics is based on one's own system.

Where did this value system originate? What happens if one value system is different from another? Fortunately, certain universal guiding principles are agreed on by virtually all religions, cultures, and societies. At the very root of all principles is that all people's rights are important and should not be violated. This belief is central to civilized societies; without it, chaos would reign.

Today, many people have few moral absolutes, they decide situationally whether it is acceptable to steal, lie, or drink and drive. They seem to think that what is right is whatever works best for the individual. In a country blessed with so many diverse cultures, you might think it is impossible to identify common standards of ethical behavior. However, among sources from many different times and places such as the Bible, Aristotle's *Ethics,* William Shakespeare's *King Lear,* the Koran, and the *Analects* of Confucius, you'll find the following basic moral values: integrity, respect for human life, self-control, honesty, and courage. Cruelty is wrong. All of the world's major religions support a version of the Golden Rule: Do unto others as you would have them do unto you.[22] Forte Hotels International for many years adopted the belief of Lord Forte that we should take care of our guests as we would like to be taken care of. Today, we should continue to uphold that standard.

The foreword to *Ethics in Hospitality Management,* edited by Stephen S. J. Hall, Robert A. Beck Professor Emeritus at Cornell University, poses the age-

[21] Angelo M. Rocco and Andrew N. Vladimir, *Hospitality Today: An Introduction.* East Lansing, MI: The Educational Institute, American Hotel and Motel Association, 1991, p. 390.

[22] Christina Holf Sommers, "Are We Living in a Moral Stone Age?" *USA Today,* March 1, 1999; Barbara Frank, "Knowing Yourself Is the First Step," *Toronto Sun,* April 17, 2000, p. 54; and Jack Kemp, "A Golden Age to Sustain," *The Washington Times,* January 3, 2001, p. A13, as cited in William Nickels, James M. McHugh, and Susan M. McHugh, *Understanding Business,* 6th ed. Boston: McGraw-Hill Irwin, 2002, p. 96.

old question: "Is overbooking rooms ethical? How does one compare the legal responsibilities of the innkeeper to the moral obligation?" He adds that to compound the situation further, what is a "fair" or "reasonable" wage? A "fair" or "reasonable" return on investment? Is it "fair" or ethical to underpay employees for the benefit of the investors?

"English Common Law left such decisions to the 'reasonable man.' A judge would ask the jury, 'Was this the act of a reasonable man?'"[3] Interestingly, what is considered ethical in one country may not be in another. For example, in some countries it is considered normal to bargain for rooms; in others, bargaining would be considered bad form.

Ethics and morals have become an integral part of hospitality decisions, from employment (equal opportunity and affirmative action) to truth in memos. Many corporations and businesses have developed a code of ethics that all employees use to make decisions. This became necessary because too many managers were making decisions without regard to the impact of such decisions on others. Hall is one of the pioneers of ethics in hospitality; each year, he organizes a scholarship for an essay on a topic related to ethics in hospitality. Hall also developed a code of ethics for the hospitality service and tourism industry:

1. We acknowledge ethics and morality as inseparable elements of doing business and will test every decision against the highest standards of honesty, legality, fairness, impunity, and conscience.
2. We will conduct ourselves personally and collectively at all times so as to bring credit to the service and tourism industry at large.
3. We will concentrate our time, energy, and resources on the improvement of our own products and services and we will not denigrate our competition in the pursuit of our success.
4. We will treat all guests equally regardless of race, religion, nationality, creed, or sex.
5. We will deliver all standards of service and product with total consistency to every guest.
6. We will provide a totally safe and sanitary environment at all times for every guest and employee.
7. We will strive constantly, in words, actions, and deeds, to develop and maintain the highest level of trust, honesty, and understanding among guests, clients, employees, employers, and the public at large.
8. We will provide every employee at every level all of the knowledge, training, equipment, and motivation required to perform his or her tasks according to our published standards.
9. We will guarantee that every employee at every level will have the same opportunity to perform, advance, and be evaluated against the same standard as all employees engaged in the same or similar tasks.

---

[23]Stephen S. J. Hall (ed.), *Ethics in Hospitality Management: A Book of Readings.* East Lansing, MI: The Educational Institute, American Hotel and Motel Association, 1992, p. 75.

10. We will actively and consciously work to protect and preserve our natural environment and natural resources in all that we do.
11. We will seek a fair and honest profit, no more, no less.

Robert Hass, CEO of Levi Strauss & Co., has an interesting comment on corporate ethics and value: "Companies have to wake up to the fact that they are more than a product on a shelf. They're a behavior as well."[24]

Some corporations use a statement of aspirations to define shared values that will guide both workforce and corporate decisions. For example, at Levi Strauss, each employee is expected to take a part in the so-called core curriculum series of training programs that deal with values, ethical practices, empowerment, and an appreciation of diversity. The purpose is to release the enormous power of involved employees.

Ethical Dilemmas in Hospitality

In the old days, certain actions may not have been considered ethical but management often looked the other way. A few scenarios follow that are not seen as ethical today and are against most companies' ethical policies:

1. As catering manager of a large banquet operation, the flowers for the hotel are booked through your office. The account is worth $15,000 per month. The florist offers you a 10 percent discount. Do you accept this? If you accept this, with whom do you share it?
2. As purchasing agent, you are responsible for procurement of $5 million worth of perishable and nonperishable items for a major restaurant chain. To get your business, a supplier offers you a substantial bargain on a house. You can live in the house, which will be under another person's name, for as long as you continue to buy from this supplier. The quality of this supplier's products and services is equal to that of other suppliers. What should you do with the offer?
3. An edict has recently come from the executive committee of the hotel that reservations from a certain part of the world were only to be taken through the embassy because the hotel had experienced severe problems with guests from this part of the world. On one occasion, one of the occupants of a suite had sent a servant to the park to collect wood, which they then used to make a fire in the room in order to prepare food. They wondered why bells were ringing and why fifteen fire trucks had arrived. Now a group of well-dressed men from the country mentioned in the edict approaches you, offer greetings, and say that their boss, a very distinguished individual, would like to stay for an indefinite period. They produce a briefcase full of $100 bills as a deposit. You decline, stating that the hotel is full, which it is not. What should you have done?

These and other ethical dilemmas are not always simply right or wrong.

[24]Jim Impoco, "Working for Mr. Clean Jeans," *U.S. News and World Report,* **115,** 5, August 2, 1993, p. 50.

Post 9–11: Disaster Management and Leadership

Hank Christen and Paul Maniscalco

Managing a facility during a disaster is the most demanding management challenge of an executive's career. Historically, many hospitality facilities have been damaged or destroyed in attacks or disasters. In the World Trade Center disaster, the Millennium and Marriott Hotels were destroyed with the towers. The MGM Grand Hotel fire resulted in major damage, with multiple deaths and injuries to the resort staff. Miami hotels and resorts were lost in hurricane Andrew. Less spectacular disasters—natural, technological, and man-made—severely affect the hospitality industry daily.

Disaster management usually begins abruptly and without warning. The important realities are:

✔ A chaotic and emotional environment
✔ No time for consensus
✔ Necessity for making fast, high-stakes decisions with inadequate data
✔ Members of the manager's employee team may be injured or dead

A hospitality manager needs to realize that he or she relinquishes management authority when emergency professionals arrive. Emergency response agencies (fire, police, and emergency medical services) use a national disaster management model called the *incident management system (IMS)*. The director of an incident is called the *incident manager* (or the *incident commander*). The incident manager (IM) has total responsibility and authority for the management of tactical operations. It is important for the hospitality manager to assume the role of technical advisor and liaison to the local incident management staff.

Hospitality managers and their staffs possess information that is essential to the local IM:

✔ Architectural drawings of the facility and related infrastructure
✔ Knowledge of facility utilities such as gas, electrical power, and water
✔ Knowledge of the heating, ventilation, and air conditioning systems
✔ Knowledge of security operations and procedures
✔ Information related to facility supplies such as food, water, building materials, and sheets/blankets

In essence, the hospitality management team is a valuable resource to support local incident management teams. The hospitality support team should be organized according to the IMS template, namely, the following five major functions:

1. Manager and staff. The staff includes a safety officer, a liaison officer to integrate with on-scene agencies, and a media representative to coordinate with the local public information officer.
2. Operations director, who ensures effective operations of hospitality and guest services insofar as possible.
3. Logistics director, who provides logistical support such as communications, food/water, supplies/equipment, and relevant infrastructure to emergency responders.
4. Planning director, who assists the facility manager in developing an internal incident action plan and coordinates with the IMS planning section chief.
5. Administration/finance director, who maintains all records and documents relating to a disaster, including financial expenditures and tracking of employee compensation/workmen's compensation.

Critical Factors

✓ Disasters begin abruptly; plan ahead.
✓ Staff and employees have expertise and information that is critical.
✓ During a crisis, leadership is as important as management.

During a disaster, a hospitality manager must lead as well as manage. Inspirational leadership extends beyond basic management principles. Leadership requires visibility and personal contact. When possible, the manager should give instructions and orders personally. It is important for the team to see the manager working with them; the manager must try to make personal contact with as many of his or her people as possible. The manager must positively reinforce the people he supervises, and must forgive their mistakes.

It is vital that the manager project confidence and stability. He or she must make every effort to stay emotionally level. Finally, it is the manager's responsibility to keep everyone informed, even when the news is bad. People will fill an information vacuum with rumors if they are not informed.

Figure 14–7 *Hilton's Corporate Mission (Courtesy of Hilton Hotels Corporation, Beverly Hills, California.)*

To be recognized as the world's best first-class hotel organization, to constantly strive to improve, allowing us to prosper as a business for the benefit of our guests, our employees, and our shareholders.

Fundamental to the success of our mission are the following:

PEOPLE:
Our most important asset. Involvement, teamwork, and commitment are the values that govern our work.

PRODUCT:
Our programs, services, and facilities. They must be designed and operated to consistently provide superior quality that satisfies the needs and desires of our guests.

PROFIT:
The ultimate measure of our success—the gauge for how well and how efficiently we serve our guests. Profits are required for us to survive and grow.

With this mission come certain guiding principles:

QUALITY COMES FIRST:
The quality of our product and service must create guest satisfaction; that's our number one priority.

VALUE:
Our guests deserve quality products at a fair price. That is how to build business.

CONTINUOUS IMPROVEMENT:
Never standing on past accomplishments, but always striving—through innovation—to improve our product and service, to increase our efficiency and profitability.

TEAMWORK:
At Hilton, we are a family, working together, to get things done.

INTEGRITY:
We will never compromise our code of conduct—we will be socially responsible—we are committed to Hilton's high standards of fairness and integrity.

Three key categories of questions need to be answered when making decisions:

1. Is it legal? Will I be violating either civil law or company policy?
2. Is it balanced? Is it fair to all concerned in the short term as well as the long term? Does it promote win–win relationships?
3. How will it make me feel about myself? Will it make me proud? Would I feel good if my family knew about it?

Social Responsibilities in Business

Ethics is broadly concerned with how persons or organizations act, or should act, in relation to others. The so-called breakdown of socially acceptable behavior appears to be a universal problem. Whatever the cause, this malaise has affected business, government, and society.

In recent years, society's interest in, and awareness of, **social responsibility** has increased enormously. For example, the "greening" of North America has led to a decrease in the use of hazardous chemicals, including some pesticides. The protection and preservation of the environment has become a major issue for most of the population.

Social responsibility, however, goes beyond doing away with nonbiodegradable fast-food containers to becoming involved in the community in which a company or one of its hospitality-tourism operations is located. This is known as giving something back to the community. For example, consider Hilton's corporate mission (Figure 14–7).

Trends in Leadership and Management

- ✔ Leading a more diverse group of associates
- ✔ Many entry-level employees do not have basic job skills
- ✔ An increasing need for training
- ✔ The need to create leaders out of line managers
- ✔ Managing sales revenue all the way to the bottom line
- ✔ Establishing independent business units to make their own profit, or subcontracting out that department
- ✔ Instead of keeping a person on payroll for a function that is only needed occasionally, outsourcing that service to specialists
- ✔ Cutting down on full-time employees and hiring more part-time employees to avoid paying benefits
- ✔ An increasing challenge to keep up with technological advances and their benefits
- ✔ Social and environmental issues continue to increase in importance

Case Study

Performance Standards

Charles and Nancy both apply for the assistant front office manager position at a 300-room upscale hotel. Charles has worked for a total of eight years in three different hotels and has been with this hotel for three months as a front office associate. Initially he had a lot of enthusiasm. Lately, however, he has been dressing a bit sloppily and his figures, cash, and reports have been inaccurate. In addition, he is occasionally "rattled" by demanding guests.

Nancy recently graduated from college, with honors, with a degree in hospitality management. While attending college, she worked part-time as a front desk associate at a budget motel. Nancy does not have a lot of experience working in a hotel, or in customer service in general, but she is quite knowledgeable as a result of her studies and is eager to begin her career.

It appears that Charles would have been considered a prime candidate for the office manager position, because of his extensive experience in other hotels and his knowledge of the hotel's culture. In view of his recent performance, however, the rooms division manager will need to sit down with Charles to review his future career development track.

Discussion Questions

1. What are the qualifications for the job that should be considered for both applicants?
2. How should the discussion between the rooms division manager and Charles be handled? Make specific recommendations for the rooms division manager.
3. Who would be the best person for the job? Why?

Case Study

Reluctant to Change

You have just been appointed assistant manager at an old, established but busy New York restaurant. Your employees respond to your suggested changes with, "We have always done it this way." The employees really do not know any other way of doing things.

Discussion Question

1. How should you handle this situation?

Career Information

Leadership and Management

As a college graduate, you will be expected to fill a leadership role when you complete your education. It is more than likely that you will be working with hourly wage employees ranging from minimum-wage employees to skilled professionals. These are people who may have been working for the company for years and are extremely good at what they do.

So, are we all leaders and can we develop our leadership skills? We all have leadership capabilities and, yes, we can develop our leadership skills. Leadership begins with each of us. We need to define our vision, mission, goals, and objectives. However, leadership is more than just defining goals, it is how we go about doing this. But you've got to know where you're going and how to get there. Then it's just a matter of becoming a believer.

Leading these employees is your challenge as a manager. This means gaining their confidence and trust. Unless you know what you are doing, it is difficult—if not impossible—to accomplish. Part of being an effective leader is not asking anybody to do anything that you would not do yourself. Motivating employees is much easier when you have a real appreciation for their jobs and this is where your work experience in college will pay off. You will have a much keener insight into your employees' jobs if you have done what they are doing. Your experience will help you with the difficult and challenging task of keeping your employees motivated and working together as a team.

Your college education is important, but a valuable part of that education comes from your work experience while in college. Upon graduation, if your experience reflects your desire, you will possess the necessary skills and ability to excel as a manager for the hospitality industry.

Courtesy of Charlie Adams.

Summary

1. Leadership is defined as the process by which a person is able to influence the activities and outcomes of others in a desired way.
2. Contemporary leadership includes transactional and transformational types of leadership.
3. Increased demands placed on hospitality leaders include ownership, corporate, regulatory, employee, environmental, and social interests. Leaders must balance results and relationships.
4. Managing is the process of coordinating work activities so that they are completed efficiently and effectively with and through other people.
5. Leaders, according to Drucker, realized four things and behaved in much the same way.
   (a) A leader is someone who has followers—some people are thinkers, and some are prophets.
   (b) An effective leader is not someone who is loved or admired, but rather someone whose followers do the right things. Popularity is not leadership; results are.
   (c) Leaders are highly visible. Leaders set examples.

   (d) Leadership is not about rank, privileges, titles, or money. It is about responsibility.
6. There are six key management functions: planning, organizing, decision-making, communicating, motivating, and controlling. However, in addition from these functions, managers occasionally have to fill roles such as figurehead, leader, spokesperson, or negotiator.
7. The difference between management and leadership is that the former is the formal process in which organization objectives are achieved through the efforts of subordinates, and the latter is the process by which a person with vision is able to influence the behavior of others in some desired way.
8. Ethics, a set of moral principles and values that people use to answer questions about right and wrong, must be incorporated into management behavior as well. Ethics and morals have become an integral part of hospitality decisions, and the scenarios that are considered unethical today are against most companies' ethics policies.

Key Words and Concepts

Communication
Controlling
Decision making
Effectiveness
Efficiency
Ethics
Frontline managers
Leader-managers
Leadership
Management
Middle managers
Motivating
Organizing
Planning
Social responsibility
Top managers
Transactional leadership
Transformational leadership

Review Questions

1. What kind of leader-manager will you be?
2. Give examples of the management functions as they apply to the hospitality industry.
3. Discuss the changing role of managers.

4. Define leadership and name the essential qualities of a good leader.
5. Distinguish between transactional and transformational leadership.

Internet Exercises

1. Organization:
   Web site:
   Summary:
   Click on the "Careers" icon and scroll down to "General Management." Answer the following questions.
   (a) What are the requirements for becoming a GM, and what tips does Wet Feet.com have to offer?
   (b) The "Career Overview" section illustrates several attributes that managers have in common. In groups, list these attributes and discuss their significance.

2. Organization:
   Web site:
   Summary:
   Find the section entitled "AMA Research." Choose two current reports. Read through these and make a bulleted list of the key information. Then write a description of how this information might affect the way a hospitality manager plans, organizes, makes decisions, communicates, motivates, and controls.

3. Organization:
   Web site:
   Summary:
   Click on the "About Us" icon. Then click on "Other Ritz-Carlton Businesses." Now go to the "Ritz-Carlton Leadership Center" and answer the following questions.
   (a) What is Ritz-Carlton's Leadership Orientation?
   (b) What are the seven habits of highly effective people?

Wet Feet.com
http://wetfeet.com
Wet Feet.com is an organization dedicated to helping you make smarter career decisions. Wet Feet.com provides inside insight on jobs and careers for both job seekers and recruiters. By all means take the time to check this one out!

American Management Association
http://www.amanett.org
The American Management Association (AMA), a practitioner-based organization, offers a wide range of management development programs for managers and organizations.

Ritz-Carlton Hotel Company
http://www.ritzcarlton.com
Ritz-Carlton hotels are known for their superior luxury and service in the hospitality industry. This particular web exercise illustrates how the Ritz-Carlton maintains its culture of service excellence. Let's take a look at the Ritz-Carlton Leadership Center.

Apply Your Knowledge

Position Requirements: Your resort has management vacancies for the following positions: executive chef, executive housekeeper, and front office manager. List the traits and characteristics that you consider essential and desirable for these positions.

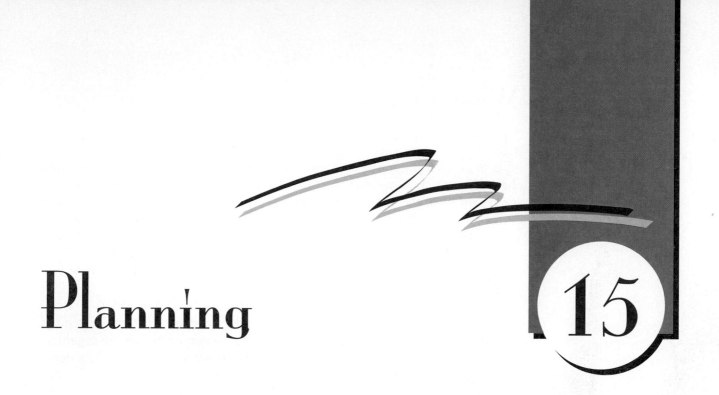

Planning

After reading and studying this chapter, you should be able to:

✔ Describe the importance of planning.
✔ Discuss the merits of the different types of planning.
✔ Explain how goals and objectives are set.
✔ Identify the seven steps in operational planning.

What Is Planning?

Things don't just happen by themselves—well, not always the way we want them to anyhow. Remember the time, on a hot day, when you walked into an ice cream store and ordered your favorite flavor, only to be told they were out if it. You were expecting to be delighted but instead were disappointed. A lack of planning was the root cause of this negative experience. Someone forgot to order or did not order the flavor of ice cream in time for you to enjoy it. This is an example of simple but important planning. There are, as we shall see, more complex forms of planning.

Planning involves selecting the various **goals** that the organization wants to achieve and the actions **(objectives)** to be taken that will ensure those goals are accomplished. In organizations, executives determine where the organization is and where it wants to go. Goals are established for each of the **key operating areas.** In the hospitality industry these would include guest satisfaction, employee satisfaction, productivity, food and beverage preparation and service, marketing and sales, operating ratios, human resources, physical property, and finances. Objectives or strategies are then planned to ensure that the goals are met or exceeded. All managers do some form of planning, whether informal or formal. With informal planning, nothing is written down, and there is little or no sharing of goals with others in the organization. The owner has a vision of what she or he wants to accomplish and just goes ahead and does it. This is frequently the situation in small businesses; however, informal planning also goes on even in larger organizations. The problem with informal planning is that it lacks continuity.

Formal planning occurs when specific goals covering a period of up to several years are identified and shared with all associates and objectives or strate-

Executive Committee Planning the Future Direction and Performance of "Their" Property
(Courtesy Evans Hotels.)

gies are developed stating how each goal will be reached. When planning is discussed in this chapter, we are referring to formal planning. Several types of planning exist; we will look at the main ones used in the hospitality industry.

Think back to the summer trip abroad to France that was introduced in the previous chapter. Your plans might include the following: how you plan to get to the airport, your airline and flight times, the airport of arrival, how you'll get into Paris, your hotel, and the itinerary of what to do each day in each city visited. Think for a moment: What if you didn't plan? The group would not know what flight to take or, on arrival in France, how to get into central Paris and then how and where to find a place to stay. This would be chaotic and stressful, to say the least. Now think of your career plans. Perhaps your goal is to have a successful career in one of the many areas of hospitality management. Successfully completing your degree along with work experience would be the objectives that would facilitate your goal accomplishment. So, we can see that planning provides direction and a sense of purpose.[1] Remember the wonderful line in *Alice in Wonderland* when Alice is lost and asks the Mad Hatter which way to go? The Mad Hatter asks her where she wants to go. Alice replies "I don't know—anywhere." The Mad Hatter then explains, "If you don't know where you're going, any path will get you there."

Planning can also help identify potential opportunities and threats. Planning helps facilitate the other functions of management: organization, decision making, communication, motivation, and especially control, because planning establishes what needs to be done and how it is to be done and control looks at how well we have done compared to how well we expected to do.[2]

The Purpose of Planning

Planning gives direction not only to top management, but to all associates as they focus on goal accomplishment. The purpose of planning is to determine the best strategies and goals to achieve organizational goals. Figure 15–1 shows the hierarchy of planning in organizations. Notice how top executives do most of the strategic planning and first line managers do most of the operational planning.

Planning provides the road map of where the organization is going. Planning also helps coordinate the efforts of associates toward goal accomplishment. Planning assists in risk reduction by forcing managers to look ahead and anticipate change so they can plan scenarios to react to those potential changes.

---

[1]This draws on Gary Dessler, *A Framework for Management.* Upper Saddle River, NJ: Prentice Hall, 2002, p. 99.

[2]Ibid, p. 100.

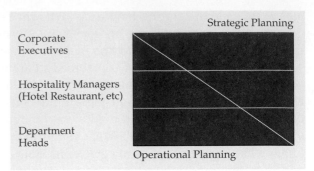

Figure 15–1 *The Hierarchy of Planning in Hospitality Negotiations*

Strategic Planning

The two main categories of plans are strategic (long-term) plans and operational (short-term) plans. Associated with strategic plans are business plans or feasibility studies, which deal with the structure of the plan and provide the details necessary for obtaining finance or other approvals for the operation. At the other end of the planning spectrum is, for example, the short-term operational plan for a function at a convention center. The services manager plans the layout of the room for client approval and then plans the method of service in accordance with client needs.

Given that strategic plans are the long-range plans for an organization, let us begin with those.

Strategic Planning and Strategic Management

Strategic planning creates the long-range plans that steer an organization toward its goals in the accomplishment of its mission and vision. The strategic planning process involves top management who, in simple terms, identify where the organization is and where it wants to go. There is a strong link between strategic planning and strategic management. The planners figure out what to do and management implements the plan.

How does a large hotel or restaurant company with the mission of being a global entity determine which markets to focus on? Should they focus on expansion in Canada, Europe, Latin America, or Asia? Which market would be more beneficial? And can they enter more than one market at a time? What will the method of entry into these markets be? Will a strategy appropriate for one country work in another? Pick up a copy of *The Wall Street Journal, Business Week,* a hospitality trade magazine, or a major newspaper and you are bound to find an article on or reference made to business strategy. In the hospitality industry, strategies are devised that become the road map of how to succeed in increasing guest satisfaction, gaining market share, increasing profits, and so on.

Strategic management develops the mission, goals, objectives and strategies by identifying the business of the corporation today and the business it wants for the future, and then identifying the course of action it will pursue, given its strengths, weaknesses, opportunities, and threats (internal and external environments).

Strategic management is a critical part of planning and the management process. There are three main strategic management tasks: First is the development of a vision and mission statement, second is translating the mission into strategic goals, and third is crafting objectives or a strategy (course of action) to move the organization from where it is today to where it wants to be.

Given the frequency of change in the environment, managers must conduct effective strategic planning in order to respond to the challenges of managing in a highly competitive environment. For example the terrorist attack of September 11, 2001, highlighted the need for business to craft effective strategic plans that allow them to respond to such surprises. In other words, a good strategic plan should include detailed prescriptions of how a business wishes to implement its mission in the highly competitive environment coupled with allowances for responding to extraordinary events.

A direct link exists between the mission of the organization and strategic management—they complement each other. Strategic planning involves creating the long-term strategy for how the organization will meet its mission. The job of strategic management is to translate the mission into strategic goals.

The difference between strategic planning and strategic management is that strategic planning is a systematic process whereby the top management of an organization charts the future course of the enterprise. Strategic management is the process of shepherding the organizational strategic plan and acquiring the necessary resources and capabilities to ensure successful implementation of the plan in the context of emergent situations caused by the level of environmental turbulence.[3]

A strategy is the "how to" action necessary to accomplish goals and missions. In the hotel industry, for instance, strategic issues have the following characteristics[4]:

✓ Strategic issues require decisions about them to be made by top management because those decisions affect many areas of a corporation's operation.

✓ Strategic issues involve the allocation of large amounts of resources. Resources must be found that will commit the organization to make a reasonable return on investment.

✓ Strategic issues are likely to affect the long-term prosperity of the business. Strategic decisions commit an organization to certain markets,

---

[3]Personal conversation with Alfred O. Lewis, D.B.A., May 15, 2002.

[4]Adapted from John A. Pearce and Richard B. Robinson, Jr., *Strategic Management.* Homewood, IL: Richard D. Irwin, 1994, p. 322.

services, products, and technologies. Once these decisions are made, they are not easily reversed.

✓ Strategic issues are future oriented. They are based on what an organization predicts will happen in the future.

✓ Strategic issues usually have major multifunctional consequences that must be closely coordinated. For example, a decision by a resort's top management to add a convention/meeting facility in order to attract the convention and meeting business will affect several departments and alter the guest mix.

✓ Strategic issues require consideration of the corporation's external environment and its strengths, weaknesses, opportunities, and threats. In a fast changing business and economic environment, a careful analysis must be made to align the organization with the best strategy for successful accomplishment of its goals.

Strategic Planning Process

Most of the strategic planning taking place at the top management level is called *corporate-level strategy*. Figure 15–2 shows the strategic management process. Notice how it begins with identifying the organization's mission, goals, and objectives. It then goes on to analyze the environment and the organization's resources and to identify strengths, weaknesses, opportunities, and threats. The organization then formulates strategies, implements them, and evaluates the results.

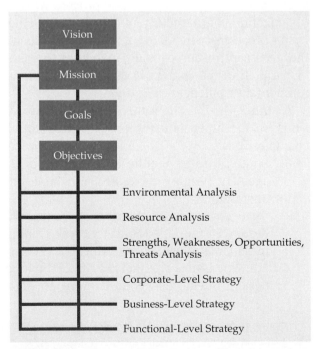

Figure 15–2 *Strategic Management Process*

Check Your Knowledge

1. Name four purposes of planning.
2. What are the two main categories of planning?
3. What are the three main strategic management tasks?

Corporate–Level Strategies

At the highest corporate level many organizations consist of a portfolio of several businesses or divisions. For instance, Disney's portfolio includes movies, theme parks, and the ABC network. Hilton Hotels' portfolio includes Conrad Hotels, Doubletree, Embassy Suites and Hotels, Hampton Inn and Hampton Inns and Suites, Hilton Hotels, Hilton Garden Inn, and Homewood Suites by Hilton. These and other companies need a corporate-level strategy to plan how to best meet the mission of the company. A few years ago, both Hilton and Marriott, after careful strategic planning, decided, in the case of Hilton, to form a separate company made up of their gaming entertainment hotels and, in the case of Marriott, sell their foodservice operations to Sodexho. This allowed both corporations to focus on best meeting their mission with their lodging operations. Hilton found that operating casino hotels was very different from operating their other hotel brands. Marriott decided that growing their hotel brands was their best strategy.

Corporations choose the number of areas of business in which they want to operate. McDonald's and KFC are focused in one area, but Hilton, Marriott, and others have several brands, ranging from full-service hotels and extended-stay hotels all the way to vacation ownership and senior living. Most companies want to grow and need to plan a strategy for that growth. There are four growth strategies. **Market penetration** aims to increase market share by promoting sales aggressively in existing markets. **Geographic expansion** is a strategy in which a company expands its operations by entering new markets—this is in addition to concentrating on existing markets. An example would be Hilton entering and enhancing its position in the Chinese market by entering into an agreement with Air China, China's leading air carrier. The agreement allows for cross-participation in Hilton Honors, Hilton's guest reward program, and Air China's Companion Club. The aim of the partnership between one of the world's most recognized hotel brands and China's leading airline is to provide enhanced global service for the increasing number of business travelers in China and to address the strong competitive situation with international airlines in the local business travel market after China's entry into the World Trade Organization.[5]

---

[5]*http://www.apn.btbtravel.com/s/Editorial-Hotels-And* -Resorts.asp? ReportID=31401.

Personal Profile: Roger Huldi

Roger Huldi, director of food and beverages at the Sheraton Hotel and Resort in San Diego, California. Huldi believes that the most important elements in planning are to have clear goals and clear objectives. You need to know what the outcome should be before planning the process.

For the food and beverage (F&B) field, the goal-setting process is done by the economic community and by corporate headquarters. The objectives are to increase sales and improve customer satisfaction while simplifying the process and standardizing. Examples of standardized plans are menu pricing, how to price in general, supply information, and discounts that are worked out by the corporation. Standardized plans are created by an F&B director with a controller setting the guidelines. These plans might also be handed down by headquarters. As a specific plan, the director gave the example of planning all detailed functions and duties for each staff member involved in an event. Then the outlet manager will utilize a single-use plan for how to set up the initiative. Standing plans track sales and are used to reorder menus and train staff at regular intervals.

A good example of a situation in the Food and Beverage Department is one that requires a lot of coordination between the departments within the same hotel as well as other hotels. Imagine that new staff has just been interviewed, tested, and has now signed on. The whole staff is gearing up for a busy season. The hotel is completely booked and, for this reason, a massive amount of staff is on duty. However, a massive cancellation has occurred, and now the hotel is completely overstaffed. The Food and Beverage Departments went through restructuring. They needed to figure out, first of all, what to expect, that is, future projections for the occupancy level for the rest of the year. Then they needed to know how many staff to keep so they could get the work done yet not adversely affect guest satisfaction. Last, they needed to determine the time frame and cost for layoffs, so as not to get involved in a legal issue. After these main decisions have been made, the director must decide how to communicate all this to his staff and who to make responsible for what.

(Courtesy of Roger Huldi.)

A new development in e-business related to planning is the performance management process. This process allows performance evaluations for the managers to be done on-line, reducing paperwork and saving valuable time for everybody involved. The same program also sets goals for the managers depending, of course, on given facts, such as occupancy of the hotel, budget allowance, and staff available.

Another efficiency program is the optimal business model. In this computer program, all the manager has to do is enter the occupancy of the hotel and from there the program will calculate the expense revenue, room budgets, payroll per quarter, and so on. Everything is calculated in proportion to room occupancy.

The third form of growth strategy is **product development,** such as Hilton's Garden Inn or a new restaurant menu item. The fourth type of growth strategy is **horizontal integration,** which is the process of acquiring ownership or control of competitors with similar products in the same or similar markets. Hilton's purchase of Promus Corporation (Embassy Suites) was an example of horizontal integration.

Strategic alliances or **joint ventures** are yet other methods for a corporation to fulfill its mission. They work like this: American Airlines has as its mission "To be the world's leading airline by focusing on industry leadership in the areas of safety, service, network, product, technology, and culture." They wanted to expand operations into Asia and Europe—the two main air travel growth areas—but lacked the resources necessary for opening up routes to several additional countries, and were not allowed to do so anyway by foreign governments because of the competition it would bring to national airlines. So American Airlines formed a "One World" alliance with several other airlines including Aer Lingus, British Airways, Cathay Pacific, Finnair, Iberia Airlines, LanChile, and Quantas and more than twenty affiliate carriers to feed each other passengers, code share some flights, and share resources, thus saving money and offering the consumer a better deal with the economy of scale.

Another strategy is **diversification** where companies expand into other types of business—related or unrelated. Celebrity chef Emeril "Bam" Lagasse's expansion into TV dinners is an example of diversification.

Strengths, Weaknesses, Opportunities, and Threats Analysis

A major strategic planning technique that is widely used in the hospitality and tourism industry is a **SWOT analysis:** an analysis of strengths, weaknesses, opportunities, and threats. A SWOT analysis is used to assess the company's internal and external strengths and weaknesses, to seek out opportunities, and to be aware of and avoid threats. A SWOT analysis is conducted in comparison with a company's main competitors. This makes it easier to see the competitors' strengths, weakness, opportunities, and threats. It also makes it easier to plan a successful strategy. Each operator can decide what the key points are for inclusion in the SWOT analysis. The four *P*'s of marketing—place (or location), product, price, and promotion—are a good place to begin. All plans need to be implemented; Figure 15–3 shows how plans follow goals and strategy. Strategic plans are implemented through action plans, operating plans, and standing plans.

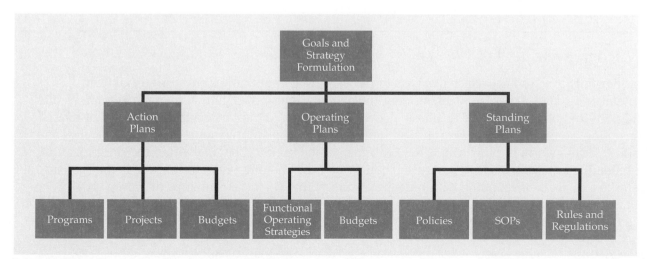

Figure 15–3 *How Plans Follow Goals and Strategies*

Environmental Scanning and Forecasting

Environmental scanning is the process of screening large amounts of information to anticipate and interpret changes in the environment. Environmental scanning creates the basis for forecasts. **Forecasting** is the prediction of future outcomes. Information gained through scanning is used to form scenarios. These, in turn, establish premises for forecasts, which are predictions of future outcomes. The two main types of outcomes that managers seek to forecast are future revenues and new technology breakthroughs. However, any component in the organization's general or specific environment may receive further attention. Both Marriott International and Magic Mountain's sales levels drive purchasing requirements, production goals, employment needs, inventories, and numerous other decisions. Similarly, your university's income from tuition and state appropriations will determine course offerings, staffing needs, salaries, and the like. These examples illustrate that predicting future revenue is a crucial first step in planning for success.

As you can imagine, the forecasting done by the president of Hilton Hotels is very different from the forecasting done by a restaurant manager or department head. The president of Hilton needs to assess the broad economic, political, social, cultural, technological, and financial implications that might impact any forecast. For instance, should Hilton open a hotel in Providence, Rhode Island, or a different city? The desire of Hilton to have a presence in these markets must be considered along with the economic and other environmental factors in each market location. The president must also consider the probability of success of the new property. Another scenario is that of the president of a major chain restaurant corporation trying to forecast in a changing business environment. What if minimum wage were to be increased? What if health care were mandated? How would these changes affect the corporation?

Recovery Strategies

World events can, and do, cause planners to pay serious attention to recovery strategies. The September 11, 2001, terrorist attack on the United States forced hospitality corporations to assess their situations and plan to improve business. According to Frank Nardozza, managing director of KPMG Consulting, some companies went into an immediate action plan of battening down the hatches and waiting for the storm to blow over. They looked at all the capital spending within their organizations and identified those items that were discretionary or fixed and put a moratorium on them. They also identified all areas of spending within the organization that could be contained or placed on a moratorium basis and redirected spending toward those activities that had the immediate short-term effect of driving up occupancies and room rates.[1]

[1] John P. Walsh, "Industry Leaders Plot Recovery Strategy," Hotel Management, **216**, 18, October 15, 2001, pp. 1, 29.

Operational Planning

How Do Managers Plan?

Planning is the first of the management functions so it is the one that establishes the basis for the other functions. In fact, without planning how would managers know how or what to organize, decide on, communicate, motivate, or control? So how do managers plan? That's what this next section is all about. Planning involves two main parts: goals and objective. **Operational plans** are generally created for periods of up to one year and dovetail with the strategic plan. We have seen that strategic planning takes place at the top management level; now we look at the operational midlevel and supervisory level and see that most hospitality managers have a shorter planning horizon. Strategic planning at the hotel does not concern itself with questions such as what businesses should the company be in, horizontal integration, vertical integration, or other business- or corporate-level strategies.[6] Most hotel,

A Hotel Department Head Meeting Planning for Upcoming Events (Courtesy Evans Hotels.)

[6]Eddistone C. Nebel, *Managing Hotels Effectively: Lessons from Outstanding General Managers.* New York: Van Nostrand Reinhold, 1991, p. 86.

restaurant, and other hospitality managers plan for periods from hourly, daily, weekly, monthly, and up to 90 days. A hotel department head meeting is a typical example of midlevel managers planning the various topics that make a hotel run successfully.

Operational plans provide managers with a step-by-step approach to accomplish goals or objectives. The overall purpose of planning is to have the entire organization moving harmoniously toward the goals. These are the seven steps in operational planning:

1. *Setting objectives.* The first step in planning is identifying expected outcomes, that is, the goals and objectives. The goals should be specific, measurable, and achievable.
2. *Analyzing and evaluating the environment.* This involves analyzing political, economic, social, and other trends that may affect the operation. The level of turbulence is evaluated in relation to the organization's present position and the resources available to achieve goals.
3. Determining alternatives. This involves developing courses of action that are available to a manager to reach a goal. Input may be requested from all levels of the organization. Group work is normally better than individual input.
4. *Evaluating alternatives.* This calls for making a list of advantages and disadvantages of each alternative. Among the factors to be considered are resources and effects on the organization.
5. *Selecting the best solution.* This analysis of the various alternatives should result in determining one course of action that is better than the others. It may, however, involve combining two or more alternatives.
6. *Implementing the plan.* Once the best solution is chosen, the manager needs to decide the following:
   - ✓ Who will do what?
   - ✓ By when?
   - ✓ What resources are required?
   - ✓ At what benefit?
   - ✓ At what cost?
   - ✓ What reporting procedures will there be?
   - ✓ What authority will be granted to achieve goals?
7. *Controlling and evaluating results.* Once the plan is implemented, it is necessary to monitor progress toward goal accomplishment.

Some plans are made to be used once, and others over and over. **Programs** are established to set out in an orderly fashion all the steps in a major one-time project. In contrast, **standing plans** are used repeatedly, as the need arises.[7]

---

[7]Ibid, p. 100.

Operational Goal Setting

Goal setting is the process of determining outcomes for each area and associate. In Chapter 1, we looked at organizational vision, mission, goals, and objectives. Once the vision and mission have been determined, organizations set goals in order to meet the mission. The goals are set for each of the key operating areas mentioned earlier. No one can work effectively without specific goals and monthly evaluation reports to gauge whether the effort is moving toward goal accomplishment, or whether adjustments must be made to change course.[8] Examples of the goals and information a sales department should record and analyze each month follow:

Group Room Nights
✓ Booked this month and year-to-date by market segment and salesperson
✓ Actual consumed room nights this month and year-to-date by month, by market segment, and on the books for months to come
✓ Actual average group room rates by month, year-to-date and on the books for months to come

Individual Room Nights
✓ Actual consumed room nights by month and year-to-date by market segment
✓ Local corporate clients—actual consumed individual and group room nights by month and year-to-date
✓ Occupancy—actual by month and year-to-date
✓ REV PAR—actual by month and year-to-date
✓ Packages—number sold for each type by month, year-to-date, and zip code origin[9]

Another example would be setting productivity goals. *Productivity* refers to the amount of labor it takes to do a particular task. Productivity is measured in labor costs, which are expressed as a percentage of sales, for each department. Because labor costs are the highest of the operational costs, it is critical to keep them in line with budget. Productivity and labor costs can be compared from one operation to another, so we can determine which is more efficient. So, the goal for a family restaurant's labor costs is 23 percent of sales. Now, if sales goes up, then so too can the labor cost—but proportionately. What if sales go down, however? Then, so too should labor costs—again, also proportionately. The skill of management is to operate efficiently and effectively. It is easy to operate a hospitality business when it is busy; the skill comes in running a hospitality business that is only operating at, say, 50 to 60 percent capacity or, worse still, even less.

---

[8]Tom McCathy, "Good Reporting Is a Marketing Must," *Lodging Hospitality,* **56,** 15, November 14, 2000. p. 14.
[9]Ibid.

Expressing goals in specific, measurable terms is important because that allows us to measure our progress toward goal accomplishment. Goals are set for each of the key result areas; an example would be profit of $100,000 per month, using the area to be measured, such as sales, then a yardstick, such as sales revenue. A time by which the goal is to be met is also identified, as is the individual who is to be responsible for its accomplishment.

Planning expert George Morrisey presents a four-point model for use in formulating goals[10]:

1. to (action/verb)
2. the (single measurable result)
3. by (target date/time span)
4. at (cost in time and/or energy)

Figure 15–4 presents several examples of well-stated goals. Notice how the model allows for objectives to state how the goals will be met.

Operational Objectives

Objectives state how the goals will be met. In the example given in Figure 15–4, to achieve a food cost percentage of 28.5 percent by October 15 and maintain it until further notice at a cost not to exceed $100 or ten working hours, the food and beverage director and executive chef will need to do the following:

✔ Cost all menu items to achieve the desired food cost percentage. By having the menu items priced and their costs calculated.

✔ Control portion sizes by establishing an exact portion for each menu item and watching to see that it is adhered to.

✔ Ensure that regular and spot checks are done on inventory and the food cost is calculated correctly. Take a physical count of all food items accurately, including all items in the freezers, in the kitchen, the storeroom, banquet kitchen, etc., and calculate their costs accurately.

✔ Ensure that all sales and food costs are included in the calculations. Check that all guest food charges are included in the calculations—especially any functions for the day of the inventory if the food is included—and that the sales are also included.

Morrisey's Four-Point Model

To (1) Action/Verb	(2) Single Measurable Result
By (3) Target Date/Time Span	At (4) Cost in Time and Energy

Figure 15–4 *Examples of Well-Stated Goals and Objectives* (Adapted from Gary Dessler, *A Framework for Management.* Upper Saddle River, NJ: Prentice Hall, 2002, p. 108.

---

[10]Dessler, *Framework Management,* p. 108.

✔ Use any leftover food within 48 hours.

✔ Maintain a vigilant loss prevention program with security. Conduct checks on bags leaving the property and do not allow any bags in the kitchen.

✔ Ensure that all food sales are accounted for by checking that food sales are recorded and paid for.

Collectively, these objectives will ensure that the goal will be met. Each goal needs to have step-by-step objectives written that state how they will be met.

We can see from the preceding examples that it makes sense if the associates who are going to be responsible for achieving the goals are also the ones involved in setting them. Some years ago this concept lead to **management by objectives (MBO),** a managerial process that determines the goals of the organization then plans the objectives, that is, the how-tos of reaching the goals. With MBO, associates usually establish the goals and objectives and review them with management. MBO works because associates have been involved with the goal and objective setting and are likely to be motivated to see them successfully achieved. The MBO process generally consists of five steps:

1. *Set organizational goals.* Top management sets goals for the company.
2. *Set departmental goals.* Department heads and their superiors jointly set supporting goals for their departments.
3. *Discuss department goals.* Department heads present department goals and ask all subordinates to develop their own individual goals.
4. *Set individual goals.* Goals are set for each subordinate, and a timetable is assigned for accomplishing those goals.
5. *Give feedback.* The supervisor and subordinates meet periodically to review the subordinate's performance and to monitor and analyze progress toward her or his goals.[11]

MBO goals need to be specific and measurable, challenging but attainable just as any other goals. The main purpose of an MBO program is to integrate the goals of the organization and the goals of the associates so that they are in focus. Over the years MBO has proved very successful and has, in some organizations, been superseded by **total quality management (TQM),** which was described in Chapter 1. TQM involves not only planning but also touches on the other functions of management. The idea of improving efficiency and increasing productivity while placing a larger emphasize on quality has caught on fast. Originally designed by Japanese businesses to help reconstruct the economy after WWII, today TQM is widely applied in most industrialized countries. The hospitality industry has embraced quality management with open arms, asking for input from all levels of employees and calling for teamwork. Ultimately the customer rates the team on quality, values, and product—and the customer does not lie. An example of TQM is that of a group of associates being asked to suggest ways

[11]Philip Evans and Thomas Wurster, "Strategy and the New Economics of Information," *Harvard Business Review,* September–October 1997, p. 72.

to improve the guest experience by addressing specific challenges (actually problems, but industry professionals prefer to be positive and call them *challenges*) that the hospitality operation has in delivering exceptional service.

Take guest check-in as an example. The TQM team would include members from the front office and guest services (bell persons, etc.) who identify line-ups for check-in during the 4:00 to 7:00 P.M. time period. A challenge or problem statement is written by the group and various ways of improving the situations are presented. They might include:

- ✔ Using a special desk for airport check-ins
- ✔ Handling convention and group guest check-ins in another location (the rooming list is made up in advance and rooms allocated with keys encoded and ready for distribution to guests)
- ✔ Cross-training and utilizing associates from other departments to assist with the check-ins
- ✔ Adopting an "all hands on deck" approach to have members of management available to assist with check-ins in various ways
- ✔ Having additional help available for housekeeping to get the rooms ready more quickly

An example of TQM in the restaurant industry is that of asking servers in a restaurant for help solving the challenge of reducing the guests' waiting time for a table by turning tables more quickly during the rush periods. Once the problem or challenge statement is written, the TQM team can focus on ways to improve the guest experience by suggesting ideas to reduce the guest waiting time. The head chef might automatically take on the role of coach, as opposed to that of supervisor. Implementing TQM will have the natural outcome of teamwork, because one employee cannot improve quality on his or her own. The chef uses motivation and inspiration to keep his team in high spirits, and each employee is important in their own way. Emphasis is placed on recruiting, training, and keeping quality employees, to ensure that the TQM approach will be a success.

Benchmarking is a concept that identifies the best way of doing something and which companies excel in that area (best practices companies). The best practice is noted and emulated or even improved on by other companies. In the spirit of cooperation, companies are expected to share information so you need to give as well as receive.

The history of benchmarking begins with the 1970s.[12] Japanese companies would take trips to industrialized nations to study their large, successful industrial companies and take that knowledge home to apply to their local companies. By aggressively copying others, they were able to supersede the company being copied by improving on the success strategy. Meanwhile, benchmarking has become a global trait. Some companies are even copying companies outside of their own industry. For example, IBM carefully studied Las Vegas casinos to apply their strategy of reducing employee theft at IBM.

---

[12]Robbins and Coulter, *Management,* pp. 228–230.

How do you benchmark? First of all, a team is formed. The duty of this team is to identify companies to be benchmarked. Next they must determine the best possible way of collecting the data, which can be collected internally, as well as externally. Once collected, it must be analyzed to determine where the success lies and where the differences lie. The last step is to create an action plan on how to improve on the newly gained data; that is, what steps need to be taken to implement it.

The question to be answered is "How do these companies obtain internal information on other companies they are benchmarking?" An initial team is formed, the members of which may have contacts among customers, suppliers, or employees of the company they are planning on benchmarking. Companies oftentimes are glad to swap success stories and information with others, not only informing them but being informed about others as well. Successful companies can often be identified by the number of quality awards they have won. Also, trade associations typically know who the successful companies are, and analyzing financial data will help you determine which companies to benchmark. Also using employees who will actually implement the benchmarked changes helps ensure their commitment to service or product improvement.

Benchmarking is more of an operational tool that can be used to guide the corporate strategy as well as the business level substrategies.[13] The process in an ideal setting is to compare company operations with those of other companies that exhibit best practices. Note that oftentimes best practices would be found outside our industry grouping. The FAA has contracted with Disney to help reduce the long lines at the airports occasioned by more severe security measures due to the threat of terrorism. In many instances, the best practices adopted from without the hospitality industry sometimes have to be modified to fit our context.

Policies, Procedures, and Rules

Policies, procedures, and rules are examples of standing plans. **Policies** set broad guidelines for associates to use when making decisions. For example it is the policy of most hotels to pay the room and tax at another hotel and provide a taxi/hotel limo when "walking" a guest.

Procedures specify what to do in given situations. An example would be when a former classmate calls you to request a room for the next weekend. However, the hotel is forecasting 94 percent occupancy and company procedures, unfortunately for the friend, state that no employees or their friends may stay at complimentary or discounted rates if the hotel is forecast to be more than 90 percent occupied. Policy and procedures often go together. A **rule** is a very specific action guide that associates must follow. Consider this example: Under no circumstances shall an employee serve alcoholic beverages to minors or intoxicated guests.

[13]Personal conversation with Alfred D. Lewis, D.B.A., May 15th, 2002.

Post 9–11: Disaster and Emergency Planning

Hank Christen and Paul Maniscalco

It is unrealistic to expect any level of success in disaster operations without a formal, comprehensive emergency management plan (CEMP). A hospitality industry CEMP must meet two important objectives:

✓ Support emergency response agencies. Hospitality companies have facilities, personnel, and supplies that enhance emergency response efforts.

✓ Provide support and direction to facility recovery. Returning to normal operations is the goal; the CEMP must address the human, financial, and material resources needed for effective recovery.

An effective hospitality industry CEMP is divided into seven major functions: (1) threat assessment, (2) vulnerability analysis, (3) management, (4) operations, (5) logistics, (6) planning, and (7) administration and finance. Functions 3 through 7 of the CEMP are the five functions of the incident management system (a national benchmark) discussed in Chapter 14's sidebar, "Disaster Management and Leadership."

The threat assessment and vulnerability analysis functions are similar to the SWOT analysis (strengths, weaknesses, opportunities, and threats) discussed in this chapter. Threats are categorized into three groups: (1) natural threats: severe weather, wild land fires, earthquakes, disease outbreaks, etc. (2) technological threats: chemical spills, utility failures, explosions, urban fires, transportation accidents, cyber failure, etc. (3) man-made threats: terrorism, cyber attacks, violence, criminal activities, bomb threats, arson, etc.

Vulnerability analysis is the identification of weaknesses or deficiencies relating to a specific threat. For example, a resort in a wilderness area is vulnerable to wildfires.

The management section of the CEMP identifies the incident manager (the person in charge) during disaster operations. The incident manager may or may not be the chief executive of the organization. He or she is responsible for directing team members as well as ensuring a direct liaison between the hospitality facility and the local on-scene incident commander.

Operations are the direct and hands-on activities of hospitality industry personnel that support emergency operations and/or assist the hospitality facility in returning to normalcy. Operations cover a wide spectrum, from evacuation and security procedures to restoration of guest services and rehabilitation of the facility.

Logistics play a vital role; by definition, a disaster exhausts the resources of responders. Logistics includes facilities (buildings), communications, supplies, utilities, fuel/maintenance, food, and water. A climate-controlled room with telephones, computers, and a fax machine serves as an ideal incident command post for fire, law enforcement, and EMS command officers. Food and hot coffee from the facility's restaurants provides rehabilitation to fire fighters. Construction materials and equipment are needed during long-term rescue efforts.

A planning section is established to monitor the CEMP and develop action plans during disaster operations to facilitate response to real-time issues and surprises that emerge during disasters. Action plans are usually updated on a twelve-hour or full-day cycle as needs dictate and are less formal than the CEMP.

Administration and finance relates to the tracking of all documents and expenditures relating to the disaster event, including employee-related issues such as salary, overtime, and workmen's compensation. Documents may include computer records, video, and photographs, as well as paper files.

Critical Factors

✓ A disaster plan is a formal document.

✓ The sections of a comprehensive emergency management plan (CEMP) include a threat assessment, vulnerability analysis, management, operations, logistics, planning, and administration/finance.

✓ A CEMP must be coordinated with local emergency agencies.

Sources of low-cost disaster planning expertise include county or city emergency management office, fire departments, law enforcement crime prevention officers, the Internet, the American Red Cross, EMS offices, and the Federal Emergency Management Agency (FEMA). Conduct at least one internal exercise a year to test your plan. Evaluate your plan and make appropriate changes continuously.

Budgeting

Most of us are familiar with budgets; we learned about them when we received our first "allowance." Remember how often we had it spent before the week was up? That's why organizations plan the use of their financial resources. A **budget** is a plan allocating money to specific activities. There are budgets for revenues (sales) and costs (expenses) for capital equipment—equipment that has an expected life of several years.

Budgets are popular because they force managers to anticipate expected sales and budget expenses accordingly—that is, not to spend it all before the week's up! Budgets are used extensively in all levels of hospitality organizations from the corporate level to the smallest departments. Once an estimation of a particular department's revenues is determined, the costs are then budgeted, leaving a portion for profit. This is also called the *bottom line.* Here's an example of a budget: A restaurant expects 750 guests in a given week, at an average check of $15 this means sales of $39,250 for the week. This allows management to budget labor costs, usually to a predetermined percentage of sales (normally between 18 and 24 percent depending on the type of restaurant). Food, beverage, and other costs are budgeted in the same way. Figure 15–5 shows a detailed restaurant budget listing all the items of expenditure. Note that the column on the right-hand side is for the percentage of sales to which the dollar amount refers. This percentage is helpful in that it can be easily compared with other similar restaurant operations. In fact, restaurant companies use percentages to check on a manager's performance. If one restaurant manager gets a food cost percentage of 28.5 and another gets 33 percent, then the corporate office will be asking the latter manager questions!

Budgets are popular because they are applicable to a variety of applications and they can be used all over the world in any country. Budgets are a planning technique that force managers to be fiscally responsible. Notice that the actual and variance columns have no entries in them as yet. As soon as the period (usually monthly) is over the results can then be added and any variances recorded.

Check Your Knowledge

1. What is the difference between operational planning and strategic planning?
2. Define benchmarking.
3. Why is it important to have a budget?

Restaurant Operational Budget

Sales	Budget (Thousands)	%	Actual Variance +(–)
Food	750.0	75	
Beverage	250.0	25	
Others	0.0		
Total Sales	1,000.0	100	
Cost of Sales			
Food	225.0	30.0	
Beverage	55.0	22.0	
Others	0.0		
Total Cost of Sales	280.0	28.0	
Gross Profit	720.0	72.0	
Controllable Expenses			
Salaries and wages	240.0	24.0	
Employee benefits	40.0	4.0	
Direct operating expenses	60.0	6.0	
Music and entertainment	10.0	1.0	
Marketing	40.0	4.0	
Energy and utility	30.0	3.0	
Administrative and general	40.0	4.0	
Repairs and maintenance	20.0	2.0	
Total Controllable Expenses	480.0	48.0	
Rent and other occupation costs	70.0	7.0	
Income before interest, depreciation, and taxes	170.0	17.0	
Interest	10.0	1.0	
Depreciation	20.0	2.0	
Net Income before Taxes	140.0	14.0	

Figure 15–5 *Restaurant Budget*

Personal Profile: Tim Mulligan

Meet Tim Mulligan, area director of human resources for the Sheraton Hotels, San Diego, California. Mr. Mulligan feels that the important elements in planning are knowing what the desired outcome will be, then having the proper information followed by organization, and, last, being a good time manager to help ensure goal attainment.

Goal setting can be divided into two types: the annual goals for managers, which have to be in line with career growth, annual bonuses, etc., and annual goals for employees, which need to be stated in terms of individual development. According to Mr. Mulligan, the objectives need to be in line with the company objectives, with the individual hotel objectives, and with the personal growth objectives.

Operational plans are important in order to meet the financial goals (profit), to meet guest satisfaction goals, and to meet the employee satisfaction goals.

Specific plans are important to reach day-to-day success with goals and objectives (i.e., check-in, recruiting, hiring process, room cleaning).

(Courtesy of Tim Mulligan.)

Single-use plans are used only for special events, such as holiday parties or HR receptions.

Standing plans are annual plans, such as benefit enrollment and management screening plans. They are also used for company policies, such as tuition reimbursement or training programs.

Mr. Mulligan gave these examples for contingency factors in planning. If the occupancy of the hotel decreases, the HR department has a plan for layoffs. On the other hand, if a need to hire a significant amount of new staff exists, then the HR department has a plan in place for a mass hiring action.

Forecasting in the HR department differs from forecasting in other departments, according to the HR director. In the HR field, there is a need for more accurate information on a business level, to determine needs on a staffing level, and the need for dollar amounts for advertising, recruiting, background checks, drug tests, training, and so forth.

In response to a question about which benchmarking practices he believes are the most successful, Mr. Mulligan named turnover rates, employee retention, the employee satisfaction index, and the guest satisfaction index.

In the field of technology, a new trend in planning is the optimal business model. This model works with drivers and is based on the business practice. As an example, this model can determine the amount of hours available for scheduling and the maximum amount of money you can spend to stay within a budget. Two more trends are an on-line employee evaluation model and a goal-setting process called the performance management process.

Check Your Knowledge

1. Give an example of goal setting.
2. What are the four points of Morrisey's model to formulate goals?
3. Briefly describe the five steps of the MBO process.

Scheduling

Scheduling of associates is a planning activity that involves taking the business forecast and allocating an appropriate number of staff to give the necessary level of service. Due to the increasing cost of labor and benefits, schedules must be planned very carefully to avoid being over- or understaffed. Because the hospitality industry is operating 24/7—meaning twenty-four hours, seven days a week—we need to staff all departments, with appropriate coverage day and night.

In Chapter 1, we briefly introduced the main shifts as early or opening, middle or swing, and late or closing plus the night shift. Staffing each area or department with a necessary group of associates costs money and is necessary just to open the doors. For example, a restaurant needs a host person to greet and seat guests, a server or two, a prep cook or two, a cook or two, a dishwasher, a bartender, and a manager. This is the minimum acceptable staffing level regardless of the number of guests. The same holds true for all areas of the hospitality industry. The problem is that we never know exactly how many guests we will have, and one day can be busy and the next quiet. That's why accurate forecasting, as discussed earlier, is so important.

Now, obviously the level of service will vary from one lodging operation to another. A full-service hotel may have 24-hour bell service, whereas a limited service hotel will not offer it. An amusement park is open up to twelve hours a day and will need at least two shifts. A restaurant is open for up to twelve hours a day and may need two shifts, depending on whether it serves breakfast, lunch, and dinner. The hospitality industry, in order to keep costs down and remain competitive, uses a large number of part-time employees. Many hospitality departments have a skeleton staff of full-time employees, which are augmented by several part-time ones, as the business needs them.

Project Management

Project management means exactly that—managing a project. Project management is the task of completing the project on time and within budget. In the hospitality industry, we have a variety of projects at each level of the corporation. At the corporate level, there is, for instance, the construction of a new hotel or restaurant. At the unit level, there is the alteration or renovation of an existing building, and at the department level, there is the installation of a new piece of equipment or a new point-of-sale system. But project management is broader than these examples. What about the Senior Prom—that's a project. So are most of the catering functions that take place at convention centers and hotels.

Hospitality companies are increasingly using project management because the approach fits well with the need for flexibility and rapid response to perceived market opportunities. Sometimes an organization has a specific need for a project that does not fit into a regular planning schedule so they use project management. Project management works like this: Say the project is to become

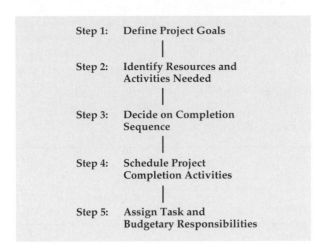

Figure 15–6 *Steps in the Project Planning Process*

more environmentally friendly. A hospitality organization will create a team of associates from various departments and challenge them to come up with a plan to accomplish the goal of becoming more environmentally friendly. Figure 15–6 shows the steps in the project planning process.

The process begins by clearly defining the project's goals. This step is necessary because the manager and team need to know exactly what's expected. All activities and the resources needed to do them must then be identified. What labor and materials are needed to complete the project? Once the activities have been identified, the sequence of completion needs to be determined. What activities must be completed before others can begin? Which can be done simultaneously? This step is actually done using flowchart-type diagrams such as a Gantt chart or a PERT network. Next, the project activities need to be scheduled. Time estimates for each activity are done and these estimates are used to develop an overall project schedule and completion date.[14]

Keeping track of who's doing what and avoiding something falling through the cracks can be major tasks. One suggestion to avoid the awkward situation of being involved in a project where an important task fell through the cracks is to create and use a differentiation document for the project team. The differentiation document, or "diff-doc," is a powerful tool that assigns responsibility for accomplishing each task and subtask in a project to a specific entity. It delineates who is supposed to program, budget, manage, design, specify, approve, supply, install, and operate every part of the development or renovation process. The document can also be expanded to include budgetary responsibility for specific tasks.[15]

[14]Robbins and Coulter, *Management,* p. 240.

[15]Jonathan C. Nehmer and Brian Bolt, "Differentiation Document Keeps Track of Who's Doing What," *Hotel & Motel Management,* **215,** 12, July 3, 2002, p. 10.

Convention Services Planning

Meet Mark Higginbotham, convention services manager, Sheraton Hotel and Resort, San Diego, California. Mark feels that important elements in planning are understanding what is needed or expected and partnering with the clients.

For the convention service manager, elements of goal setting are, first of all, what the hotel or department as well as the clients need in forecasted money and, second, the amount of space needed for the program.

His objectives are to plan and create the menu that will please the client and reach budgeted money. It also is important to work with the client to ensure that the space is acceptable but not excessive because unused space can be sold.

Specific plans coupled with single-use plans can be applied to working with a group that "maxes" out a certain space to allow multiple uses for the same room. An example of this is setting a meeting room with rounds of ten, allowing them to use the room for lunch when the other space is not available. Or to set up buffets in the foyer because the room can be set up in fifteen minutes during the break, after a meeting or prior to lunch.

According to Mr. Higginbotham, an example of having contingency factors in planning is as follows. His department always prepares for 5 percent over the count given by the client for an event to ensure that they are ready for an unexpected rise in the number of people attending. Audiovisual equipment is always stocked in pairs on the chance that a projector will go out in the middle of a program or meeting. Indoor space is always held as a backup for outdoor functions just in case the weather is bad.

A new trend in planning in convention service management is to set dates and deadlines for clients to provide a final agenda. This allows CSM personnel to plan for and release space and be better prepared to service the group by assigning additional meeting space if needed. An example is, if a client needs additional space that is not in the contract, CSM personnel will inform the client of the food and beverage value of that room. In situations where the food and beverage minimum is not met, the difference is made up with the room rental.

Trends in Planning

✔ Given today's hospitality business environment of rapid change, planning needs to be done quickly and adjusted when necessary.

✔ Technology, especially the Internet, can be used to overcome time and distance, allowing for more people to have input into the planning process. Associates can contribute to the planning process on-line instead of going to meetings.

Case Study

As a member of senior management for a twenty-unit local restaurant or hotel chain, you have been asked to plan the corporate expansion. You need to draw up a plan of how best to expand. Consider how other chains plan their growth. Write down all the options, then make recommendations.

Career Information

Planning is an integral part of any career. Someone has to plan the strategic direction of all hospitality corporations. Likewise, midlevel and lower level managers, in order to be successful, need to plan and reevaluate plans. The larger corporations have planning departments, but operational experience is necessary before moving up to the corporate planning area.

Summary

1. Planning involves selecting the various goals that the organization wants to achieve and the actions (objectives) that will ensure the organization accomplishes the goals.

2. Goals are set for each of the key operating areas.

3. Planning gives direction, not only to top managers, but to all associates as they focus on goal accomplishment.

4. Strategic (long-term) planning and strategic management involve the process of identifying the business of the corporation and the business it wants for the future, and then identifying the course of action it will pursue, given its strengths, weaknesses, opportunities, and threats.

5. There are three main strategic management tasks: developing a vision and mission statement, translating the mission into strategic goals, and creating a strategy or course of action to move the organization from where it is today to where it wants to be.

6. Strategic planning and management take place at the higher levels of management. This is known as corporate-level strategy.

7. There are four growth strategies: market penetration, geographic expansion, product development, and horizontal integration.

8. A strengths, weaknesses, opportunities, and threats (SWOT) analysis is a key strategic management technique.

9. Environmental scanning is the process of assessing information about the economic, social, political, and technological environment to anticipate and interpret changes in the environment.

10. Operational plans are generally for periods of up to one year and dovetail with the strategic plan.

11. There are seven steps in operational planning: setting objectives, analyzing and evaluating the environment, determining alternatives, evaluating alternatives, selecting the best solution, implementing the plan, and controlling and evaluating results.

12. Benchmarking is a concept that identifies the best way of doing something and which companies excel in the area under study.

13. Policies, procedures, and rules are examples of standing plans. Policies set broad guidelines, procedures specify what to do in given situations, and rules are very specific action guides that associates must follow.

14. Budgets are plans allocating money for specific activities. They are popular because they force managers to anticipate expected sales and budget expenses accordingly.

15. Goal setting is determining the outcomes for the organization and associates.

16. Objectives state how the goals will be met. Management by objectives is a managerial process that determines the goals of the organization then plans the objectives.

17. Project management is the task of completing a project on time and within budget.

Key Words and Concepts

Benchmarking
Budget
Diversification
Environmental scanning
Forecasting
Geographic expansion
Goal setting
Goals
Horizontal integration

Joint ventures
Key operating areas
Management by objectives (MBO)
Market penetration
Objectives
Operational plans
Policies
Procedures

Product development
Programs
Project management
Rule
Scheduling
Standing plans
Strategic alliances
Strategic management
Strategic planning

SWOT (strengths, weaknesses, opportunities, and threats) analysis
Total quality management (TQM)

Review Questions

1. What does planning involve?
2. How are goals and objectives different?
3. What is strategic planning?

4. What is the distinction between SWOT analysis and environmental screening analysis?
5. Why do companies use policies, procedures, and rules?

Internet Exercise[16]

You've been hired as a summer intern in the business intelligence department by a major fast-food chain. Your manager has asked you to compile information on four of the company's most important competitors. Specifically, she'd like to find out about (1) any new products these competitors have or may be introducing, (2) annual sales and profits for the last five years, and (3) other strategic changes the competitors may be planning. Go online to the competitors' websites and obtain as much information as possible.

Apply Your Knowledge[17]

Benchmarking can be an important tool and source of information for managers. It can also be useful to students, as you'll see in this team-based exercise. In your small group, discuss study habits that each of you has found to be effective from your years of being in school. As a group, come up with a bulleted list of at least eight effective study habits in the time allowed by your professor. When the professor calls time, each group should combine with one other group and share ideas, again in the time allowed by the professor. In this larger group, be sure to ask questions about suggestions that each small group had. Each small group should make sure it understands the suggestions of the other group with which it is working. When the professor calls time, each small group will then present and explain the study habit suggestions of the other group it was working with. After all groups have presented their suggestions, the class will come up with what it feels are the "best" study habits of all the ideas presented.

[16]Modified from Robbins and Coulter, *Management*, p. 245.
[17]Ibid.

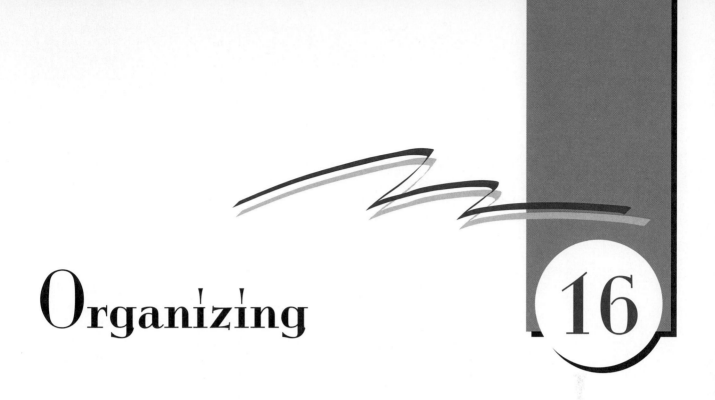

Organizing

16

After reading and studying this chapter, you should be able to:

- ✓ Define organizational structure and organizational design.
- ✓ Explain why structure and design are important to an organization.
- ✓ Describe the key elements of organizational structure.
- ✓ Differentiate between mechanistic and organic organizational designs.
- ✓ Explain team-based structures and why organizations use them.
- ✓ Describe matrix structures, project structures, independent business units, and boundaryless organizations.

From Planning to Organizing

Howard Schultz, head of Starbucks Corporation,[1] knows that with more than 2,200 Starbucks stores in the United States, organizing the company is no easy task. Such an organization needs training departments to turn college students into café managers (who know, for example, that every espresso must be pulled within twenty-three seconds or be thrown away), departments that sell coffee to United Airlines and supermarkets, and a way to manage stores in locations as far away as the Philippines and China. How to organize is, therefore, not an academic issue to Howard Schultz. He has discovered that planning and organizing are inseparable. When his company was small, its strategy focused on high-quality coffee drinks provided by small neighborhood coffeehouses. This strategy in turn suggested the main jobs for which Schultz had to hire lieutenants, for example, store management, purchasing, and finance and accounting. Departments then grew up around these jobs.

As Schultz's strategy evolved to include geographic expansion across the United States and abroad, his organization also had to evolve. Regional store management divisions were established to oversee the stores in each region. Today, with Starbucks coffee also sold to airlines, bookstores, and supermarkets, the company's structure is evolving again, with new departments organized to sell to and serve the needs of these new markets. What Schultz discovered is that the organization is determined by the plan; that is, strategy determines structure.

The Purpose of Organizing

The purpose of **organizing** is to get a job done efficiently and effectively by completing these tasks:

- ✔ Divide work to be done into specific jobs and departments.
- ✔ Assign tasks and responsibilities associated with individual jobs.
- ✔ Coordinate diverse organizational tasks.
- ✔ Cluster jobs into units.
- ✔ Establish relationships among individuals, groups, and departments.
- ✔ Establish formal lines of authority.
- ✔ Allocate and deploy organizational resources.

---

[1]This draws on Gary Dessler, *A Framework for Management.* Upper Saddle River, NJ: Prentice Hall, 2002, pp. 147–148.

This chapter covers these important aspects of organization, but first we need to know what organization is. Organization refers to the arrangement of activities so that they systematically contribute to goal accomplishment. No one person can do all the things necessary for a hospitality organization to be successful. Imagine just one person trying to do all the different tasks that make a restaurant meal memorable.

Defining Organizational Structure

In the past few years, organizational structures have changed quite a bit. Traditional approaches were questioned and reevaluated as managers searched for structures that would best support and facilitate employees doing the organization's work. The structure needs to be efficient but also have the flexibility that is so necessary in today's dynamic environment. The challenge for managers is to design an organizational structure that allows employees to efficiently and effectively do their work.

An **organizational structure** is like a skeleton in that it lends support to the various departments in an organization. It provides the total framework by which job tasks are divided, grouped, and coordinated. In today's leaner and meaner hospitality business environment, organizations are flatter, meaning they have fewer levels of managers. They are also structured to better fulfill the needs of the guests. A typical example is the change of mind-set that turned the traditional organizational chart upside down, as shown in Figure 16–1. The general manager used to be at the top of the organizational chart and the frontline associate at the bottom—the guest never appeared on the chart! Now we have the guest at the top of the inverted pyramid and the general manager at the bottom. Given higher labor costs, there are also fewer associates to do the same amount of work. Organizations have had to become more flexible in their desire to delight the guest. Some hotels have created rapid reaction teams of associates who respond to urgent guest needs. These teams are from several different departments but come together in an effort to please the guest. More about this type of team and other teams are discussed later in this chapter.

Work Specialization and Division of Labor

You may recall the humble beginnings of Marriott International as a Hot Shoppe. Mr. and Mrs. Marriott probably decided what was going to be on the menu, then they purchased the food, cooked it, and served it. They also collected the money and made sure everything was to their guests' liking. It's fun and stimulating to have your own business and see the results of food well prepared and served and gratified guests returning. The challenge, however, is that as the demand for additional products or services increases, it becomes more

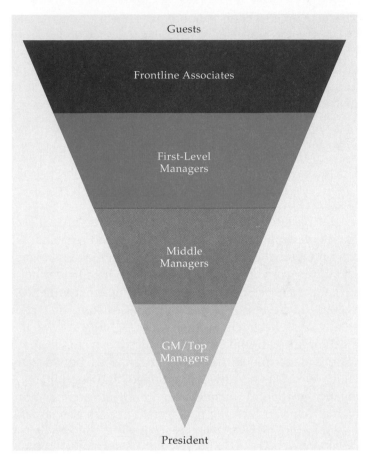

Figure 16–1 *The New "Upside-Down" Organizational Chart*

and more difficult for individuals or small groups to increase their output without changing the way they are organized.[2] Now consider the organizational structure of Marriott International today.

Today, work specialization is used to describe the extent to which jobs in an organization are divided into separate tasks. One person does not do the entire job. Instead, it is broken down into steps and a different person completes each step. In the hospitality industry, we use work specialization in various departments, but not to the extent that heavy industry does. The reason is that in the hospitality industry, we are not producing a commodity, so the line cook is likely to continue to prepare a variety of different dishes. However, the concept does apply to a banquet kitchen when a line is created to plate the food. In such a situation, each person will add a particular part of the meal to the plate and someone will check it and place it in the heated rolling cart. In other departments, such as housekeeping, work specialization has some application:

[2]Eddystone C. Nebel, *Managing Hotels Effectively: Lessons from Outstanding General Managers.* New York: Van Nostrand Reinhold, 1991, p. 112.

*Work Specialization
Allows Professionals to
Focus on Their Specialty*
(Courtesy Evans Hotels.)

In making up guest rooms, housekeepers may work in pairs with each specializing in a particular task. However, because the tasks are very repetitive, housekeepers prefer to do more than one task to avoid boredom.

Departmentalization

We are all familiar with governmental departments such as the Department of Motor Vehicles and Department of Labor, and your college probably has departments of admissions, financial aid, and student affairs, to name just a few. Once jobs have been divided up by work specialization, they have to be grouped back together so that the common tasks can be coordinated. This is called **departmentalization.** Every organization has its own form of departmentalization according to its needs. The organization's structure is shown in its **organization chart** (Figure 16–2).

Departments are created to coordinate the work of several associates in a given area. An example is housekeeping in a hotel or marketing and sales for a convention center. The main question facing company presidents is "What form of organization will best meet the organization's goals?" Should it be organized by function, product, service, guest, or territory, or by a combination of these?

The simplest form of departmentalization is by **function.** A large hotel rooms division has a reservations department, uniformed service department, front desk, communications department, concierge, housekeeping, and so on—each with its own specialized function.

Choice Hotels International departmentalizes its lodging properties by **product** in the form of brands: Comfort Inns, Comfort Suites, Quality Hotels, Sleep Inns, Clarion, MainStay Suites, Econo Lodge, and Roadway Inns. Each brand

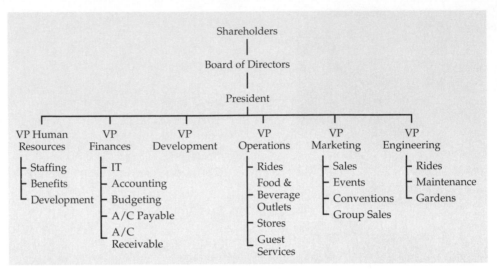

Figure 16–2 *Organization Chart for a Theme Park*

attracts a slightly different target market and offers slightly different services and is managed independently.

Sodexho and ARAMARK, both huge multinational corporations, with billions of dollars in sales, departmentalize by **guest** needs. They have departments or divisions for education, business and industry, health care, and so on. The sales department of a convention and visitors bureau may departmentalize itself by market served: travel industry, medical, legal, insurance, leisure travel, incentive travel, or military.

Many of the larger companies departmentalize by **territory** when they have representation in several states, provinces, and countries. Avis car rental has representation in a number of states, provinces, and countries. They recognize that each geographic market has its own nuances.

Authority and Responsibility

Authority is closely associated with chain of command because it gives the right to managers to exercise their power in a given situation. Authority should be commensurate with responsibility. In other words, managers should only exercise power in accordance with their position. In any organization, there is a two-way obligation regarding authority: Managers can expect their associates to do the work required and, in return, associates need to perform their duties by working efficiently and effectively. In recent years, managers have increasingly empowered associates to make more decisions—this is particularly so in the hospitality industry. We have to ensure that our guests are delighted. Some companies have empowered their employees to do whatever it takes to please the guest, even to the extent of **comping** a room if necessary.

In the hospitality industry it is very important to not only have formal authority but also respect. Associates are quick to gauge a new supervisor's or manager's credibility to see how much they know and to determine if they are able to help out by "getting their hands dirty" in an emergency. Someone who has "been there" is likely to gain the associates' respect if they are able to step in and help out during a crisis. Managers are often given authority but lack the in-depth knowledge of the department to really be able to lead by example. Simply put, "You've got to know your onions." Without credibility and therefore respect, it is much more difficult for associates to work with managers to get the job done. Thus many companies require that a newly appointed manager have experience in the area or at least an accelerated apprenticeship in the area he or she will be responsible for, thus building up the credibility of the new manager.

When authority is delegated so also should commensurate **responsibility** be delegated. That means that when one is given "rights," one also assumes an obligation to achieve objectives by performing required activities.[3] Responsibility means that you are responsible for the performance of your operation and the associates who work with you. That can sometimes be a big responsibility. What if an associate serves an alcoholic drink to a guest who is intoxicated and that guest later goes and gets into an automobile and drives off, only to have an accident, injuring not only themselves but also another innocent party. Are you responsible? *Yes!* As manager of the department or restaurant you are not only responsible but also liable.

Check Your Knowledge

1. Why is organizing important?
2. What are the drawbacks of work specialization?
3. Describe ways managers can departmentalize work activities.

Chain of Command

Organization charts not only show the structure and size of the organization but also the **chain of command** (Figure 16–3). Departments are clearly indicated, and titles may be used to show the position each associate has. The chain of command begins at the top of the organization, in the case of a large publicly traded company like Marriott International, with the board of directors, who are elected by the shareholders. The board of directors selects a president (chief executive officer, CEO), and the president selects the top executives

---

[3]Robert N. Lussier, *Management Fundamentals*. Cincinnati, OH.: South-Western College Publishing, 2000, p. 187.

Chain of Command for a Hotel

Board of Directors
↑ ↓
CEO/President
↑ ↓
Top Executives (CFO, VP, etc.)
↑ ↓
Regional/Area Vice Presidents
↑ ↓
General Manager
↑ ↓
Directors (Director of Rooms Division,
Director of Food and Beverage, etc.)
↑ ↓
Department Heads (Executive Chef, etc.)
↑ ↓
Supervisors
↑ ↓
Frontline Associates

Figure 16–3 *An Example of a Hotel's Chain of Command*

like the chief financial officer (CFO), vice president of marketing, and so on. The president and the executive team develop plans that are presented to the board for approval and then implement those plans. The chain of command is helpful for associates who have questions or need advice, because they will know whom to ask. Similarly, they know to whom they are responsible for their work performance. The chain of command should flow from the top to the bottom of the organization and up from bottom to top. This is usually illustrated by lines of authority that indicate who is responsible for what or over whom.

The Customer Is God

An industry consultant was once in Japan giving a seminar with another colleague. The colleague began by saying that in business today the customer is king, and as he said that a gentleman rushed down from the back row and grabbed the microphone and told the audience that the customer is not king but God! The gentleman was the company president. Reflecting on this unusual happening, the consultant realized just how much the Japanese revere their guests.

Increasing Span of Control

The question is often asked, "How many associates can a manager supervise?" The answer used to be between eight and twelve. Now, however, the answer is likely to be twelve to eighteen. The reason for this increase in span of control is that organizations needed to become more competitive with not only other U.S. companies but foreign ones too. Consider the cost savings realized by eliminating levels of management: If there are two organizations both with 4,000 employees and one organization has a span of control of, say, ten and the other, fifteen, the wider span of control will have fewer levels of management and lower costs because there will be fewer managers. But how much will that save? Well, if the average manager makes $65,000 a year, then the total savings would be $8.66 million. Having said that many hospitality corporations have increased their span of control, it is also fair to say that they realize that there is a point when associates become overburdened by the number of people reporting to them. At that point, managers don't have the time to give advice nor do they have time to properly supervise their associates, so standards decline. So, what factors determine the appropriate span of control? It depends on the type of work being done. Is it straightforward or complex? Are the associates highly skilled and well trained or is there a training need? Other factors include the degree to which standardized procedures are in place, the information technology available, the leadership style of the manager, and how experienced the manager is in the area of concern.

Empowerment

Given the increasing span of control, **empowerment** has become an industry norm. As managers delegate more authority and responsibility, associates have become empowered to do whatever it takes to delight the guest. Frontline associates are in a better position to know guests' wants and needs than management, so it makes sense to empower them to take care of delighting guests. In the old days, associates had to check with management before making a decision to ensure guest delight. Let's look at an example. A guest and his wife check into a hotel that advertises a room rate that includes a buffet breakfast. Unfortunately, the wife catches a nasty virus and is not well enough to go down to enjoy the buffet breakfast. Her husband says that he will call her to let her know what's offered at the buffet, so she can choose something and he can bring it up for her. He goes down to the restaurant and dutifully calls her to tell her what's available; she lets him know that she wants scrambled eggs and bacon. When the husband explains to a server that his wife is sick and is not able to come down for the buffet and asks the server to give him a tray so he can carry up her breakfast, the server listens and goes and finds another

Empowerment Allows Associates to Own the Guest Request and Check to See That It Has Been Fulfilled
(Courtesy Evans Hotels.)

Personal Profile: Jody Nicholas

Jody Nicholas was born in Zambia, a Third World country located in South Central Africa. His family then moved to neighboring Botswana where Jody completed his primary education before going to the International School of South Africa, a boarding school about three hours drive from Johannesburg.

It was in boarding school that Jody believes he acquired the discipline and mental skill set for dealing with people of different cultures, developing a team frame of mind and understanding the importance of being a team player. "I remember always being the negotiator or mediator in school, and always enjoying being a part of that process." It was Jody's service frame of mind and business mentality that would lead him to a career in hospitality.

At the age of sixteen, Jody was in his senior year at high school when his father confronted him with a challenge: "Do well in high school, son, and you can go to college anywhere you want." Jody jumped on this challenge and before long was accepted to the

(Courtesy of Jody Nicholas.)

United States International University (now Alliant International University) in San Diego, California, where he studied hotel and restaurant management with a concentration in marketing.

Jody became student ambassador for the university's hotel program and assistant to the director of the hotel school. He also received a presidential scholarship for academic excellence along with an additional scholarship through Prentice Hall for whom he did research to be used in various hotel and restaurant management books. Jody's greatest achievement to date was in 2001 in Chicago when he received the Salute to Excellence Award at the National Restaurant Association Convention where the nation's top hotel and restaurant students are recognized for their hard work and dedication to the hospitality industry.

Before graduating, Jody completed two internships, one with the Holiday Inn in Carlsbad and the second with the Residence Inn by Marriott. Jody believes that completing these internships was fundamental in gain-

more senior server, but not the manager. The husband then explains all over again and once more asks for a tray. This time he is told that food cannot be taken upstairs. The husband then says "My wife is sick and needs something to eat and drink. We've already paid for it. . . . Get the manager here now!" The server later comes over to say that the duty manager says the husband can choose anything from the cold section of the buffet but not the hot part. That does it. The guest demands the general manager, not the duty manager, be summoned. You get the picture. All of this could have been avoided if only the associates had been empowered to use a little discretion.

Centralization and Decentralization

Some organizations make most of the decisions at the corporate office and inform unit managers of them. This process is called **centralization.** If the top managers make the organization's key decisions with little or no input from subordinates, then the organization is centralized. Other organizations make most of the decisions at the unit level, or with input from associates. This is **decentralization.** In reality, organizations are never completely centralized or ing a more practical perspective of the industry and complemented the theoretical knowledge he gained throughout his studies.

In June 2001, Jody graduated magna cum laude and received the university's Outstanding Bachelor of Science Award. He is currently the front office supervisor at the largest Residence Inn by Marriott, located in La Jolla, California. He has recently been given the opportunity to attend Marriott's management training program.

Jody is grateful for the various mentorships that he has received throughout the years, in particular for those of Ana Lora and Kathy Muth. The outstanding leadership and guidance that these two have provided have been instrumental to Jody's progress, especially in front office operations. Jody also recognizes the motivation of Greg Albertini, who has helped Jody develop a greater understanding of the industry as a whole and, in a short period of time, "pounded" the vitality of laying a foundation on which to build Jody's career.

Jody is confident that he is well on his way to becoming a general manager and sees himself climbing the corporate ladder of Marriott International and joining its franchise and development branch, where he hopes to help the company strategically expand its hotel base, worldwide recognition, and management dominance.

At twenty-three years of age, Jody feels that he is only beginning to get his feet wet, but offers this advice to others in the pursuit of their dreams:

1. *Get an education.* This will give you the discipline and maturity to develop your communication skills, enhance your understanding of different cultures, and most of all do networking. These days, we have all come to appreciate the importance of knowing the right people and building the right relationships.
2. *Pay your dues.* For those of you in school, do internships and join various organizations or clubs. Gain a level of practical experience that will complement your studies and make you more marketable in this competitive industry.
3. *Progress and development.* Develop your team and position your team members to be successful. Give them the necessary tools so that they too can progress. The most legitimate way to progress is to train those people around you to replace you. Few managers have this mentality and prefer to be complacent and remain in their comfort zone.
4. *Sincerity.* Be sincere in everything you do. Have a sincere desire to improve your class, team, family, or business by showing sincerity in the way you listen, appreciate, condemn, and praise; you'll be amazed at the impact such an approach will have on those around you.

The world is yours! Best of luck,
Jody Nicholas

---

decentralized because they could not function if *all* decisions were made by the CEO, nor could they function properly if *all* decisions were made at the lowest level. Figure 16–4 illustrates the difference between a centralized and a decentralized organization.

Many companies have become more centralized in an effort to save costs and improve service to associates. Due to the rapid changes in the hospitality business, organizations are becoming more flexible and responsive. This means the organizations are becoming more decentralized. A good example is Choice Hotels' restructuring of their franchise services. They have centralized franchising services under one umbrella and created one brand management position that oversees the company's eight brands. As a result, the company closed five market offices, at a cost savings of $2.5 million in corporate overhead a year plus $4 million a year in the operations of its marketing and reservations departments.[4]

---

[4]Ruthanne Terrero, "Choice Spends to Restructure Franchise Services," *Hotel Business,* **11,** 1, January 7–20, 2002, p. 3.

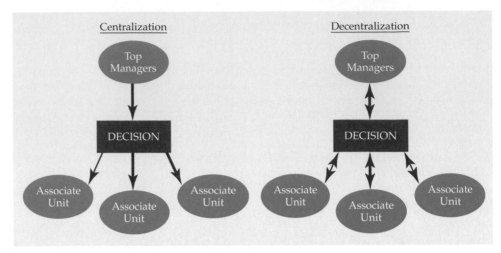

Figure 16–4 *Centralization versus Decentralization in an Organization*

In large companies especially, lower level managers who are "closer to the action" and typically have more detailed knowledge about problems and how best to solve them are empowered to delight the guest.

Check Your Knowledge

1. How are the chain of command and span of control used in organizing?
2. Describe the factors that influence greater centralization and those factors that influence greater decentralization.

Organizational Design Decisions

Organizations are structured in different ways depending on which structure best suits their needs. A company with 20 associates will look very different from one with 10,000 associates. But even organizations of comparable size don't necessarily have similar structures. What works for one organization may not work for another. How do managers decide which is the best structure for them? That decision depends on certain contingency factors that we are about to discuss.

Mechanistic and Organic Organizations

Mechanistic and organic organizations are described in Figure 16-5. The **mechanistic organization** is a rigid and tightly controlled structure. It's characterized by a relatively high degree of job specialization, rigid departmentalization, many layers of management, narrow spans of control, high formalization, centralized decision making, a limited information network (mostly downward communication), and little participation in decision making by lower associates. This combination of elements results in what is called a *tall organizational structure.*[5]

With mechanistic organizations, there is a strong adherence to the unity of command principle and a formal hierarchy of authority, with each person controlled and supervised by one supervisor. Keeping the span of control small at increasingly higher levels in the organization creates tall impersonal structures. As the distance between the top and bottom of the organization expands, top management increasingly imposes rules and regulations. Top management substitutes rules and regulations because they cannot easily enforce control. It is top management's aim for mechanistic organizations to be well oiled by rules, regulations, and routinization. The intention is to minimize the impact of personalities and judgments that might allow inefficiencies. Standardization is expected to lead to stability and predictability because confusion and ambiguity are eliminated.

In the hospitality industry, none of the organizations is completely mechanistic in structure; however, some are predominantly mechanistic—you may be working or have worked in the past for one of them. They are not necessarily all bad, but they are not the preferred type of organizational structure in today's rapidly changing environment.

An **organic organization** is in direct contrast with the mechanistic form. It is low in complexity, low in formalization, and decentralized. The organic organization is a highly adaptive form that is as loose and flexible as the mechanistic

Mechanistic Organization	*Organic Organization*
High specialization	Division of labor
Rigid departmentalization	Adaptive, flexible departmentalization
Narrow span of control	Few formal rules, little supervision
High formalization	Low in formalization
Limited information network	Low in complexity
Centralization	Decentralization

Figure 16–5 *Mechanisitic and Organic Organizations*

[5]Larry J. Gitman and Carl McDaniel, *The Future of Business.* Cincinnati, OH: South-Western College Publishing, 2000, p. 237.

organization is rigid and stable. The loose structure allows it to change rapidly as needs require. Organic organizations use division of labor, but the jobs are not standardized. Associates are professionals who are technically proficient and trained to handle diverse problems. They need very few formal rules and little direct supervision because their training has installed in them standards of professional conduct. For instance, when given a recipe a competent professional chef does not need to be given procedures on how to use it. Most problems can be solved after conferring with colleagues. Professional standards guide associates' behavior. The organic organization is low in centralization in order for the professional to respond quickly to problems and because top management cannot be expected to possess the expertise to make necessary decisions.

Most hospitality organizations are based on a combination of the two organizational structures. It is also likely that the larger an organization becomes, the more mechanistic it will be. An independent restaurant is more likely to use associates' opinions and be adaptable. Communication is likely to be more informal and to some extent authority may be decentralized. A larger restaurant chain is more likely to have more rigid hierarchical relationships, fixed duties, formal communication channels, and centralized decision making.

Coordination of Activities

When there are only a few associates in an operation, everyone can catch up quickly, but as the business expands, problems can and do occur unless there is good **coordination of activities.** The hospitality business is fast paced—guests want something now or even sooner! Departments need to communicate quickly and often to keep up with guest requests. You may have experienced an occasion when something did not go as planned—perhaps it was the check-out delay at your hotel or there were charges on your folio that were not yours—but now you're in a rush to get to the airport. You get the picture—someone made a mistake!

Coordination of Different Functions and Areas Is Critical in Exceeding Guest Expectations—an Event Coordinator Goes over the Event Plan with Service Associates

Contingency Planning

Top managers give a lot of thought to designing an appropriate structure. What that appropriate structure is depends on the following factors: the organization's strategy, size, technology, and degree of environmental uncertainty. Structure should follow strategy and be closely linked.

An organization's size generally affects its structure. Larger organizations tend to have more specialization, departmentalization, centralization, and rules and regulations than do small organizations. If there are 30 associates at one hospitality company and 300 at another, then the one with 300 will have more departments and be more mechanistic.

Every organization has some form of technology that relates to structure. Consider a hotel company that has a central reservations center. It can hold the inventory of all the hotels in the chain and be far more efficient in offering available rates and rooms to callers and also make the inventory available to travel agents and Internet travel organizations. A central reservations center can also do a better job of controlling and maximizing revenue for the available rooms than a bunch of decentralized centers.

Technology has enabled restaurant chains to transfer data and store menus and operations and training manuals via the Internet. In some cases this has led to a change in organizational structure. In the hospitality industry, technology has tended to aid the existing structure to perform better—sometimes with fewer associates. A convention center may have the latest software program for reserving and allocating space but it will not significantly change the organization's structure—someone still needs to take the guest requests and enter them into the program.

Contingency factors deal with what hospitality organizations refer to as the *what-ifs.* What if "such and such" happens? The company plans and organizes for several possible outcomes. After the terrorist attack on September 11, 2001, many hospitality companies immediately planned and organized for a drastic drop in business. Departments were greatly reduced, reorganized, or even closed in an effort to reduce the losses.

Check Your Knowledge

1. Describe the differences between mechanistic and organic organizations.
2. Discuss the importance of coordination of activities and contingency factors.

Contemporary Organizational Designs

Team-Based Structures

In response to competitive market demands for being lean, flexible, and innovative, managers are finding creative ways to structure and organize work and to make their organizations more responsive to guest needs. The first of the contemporary designs is a **work team structure;** either the complete organization or a part of it is made up of teams that perform the duties necessary to delight the guest (Figure 16–6). This concept is, like many, borrowed from business but has relevance for hospitality managers. Perhaps the best use of this concept for hospitality managers is with TQM, which you may remember we introduced in Chapter 1. Basically, teams of mostly frontline associates take on the challenge of improving guest services and products. At first, these teams are often made up of associates from one department but later can be made up of associates from different departments. This actually improves coordination between departments. Sales departments can also work well in teams and so can the banquet kitchen and for that matter most departments in a hospitality operation. However, the team is more likely to consist of associates from one department as opposed to associates from several departments. In any event, teams tend to be more productive. There are two main types of work teams: integrated and self-managed. Integrated work teams are given a number of tasks by the manager, and the team gives specific assignments to members.

Figure 16–6 *The Four Types of Contemporary Organizational Designs*

*Team-Based Structures
Can Be Made Up of Part
or All of the Company*
(Courtesy of Sodexho.)

Self-managed work teams are assigned a goal, and the team plans, organizes, leads, and controls to achieve the goal.[6]

Matrix and Project Structures

The **matrix structure** is an organizational structure that assigns specialists from different departments to work on a project; for example, a new attraction, restaurant, or hotel opening. The specialists come together to pool their knowledge and experience to work on the project. During this time they may have two bosses: their normal department head plus the project manager. To work effectively, project managers and department heads need to communicate on a regular basis. Matrix structures are appealing to organizations that want to speed up the decision-making process or get projects accomplished more quickly.

A matrix organization, however, does not work for everyone. They can be disruptive because the participants need to take a leave from their current position and then, once the project is completed, they need to return to their original position. Additionally, having more than one manager can be frustrating. **Project structures** are ones in which employees continuously work on projects. Unlike a matrix structure, members of a project do not return to their departments after project completion. They go on to the next project. An example of a project structure in the hospitality industry would be a pre-opening team for attractions, hotels, resorts, and restaurants. Teams of employees become part of the project team because they have specific knowledge and expertise. Once the project is complete the members go on to the next project.

Independent Business Units

Some hospitality companies have adopted the concept of **independent business units (IBUs)** to encourage departments to not only delight the guest but

---

[6]Robert N. Lussier, *Management Fundamentals.* Cincinnati, OH: South-Western College Publishing, 2000, p. 198.

also to watch the money all the way to the bottom line. In other words, the IBU becomes its own independent business and makes decisions accordingly with little or no need to get approval for routine operational decisions. The unit can implement strategies that will improve guest satisfaction or reduce costs by finding a quicker or better way of doing something. Forming IBUs is an excellent strategy to get associates to realize the total picture of revenue and expenses for a department. It forces associates to engage in all elements of management to make a profit. IBUs also enable management to seriously look at departments not making sufficient profit contribution, with a view toward making changes and improvements or eliminating the department. Departments that once made a loss are now making a profit as a result of the company installing an IBU system of organizational design.

Boundaryless Organizations

Another contemporary approach to organizational design is the **boundaryless organization,** an organization whose design is not defined by, or limited to, the horizontal, vertical, or external boundaries imposed by a predefined structure.[7] The term was coined by Jack Welch, former chairman of General Electric, who wanted to eliminate vertical and horizontal boundaries within GE and break down external barriers between the company and its customers and suppliers. This idea may sound odd, yet many of today's most successful organizations are finding that they can most effectively operate in today's environment by remaining close to the guest and being flexible and unstructured. The boundaryless organization seeks to eliminate the chain of command, to have appropriate spans of control, and to replace departments with empowered teams. Hospitality organizations are moving in this direction but are not there yet. Some might feel that this is not a concept that will work for hospitality organizations, whereas others might think it's a great idea. Hospitality companies recognize that it is important to stay close to the guest but are challenged to create a boundaryless organization.

Teams and Employee Involvement

Teams are task-oriented work groups; they can either be formally appointed or may evolve informally. We all work with others, to a greater or lesser extent, in order to meet or exceed goals. Both formal and informal teams make important contributions to the company and to associates' need satisfaction. For example, an informal team from one hotel saved the company more than $250,000 a year after the team made a proposal about energy savings. Each

[7]See, for example, G. G. Dess, A. M. A. Rasheed, K. J. McLaughlin, and R. L. Priem, "The New Corporate Architecture," *Academy of Management Executive,* August 1995, pp. 7–20. As cited in Robins and Coulter, *Management,* p. 271.

Post 9–11: Principles of Organization for Disaster Operations

Hank Christen and Paul Maniscalco

The development of a comprehensive emergency management plan (CEMP) is based on a functional organization, not a hierarchy. The normal top-down flow of orders, instructions, and information through multiple levels of management (a hierarchy) does not translate effectively to disasters. The function, not the title or level of the player(s), is the key.

Disaster management is organic, loose, and flexible. The first principle of this function-based system is **decentralization.** It is a "flat system" with only three layers: manager/staff, functional directors (operations, logistics, etc.), and sectors. Sectors are established as needed to support the primary functions (example: a food/water sector assigned by the logistics director).

The second key principle is **chain/unity of command.** Someone is in charge, there are functional directors, and there are sector leaders. Information and direction flows from the manager to the functional directors, to the sector leader, and vice versa. *Bottom-up information flow is as relevant in a disaster as top-down information flow.* Sector leaders who are physically involved often have more knowledge and insight into specific problems than the boss at the top. Senior managers must empower their subordinates and trust them.

The third key principle of organization is **span of control.** The span of control in disaster operations is much narrower than in normal business management. A span of control of three to four should be maintained. The environment is stressful, with poor communications, inadequate resources, and short decision times.

An effective organizational tool to keep the span of control within limits is *branching:* dividing a functional level into two or more segments called branches. For example, the logistics director can divide responsibilities into two areas: service branch, responsible for communications and food/water; and support branch, responsible for facilities, supplies, and maintenance.

The incident manager needs a staff (called the *management staff*) for assistance. The three key positions on the management staff are:

- ✓ Liaison—serves as a point of contact with emergency responders and other involved agencies, companies, or organizations

- ✓ Public information—coordinates with the local public information officer; drafts and implements public information strategy
- ✓ Safety officer—coordinates with incident safety officer; responsible for safety monitoring of all employee activities; *has authority to suspend unsafe procedures or practices*

During emergency activities, the planning director must maintain a disaster organizational chart listing positions and names of employee assignments. Organizational restructuring and personnel assignments must be charted during each briefing period to ensure that all team members fully understand their positions: whom they direct, and whom they report to. A preprinted (legal size: 8½" × 14") chart showing sector boxes under each functional box needs to be developed. As sectors are established or disbanded, they should be added to or deleted from the chart. A bulletin-board-size (4' × 6') chart (use dry-erase material) should be posted in the internal management center. A disaster demands a very flexible and organic structure; sectors are frequently established and dismantled in response to unpredictable event dynamics.

> **Critical Factors**
> - ✓ Focus on functions instead of a hierarchy.
> - ✓ Maintain a flat organizational structure.
> - ✓ The ideal span of control is three or four operations.
> - ✓ Utilize a disaster organizational chart.

Job descriptions are another organizational tool that helps to ensure effective disaster management. All positions must be defined. The descriptions should be brief and concise. Employees should be assigned to functions and sectors based on their skill sets. For example, a maintenance director is a good choice for the position of logistics director. An individual may shift jobs during emergencies; for example, a marketing manager with previous military planning experience is the logical choice for planning director during an emergency. It is imperative that everyone understand their roles in the crisis setting, especially if roles change from normal assignments.

team member not only received a sizable bonus but their employee satisfaction scores were significantly higher than those of associates who did not participate in the team.

Teams are great for doing work that is complex, interrelated, or of a volume larger than one person can handle. Harold Geneen, while chairman of ITT, said, "If I had enough arms and legs I'd do it all myself." We all know that associates cannot do everything themselves due to limitations of arms and legs, time, expertise, knowledge, and other resources. There is a certain "buzz" in a restaurant on a busy Friday night; when the kitchen is getting "slammed" you know what teamwork is or isn't!

The funny thing about teams, as you have probably experienced by now, is that you don't always get to choose who you work with—just like when you do term papers and projects in teams. And even when you do get to choose classmates, it sometimes doesn't work out. They don't do their fair share or something else doesn't work. Yet in the hospitality industry we are constantly working in teams to exceed guest expectations. So how can we make teams more effective?

Group Dynamics

Why are some groups more successful than others? Why does a team of mediocre players sometimes beat a team of superior players? You've probably experienced a situation in which, when seemingly against all odds, a team excels. Remember the survival programs on television in the early 2000s? A group of people was dropped off in some remote place and over a period of time the group members had to survive as teams, *but* they could vote people "off the island." Wow, what if we did that in the hospitality industry?

Why and how this happens is called *group dynamics* and includes variables such as the abilities of the group's members, the size of the group, the level of conflict, and the internal pressures on members to conform to the group's norms. Sometimes external influences inhibit the group's performance. Corporate may dictate policies that make it more difficult for the group to succeed or there may be a shortage of resources. One of the fascinating aspects of group dynamics is the members of the group. You may have experienced a group project at college. Sometimes you got to choose whom you worked with and sometimes your group members were selected randomly. Which worked best?

How Companies Use Teams at Work

Hospitality companies use teams at work in a variety of ways. One way is to structure the organization into teams from the start. Instead of calling them departments, they are called teams. This implies, of course, that employees need to be **team players,** something so necessary in the fast-paced hospitality industry. Another way in which management can use teams is through total quality management (TQM) programs that involve associates working in teams to constantly improve the guest experience. Teams are formed either from individual departments or from several different departments. They choose an area of the operation that needs improvement, usually one of guest concern, and proceed to make changes that will benefit the guest. TQM teams have made important contributions to the industry and continue to do so.

Self-managed teams make decisions that were once made by managers. This saves managers time, allowing them to concentrate on more important things. An example was given in Chapter 4: Hotel housekeepers who score highly on room inspections no longer need to have their rooms checked by a floor housekeeper. These teams of housekeepers actually receive a bonus for superior performance and the hotel saves the salary of the floor housekeepers. Self-managed teams can and do work successfully in several types of hospitality organizations from theme parks to convention centers.

How to Build Productive Teams

Building productive teams is critical to the success of any organization, especially in the service-oriented hospitality industry. In recent years, the introduction of TQM processes has significantly increased the number of teams in the hospitality industry. At the heart of TQM is process improvement, and associate participation is the heartbeat. **Productive teams** are built by giving associates the authority, responsibility, and encouragement to come together to work on guest-related improvements that will enhance not only the guest experience but also make the associates' jobs easier. Teams need leadership, which is either appointed by management or the team is allowed to choose a leader. As with any other endeavor, goals and objectives need to be set and the team given the resources it needs to accomplish those goals. It is amazing to see the enthusiasm that teams can generate as they work on improving the guest experience. Associates will come up with great ideas that can save money and provide guests with better service. Team building happens when members interact to learn how each member thinks and works. Through close interaction, team members learn to develop increased trust and openness. When a team focuses on goal setting and who will plan on accomplishing what by when, and so on, the team will likely be on its way to becoming a high-achieving team.

Job Rotation

Job rotation is an excellent way to relieve the possible boredom and monotony that can be a disadvantage of work specialization because it gives associates a broader range of experiences. Once associates have mastered the jobs they were hired to do, there is a tendency for boredom to set in. Job rotation creates interest and assists in developing associates to take on additional responsibilities. The management training programs of some of the major hospitality corporations are good examples of job rotation; graduates spend a few months in several departments before selecting an area of specialization. Even then, as a frontline manager, you are likely to move through a few departments to build up your knowledge and experience. Job rotation does create some

Corporate Profile Six Flags

Six Flags is a world-renowned theme park. The company owns and operates thirty-eight different parks spread out over North America, Latin America, and Europe. Locations include Mexico City, Belgium, France, Spain, Germany, and most major metropolitan areas in the United States. In fact, having a park in forty of the fifty major metropolitan areas in the United States has earned Six Flags the title of world's largest regional theme park company. Annually, more than 50 million visitors are reported to entertain themselves at Six Flags theme parks worldwide. The company prides itself in claiming that 98 percent of the U.S. population is within an eight-hour drive to any one of the numerous Six Flags theme parks.

Now who is behind this huge success? The founder of the first theme park was a man named Angus Wynne. He was a Texas oil baron with a vision. His vision was to create a family entertainment park that was fun as well as affordable and, most importantly, within reachable distance to where people lived. A simple amusement park was transformed into a theme park by Wynne adding innovative rides with theme presentations. His first park opened in Texas in 1961. The transformation proved to be a huge success with the public; visitors were drawn in crowds to the newly opened theme park.

The park was named after the six different flags that flew over Texas at one time, representing the six different countries that marked Texas's past history. The theme park was divided into six different regions, each modeled after the country it represented. Visitors could marvel at Spanish haciendas or French bistros, all the while in the company of Southern belles and pirates.

This ride, called Viper, is located in the Six Flags Magic Mountain theme park in Los Angeles. It is reported to be the world's largest looping roller coaster. It is 188 feet high, with seven loops that turn you upside down at the speed of seventy miles per hour. (Courtesy of Six Flags Magic Mountain.)

Today, Six Flags has a licensing agreement with DC Comics and Warner Bros. This means characters such as Batman, Superman, and Bugs Bunny and the gang can be found wandering around the parks and having their pictures taken with park visitors. With fantastic rides and show-stopping entertainment, the parks have become one of the first-choice amusement parks for entertainment-seeking families and individuals.

Funding for expansion of the company was drawn primarily from the profits made from the first successful parks opened, including the first one in Texas. In 1996 Six Flags went public for the first time, meaning it allowed the public to purchase its stock as opposed to hand-picked private investors. The shares were sold at $18 each, and their purchase totaled nearly $70 million. Only one year later the company had raised $200 million with its public offering. With these kinds of funds, Six Flags continued purchasing land or old amusement parks and turning them into Six Flags theme parks, rapidly expanding their reach.

In 2000, the parks had become so successful and had such a high income that large corporations, including AOL, Kodak, and Univision, signed major sponsorship deals with Six Flags. One year later Perrier and Pringles joined the sponsorship team.

The current management team has been in effect since 1994. President Gary Story serves simultaneously as the chief operating officer and director. He was the company's executive vice president before his promotion to president. The CEO of the company is Kieran E. Burke, former president of Six Flags from 1989 to 1994. He also serves as director and chairman of the board. With the management team going strong and further expansion planned, the future success of Six Flags looks rosy.

additional costs, mostly in the area of training and reduced productivity, because as associates move into new positions, they need time to become proficient in their new roles. A major benefit of job rotation is that associates become well rounded in the operation of the corporation, and many associates are promoted as a result of gaining the additional knowledge and experience.

Job Enlargement and Job Enrichment

Job enlargement increases the scope of the associates' work. Originally, it was intended as a way of maintaining interest in the work; more recently, it has become an economic necessity. Today, hospitality management professionals have more work and responsibilities than ever before—that's why workplace stress has become an issue. However, no one in the hospitality industry can say that his or her job is uneventful. In our business no two days are alike and, for many, that's one of the fascinations of the hospitality business, despite the increased workload. **Job enrichment** adds some planning and evaluating responsibilities to a position. It gives associates greater control over their work by allowing them to assume some tasks typically done by their supervisors.

Trends in Organizing

- ✔ Computerized scheduling programs save the organizer time and limit the error margin for being over- or understaffed.
- ✔ The fact that recipes are just a click away on the Internet helps speed the organizational process tremendously.
- ✔ The new dynamic of multitasking has caused a drastic change in the organizational chart. For example, today, front desk workers are responsible for much more than just checking guests in and out. Through multitasking, they simultaneously act as phone operators, customer service agents, tour guides, and occasionally concierges.
- ✔ A new trend following the September 11, 2001, tragedy is to decentralize organizations.
- ✔ Reduced occupancies at most hotels have led to a reduction in staff and managerial positions. This, in turn, has led to more decentralized organizations with fewer levels of management.

Case Study

Club Mediterranee is an international French-based company that has about sixty Club Med vacation villages around the world. The company originally functioned as a matrix organization: Each village manager reported both to a country manager and to a number of different directors. Directors worked out of company headquarters, and each director had primary responsibility for some facet of Club Med operations and marketing. This structure, however, proved less than satisfactory. Club Med, for example, prides itself on providing village arrangements that reflect *local* atmospheres—a difficult feat for directors to achieve from remote locations.

Discussion Question

1. How would you restructure Club Med?

Career Information

The executive chef of the Sheraton Hotel in San Diego, Steve Black, has commented on what he believes tomorrow's managers need in terms of skills, and his thoughts are definitely a dose of common sense. From his job experience, there always seemed to be a lack of common sense as well as basic people skills, both of which are important to managers. Also important is hands-on work, which translates into loads of experience.

Always popular advice on managerial positions relating to organization, is to be trained in multitasking. Instead of being knowledgeable in one job position, try to advance yourself into a position where you are able to perform the job duties of three or four positions, if necessary. Expand on training and, when gaining experience, ask to be put in a new department in order to learn new skills.

Summary

1. The purpose of organizing is to get jobs done efficiently and effectively.
2. Goals are accomplished by organizing the work to be done into specific jobs and departments; assigning tasks and responsibilities associated with individual jobs; coordinating diverse organizational tasks; clustering jobs into units; establishing relationships among individuals, groups, and departments; establishing formal lines of authority; and allocating and deploying organizational resources.
3. Organizational structure is the total framework through which job tasks are divided, grouped, and coordinated.
4. Organizational structure is divided into these parts: work specialization, departmentalization, authority and responsibility, chain of command, delegation, increasing span of control and empowerment, and centralization and decentralization.
5. Organizational designs and decisions consist of mechanistic and organic organizations, coordination, contingency factors, common organizational design, contemporary organizational design IBUs, and the boundaryless organization.
6. Teams are task-oriented work groups; they can either be formally appointed or may evolve informally.

Key Words and Concepts

Authority	Division of labor	Matrix Structure	Responsibility
Boundaryless organization	Empowerment	Mechanistic organization	Self-managed teams
Centralization	Function	Organic organization	Team player
Chain of command	Guest	Organization chart	Teams
Comping	Independent business unit	Organizational structure	Territory
Contingency factors	(IBU)	Organizing	Work specialization
Coordination of activities	Job enlargement	Product	Work team structure
Decentralization	Job enrichment	Productive teams	
Departmentalization	Job rotation	Project structure	

Review Questions

1. Would you rather work in a mechanistic or an organic organization? Why?
2. Looking to the future, which is the best organization structure for a theme park? A fifty-room resort? A mid-priced Italian restaurant? An economy 100-room hotel? A 3,000-room casino hotel?
3. Describe a team-based structure.
4. Compare and contrast a matrix structure and a project structure.
5. When might an organization design its structure around independent business units?

Internet Exercise

Go to the web site of three major public companys of your choosing and examine how the company is organizationally structured. What different types of product offerings do they have? In how many countries or regions are they represented? What kind of divisions do they have? Have different types of guest groups been identified?

Apply Your Knowledge

Mini Project: This project is based on a real-life experience of the executive chef at the Sheraton Hotel in San Diego. The project is to organize an off-site event, which is an event planned and organized by the Sheraton staff but it does not take place at the hotel itself.

The Sheraton typically caters the annual San Diego Zoo fund-raiser every year. The attendance for this event is roughly 1,000 people. The caterers organize and cater a reception followed by dinner. Your challenge is to plan this off-site event using planning techniques and organizational skills learned.

Communication and Decision Making 17

After reading and studying this chapter, you should be able to:

✔ Define communication.

✔ Improve your interpersonal communication.

✔ List barriers to effective interpersonal communication and how to overcome them.

✔ Differentiate between formal and informal communication.

✔ Explain communication flows and networks.

✔ Outline the eight steps in the decision-making process.

✔ Understand why managing is a synonym for decision making.

✔ Know the difference between rational, bounded rational, and intuitive decisions.

✔ Identify the situations in which a programmed decision is a better solution than a nonprogrammed decision.

✔ Differentiate the decision conditions of certainty, risk, and uncertainty.

✔ Describe the different dimensions of decision-making styles.

Managerial Communication

Communication is the oil that lubricates all of the other management functions of forecasting, planning, organizing, motivating, and controlling. Additionally, because managers spend a high percentage of their time communicating, the communication function becomes doubly important. Managers interact with others throughout the day by the following means:

✔ Personal face-to-face meetings

✔ Telephone

✔ Mail/fax

✔ Memos, reports, log books, and other internal/external written communication

✔ E-mail, Internet web sites

The simplest method of communication involves a sender, a message, and a receiver. However, merely sending a message cannot ensure that the message will be received and understood correctly. Several factors can lead to distortion of the message, such as noise interference or poor listening skills and inappropriate tuning. During the middle of a busy lunch service is not the right time to be asking the chef a question about the company's policy on sick-pay benefits. In this chapter we explore these various barriers to effective communication and the importance of good communication to a manager.

What Is Communication?

The definition of communication is the exchange of information and the transmission of meaning.[1] The essence of communication is the exchange of information. In other words, if no exchange has taken place, then no communication has taken place. Another important aspect of communication is understanding the meaning. The sole transfer of information is not enough to ensure successful communication; the actual meaning must be understood as well. A manager passing along information to an employee in Spanish will find that information of little use if the employee does not understand Spanish. Good communication is not necessarily agreeing with the message being conveyed, but rather an understanding of the message.[2] Perfect communication results when a sender communicates a thought or idea and the receiver perceives it exactly as envisioned by the sender. Just because the receiver does not agree with the message does not mean that the communication process has failed. You can disagree with something while at the same time fully understanding it.

---

[1]Gary A. Dessler, *A Framework for Management,* 2nd ed. Upper Saddle River, NJ: Prentice Hall, 2002, p. 282.

[2]C. O. Kursh, "The Benefits of Poor Communication," *Psychoanalytic Review,* Summer–Fall 1971, pp. 189–208, as cited in Stephen P. Robbins and Mary Coulter, *Management,* 7th ed. Upper Saddle River, NJ: Prentice Hall, 2002.

Managerial communication includes two different types: **Interpersonal communication** occurs between two or more individuals, and **organizational communication** includes all the different forms, networks, and systems of communication that occur among individuals, groups, or departments within an organization.

Interpersonal Communications Process[3]

Communication between two or more people is described as interpersonal communication. The **interpersonal communications process** is made up of seven elements: the communication source, the message, encoding, the channel, decoding, the receiver, and feedback (Figure 17–1). Before communication can take place, a **message** must exist and be conveyed. This message is dispatched from the sender and passed to the receiver. The message will travel in converted form because it has to be **encoded** and then passed by way of a medium, a **channel,** from the sender to the receiver. It is then retranslated by means of **decoding.** When successful communication has taken place, the receiver will give **feedback** to the sender that he or she has correctly understood the message being conveyed. The ultimate result of this process is that meaning is transferred from one individual to another.[4]

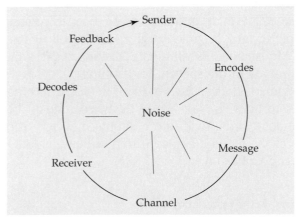

Figure 17–1 *Interpersonal Communications Process (Derived from Stephen P. Robbins and Mary Coulter,* Management, *7th ed. Upper Saddle River, NJ: Prentice Hall, 2002, p. 283.)*

[3]Draws on Robbins and Coulter, *Management,* pp. 283–284.

[4]D. K. Berlo, *The Process of Communication.* New York: Holt, Rinehart & Winston, 1960, pp. 30–32, as cited in Robbins and Coulter, *Management,* p. 283.

Noise is often a part of the interpersonal communication process. Noise can consist of various activities going on in the background, sounds of machinery or coworkers, or it can even be as simple as static in the telephone line or illegible print. Therefore, noise is considered a somewhat constant disturbance in the communications process and the cause of distortions of the message. Each element in the process can be influenced and distorted by disturbances.

The sender conveys a message by encoding it. During this process, four major things could go wrong and distort the message. The sender can have too little or too much knowledge. He or she can't communicate what he or she does not know.

However, if the proper explanations aren't given, the receiver could falsely interpret the message. Too much knowledge might cause the message not to be understood at all. Preexisting attitudes and the cultural system of the sender can influence the encoding of the message as well. Attitudes and beliefs about subject matters will leave their traces in the message and may be picked up by the receiver.

The message itself, such as a written document, an oral speech, or gestures and facial expressions, can be influenced by disturbances. Noise will influence listening skills during an oral speech. Faulty equipment can lead to disruption of the message if it is conveyed through e-mail or fax. Symbols such as pictures, words, and numbers that are selected by the sender to convey his or her message can be influenced by noise.

The channel used to convey the message is important to the whole communications process. If you choose to use an oral speech to communicate with a person who has a hearing impairment, naturally the message will not be understood as the sender intended it to be. Whether the sender chooses to use an office memorandum, a phone call, e-mail, gestures, or pictures to convey the message will play a large role in how accurately the receiver will understand it. Using two channels can sometimes eliminate distortion; an oral speech followed by a written summary of the speech, for example.

The receiver is limited by the same factors as the sender. If he or she has too little knowledge of the subject, distortions will take place. Likewise, if he or she has too much knowledge, too much can be read into a simple message. The preexisting attitudes and beliefs of the individual play a role in how distorted the message will be after the decoding has taken place.

Ways of Communicating Interpersonally

Managers can communicate in various ways. Examples include face-to-face, telephone, e-mail, fax, group meetings, memos, formal presentations, bulletin boards, mail, employee publications, and computer-, video-, and teleconferencing. All of these ways to communicate use oral or written symbols to convey a message.[5] There are other ways to communicate, however.

---

[5]Robbins and Coulter, *Management,* p. 286.

Managers May Choose to Communicate Their Messages by Means of E-Mail

Nonverbal communication is communication without words. Taking examples from everyday life shows how important and frequent nonverbal communication is. Ambulance sirens, a honking horn, the school bell, or the sound of a ringing phone all communicate something to us without using any words. Similarly, gestures, actions, and the type of clothes worn communicate messages to us. A person wearing a police uniform tells us he belongs to the police force. In the same manner the type of car a person drives or the size of a house conveys to others a message about that person. All of these forms of communication are nonverbal.

Body language is facial expressions, gestures, and any other ways of communicating a message with your body. For example, if a person smiles or laughs, a message of joy or friendliness is conveyed. In the same manner, rolling of the eyes indicates disbelief or even annoyance. Emotions are typically conveyed purely by body language.

Verbal intonation is the use of the voice alone to give emphasis to certain parts of a phrase or words. For example, consider the phrase "What are you

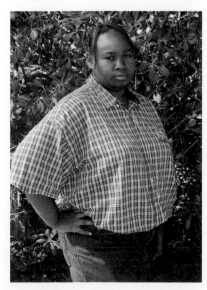

Facial Expressions, a Part of Body Language, Convey Different Meanings

doing?" An abrasive, loud intonation of the voice will indicate that the person is upset, angry, and even defensive. However, if the same sentence is said in a smooth, soft voice it will be understood as real interest, and even concern, or a friendly inquiry. Verbal intonation is almost more important than the actual words being said. A common saying is that it is not what you say, but how you say it. This is a very important fact that managers should take note of.

Check Your Knowledge

1. What is the difference between interpersonal and organizational communication?
2. What are three ways of communicating interpersonally?
3. Describe the interpersonal communications process.

Barriers to Effective Interpersonal Communication[6]

Many elements can influence interpersonal communication. Some of the major barriers are discussed next.

Perception

Everybody perceives thing differently. This is due to different backgrounds, upbringing, personal experiences, and major influences in their lives. No two people are alike and neither is their perception. Whereas one person may be optimistic and perceive a message in a positive light, another may be a pessimist and see only negative aspects of the message. Unwanted news is easily screened out and forgotten about, while things we want to hear are remembered for a longer period of time.

Semantics

The actual meaning of words, or **semantics,** is the cause of many failed communication efforts. The literal meaning of words and the actual meaning can be two different things, but can be expressed in the same way. For instance, if a restaurant manager tells a server to make the guests feel comfortable, she doesn't necessarily mean that the server will bring pillows, blankets, or even beds into the dining area. The manager may have meant to make the customers feel comfortable in a nonphysical way, by attending to them, making sure they are satisfied with their order, and making sure their water glass is

---

[6]Draws on Dessler. *A Framework for Management,* pp. 284–285; see also Robbins and Coulter, *Management,* pp. 288–291.

refilled promptly. Using **jargon,** specialized terminology or technical language that may be used widely within an organization, may be ineffective if used with new employees or people who are not familiar with it.

Nonverbal Communication

Nonverbal communication, communication through body language, is a typical means of communication. However, it can also be considered a barrier to effective communication. The weight of the decoding of a message lies with the nonverbal communication rather than on the actual encoded message. "It has been estimated that in a conversation involving two people, verbal aspects of a message account for less than 5% of the meaning, whereas nonverbal aspects of a message account for 95% of the meaning" one expert said.[7] For example, if a supervisor comes to work in the morning disgruntled about morning traffic, the subordinates might misinterpret the angry facial expression as the supervisor being dissatisfied with their work although he never literally said so.

Here are a few common interpretations of nonverbal communication from an expert's list that you probably use during everyday conversations: Biting your lips typically indicates anxiety; scratching your head shows confusion or disbelief; hand wringing is a strong sign of feeling uncomfortable in a situation, almost to the point of panic; and sighing is interpreted as boredom or a sign of distress.[8] Next time you have a conversation with someone, take note

Nonverbal Communication as a Barrier to Effective Communication

[7]R. Wayne Pace and Don Faules, *Organizational Communication.* Upper Saddle River, NJ: Prentice Hall, 1989, as cited in Dessler, *Framework for Management,* p. 284.

[8]Douglas M. McGregor, "The Human Side of Enterprise," in Michael Matteson and John M. Ivancevich (eds.), *Management Classics,* Santa Monica, CA: Goodyear, 1977, as cited in Dessler, *Framework for Management,* p. 284.

of your own nonverbal communication: what you are expressing with gestures and facial expressions.

Misinterpretations of nonverbal communication are especially dominant in cross-cultural communication. Gestures and expressions mean different things in different cultures. For example, it is considered impolite to make direct eye contact with the person speaking in most Asian and African countries, whereas it is considered polite to look the speaker in the eye in most Western cultures.

Ambiguity

Ambiguity, vagueness, or uncertainty can occur in a message being conveyed. A message may be ambiguous, meaning the person receiving the message is uncertain about the actual meaning. If a manager asks an employee to come to her office as soon as possible, it could mean immediately or next week when the employee has some free time. When the words of a message are clear, but the intentions of the sender aren't, ambiguity occurs. The employee may be unclear as to why the manager wants to see him in the office now. Ambiguity might also be described as the receiver's uncertainty about the consequences of the message. The employee might ask, "What will happen if I don't go to her office immediately?"

Defensiveness

When people feel that they are being verbally attacked or criticized, they tend to react defensively. The reaction could be making sarcastic remarks, being overly judgmental, or simply screening out the unpleasant parts of the conversation. This often happens when employees refuse to realize personal flaws; using defense mechanisms helps them screen out the negative image of themselves and they will be able to keep their self-esteem. However, acting defensively is a barrier to effective communication.

Overcoming Barriers to Effective Interpersonal Communication

Because the barriers to effective interpersonal communication just discussed do exist, there are ways to improve on the communication to largely overcome them. An essential part of a manager's job is to be an effective communicator. The following suggestions should help make interpersonal communication more effective.

Use Feedback[9]

Right off the bat, utilizing feedback, the last step in the communications process, will eliminate misunderstandings and inaccuracies regarding the mes-

---

[9]Draws on Dessler, *Framework for Management,* p. 291.

sage being conveyed. The feedback can be verbal or nonverbal. After the receiver has decoded the message, the sender should make sure the message has been understood. It can be as simple as asking the employee: "Did you understand what I said?" The ideal response to this question will be more than a yes or no answer. The best form of verbal feedback is a quick restatement and summary of the message that has been conveyed: "You said you switched my shift tomorrow to the night shift." This way the sender can be sure his message has been correctly understood.

The nonverbal form of feedback consists of various reactions to a message. First off, the sender can watch for nonverbal cues as to whether the message has been understood or not. Eye contact, facial expression, scratching the head, or shrugging of shoulders all can indicate how accurately the message has been received and understood. Furthermore the actual actions following the message can be used as feedback. A manager telling her staff about a new serving procedure will find out how accurately her message has been understood by watching the staff to see if they follow the new procedure or not. If some servers do not follow the new procedure, the manager will have to clarify or restate the message.

Active Listening[10]

There is a difference between hearing and actually listening. You might hear what your manager is saying, but did you really listen? Hearing is passive, and listening is an active act of understanding and responding to the words being said. The first step to **active listening** is to listen for the total meaning. For example, if a manager tells his employee that the room occupancy is down this quarter, instead of responding by saying, "Don't worry, it'll be fine," the employee recognizes that a problem exists. The second step is to reflect the feelings. This is an important step for the sender of the message because it helps him communicate the emotional part of his message. The receiver would reflect it by saying something like "This situation must be stressful for you." The last step is to note all nonverbal cues and respond to them. These cues might include hand gestures or facial expressions.

Avoid Triggering Defensiveness

Defensiveness is one of the main barriers to effective communication. By avoiding the tendency to criticize, argue, or give advice to a subordinate, defensive behavior can be avoided. Humans don't like being criticized, because that diminishes their self-image. Phrases that convey blame or finger pointing are typically useless. The receiver will respond by arguing or storming off, and the communication has largely failed. A solution to this is to wait for a cooling-off period so that both parties can regain their composure. Generally, managers should avoid overly negative statements.

---

[10]Draws on Robbins and Coulter, *Management,* p. 286.

Check Your Knowledge

1. Define semantics.
2. Explain ambiguity as it relates to communication barriers.
3. What are three ways of overcoming communication barriers?

Organizational Communication

Organizational communication is necessary in managerial communication. The fundamentals include formal communication versus informal communication, communications flow patterns, and formal and informal communication networks.

Formal and Informal Communication

The two major forms of organizational communication are formal and informal communication. **Formal communication** is used by managers to communicate job requirements to their employees. It follows the official chain of command. Formal communication occurs when, for instance, a manager tells an employee his or her schedule for the following week. The subject matter is always job related and seen as essential to the employment.

Informal communication does not follow a company's chain of command or structural hierarchy. The subject matter may be job related but may not be essential to performing job duties. Examples of informal communication are employees talking at the water fountain, lunchroom, or at company events. In every organization employees form relationships with each other, whether as acquaintances or as actual friendships. Employees use informal communication to satisfy their need for social interaction and it can also improve an organization's performance, through better employee relationships and by having a faster, more efficient communications channel.[11] The 'grapevine' is a form of informal communication.

Communication Flows and Networks

Communication flows in various directions: upward, downward, laterally, diagonally, and so on, as discussed next.

---

[11]Ibid, pp. 293–296.

Upward Communication

Upward communication takes place when managers, or simply superiors, rely on their subordinates for receiving information. It flows upward from employees to managers. This type of communication is important to managers because it helps them determine the satisfaction level of their employees and how they feel about their jobs, the organization in general, or problems with coworkers or even the manager himself. Some managers even encourage their subordinates to give them ideas about how to make improvements in the organization. Some examples of upward communication include manager performance reports, employee surveys, suggestion boxes, and informal group sessions with other coworkers.

Downward Communication

Communication flowing down from supervisor to employee is considered **downward communication.** Managers use this type of communication for various purposes: to inform employees of company policies, procedures, employee evaluations or job descriptions, and to discuss the future of the employee. Downward communication is often used by their managers to inform, direct, coordinate, and evaluate employees.

Lateral Communication

Communication that takes place between the employees of a company who are on the same hierarchical level in the organization is called **lateral communication.** This type of communication is used by employees to discuss their environment and the organization in general. Lateral communication is also used by cross-functional teams to facilitate communication. The important thing to remember is to always let the supervisor know about decisions made through lateral communication.

Diagonal Communication

Communication that takes place between employees who are on different hierarchical levels and in different departments of the organization is called **diagonal communication.** An example of this type of communication is that of a chef communicating with a front desk receptionist. The two employees are not on the same level nor are they in the same department of a hotel. Through e-mail almost every employee is able to communicate efficiently with any other employee in the same organization. However, as with lateral communication, the employees must make a point to update their managers on decisions made during this type of communication.

Two of the forms of communication flow, vertical and lateral, can be combined in various forms. These new forms are called **communication networks.** The most common are chain, wheel, and all-channel (Figure 17–2), as well as the grapevine.

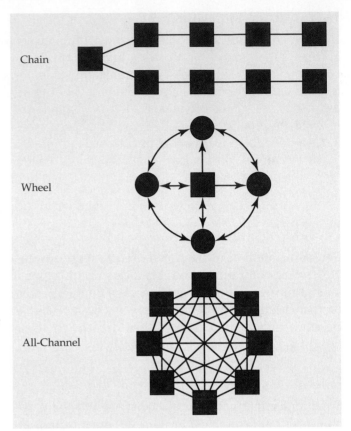

Figure 17–2 *Three Organizational Communication Networks (Derived from Stephen P. Robbins and Mary Coulter,* Management, *7th ed. Upper Saddle River, NJ: Prentice Hall, 2002, p. 295.)*

Chain, Wheel, and All-Channel Communication Networks[12]

Communication in a chain network flows according to the existing chain of command of an organization. This includes downward as well as upward communication flow. This type of network is highly accurate, no information can be lost, and the path the message travels is precise. On the downside, the chain network is only moderately fast and moderately popular with employees.

The wheel network is a network in which communication flows between a strong leader and each individual in a group or team. In this network the coworkers do not need to communicate with each other; they communicate solely with their leader. The advantage to this type of communication is that it is relatively fast in speed and accuracy. However, this type of communication is usually not very popular with employees.

The all-channel communication network is differentiated from others by its freely flowing communication between all members of a group or team. This means the leader communicates with her employees, as well as the employees under her, and with their leader. This type of network is very popular with

---

[12]Ibid, pp. 294–295.

employees, and the speed at which messages travel is almost supersonic. However, the accuracy of the message is not always at 100 percent.

One thing to remember is that every unique situation will require a different communication network. No one network is perfect for every situation.

The Grapevine

This type of communication network may be the most popular and important in an organization. One survey reported that 75 percent of employees hear about matters first through rumors on the grapevine.[13] The definition of the grapevine network is an informal organizational communication network. This network is an important source of communication for the managers of an organization. Through the local informal grapevine, issues that employees consider a reason for stress and anxiety are made known. This network acts as a very effective feedback mechanism and as a filter that sorts out only the issues that employees find important. The negative aspect of this communication network is the occasional rumor that travels through it. This is pretty much unavoidable; however, successful managers can eliminate the negative impact of rumors. This can be done by speaking openly and honestly with employees about any negative feelings or important decisions that are made.

Check Your Knowledge

1. Define informal communication.
2. What is the difference between lateral and diagonal communication?
3. Elaborate on the wheel communication network.

Decision–Making Process

All individuals in organizations small or large are faced with the task of decision making. This can involve decisions as simple as where to go to lunch today or complex decisions such as the best place to locate a new franchise. A comprehensive, detailed **decision-making process** is utilized when faced with making a complex decision. However, the same model can also be used for simple decisions.

---

[13]"Heard It through the Grapevine," cited in *Forbes*, February 10, 1997, p. 22, as cited in Robbins and Coulter, *Management*, p. 293.

Personal Profile: Patricia Tam

Vice President of Halekulani Corp., Waikiki, Hawaii

Patricia Tam is a role model to everyone who wants to pursue a career in the hospitality industry. It is not hard to see why. Patricia is a woman of great ambition and ability. She has proved herself capable of succeeding at almost anything she attempts to do.[1]

Patricia is of Chinese heritage and was brought up in Hawaii. During her childhood years, her ambition was to become an English teacher. Entering the hospitality industry never entered her mind. In fact she didn't stay in a hotel until she was a young adult: "I was going along with some friends to the mainland for one of the first times I'd been off the island."

When she finished college at age twenty-three, she became proprietor of a bakery. She was then recruited by Amfac Corp. to open a bakeshop at its Royal Lahaina hotel on Maui in 1975. She says, "When I opened the bakeshop there, I liked the whole aura of resort life, not just because of the guests' experience, but because of the beach and the large infrastructure." She enrolled in the resort's management training program, which would be the start of a long and successful career journey in the lodging industry.

(Courtesy Patricia Tam.)

Patricia started working at the Halekulani in 1983. Halekulani was first constructed in 1907 as a beachfront home accompanied by five bungalows. In 1983, it reopened as a 466-room low-rise complex. It is Waikiki's premier five-diamond resort.

When Patricia became general manager of Halekulani, the situation was less than desirable. She was promoted in the post-Gulf War period, and the once glorious Pacific destinations had stagnated. Because most of Hawaii's visitors were Asian, Japan's ongoing recession added to the difficult times. In the 1960s, Hawaii experienced its tourist boom years. But during the early 1990s, Hawaii had to fight for every bit of the global destination market it could capture. Patricia says, "We're sitting in an arena right now where the first one to the finish line is the winner. And I think that it's more exciting to be working in this business now than it would have been in the boom years, when all you had to worry about was how many people you couldn't accommodate tonight."

Patricia realizes that the hotel business can make either a profit or loss. "I think for a lot of us who get into the business, we see the fun part of it: the bartending, the wait help, the restaurant excitement, the chance to meet really fabulous people from around the world. We see one side of the vision of what luxury properties are all about," she explains. "But there's the other side of it, which is that it is a business and, what do businesses do? They've got to make money."

Patricia believes that outstanding guest services make a good hotel and maintain guest loyalty. She pays careful attention to detail and perfection and lets nothing pass her by. Even guest complaints are discussed one by one. She says, "You can get so worked up about the attention to detail that unless you're communicating with staff, it can be pretty challenging for them in terms of how to keep this hotel perfect. Not everybody knows how. But everybody tries to keep it that way." Maintaining her great reputation as a general manager as well as the hotel's reputation as a superior destination is her drive for perfection. John Sharpe, president of the Toronto-based Four Seasons hotel, nominated Patricia to be Hotelier of Halekulani, meaning "house benefiting heaven," was voted best hotel in the world by *Gourmet* magazine. It has held its AAA five-diamond rating since 1986. It was a finalist for Conde Nast Traveler's 1996 Reader's Choice "Best Tropical Resorts" award and ranked in the top three hotels in the country in Zagat's U.S. hotel, resort, and spa survey of 1995–1996. Its well-known restaurant, La Mer, is Hawaii's only AAA-rated five-diamond restaurant, and has been known as such since 1991.

Patricia served as a hotel assistant manager, room's division director, and acting general manager, and also general manager of Halekulani's adjacent sister property, the four-diamond Waikiki Parc hotel. Then finally, in 1993, she became the general manager of Halekulani. Through it all, she always wanted more. She says, "I could work the operations in a very good management way, but I never had to be the person responsible for the final decision-making on a lot of things. The challenge, the intimidation of that process, coming back over as the general manager, was quite overwhelming to me. But that was also my proudest moment because that's when I realized that I really had to buckle down." The readers of *Hotels* magazine named Patricia the 1999 Hotelier of the World.

As for her personality, Patricia is a very genuine person who doesn't credit only herself. She doesn't forget that her success depends on an ongoing and mutually beneficial relationship between Halekulani's owner, Halekulani Corp., and herself. She says, " I always look at it as a kind of management proposition where you can

always learn every day." She adds, "Every day you can learn something new, not only about how to maintain a luxury property, but how to develop it and take it to the next level, because that's what it's all about."

---

[1] This profile draws on Tony De la Cruz, "Independent Hotelier of the World, Patricia Tam, Reaching for Resort Perfection," *Hotels,* **33,** 11, November 1999, pp. 64.

The decision-making process consists of eight major steps (Figure 17–3):

1. Identification and definition of problem
2. Identification of decision criteria
3. Allocation of weights to criteria
4. Development of alternatives
5. Analysis of alternatives
6. Selection of alternative
7. Implementation of alternative
8. Evaluation of decision effectiveness

This model can be used for most decisions from simple ones, such as what to buy for dinner, to complex corporate decisions about new marketing strategies. So let's take a closer look at each step of the decision-making process.

Step 1: Identification and Definition of Problem

Let's say that we are experiencing a discrepancy between current and desired results. In this case, the decision-making process begins with identifying and defining the problem(s). It is not always easy to identify the problem because other issues may muddy the waters. In a hotel setting, problem situations can be identified with respect to, say, guest check-in. In some of the larger city-center, convention-oriented hotels, long lines of guests are frequently waiting to check into the hotel. Defining this problem is best done by writing a problem statement: The problem is that it takes too long for guests to register. Once the problem has been accurately stated, it becomes easier to move to the next step in the decision-making process.

Another example comes to us from Herb Kelleher, former president of Southwest Airlines, when he made the decision to remove the closets at the front of Southwest planes. This was in response to a problem: It took too long

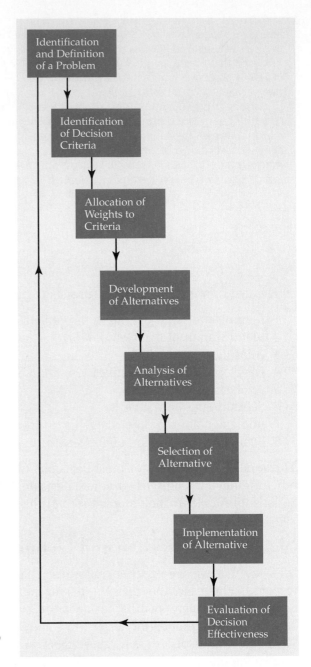

Figure 17–3 *Eight-Step Decision-Making Process*

to turn around the planes. To be competitive and successful, it is necessary to reduce the turn-around time in order to squeeze more flights into each day. The situation that caused or contributed to the turn-around problem was that the first people on the plane typically went to the closets first and then grabbed the nearest seats. On landing, the departing passengers were held up

Southwest Airlines Operations (Courtesy of Southwest Airlines.)

while the people in the front rows rummaged through the closets for their bags. The airline now turns around about 85 percent of its flights in twenty minutes or less and is one of the most profitable airlines.

Step 2: Identification of Decision Criteria

Once the problem has been identified and defined, we need to determine the criteria relevant to the decision. Suppose the problem is that we are hungry; then the decision criteria might be the following:

1. What type of food would we prefer?
2. How much time do we have?
3. How much do we want to spend?
4. How convenient is parking?
5. What is the restaurant's reputation?
6. How is the food quality?
7. How is the service?
8. How is the atmosphere?

These criteria must have been developed by a group that wants to eat out at a restaurant. Criteria that are not identified are usually treated as unimportant.

Step 3: Allocation of Weights to Criteria

To the decision makers, the decision criteria all have differing levels of importance. For instance, is the expected cost of the meal more important than the atmosphere? If so, a higher weight should be attached to that criterion.

One method used to weight the criteria is to give the most important criterion a weight of ten and then score the others according to their relative importance. In the meal example, the cost of the meal might receive a weight of ten, whereas the atmosphere might be awarded a weight of six. Table 17–1 lists a sample of criteria and weights for restaurant selection.

Table 17–1 Criteria and Weight in Restaurant Selection	
How much do we want to spend?	10
What type of food would we prefer?	8
How much time do we have?	6
How is the food quality?	9
How is the atmosphere?	6
How is the service?	7
How convenient is parking?	6
How is the restaurant's reputation?	6
How far do we want to go to a restaurant?	7

Step 4: Development of Alternatives

In developing alternatives, decision makers list the viable alternatives that could resolve the problem. No attempt is made to evaluate these alternatives, only to list them. Using the restaurant scenario, the alternatives are shown in Figure 17–4.

Step 5: Analysis of Alternatives

The alternatives are analyzed using the criteria and weights established in steps 2 and 3. Table 17–2 shows the values placed on each of the alternatives by the group. (It does not show the weighted values.) The weighted values of the group's decision about which restaurant to go to are shown in Table 17–3.

Once the weighted values are totaled, we can see that Pizza Hut and Wendy's are the restaurants with the highest scores. Notice how these are not the restaurants with the highest scores before the weighted values were included.

Step 6: Selection of Alternative

The sixth step involves the selection of the best alternative. Once the weighted scores for each alternative have been totaled, it will become obvious which is the best alternative.

Step 7: Implementation of Alternative

We next need to ensure that the alternative is implemented so that the decision is put into action. Sometimes good decisions fail because they are not put into action.

Step 8: Evaluation of Decision Effectiveness

The final step in the decision loop is to evaluate the effectiveness of the decision. As a result of the decision, did we achieve the goals we set? If the deci-

KFC

Taco Bell

Pizza Hut

McDonald's

Applebee's

The Olive Garden

Wendy's

Figure 17–4 *Restaurant Alternatives*

Table 17–2
Analysis of Alternatives

	KFC	Taco Bell	Pizza Hut	McDonald's	Applebee's	Olive Garden	Wendy's
Price	9	10	10	10	7	7	9
Type of food	7	8	9	8	8	9	9
How much time	9	9	7	10	7	6	10
Quality of food	7	7	8	7	8	8	8
Atmosphere	7	7	8	7	9	9	7
Service	6	6	7	7	8	9	7
Convenient parking	10	10	10	9	10	10	10
Restaurant reputation	8	8	8	7	8	9	8
How far away	8	8	8	10	7	7	8
Total	71	73	75	76	72	74	75

Table 17–3
Weighted Values Analysis

	KFC	Taco Bell	Pizza Hut	McDonald's	Applebee's	Olive Garden	Wendy's
Price	90	100	100	100	70	70	90
Type of food	56	64	72	64	64	72	72
How much time	54	54	42	60	42	36	60
Quality of food	63	63	72	63	72	72	72
Atmosphere	42	42	48	42	54	54	42
Service	42	42	49	49	56	63	49
Convenient parking	60	60	60	56	60	60	60
Restaurant reputation	48	48	48	42	48	54	48
How far away	56	56	56	70	49	49	56
Total	511	529	547	546	515	530	549

sion was not effective, then we must find out why the desired results were not attained. This would mean going back to step 1. If the decision was effective, then no action, other than recording the outcome, needs to be taken.

Check Your Knowledge

1. What are the eight steps in the decision-making process?
2. Give an example of a problem statement along with at least five decision criteria questions to ask.

Post 9-11: Communicating During Disasters

Hank Christen and Paul Maniscalco

Communication during a disaster requires complex interactions. If communications are not effective, myriad problems for the organization result, including irreparable harm to the organization's reputation, significant fiscal harm, and drastically reduced organizational business opportunities after the event.

Many hospitality industry managers fail to grasp the importance of preventing significant damage to their organization's reputation and future business prospects due to disasters, a situation is further complicated by a lack of familiarity with successful crisis communication techniques. The manager must confront events that are emergent and fluid, make quick and effective decisions, and communicate effectively and expeditiously, especially to the media.

> **Critical Factor:** The Dupont Plaza Hotel fire and TWA Flight 800 exemplify miscue and poor message delivery. Media evaluation of the industries involved was brutal because the managers had failed to release "good and timely" information to the families.

Fundamental components of effective disaster communication are: (1) defining the disaster/crisis, (2) assembing a communication team, (3) designating and training a spokesperson, and (4) releasing a statement.

1. **Define disaster/crisis for the organization.** A disaster or crisis is any situation that threatens the health, safety, integrity, or reputation of the organization and its employees or patrons. Usually it originates as an unusual event or emergency such as accident, crime, fire, flood, natural, technological, or manmade disaster. It also is a situation in which the media or the public perceives that the organization did not react to a critical situation in a timely or appropriate manner.
2. **Assemble a disaster/crisis communication team.** This team is responsible for writing the organizational communication response delivered during an incident. The team should be composed of key individuals: the Chief Executive Officer or top manager at the facility, the head of public relations, the operations manager, the director of

safety and/or security, legal counsel, and the area manager involved in the crisis (an ad hoc assignment in emergent situations).
3. **Designate and train an organizational spokesperson.** Every hospitality management team should have at least one person solely responsible for speaking to the media to represent the organization during a crisis. The organization must speak with a single voice. The speaker needs to be professional, reassuring, and factual, and must have appropriate orientation and education on media relations.
4. **Research the facts, craft a reference sheet, and release a statement.** After researching the events and confirming facts, an event reference sheet should be crafted. It should contain an incident summary, including confirmed particulars, for media release; it should be updated as events or responses change. Collaboration with legal counsel is also necessary to ensure compliance with privacy and organizational security.

Expeditious communication is also critical. Prompt delivery helps to control event interpretation and present the organization's version of the incident. The first statement must identify who, what, where, and when (the four *W*'s). Only confirmed facts received from competent authorities should be given, and the legality of a release should be confirmed before it is issued. The speaker should not speculate.

Providing the four *W*'s and showing compassion and concern for those involved (public and employees) during initial media interactions is the basis of successful communication. Demonstration of genuine compassion and concern secures patron and employee confidence and loyalty. The spokesperson should take the initiative to share information and engender an open and inclusive environment; otherwise, alienated patrons or employees will not be supportive during the company's recovery.

> **Critical Factor:** Release of legal and medical information should be coordinated with the appropriate medical authority. Failure to do so may compromise an investigation or medical privacy protections afforded by law.

How Managers Make Decisions

Managers are the prime decision makers in any organization. Although all employees are faced daily with decisions, the choices a manager makes most reflect and influence the future of the organization. Decision making is a large part of all four primary managerial functions: planning, organizing, leading, and controlling. Therefore, managing is sometimes used as a synonym for decision making.[14]

Making Decisions: Rationality, Bounded Rationality, and Intuition

The first criterion for making a decision is that it must be rational. Several assumptions are made to define what a rational decision really is. First, the decision itself would have to be value maximizing and consistent within natural constraining limits. This means that the choice made must maximize the organization's profitability. Tying in with this is the natural assumption that the manager making the decision is pursuing the organization's values and profitability, not his or her own interest.

One assumption of **rationality** as it relates to the decision maker is that he or she is fully objective and logical. When making the decision, a clearly stated goal must always be kept in mind. This goes hand in hand with starting with a problem statement.

Assumptions of rationality can be successfully met under certain conditions. These include being faced with a simple problem, having clearly defined goals, limited alternatives, minimal time pressure, low cost for seeking and evaluating alternatives, an organizational culture supporting risk taking and innovation, and measurable and concrete outcomes.[15] Unfortunately, some decisions that must be made do not apply to these conditions; this is where bounded rationality comes into play.

Bounded rationality suggests that managers make decisions based on the decision-making process that is bounded, or limited, by an individual's ability to

Rational Decision Making

Professional managers at the Sheraton Hotel and Resort in San Diego provided us with a real-life problem that deals with making rational decisions: How much space should we reserve for large parties? For example, if a group of 500 reserves a room, and only 300 show up, the other 200 spaces are basically "dead space," which could have been rented out to another party of 200 people. To protect themselves from this kind of dilemma, the hotel has attached a food and beverage price to each room. If you reserve the room, the food and beverage price is charged automatically, even if the guests don't show up.

[14]H. A. Simmon, *The New Science of Management Decision.* New York: Harper & Row, 1960, as cited in Robbins and Coulter, *Management*, p. 165.

[15]F. A. Shull, Jr., A. L. Delbecq, and L. L. Cummings, *Organizational Decision Making*, New York: McGraw-Hill, 1970, as cited in Robbins and Coulter, *Management.*

process information.[16] Managers know that their decision-making skills are based on their own competency, intelligence, and last, but not least, their rationality. They are also expected to follow the decision-making process model. However, certain aspects of this model are not realistic with respect to true-life managerial decisions, which are made with respect to bounded reality. This comes into play, for example, when decision makers cannot find all of the necessary information to analyze a problem and all of its possible alternatives. Therefore, they find themselves **satisficing,** or accepting, a solution that is just "good enough," rather than maximizing. Consider this example: A chef for a major hotel chain has to prepare a banquet for fifty people. On the menu is half a chicken for every guest, which means that the chef needs 100 whole chickens for this banquet. He purchases the chickens at a market twenty-five miles away where he has made the same purchase before for $60. Because he has made purchases from this market before he knows the quality of the food they sell. What the chef did not know was that there was a free-range chicken farm only ten miles away that would have sold him the 100 chickens for the same price. Instead of researching his alternatives, the chef satisficed himself with the first option that came to mind and settled on it, assuming it was probably not the best but "good enough." This behavior is rationally bounded because the best solution to be found was bounded by the chef's ability to research all alternatives instead of settling on the first acceptable one that came to mind.

Most decisions that managers make are not based on perfect rationality due to various factors, such as time constraints on researching all possible solutions or lack of resources to do the research. Therefore, the decisions are typically based on bounded rationality. In other words, they make decisions based on alternatives that are just satisfactory. At the same time, though, the decision maker will be strongly influenced by an organization's culture, power considerations, internal politics, and an **escalation of commitment.** An escalation of commitment occurs when commitment to a previous decision is increased despite evidence that it may have been wrong.[17] For example, consider the demise of the Planet Hollywood Restaurant chain. At the launch of the chain, the team of marketing professionals deemed it economically sensible to set a

---

[16]See N. McK. Agnew and J. L. Brown, "Bounded Rationality: Fallible Decisions in Unbounded Decision Space," *Behavioral Science,* July 1986, pp. 148–161; B. E. Kaufman, "A New Theory of Satisficing," *Journal of Behavioral Economics,* Spring 1990, pp. 35–51; and D. R. A. Skidd, "Revisiting Bounded Rationality," *Journal of Management Inquiry,* December 1992, pp. 343–347, as cited in Robbins and Coulter, *Management,* p. 247.

[17]See B. M. Staw, "The Escalation of Commitment to a Course of Action," *Academy of Management Review,* October 1981, pp. 577–587; D. R. Bobocel and J. P. Meyer, "Escalating Commitment to a Failing Course of Action: Separating the Roles of Choice and Justification," *Journal of Applied Psychology,* June 1994, pp. 360–363; C. F. Camerer and R. A. Weber, "The Econometrics and Behavioral Economics of Escalation of Commitment: A Reexamination of Staw's Theory," *Journal of Economic Behavior and Organization,* May 1999, pp. 52–82; V. S. Rao and A. Monk, "The Effects of Individual Differences and Anonymity on Commitment to Decisions," *Journal of Social Psychology,* August 1999, pp. 496–515; and M. Keil, "A Cross-Cultural Study of Escalation of Commitment Behavior in Software Projects," *MIS Quarterly,* June 2000, pp. 299–326, as cited in Robbins and Coulter, *Management,* p. 157.

high price on their burgers and other food items. The restaurant set out to be a novelty establishment, although the target customers were middle-class citizens. Although it was evident that the decision to have high-priced products in a middle-class establishment was doomed for failure from the beginning, the decision makers stuck with it. The inevitable took place, and Planet Hollywood went belly up and was forced to close its chain with locations all around the world. The negative consumer reaction was predictable, but the decision makers escalated their commitment to the set prices even though it was a bad decision. Rather than search for new alternatives, they did not want to admit to making a bad decision and simply increased their commitment to the original one.[18]

Using rationality and common sense to influence decision making is very important—we must not forget the role of plain and simple human intuition. Intuition is used in everyday life, for decisions such as not grabbing a hot baking pan with your bare hands. It ranges all the way to the corporate level, where managers often utilize their own intuition when making corporate decisions. **Intuitive decision making** is a subconscious process of making decisions on the basis of experience and accumulated judgment. Five different identified aspects of intuition comply with the different types of decisions made. The first is a values- or ethics-based decision. Managers will recall the ethics system they were raised with and base their decisions on personal morals. The second is an experience-based decision. Through trial and error the manager has gained experience and will base a decision on past learning. Affect-initiated decisions are those that are based on a manager's emotions and feelings. The fourth type is a cognitive-based decision. The manager's previous training, learned skills, and gained knowledge influence the decision-making process. Last, the manager utilizes his or her subconscious mind to retain data and process it in such a way that it will influence the type of decision he or she will make.

Intuition and rationality are separate but are often used in combination in most decision making. The two complement each other to offer the manager an ideal solution for the decision-making process. As an example, consider a manager who has to make a decision on a situation that is similar to one he has come across in the past. Instead of using careful analytical rationality, he will make a decision based on a "gut feeling" and act quickly with what appears to be limited information. The decision is ultimately made based upon his experience and accumulated judgment. In a survey of managers and other employees in high positions, it was revealed that decisions based on gut feelings were quite common. In fact one-third of them placed emphasis on utilizing their intuition over cognitive problem solving and rational decision making.[19]

[18]"Why Planet Hollywood Bombed," personal conversation with John Trombold, May 18, 2002.

[19]V. Pospisil, "Gut Feeling or Skilled Reasoning?" *IW,* March 3, 1997, p. 12, as cited in Robbins and Coulter, *Management,* p. 158.

Check Your Knowledge

1. List criteria for making a rational decision.
2. Give an example of satisficing.
3. What are the five aspects of intuition?

Types of Problems and Decisions

There are several different types of decisions that match different types of problems. They are applied as solutions depending on the various situations that arise. The managers that are aware of these differences are able to use them to their advantage.

The two major types of decisions are programmed decisions and nonprogrammed decisions. A **programmed decision** involves situations that recur on a regular basis, allowing the response to be a handled with a "programmed" response. In a programmed decision, the response will occur on a repetitive basis; for example, when the number of New York steaks goes below a specified number, an order for more is automatically placed. Programmed decisions generally become a standard operating procedure. Alternatives are not necessary most of the time, because the problem statement is familiar and, therefore, the solution is in close reach due to past successful decisions made. The response to a shortage of New York steaks is simply a reorder; the alternatives are truly limited. A programmed decision is made in response to a recurring problem; the approach to dealing with it has become repetitive and therefore does not require a careful analysis.

A **nonprogrammed decision** is nonrecurring and made necessary by unusual circumstances. The type of problem that induces a nonprogrammed decision is a poorly structured problem. These types of problems are usually new or unusual to the decision maker. More often than not, the information on the problem is incomplete or unavailable. This generally increases the difficulty gradient of finding an appropriate solution. Most importantly though, the problem is unique and nonrecurring, such as which computer hardware and software a restaurant should install, or whether to expand by franchising or by company-owned restaurants. These are distinctive decision situations that are not likely to recur for several years and require a custom-made decision.

The more sophisticated a company is, the more programmed decisions are made. Many large corporations have policy and procedure manuals to guide man-

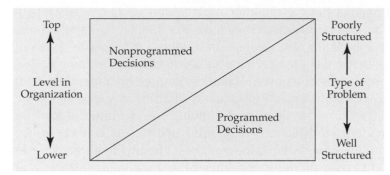

Figure 17–5 *Nonprogrammed and Programmed Decisions (Derived from Stephen P. Robbins and Mary Coulter,* Management, *7th ed. Upper Saddle River, NJ: Prentice Hall, 2002, p. 161.)*

agerial and supervisory decision making. Nonprogrammed decisions call for greater analysis, innovation, and problem-solving skills. Figure 17–5 diagrams programmed and nonprogrammed decisions and the level in the organization.

Decision-Making Conditions

In a perfect world, we would have all the information necessary for making decisions. However, in reality, there are some things that are unknowable. This leads us to decision-making conditions. Decision making includes three major conditions: certainty, risk, and uncertainty. These three conditions all have individual characteristics that define each.

The ideal situation for making a decision is one of **certainty.** A decision of certainty includes having knowledge of all of the alternatives and therefore having no risk involved when making a decision, since the outcome is known. A good example for this condition is illustrated by a hotel investment specialist who is allotted a share of the hotel's profit. The investor's options are clear and defined, he knows exactly how much interest is earned on bonds, and also how much interest is offered by various banks, the security issues, and how many years it will take for them to mature.

Making a decision that involves **risk** is one of the most common situations. Here the decision maker is not certain of the outcome of the situation. However, through personal experience, or a simple "gut feeling," she is able to estimate the probability of the outcome. Although not all alternatives are properly researched, by using historical data, probabilities can be assigned to various alternatives and the best probable outcome ultimately chosen. This is called a risk condition as it relates to decision making and is characterized by having some knowledge of the outcome of the various alternatives, combined with the element of unpredictability.

For example, a popular hotel is thinking about adding on family apartments to its property. So far the largest room they have is a double; the family rooms would need to have beds for four people along with a kitchenette. Perusing past historical data helps make the decision somewhat clearer. In the past year alone, 40 percent of all customers were families of three or more. Reviewing the customer comments, the demand for a family apartment is relatively large. Although the construction of an apartment building will cut into the revenue, the rental profit made from these more expensive apartments is likely to outweigh costs in less than three years. Also, the hotel is hoping to attract an even larger family crowd to their property once they offer apartments. Although all of the past data is valuable information and can to some extent predict the future, a factor of risk involved, because there is always some level of unpredictability about the future.

Uncertainty situations are characterized by having to make a decision when the outcome is not certain and when reasonable outcome estimates can't be made either. These situations often arise when alternatives to the decision are limited due to lack of adequate information. Although conditions of uncertainty are not as common as situations of risk, managers still find themselves confronted with uncertainty in decision-making situations.

Check Your Knowledge

1. What is the difference between programmed and nonprogrammed decisions?
2. Give one similarity between risk and uncertainty decision-making conditions.

Decision–Making Styles

What are the different approaches to making decisions? One perspective proposes that managers differ along two dimensions as it pertains to the way they approach decision making.[20] The first dimension is the **way of thinking.** Decision makers differ in their way of thinking; some are rational and logical while others are intuitive and creative. The rational type of decision maker will look at the information in order. He will organize the information and make

---

[20]A. J. Rowe, James D. Boulgarides, and Michael R. McGrath, *Managerial Decision Making, Modules in Management Series,* Chicago: SRA, 1984, pp. 18–22, as cited in Robbins and Coulter, *Management,* p. 165.

sure it is logical and consistent. Only after carefully studying all of the given options will he finally make the decision. An intuitive thinker, on the other hand, can look at information that is not necessarily in order. This person is able to make quick decisions based on her spontaneous creativity and her intuition. Although a careful analysis is still required, these types of people are comfortable looking at all solutions as a whole as opposed to studying each option separately.

The second dimension about which people differ is each individual's **tolerance for ambiguity.** The managers who have a high tolerance for ambiguity are lucky in that they save a lot of time while making a decision. These individuals are able to process many thoughts at the same time. Unfortunately, some managers have a low tolerance for ambiguity. These individuals must have order and consistency in the way they organize and process the information, so as to minimize ambiguity.

When reviewing the two dimensions, way of thinking and tolerance for ambiguity, and their subdivisions, four major decision-making styles become evident:

1. The **directive style** entails having a low tolerance for ambiguity as well as being a rational thinker. The individuals that fall into the category of having a directive decision-making style are usually logical and very efficient. They also have a primary focus on the short run and are also relatively quick decision makers. Directive decision makers value speed and efficiency, which can cause them to be remiss in assessing all alternatives, such that decisions are often made with minimal information.

2. Decision makers that fall into the category of having an **analytic style** have a large tolerance for ambiguity. Compared to the directive decision maker, these people require more information before making their decisions and, consequently, they consider more alternatives. Individuals with an analytic style are careful decision makers, which gives them leeway to adapt or cope to unique situations.

3. Decision makers who have a **conceptual style** pertaining to their decision-making skills look at numerous alternatives and are typically very broad in their outlook. Their focus is on the long run of the decision made. These individuals are typically creative and often find creative solutions to the problem with which they are dealing.

4. Decision makers who work well with others are said to have a **behavioral style** of decision making. This entails being very receptive to suggestions and ideas from others as well as being concerned about the achievements of their employees. They commonly communicate with their coworkers through meetings. These individuals try to avoid conflict as often as possible, because their acceptance by others is very important to them.

"No . . . I mean, yes."

A former CEO always said "no" first because he could always change his mind to "yes" later. Today it might be better to say, "Let me get back to you on that request" or "Let's discuss this—can you meet with me on Monday at 10 A.M.?"

At least one of these decision-making styles is always utilized by managers. However, it is also quite common for a decision maker to combine two or more styles to make a decision. Most often a manager will have one dominant decision-making style and use one or more other styles as alternates. Flexible individuals will vary their decision-making styles according to each unique situation. If the style is to consider riskier options (analytic style) or if the decision is made based on suggestions from subordinates (behavioral style), each style will eventually bring the decision makers to the optimal solution for the unique problems they are facing.

Check Your Knowledge

1. Name the two dimensions of decision-making styles.
2. Briefly describe the conceptual style of decision making.

Trends in Communication and Decision Making

✔ Trends such as improving technology to aid with communication are likely to continue. Voice mail, e-mail, and the Internet will increasingly assist hospitality managers and associates with speedier communications. All-way radio connectivity, which allows associates to communicate live, enables them to better serve the needs of discriminating guests.

✔ An integral part of management's decision-making process is the management support system (MSS). The MSS has two distinctive elements, the management information system (MIS) and the decision support system (DSS). The MIS provides managers with all information needed to routinely run the business, thus it is of great value in making routine decisions. Usually included in the information flow are daily or monthly sales data, daily inventory, and employee hours and salaries, to name a few of the pertinent facets of information. The DSS, unlike the MIS, which deals with structured, routine business information, is designed to offer the manager information to assist in solving the non-routine problems. The DSS processes both internal and external data.

Corporate Profile: Starwood Hotels

Starwood, a leading hotel and resort corporation that owns the Sheraton, Westin, and St. Regis hotels, has recently adopted a software system designed for solving problems. It is called the Six Sigma program and promises the user more efficiency with a higher profit return. Typically a few employees, termed "Black Belts," are trained in problem solving and how to use the Six Sigma program. One "Master Black Belt" is a highly trained individual in an upper-level position. These individuals are responsible for carrying out the decision-making process or leading the corporation through the process.

The process entails five major steps. The first step is to construct a problem statement and, second, to identify the steps needed to solve the problem. Then a problem-solving team is created. Typically, there are four members per team. Next a complete analysis is conduct-

(Courtesy of Sheraton San Diego Hotel & Mariha.)

ed followed by the actual implementation of the solution. Constant control and monitoring of the implemented solution is the last step. This will prevent any fatal errors or mishaps during the last phase.

New technology is being used for decision making. One computer program, called Hotel Expert, is used to track guests at various Starwood properties throughout the nation to create a consumer profile. Security issues are also logged on this program as well as front desk issues, to ensure optimal costumer service. KEIO is a program that keeps track of the preferred customers. It logs food preferences, birthdays, room preferences, favorite TV programs, and so on for frequent guests, again to ensure optimal customer service. In this way the Starwood property will be able to surprise preferred customers by upgrading their rooms for birthdays or anniversaries.

Case Study

Guests at a busy eight-story four-star hotel are constantly complaining about having to wait too long for the elevator. At 8:00 A.M. some of the elevators are in use by the housekeeping department whose associates are going up to begin work on the guest rooms. At the same time, room service has an elevator blocked off to serve in-room breakfasts because the kitchen and the banqueting departments are using the service elevators. Then, at about 10:30 A.M. the housekeepers use the elevators to go down for their morning break. The general manager recognizes your potential and asks you to come up with suggestions to take care of the problem/challenge.

Career Information

The ability to make good decisions and communicate those decisions is a necessary skill. Industry practitioners frequently make decisions based on "what's more expedient" and cost–benefit analyses or, better yet, decisions that don't cost money. Future hospitality managers are advised to work with corporations of excellence and be mentored by managers of distinction. There is so much to learn and we need all the help we can get. We are often faced with important career decisions: "Should I go and work for Company A or B?" One suggestion is to get a piece of paper and put a line down the center. Put all the positive things about the company or the position you are considering on the left side and all the negative things on the right side. You will likely soon realize which is the best decision.

Summary

1. The definition of communication is the transfer and understanding of meaning. Managerial communication is divided into two categories: interpersonal communication and organizational communication. Interpersonal communication takes place between two or more people, and organizational communication consists of all the networks and systems of communication that exist in an organization.

2. The interpersonal communications process can be disrupted or fail based on several factors. To improve on your interpersonal communication skills, you need to eliminate as much noise during the communications process as possible; that is, close the door to your office or move to a quiet space in the building. Inform yourself about how knowledgeable the receiver is on the subject. Be sure to provide adequate explanations if the knowledge is limited. Last, pick the appropriate channel of communication to ensure successful conveyance of the message.

3. Barriers to effective interpersonal communication include misunderstood perception, misuse of semantics, misguided use of nonverbal communication, ambiguous messages, and defensiveness. Ways to overcome these barriers are through use of feedback, active listening, and avoiding defensiveness.

4. Managers use formal communication to communicate job requirements to their employees. It follows the official chain of command. Informal communication does not follow a company's chain of command or structural hierarchy. The subject matter is typically not job related and is not essential to performing job duties.

5. Communication flows are part of the organizational communication process. Upward communication flows from the employees to the manager. Downward communication flows from manager to employees. Lateral communication takes place among employees who are on the same organizational level. Diagonal communication cuts across organizational levels as well as work areas. The four different types of communicational networks are the chain, the wheel, the all-channel, and the grapevine networks.

6. The decision-making process consists of eight steps: (1) identification and definition of problem, (2) identification of decision criteria, (3) allocation of weights to criteria, (4) development of alternatives, (5) analysis of alternatives, (6) selection of alternative, (7) implementation of alternative, and (8) evaluation of decision effectiveness.

7. Although all employees in a company make decisions on a regular basis, in the end it is the manager's decisions that count. His or her decisions usually represent the final word and are valued as "the right decision." Decision making is a large part of all four primary managerial functions: planning, organizing, leading, and controlling. Hence, word of mouth is that managing is a synonym for decision making.

8. A rational decision is based on the following assumptions: The decision is value maximizing, is within natural limits, and the manager making the decision is fully objective, logical, and has the organization's economic interest in mind. As a result, the rational decision-making problem is simple, has clearly defined goals, limited alternatives, minimal time pres-

sure, low cost for seeking and evaluating alternatives, an organizational culture that supports risk taking and innovation, and measurable and concrete outcomes. Bounded rationality suggests that managers make decisions that are bounded by an individual's ability to process information. Managers often cannot possibly analyze all available information and all alternatives, therefore, they typically satisfice rather than maximize. Finally, intuitive decision making is a subconscious process of making decisions on the basis of experience and accumulated judgment, including ethics learned.

9. Programmed decisions require a problem situation that is a frequent occurrence, allowing the response to be handled with a routine approach. Programmed decisions generally become standard operating procedures. A nonprogrammed decision is nonrecurring and made necessary by unusual circumstances. These types of problems are usually new or unusual to the decision maker. More often than not, the information on the problem is incomplete or unavailable.

10. The decision condition of certainty includes having knowledge of all of the alternatives and, therefore, having no risk involved when making a decision, since the outcome is pretty much known. Uncertainty situations are characterized by having to make a decision when the outcome is not certain and when at the same time reasonable outcome estimates can't be made either due to lack of adequate information. In the risk situation the decision maker is not certain of the outcome of the situation. However, through personal experience, historical data, or a simple "gut feeling," he or she is able to estimate the probability of the outcome.

11. Decision-making styles vary depending on a person's way of thinking, meaning rational or intuitive, and a person's tolerance for ambiguity, which can be low or high. Combinations of these differences give us the directive style (low tolerance for ambiguity and rational way of thinking), the analytic style (high tolerance for ambiguity and rational way of thinking), the conceptual style (high tolerance for ambiguity and intuitive way of thinking), and, last, the behavioral style (low tolerance for ambiguity and intuitive way of thinking).

Key Words and Concepts

Active listening
Allocation of weights to criteria
Analysis of alternatives
Analytic style
Behavioral style
Body language
Bounded rationality
Certainty
Channel
Communication
Communication networks
Conceptual style
Decision-making process

Decoding
Development of alternatives
Diagonal communication
Directive style
Downward communication
Encoding
Escalation of commitment
Evaluation of decision effectiveness
Feedback
Formal communication
Identification and definition of problem

Identification of decision criteria
Informal communication
Implementation of alternative
Interpersonal communication
Interpersonal communications process
Intuitive decision making
Jargon
Lateral communication
Message
Nonprogrammed decision

Nonverbal communication
Organizational communication
Programmed decision
Rationality
Risk
Satisficing
Selection of alternative
Semantics
Tolerance for ambiguity
Uncertainty
Upward communication
Verbal intonation
Way of thinking

Review Questions

1. The most important aspect of a manager's job is typically described as decision making. Why do you believe this is so? Explain.

2. When reviewing some important decisions you have made, would you describe them as mostly rational or intuitive decisions? What are the characteristics of each? How does intuition affect the decision-making process?

3. During the communications process, if the receiver disagrees with the sender, does this always mean that the message has not been properly understood? Or could it mean something else? Explain.

4. How can the grapevine network be used to a company's advantage?
5. When communication is not effective, is it always the fault of the receiver? Discuss all options.

Internet Exercise

Developing alternatives for making decisions often requires associates to be creative. Using the Internet, find three sites that offer ideas on how to improve creativity. Then write two or three paragraphs explaining what role creativity should play in decision making and what you learned from your search about how you can be a more creative decision maker.[21]

Apply Your Knowledge

Select a hospitality-related problem and write a problem statement. Then, using the decision-making steps, show how you would solve the problem.

[21] Adapted from Robbins and Coulter, *Management* p. 171.

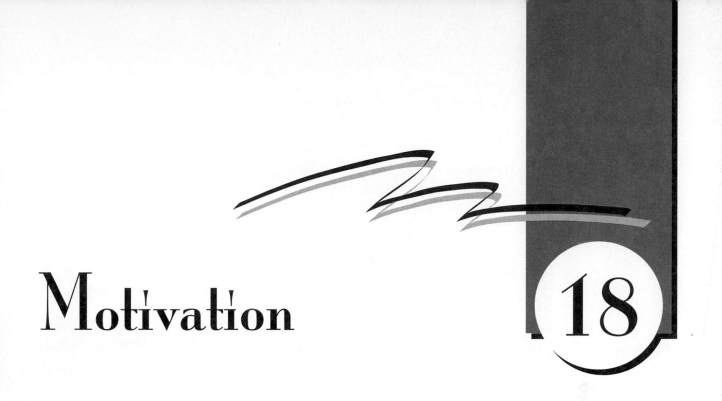

Motivation

18

After reading and studying this chapter, you should be able to:

✔ Define motivation.
✔ Describe three early motivation theories.
✔ Know how to use goals, reinforcers, referents, or expectations to motivate employees.
✔ Understand the challenge managers face in motivating today's diverse workforce.
✔ Identify ways to motivate the diverse workforce.

What Is Motivation?

Motivation is the art or process of initiating and sustaining behavior toward certain goals. Motivating people is all about inspiring them to do something because they want to do it, not because someone tells them to do it. As the American and Canadian hospitality and tourism industries have right-sized the organizational structure by reducing the number of levels of management, the need for motivation has increased. Hotel general managers say that their biggest challenge is how to motivate employees. This chapter should help you understand your own motivation and influence that of those you will lead in the future.

A number of theories about motivation have been developed over the years by experts in motivational psychology. Each has made a contribution to where we are today.

McGregor's Theory X and Theory Y

This motivational approach draws on Douglas McGregor's theories. He classified human nature into two categories, based on a set of assumptions: Theory X and Theory Y.[1] **Theory X** describes people in primarily a negative view. The employee that falls under this category is typically a pessimist, has little ambition, generally dislikes work, tries at every cost to avoid responsibility, and needs constant supervision and control to be effectively productive. Unfortunately, some of those employees may be in the hospitality industry! Theory X managers are dictators and behave like tyrants, which is often described as "my way or the highway." **Theory Y,** on the other hand, paints a positive picture of people. Employees that fit the Theory Y profile are primarily optimistic, enjoy working, seek out responsibilities, need little supervision, and typically have a lot of ambition. The typical employee is more likely to have a Theory Y personality. Therefore, McGregor theorized that giving employees more responsibilities, letting them be part of the decision-making process, and giving them challenges would lead to higher motivation in the workplace.

McGregor's theories cannot be proven, because they are based on assumptions of certain behaviors. There is no guarantee that altering your behavior and treating people according to Theory Y assumptions will improve motivation.

Herzberg's Motivation–Hygiene Theory

A widely accepted and influential theory of motivation is Frederick **Herzberg's motivation and hygiene factors** theory. While studying managers in the work

---

[1] D. McGregor, *The Human Side of Enterprise*, New York: McGraw-Hill, 1960, as cited in Robbins and Coulter, *Management*, p. 426.

environment, psychologist Frederick Herzberg concluded that two separate and distinct sets of factors influenced individual motivation. Herzberg referred to these groups of factors as *satisfiers* and *dissatisfiers,* or *motivators* and *hygiene factors.* **Motivators** are the intrinsic factors that increase job satisfaction and, hence, lead to increased motivation in employees. Herzberg identified the motivators as follows:

1. Work itself
2. Recognition
3. Responsibility
4. Achievement
5. Growth
6. Advancement

The **hygiene factors,** on the other hand, were identified as factors that eliminate job dissatisfaction but fail to motivate. Although dissatisfaction is largely eradicated, the employees are not satisfied either. The hygiene factors are as follows:

1. Company policies and administration
2. Salary
3. Working conditions
4. Relationships with supervisors
5. Relationships with peers
6. Relationships with subordinates
7. Security
8. Status

The main premise of Herzberg's theory is that if the hygiene factors are not met, it is unlikely that much motivation will occur, no matter how many of the motivators are met. However, once the hygiene factors have been met, significant motivation will occur once the motivator factors are present.

Table 18–1
Herzberg's Motivation and Hygiene Factors

Motivators	Hygienes
Work itself	Company policies and administration
Recognition	Salary
Responsibility	Working conditions
Achievement	Relationships with supervisors
Growth	Relationships with peers
Advancement	Relationships with subordinates
	Security
	Status

Source: John Walker, *Introduction to Hospitality,* 3rd ed. Upper Saddle River, NJ: Pearson Education, 2002.

Maslow's Hierarchy of Needs

Maslow's theory of the hierarchy of needs has influenced motivational techniques for many years. The theory suggests that there are five basic needs or motives common to adults:

1. *Physiological needs,* which are necessities for life, including food, air, and fluids, all of which are essential to our physical existence
2. *Safety needs,* which provide us with the security and assurance that our physiological needs will be met in the future
3. *Love and belonging needs,* which are social needs such as the need for affection and the need for acceptance by others
4. *Esteem needs,* which are the needs of self-respect and respect from others
5. *Self-actualization needs,* which are the need for self-fulfillment and the need to reach one's potential

Figure 18–1 shows Maslow's five needs together with examples of how each might be satisfied in an organizational setting.

Although Maslow's theory was first proposed in 1943, it is still widely and highly regarded as having a significant influence on management and employee motivation.

Now let's relate Maslow's theory to practical hospitality applications. Ask any poor student with unmet physiological and security needs about what motivates them. They will most surely say money and security. So, wages, benefits, and job security are important and motivating to the lower level needs.

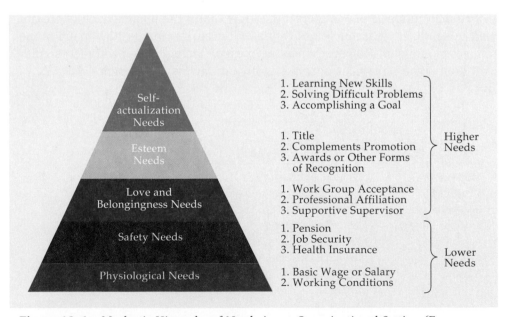

Figure 18–1 *Maslow's Hierarchy of Needs in an Organizational Setting (From Donald D. White and David A. Bednar,* Organizational Behavior: Understanding and Managing People at Work, *2nd ed. Boston: Allyn and Bacon, 1991, p. 149.)*

But, once those needs have been met by a certain level of job performance, they cease to be motivators for greater job-related efforts. If an associate is to go beyond a minimum level of achievement, then management must appeal to higher order needs.[2] Moving up to social and affiliation needs, the hospitality industry has no problem in fulfilling their needs. Hospitality associates work in departments that have built-in groups or teams, allowing for plenty of social interaction. Now, of course, that can be good or bad depending on the "climate" or culture in the department—but then it's up to management to make it a positive working experience. A win–win situation exists when associates identify with the department and organization and, better yet, when they feel accepted and that they belong. In such a case, they will be motivated to achieve organization and personal goals.

In the social affiliation context, outstanding managers care for their associates and offer praise in public by having award and recognition ceremonies. Additionally, managers who do something unexpected like give tickets to a baseball game to an associate who is a fan increase the associate's feeling of belonging.

Make everyone a winner. As a manger, if you can remove obstacles and make your team winners by providing a good climate, incentives, and rewards, you will have a motivated group.

Managers can help motivate associates' natural need for self-esteem by giving them the opportunity to be a winner. Consider this example: One day I was walking through the hotel lobby with a GM of the Westgate Hotel. He bumped into his director of marketing and introduced her as the most professional and best DOM he had ever worked with because she was able to "fill rooms" even in a difficult economy. George went on for a few minutes and was so enthusiastic in his praise that it must have been a perfect self-esteem builder for the director of marketing.

Self-actualization is also the need to achieve, and the need to achieve is a motivator. Maslow felt that people's ultimate need is achievement for its own sake; this is self-actualization.[3] Self-actualization is

---

"Bowling for Motivation?"

Ken Blanchard, a beloved leader-manager, best-selling author, and marvelous presenter, tells a story about motivation.[1]

Dave is a below-average worker—not really motivated. But on Wednesday nights he is the star of the bowling team. If you could only see him then, not only is he very motivated, but he motivates others. Now, just for a moment, suppose he was about to bowl and for some unknown reason he did not get a strike. How do you think he would feel if his manager were to say, "Dave you knocked down only six pins. Why didn't you get them all?" Or worse still, what if the manager were to put a curtain halfway down the lane so Dave could not see what he was aiming at. Yes, you see the analogy. All too often, management spoils any chance of motivating associates by not setting clear goals and objectives. Then they compound the problem by asking why the associate knocked down only so many pins and not all of them. Regrettably, this kind of situation still occurs—maybe you have similar personal experiences.

[1]Ken Blanchard, presentation to the National Restaurant Association, May 18, 2001.

The Journey *Is* Important

Someone once said that if a person isn't having fun trying to get to the top that the trip really isn't worth it. In other words, the journey is as important and satisfying as the destination.

---

[2]Gerald Goll, "Management Misperceptions: An Obstacle to Motivation," *PIC Hospitality Review*, Spring 1989, **7**, 1, pp. 85–91, as cited in Eddeystone C. Nebel, *Managing Hotels Effectively, Lessons from Outstanding General Managers.* New York: Van Nostrand Reinhold, 1991, p. 217.

[3]Nebel, *Managing Hotels Effectively*, p. 184.

expressed in several ways, such as "Developing service excellence" or "We are ladies and gentlemen serving ladies and gentlemen" or "We try harder."

Contemporary Theories of Motivation

Plenty of hypotheses exist about motivation—what drives humans to do something they don't have to do. The following motivational theories are not necessarily the most popular, but have been tested and proven by researchers.[4] However, they may also not be as well known as the earlier motivation theories just discussed. These include the goal-setting theory, reinforcement theory, equity theory, and expectancy theory.

Goal-Setting Theory

Both companies and individuals are better off when they set goals. Even if they are not all reached, the results will be better than if no goals were set. As a result, many companies have included some form of **goal-setting theory** as part of their reward and recognition programs.

Goal setting is a key element in management by objective (MBO) and total quality management (TQM). With MBO, goals are generally set by employees, in conjunction with managers. Once the employees have set the individual and group/departmental goals, management approves the goals. Employees are far more likely to achieve and even exceed goals that they have had a hand in setting than they are to achieve goals handed down from above. TQM and empowerment have contributed greatly to employee motivation. Figure 18–2 illustrates the goal-setting theory.

Reinforcement Theory[5]

The main ideology behind **reinforcement theory** is that behavior is a function of its consequences. This theory argues that human behavior is caused by external factors, rather than internal factors, as suggested in the goal-setting theory. The factors that control the behavior are called **reinforcers,** consequences that are given immediately after a certain behavior takes place in order to ensure that the behavior will be repeated.

This is one of the few theories that focuses primarily on action alone. It ignores factors such as goals, needs, or expectations and instead rewards actions alone. An example of reinforcement theory is that of a publishing com-

---

[4]See R. Albanese and D. D. Van Fleet, "Rational Behavior in Groups: The Free-Riding Tendency," *Academy of Management Review*, April 1985, pp. 244–255, as cited in Robbins and Coulter, *Management*, p. 432.

[5]Draws on Robbins and Coulter, *Management*, pp. 432–433.

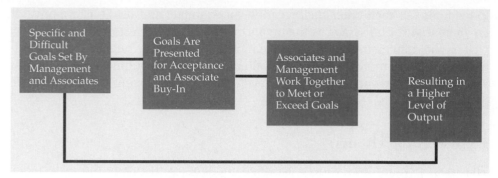

Figure 18–2 *Goal-Setting Theory*

pany that rewards its authors for every submitted chapter. An advance check is sent to the authors when the completed chapter is received, which proves to be an incentive for the writers to continue their writing and submitting the chapters on time. B. F. Skinner explained the psychological explanation for this motivator as follows: Rewards given to people for positive behavior ensure that the action will be repeated. The sooner after the desired action the reward is given, the more effective it will be. Behavior that is punished or not rewarded is less likely to be repeated.[6]

Equity Theory

Equity theory relates to the exchange of individual contributions for organizational rewards. It was developed by J. Stacey Adams. Equity theory suggests that an individual's motivation relies on three important variables:

1. The inputs an individual perceives she or he is contributing
2. The outcome (rewards) an individual perceives she or he is receiving
3. The way in which an individual's inputs and outcomes compare to the inputs and outcomes of another person[7]

Many of us tend to evaluate our own efforts in comparison with outcomes/rewards and then compare them to the outcomes/rewards of others doing similar activities. Our motivation is likely to be affected positively or negatively by our level of satisfaction based on the comparison.

The timings that people compare themselves to are called the **referents.** They are a very important part in the equity theory, and include **other, system,** and **self.** The *other* category entails other individuals with similar jobs, typically on the same hierarchical level, as well as friends, neighbors, and associates.

---

[6]M. Beyerlein and C. Harris, "Introduction to Work Teams," presentation at 9th Annual International Conference on Work Teams, 1998, as cited in Robbins and Coulter, *Management*, p. 411.

[7]Donald D. White and David A. Bednar, *Organizational Behavior: Understanding and Managing People at Work,* 2nd ed. Boston: Allyn and Bacon, 1991, pp. 407–412.

Individuals tell each other their salaries, for example, and use it as a motivator for themselves. The *system* is the organizational pay policies and procedures as well as the administration of the system. The *self* category refers to the individuals themselves; more precisely, the ratio of input versus output. A person's past jobs, salaries, personal contacts, and even family commitments all motivate the person to perform.

Expectancy Theory

The most popular and widely accepted motivation theory is the expectancy theory.[8] Developed by Victor Vroom, **expectancy theory** is based on the premise that people will put out effort equivalent to the perceived rewards. If people think they are definitely going to receive rewards, they are more likely to be motivated and give the extra effort required to achieve the goals that lead to those rewards. Bonuses utilize the expectancy theory of motivation. For example, if a foodservice manager meets or exceeds a predetermined level of profitability, she will receive financial and possibly other bonus incentives.

The typical expectancy model is simplified in Figure 18–3. It includes the following steps: personal effort leads to personal achievement, which brings organizational rewards, and ultimately leads to individual goals.

The expectancy theory has three main relationships. The first is the expectancy or effort–performance linkage.[9] It is described as the probability that if a certain amount of effort is exerted, a certain amount of performance will ultimately be achieved by the individual. The second variable is the instrumentality or performance–reward linkage. This is the degree to which a person believes that his performance on a particular level will actually help him attain the desired outcome. The last relationship is that of valence or the attractiveness of the reward. This is the value or importance that the individual places on the reward that can be achieved from the job being done. Valence considers the goals as well as the needs of the individual.

Just "Plane" Smart

There are many great stories about Herb Kelleher. Consider the time Southwest was being threatened by an aviation services company over the advertising slogan "Plane Smart." Instead of incurring huge attorneys' fees and dealing with months-long litigation, the two CEOs agreed to settle the matter with an arm-wrestling contest. Herb actually lost the contest, but the other CEO had so much fun that the lawsuit was dropped. Both companies saved a bundle in legal fees.

Figure 18–3 *Expectancy Model.* (Modified from Walker, *Introduction to Hospitality* 3/e, Upper Saddle River, NJ: Prentice Hall, 2002, p. 569.)

[8]V. H. Vroom, *Work and Motivation.* New York: John Wiley, 1964, as cited in Robbins and Coulter, *Management,* p. 438.

[9]Stephen P. Robbins, *Management,* 3rd ed. Englewood Cliffs, NJ: Prentice Hall, 1991, pp. 438–439.

Personal/Corporate Profile: Herb Kelleher

Herb Kelleher, who recently gave up the titles of president and CEO to two other Southwest executives, is the living embodiment of the phrase *one of a kind*. With his charismatic personality, he is a person who leaves a distinctive mark on whatever he does.

Since the birth of Southwest Airlines in 1971 as a tiny Texas commuter airline with four airplanes, Herb Kelleher—simply Herb to even his most distant acquaintances—has nurtured Southwest Airlines into the seventh largest airline, with revenues of more than $5.5 billion a year. The company has been profitable every year since 1973. When other carriers lost billions or were struggling with bankruptcy during the early 1990s, Southwest was the only company that remained consistently profitable—a record unmatched in the U.S. airline industry—cheerfully pursuing its growth plans by buying more planes, expanding into new cities, and hiring personnel. Southwest is also a model of efficiency: It is an eleven-time winner of the U.S. Department of Transportation's Triple Crown, a monthly citation for the best on-time performance, fewest lost bags, and fewest overall complaints. Kelleher's operation, based on flights covering relatively short distances for prices that are sometimes shockingly low, is likely to experience rapid growth and become even more of a leading power.

One of the keys to this success lies in the company's mission. Southwest Airlines aims at providing cheap, simple, and focused airline service. Kelleher devoted enormous attention to thousands of small decisions, all designed to achieve simplicity. Among these small but tremendously strategic decisions were the removal of closets at the front of the planes to improve passengers' speed in boarding and departing, and no onboard food, except snacks, which is justified by the short distances the flights cover on average (about 400 miles). Southwest also refused full participation on computerized reservations systems used by travel agents. More than 80 percent of all Southwest tickets are sold directly to customers, saving the company millions annually. There is no assigned seating, no first-class seating.

(Courtesy of Southwest Airlines.)

Planes have been standardized: Southwest only operates one type of aircraft, the 737, which simplifies flight crew training and maintenance personnel training.

These relatively minor privations have their positive counterpart in the fact that Southwest ground crew can turn around a plane at the gate in about twenty minutes! The airline's customers especially appreciate its low fares and on-time schedules.

Who is behind all this? The airline's success is credited to Kelleher's unorthodox personality and entrepreneurial management style. Born and raised in New Jersey, he was the son of the general manager of Campbell Soups Inc. He began to show leadership qualities as student body president both in high school and in college. From his original idea of becoming a journalist, Kelleher shifted his goal to the practice of law. By the mid-1960s, he was successfully practicing in San Antonio, Texas, his wife's hometown. However, he was always seeking the possibility of starting a venture of his own. The big chance came in 1966, when a banker client, Rollin King, suggested that Texas needed a short-haul commuter airline. That was the trigger: Southwest was born in 1971.

Steve Lewing, a Gruntal & Co. analyst, describes Kelleher as "brilliant, charming, cunning and tough."[1] He is, indeed, a unique character. He is a man characterized by a strong sense of humor, who has appeared in public dressed as Elvis, who "has carved an antic public persona out of his affection for cigarettes, bourbon, and bawdy stories."[2]

The CEO, like all great leaders, never stepped into an ivory tower. While CEO, Herb directly supervised his business, personally approving expenses over $1,000. His outstanding hands-on efforts also led to unusually good labor-management relations, on the basis of the motto "People are the most important of resources." In fact, he managed to establish very strongly that old bond of loyalty between employees and their company that may have disappeared elsewhere in the American corporate environment.

He still represents some sort of a father figure to his employees, as well as the jester, the "Lord of Ha-Ha."

continued

This personal feature is and must be, reflected in his personnel: "What we are looking for, first and foremost, is a sense of humor," says Kelleher, "and then people who have to excel to satisfy themselves."[3] The effort that he gets out of his employees makes the real difference. Unlike workers at most other carriers, Southwest employees are willing to pitch in whatever needed. For example, a reservations sales clerk in Dallas took a call from an anxious customer who was putting his eighty-eight-year-old mother aboard a flight to St. Louis. The woman was quite frail, the fellow explained, and he wasn't quite sure she could handle the change of planes in Tulsa. "No sweat," replied the clerk, "I'll fly with her as far as Tulsa and make sure she gets safely on the St. Louis flight."

Kelleher's outstanding leadership ability is also demonstrated by his long-term thinking. He gathered a top-rank team of successors, which will guarantee the airline's future prosperity. Kelleher is the type of leader who inspires, the amiable uncle to refer to, the cheerleader who motivates, and the clown who makes fun.

---

[1]Kenneth Labich, "Is Herb Kelleher America's Best CEO?" *Fortune*, **129,** 9, May 2, 1994, p. 52.
[2]Ibid.
[3]Ibid.

Check Your Knowledge

1. What are the characteristics of a Theory Y employee?
2. What are reinforcers?
3. Describe the goal-setting theory.
4. Give an example of expectancy theory.

Motivating a Diverse Workforce

With today's diverse workforce, managers must be highly flexible to keep all of their employees motivated. A basic example of the differences in the workforce is what is important for women versus men. Men typically place more importance on autonomy in their jobs, whereas women place more importance on good interpersonal relationships and flexible work hours.[10] The most important part for managers to remember is that every single one of their employees is an individual with a different background. The goals and needs of an employee who is older working solely for retirement income will be very different from the goals and needs of an employee who may be a single parent,

---

[10]J. R. Billings and D. L. Sharpe, "Factors Influencing Flextime Usage Among Employed Married Women," *Consumer Interests Annual*, 1999, pp. 89–94; and I. Harpaz, "The Importance of Work Goals: An International Perspective," *Journal of International Business Studies*, First Quarter 1990, pp. 75–93, as cited in Robbins and Coulter, *Management*, p. 443.

working full time to support a family. Due to employees' varied needs and goals, the motivators will be different as well as the ultimate reward.

How do we motivate this diverse workforce? Several incentive programs can be used, including offering employees flexible working schedules, of which there are many different types. They are primarily designed to accommodate employees who have other duties and or responsibilities apart from their careers. Such a schedule appeals particularly to single parents, people who need to take care of sick family members, or women who enter the workforce after giving birth.

Let's start with a discussion of the **compressed workweek.** This schedule allows employees to work fewer days a week and make up the hours by working longer on the days they do go to work. One form of this is to work ten hours a day, and only four days a week. Another name for it is the 4–40 program. The conditions and hours of the compressed workweek vary from organization to organization to fit each individual's needs.

The **flextime** schedule allows for more flexibility than the compressed workweek. It is also known as **flexible work hours.** This system is designed by organizations to allow employees to make their own individual schedule to fit their needs. A required number of hours have to be worked during the week, but the individual is free to schedule the hours as they please within limitations. The most common limitation is certain core hours that each employee must work; however, starting times, ending times, and lunch hours are flexible. Flextime is one of the most desired benefits employees ask for when they are hired.[11]

Job sharing is the term used to describe a situation in which two or more people share one job. This type of motivation for the workforce is very effective when it comes to parents or retirees who do not want a full-time job, yet want the demands of one.

When Managing a Diverse Workforce, the Need for Diversity Training Often Arises (Courtesy of Sodexho.)

[11]"Health Club Memberships, Flextime Are Most Desired Perks," *Business West,* September 1999, p. 75, as cited in Robbins and Coulter, *Management,* p. 443.

Last, there is the option of **telecommuting.** This option has been made possible only recently with the advances made in technology. Employees are able to complete their job duties from home through the use of computers, the Internet, phones, cell phones, and faxes. This form of employment is very convenient, because employees have flexible hours, can wear whatever they please since they work mostly from home, reduce their commute, and have few workplace interruptions. Although this form of work relief is common in many industries, its applicability in hospitality is somewhat restricted in the sense that many positions in hotels and restaurants are labor-intensive, high customer contact jobs (front desk, servers, host/hostess, housekeeping, etc.); this, however, does not preclude its use in the back of the house where actual face-to-face guest contact is not necessary. For instance, sales and catering personnel could work from home, providing they have computer access to the property.

Pay-for-Performance Programs[12]

The **pay-for-performance** program is one of the most popular and widely known methods of motivation. It can be described as any method that relates pay to the quantity or quality of work an employee produces. Examples include a chef meeting the food cost percentage and the engineering department meeting safety goals.

Piecework Pay Plan

The first type of pay-for-performance plan we are going to look at is the **piecework pay plan.** This plan pays the employee according to an actual amount or "piece" of work produced. The employee receives a set amount of money for every piece produced. One example of this is to offer servers an extra percent of sales of a specific wine. Thus the server will be motivated to upsell and, by doing so, the guest perceives that the server is paying special attention to them.

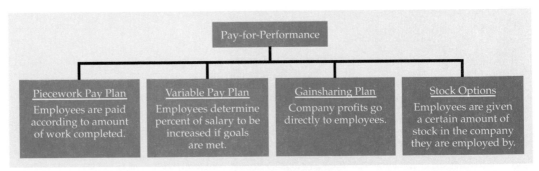

Figure 18–4 *Pay-for-Performance Programs*

---

[12]Draws on Gary A. Dessler. *A Framework for Management,* 2nd ed. Upper Saddle River, NJ: Prentice Hall, 2002, pp. 265–267.

Another method is to determine what the average check is for each station, and for each increase (say, $5 over average) the server receives a bonus or recognition as server of the day, week, or month.

The success of this type of motivation can be explained by Vroom's expectancy theory. The theory states that the employee will be motivated and perform well if he has knowledge that a reward will follow. Money is the reward in our example, and will motivate the server to suggest the wine to his customers.

Variable Pay Plan

Another form of pay-for-performance programs is the **variable pay plan,** which is much like gambling. The employee gets to put up a voluntary percentage of her base salary. Let's say 6 percent. If the company's goals for the particular department the employee is working in are met, she will receive that 6 percent of her salary and, depending on company policies, it might be doubled or tripled. However, if the goals are not met, the employee loses the 6 percent of her salary. Perhaps this would be an interesting concept to try in Las Vegas?

This theory can again be explained by looking at Vroom's expectancy theory. The employee not only expects to get a reward if she meets the company's goals, but also expects to lose a part of her salary if the goals are not met. This would be a negative expectancy.

Gainsharing Plan

When employees are able to directly benefit from a company's profits or gains, the motivational theory is called a **gainsharing plan.** To implement this program, the employer must first of all choose a unit of measure. An example would be cost per unit produced. Next a funding formula is calculated, such as "Forty-seven percent of savings go to employees." Based on individual performance, management then decides how the savings are distributed among employees. If it so happens that an employee is able to achieve cost savings in line with his individual performance goals, the resulting gains are shared with him.

A good hospitality example is the upselling that is done at the front desk. A guest with a reservation for a standard room that is persuaded by the front desk employee to upgrade her room to a luxury suit is being upsold. The front desk employees are promised 50 percent of the profit made from upselling, and this profit is then justly divided among the employees by the department manager. Another example is the energy cost-saving programs that are implemented by hotels. They have certain guidelines that the employees must follow, such as switch off the freezer for certain hours during the day, turn off all lights and electric appliances after cleaning a room, or turn down the heater or air-conditioning during peak energy hours. Employees who follow these guidelines are rewarded by a promised 45 percent of the money saved as a result of the electricity cutbacks. Managers are then given the task of justly dividing the 45 percent among the employees.

(Courtesy of Starbucks Coffee Company.)

Stock Options

A pay-for-performance program that almost all companies have implemented in the past twenty years is the **stock option plan.** Employees are given a certain amount of stock in that company either as a reward for good work or as an incentive to get hired. The employee understands that through his hard work, the performance of the entire company will go up, and so will the stock price. The employees are motivated to make the company successful, so that they can sell their stock and make some money. Starbucks is an excellent example of a company that uses a stock option plan. The theory of their employment practice is that every single employee is viewed as a partner. When hired, employees receive stock options and are, therefore, considered part owners of the company. Through hard work and performance the stock price will rise—and so will their ultimate reward.

Open–Book Management

As a way of motivating their employees, companies sometimes implement an **open-book management** policy. The book that is open is actually the company's financial records and statements. The theory behind this practice is to let the employees see the direct result of their spending habits and therefore create an interest in each employee to behave as economically and efficiently as possible, thereby saving the company more money and ultimately increasing profit. Naturally employees without a financial background will have to attend courses in how to read and make sense of the financial statements. The idea is to treat them like partners, rather than just employees, and have them see the bottom line of the company's financial assets and pitfalls. A study conducted by Ernst & Young LLP shows that employees who are treated more like business partners are more likely to be productive and motivated.[13]

---

[13]R. C. Yafie, "Pass the 10Q, Partner," *Journal of Business Strategy,* January–February 1996, pp. 53–56; and J. P. Schuster, J. Carpenter, and J. P. Kane, *The Power of Open-Book Management,* New York: John Wiley, 1996, as cited in Robbins and Coulter, *Management,* p. 446.

In today's multibillion-dollar-profit, multimillion-employees-type companies, it is hard for employees to see their company's big picture. All they see and know is their own department and how their individual performances affect their direct supervisor as opposed to how it relates to the whole company's performance and profit margin. This is when open-book management makes a huge impact. Employees are able to see the link between their performance, the company's operational results, and ultimately the profit margin and where the company stands in relation to their competitors. All of this just by showing and having them understand the financial statements, or "the books."

Check Your Knowledge

1. What are some examples of a flexible work schedule?
2. How do pay-for-performance programs work?
3. Define open-book management.

Motivating the New Workforce

The "new workforce" of today includes a number of employees who have special employment endorsements. They require special attention when it comes to conventional motivation plans. We are going to look at the following groups that make up the "new workforce": professional employees, and low-skilled, minimum-wage employees.

Motivating Professionals

The growing group of professional workers includes a typically college-level-educated, specialized, and, most importantly, well-paid workforce. The challenge is how to motivate these employees, because they seem to have a great deal of intrinsic satisfaction in their jobs already.

A somewhat stereotypical description of professional employees is that their jobs are pretty much the center of their lives. Their motivation is to improve their job skills and find creative solutions to ever more complex problems. What drives these types of workers is typically not money, since they are paid quite well; it is more the acknowledgment of their peers and superiors of their outstanding work. Do you see why it might be a challenge to motivate this workforce?

Instead of monetary rewards, such as bonuses or stock options, this type of employee can be motivated intellectually. Courses, new training programs, and conferences on their particular field of expertise are very important to professionals because they need to keep themselves updated and learn new

Post 9-11: Motivating Individuals in Your Organization for Disaster Preparedness

Hank Christen and Paul Maniscalco

Motivation for disaster preparedness begins with convincing staff and employees that they have a problem, namely emergency events. The manager must nurture a culture that ensures employees that they are part of the solution to that problem. Employees must understand that their performance in a disaster affects their well-being, and may possibly save their life.

When developing a disaster emergency response plans, serious consideration should be given to involving representatives from all areas, as it should when implementing any managerial initiative. All departments and a cross-section of employees (managers, supervisors, and line personnel) should be included. Representatives of employee or collective bargaining organizations may also be invited to participate. Such inclusion affords the manager and the organization the opportunity to lay the foundation for a sense of ownership in the process—a useful motivational tool from the very beginning.

A technique that encourages employee representation is involvement of all employees in the threat assessment and vulnerability analysis component of your planning process. Employees should be stimulated to identify threats and vulnerabilities (an ongoing process) and rewarded for good ideas. Rewards should be tangible and immediate for nonmanagement team members; a day off, gift certificates, dinner for two (at another facility), or cash are examples of appropriate rewards. Positive employee contributions should be noted on job evaluations.

Contingency plans should not be dependent upon the manager always being onsite or available to get to the property. It is critical that disaster planning team members feel a sense of ownership of the situation in order to ensure that, when crisis strikes, the plan is implemented effectively and appropriately.

Critical Factor: All stakeholders should be involved in the planning process in order to achieve effective emergency response. Employees' ownership of the situation will ensure a sustainable motivation for preparedness.

The next step in becoming motivated for emergency preparedness is understanding the mission's value. Benefits of an effective emergency preparedness plan include:

- ✔ A safer workplace for you, your peers, and your patrons
- ✔ Saved lives and a reduction in suffering of your coworkers and customers
- ✔ A better chance of resuming business after an event
- ✔ Protection of the reputation of your company

Once co-workers and employees understand the value of adopting a sustainable disaster response plan and the plan has been crafted, it must be exercised in order to evaluate projected responses and activities. Exercises provide an opportunity to truly engage team members and heighten their interest and motivation about disaster preparedness. A properly structured exercise evolution creates a highly interactive process that allows the team members to role-play at the highest levels and enables management to identify flaws in the plan. It is an opportunity for disaster planning members to shine and show their skills.

Critical Factor: Exercises are a valuable tool for reinforcing orientation to the disaster response plan and for motivating the team to sustain interest in readiness.

Training is also a motivator. Creativity in using various multi-media formats can eliminate the boredom that employees frequently associate with training. Videos and case studies of real-world events in similar companies or facilities should be employed. The use of as many graphics and visuals as possible will preclude a bland lecture format. Speakers from local agencies and from the hospitality industry who have experienced disasters may be scheduled. Finally, employees should be rewarded for training accomplishments to help ensure their sustained interest in readiness.

An Employee of the Month (Courtesy of Sodexho.)

techniques as soon as they come out in order to stay on top. These training courses and seminars can be used as rewards for good job performance and as incentives to work harder. Additionally, autonomy can be used as a reward and as a sign of trust in the employee for motivation purposes. Let employees schedule their own workweek in ways they find productive, and give them autonomy on new, challenging projects. Recognition in the form of rewards will give them a feeling of importance and also demonstrate sincere interest in their successes.

Motivating Low-Skilled, Minimum-Wage Employees

Some of the workforce is not highly educated, not well trained, and not pure professionals. In real life, every manager has to deal with employees who have a minimum skill level, little education, and are paid minimum wage. More salary, the typical motivator for employees, is not a solution, because the company usually cannot afford to raise the salary of low-level employees. Motivating this workforce is one of the hardest tasks managers have to face.

One motivator apart from money that works particularly well with minimum-wage workers is recognition. Employee recognition programs can include certificates, plaques, award ceremonies, celebrations recognizing employees' achievements, or gift certificates. When you walk into Burger King, for example, you will see a designated wall hung with plaques indicating who the employee-of-the-month is. As long as this kind of public praise is sincere and given for legitimate reasons, it works well as a motivator.

In accordance with expectancy theories and job design, there is one other vital way to motivate minimum-wage employees. By empowering frontline workers with more authority in their jobs, they generate feelings of importance and responsibility for the company's success. Empowerment of employees enhances their motivation, due to the fact that they are able to learn new skills, gain experience in autonomy, realize the task significance and identity, and receive feedback. In addition, the employee is able to see the direct success of their performance. They are able to see the link between job performance and the success of the company, which translates into their pay. Although motivating low-skill, minimum-wage employees can be a rather difficult task, there are options to achieve motivation.

From Theory to Practice: Additional Suggestions for Motivating Employees[14]

Motivational theories sound good on paper, but how well do they apply in real-life situations? Translating motivational methods from theory into practice is every manager's individual challenge. However, this chapter should help you gain knowledge and an understanding of how to motivate various employees. The following is a summary of suggestions of the essence of motivating employees.

1. *Recognize individual differences.* It is important to realize that each employee is different. That is, each person has different factors that motivate him. Different attitudes, needs, and personality traits account for the individuality of every employee.
2. *Match people to jobs.* To match the character of each employee with the type of job that best suits their needs and wants is a very important factor in employee motivation. An example of this is to match a professional, with a high level of education and skill for problem solving, with a job that gives her maximum autonomy, room to grow, and challenging goals.
3. *Use goals.* The goal-setting theory plays a large role in motivating employees. Each manager should provide employees with specific goals and feedback on how well they are doing in achieving those goals. The method of setting these goals can vary from person to person. For some workers it is more effective if they are part of the process of goal setting and in some instances are able to set goals for themselves. Other persons work better when their supervisor provide them with clear, determined goals and they have no say in what those goals will be.
4. *Ensure that goals are perceived as attainable.* The important fact to remember when identifying goals for employees is to make them clearly attainable to the employee. If goals are set at an unrealistic level, it is pointless to the employee to even try to achieve them. This ultimately leads to a lack of motivation. Managers must reinforce that if the employees increase their efforts, they will be able to achieve their goals.
5. *Individualize rewards.* Just as employees all have different characteristics and qualities, they all need different motivator factors for higher performance. For example, money can motivate a minimum-wage worker to achieve higher goals, but it will do little for a worker who is already well compensated and enjoys a challenge. Individualized rewards include more autonomy, promotions, more pay, participation, recognition, and work challenges.

[14]Draws on Robbins and Coulter, *Management,* p. 454.

6. *Link rewards to performance.* Sometimes it is not as clear as one would think that the rewards employees receive are a direct result of their performance. It is important to show employees that their rewards are due to their individual achievement, rather than that of others. It is also important that managers increase the visibility of rewards, to see that they are attainable.

7. *Check the system for equity.* Employees should be aware of the fact that their individual input is rewarded by their individual output. Input must always equal output. This means that if an employee has a higher skill level and experience, he will ultimately be paid higher and given more responsibility than an employee who is below the skill level and has no experience. This ensures that the motivation of the employee will stay high, since he is aware that he cannot compare his reward to that of others who are not on the same level.

8. *Don't ignore money.* Although we said that not all workers are motivated by monetary rewards, it is essential to remember that money is the primary reason most people work. Therefore, performance-based wage increases, piecework bonuses, and other pay incentives are an essential part in motivating most employees. We can state the obvious: If it weren't for the money no one would show up for work. So what better method to have people show up to work more often than by giving them more of what they want—money?

Check Your Knowledge

1. What is the challenge in motivating professionals?
2. How can a manager successfully motivate minimum-wage employees?

Trends in Communicating and Motivating

✔ Understanding the "emotional" aspects of motivation will change the way we manage. Emotional intelligence refers to skills in intra- and interpersonal relations. In the future, managers will view employees from a deeper emotional standpoint rather than on the surface level.

✔ Increased globalization is making the hospitality workplace even more diverse. Individual differences go past traditional demographics to varying deep-level attitudes and beliefs, particularly with nontraditional cultures that are relatively new to the United States. For example, cruise lines are recruiting extensively from Eastern European countries, forcing managers to change the way they interact with employees.

✔ Advancing employee skills will help to satisfy needs, particularly in the "new workforce." The "Generation X" group and the younger "Generation Y" group are very concerned with increasing marketability through learning and developing. Managerial efforts to develop skills and knowledge will help in this regard.

✔ Economic challenges are forcing hospitality organizations to operate "leaner." Hospitality managers will be forced to develop quick, inexpensive methods of maintaining workplace morale. Rather than greater resources to motivate, creativity will be the key.

✔ The advent of telecommuting will change how we motivate employees. Many teams are now "virtual," meaning that face-to-face interaction between supervisors and employees is decreasing. Managers in the future will need to motivate from afar.

Case Study

Michelle Williams recently graduated with a bachelor's degree in hospitality management and has been hired as the front desk manager in a medium-sized hotel located in New York City. The hotel's clientele is truly international and so is its staff, which originates from more than twenty different nations. Many of the employees speak more than one language, often at work. Michelle is from the midwestern United States and has had little experience in managing and motivating a multicultural work group. Indeed, she knows little or nothing about many of the cultures she is surrounded by.

One challenge put to Michelle when she was hired was to give a "lift" to the staff and try to create more of a team atmosphere. Currently, the employees at the front desk operate as a bunch of individuals, with little sense of teamwork. It seems as though the differences in culture are preventing the group from getting closer. As a result, the atmosphere at the front desk is cool and functional, rather than warm and friendly.

In addition, Michelle must contend with a number of employee problems if the department is going to function properly. For example, Maria, who originally comes from Spain, is excellent with customers but often comes to work late. Even when confronted by past supervisors about her lateness, Maria failed to see this as a real problem. Bjorn is a Norwegian hospitality student working part time in the hotel. Although Bjorn is always on time and works very efficiently, his demeanor with the customers is lacking. Oftentimes, guests and coworkers perceive him as being aloof or standoffish. Bjorn rarely smiles at guests. Finally, Peng from Hong Kong is very diligent about his work and gives 100 percent to any task he is given. Unfortunately, Peng has some difficulty speaking English and has little confidence in his speaking ability. As a result, he tends to rush through interactions with guests and limits his conversations, saying only what he must to complete the task.

Discussion Questions

If you were in Michelle's place as the new front desk manager, what methods would you use to answer the following?

1. How will you address each of the work-related problems and motivate Maria, Bjorn, and Peng?
2. How will you facilitate a greater understanding of differences in national culture among the team members at the front desk?
3. Decide on how to build a sense of teamwork with this multicultural group.

Career Information

In a career sense, motivation is personal, it must begin with ourselves. If we are motivated, we can also have a positive motivational influence on others. We don't have a career in motivation, but without motivation we don't have a career. Throughout our careers it is important to stay informed about the latest motivational techniques and to continually find out what motivates our staff. To determine that, you've got to ask them.

Summary

1. Motivation is the art or process of initiating and sustaining behavior toward certain goals. Motivating people is basically inspiring them to do something because they want to do it, not because someone says to do it. The motivational process begins with a need or a demand that is not met. This creates an uncomfortable situation. The person who experiences this need will search for goals that, if obtained, will satisfy that need or demand, therefore, eliminating the uncomfortable situation.

2. Three early motivation theories are McGregor's Theory X and Theory Y, Herzberg's motivation-hygiene theory, and Maslow's hierarchy of needs. McGregor's theory states that there are two kinds of employees. The X person is a pessimist, with a negative attitude toward work, while the Y person is positive and willing to put time and energy into work. Herzberg's theory suggests that hygiene factors actually reduce employee dissatisfaction, while motivators take it a step further and produce job satisfaction. Maslow's hierarchy states the five needs that humans thrive for in a hierarchical pattern: the most basic first, physiological; then safety; social; esteem; and the highest, self-actualization.

3. Having the employee be an active participant in setting goals actually acts as a motivator to achieve these goals. Employees are far more likely to achieve and even exceed goals that they have had a part in setting than they are to achieve goals prescribed from above. Reinforcers are used in reinforcement theory to motivate employees. They are given to employees as a reward for positive behavior, to make sure it will be repeated in the future. Referents, in the equity theory, are the "others" that people compare themselves to. Employees compare their job's inputs–outcomes ratio to those of their coworkers. Seeing that others work harder or are given more responsibilities acts as a motivator. Expectancies as motivators is based on the premise that people will put out effort equivalent to the perceived rewards. If people think they are definitely

going to receive rewards, such as bonuses, they are more likely to be motivated and give the extra effort required to achieve their goals.

4. Managers face a challenge with motivating today's workforce because workers' characteristics are varied; they come from different backgrounds and have different needs and goals. Examples of these employees include immigrants, seniors, young professionals, and minimum-wage employees. Managers must be highly flexible to keep all of their employees motivated.

5. One way to motivate people is to offer a flexible workweek. This can include a compressed workweek, flextime, job sharing, or telecommuting. Another motivational strategy is to have a pay-for-performance program. With a piecework pay plan, variable pay plan, gainsharing, or a stock option plan, employees get paid more or less depending on their job performance. Finally, open-book management policy, in which a company's financial records and statements are open for any employee to view, is considered a motivational strategy because employees see the direct results of their work in the company's assets and are motivated to work harder.

Key Words and Concepts

Compressed workweek	Herzberg's motivation and	Other (in equity theory)	Stock option plan
Equity theory	hygiene factors	Pay-for-performance	System (in equity theory)
Expectancy theory	Hygiene factors	Piecework pay plan	Telecommuting
Flextime/flexible work	Job sharing	Referents	Theory X
hours	Motivation	Reinforcement theory	Theory Y
Gainsharing plan	Motivators	Reinforcers	Variable pay plan
Goal-setting theory	Open-book management	Self (in equity theory)	

Review Questions

1. Why is motivation such an important part of everyday work? Managers are always concerned about new ways to motivate their employees. Explain the importance.

2. Use an example from the hospitality industry to illustrate each of the three early motivational theories.

3. Depict the main obstacles that exist when motivating low-level employees, such as the housekeeping staff of a hotel. Give specific examples. What is different from this situation versus motivating professionals, such as the head chef?

4. How can the early motivational theories be related to motivating a diverse workforce?

5. What motivational technique would work best for your own individual demands? Which technique would be less effective? Explain your answer.

Internet Exercise

Go to the web site http://www.employee-motivation-hq. com and click on the section titled "Secret of Motivation." Then answer the following questions:

1. What are the two things employees really want most from their jobs?

2. What factors draw us to the best organization and keep us there performing at peak effectiveness?

3. According to the national study of the changing workforce, published by the Families and Work Institute, what factors have the highest and lowest impact on job satisfaction?

Apply Your Knowledge

Interview three hospitality associates—preferably one manager, one supervisor, and one associate—to find out what motives them.

Control

19

After reading and studying this chapter, you should be able to:

✔ Define control.
✔ Give reasons why control is important.
✔ Describe the four-step control process.
✔ Distinguish among the three types of control.
✔ Explain the important financial controls.
✔ Describe the qualities of an effective control system.
✔ Outline the contemporary issues in control.

Ever get to the end of the week or month and find that you've run out of money? Well, we all have, and, yes, it's because we did not exercise proper control. But control is not only about keeping our finances in order—it has a much more broad and important role to play in hospitality management. All hospitality managers need to use a variety of control measures to check and see if the results they achieve are in line with expectations and, if not, to take corrective actions. The control process even sets the parameters for managerial action by setting up control by exception, meaning that managers only take action if the results are outside the acceptable range. Control is often used in conjunction with techniques such as total quality management by allowing associates and management to establish guest service levels.

Control is about keeping score and setting up ways to give us feedback on how we are doing. The feedback leads to corrective action, if necessary. If, for instance, a chef and restaurant manager forecast 250 covers and 320 actually come, then they will have to "prep" more food items in a hurry and guide servers to recommend certain dishes in order to avoid 86'ing too many menu items. These and the many other examples we will read about in this chapter are all control related.

Control has close links to each of the other management functions, especially planning, which, as we know, includes setting the goals and making plans on how to reach the goals.

What Is Control?

What control does is provide a way to check actual results against expected results. Action can then be taken to correct the situation if the results are too far from the expected outcome. If labor costs are 26 percent and they were expected to be 23 percent, the difference is only 3 percent, but that 3 percent could add up to thousands of dollars.

Control is the management function that provides information on the degree to which goals and objectives are being accomplished. Management engages in controlling by monitoring activities and taking corrective actions whenever the goals are not being met. An effective control system ensures that activities are completed that lead to the attainment of the organization's goals.

Control is far broader than you might think. It's not just about checking on outcomes; it is also about providing guidelines and mechanisms to keep things on track by making sure there are "no surprises" when the results are known. Control is also about keeping your eyes and ears open. Every place seems to have someone who steals so, as an old Swiss hotel manager mentor said to me in his heavy accent, "John, before you can stop someone else stealing the chicken, you must first know how to steal the chicken." The best way to avoid these losses is to have a really tight control system.

Why Is Control Important?

Why is control so important? Control is important because it's the final link in the management functions. It's the only way managers know whether organizational goals are being met and, if not, why not. Controlling is involved with planning, organizing, and leading. Figure 19–1 shows the relationship between controlling and the other management functions.

Goals give specific direction to managers. Effective hospitality managers need to constantly follow up to ensure that what others are supposed to do is, in fact, being done and goals are being met. Managers need to develop an effective control system—one that can provide information and feedback on employee performance. An effective control system is important because managers need to delegate duties and empower employees to make decisions. But, because managers are responsible for performance results, they also need a feedback mechanism, which control provides.

Given that management involves leading, planning, organizing, communicating, motivating, and controlling, one might easily get the impression that maintaining control is just something managers do after they are finished planning, organizing, and leading. For example, controlling always requires that

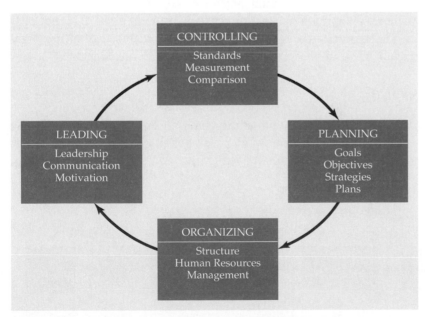

Figure 19–1   *Relationship between Controlling and the Other Management Functions* (Modified from Stephen P. Robbins and Mary Coulter, *Management,* 7th ed. Upper Saddle River, NJ: Prentice Hall, 2002, p. 498)

some desirable outcomes such as targets, standards, or goals be set. Similarly, much of what managers do when they have their leadership hats on involves making sure that employees are doing and will do the things they are supposed to do. However, as we learned in the chapter on motivation, the sort of self-motivation that derives from empowering teams and putting them in charge is often the better alternative.

Check Your Knowledge

1. Define control.
2. Why is control important?

The Control Process

The **control process** is a four-step process of setting standards, measuring actual performance, comparing actual performance against those standards, and taking managerial action to correct deviations or inadequate performances (Figure 19–2). These standards are the specific goals created during the planning process against which performance progress can be measured.

Setting Standards

In the hospitality industry, setting standards generally means establishing the levels of service, the quality of food and beverages offered, employee performance levels, and return on investment. Standards are normally set in terms of

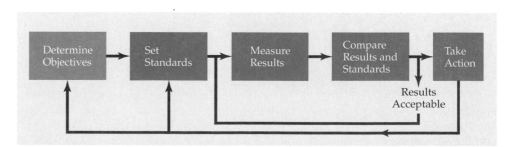

Figure 19–2 *The Control Process*

quantity, quality, finances, or time. A caterer has to determine the quantity or number of guests to serve at a function. If the caterer purchases food for too many guests, then food will be left over, but if they prepare for too few guests then there will not be enough food. When a chef purchases food items, they are controlled upon arrival to ensure that the right quality is being delivered. Budgets are used in controlling financial expenditures and time is used to, for example, control labor costs—a cook should only take a certain number of minutes to prepare a batch of pasta and vegetables.

A word of caution: When developing a method of measurement, one must be absolutely sure first that the goals are indeed measurable. Now, as convoluted as that may sound, let's illustrate the point.

Suppose after careful planning, with input from staff, all agree that labor costs are too high, at 28 percent. So the decision is made to reduce labor costs and that becomes a stated goal—one that is hard to object to. At the end of the month, the kitchen still has a labor cost of 28 percent, so they have not achieved the goal. During your discussion with the personnel responsible, they claim that their plan to reduce labor costs will not be effective until 2 months hence. You remind them that the goal was to reduce labor costs, they agree that it was, and you point out that last month's labor cost and this month's are the same. Who is correct here? Answer: neither. The goal of reducing labor costs is inadequate and it is not measurable or attainable on your part. The kitchen staff has put a plan into effect that they feel will reduce labor costs by the end of the following month; they feel they are doing all that you asked. The dilemma is that the goal lacks specificity. Had the goal been to decrease labor costs to 24 percent by the end of February, it would be measurable and attainable. Then we could say to the kitchen staff that they hadn't met the stated goal, but since we didn't quantify the goal, they are correct.

Information for Control Purposes Can Be Acquired by a Variety of Methods, Including the Telephone. (Courtesy of Evans Hotels.)

Measuring

Managers must first know what they are **measuring** and how they are measuring it before they can measure expected performance. Personal observation, by monitoring subordinates to make sure things are done right, is the simplest and most common way of comparing actual performance to standards. So, the chef can see if the cook is cutting, slicing, and dicing correctly and if the right amount is being prepared according to the standardized recipe.

Direct Supervision

The purpose of direct supervision is to detect problems of associate-specific actions as they occur and to make corrections immediately in order to keep associate actions in line with management expectations.

How We Measure

Four common sources of information frequently used by managers to measure actual performance are personal observation, statistical reports, oral reports, and written reports.

Management by walking around (MBWA) is the best way to make personal observations. MBWA is a phrase used to describe when a manager is out in the work area, interacting directly with associates and exchanging information about what is happening. MBWA can pick up factual omissions, facial expressions, and tones of voice that may be missed by other sources. Front office managers will not be aware of how guests are being checked in during the busy early evening check-in period if they are in their offices at that time.

Statistical reports provide information in the form of data that measure results and can be used for comparative purposes. They also use charts, graphs, and other displays that are easy to visualize. Some managers keep charts on the key result areas and plot the department's progress. Others place safety charts on the associate notice board. These charts visually display the importance of safety and the number of accident-free days, which is another type of goal often sought.

Control information can be acquired through oral reports, conferences, meetings, one-on-one conversations, or telephone calls. The advantage of oral control reports is that they can be both quick and allow instant feedback in the form of a two-way conversation. A manager can inquire about the status of a function and get immediate feedback from the banquet captain. In the often fast-paced hospitality industry, oral control communication is often more effective than other forms of communications. Every time a restaurant service team has an "alley rally" they are, in part, using oral control communications to let servers know what to sell, what the specials are—so guests can be encouraged to order them—instead of "slamming" the kitchen with multiple à la carte orders.

Written reports are also used to measure performance. Like statistical reports, these are slower yet more formal than personal observation or oral reports. Written reports generally have more information than oral ones and are usually easy to file and retrieve. General managers usually expect to see the "daily report," which gives details of the performance results from yesterday, on their desks as they walk into their offices. However, they also want a verbal report from any department they may visit on the way to the office, like "Did we sell out last night?"

Given the varied advantages of each of these measurement approaches, comprehensive control efforts by managers should use all four.

What We Measure

We measure the results to see how they compare with expectations. What we measure is more critical than how we measure—what if we are measuring the wrong thing? The results we measure include guest satisfaction, labor costs, food and beverage costs, employee satisfaction, rooms and room rates, bed sheets, energy costs, insurance, labor turnover, and so on.

In simple terms, we measure labor costs because they are the highest of the variable costs. Did we meet our goal of a 24 percent labor cost reduction? Next, did we meet our goal of a 28 percent food cost? To find out if we met our goals, we would need to set up control measuring procedures regarding the daily monitoring of labor costs. Estimates of sales are given to department heads who then plan and organize their labor costs accordingly. In other words, if you know your sales you can then control your labor costs to the 24 percent. For example, for food and beverage cost control we would scrutinize ordering, purchasing, storing, issuing, preparing, and serving of the various food items. We would take inventory, calculate the actual cost of the food, and express the cost as a percentage of sales. Remember, it's the cost over sales times 100.

Whenever performance results can be measured, it is desirable to consider a results-accountability system. Some control criteria are applicable to any management situation. For instance, because all managers, by definition, coordinate the work of others, criteria such as employee satisfaction or turnover and absenteeism rates can be measured.

Most managers have budgets set in dollar costs for their area of responsibility. Keeping costs within budget is, therefore, a fairly common control measure. However, one of the main purposes of control is to influence behavior. As such, a results-accountability control system must be able to detect deviations from desired results quickly enough to allow for timely corrective management action.

Having timely information and acting on that information is crucial in avoiding the following situation: Why is it that at some hospitality operations each month's income statement results take almost a month to complete? Due to the delay it takes to produce the results, thousands of dollars are lost before any problems can be fixed.

Effective Managers

Effective managers first control the "big ticket" items that will be costly if not controlled. Once the more costly items are under control, they can move on to other, less costly items.

Comparing Results

Comparing results with expectations shows the amount of variation between actual performance and the standard or expected results. Some variation is generally seen between the expected and the actual results—but how big is the variation? The range of variation is the acceptable difference between the actual and expected results.

Managers are concerned with the size and direction of the variance. Let's look at an example: If guest surveys show that one department is not performing up to expectations, then management would make decisions to have the problem fixed. But what if that didn't work? Then more drastic action would be necessary. Meanwhile the survey scores would continue to drop. Management would quickly find out in which direction and how fast the barometer of guest satisfaction was moving.

Taking Managerial Action

The final step in the control process is taking managerial action. **Correcting actual performance** is used by managers if the source of the performance variation is unsatisfactory. For instance, **corrective action** might include changing the way the job tasks are done, changing strategy (doing different tasks), changing structure (changing supervisors/managers' compensation practices), changing training programs, redesigning jobs, or firing employees.

A manager who decides to correct actual performance then has to make another decision: Does she or he use **immediate corrective action,** which corrects problems at once to get performance back on track, or **basic corrective action,** which looks at how and why performance has deviated and then proceeds to correct the source of deviation? Many managers say they don't have time to take corrective action, yet they are the ones perpetually "putting out fires."

Effective managers analyze deviations and, when the benefits justify it, take the time to pinpoint and correct the causes of variance. This kind of control begins with effective associate selection and training. Hiring the right person for the job and ensuring that associates are properly trained increase the chances that they can be trusted to do the right thing.

Good communication is critical to associate control for a number of reasons. The most important reason is that good communication helps associates understand what is expected of them. Employee performance reviews take on added significance when viewed from the control perspective. Rather than a method of reviewing past performance, they become a control technique. By rewarding and praising desired behavior, management can use performance reviews to shape future behavior. The opposite will be true of undesirable behavior. Performance reviews are also a good time to consider training, reassignment, raises, and promotion decisions.

It is important to note the motivating influences of raises and promotions and how they act as a form of control. Granting raises and awarding promotions based solely on operating results criteria and desired behavior send an important

Who Do We Bill?

A fun lack of control story happened at a five-star hotel restaurant close to Christmas, when a guest signed the check for his table's extravagant business lunch "S. Claus." The server, thinking that the guest had signing privileges, gave the check to the restaurant cashier, who in turn sent it up to the billing office so that it would go out to the client at the end of the month. Three days later, the check came back to the restaurant with the question "Which company is he with?"

Check Your Knowledge

1. What are the elements of the control process?
2. Briefly describe the four common sources of information managers use to measure employee performance.
3. Explain the difference between immediate corrective action and basic corrective action.

message to all associates. Those actions say that performance and behavior are being monitored and are the basis for personnel decisions. In this way employee actions are controlled.

Types of Control

Managers can use controls *in advance* of an activity (feedforward control), *during* the activity (concurrent control), and *after* the activity (feedback control) has been completed. Figure 19–3 shows the three types of control.

Feedforward control focuses on preventing anticipated problems since it takes place in advance of the actual work activity. For example, by carefully explaining the policy on billing for catering functions, a catering manager uses

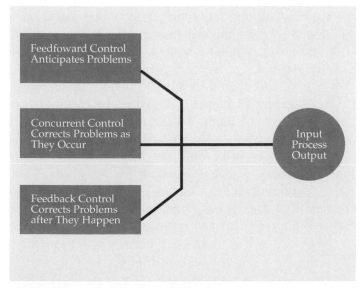

Figure 19–3 *Three Types of Control*

feedforward control to explain to the client that an accurate number of people attending the function must be given in order for the correct space to be allocated for the function. A follow-up number is to be given three months, one month, and two weeks prior to the event, and final guaranteed numbers are required forty-eight hours prior to a function. This is the number for which food is purchased, prepared, and charged for accordingly. By working closely with the client, the catering manager ensures that there are no surprises.

In the kitchen, recipes are an example of feedforward control; they prescribe the quantity of each ingredient necessary to make a particular dish. Recipes also help with consistency by making each dish look and taste the same. (Now that could be good or bad!) Without recipes we know the result is going to be a disaster.

Another example of feedforward control occurred when McDonald's opened in Moscow. McDonald's sent quality control experts to help Russian farmers learn techniques for growing high-quality potatoes and bakers to teach processes for baking high-quality breads. Why? Because McDonald's strongly emphasizes product quality no matter the geographic location. They want a McDonald's cheeseburger in Moscow to taste like the one in New York.[1]

Airlines do preventive maintenance on their aircraft; restaurants do the same on their kitchen equipment and dishwashers to prevent any breakdowns during operation. Resorts and hotels also conduct preventive maintenance on the building, the air conditioning system, and so on. These are all examples of feedforward controls.

Feedforward controls are helpful in that they encourage managers to *prevent* problems rather than *react* to them. The challenge is that feedforward controls take more time to organize than the other types of control, yet they save time in the long run.

Concurrent control is a type of control that takes place while a work activity is in progress. When control is enacted while the work is being performed, management can correct problems before they

Corporate Control

The catering manager of a large convention and banqueting department received a memo stating that no overtime could be worked unless the F&B director authorized it in advance. Now, for a busy department that did thousands of dollars in business every day and was responsible for most of the F&B Division's profit, that memo from the corporate office was not well received—how could they prevent clients from changing their minds at the last minute—and how dare they impose on our operation in this way? In retrospect, the department was caught up in a blanket policy to reduce labor costs by utilizing feedforward control and it worked because many of the not-so-profitable departments were abusing overtime payments to their associates. The convention and banqueting department services manager planned and scheduled the work more effectively and the catering managers were able to persuade the clients to avoid last minute room changes by explaining that it would involve additional changes at overtime rates. Incentives were also given to clients to select room setups that would involve fewer complete room changes (from a dinner to a classroom setup when a cabaret might be equally as suitable). Substantial company-wide savings were made and the conference and banqueting department did react positively to the change (after a brief period of complaining). They also saved several thousand dollars, which, of course, went straight to the bottom line.

[1]Stephen P. Robbins and Mary Coulter, *Management* 7/e. Upper Saddle River, NJ: Prentice Hall, 2002, p. 505.

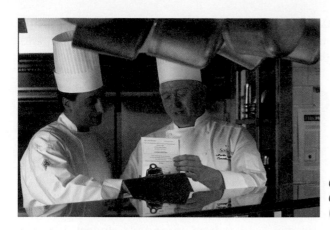

*Chefs Frequently Use
Concurrent Control*
(Courtesy of Sodexho.)

become too costly. The best form of concurrent control is direct supervision, when a manager can concurrently monitor the actions of associates and correct problems as they occur. Although some delay results between the activity and the manager's corrective response, the delay is minimal. For instance, you may have experienced concurrent control when using a computer program such as word-processing software that alerts you to misspelled words or incorrect grammatical usage. In addition, many organizational quality programs rely on concurrent controls to inform workers if their work output is of sufficient quality to meet standards. Chefs use concurrent control when checking on how a recipe is being prepared; the cook can be guided on the correct consistency of a product.

Feedback control, the most popular type of control, takes place after the activity is done. For example, financial statements are examples of feedback control. If, for instance, the income statement shows that sales revenues are declining, the decline has already occurred. The manager's only option is try to determine why sales decreased and to correct the situation.

Feedback control is helpful in hospitality industry situations where a number of activities repeat themselves: Guests make reservations, are welcomed, checked in, roomed, wined and dined, and so on, so resorts and hotels have developed several controls that help measure and report on these activities. These controls include guest surveys, comment cards, and outside checkers who stay at a property and give a detailed report to management on their findings.

Feedback control has two advantages over feedforward and concurrent control. First, feedback provides the managers with meaningful information on how effective their planning efforts were. Feedback that indicates little variance between standard and actual performance is evidence that the planning was generally on target. If the deviation is significant, a manager can use the information when formulating new plans to make them more effective. Second, feedback control can enhance employee motivation. Associates generally want information on how well they have performed.

Remember the profile of T.G.I. Friday's earlier in this book, where the food cost percentage was expected to be 27 percent and the actual was 27.2 percent, meaning the variance was 0.2 of a percentage point. That is feedback control. When a theme park forecasts an attendance of 30,000 on a particular day and the actual comes in at 32,000, that's feedback control.

Other Types of Control

Food and Beverage Controls

Ask any food and beverage operator about controls and you are likely to get a serious look followed by a comment about how important control is to the operation. Lots of money can be made or lost depending on how tight the control is. Most operations will take inventory and calculate the food and beverage costs expressed as a percentage of sales at least once, sometimes twice, a month. A glance at this book's index will indicate several pages where food and beverage controls are discussed in detail, so here we will look at control from a management perspective.

When you become a manager and assume responsibility for controlling food and beverage items, the first thing to do is to get the locks changed because you have no idea who has access to what. The second thing is to review all control procedures. If you really want to exercise tight control, then insist that all orders have your signature or approval—that way, you know what should be received. Next, the stores need to be under the authority and responsibility of one person who is held accountable for all items under their control.

Check Your Knowledge

1. When is feedforward control used?
2. What is the difference between concurrent control and feedback control?

Operational Financial Controls

At the operational level in the hospitality industry, our financial controls mainly consist of **budgets** and **income statements.** Budgets "guestimate" the sales figure for the month/year and allow for up to a specific dollar amount to be spent on any cost of goods sold or controllable costs item. Just preparing the budget has a control-like effect on managers. They are responsible for the financial outcome of their departments and rely heavily on budgets. Instead of just allowing departments to budget the same amount year in and year out, the concept of **zero-based budgeting** has managers begin with a budget of zero dollars and justify all the cost of goods sold, controllable costs, and capital expenditures (things like equipment) they plan on making so that there will be an appropriate amount of profit. Refer to Figure 15–5 in Chapter 15 for an example of a restaurant budget.

Income statements show the actual sales and expenditures for a month/year. They are used extensively in the hospitality industry as a means of control because we are results driven. Managers use the results for controlling the next period's performance. For example, if the results of the beverage department come in below expectations, then corrective action in the form of increased spot-checks would immediately be instigated along with more frequent inventory checks. Figure 19–4 shows a hotel income statement.

As stated earlier, but worth repeating, good managers first control the "big ticket" items that will be most costly if not controlled. Once the most costly items are under control, they can move on to controlling other items. Looking at the labor costs in Figure 19–4, we can see that payroll is the largest of the controllable costs. Labor costs, like any other, need to be controlled in line with sales. Each department will have its own desired labor cost expressed as a percentage of sales. If sales go up, it is easier to control labor costs. However, if sales go down, then the skill of management is to "control" labor costs to avoid losing more than absolutely necessary. Management also needs to be fair with associates. After the September 11, 2001, tragedy, Marriott set an example at many of their hotels and resorts by not laying off any associates—they instead reduced everyone's hours—this did a lot to keep their associates loyal.

In managerial accounting, food and beverage costs are the next largest to be controlled after labor costs. Attractions like Sea World, clubs, resorts, hotels, and restaurants all offer food and beverages to their guests. All food and beverage items need to be costed and priced in advance to yield a certain percentage— let's say 24 percent. We all know that these percentages will vary from one organization to another—the point is that both food and beverage departments need to be "controlled" to produce the expected results, and income statements provide the feedback, written report-type of control.

Things like recipes, portion control, proper purchasing, storage, issuing, and preparation of all food and beverage items will help ensure that the items reach the guest correctly. Next, we need to ensure that all monies reach the bank— no fingers in the cash register! No bags in the kitchen, no internal trades between departments. A proper system must be in place for recording all sales and ensuring that the correct amount is received from guests. Several point-of-sale systems and front- and back-of-the-house systems are available from which hospitality operators can choose. They assist the control process in making the job easier.

INCOME STATEMENT
APRIL 2002

	CURRENT MONTH						YEAR TO DATE					
	CURRENT	%	BUDGET	%	LAST YR	%	CURRENT	%	BUDGET	%	LAST YR	%
REVENUE												
ROOMS	291,371	61.5%	310,270	66.3%	312,768	66.5%	1,106,897	63.5%	1,150,835	66.1%	1,167,731	64.3%
FOOD	136,868	28.9%	111,503	23.8%	108,176	23.0%	453,192	26.0%	414,868	23.8%	449,848	24.8%
BEVERAGE	22,830	4.8%	23,717	5.1%	26,470	5.6%	90,041	5.2%	84,787	4.9%	100,355	5.5%
TELEPHONE	5,473	1.2%	4,593	1.0%	6,686	1.4%	18,634	1.1%	17,390	1.0%	28,852	1.6%
SUNDRIES	367	0.1%	651	0.1%	798	0.2%	2,020	0.1%	2,368	0.1%	2,868	0.2%
OTHER INCOME	16,605	3.5%	17,270	3.7%	15,109	3.2%	72,914	4.2%	71,108	4.1%	66,559	3.7%
TOTAL REVENUE	473,514	100.0%	468,004	100.0%	470,007	100.0%	1,743,698	100.0%	1,741,356	100.0%	1,816,213	100.0%
DEPT EXPENSES												
ROOMS	68,874	23.6%	68,671	22.1%	63,403	20.3%	272,356	24.6%	273,771	23.8%	246,979	21.2%
FOOD	138,332	101.1%	115,108	103.2%	96,580	89.3%	468,515	103.4%	427,109	103.0%	398,509	88.6%
BEVERAGE	12,809	56.1%	11,080	46.7%	11,464	43.3%	46,567	51.7%	41,676	49.2%	49,675	49.5%
TELEPHONE	4,636	84.7%	4,867	106.0%	5,628	84.2%	20,543	110.2%	19,793	113.8%	21,234	73.6%
SUNDRIES	213	58.0%	418	64.2%	990	124.1%	1,957	96.9%	1,578	66.6%	2,744	95.7%
OTHER INCOME	10,531	63.4%	12,741	73.8%	12,956	85.8%	43,047	59.0%	56,513	79.5%	44,364	66.7%
TOT DEPT EXPENSES	235,395	49.7%	212,885	45.5%	191,021	40.6%	852,985	48.9%	820,440	47.1%	763,505	42.0%
DEPT PROFIT	238,119	50.3%	255,119	54.5%	278,986	59.4%	890,713	51.1%	920,916	52.9%	1,052,708	58.0%
UNDIST EXPENSES												
ADMIN & GENL	47,054	9.9%	38,531	8.2%	43,762	9.3%	206,582	11.8%	168,784	9.7%	184,744	10.2%
MARKETING	26,619	5.6%	30,139	6.4%	15,458	3.3%	91,079	5.2%	88,953	5.1%	57,023	3.1%
REPAIR & MAINT	26,767	5.7%	39,621	8.5%	37,668	8.0%	142,323	8.2%	165,966	9.5%	130,646	7.2%
GROUNDS	22,662	4.8%	26,650	5.7%	29,897	6.4%	108,114	6.2%	107,024	6.1%	95,284	5.2%
UTILITIES	20,494	4.3%	26,785	5.7%	19,010	4.0%	85,988	4.9%	99,652	5.7%	83,380	4.6%
TOT UNDIST EXP	143,596	30.3%	161,726	34.6%	145,795	31.0%	634,086	36.4%	630,379	36.2%	551,077	30.3%
GROSS OPER PROFIT	94,523	20.0%	93,393	20.0%	133,191	28.3%	256,627	14.7%	290,537	16.7%	501,631	27.6%
FIXED EXPENSES												
PROP TAXES	5,734	1.2%	5,734	1.2%	5,099	1.1%	27,015	1.5%	26,983	1.5%	24,443	1.3%
INSURANCE	2,622	0.6%	2,622	0.6%	1,700	0.4%	10,488	0.6%	10,488	0.6%	6,800	0.4%
INTEREST	1,220	0.3%	1,252	0.3%	1,345	0.3%	4,944	0.3%	5,008	0.3%	5,442	0.3%
INCOME TAXES	0	0.0%	0	0.0%	0	0.0%	0	0.0%	0	0.0%	0	0.0%
DEPREC	26,000	5.5%	26,000	5.6%	26,000	5.5%	104,000	6.0%	104,000	6.0%	100,000	5.5%
TOT FIXED EXP	35,576	7.5%	35,608	7.6%	34,144	7.3%	146,447	8.4%	146,479	8.4%	136,685	7.5%
NET INCOME	58,947	12.4%	57,785	12.3%	99,047	21.1%	110,180	6.3%	144,058	8.3%	364,946	20.1%

	CURRENT	BUDGET	LAST YR		CURRENT	BUDGET	LAST YR
ROOMS AVAIL	2,580	2,580	2,670		10,320	10,320	10,680
ROOMS OCCUPIED	1,495	1,670	1,797		5,747	6,078	6,529
OCCUPANCY %	57.9%	64.7%	67.3%		55.7%	58.9%	61.1%
AVG RATE	$151.63	$147.30	$141.56		$147.84	$147.09	$142.50

Figure 19–4 *Hotel Income Statement* (Courtesy of Hospitality Concepts, San Diego.)

Corporate Profile: Sodexho

Sodexho is a North American leading food and facilities management services company.[1] This company is also a member of the international Sodexho Alliance that was founded in 1966 by a Frenchman named Pierre Bellon with its first service provider in Marseille, France. Primarily serving schools, restaurants, and hospitals, the company soon became internationally successful by signing deals with Belgian food service contractors. In 1980 after considerable success in Europe, Africa, and the Middle East, Sodexho Alliance decided to expand its reach into North and South America. In 1997 the company joined with Universal Ogden Services, a leading U.S. remote-site service provider. The empire grew a year later when Sodexho Alliance and Marriott Management Services merged. The merger created a new company called Sodexho Marriott Services. Listed on the New York Stock Exchange, the new company became the market leader in food and management services in the United States. At that time, Sodexho Alliance was the biggest shareholder, holding 48.4 percent of shares on the company's capital. In 2001, however, Sodexho Alliance acquired 53 percent of the shares in Sodexho Marriott Services, which changed its name to simply Sodexho.

Today, Sodexho Alliance has over 270,000 employees at 6,000 sites in 70 countries. In the United States there are 130,000 employees. The goal of Sodexho is to improve the quality and life of customers and clients all over the United States and Canada. They offer outsourcing solutions to the health care, corporate, and education markets. This includes the following services: housekeeping, groundskeeping, food service, plant operation and maintenance, and integrated facilities management.

Sodexho's mission is to create and offer services that contribute to a more pleasant way of life for people wherever and whenever they come together. Its challenge is to continue to make its mission and values come alive through the way in which employees work together to serve the clients and customers. The values of Sodexho are service spirit, team spirit, and spirit of progress.

A leading provider of food and facilities management services in North America, Sodexho provides their services at more than 6,000 locations, including corporations, colleges and universities, health care organizations, and school districts. They are always looking to develop talent. Sodexho offers internships in food service and facilities management businesses as well as in staff positions such as finance, human resources, marketing, and sales. Sodexho believes that workforce diversity is essential to the company's growth and long-term success. By valuing and managing diversity at work, Sodexho can leverage the skills, knowledge, and abilities of all employees to increase employee, client, and customer satisfaction.

(Courtesy of Sodexho.)

---

[1]Draws on Sodexho USA home page, http://www.sodexhousa.com/about_us.html.

Qualities of an Effective Control System

Effective control systems tend to have certain characteristics in common.[2] The importance of these qualities varies with the situation; effective control systems have ten characteristics (Figure 19–5).

1. **Accuracy.** An effective control system is reliable and produces valid data.
2. **Timeliness.** An effective control system provides timely information.
3. **Economy.** An effective control system must be economical to operate.
4. **Flexibility.** An effective control system is flexible enough to adjust to changes and opportunities.
5. **Understandability.** The users can understand an effective control system.
6. **Reasonable criteria.** Control standards must be reasonable and attainable.
7. **Strategic placement.** Because managers can't control everything, they must choose to control those factors that are strategic to the organization's performance.
8. **Emphasis on exceptions.** Managers can't control all activities; control devices should call attention only to the exceptions.
9. **Multiple criteria.** Measures decrease tendencies toward a narrow focus.
10. **Corrective action.** The control system not only indicates significant deviations, but also suggests appropriate corrective action.

Experienced managers use effective controls by exception, meaning that if the results are outside the acceptable predetermined limits, then they take action; otherwise they concentrate on something else.

Accuracy	*Reasonable Criteria*
Timeliness	*Strategic Placement*
Economy	*Emphasis on Exceptions*
Flexibility	*Multiple Criteria*
Understandability	*Corrective Action*

Figure 19–5   *Ten Characteristics of an Effective Control System*

[2]W. H. Newman, *Constructive Control Design and Use of Control Systems*, Upper Saddle River, NJ: Prentice Hall, 1975, p. 33.

Contingency Plans and Control

The most important contingency plan factor that affects the design of an organization's control system is the size of the organization. The control system should vary according to the organization's size. A small organization relies more on informal and personal control approaches. Here, concurrent control (direct supervision) is probably the most cost effective. However, as organizations increase in size, direct supervision is likely to be supplemented by an expanding formal control system of reports, regulations, and rules. Very large organizations will typically have highly formalized and impersonal feedforward and feedback controls. Contingency plans and control cover the "what if's"—what if our sales dip 8 percent—what will we do? Reduce associate hours, reduce expenditures and attempt to boost sales.

As you move up in the organization's hierarchy, there is a greater need for several different types of control; this reflects increased operational complexities. Additionally, the greater the degree of decentralization, the more managers will need feedback on employees' decisions and performance results. Managers who delegate the authority for making decisions and performing work are still ultimately responsible for the actions of those to whom it was delegated.

The importance of an activity influences whether and how it will be controlled. However, if an error can be highly damaging to the organization, extensive controls are likely to be implemented. It simply makes sense to control the big ticket items.

Adjusting Controls for Cultural Differences[3]

Control is used quite differently in other countries. The differences in organizational control systems of global organizations are seen primarily in the measurement and corrective action steps of the control process. In a global hospitality corporation, managers of foreign operations tend to be controlled less directly by the home office, for no other reason than that distance keeps managers from being able to observe work directly. Because distance creates a tendency to formalize controls, the home office of a global company often relies on extensive formal reports for control. Global companies rely on the power of information technology to provide speedy control reports of results.

Technology's impact on control also can be seen when comparing technologically advanced nations with less technologically advanced countries. In

[3]Ibid, p. 510.

Post 9–11: Control and Command in Time of Disaster

Hank Christen and Paul Maniscalco

Before any emergency or disaster occurs, an organization's responsibility for the control of the situation and for the command of each organizational element need to be clearly specified in the emergency/disaster plan. Individual departments and contractors (who provide goods and services) are integral to ensuring the organization's continued operation, reputation management, and event survivability. One of the most important tasks is defining control of the organizational response to the event in the planning phase. Once this requirement has been identified, the next step is to implement an interim command and control framework that functions as the highest authority responsible for management of the event.

This command configuration places critical departments and subunits under the control of a single authority—the person onsite ultimately in charge of all the organization's resources—the incident commander. This new organizational structure is designed for the sole purpose of resolving the crisis, and it is in effect only in times of emergency. After the crisis has been resolved, the command structure relinquishes its authority to the standard daily managerial configuration. Even though this command structure serves at the direction of the organization and depends upon it for logistical support, its characteristics and qualities are unique to itself and to the mission.

The incident command structure requires an effective command and control design—a system providing for critical department interaction and assuring that all efforts are directed toward achieving a common goal. Without a robust, sustaining support mechanism, the chain of command and communications are fragmented, confusing, and vastly ineffective. By establishing a control mechanism in advance, the organization's command structure is highly adaptable for large and small-scale emergencies and is flexible enough to integrate resources from different corporate and vendor areas. Several critical issues should be considered when designing a command and control system:

✔ Every emergency event demands a structured plan. While more minor emergencies generally do not require a fully scripted response, some guidance is required in all emergency scenarios. Without a response plan, the organization's incident commander is unable to seek the advice and employ the expertise of subordinate commanders.

✔ The command structure must provide a manageable span of control to be effective. Without a manageable span of control, the incident commander quickly becomes overloaded with data and requests. This phenomenon is frequently referred to in the emergency response field as OBE, "overwhelmed by events." OBE *must* be avoided. Early recognition of span of control issues enables the manager to assign subordinate commanders and avoid OBE.

✔ Comprehensive resource management, distribution, and accountability are also required. Some required resources may have a limited service time, and replacements must be arranged for. Radio batteries must be exchanged and recharged. Repair parts from distant locations may be needed. Personnel must be fed and relieved. These factors demand that the incident manager assign a current status condition to all resources and provide for efficient operation.

✔ Communications systems must be reliable, efficient, and secure. Frequently facility communications are disabled due to the incident. The result is an inability to communicate, control, and prioritize subordinate tasking. In the military, communications is called "the voice of command." Commanders who cannot communicate cannot control. The manager should work with the organization's security department and enhance their radio capacity so that internal resources are in place to sustain crisis communications.

Critical Factors
- Control begins with a structured plan.
- A narrow span of control should be maintained to avoid OBE (overwhelmed by events).
- Operational control is not possible without effective communications.

countries such as the United States, Japan, Canada, the United Kingdom, France, Germany, and Australia, managers of global companies use indirect control devices, particularly computer-related reports and analyses in addition to standardized rules and direct supervision, to ensure that work activities are going as planned.

In less technologically advanced countries, managers tend to rely more on direct supervision and highly centralized decision making for control. Also, constraints on what corrective actions managers can take may affect managers in foreign countries because laws in some countries do not allow managers the option of choosing the facilities, laying off employees, taking money out of the country, or bringing in a new management team from the outside country.

Contemporary Issues in Control[4]

One issue that can arise as managers begin to design efficient and effective control systems include technological advances in computer hardware and software that have made the process of controlling much easier, but these advances have brought with them difficult questions regarding what managers have the right to know about employee behavior. Another issue is workplace privacy.

Workplace Privacy

If you work, do you think you have a right to privacy at your workplace? What can your employer find out about you and your work? You might be surprised by the answer. Why do managers feel they must monitor what employees are doing? A reason is that employees are hired to work, not to surf the web checking stock prices, placing bets at online casinos, or shopping for presents for family or friends.

Recreational on-the-job web surfing has been said to cost a billion dollars a year in wasted computer resources and billions of dollars in lost work productivity.[5] Another reason why managers monitor employee e-mail and computer usage is that they don't want to risk being sued for creating a hostile workplace environment because of offensive messages or an inappropriate image displayed on a coworker's computer screen. Concern about sexual harassment is one of the reasons why the companies might want to monitor or keep the backup copies of all e-mail. This electronic device can help establish what actually happened if an incident arises and can help managers react instantly. Managers

---

[4]Ibid, pp. 511–517.

[5]L. Guernsey, "The Web: New Ticket to a Pink Slip," *The New York Times,* December 16, 1999, pp. D1 + ; and K. Naughton, "CyberSlacking," *Newsweek,* November 29, 1999, pp. 62–65, as cited in Robbins and Coulter, *Management,* p. 513.

Increased Use of Computers at the Workplace Poses Risk for Privacy Issues

also need to be certain that employees are not inadvertently passing information on to others who could use that information to harm the company.

Employee Theft

Would it surprise you to know that up to 85 percent of all organizational theft and fraud is committed by employees, not outsiders?[6] Any unauthorized taking of company property by employees for their personal use constitutes employee theft, from fraudulent filing of expense reports to removing equipment, software, and office supplies from the company premises. Hospitality businesses have long faced serious losses from employee theft caused by loose financial controls, especially at the start-up of a business.

Why do employees steal? There are several perspectives. The industrial loss prevention professionals suggest that people steal because the opportunity presents itself through lax controls and favorable circumstances. Some people have different social financial problems or pressures such as gambling debts. People steal because they can rationalize whatever they're doing as being correct and appropriate behavior. Each of these approaches provides compelling insights into employee theft and has been instrumental in creating programs designed to

A Prepay Restaurant

There is a great hole-in-the-wall restaurant in New York City where arguably the best front-end control system is in place. Servers have to pay the cooks for the guest's food—so you know that they will get the money from the guests.

---

[6]A. M. Bell and D. M. Smith, "Theft and Fraud May Be an Inside Job," *Workforce Online* (http://www.workforce.com), December 3, 2000, as cited in Robbins and Coulter, *Management*, p. 514.

deter it. We can apply the concept of feedforward, concurrent, and feedback control to identify measures for deterring or reducing employee theft.[7]

Workplace Violence

Factors contributing to workplace violence include employee stress caused by long working hours, information overload, daily interruptions, unrealistic deadlines, and uncaring managers. Even office layout designs where employees work with noise around them have been cited as contributing to the problem.[8] Others described dysfunctional work environments characterized by the following as primary contributors to the problem:[9]

- ✔ Employee work driven by time, numbers, and crises
- ✔ Rapid and unpredictable changes in which instability and uncertainty plague employees
- ✔ A destructive communication style in which managers communicate in an excessively aggressive, condescending, explosive, or passive-aggressive style
- ✔ Excessive workplace teasing or scapegoating
- ✔ Authoritarian leadership with a rigid, militaristic mind-set of managers versus employees; employees not allowed to challenge ideas, participate in decision making, or engage in team-building efforts
- ✔ Double standards in terms of policies, procedures, and training opportunities for managers and employees
- ✔ Unresolved grievances because there are no mechanisms or only adversarial ones in place for resolving them, dysfunctional individuals may be protected or ignored because of long-standing rules, union contact provisions, or reluctance to take care of problems
- ✔ Emotionally troubled employees and no attempt by managers to get help for these people
- ✔ Repetitive, boring work in which there is no chance of doing something else or of new people coming in
- ✔ Faulty or unsafe equipment or deficient training that keeps employees from being able to work efficiently or effectively
- ✔ A hazardous work environment in terms of temperature, air quality, repetitive motions, overcrowded spaces, noise levels, excessive overtime, and so forth; to minimize costs, no additional employees are hired when overload becomes excessive, leading to potentially dangerous work expectations and conditions
- ✔ A culture of violence in which there's a history of individual violence or abuse, violent or explosive role models, or tolerance of on-the-job alcohol or drug abuse

---

[7]Ibid, p. 514.

[8]R. McNatt, "Desk Rage," *Business Week,* November 27, 2001, p. 12, as cited in Robbins and Coulter, *Management,* p. 516.

[9]M. Gorkin, "Key Components of a Dangerously Dysfunctional Work Environment," *Workforce Online* (http://www.workforce.com), December 3, 2000.

Personal Profile: Michael R. Thorpe

The Leader of the Future Will Be a Holistic One

Michael R. Thorpe, who has successfully earned a bachelor of science degree in hotel and restaurant management at the United States International University, is an outstanding example of the leadership skills that can be acquired throughout the school and college career.

Mike's leadership abilities developed from an early age, with his involvement in the Boy Scouts of America. Looking back at that memorable time, Mike recognizes how important it is for a leader to be a good role model. He emphasizes the fact that it is necessary to make a sharp distinction between "good" leaders and "bad" leaders, thus establishing a learning process that is based on the identification of both "shoulds" (positive examples, experiences, activities, skills) and "should-nots" (mistakes, negative attitudes). Michael's experience with the Boy Scouts was one that provided him with fundamental values and skills, which were acknowledged when he achieved the rank of Eagle Scout.

(Courtesy of Michael Thorpe.)

In high school as well as in college, Mike's leadership skills were progressively developed and utilized. He believes that the key to learning is involvement. In fact, he always took part in school activities, also emphasizing the importance of maintaining a broad horizon of interests. In particular, Michael chose to actively participate in a variety of extracurricular activities, including academic, service-oriented, and sports organizations. He stressed the belief that there is a strict correlation among such fields that shapes the overall personality of the leader. "The leader of the future will be a holistic one," Mike says.

Michael's involvement in academic organizations, such as the student body government council; in sports, as captain of the football team and vice president of the football club; and in service-oriented enterprises, such as the Hosteur's Society HRTM Club, to which he was elected president, helped him develop the necessary skills for high-quality interaction with people. He learned that a good leader is someone who is able to gather a group of individuals and coordinate each single talent, skill, propensity, and personality into a successful team, joining forces in the pursuit of one common goal. Each member of the team must be fulfilled in his or her need for belonging, personal satisfaction, recognition, and so on. To accomplish this task, Mike understood that a leader must also be extremely respectful of each individual's personal life, needs, problems, cultural background, and diversity, setting aside personal likes and dislikes. Diversity also provides an opportunity for the leader to learn from the people he or she guides, an opportunity that every leader must have the humility and willingness to pursue.

In Mike's words, the leader must act as a "glue" that unites people, and the organizer who finds the "right place" for each individual, a place in which he or she will be able to excel and perform at his or her full potential.

Work experience throughout his college career has also taught Mike that workers will function at their best in a work environment that is appealing and challenging, and that provides them with the right tools—in terms of knowledge, motivation, rewards, and climate—to produce the optimal outcome.

To achieve such results, Michael excludes, as much as possible, the carrot-on-a-stick approach. He feels that such a method is a superficial remedy that doesn't get to the root of the problem—and thus doesn't solve it—and doesn't consider that a leader deals with human beings intrinsically characterized by a distinct intelligence and personality. Furthermore, when dealing with subordinates' failures or mistakes, Michael prefers to approach the person(s) in question from his or her point of view, trying to understand what the cause of the inefficiency might be and trying to establish whether that person's poor performance is determined by his own possible leadership mistake.

Mike greatly respects a leader who creates a sense of cooperation, community, and teamwork. Just like in a family, the leader should step down from an intolerable ivory tower, and be open to each member of the team, to listen and be willing to help with possible personal problems, emphasizing the importance of the open communication. And as in a family, the leader must be the caring parent who can also progressively impose discipline and obtain the results expected depending on the members' potential.

Mike understands the role of a father, because he has a three-year-old who represents, among other things, the ultimate challenge for leadership. "Workers' livelihoods do depend on the employer/leader."

This list may not look like the place you work, but some of these factors appear in a good many corporations especially with the pressure of making a profit in the increasingly competitive "24-7-365" environment.

Control is critical in the hospitality industry because we need to know how we are doing all the time. We need to know if goals are being met and standards reached or exceeded. According to the situation, well-managed hospitality businesses use a variety of controls to provide the necessary information to management for decision-making purposes.

Check Your Knowledge

1. Briefly explain zero-based budgeting.
2. List the qualities of an effective control system.
3. What are some contributors to workplace violence?

Trends in Control

Increasing use of technology for control helps not only with making the job of control easier but also much quicker. Quicker results mean decisions to make necessary changes are made sooner, thus avoiding further losses.

Handheld devices that take inventory are an example of how technology can assist management with inventory taking.

Case Study[1]

Ritz-Carlton is an outstanding hotel in providing luxury service to its guests. In contrast with the standard goals of ordinary business hotels—to provide a home away from home—the Ritz-Carlton Hotel company decided to take it a step further and provide luxury accommodation to industry executives, meeting and corporate travel planners, and other affluent travelers. The chain is Atlanta based and runs twenty-five luxury hotels that pursue excellence in each market.

Recently the hotel company was awarded the U.S. government's Malcom Baldrige National Quality Award. The award praised Ritz-Carlton for its participatory leadership, thorough information gathering, coordinated planning and

continued

execution, and trained workforce that was ready to "to move heaven and earth" to satisfy their customers. Thinking about control, what types of control mechanisms did Ritz-Carlton need to achieve excellence?

The corporate motto is "Ladies and Gentlemen serving Ladies and Gentlemen." All employees are expected to practice the company's "Gold Standards." These standards are made up of a service credo and the basics of premium service, including processes for solving any problem guests may have.

The difference between this luxury chain and other hotel companies is that their employees are "certified" after the common basic orientation followed by an on-the-job training. This certification to work for Ritz-Carlton is reinforced daily by frequent recognition for achievement, performance appraisal, and daily "lineups." Annual surveys are given to make sure the employees know the quality standards the hotel company expects of them as well as to determine their level of satisfaction with the company. One year 96 percent of the employees surveyed ranked excellence in guest services as their primary duty. Workers are empowered by the company to do whatever it takes to solve any sort of problem a customer might encounter. Employees are required to assist their coworkers in dealing with a guest satisfaction issue leaving no room for any excuse as to why a customer problem was not solved on the spot. In this way, the guest is truly treated as a king; guest satisfaction comes first—always.

Discussion Question

1. In what ways does Ritz-Carlton utilize control to ensure high-quality service?
2. How does the company maintain and foster its employees' high level of commitment?

---

[1] Adapted from Gary Dessler, *A Framework for Management.* Upper Saddle River, NJ: Prentice Hall, 2002, pp. 376–377.

Career Information

To control the direction that life takes you is to end up where you wanted to be. The control process will help you to set a career path that is definable and predictable. You can then have a clear understanding of what you are doing and how well you are doing it. If you are meeting the standards that you have made for yourself, you will be rewarded in your long-term career.

Summary

1. Control is the management function that provides information on the degree to which goals and objectives are being accomplished.
2. Control is important because it's the final link in the management function. An effective control system is important because managers need to delegate duties and empower employees to make decisions.
3. The control process can be described as setting standards, measuring actual performance, comparing actual performance against those standards, and taking managerial action to correct deviations or inadequate performances.
4. Managers can use controls *in advance* of an activity, which is called feedforward control; *during* the activity, which is concurrent control; and *after* the activity, called feedback control.
5. Budgets and income statements are primarily used for financial control. Budgets "guestimate" the sales figure for the month/year and allow for up to a specific dollar amount to be spent on any cost of goods sold or controllable costs item. Income statements show the actual sales and expenditures for a month/year.
6. Effective control systems have ten characteristics: accuracy, timeliness, economy, flexibility, understandability, reasonable criteria, strategic placement, emphasis on exceptions, multiple criteria, and corrective action.
7. Contemporary issues in control include the increasing use of technological advances, which raise the issue of workplace privacy. Additionally workplace violence and employee theft are issues in the control process.

Key Words and Concepts

Accuracy
Basic corrective action
Budget
Concurrent control
Control
Control process
Correcting actual
  performance

Corrective action
Economy
Emphasis on exceptions
Feedback control
Feedforward control
Flexibility
Immediate corrective action

Income statement
Management by walking
  around (MBWA)
Measuring
Multiple criteria
Reasonable criteria

Strategic placement
Timeliness
Understandability
Zero-based budgeting

Review Questions

1. Imagine a restaurant that is lacking any kind of control. Describe the negative and positive aspects of this environment and then answer the following question: Why is control necessary?
2. If you were a manager of a Hilton Resort in the Bahamas, what way of measuring actual employee performance would you utilize and why? What are the pros and cons of your chosen method?
3. Explain the three different types of control. Think of a situation where you have been controlled. Which type of control works best for you?
4. Describe how you envision an effective control system. What types of control would you use? How would you measure employee performance? How would you keep employee theft under control? What about workplace violence? Which operational financial control would you implement?

Internet Exercise

Go to http://www.strategicfinancemag.com/2001/05h.htm and answer the following questions:

1. What are the causes of workplace violence?

2. How would have you handled the McDermott situation? Why?

3. What should you do if you ever get fired?

Apply Your Knowledge

Go to http://www.epolicyinstitute.com/disaster/stories.html and answer the following questions:

1. Do you think that it's fair for employers to monitor their employee's e-mails?

2. What would you do if you caught your boss reading your e-mails?

Hospitality Industry Technology

After reading and studying the chapter, you should be able to:

✔ Identify the characteristics of information technology and information systems in the hospitality industry.

✔ Identify the different types of information systems.

✔ Differentiate between information technology use in hotels and restaurants.

✔ Apply the importance of information systems to the hospitality industry.

✔ Relate hospitality industry technology to management, such as property management systems.

What Is Hospitality Industry Technology?

Hospitality information systems (HIS) are a collection of components that work together to provide information help in the operations and management of a hospitality organization.[1] In the hospitality industry, information technology systems are primarily computers and telephone systems, but can be software applications and hardware that are used in a variety of locations in various sectors of the industry. This chapter examines the technology used in the hospitality industry today.

In the hospitality industry, information systems make use of computers and telephone systems to provide guest services, to make business processes more effective, and to perform decision-making functions for managers (Figure 20–1). The computers, communications equipment, and other technology used in information systems are called **information technology (IT).** Computer information systems give hospitality managers an advantage because they reduce the chance of error. These systems allow managers to control an entire property at the touch of a button. For example, computerized systems can now help monitor work as it is being done, thereby warning associates about obvious or like-

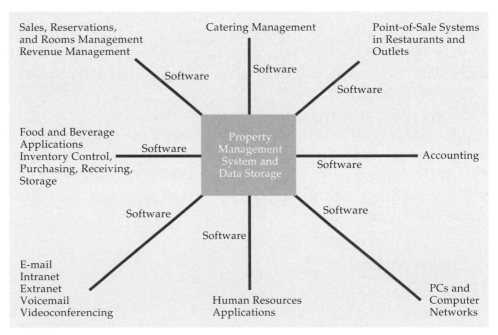

Figure 20–1 *Components of Hospitality Information Technology*

[1]Robert C. Nickerson, *Business Information Systems*, Upper Saddle River, NJ: Prentice Hall, 2001, p. 4.

ly errors before those errors cascade to create additional errors elsewhere.[2] In housekeeping operations, housekeepers can be notified in advance of guest requests before guests check into the hotel. How do they know what the guest might request in advance? Some hotels, restaurants, and especially casinos keep information on guest likes and dislikes. This helps create a comfortable and predictable environment for guests and at the same time it saves time and provides efficiency in the housekeeping department.

Types of Hospitality Industry Technology Systems

The hospitality industry utilizes various systems and technologies in order to serve guests more efficiently and effectively. The systems include work group information systems, electronic mail, organizational information systems, and global information systems.

Work Group or Group Information Systems

Many hospitality businesses today have **work group information systems.** These systems allow groups of associates within a department to share data and information that help manage the department's functions. These systems sometimes utilize a **local-area network (LAN)** in which the employees of a business can communicate and work with one another simultaneously via different computers within a complex or campus of buildings. LANs allow a large number of people to communicate and exchange messages within seconds. These LAN connections are adopted by large businesses and, in conjunction with **wide-area network (WAN)** connections, allow franchises to link with one another over considerable distances. In large franchises, many people are trying to communicate with one another and these work groups can communicate faster with high-speed access within and outside of the businesses.

Electronic Mail

Electronic mail (e-mail) is a type of work group information system that allows the staff and guests to communicate from different locations. Messages can be posted and retrieved within seconds by the use of e-mail. A number of hotels provide in-room connections that allow guests to check their e-mail.

With e-mail, letters and memos that normally would be sent on paper are transmitted electronically, from one computer in the network to another. For

[2]Steven Alter, *Information Systems, The Foundation of E-Business,* Upper Saddle River, NJ: Prentice Hall, 2002, p. 14.

example, Sheraton Hotels use a system called Geac, which allows departments such as guest reservations or communications to post messages for guests that are received within seconds. This system allows information to be shared within the network. Many hospitality organizations use Microsoft Outlook or Lotus Notes for calendaring and scheduling—these are called *groupware.*

Electronic mail work groups can be used for many operations of a hospitality business such as reservation confirmations for guests and interorganizational messages for associates.

Organizational Information Systems

Organizational information systems are used throughout a company and can be accessed by a number of associates. They may also be called **enterprise information system.** These systems are controlled by several computers, which are separated by long distances. Examples of these systems would be payroll, time and attendance, guest history, or reservations systems. Many benefits accrue from using organizational information systems for payroll. Many companies today do not use the traditional time cards; instead they use an electronic system that scans time cards. A system such as this supplies hourly data to the payroll branch, which could be located across the country. This facilitates the timely distribution of employee paychecks each pay period.

An enterprise system is a customized service module that is used by, for instance, a hotel chain's multiple outlets in various locations. The Fairmont Hotel chain uses PeopleSoft, a program that allows Fairmont Hotel associates to access the same information regardless of which hotel they are located at.

Global/International Information Systems

Companies that do business outside their own country are called international businesses.[3] These worldwide businesses have information systems that allow them to stay linked; these systems are called **global** or **international information systems.** If international companies are to communicate and make transactions effectively, they must use international information technologies and systems.

High-speed Internet service is one form of information technology that these businesses can utilize. With the help of the Internet and computer-based software, companies can speed transactions between one country and another. An example of a company that provides such services is Wayport High-Speed Internet Solutions. Wayport High-Speed Internet Solutions for Hotels is a provider of high-speed wireless and wired Internet service for hotels and their guests. The Wayport service allows hotel guests to connect to the Web, e-mail, and the guest's corporate networks at speeds up to fifty times faster than traditional modem connections. This results in a competitive edge when targeting

---

[3]Nickerson, *Business Information Systems,* p. 16.

business guests, because it enables reduced PBX/voice trunk (long-distance) saturation and cost, property differentiation, and brand enhancement.[4] Typically these are the benefits businesses may receive by using high-speed Internet access for transactions.

Check Your Knowledge

1. What does LAN stand for?
2. Briefly state the purpose of HIT.
3. Give some examples of what electronic mail work groups are used for.

Hospitality Information Processing

Hospitality businesses process **data** (simple facts) into useful **information** (organized data). Information can be used to enter guest reservations, collect guest information, bill guests, and so forth. This information can be entered into a computer **database** in which the data are stored for future reference, and the front desk and accounting departments can share it. For instance, guest payments must be recorded and transmitted from the initial sale at the front desk, to accounting, where they are documented for legal purposes. The term **information sharing** refers to business processes that operate independently accessing each other's data.[5]

Hospitality businesses worldwide use **electronic data interchange (EDI)** to transfer business data such as purchase orders and requests from a hotel to a supplier. Hotels use EDI to execute orders for various departments within the business. "EDI eliminates delays and increases accuracy by providing electronic transmission of data between the guest's computer and the supplier's computer."[6] These highly advanced EDI systems enable hospitality businesses to reduce costs and work more efficiently.

Some hotel companies, like Choice International, have tried to develop their own high-speed Internet provider but realized that such a project presents too many challenges so they have opted to go with a company specializing in providing high-speed connections. Considering that Choice has more than 3,300

---

[4]Wayport, Inc., *Wayport High-Speed Internet Solutions for Hotels.* Austin, TX: Author, 2001, handout.

[5]Alter, *Information Systems,* p. 102.

[6]Ibid, p. 184.

hotels (Comfort Inn, Comfort Suites, Clarion, Quality, Econo Lodge, Sleep Inn, Roadway Inn, and Mainstay Suites franchises), it is remarkable that they were able to find an application service provider called Viator who could provide access to all franchisees.

Daniel Rothfield, Choice's senior VP of partner services, says that Viator provides hardware and software from leaders in the technology industry; customized, turnkey programs to fit each property's specific needs. Viator has a proven track record of installations, plug-and-play usage, and purchase or leasing options including use of existing wiring and connectivity when possible. Systems can be financed at a minimal charge to guests or at no charge to guests for those franchisees that absorb the nominal costs.[7]

Hotel Information Technology Systems

Information technology has helped hotels reach one of the main goals of a hotel: to deliver exceptional guest satisfaction. Some hotels have utilized technology for many years. The first hotel to use a computer was the New York Hilton in 1963. This was the first computer-automated guest room management system, but it was very inefficient because front desk clerks had to use key punch cards to record information and then process these cards in a batch at a later time.[8] Fortunately, hospitality information technology has progressed and today several efficient systems are fast becoming industry standards.

Property Management Systems

The **property management system (PMS)** is the hub of information processing in a hotel.[9] A property management system is a computer-based lodging information system that relates to both the front office and back office activities. Property management systems are used to help complete many tasks within a short period of time. Hotels with a large number of guests and employees to serve and inform predominantly use these systems. A PMS will aid a property to become more efficient with time, which is an important factor for guests who demand personal attention and fast service.

The property management system can interface with many other modules or applications. One application of the PMS in the front office is the room management module. A **room management module** tracks the status of rooms, which can assist the housekeeping department with their duties.[10] "The hotel

---

[7]Nickerson, *Business Information Systems*, p. 4.

[8]P. J. Sheldon, *Tourism Information Technology.* New York: CAB International, 1997, pp. 110, 114, 118.

[9]Ibid., p. 114

[10]Ibid., p. 118

*A Popular Property
Management System
(Courtesy of MICROS
Systems, Inc.)*

room master in the PMS contains data on each room such as room number, room type, room features, room rates, locations and the status of each room." Knowing the status of each room definitely helps the housekeeping department know what work has to be done, what work is in progress, and what work has been completed.

Another front office module is a **guest accounting module.** "A guest accounting module increases the hotel's control over guest accounts and significantly modifies the night audit routine."[11] Other functions of a PMS are electronic locking systems, energy management systems, and call accounting systems.

There are many potential users of a PMS. Any manager making strategic decisions could utilize the information provided by a PMS. Some property management systems even offer microcomputer interfaces so that the information from the PMS can be downloaded onto a personal computer to be utilized by a number of business applications.

Companies such as INNfinity Hospitality Systems and Palm Hospitality Technologies Inc. have joined to create property management systems that help hotels to modernize with very little cost.[12] This new PMS-WOM (wireless operations management) system provides hotels with a Windows-based PMS from INNfinity, the JiHi (Just in-time Housekeeping Integrated) solution from Palm Hospitality Technologies for wireless housekeeping, minibar and[13]

---

[11]M. Kasavana and J. Cahill, *Managing Computers in the Hospitality Industry*, Lansing, MI: Educational Institute of the American Hotel and Motel Association, 1992, pp. 12, 13, 115–117.

[12]INNfinity Hospitality Systems and Palm Hospitality Technologies, Inc. Marketing Departments, *The World's First Fully-Integrated PMS and Wireless Operations Management System.* Quebec, Canada: Author, 2000, handout.

[13]Ibid.

maintenance/guest requests, and high-speed T1 Internet access for a complete in-hotel wireless network for all meeting/guest rooms and common areas.

An example of how technology is assisting hospitality operators is given by the Washington Duke Inn & Golf Club in Durham, North Carolina, which has revamped its audit process, eliminating the night audit and moving to an audit every five days. Using Hospitality Technology Solutions' automated hotel audit, they have gone from two night auditors seven days a week plus an hour of day audit to one person who performs the entire process, including management reports, in approximately fifteen hours a week.[14]

Another example is the four star Château Cartier Relais Resort, Ontario, Canada, which is a convention resort property that uses the Northwind Maestro PMS system. They found that it has helped streamline the sales and catering bookings, and they have used its yield management feature to better manage inventory and maximize revenue for year-round packages. The system also creates detailed guest history reports. The sales and catering staff have been able to increase the amount of bookings by 15 percent by switching to a single computerized system from a more paper-oriented system. The ADR is up 7 percent this year due to new yield management practices.[15]

Some hotels use an express check-in process that allows guests to conveniently check in and check out via a touch screen that interfaces with the hotel's property management system without associate assistance. A booth in the lobby allows guests to input their reservation details or provide data from an inserted card or touch-screen selections. Based on the information given, a series of tasks is then completed and after obtaining an electronic signature, an electronic room key is then encoded and dispensed. A printout of guest stay information including room type, rate, and departure date is printed. Guests may also use the booth to check out.[16]

NCR and others also offer a self-service check-in system. A kiosk utilizes a colorful graphical interface and intuitive touch-screen technology to guide the guest through the check-in process. It is ideal for full-service properties, where large groups may be checking in simultaneously, and for extended-stay properties that have limited after-hours personnel. Not only does this kind of technology save time for guests, it can also save properties money.[17]

Perhaps the ultimate in guest convenience is the wireless curbside guest check-in made possible by the Ving Card system. This recent technological advance allows guests to go right to their rooms from curbside. The system is capable of interfacing with existing PMS systems to fully integrate property management, reservations, and guest service functions. With a portable keycard encoder and MICROS's OPERA Palm, a wireless handheld device

[14]"Washington Duke Inn Revamps Its Audit Process for Better Efficiency," *Hotel Business,* March 29, 2002, http://www.hotelbusiness.com/links/archive_view.asp?id=1468.

[15]http://www.hotelbusiness.com/links/archive_view.asp?ID=14159.

[16]MICROS home page, http://www.micros.com.

[17]Personal correspondence with Rebecca Brien, May 15, 2002.

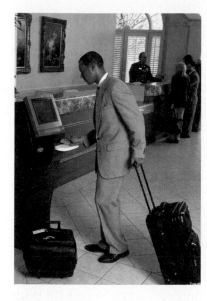

VingCard VISION Is a Full-Featured, Functionally Rich Access Control System (Courtesy of VingCard Elsafe, Inc.)

with real-time database access, the system works seamlessly to provide the ultimate guest convenience.[18]

Some property management systems use Microsoft Windows to move data between applications and to share information—a process called *information sharing.* Information sharing permits menu-driven interface with other systems such as advanced reservations, room inventory, self-check-in/out, night audit, guest accounting, city ledger, group handling, travel agency accounting.[19] All of these systems are designed to improve guest service. But beware: Management needs to ensure that the front desk associate doesn't just look down while keying in the guest name and other details without ever really looking up at the customer. Yes, the hotels that will be successful in the next few years are the ones that go out of their way to make guests really feel welcome and give a high-tech, yet high-touch service.

Energy Management Systems

Technology is used to extend guest in-room comfort by means of an energy management system. Passive infrared motion sensors and door switches can reduce energy consumption by 30 percent or more by automatically switching off lights and air conditioning, thus saving energy when the guest is out of the room. Additional features include:

- ✔ Room occupancy status reporting
- ✔ Automatic lighting control
- ✔ Minibar access reporting

[18]VingCard press kit, May 2002.

[19]http://www.globalaz.com/prod.02.htm#Fund%200for%20Yourself.

✔ Smoke detector alarm reporting
✔ Central electronic lock control
✔ Guest control amenities

Due to increasing energy costs, some operators are installing software programs that will turn off nonessential equipment during the peak billing times of day (utility company's charges are based on peak usage). Hospitality operators can save money by utilizing this type of energy saving software to reduce their energy costs.

Call Accounting Systems

Call accounting systems (CAS) track guest room phone charges. Software packages can be used to monitor where calls are being made and from what phones on the property. To track this information, the CAS must work in conjunction with the PBX (telephone) and the PMS. Call accounting systems today can be used to offer different rates for local guest calls and long-distance guest calls. The CAS can even be used to offer discounted calling during off-peak hours at the hotel.

Guest Reservation Systems

Before hotels started using electronic means to book reservations, they used to receive reservations by letters, telegrams, faxes, and phone calls.[20] Airlines were the first industry to start using global distribution systems (GDS) for reservations[21] (Figure 20–2). Global distribution systems are electronic markets for specific travel and tourism components. Initially, hotels offered reservations through airline GDSs, but the rigid structure of the older (legacy) GDS databases soon became obsolete for the hotel industry. Hotels could only publish a few rates for each type of room they offered. When a travel agent would search for rooms, some hotels would automatically be eliminated from the search because they couldn't publish all of their rates.

Eventually, hotels and brand chains began receiving reservations in central offices called **central reservation offices (CRO).** These offices could handle several properties' reservations. Later, hotels developed **central reservation systems (CRS)** that could handle a lot more information than the older global distribution systems and they could be integrated with a property management system. Two types of central reservation systems are in use: affiliate and nonaffiliate systems. Affiliate systems are central reservation systems in which all participating properties are contractually related.[22] A nonaffiliate reservation system refers to a subscription system that links independent properties. A

[20]P. O'Connor, *Electronic Information Distribution in Tourism and Hospitality.* Cergy Pontoise, France: CABI Publishing, 1999, pp. 14, 15, 27, 28.

[21]Tesa, *New Technologies.* May 14, 2002, http://www.tesalocks.com/hotel/fh3.htm.

[22]Kasavana and Cahill, *Managing Computers.*

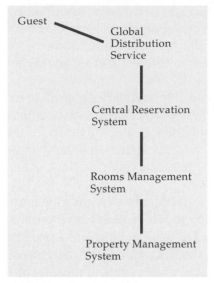

Figure 20-2 *Sequence and Relationships of a Hotel Guest Reservation*

hotel subscribes to the system's services and takes responsibility for updating the system with accurate room availability data. Nonaffiliate systems generally provide the same services as affiliate systems, thus enabling independent hotel operators to gain benefits otherwise available only to chain operators.

A central reservation system houses the electronic database in the central reservation office. Hotels provide room rates and availability information to the CRO usually by data communication lines. This automatically updates the CRS so that guests get the most up-to-date information when they book through the central reservation office.[23] Guests instantly receive confirmation of their reservation or cancellation.

The hotel benefits from using a central reservation system. With such a system, hotels can avoid overselling rooms by too large a margin. The CRS database can also be used as a chain or individual property-marketing tool because guest information can easily be stored. A CRS can also provide yield management information for a hotel. The more flexible a central reservation system is, the more it will help with yield management. For example, when demand is weak for a hotel, rates will need to drop to increase reservations and profitability. When demand is higher, the hotel can sell room rates that are closer to the rack rate.

A CRS can be used in several areas of a hotel. If a hotel has a reservations department, the terminals or personal computers in that department can be connected to the central reservation system. It would also be important for front desk employees to have access to the CRS. The reason for this is because they will need to know what the hotel has available because they may need to

---

[23]Caterease, *Catering & Event Management Software.* Naples, FL: Author, 2001, handout.

book rooms for walk-ins who don't have reservations. Constant communication back and forth is needed between the central reservation system and the front office and reservations department. Certain managers who are the decision makers in the hotel will also use the system to forecast and set pricing for rooms and different amenities.

When choosing a central reservation system, several factors need to be assessed. First, it would be essential to determine whether the property will be part of an affiliate system or nonaffiliate system. The size and the design of the database is a crucial decision. Hotels should choose a system that can handle the amount of data they want to keep track of, and it should have the capability to be modified in the future.

Hotels can use other forms of technology to facilitate reservation systems. Several companies offer an **application service provider (ASP)** environment that can deliver a complete booking system tied to the hotel's inventory in real time via the Web. One operator, Paul Wood of the El Dorado Hotel in Santa Fe, New Mexico, says that he simply went to the ASP's Web site and put in a promotional corporate rate for the summer, and the same day, he started seeing reservations coming in with that code. After a few months, bookings were up 3 percent over the previous year.

Reservations are still being made over global distribution systems and through other channels via the Internet. About 15 percent to 20 percent of all bookings are made via third-party Internet channels, including GDS players and consumer e-commerce sites such as Travelocity and Priceline. Another 5 percent come in over the hotel's own Web site.[24] Reservation systems that utilize the Web are usually referred to as **web reservation systems (WRS).**

Cendant, which owns AmeriHost Inn, Days Inn, Howard Johnson, Knights Inn, Ramada, Super 8, Travelodge, Villager, and the Wingate Inn chains, is investing $40 million in Trip.com, its travel–hotel–rental car Web site, to raise awareness of its site and make it more appealing to leisure travelers. Previously it was aimed at business travelers, but since September 11, 2001, with business travel considerably down, the shift in focus became necessary.[25] Many hotel companies are now finding that about 5 percent of their chain-wide bookings are via the Internet. Even more promising is that each room being sold costs the hotel less than it would through conventional call-center bookings. Marriott, for example, can process an online booking through its Web site for about $3.50 versus $5.00 for a telephone transaction.[26]

Billing Guests

Hospitality businesses today seek to obtain the most high-speed and reliable computer systems they can afford that allow them to bill their guests without

---

[24]http://www.htmagazine.com/archive/Nov2001/Nov2001_5.html.

[25]CNN, April 29, 2002.

[26]http://www.htmagazine.com/archive/Nov2001/Nov2001_5html.

delay. Fast access to guests' accounts is required by large hotels due to their high priority for guest satisfaction (no lineups at checkout).

Billing guests has become much easier with the aid of computers. Billing guests can be a long process if information technologies are not used to complete transactions. Property management systems aid large hotels to make faster transactions and provide a more efficient service to their guests. These systems help the hospitality associates bill their guests within seconds.

Some hotels utilize software that enables guests to check and approve their bills by using the TV and remote, thus avoiding the need to line up at the cashier's desk to check out. A copy of their bill is then mailed to their home address.

Security

Each and every business in the hospitality industry offers some sort of security for their guests and employees. Peace of mind that the hotel or restaurant is secure is a key factor in increasing guest satisfaction. Security is one of the highest concerns of guests who visit hospitality businesses. Hospitality information technology systems include surveillance systems in which cameras are installed in many different areas of the property to monitor the grounds and help ensure guest safety. These cameras are linked directly to computers, televisions, and digital recorders, which helps security teams keep an eye on the whole property.

Recent technological advances have produced electronic door locking systems, some of which even offer custom configurations of security and safety. Guest room locks are now capable of managing information from both magstripe and smart cards simultaneously. From the hotel's point of view, one of the main advantages of this kind of key is that the hotel knows who has entered the room and at what time because the system can trace anyone entering the room.

In-room safes can now be operated by key cards. Both systems are an improvement on the old metal keys. Even smarter safes use biometric technology that includes the use of thumbprints or retina scans to verify a user's identity.

Guest Comfort and Convenience

Hotels provide guest comfort and convenience in order to maintain a home-away-from-home feeling for their guests. Hotels will receive recognition

> ### The Venetian Goes High Tech
>
> The Venetian Resort–Hotel–Casino in Las Vegas has put the Res.Net system on its in-house servers, according to Chris Stacy, Internet marketing manager at the 3,036-room (and growing) Venetian. After a recent customization, the system is taking in about 7 percent of all reservations. Best of all, payment to the software vendor is about half the rate paid to a GDS.
>
> Visitors input an arrival date and the system returns a room image and a room rate, plus an up-sell message suggesting a room upgrade. Surprisingly, about 80 percent of visitors select the up-sell. Now, the Venetian is building its online capacity to handle the increased complexities of booking inclusive packages and meetings, which is 40 percent of the hotel's business.[27]

Electronic Lock (Courtesy of VingCard Elsafe, Inc.)

[27]Ibid.

because they provide many additional in-room services and amenities for their guests, such as dining, television, telephones, Internet connections, minibars, and hygiene products. These amenities help provide a cozy experience for the guest. Many other services can be provided outside of the rooms such as swimming pools, massages, fine dining, postal services, and meeting space. Other services are provided to suit the demands of all types of guests, a concierge and business center, for example.

Hotels communicate with many entities to provide services for their guest. Some companies offer creative solutions to hotels for enhanced in-room services for guests. Sprint InSite with KoolConnect Interactive Media has created a product that provides many services to the guest from just one supplier. Services include Internet access and e-mail, movies on demand, music on demand, games on demand, hotel and concierge services, special promotions, advertising, travel planning, feedback from guests, and customer support. All of these services aid hotels in fulfilling guest demands. Sprint states, "Build loyalty and promote business retention by enhancing the overall quality-of-visit for your guest."[28] Play Stations and video games are also a part of the technology-based guest amenities.

Sales and Marketing

One of the main ways to implement technology for sales and marketing is through databases. A database is a piece of software that instills a formal structure on data organized for users. Using a **database management system (DBMS),** a database can be accessed and queried to search for records with certain qualities. In the case of sales and marketing, a database of customers could be gathered to determine which customers should be contacted for promotions or which customers have already been contacted.

One company that specializes in such products is Pegasus Business Intelligence. "Pegasus Business Intelligence provides answers to marketing questions through data warehousing, industry wide statistics and marketing consulting services."[29] Another popular topic in sales and marketing is **customer relationship management (CRM).** CRM provides a way to keep track of guest preferences and to find new and repeat guests that are your target market. CRM can involve a stand-alone system or a system that is integrated with your PMS.[30]

E-mail and voice mail can be an effective marketing tool. For example, frequent users may receive e-mails about upcoming events and special offers.

[28]Sprint InSite with KoolConnect Interactive Media, Overland Park, KS, 2001, handout.

[29]http://hospitalityupgrade.com/, May 14, 2002.

[30]John Schweisberger and Amitava Chatterjee, "Small Hotels and CRM," http://www.hospitalityupgrade.com, May 15, 2002.

Once a company has guest e-mail addresses they can send information that may be helpful to the guests.

The Internet is also used in the marketing of a property or restaurant by allowing prospective guests to go on a virtual tour of the property or check out the restaurant's menu.

Catering

Hospitality businesses provide various services for all types of guests, one being catering and event management, in which large groups of people arrive on a certain date and need catering services for their meetings and conventions. **Information systems (IS)** and technology have advanced this ability to large hotels seeking to enhance their catering management as a way to increase revenue. Catering has become much easier and efficient with the aid of computer systems and Internet-based software.

Software companies have realized the importance of the market for catering and event management to both small and large businesses. Caterease catering and event management software has created a program that allows hotel managers to reserve meeting space and rooms for their future guests. Caterease is one of the largest software providers to the leading hotel brands worldwide. The guest rooms manager module helps hotels, motels, and inns keep track of all of their sleeping accommodations, blocks guest space, links reservations to event contracts, and runs detailed reports.[31]

Delphi is another leading hospitality industry software provider for automating the sales, marketing, and catering processes of large properties. The Delphi program has long been popular with industry professionals who use it for a variety of applications, from scheduling and priority setting to function diary and banquet event orders. **Computer information systems (CISs)** allow software companies, such as Caterease and Delphi, to create highly advanced systems to make hospitality businesses more efficient.

Check Your Knowledge

1. Name the nine different areas of hotel information technology systems.
2. What is the primary use for a PMS? What are the other uses?
3. How does technology influence catering? Name a software program that can be applied to catering.

[31]Caterease, *Catering & Event Management Software.*

Restaurant and Foodservice Information Technology Systems

The foodservice industry has benefited from the use of information technology. Proper implementation of information systems aids large and small restaurants and foodservice businesses in providing more efficient services to their guests and more control to prevent losses.

As a listing of the Top 100 independent restaurants illustrates,[32] technology does make a difference. It lets operators drive down costs, helps them serve guests with more panache, and gives them additional time to put toward the care and feeding of customers. Guest satisfaction is a high priority, if not the highest, in the food service world. Guests with all sorts of demands can be satisfied by a restaurant that provides efficient and effective service. Businesses, in order to achieve higher revenues and therefore a successful future, must constantly seek out new ideas to increase the efficiency of their systems and achieve guest satisfaction.

In the restaurant and foodservice industry IT is divided into **front- and back-of-the-house operations.** The front-of-the-house system includes the point-of-sale system, kitchen display systems, and guest services solutions. The back of the house systems are also called product management and include inventory, food costing, labor management, and financial reporting.

Front-of-the-House Restaurant Systems

Point-of-Sale Systems

Point-of-sale (POS) systems are very common in restaurants and other foodservice settings such as a stadium, theme park, airport, or cruise ship. These systems are also used by hotel properties that have food and beverage and retail outlets. They are used to track food and beverage charges and other retail charges that may occur at a hotel or restaurant. A point-of-sale system is made up of a number of POS terminals that interface with a remote central processing unit. These terminals may also have their own microprocessors so that processing can be done at the terminal, and all the terminals are networked.[33] This enables a property to operate without a central processing unit. POS systems built in this fashion are called microbased POS systems.[34] A POS terminal may be used as an electronic cash register too. The POS system is usually interfaced with a property management system at a hotel to record guest transactions dur-

---

[32]Margaret Sheridan and Janice Matsumoto, "R&I Special Report, 2000 Top 100," http://www.rigmag.com/007/sr.htm, April 1, 2000.

[33]Kasavana and Cahill, *Managing Computers.*

[34]Ibid.

Point-of-Sale System
(Courtesy of MICROS
Systems, Inc.)

ing their stay at the hotel. Terminals can be placed anywhere in the hotel or restaurant where transactions are taking place. For example, a hotel may have POS terminals at the front desk, at food and beverage outlets, and at any retail outlet in the hotel. A restaurant may have terminals at server stations or at the host station. Many POS systems in use today have graphical user interfaces and touch-screen terminals and run off of a variety of operating systems.

POS systems have many uses and users. In the hotel, front desk managers and employees are some of the most frequent users of a POS system because they have the most contact with guests and guest transactions. They very often have the authority to remove additional room charges or charge the guest for additional services as appropriate. Other users of this system could be room service managers and employees. In a restaurant, both the managers and the wait staff could use the POS to keep track of sales and guest checks.

MICROS, a leading software, hardware, and enterprise systems provider, offers Restaurant 3000, a modular suite of applications that encompasses front-of-the-house, back-of-the-house, and enterprise systems. The popular 3700 POS is a Windows-based touch-screen system where client terminals are networked to a central POS server. Transactions are rung at the terminal and posted into the database for later analysis and reporting. The 3700 POS will support a network of kitchen printers so that orders can be presented to line cooks and chefs for food preparation.

This POS system also supports use of a wireless personal digital assistant as an order-taking device so that servers can take orders directly from the guest tableside. Mobile handheld devices can greatly speed the processing of orders to the kitchen and ultimately increase revenues due to faster table turns.

Various hardware and software POS solutions are available. Among the computer-based programs used is e-Revelation from InfoGenesis. It is a computer-based POS system that claims to reduce costs and increase efficiency for the hospitality world. "Whether you manage a single restaurant, a chain

Corporate Profile: MICROS Systems

MICROS Systems, Inc., is one of the global leaders in hospitality technology, specializing in producing and selling a variety of hospitality management systems and POS systems.[1] The POS systems help restaurants, hotels, resorts, casinos, stadiums, airports, and the entertainment industry to manage product costs, customer price sensitivity, and employees and to maintain margins.[2] Their mission is to develop products for the hospitality industry that will help the industry increase efficiency, reduce operating costs, and raise the level of service for customers.

Founded in 1977, Micros has served the industry for more than twenty years.[3] Combined with its international subsidiary, Micros Fidelio, the company has offices all around the world, including Asia Pacific, Europe, Africa, Middle East, and Latin America, with corporate headquarters in Columbia, Maryland. The companies have installed more than 120, 000 systems for the hospitality industry in 130 countries.

(Courtesy of MICROS Systems, Inc.)

For the lodging sector of the hospitality industry, Micros offers a centralized reservation system and customer information systems. Their table service restaurant customers have a variety of technological products from which to choose that help make running their businesses easier and faster with fewer errors. Four different categories of software products are offered: POS systems, enterprise office systems, restaurant operations systems, and corporate applications.

The newest technology they offer is the 9700 Hospitality Management System (HMS). This POS system combines front end and back office restaurant service to cut down time, especially in large businesses. The 9700 HMS can run reports and automate system utilities while simultaneously being used by personnel. The system runs on of restaurants, or a combination of fine dining, hotel room service, lounge and gift shop operations, e-Revelation is based on the point-of-sale solution used by the hospitality industry throughout the world."[35]

The new 1,000-room Westin Diplomat Resort & Spa has installed the e-Revelation POS. The POS terminals manage the F&B transactions, and handheld terminals offer more convenience to guests. The Diplomat felt this POS system best fit its needs. Steve Hicks, director of information technology, said that it's all about how the system can help improve the guest experience.[36]

When buying a POS system, several factors need to be considered to ensure you choose and implement the best system. According to Kasavana and Cahill, the size and type of operation play an important role in choosing a proper system.[37] Fewer terminals are needed in a limited service property than in a larg-

---

[35]InfoGenesis, *e-Revelation, The Power of ASP-Based POS.* Santa Barbara, CA: Author, 2000, handout.

[36]http://www.hotelbusiness.com/links/archive_view.asp?ID=14461.

[37]Kasavana and Cahill, *Managing Computers.*

the Microsoft Windows NT application and employs structured query language (SQL), an industry-standard method for accessing database information, so data can be stored with most available software packages.

Another feature for restaurants is product management software, which allows operators to customize their application screens to fit their requirements. They can tailor file content or form names and change screen layouts.

The flexible Inventory Management system:

- ✔ Supports multiple costing methods
- ✔ Supports units and counting locations
- ✔ Maintains perpetual inventory balances
- ✔ Supports scheduled count tasks for end-of-period inventories and unlimited ad hoc inventories
- ✔ Allows detailed recipe management of up to four recipes and cost assignments per POS menu item
- ✔ Supports batch recipes and subrecipes
- ✔ Allows real-time depletion of inventory based on sales items

MICROS has developed a software program called Labor Management that allows hospitality businesses to maintain human resources files, support payroll processing, and generate staff schedules for multilevel operations. Labor Management

- ✔ Allows edits to POS time cards with an audit trail
- ✔ Supports vacation, sick, and other earnings or benefits information
- ✔ Generates reports on scheduled versus actual labor costs and can be integrated with MICROS

3700 POS systems' time and attendance information

- ✔ Manages centralized employee information including personal data, I-9 documentation, and tax filing data for federal, state, and local agencies
- ✔ Facilitates employee reviews and evaluations and maintains schedule availability and requests
- ✔ Reviews scheduling costs for regular and overtime hours
- ✔ Calculates labor costs by location, job, or category
- ✔ Enforces minimum-wage rates, tip credits, and overtime regulations

MICROS Systems, Inc., has become a profitable industry leader in hospitality technology. The company's approach to global business opportunities has definitely contributed to its expansion. Today, MICROS offers its products in multiple languages and translates the price of its products into multiple currencies. Globalizing the enterprise and continuing to produce superior technological products has translated into continued success and $325.4 million in revenue in 2001.[4]

---

[1]MICROS home page, http://www.micros.com.
[2]*4th Annual Restaurant Industry Technology Study: Creating Business Value through Collaborative Technology.* Hospitality Technology and CSC, 2002, pp. 16–17.
[3]MICROS home page.
[4]MICROS press kit, May 2002.

er hotel or resort, where terminals may be needed in many different locations. Security of the POS is another concern. If guests are able to charge many services and items to their rooms, it is necessary to ensure the guest's identity is valid and authorizes them to bill to their room. Sometimes systems will require a user to enter a reference code or a guest's last name to make sure that the room and name match. There could be two accounts under one room number. In addition, some systems require guests to provide a room key card on which is encoded material about the guest's portfolio. The guest may still have to provide a room number and name along with the card. The card can then be swiped to complete the transaction.

Choosing a POS

One of the most crucial IT decisions is choosing the right POS system. Each hardware/software package has its own unique characteristics and, despite claims to the contrary, there is no such thing as one size fits all, nor, unfortunately, is there a single template or criteria list to peruse when selecting a POS

Wireless POS System

Peter Perdikakis is the owner of two Skyline fast-casual restaurants in Cincinnati. The restaurants are unusual in that the kitchen is open and visible to diners. Servers used to simply yell the orders across the steam table. Peter says, "You eat off china and have silverware, but it's very fast—typically you get your order about two minutes after it's ordered. Other POS systems slowed this process down, because the servers had to go over to a terminal and write down the order," which is why Peter became interested in wireless. When he wanted to expand his operations he selected a Pocket POS system from PixelPoint, consisting of two primary fixed terminals (one at a drive-through window and one at the check-out station), three handheld units for use on the dining floor, and another fixed unit for the back office.

The PixelPoint wireless POS system allows the servers to use a handheld PDA, which operates on the Windows CE platform, to send orders to the kitchen. Given that wireless POS systems speed up orders, their use in restaurants is likely to be on the increase.

system.[38] Some universal criteria do, however, apply to POS system selection. This decision should not be rushed.

Start by identifying your unique needs so that you can determine which available systems can accommodate them. Mike Gaston, MIS director for the Copper Cellar Corporation, which operates twelve restaurants based in Knoxville, Tennessee, came up with this list of requirements for his company's new Squirrel for Windows NT POS system[39]:

✔ Easy for wait staff to learn
✔ Easy for managers to learn and use so data can be collected smoothly, distributed properly, and applied chain-wide even by wait staff without computer literacy
✔ Compatible with the custom-developed financial application in the main office
✔ Uses Microsoft Windows NT operating system and SQL server database architecture
✔ Scalable over time as Copper Cellar Company and its units grow

Other considerations include system performance and speed. For example, can the system provide real-time data to the home office of a large chain restaurant operation? Chevy's Fresh Mex, a 166-unit chain, selected its POS system largely because of its enterprise capabilities. The system allows the director of restaurant support to analyze remotely the entire chain in real time—something very useful when restaurants are in different time zones.

[38]http://www.htmagazine.com/archive/Oct2001/Oct2001_2.html.
[39]Ibid.

Kitchen Display Systems

Kitchen display systems further enhance the processing of orders to and in the kitchen. Printers in the kitchen are replaced with video monitors and present orders to kitchen associates along with information on how long orders are taking to be prepared. Orders change color or flash on the monitor, which alerts kitchen associates to orders that are taking too long. Kitchen monitors are widely used in quick-service restaurants, but are also gaining momentum in table service restaurants. Kitchen video systems also post order preparation times to a central data base for later reporting and analysis by management to determine how the kitchen is performing.

Guest Services Solutions

Guest services solutions are applications that are designed to help a restaurateur develop a dining relationship with guests. Applications include a frequent diner management program, delivery management with caller ID interface, and guest accounts receivable to manage home accounts and gift certificate management. All of these applications are accessed through the POS system and give restaurateurs the opportunity to offer their guests convenience, while allowing the restaurateurs to track who their best customers are. Guest activity is posted into the central database and management can develop targeted marketing programs based on this information.

Check Your Knowledge

1. What do front-of-the-house systems entail?
2. What criteria need to be considered when choosing a POS system?
3. Briefly define guest services solutions.

Back-of-the-House Restaurant Systems

For restaurant operators, selecting a back-of-the-house application is a complex decision. There is no cookie-cutter model for creating criteria because there are too many variables. Nationally owned chains' and franchisers' requirements differ from those of a neighborhood restaurant. Back office applications that control costs, manage inventories, and optimize labor are instrumental tools that allow operators to pull data from the POS application to generate reports for analysis.[40] Back-of-the-house systems are also known as product manage-

[40]Nickerson, *Business Information Systems,* p. 4.

ment systems and include inventory control and food costing, labor management, and financial reporting features.

Inventory Control and Food Costing

Product management applications provide restaurateurs with the ability to track all aspects of their inventory. Food cost menu items sold through the POS system are linked to recipes, which are made up of inventory items. Each time an item is sold, the appropriate inventory items are automatically depleted through the software application. For example, when a hamburger is sold, the inventory is depleted by one hamburger patty, one bun, one slice of tomato, one ounce of lettuce, and one ounce of onion. The system can automatically determine when inventory levels are low and it is time to place an order. Restaurateurs can set par levels for stock based on forecasted business to allow the system to generate the proper reorder quantities.

Restaurant managers periodically take a physical inventory count and enter that into the system to determine if there are any variances. Variances occur due to spoilage, waste, improper recipes, or theft. Inventory variance reports are critical to analyzing the profitability of a restaurant. When new items are received into inventory, they are entered into the system and, along with information about the cost of those items, the systems allow restaurants to then determine the food cost of their menu items.

In the restaurant and food service industry, inventory control must be accurate and monitored in a timely fashion. Inventory must be carefully managed due to the various types of foods restaurants handle. Perishable and nonperishable foods must be properly handled in order to provide fresh dishes on the menu. Information systems provide inventory control software to help foodservice associates manage their supply. Computer-based software determines reorder points to help eliminate low inventory levels, which can lead to inadequate service for restaurant guests. Companies **purchasing stock and materials** must determine proper stock levels, accurate ordering points, and approved vendor lists. This is all a part of the reorder process and can be handled by any number of available ISs.

Managers' tasks in the foodservice industry are continually changing due to advances in technology. "In the back of the house, laser bar-code scanning technology is accelerating the often-grueling inventory process. 'For foodservice packaging with its irregular surfaces, laser scanners are the way to go,' says Pierce Johnson, president of a technology company based in Oak Park, Illinois. Laser scanners are not affected by frost and result in fewer misreads than contact scanners, according to Johnson. This efficiency is noticed at Hyatt Regency Kauai where laser scanners have cut the quarterly inventory time nearly in half during the past year, according to Al Garces, director of purchasing."[41]

[41]Katie Parter, "Operations, Happy Scanning," http://www.rimag.com/015/Ops.htm, August 1, 2000.

Personal Profile: Ed Rothenberg

Working in, studying, and excelling in the hospitality industry can open up a wide variety of career choices and opportunities for a student. I started in the hospitality industry at age sixteen. Today, I have been at MICROS Systems, Inc., for more than nine years. I am the vice president of restaurant product development, reporting directly to the CEO and responsible for a fifty-five-person development group charged with creating software and hardware products for the hospitality industry. Reflecting on the path I took to get here, I consider myself fortunate to be able to combine two exciting interests in my life, technology and hospitality. So far they have come together to become a very successful and rewarding career.

My introduction to the hospitality industry was in high school; I found a challenging and interesting job working for a local farm that specializes in catering picnic-style events for large gatherings. Smokey Glen Farm is family owned and operated, and hosts events such as company picnics, weddings, business meetings, and family reunions for up to 7,000 guests at a time on their ninety-eight-acre farm in Gaithersburg, Maryland. It was at Smokey Glen that I learned to appreciate the business of entertaining people. Some key principles I learned early on from that job stayed with me well beyond my time at Smokey Glen: *Hustle, work hard, take care of your customers, exceed their expectations, work as a team, and take personal responsibility for ensuring success.* I knew these were the basic concepts of the hospitality industry, but as I later found out, they also applied to every job I've had, even outside the industry. I worked for Smokey Glen Farm through college and during that time I moved into a management position; in that position I gained insight into the management requirements needed to lead a large and successful hospitality operation. As I attended college, I continued to work in various jobs in the restaurant industry.

I graduated from the University of Maryland with a bachelor's degree in government and politics and decided to continue to work in the hospitality industry. At that time I felt that the hospitality industry would keep me interested for the rest of my life; I even planned on opening my own restaurant. As a hobby I became interested

(Courtesy of Ed Rothenberg)

in computers, particularly software, and began to experiment with some software development efforts that helped to run a restaurant. My interest in software development grew to the point where I decided to go back to school, and in 1993 graduated from the University of Maryland with another bachelor's degree in computer science. I wanted to find a way to combine my interest in technology and hospitality into a career. One day, I noticed a classified ad in the *Washington Post* looking for a "restaurant manager that knows the UNIX operating system." This led me to MICROS Systems.

My career with MICROS began in the spring of 1993. MICROS was about to launch a new product called the 8700 Hospitality Management System, a UNIX-based point-of-sale system targeting restaurants, hotels, and casinos. I had found a way to combine my education and hospitality experience and I was very excited about the opportunity. My first position with MICROS was as a systems installer. I traveled the world installing the MICROS 8700 system in hotels, casinos, stadiums, theme parks, and airports. It was the best experience. I developed a deep understanding of exactly how MICROS customers use our technology to run their business. I had the opportunity to work with all levels of restaurant and management staff and gained a better understanding of how different technical solutions enable a restaurant to run more efficiently.

I worked as a system installer for MICROS Systems for about two years and then moved into a position as a sales engineer in our Major Account Sales Group. Our Major Account Sales Group is responsible for developing relationships with major restaurant chains and providing products to them. My role as a sales engineer was to provide technical support to the sales process, working with prospective customers to understand and meet any complex requirements that they might have. The experience I gained working with the Major Account Sales Group gave me insight into the sales process, as well as the customers' evaluation and decision-making processes used to select their technology solutions. I stayed in this position for about two years, before moving into MICROS Systems Product Development Group.

The MICROS product development culture relies heavily on employees with hospitality experience.

continued

MICROS's belief is that it is better to hire a person with hospitality experience and train them about technology than it is to hire someone with technical experience and get them to understand the requirements of the hospitality industry. More than 50 percent of the employees in our product development group have hospitality experience and participate in the design, development, test, and documentation of our products. We feel this is critical for us to create products and technology that are appropriate for the hospitality industry. The same is true for other areas of the company; our customer service, sales, installation, and support staff all have significant hospitality industry experience. With my technical background, experience in installing and selling our systems, and hospitality experience, the product development group was a perfect fit for my experience and interest.

In 2002, I graduated from an executive program at the University of Pennsylvania with a master's degree in technology management. This intense three-year program sponsored by Penn's Engineering School and the Wharton Business School provided an excellent education and perspective in various aspects of managing the business of technology, and also served to validate many of the experiences I had. My formal education has greatly improved my thinking in the area of product strategy, leadership, and management. Armed with this education, I am more effective leading and managing MICROS's product development efforts.

Everybody has seen the book by Robert Fulghum *All I Really Need to Know I Learned in Kindergarten.* Well, I think I can safely say that the most important things I need to know about business I learned from working in the hospitality industry. Everything I learned as a high school student working for a family-owned catering operation, I apply to my position as vice president of a large product development group for a multimillion-dollar international company. *Work hard, hustle, take care of the customer, exceed expectations, work as a team, and above all take personal responsibility for ensuring success.* I approached each successive position in life as an opportunity to learn something new about business, leadership, management, or some aspect of being successful. When I didn't feel I was learning enough, I went back to school to get exposed to new information and perspectives that aided in my growth. I benefited from several mentors along the way, both inside and outside of business, and I never turned down an opportunity to face a new challenge, take on additional responsibility, or learn something new. The hospitality industry has been a challenging and rewarding career for me. I look forward to working with restaurant operators for years to come, bringing them new technologies and products to make their restaurants run better.

Labor Management

Most front-of-the-house systems have the ability to track employee working time. A back-of-the-house labor management package adds the ability to manage all of a restaurant's payroll and human resource information. A labor management system includes a human resources module to track hiring, employee personal information, vacation, I-9 status, security privileges, tax status, availability, and any other information pertinent to employees working at the restaurant. A labor management system would also include scheduling capability so that managers can create weekly schedules based on forecasted business. Schedules would then be enforced when employees check in and out so that labor costs can be managed.

The labor management package also presents actual work time and pay rates to a payroll processor so that pay-checks can be cut and distributed. It also collates tips data and receipt data from the front of the house so that proper tip allocations can be reported according to IRS guidelines.

Financial Reporting

Back-of-the-house and front-of-the-house systems post data into a relational database located on the central server. The restaurant manager uses these data for reporting and decision making. Profit and loss reports, budget variances, end-of-day reports, and other financial reports are generated from the central database. Financial management reporting needs to be flexible so that restaurant operators can manipulate it in ways that are useful to them.

It is also important to get reports during the day in real time as the day unfolds, so that restaurateurs can make decisions before profit is lost. Some reporting packages provide a graphical representation of the financial data displayed continuously on a monitor so that critical restaurant data are always available. This type of reporting provides restaurants with a real-time "heartbeat" for their operations.

Both back-of-the-house and front-of-the-house systems must be reliably linked so that POS food costs, labor costs, service times, and guest activity can be analyzed on the same reports. Restaurant management can then make critical business decisions armed with all necessary information.

Personal Digital Assistants

Personal digital assistants (PDAs) help hospitality businesses stay effective and efficient by improving time management and helping with faster service. For example, computer systems are used today in restaurants to transmit orders to the kitchen and to retrieve and post guest payments. These actions took extra time in the past, when the computer systems were placed at a distance

Pocket PC Used in Restaurants (Courtesy MICROS Systems, Inc.)

Post 9–11: Digital Disasters

Hank Christen and Paul Maniscalco

The hospitality industry has witnessed the computerization of security, reservation, telecommunication, inventory management, financial, and energy management systems. Computer systems and the fiscal well-being of a contemporary hospitality organization have become inextricably linked. But what happens to the operation if the computer systems are disabled or destroyed by criminals or disgruntled workers?

> **Critical Factors:**
> ✔ Computers provide greater accountability, efficiency, and economy to hospitality operations worldwide.
> ✔ The hospitality industry is extremely computer dependent.
> ✔ Protection of the organization's electronic infrastructure is vital.

Let's take a look at the fundamental components of an efficient hospitality industry technology security program.

1. **Anti-virus software should be installed and kept up to date.** Anti-virus software programs are designed to protect computers against known viruses. Anti-virus programs should be updated frequently—the more frequently, the better.

2. **E-mail from unknown sources should not be opened.** A significant portion of hostile entries into computer systems are the result of e-mail from unknown senders being opened. The safest thing to do is to delete the entire e-mail and all attachments. Even if the e-mail sender is known, caution should be exercised with unusual messages; a colleague could unintentionally send a virus. The "I Love You" virus that spread to millions of people in 2001 is a great example.

3. **"Safe" passwords should be chosen and assigned.** Passwords are secure only if they are difficult to figure out and are not shared. The basic rules for passwords are: (1) Passwords should be a minimum of eight characters, be as random as possible, and use a combination of uppercase and lowercase letters and numbers (for example: CsO1n2Ie). (2) Passwords should be changed on a regular basis—at least every 90 days. (3) Access to your password should not be granted to anyone!

4. **The computer system should be protected from intruders by using firewalls.** Intruders can manipulate data, steal funds, and damage equipment. A firewall creates a protective barrier between a computer system and the outside world, preventing unauthorized persons from gaining access to a computer while it's connected to the Internet.

5. **Backdoor dial-in numbers should be changed regularly.** Many computer systems have dial-in access so members of the organization can update programs from remote locations. Frequent changing of this dial-in number helps decrease the chances of unauthorized access to the system.

6. **Users should disconnect from the Internet when not in use.** The Internet is a two-way street: a computer transmits *and receives* information. Disconnecting from the Internet when no longer needed diminishes the chance that an unintended person is able to access a computer remotely.

7. **Computer data should be backed up frequently.** Backup data should be stored at a different site. For networked systems, backup copies of data files should be kept on another computer or server in the network. Important data backups should be done weekly. For large server farms, IT personnel should consider the frequency with which they back up their files to ensure data protection.

8. **Security protection update patches should be downloaded when available** in order to prevent hackers from attacting a computer.

9. **Employees should know what to do if their computer becomes infected.** In small organizations, everyone should be familiar with how to update virus protection software and how to download security patches from vendors. In large organizations, the information technology department should provide regular security updates in order to gauge improvements needed.

> **Critical Factor:** Loss of computer access or control can result in significant financial losses and damage to assets.

from the server. PDAs have been created to allow servers to control their business with their fingertips.

InfoGenesis has partnered with Symbol Technologies to create a handheld POS terminal that offers high-speed transmissions to various departments. Many benefits are gained from using handheld or PDA devices. "Using a wireless handheld communication device, each server transmits orders directly from the table to the POS terminal. No time is wasted writing down orders and then having to re-enter them at a fixed computer terminal. When it comes time to pay, credit cards can be swiped and processed right at the table, increasing the customer's security and saving more time. Servers have an entire menu at their fingertips, alleviating the need for memorization and reducing training time."[42] These handheld computer systems allow restaurants to work efficiently with their guest and employees.

An anticipated advance in "tablet" technology is expected to send PDAs the way of pneumatic tubes, wooden racks, and light bulbs. The problem with PDAs is that they're clumsy and the screens are just too small. Scrolling horizontally and vertically is cumbersome. Tablets look like simple, small LCD screens, yet they contain high-powered computers. The tablet can be plugged into (seated on top of) folding keyboards, and takes advantage of touch-screen technology, handwriting recognition, wireless Internet and Bluetooth technology, and, of course, includes all the plug-in features of newer desktops.

One of the leading software providers to restaurant operators is Restaurant Technology, Inc. (RTI). RTI was founded by two restaurant owners who understand the accounting applications that operate from a central platform known as the Restaurant Financial System. Working together, their accounting programs form an integrated system, with these modules:

✔ Accounts payable
✔ Check reconciliation
✔ Daily store reporting
✔ General ledge
✔ Payroll
✔ Time keeping

PDAs can also be used in the hotel setting. Oftentimes, PDAs can be integrated with a PMS to give housekeepers real-time information about which rooms need to be cleaned and which rooms are not occupied. In the same way, as housekeepers complete the cleaning of a room, they can send a wireless signal to the front desk to affirm that the room is ready to be occupied.

[42]InfoGenesis, *Point of Sale for Hospitality and Foodservice, Benefits of Handheld Technology.* Santa Barbara, CA: May 18, 2002, handout.

Check Your Knowledge

1. Explain in what ways advances in technology aid the inventory process in restaurants.
2. What are back-of-the-house systems also known as?
3. What are the benefits of using a PDA?

Count Your Dimes and Pennies

State-of-the-art technology helps prevent theft, but digital cameras, electronic safes, and alarm systems are only part of the solution. As one operator, Pine Luongo, creator of concepts such as Coco Pazzo, Tuscan Square, and Le Madri, says, "If you want to earn $10,000, count dimes and pennies. It's that simple."[1] Food inventory is done daily by computer and weekly by human hands. Other systems Pine's restaurants use are surveillance cameras, especially at the multilevel operations such as Centolire in New York City. Cameras frame exits and entrances, professional kitchens, wine cellars, and storage areas. Several chain operations have remote digital video systems, which allow senior managers with compatible software to monitor the daily activities of business and employees at any unit in the network.

---

[1]Margaret Shendan, "Remote Control: Surveillance, Inventory Tracking Are Among Multiple Roles to Loss Prevention for Operators," *Restaurant & Institutions*, November 15, 2001, p. 63.

Trends in Hospitality Industry Technology

- ✔ Online travel purchasing is rising dramatically.
- ✔ Online restaurant reservation sites provide a place for independent restaurants to advertise and book reservations.
- ✔ Customer relationship management (CRM) is becoming a popular technology topic for large and small hospitality companies alike.
- ✔ Use of PDAs in the hospitality industry is likely to increase.

Case Study

John is the general manager of a resort hotel with 500 rooms. The hotel uses a POS system for its several restaurants and spa. However, none of the charges from the spa or restaurants can be posted to a guest's room bill. John wants to look at figures to see how much the average guest staying in his hotel spends in the spa and restaurants. In addition, guests often don't understand why they can't charge something from the spa to their room. To make matters worse, because there are several restaurants, the receiving department often gets confused as to which restaurant the food orders are going to. For the past week, one of the restaurants has run out of several hot menu items because one of the other restaurants received their food orders from the receiving department. When John goes to look at hotel revenues for the week, the database that houses all the guest transactions crashes.

Discussion Questions

1. What kind of systems should be installed on John's property to remedy this situation?
2. What considerations must John look at before installing this system?

Case Study

Lisa is a proprietor and owner of a popular restaurant in town. She would like to install a POS system to take care of guest bills and to simplify order taking for her wait staff and order receiving for her chefs.

Discussion Questions

1. If you were consulting Lisa, where would you tell her to look for a cost-effective system?
2. If you were in Lisa's position, what kind of POS system would you choose? What does this particular product offer over other possible systems?

Career Information

There are a variety of career opportunities in the technology sector of the hospitality industry. If you are interested in this side of the hospitality industry, it would be best to gain some additional education in the field of information systems. If you are technologically savvy, numerous jobs are available in web design, product development, implementation of systems, and so on. Many companies specialize in hospitality technology products and services and are looking for people who have a background in hospitality and technology. Job postings for technology positions can be found at http://www.hospitalityupgrade.com. Go to http://www.hospitalityupgrade.com, click on the "Jobs" icon to look at current job postings of numerous vendors. Technology jobs are also offered through corporate hotels. Hilton, Hyatt, and Marriott are three corporate hotel chains that offer information systems positions. These positions are listed on their job databases, which can be searched through their web sites (http:// www.hilton.com, http://www.hyatt.com, http://www. marriott.com). Jobs in technology or information systems are not limited to the places mentioned—the possibilities are endless.

Summary

1. Hospitality industry technology is characterized by making operations quicker and more efficient. The use of information systems allows many operations to be completed quickly with little chance for error.

2. Information systems are a collection of components that work together to provide information help in the operations and management of an organization.

3. Information technology in hotels and in restaurants differ primarily in the use and purpose of the software systems. Hotels largely utilize technology for accurate guest reservations, billing, and guest comfort and convenience, because in the lodging section of the industry many guests today demand high-speed connections in their rooms and faster check-in and check-out services. In the restaurant business, however, technology is used primarily to provide more efficient ways to process food orders and service, using different POS systems. Technology is used for more accurate inventory control measures as well.

4. The different types of information systems include work group or group information systems, electronic mail work groups, organizational information systems, and global/international information systems.

5. The term *information sharing* can be explained as information that can be accessed by each independently processed department in a business. For example, the front desk and accounting may share the same software, for example, guest payments. These payments must be recorded and transmitted from the initial sale at the front desk, to accounting, where the sale is documented for legal purposes.

6. The importance of information systems is to provide a variety of services to guests that make the customer experience more enjoyable by making it quicker and more efficient with fewer errors. In hospitality this is particularly important, due to the size of most hotels. Systems such as PMS are designed to aid large properties to become more efficient with time, which is an important factor for guests who demand faster service.

7. Hospitality industry technology involves management systems, such as the PMS. This system is used to help employees complete many tasks within a short period of time. Another example is organizational information systems, which take care of the payroll and other internal functions that belong to management.

Key Words and Concepts

Application service provider (ASP)

Back-of-the-house operations

Call accounting system (CAS)

Central reservation office (CRO)

Central reservation system (CRS)

Computer information system (CIS)

Customer relationship management (CRM)

Data

Database

Database management system (DBMS)

Electronic data interchange (EDI)

Electronic mail (e-mail)

Enterprise information system

Front-of-the-house operations

Global (international) information systems

Guest accounting module

Hospitality information system (HIS)

Information

Information sharing

Information systems (IS)

Information technology (IT)

Local-area network (LAN)

Organizational information system

Personal digital assistant (PDA)

Point-of-sale (POS) system

Property management system (PMS)

Purchasing stocks and materials

Room management module

Web reservation system (WRS)

Wide-area network (WAN)

Work group information system

Review Questions

1. Describe how technology aids guest comfort and convenience.
2. Name and briefly explain the different types of hospitality industry technology systems.
3. Explain the function of a POS system. How does it aid the restaurant business?
4. What are some ways in which IT has improved guest reservations systems and software?
5. In what ways is the rapid increase in hospitality industry technology systems affecting hospitality businesses? What about the hospitality industry economy?

Internet Exercises

Hospitality Upgrade (http://www.hospitalityupgrade.com) is a great web site that offers useful information about information technology in the hospitality industry. Under the "Find a Vendor" section of the web site, choose a vendor to research.

(a) What information systems/information technology does the company specialize in?
(b) What are some examples of the products or services they offer?
(c) Where has the company done recent installations?

Apply Your Knowledge

1. What information systems are used in hotels? What information systems are used in restaurants? What systems can be used in both settings?
2. In a group, choose a restaurant, foodservice business, or hotel. Analyze the company's business needs and what information systems would be helpful for your particular business to function.

Glossary

A

Accounting director The person in charge of accounting and money-related topics.

Accounts payable Accounting system that lists balances that are owed to someone and still need to be paid; source of funds.

Accuracy A precise and effective control system—one that is reliable and produces valid data.

Active listening Listening for full meaning without making premature judgments or interpretations.

Actual market share The market share that a business actually receives compared with the fair market share, which is an equal share of the market.

ADA *See* Americans with Disabilities Act.

ADR *See* Average daily rate.

Age Discrimination in Employment Act Act that protects individuals over 40 years of age from age discrimination in matters of hiring, discharge compensation, or other terms of employment.

Agenda 21 A charter produced during the 1992 Earth Summit held in Rio de Janeiro, Brazil, that addresses issues pertaining to the environment and sustainable development and is intended to prepare the world to successfully meet the challenges of the twenty-first century.

AHMA American Hotel and Motel Association.

Airport hotel A hotel that is classified as a luxury, midscale, economy, or suite hotel that is located near an airport and caters to travelers.

Á la carte 1. A menu on which food and beverages are listed and priced individually. 2. Foods cooked to order compared with foods cooked in advance and held for later service.

Alcohol Naturally occurring and easily synthesized compound that induces intoxication when consumed.

All-channel network Free-flowing communication between all members of a group or team.

Allocation of weights to criteria Allocating different levels of importance to decision criteria according to a weighting method.

Allocentric Psychological term referring to someone who enjoys varied and unfamiliar activities.

All-suite extended-stay hotel A hotel that is classified as a luxury, midscale suite hotel.

Ambiance The combined atmosphere created by the décor, lighting, service, possible entertainment (such as background music), and so on, that enhances the dining or lodging experience.

Ambiguity Vagueness or uncertainty; can occur in three aspects of a message: the actual meaning of the message, the sender's intentions, and the reader's perceptions of the message.

Amenities Features that add material comfort or convenience to a guest's stay, for example, hair shampoo, an iron and ironing board in each room, and an in-room coffee maker.

American service Food is dished onto individual plates and served to guests.

Americans with Disabilities Act (ADA) Act that prohibits discrimination against persons with disabilities and stipulates that employers must make "readily achievable" modifications to their premises and to work practices and working conditions for those with disabilities.

Analysis of alternatives Analyzing alternatives according to the "weights to criteria" method.

Analytic style A decision-making style characterized by a high tolerance for ambiguity and an intuitive way of thinking.

Aperitif A fortified wine flavored with one or more herbs and spices, usually consumed before a meal.

Apollo Name of a commonly used airline reservation system.

Application service provider (ASP) Delivers a complete booking system tied to the hotel's inventory in real time via the Internet.

Atmosphere   The combination of mood, lighting, furnishings, and music that creates an immediate conscious as well as subconscious effects on guests.

Authority   The rights inherent in a managerial position to tell people what to do and to expect them to do it.

Average daily rate (ADR)   One of the key operating ratios that indicates the level of a hotel's performance. The ADR is calculated by dividing the amount of dollar sales by the number of rooms sold.

Average guest check   The average amount each group spends. Mostly used in a restaurant setting.

B

Baby boomers   Anyone born in the twenty-year period from 1946 through 1965. Baby boomers represent the largest segment of the population—about eighty-one million United States residents in 1990. Baby boomers travel more frequently than their parents and regard travel as a necessity rather than a luxury.

Baccarat   A traditional table game in which the winning hand totals closest to nine.

Back-of-the-house operations   Refers to the support areas behind the scenes in a hotel or motel, including housekeeping, laundry, engineering, and foodservice. Also refers to individuals who operate behind the scenes to make a guest's stay pleasant and safe.

Balance sheet   Reflects how a business's assets and liabilities relate to the owner's equity at a particular moment in time.

Banquet   A formal dinner.

Bar mitzvah   A Jewish religious ritual and family celebration commemorating the religious adulthood of a boy on his thirteenth birthday.

Basic corrective action   Action that looks at how and why performance deviated and then proceeds to correct the source of deviation.

Batch cooking   The cooking of food in quantities for consumption throughout a meal period. Used in noncommercial foodservice to avoid putting out all the food at 11:30 and having it spoil. Batches are cooked for readiness at 11:30, 12, 12:30, etc.

Bat mitzvah   A Jewish religious ritual and family celebration commemorating the religious adulthood of a girl on her thirteenth birthday.

Bed and breakfast   A rate that combines a night's accommodation with breakfast the following day. The breakfast can be either a full breakfast or continental breakfast.

Behavioral style   A decision-making style characterized by a low tolerance for ambiguity and an intuitive way of thinking.

Benchmarking   The search for the best practices among competitors or noncompetitors that lead to their superior performance.

Bet   An amount wagered or put into play during a gaming activity.

Beverage cost percentage   Similar to food cost percentage, except it relates to beverages.

Big 6   Casino game involving a wheel spun by a dealer in which players wager on six possible outcomes.

Blackjack   A table game in which the winning hand is determined by whether the dealer or the player gets cards that add up to a number closest to or equal to 21 without going over.

Boardroom-style meetings   A type of meeting setup designed for a small number of participants who will sit around a rectangular table.

Body language   Gestures, facial expressions, body postures, and other movements of the body that convey meaning, such as the emotional state and attitude of the person.

Bonding   A recreational process by which people form relationships built on the experiences they have enjoyed together.

Boundaryless organization   An organization whose design is not defined by, or limited to, the horizontal, vertical, or external boundaries imposed by a predefined structure.

Bounded rationality   Behavior that is rational within the parameters of a simplified decision-making process, which is limited (or bounded) by an individual's ability to process information.

Brigade   A team of kitchen personnel organized into stations.

Budget   A numerical plan for allocating resources to specific activities.

Budgeting   The process of forecasting sales and costs.

C

Cage   An area under the control of a casino cashier in which cash is exchanged for chips and coins.

California menus   Menu from which guests can order any item on the menu at any time of the day.

Call accounting system (CAS)   A system that tracks guest room phone charges.

Call package   In bar operations, it is the group of spirits that the bar offers to guests who ask for specific name brands.

Capture rate   A term used in hotel food and beverage to describe the number of hotel guests who use the food and beverage outlets.

Casino   An area in which gaming activities take place involving table games and slot machines.

Casino hotel   Hotel that combines accommodations with gambling.

Casual dining   Relaxed dining; could include restaurants from several classifications.

Catastrophe plans   Plans to maximize guest and property safety in the event of a disaster.

Catchment area   The geographical area that falls within a specific radius established to determine the size of a restaurant's market (usually one to five miles).

Catering   Part of the food and beverage division of a hotel that is responsible for arranging and planning food and beverage functions for conventions and smaller hotel groups, and local banquets booked by the sales department.

Catering director   Head of all catering operations.

Catering service manager   Head of the catering services department.

CBX   The telecommunications department. Also called PBX.

Celebrity restaurants   Restaurants that are owned, or partially owned, by celebrities.

Central reservations system (CRS)   A reservation system that is commonly used in large franchises to connect their reservation systems with one another; allows guests to call one phone number to reserve a room at any of the chain properties.

Central reservations office (CRO)   The central office of a lodging company, where reservations are processed.

Centralization   The degree to which decision making is concentrated at a single point in the organization.

Certainty   The condition of knowing in advance the outcome of a decision.

CFA   Culinary Federation of America.

Chain network   Within this network, communication flows according to the existing chain of command of an organization, including upward and downward communication flow.

Chain of command   The continuous line of authority that extends from upper organizational levels to the lowest levels in the organization and clarifies who reports to whom.

Champagne   Sparkling wine made in the Champagne district of France.

Channel   The medium along which a message travels.

Charter of Sustainable Tourism   A result of the World Conference on Sustainable Tourism held in Spain in 1995; recognizes the objective of developing a tourism industry that meets economic expectations and environmental requirements, and respects not only the social and physical structure of the location, but also the local population.

Chef tournant   A chef who rotates the various stations in the kitchen to relieve the station chefs.

Chefs de partie (shef de par-tée)   Also known as station chef. Produces the menu items for a station under the direct supervision of the chef or sous chef.

Chief steward   Person in a hotel, club, or foodservice operation responsible for the cleanliness of the back of the house and dishwashing areas and for storage and control of china, glassware, and silverware.

CHRIE   Council on Hotel, Restaurant, and Institutional Education.

City center hotel   A hotel located in a city center.

City ledger   A client whose company has established credit with a certain hotel. Charges are posted to the city ledger and accounts are sent once or twice monthly.

Civil Rights Act of 1964   Act that bans discrimination based on race, religion, color, sex, and natural origin.

Class III gaming   A class of gaming created by the Indian Gaming Regulatory Act that includes most casino games. For a state to have class III gaming, casino gaming must be legalized for commercial (non-Indian) gaming operators and must be conducted in conformance with a contract, or agreement, between state governments and the tribes.

Classroom-style meetings   A type of meeting setup generally used in instructional meetings, such as workshops.

Clinic   A form of meeting whose attendees learn by doing.

Club   Association of persons with some common objective, usually jointly supported and meeting periodically.

Cold calling   A type of prospecting whereby sales representatives call on individuals or organizations and have no idea if these people will turn out to be true sales prospects.

Commercial foodservice   Operations that compete for customers in the open market.

Commission cap   Limits the amount of commission earned by travel agents booking airline tickets. The caps were imposed in 1995, changing commissions to $25 each way for domestic flights and reducing commissions for international flights from 11 to 8 percent.

Communication   The exchange of information and the transmission of meaning.

Communication flows   Within an organization, communication can flow in upward, downward, lateral, and diagonal directions.

Communication networks   The variety of patterns of vertical and horizontal flows of organization communication.

Communication source   The original sender of a message.

Comparing results with expectations   Indicates actual performance by showing the amount of variation between standards and reality.

Comparison matrix   Used to analyze the competitions' strengths and weaknesses to help determine which strategies to use in a marketing action plan.

Compensation   Remuneration including salary, wages, and benefits.

Competitor analysis   An analysis of competitors' strengths and weaknesses.

Comping   Offering a complimentary service without charge.

Compressed workweek   A workweek in which employees work longer hours per day but fewer days per week.

Computer information system (CIS)   An information system that uses electronic computing technology to create the information system.

Concept   The elements in a foodservice operation that contribute to its function as a complete and organized system serving the needs and expectations of its guests.

Conceptual style   Decision-making style that involves considering numerous alternatives in order to find creative solutions for the problem.

Concierge   A uniformed employee of a hotel who has a desk in the lobby or on special concierge floors and answers questions, solves problems, and performs the services of a private secretary for the hotel's guests.

Concurrent control   A type of control that takes place while a work activity is in progress.

Confirmed reservations   A reservation made by a guest that is confirmed by the hotel for the dates they plan on staying.

Contingency factors   Deal with what hospitality organizations refer to as "what if's." The four contingency factors are the organization's strategy, size, technology, and degree of environmental uncertainty.

Contingency perspective   An approach that says that organizations are different, face different situations (contingencies), and require different ways of managing.

Contractors   Companies that operate a foodservice for the client on a contractual basis.

Contribution margin   Key operating figure in menu engineering, determined by subtracting food cost from selling price as a measure of profitability.

Control   The process of monitoring activities to ensure that they are being accomplished as planned and correcting any significant deviations.

Control process   A three-step process including measuring actual performance, comparing actual performance against a standard, and taking managerial action to correct deviations or inadequate standards.

Controllable expenses   Expenses that can be controlled by means of cost-effective purchasing systems, a controlled storage and issuing system, and strict control of food production and sales. This is usually watched over by management.

Controller   Head accountant who manages the accounting department and all financial dealings of a business.

Controlling   The provision of information to management for decision-making purposes.

Convention   Generic term referring to any size of business or professional meeting held in one specific location, which usually includes some form of trade show or exposition. Also refers to a group of delegates or members who assemble to accomplish a specific goal.

Convention center   Large meeting place.

Convention hotel   Large hotel that provides accommodation for attendees at conventions; usually located near a convention center.

Conventions and visitors bureaus   1. Organizations responsible for promoting tourism at the regional and local level. 2. A not-for-profit umbrella organization that represents a city or urban area in soliciting and servicing all types of travelers to that city or area, whether for business, pleasure, or both.

Coordination of activities   The process of achieving unity of action among interdependent activities.

Corporate culture   Governs how people relate to one another and their jobs. The overall style or feel of a company.

Corporate philosophy   The core beliefs that drive a company's basic organizational structure.

Corporate travel agencies   Also known as outplants, corporate travel agencies specialize, either partly or wholly, in handling corporate or government accounts.

Corporate travel manager   Individuals employed by corporations, associations, government agencies, and other types of organizations to coordinate the organization's travel arrangements.

Correcting actual performance   Approach used to correct negative variation from work standards if its source lies in unsatisfactory work; might include redefining job tasks, changing work compensation, training programs, or laying off staff.

Corrective action   Action that is tending or intended to correct.

Covers   The guest count of a restaurant.

Creative financing   The cross-collateralization of several properties.

Cuisine   Food cooked and served in styles from around the world.

Curbside appeal   Visual appeal/cleanliness designed to encourage people to dine in a particular restaurant.

Currency fluctuations   Changes in the value of one currency compared to another or of one currency compared to itself.

Customer relationship management (CRM)   Business attempting to "manage" the relationship with their customers or guests for long-term mutual benefit.

Cyclical menu   Menu that repeats itself over a period of time, usually every ten, fourteen, or eighteen days.

D

Daily report   A report prepared each day to provide essential performance information for a particular property to its management.

Data   Raw, unanalyzed facts.

Database   A collection of data arranged for ease and speed of retrieval, such as by a computer.

Database management system (DBMS) A system for managing databases.

Decentralization The degree to which lower level employees provide input or actually make decisions.

Decision making The process of choosing a course of actions among alternatives to solve a specific problem.

Decision-making conditions These conditions include certainty, risk, and uncertainty.

Decision-making process The process of developing and analyzing alternatives and choosing from among them.

Decoding Retranslating a sender's message.

Defensiveness Response to verbal attacks or criticism; defensiveness may take the form of sarcastic remarks, being overly judgmental, or intentionally not hearing the unpleasant parts of the conversation.

Demographics Statistical study of the characteristics of human populations.

Departmentalization The process through which an organization's activities are grouped together and assigned to managers; the organization-wide division of work.

Desk clerk An employee who works at the front desk to register guests; supplies rates, information, and guest reports.

Destination Location where travelers choose to visit and spend time.

Destination-management company Organization in charge of developing and implementing tourism programs.

Development of alternatives Listing possible alternatives that could resolve a problem.

Diagonal communication Communication that cuts across work areas and organizational levels.

Dinner house restaurant Restaurant that has a casual, eclectic décor that may promote a particular theme.

Directive style A decision-making style characterized by a rational way of thinking and low tolerance for ambiguity.

Diversification A corporate strategy whereby managers try to better utilize their organization's resources by developing new products and new markets.

Diversity An increase in the heterogeneity of an organization through the inclusion of different ethnic groups.

Division of labor The breakdown of jobs into narrow and repetitive tasks.

DOC Director of catering.

Downward communication Communication flow within the organization from supervisor or manager to employees.

Dram shop legislation Laws and procedures that govern the legal operation of establishments that sell measured alcoholic beverages.

Drop Total amount wagered in a casino during a period of time.

Du jour French expression used in menus, meaning "of the day."

E

Economical Effective work with the least amount of resources or input.

Economics The science relating to the production, distribution, and use of goods and services.

Economy/budget hotel A hotel that offers rooms at lower rates compared to midscale or upscale hotels.

Ecotourism Responsible travel to natural areas that conserves the environment and sustains the well being of the local people.

EEO *See* Equal employment opportunity.

EEOC *See* Equal Employment Opportunity Commission.

Effectiveness Completing activities so that organizational goals are attained; also referred to as "doing the right things" or "getting things done."

Efficiency Getting the most output from the least amount of inputs; also referred to as "doing things right" or "getting things done well."

Eighty-sixed ("86'ed") A restaurant expression meaning an item is canceled or no longer available.

Elastic Demand changes with economic conditions.

Electronic data interchange (EDI) A way for organizations to exchange standard business transaction documents using direct computer-to-computer networks.

Electronic mail (e-mail) The instantaneous transmission of written messages on computers that are linked.

Emphasis on exceptions The practice of not questioning a certain routine or way of doing as long as everything goes well. Only cases of exceptions to routine, such as problems or complaints, have the potential to change the routine.

Employee right to know Per U.S. Senate Bill 198, information about chemicals must be made available to all employees.

Employee training For many organizations, an ongoing activity that is conducted by a training department, a training manager, or by line management or specially selected individuals within each department.

Empowerment The act of giving employees the authority, tools, and information they need to do their jobs with greater autonomy.

Encoding Converting the message into symbolic form.

Engineering director Head of the engineering and maintenance department and supervisor of its employees; may also maintain the hotel blueprints.

Enterprise information system *See* Organizational information system.

Entremetier (awn-truh-mit-tee-háy) Vegetable chef.

Entrepreneur Individual who creates, organizes, manages, and assumes the risk of an enterprise or business.

Environmental analysis An analysis of how the uncontrollable and controllable factors will affect a hospitality and travel organization's directions and success. It is an element of situation, market, and feasibility analyses, and provides a foundation for long- and short-term marketing plans.

Environmental scanning The screening of large amounts of information to anticipate and interpret changes in the environment.

Equal employment opportunity (EEO) The legal right of all individuals to be considered for employment and promotion on the basis of their ability and merit.

Equal Employment Opportunity Commission (EEOC) Organization that individuals may turn to if they feel that they have been discriminated against by an employer.

Equal Pay Act An act that prohibits discrimination in which employers pay men more than women for jobs requiring substantially equal skills, effort, and responsibility.

Equity theory The theory that an employee compares his or her job's inputs–outcomes ratio with that of relevant others and then corrects any inequity.

Escalation of commitment Increased commitment to a previous decision despite evidence that it may have been wrong.

Ethics The study of standards of conduct and moral judgment; also, the standards of right conduct.

Ethnic restaurants A restaurant featuring a particular cuisine such as Chinese, Mexican, or Italian.

European plan An accommodation-only rate that includes no meals.

Evaluation of decision effectiveness Determine whether specified goals have been achieved.

Executive chef The head of the kitchen.

Executive committee A committee of hotel executives from each of the major departments within the hotel generally made up of the general manager, director of rooms division, food and beverage director, marketing and sales director, human resources director, accounting and/or finance director, and engineering director.

Exempt employees Those employees who under Section 13(a)(1) of the Federal Minimum Wage Law are not required to be paid overtime. This is because they are primarily engaged in managerial or administrative functions.

Expectancy theory The theory that an individual tends to act in a certain way based on the expectation that the act will be followed by a given outcome and on the attractiveness of that outcome to the individual.

Expense accounts Accounts primarily used for entertaining purposes.

Exposition Event held mainly for informational exchanges among trade people. Large exhibition in which the presentation is the main attraction as well as being a source of revenue for an exhibitor.

F

Fair Labor Standards Act of 1938 Established a policy for minimum wage and a maximum length for the workweek.

Fair market share A market share based on each business receiving an equal share of the market.

Familiarization (fam) trips Free or reduced-price trip given to travel agents, travel writers, or other intermediaries to promote destinations.

Feedback The receiver's response to the message that was actually received in the communication process.

Feedback control A type of control that takes place after the activity is done and uses the obtained information to remedy the situation.

Feedforward control A type of control that focuses on preventing anticipated problems since it takes place in advance of the actual work activity.

Fermentation The chemical process in which yeast acts on sugar or sugar-containing substances, such as grain or fruit, to produce alcohol and carbon dioxide.

FIFO *See* First-in, first-out.

Fine dining Upscale dining, usually with white tablecloths, à la carte menus, and table service.

Finger foods Appetizers and bits of foods that can be eaten without the aid of utensils.

Fining Process by which wine that has matured is filtered to help stabilize it and remove any solid particles still in the wine.

First-in, first-out The supplies that are ordered first are used first.

First mortgage loans The most common type of real estate loan taken out by a lender to buy property over time.

Fixed costs A cost or expense for a fixed period and range of activity that does not change in total but becomes progressively smaller per unit as volume increases.

Flexibility The ability to readily undergo change and modification.

Flextime/flexible work hours A scheduling system in which employees are required to work a certain number of hours per week, but are free, within limits, to vary the hours of work.

Floor supervisor Supervises day-to-day work of room attendants at larger motels. Also called assistant housekeepers.

Focus groups A gathering of eight to twelve people who are interviewed as a group by a facilitator.

FOM *See* Front office manager.

Food and beverage director Person responsible for the successful operation of all restaurant and kitchen duties, including guest satisfaction and profitability.

Food cost percentage A ratio comparing the cost of food sold to food sales, which is calculated by dividing the cost of food sold during a given period by food sales during the same period.

Forecasting The prediction of future outcomes.

Formal communication Communication that takes place within a prescribed organizational work agreement.

Fortified wines Wine to which brandy or other spirits have been added to stop any further fermentation or to raise its alcoholic strength.

Forum A public assembly or lecture involving audience discussion.

Franchise 1. The authorization given by one company to another to sell its unique products and services. 2. The name of the business format or product that is being franchised.

Franchisee Person who purchases the right to use or sell the products and services of the franchiser.

Franchiser An individual or company that licenses others to sell its products or services.

Franchising A concept that allows a company to expand quickly by allowing qualified people to use the systems, marketing, and purchasing power of the franchiser.

Freeway hotel Hotel that is built near a freeway.

French service Restaurant service where one waiter (a captain) takes the order, does the tableside cooking, and brings the drinks and food and the secondary or back waiter serves bread and water, clears each course, crumbs the table, and serves the coffee.

Front office manager (FOM) Person who manages the front office department.

Front-of-the-house operations Comprises all areas with which guests will come in contact, including the lobby, corridors, elevators, guest rooms, restaurants and bars, meeting rooms, and restrooms. Also refers to employees who staff these areas.

Frontline manager/supervisor Low-level manager that manages the work of line employees and has guest contact.

Full-service hotel Hotel that has restaurants, lounges, concierges, and many more facilities to cater to guests' needs.

Full-service restaurant 1. Restaurant that has more than a dozen or so main course items on the menu. 2. Restaurant that cooks food to order.

Function Assigned duty or activity.

G

Gainsharing plan A group incentive program that shares the gains of the efforts of group members with those group markets.

Gaming Wagering of money or other valuables on the outcome of a game or other event.

Gaming entertainment industry Businesses that offer games of risk as part of a total package of entertainment and leisure time activities including resort hotel, various foodservice concepts, retail shopping, theme parks, live entertainment, and recreational pursuits.

Garde manger (gar mawn-zháy) Pantry chef who prepares all cold appetizers, desserts, and salads.

GDP *See* Gross domestic product.

General manager Head manager in an organization. Ultimately responsible for the operation of the hospitality establishment and the supervision of its employees. Held directly accountable by the corporation or owners for the operation's level of profitability.

Geographic expansion A strategic growth alternative of aggressively expanding into new domestic and/or overseas markets.

Global (international) information system Information system that allows worldwide companies to stay linked, communicate with each other, and make transactions.

Globalization The spread of companies beyond their borders to several other countries.

Goal Specific result to be achieved; the end result of a plan.

Goal setting Traditionally, goals are set at the top and then broken down into subgoals for each level of the organization that works together toward the achievement of the ultimate goals.

Goal-setting theory The proposition that specific goals increase performance and that difficult goals, when accepted, result in higher performance than do easy goals.

Government-sponsored recreation Recreation paid for from government taxes; includes monies sent to cities for museums, libraries, and municipal golf courses.

Grapevine Informal organizational communication network.

Grievance A complaint filed by an employee against the employer or employer's representative.

Gross domestic product (GDP) Total value of goods and services produced within a country, minus the net payments on foreign investments.

Gross gaming revenue (GGR) The net spending of customers on gaming. This does not include spending on nongaming operations such as food and beverage, hotel rooms, and other retail expenditures.

Gross operating profit Revenues minus operating costs before taxes.

Gross operating revenue Total payments received for goods and services.

Group dynamics A very important factor for group performance; includes individual abilities of group members, the size of the group, level of conflict, and the internal pressures on members to conform to the group's norms.

Guaranteed reservations If rooms are available on guest demand, the hotel guarantees the guests rooms on those days.

Guest A person who is the recipient of hospitality in the form of entertainment, at someone's home, as a visiting participant in a program, or as a customer of an establishment such as a hotel or restaurant.

Guest accounting module A system that increases the hotel's control over guest accounts and significantly modifies the night audit routine.

Guest counts (covers)   The numbers of guest dining in a restaurant.

Guest satisfaction   The desired outcome of hospitality services.

Guest service department   Department that takes care of guests and their needs.

H

Handle   Dollars wagered, or bet; often confused with "win." Whenever a customer places a bet, the handle increases by the amount of the bet. The handle is not affected by the outcome of the bet.

Harassment   Persistent disturbing of a person verbally, physically, or sexually.

Hard count   The procedure for counting the coins and tokens removed from slot machines.

Haute cuisine   Contemporary cuisine.

Herzberg's motivation and hygiene factors   A motivation theory according to which intrinsic factors, such as achievement recognition and self-esteem, are related to job satisfaction and motivation, whereas extrinsic factors, such as hygienic conditions, are associated with dissatisfaction only and do not motivate even if excellent hygienic conditions of the job exist.

Hold   Total amount of win in a casino during a period of time.

Hops   The dried, conical fruit of a special vine that imparts bitterness to beer.

Horizontal integration   Acquiring ownership or control of competitors that are competing in the same or similar markets with the same or similar products.

Horseshoe-style room setup   A meeting room.

Hospice   An old French word meaning "to provide care/ shelter for travelers." The word *hospitality* is derived from this word.

Hospitality   1. The cordial and generous reception of guests. 2. Wide range of businesses, each of which is dedicated to the service of people away from home.

Hospitality information system (HIS)   A collection of components that work together to provide information help in the operations and management of a hospitality organization.

Host/hostess   A greeter and "seater" at the entrance of a restaurant.

Hotel general manager   Manager in a hotel organization who is ultimately responsible for the operation of the hospitality establishment and the supervision of its employees. Held directly accountable by the corporation or owners for the operation's level of profitability.

Hotelier   Keeper, owner, or manager of the property.

Housekeeping   Considered a back-of-the-house department; responsible for cleaning and servicing guest rooms.

Human resources manager or director   Manages the hotel's employee benefits program and monitors compli-

ance with laws that relate to equal opportunity in hiring and promotion.

Hygiene factors   Factors that eliminate job dissatisfaction but don't motivate.

I

Identification and definition of a problem   Identifying and defining a problem.

Identification of decision criteria   Identifying criteria important for making decisions.

Illegal aliens   Individuals who move to another country illegally, without permission to enter as either immigrants or refugees. Also called undocumented workers.

Immediate corrective action   Corrective action that corrects problems at once to get performance back on track.

Incentive travel   Marketing and management tool currently used to motivate people by offering travel rewards for achieving a specific goal.

Income statement   Lists the amount of money or its equivalent received during a period of time in exchange for labor or services, from the sale of goods or property, or as profit from financial investments.

Independent business unit (IBU)   Independent business that makes decisions accordingly, with little or no need to get approval for routine operational decisions from higher up in the organization.

Independent restaurant   Nonfranchise restaurant, privately owned.

Indian Gaming Regulatory Act   A federal act that created a statutory basis for the operation of gaming by Indian tribes in order to promote tribal economy development, self-sufficiency, and strong tribal governments.

Inflation   Increase in the volume of money and credit, resulting in a continuing rise in the general price level.

Informal communication   Does not follow a company's chain of command or structural hierarchy and the subject matter is typically not job related or essential to performing job duties.

Information   Processed and analyzed data.

Information system (IS)   A set of people, data, and procedures that works together to retrieve, process, store, and disseminate information to support decision making and control.

Information technology (IT)   Any processes, practices, or systems that facilitate the processing and transportation of data or information.

Infusion   The extraction of flavors from foods.

Inseparability   The linkage of hospitality products and services.

Installation of alternative   Put the decision into action.

Institutional foodservice   Operations that serve people who are members of particular societal institutions, such as hospitals, colleges, schools, nursing homes, the military, and industry.

Interest rate   Rate set by the Federal Reserve Bank and banks in general that determines the amount of interest charged for loans.

International information system   *See* Global (international) information system.

Interpersonal communication   Communication between two or more people.

Interpersonal communications process   Consists of seven elements: the communication source, the message, encoding, the channel, decoding, the receiver, and feedback.

Intuitive decision making   A subconscious process of making decisions on the basis of experience and accumulated judgment.

Inventory control   A way to keep track of all resources required to produce a product.

J

Jargon   The specialized or technical language of a trade, profession, or similar group.

Job description   A description of the duties and responsibilities involved with a particular job.

Job enlargement   A horizontal increase in the number of similar tasks assigned to a job.

Job enrichment   A vertical expansion of a job by adding planning and evaluating responsibilities that act as motivators and make the job itself more challenging.

Job rotation   The systematic movement of workers from job to job to improve job satisfaction, reduce boredom, and allow employees to have a broad perspective over the work processes within the entire organization.

Job shadowing   A person working in a certain field, but also training for another.

Job sharing   The practice of having two or more people split a full-time job.

Joint venture   An approach to going global that is a specific type of strategic alliance in which the partners agree to form a separate, independent organization for some business purpose.

K

Keno   A type of bingo game in which players wager on randomly drawn numbers.

Key operating areas   The most important functional areas of an organization that work and interact toward the achievement of the organization's goals.

Kitchen brigade   System of kitchen organization in which the staff is divided into specialized departments, all contributing collectively to the preparation of a meal.

Kitchen manager   Person who manages the kitchen department.

L

Labor cost percentage   Similar to food cost percentage, except it relates to labor. The formula is as follows: Labor costs divided by net sales multiplied by 100 = the labor cost percentage.

Labor intensive   Relying on a large workforce to meet the needs of guests.

Lager beer   Beverage that is normally referred to as just *beer;* it is clear, light bodied, and refreshing.

Lateral communication   Takes place between the employees of a company who are on the same hierarchical level in the organization.

Leader-manager   A style of leadership and management that is a combination of leadership and management.

Leadership   One person influencing another to willingly work toward a predetermined objective.

Leading   The process by which a person with vision is able to influence the behavior of others in some desired way.

Leads   In the convention and visitors bureaus' lingo, leads are prospective clients.

Leasing   A contract allowing the use of real estate for a number of years in exchange for rent.

Leasing arrangement   The actual leasing contract details.

Leisure   Freedom resulting from the cessation of activities, especially time free from work or duties.

Leveraged money   Loans used to finance most of the purchase price.

Liaison personnel   Workers who are responsible for translating corporate philosophy for the contractor and for overseeing the contractor to make sure he or she abides by the terms of the contract.

Local-area network (LAN)   Allows employees of an organization to communicate and work with each other simultaneously through different computers inside a complex or building.

M

Maître d'hotel   Head waiter.

Malt   Germinated barley.

Managed services   Services that can be leased to professional management companies.

Management   The process of coordinating work activities so that they are completed efficiently and effectively with and through other people.

Management by objectives (MBO)   Managerial process that determines the goals of the organization and then plans the objectives or "how" to reach the goals.

Management by walking around (MBWA)   Management style in which the manager goes out in the work area, interacts with associates, and exchanges information about work; allows the manager to pick up information communicated through body language and tones of voice, and shows employees and clients that the manager is available and cares about them.

Management contract   Written agreement between an owner and an operator of a hotel or motor inn by which the owner employs the operator as an agent (employee) to assume full responsibility for operating and managing the property.

Manager   A person who works with and through other people by coordinating their efforts to achieve organizational goals.

Managing   The formal process in which organizational objectives are achieved through the efforts of subordinates.

Marker   A type of check that documents the amount of credit extended to a casino guest.

Market demand   The demand for a product or service.

Market niche   A specific share or slot of a certain market.

Market penetration   A growth strategy to boost sales of present products by more aggressively permeating the organization's current markets.

Market segment   Smaller, identifiable groups that can be defined using any set of characteristics, such as those found in geographic, demographic, or psychographic information. Subgroups of customers who share a specific set of needs and expectations.

Market share   The share of the market that a particular operation has.

Marketing action plan   Plan based on place, product, price, and promotion; used to set realistic goals and strategies for achieving the desired results.

Marketing and sales director   Person responsible for marketing and sales for the property.

Marketing consortium or referral organization   Made up of independent hotels that refer guests to each of the other members' hotels. Offers similar benefits to franchisees, at a lower cost; properties share a centralized reservations system, image, and logo.

Marketing mix   The term used to focus on the pertinent Ps: place, price, promotion, partnership, packaging, programming, and people.

Mash tub   In the making of beer, a large stainless steel or copper container used to mix and heat water and grains.

Mashing   In the making of beer, the process of grinding the malt and screening out any bits of dirt.

Maslow's hierarchy of human needs   Theory that suggests that there are five basic needs or motives common in adults (physiological needs, safety needs, love and belongingness needs, esteem needs, self-actualization needs).

Matrix structure   An organizational structure that assigns specialists from different functional departments to work on one or more projects.

Measuring   An evaluation or basis of comparison in order to ascertain the dimensions, quantity, or capacity of something.

Mechanistic organization   An organizational design that's rigid and tightly controlled.

Meeting   Gathering of people for a common purpose.

Meeting planner   Coordinates every detail of meetings and conventions.

Megaresort   An extremely large gaming entertainment complex with thousands of guest rooms, a large gaming area, a number of ballrooms and breakout facilities, numerous food and beverage outlets including room service and banquet facilities, and numerous retail and recreational offerings.

Mentor   A person who offers advice and counsel to someone who is new to a job or career track.

Menu   A list of the chef's dishes.

Menu development   The process of determining what type of food will be offered in a restaurant.

Menu engineering   Tool in menu planning that uses the menu as a whole, not individual items that make up the menu, as a measure of profitability.

Message   A purpose to be conveyed.

Microbreweries   Small breweries that make beer.

Middle managers   Managers between the first-line level and the top level of the organization who manage the work of first-line managers.

Minibar   A small refrigerated bar in guest rooms.

Mise en place (miss en plás)   French phrase meaning "everything in its place"; state of overall preparedness; having all the necessary ingredients and cooking utensils at hand and ready to use at the moment work on a dish begins.

Mission statement   A statement of the central purpose, strategies, and values of an organization.

Motivating   The art or process of initiating and sustaining behavior toward certain goals.

Motivation   The willingness to exert high levels of effort to reach organizational goals, conditioned by the effort's ability to satisfy some individual need.

Motivators   Factors that increase job satisfaction and motivation.

Multiple criteria   An effective control system needs to take into consideration multiple criteria in order to get a more realistic grasp of the situation and narrow down tendencies.

Multiplier effect   Concept that refers to new money that is brought into a community to pay for hotel rooms, restaurant meals, and so on. To some extent, it then passes into the community when the hotel or restaurant orders supplies and services, pays employees, and so on.

Mundo Maya　A joint, ecotourism endeavor comprised of the countries in which the Mayan civilization was, and still is, found. These countries are Belize, El Salvador, Guatemala, Honduras, and the five Mexican states of Quitana Roo, Yucatán, Campeche, Tabasco, and Chiapas.

Must　A mixture of grape pulp, skins, seeds, and stems.

N

National Center for Responsible Gaming (NCRG)　The NCRG is a research and education foundation created by the gaming entertainment industry to fund gambling addiction research.

National Gambling Impact and Policy Commission Act　This act established a nine-member federal commission to assess impacts of all types of gambling in the United States.

National Restaurant Association (NRA)　The association representing restaurant owners and the restaurant industry.

National School Lunch Program　Program that provides students from a certain income level with a free lunch.

National Tourism Organization (NTO)　Organization used by national governments to promote their countries.

Networking　The process of meeting with and gathering information from an ever-expanding channel of acquaintances.

Niche　A marketing term used to describe a specific share or slot of a certain market.

Night auditing　The process of verifying and balancing the guests' accounts.

Night auditor　Person who verifies and balances guests' accounts.

Nonprogrammed decisions　A unique decision that requires a custom-made solution.

Nonverbal communication　Communication transmitted without words through body posture, gestures, and mimics.

Nouvelle cuisine　A mid-twentieth-century movement away from classic cuisine principles. Includes shortened cooking times and innovative combinations. A lighter, healthier cuisine based on more natural flavors, including herbs.

NRA　*See* National Restaurant Association.

NTO　*See* National Tourism Organization.

Nutrition education programs　Food served in school cafeterias must follow the nutrition standards set by government programs.

O

Objectives　Specific results toward which effort is directed.

Occupancy forecast　Forecast of a hotel's occupancy for a given period.

Odds　The statistical probabilities of the outcomes of a particular gaming activity.

Online　Access to a computer via a terminal.

Open-book management　A management style in which a company opens its books to the employees, sharing financial data, explaining numbers, and rewarding workers for improvement.

Operating ratios　Ratios that indicate an operation's performance.

Operational plans　Short-term plans that show the detailed daily steps of business operations.

Organic organization　An organizational structure characterized by flexible lines of authority, less specialized jobs, and decentralized decisions.

Organization chart　A chart that illustrates the organization-wide division of work by charting who is accountable to whom and who is in charge of what department.

Organizational communication　All the patterns, networks, and systems of communication within an organization.

Organizational information system　Information system that is controlled by several remote computers and can be used throughout a company and accessed by a number of associates.

Organizational structure　The formal framework by which jobs and tasks are divided, grouped, and coordinated.

Organizing　Getting the job done efficiently and effectively by arranging the activities of the enterprise in such a way that they systematically contribute to the enterprise's goals.

Orientation　A meeting that describes the operation of a business to new employees; usually occurs within the first few days of employment.

Other　Different from that or those implied or specified.

Overbooking　Lodging practice of booking 10 to 15 percent more reservations than available to combat the loss of revenue resulting from guests who make reservations but who do not arrive.

Overvalued　A property that is for sale for more money than it is worth.

P

PABS　*See* Profit analysis by segment.

Par stock　Level of stock that must be kept on hand at all times. If the stock on hand falls below this point, a computerized reorder system will automatically reorder a predetermined quantity of the item.

Partnership　Any venture in which two or more persons endeavor to make a profit.

Pathological gambling   An addiction in which there is a chronic and progressive failure to resist impulses to gamble; includes gambling behavior that comprises, disrupts, or damages personal, family, or vocational pursuits.

Pay for performance   Any compensation method based on merit or performance rather than across-the-board non-output-based pay.

PBX   The telecommunications department. Also called CBX.

Perception   The unique way each person defines stimuli, depending on the influence of past experiences and the person's present needs and personality.

Performance evaluation or appraisal   A meeting between a manager and one of his or her employees to 1. let the employee know how well he or she has learned to meet company standards, and 2. let managers know how well they are doing in hiring and training employees.

Perishability   Refers to the fact that the hospitality product has a limited lifetime; for instance, last night's vacant hotel room cannot be sold today.

Perpetual inventory   A running inventory that automatically updates itself.

Personal digital assistant (PDA)   Computer system that transmits information or orders and retrieves and posts guest payments; often used in restaurants to improve time management and allow faster service.

Piecework play plan   Payment to associates for the amount, or "piece," of work produced.

Pilferage   Stealing.

Planning   A process that involves defining the organization's goals, establishing an overall strategy for achieving these goals, and developing a comprehensive set of plans to integrate and coordinate organizational work.

PMS   *See* Property management system.

Point-of-sale (POS) system   A system used in restaurants and outlet stores that records and posts charges; consists of a number of POS terminals that interface with a remote central processing unit.

Poissionier (pwa-saw-nee-héy)   Fish station chef.

Poker   A card game in which participants play against each other instead of the casino.

Policies   A guideline that establishes parameters for making decisions.

Political analysis   An analysis of the impact that current and pending legislation may have on the organization.

Pool bar   A bar located near or, in some cases, in the pool.

Portfolio financing   The grouping of several investments with a portfolio that spreads the investment risk.

Positioning   Process of establishing a distinctive place in the market (and in the minds of potential guests).

Pour-cost percentage   Similar to food cost percentage, except used in beverage control.

Prime cost   The cost of food sold plus payroll cost (including employee benefits). These are a restaurant's largest costs.

Privilege taxes   Taxes paid by gaming companies to local, regional, and state governments for the privilege of operating a gaming business, often designated as a percentage of gross gaming revenue.

Procedures   A series of interrelated sequential steps that can be used to respond to a well-structured problem.

Product   A tangible good or intangible service produced by human or mechanical effort or by a natural process.

Product development   The strategy of improving products for current markets to maintain or boost growth.

Product life cycle   The stages of market acceptance of products and services.

Product specification   The establishment of standards for each product, determined by the purchaser. For example, when ordering meat, the product specification will include the cut, weight, size, percentage of fat content, and so on.

Production control sheet   A checklist/sheet itemizing the production.

Productive teams   Built by giving associates the authority, responsibility, and encouragement to come together to work on guest-related improvements that will enhance the guest experience and make the associates' jobs easier.

Productivity standards   Standards of measurement established to gauge employee productivity.

Profit analysis by segment (PABS)   Using a combination of marketing information and cost analysis, this process identifies average revenues generated by different market segments and then examines the contribution margin for each of the segments considering the cost of making those sales.

Programmed decisions   A repetitive decision that can be handled by a routine approach.

Programs   An organized list of procedures, events, or other pertinent information; a schedule.

Project   A one-time-only set of activities that have a definite beginning and ending point in time.

Project management   The task of getting a project's activities done on time, within a budget, and according to specifications.

Project structure   An organizational structure in which employees continuously work on projects.

Proof   Figure representing liquor's alcohol content.

Property management system (PMS)   A computerized system that integrates all systems used by a lodging property, such as reservations, front desk, housekeeping, food and beverage control, and accounting.

Psychocentric   Psychological term referring to a self-inhibited, nonadventurous person.

Psychographic research   Attempts to classify people's internal motives and behavior.

Purchasing   The act of buying all items necessary for the operation of a business.

Purchasing stocks and materials   Involves the determination of proper stock levels, accurate ordering points, and approved vendors.

Q

Quick-service restaurants Restaurants that offer quick service.

R

Rationality Consistent with or based on reason; logical. A rational decision needs to be value maximizing and consistent within natural restraining limits.

Real Estate Investment Trust (RIET) A method that allows small investors to combine their funds and protects them from double taxation that is levied against an ordinary corporation or trust; designed to facilitate investment in real estate in much the same way a mutual fund facilitates investment in securities.

Reasonable criteria Control standards in an effective control system must be attainable and realistic.

Receiver Retranslates the sender's message.

Receiving The back-of-the-house area devoted to receiving goods.

Recession A downturn in the economy.

Recreation Refreshment of strength and spirits after work; a means of diversion.

Recreation for special populations Recreation designed to accommodate persons with disabilities, for instance, the Special Olympics.

Recruitment Process by which prospective employees are attracted to an organization.

Referents The persons, systems, or selves against which individuals compare themselves to assess equity.

Reinforcement theory The theory that behavior is a function of its consequences, that is, a reward is a consequence that triggers a desired response or performance.

Reinforcers Any consequence immediately following a response that increases the probability that the behavior will be repeated.

Reorder point Point at which an item needs to be reordered so as not to run out of it by the time the next delivery is received.

Reservations department Department responsible for taking reservations.

Resort Place providing recreation and entertainment, especially to vacationers.

Resort hotel Hotel that provides recreation and entertainment, especially to vacationers.

Responsibility The obligation to perform any assigned duties.

Responsible gaming Strategies employed by the gaming entertainment industry to mitigate pathological and underage gambling, including prevention, and education and awareness programs for employees, customers, and local communities.

Restaurant accounting Usually done by the accountant, who calculates all costs and prepares taxes.

Restaurant concept The quality, location, menu, price, atmosphere, and management style for a particular restaurant.

Restaurant forecasting Process of estimating future events in the restaurant.

Restaurant manager Head of operations in a restaurant.

Rev par Revenue per available room.

Risk Those conditions in which the decision maker is able to estimate the likelihood of certain outcomes.

Rollover To roll a booking over from one occasion to the next.

Room management module A system that tracks the status of rooms, which assists the housekeeping department and the front desk with their duties.

Room occupancy percentage A key operating ratio for hotels that is calculated by finding the number of rooms occupied and dividing by rooms available.

Room rates The various rates charged for hotel rooms.

Room service The cleaning of rooms and resupplying of materials (towels, soap, etc.) by the housekeeping staff.

Roulette A traditional table game in which a dealer spins a wheel and players wager on which number a small ball will fall.

Roux A paste for thickening sauces, made from equal quantities of fat and flour.

Rules A very specific action guide that associates must follow.

Rules of order Procedural guidelines regarding the correct way to conduct a meeting.

Russian service Restaurant service in which the entree, vegetables, and starches are served from a platter onto the diner's plate by a waiter.

S

SABRE Name of a commonly used airline reservation system.

Sanitation safety The ability to keep a property in a workable, safe condition.

Satisficing Acceptance of solutions that are good enough.

Saucier (sauce-see-háy) Saute cook.

Scheduling Detailing what activities have to be done, the order in which they are to be completed, who is to do each, and when they are to be completed.

Security/loss prevention Security department that provides guest protection and retrieves lost valuables.

Segmenting Splitting the market with user groups that have common characteristics.

Selection The process of determining the eligibility and suitability of a prospective employee.

Selection of alternative Selecting the alternative with the highest "weighted" score.

Self The essential qualities distinguishing one individual from another; individuality.

Self-managed team A type of work team that operates without a manager and is responsible for a complete work process or a segment.

Self-operator Company that operates its own foodservice operations.

Semantics The study of the actual meaning of words.

Seminar A type of meeting that involves a lecture and a dialogue that allows participants to share experiences in a particular field.

Service bar A bar, usually behind the scenes of a banquet or other event, from which servers dispense drinks.

Service encounter Period of time in which a customer directly interacts with either personnel or the physical facilities and other visible elements of a hospitality business.

Sexual harassment Occurs whenever any unwanted sexually oriented behavior changes an employee's working conditions and/or creates a hostile or abusive work environment.

Shift work Normally a shift is six to eight hours of work.

Shoppers People who are paid to use a bar like regular guests, except they closely watch the operation.

Site inspection Previewing of a site (usually a convention center or hotel) to determine its suitability for the event/function/meeting being planned.

Slot machine An electronic gaming device.

Social analysis Analysis of social trends and customs used in compiling an upscale marketing plan.

Social responsibility A business firm's obligation, beyond that required by law and economics, to pursue long-term goals that are good for society.

Soft count The procedure for counting the content of each table game's drop box.

Sommelier (so-mal-ee-yáy) In a restaurant, the person with considerable wine knowledge who orders and serves wines.

Sous chef (soo shef) A cook who supervises food production and who reports to the executive chef; he or she is second in command of a kitchen.

Sous-vide (sou-veed) Air-tight pouches of prepared food that can be quickly reheated.

Span of control The number of people a supervisor/manager can effectively supervise.

Sparkling wine Wine containing carbon dioxide, which provides effervescence when the wine is poured.

Specialty restaurant Restaurant that falls under a specific category; for instance, a seafood or steak restaurant.

Spirits Another name for distilled drinks.

Spreadsheet Computerized version of an accountant's ledger book that not only records numeric information but also performs calculations with that information as well.

Standing plans Ongoing plans that provide guidance for activities performed repeatedly.

Stewarding The department in a hotel or foodservice operation responsible for back-of-the-house cleanliness in the food and beverage areas; the cleanliness of the china, cutlery, glassware; and the custody of related food and beverage equipment.

Stock option plan A plan by which employees are offered options to buy stocks in the company.

Strategic alliance An approach to the expansion of a business's activities (entering new markets) that involves a partnership with another organization(s) in which both share resources, guests, and knowledge in serving existing clients and in the development of new products and services.

Strategic management Process of identifying and pursuing the organization's strategic plan by aligning internal capabilities with the external demands of its environment, and then ensuring that the plan is being executed properly.

Strategic placement In an effective control system, managers need to put emphasis on certain factors that are vital to the system's performance.

Strategic planning Identifying the current business of a firm, the business it wants for the future, and the course of action of strategy it will pursue.

Strategy/tactics Actions taken to achieve goals.

Suggestive selling Employees suggestively sell products and services of the operation.

Suites Combined living space with kitchen facilities, or a bedroom section with an attached parlor.

SWOT analysis A strategic planning tool for analyzing a company's strengths, weaknesses, opportunities, and threats.

Symposium A formal meeting at which several specialists deliver short addresses on a specific topic or related topics.

Syndicates A group of investors.

System A set of interrelated and interdependent parts arranged in a manner that produces a unified whole.

T

Table d'hôte French for "table of the host." During medieval times, poorer travelers had to eat with the landlord and his family in the kitchen, and they were served the "ordinary" fare at a nominal cost.

Target market The market on which an operation wants to focus.

Task analysis Analysis of the tasks and job required to perform a particular job.

Taverns Establishments that serve some food but specialize in alcoholic beverages.

Team-based structure An organizational structure in which the entire organization is made up of work groups or teams.

Team player   Committed to the team's objectives, members, and goals.

Teams   Task-oriented work groups that either evolve informally or are appointed formally.

Technological analysis   An analysis of the technological changes that may impact the company.

Technology   All the uses derived from discoveries and innovations to satisfy needs; generally refers to industrial technology.

Telecommuting   A job approach in which employees work at home and are linked to the workplace by computer and modem.

Territory   The area for which a person is responsible as a representative or agent; a sphere of action or interest.

Texture   Referring to food and wine, texture is the combination of the qualities in food or wine that correspond to sensations of touch and temperature, such as softness, smoothness, roundness, richness, thickness, creaminess, chewiness, oiliness, harshness, silkiness, and coarseness.

Theater-style meeting setup   A meeting setup usually intended for a large audience that is not likely to need to take notes or refer to documents. It generally consists of a raised platform and a lectern from which the presenter addresses the audience.

Theme parks   Based on a particular setting or artistic interpretation; operates with hundreds or thousands of acres of parkland and hundreds or thousands of employees running the operation.

Theme restaurants   A restaurant distinguished by its combination of decor, atmosphere, and menu.

Theory X   The assumption that employees dislike work, are lazy, avoid responsibility, and must be coerced to perform.

Theory Y   The assumption that employees are creative, enjoy work, seek responsibility, and can exercise self-direction.

Timeliness   Occurring at a suitable time; well timed; opportune.

TIPS   Training for intervention procedures by servers. Sponsored by the NRA, TIPS is a certification program that informs participants about alcohol and the effects of alcohol on people, the common signs of intoxication, and how to help customers avoid drinking too much.

TO   *See* Tourism office.

Tolerance for ambiguity   Individuals with a high tolerance for ambiguity are very time efficient in making decisions because they are able to process many thoughts at the same time. Those with a low tolerance for ambiguity need more time to make a decision because they process information in a consistent and ordered way in order to minimize ambiguity.

Top managers   Managers at or near the top level of the organization who are responsible for making organization-wide decisions and establishing the goals and plans that affect the entire organization.

Total quality management (TQM)   A managerial approach that integrates all the functions and related processes of a business such that they are all aimed at maximizing guest satisfaction through ongoing improvement.

Tour operators   Agencies that sell tour packages to groups of tourists and usually include an escort or guide with the tour.

Tourism   Travel for recreation or the promotion and arrangement of such travel.

Tourism office (TO)   Organization in charge of developing and implementing tourism programs for an individual state. Also referred to as a destination marketing organization.

Tourists   People who take trips of 100 miles or more and who stay at least one night away from home.

TQM   *See* Total quality management.

Trade show   Event held for informational exchanges among trade people. Also called exposition.

Training   Activity that is conducted by a training department, a training manager, line management, or specially selected individuals within each department to orient and teach new employees how to perform their jobs.

Transactional leadership   A type of leadership that focuses on accomplishing the tasks at hand and on maintaining good working relationships by exchanging promises of rewards for performance.

Transformational leadership   A type of leadership that involves influencing major changes in the attitudes and assumptions of organization members and building commitment for the organization's mission, objectives, and strategies.

Transit occupancy taxes   Taxes paid by people staying in a city's hotels.

Travel and tour wholesaler   Company or individual who designs and packages tours.

Trends   Prevailing tendencies or general movements.

Triple net lease   A lease in which the lessee must pay for all alterations, insurance, utilities, and possible commercial fees (e.g., landscaping or parking upkeep, security).

Truth-in-menu laws   Provisions that prohibit misrepresentation of items being sold. They require descriptions on menus to be accurate.

Turnover rate   Calculated by dividing the number of workers replaced in a given time period by the average number of employees needed to run the business.

U

Uncertainty   A situation in which a decision maker has neither certainty nor reasonable probability estimates available.

Understandability   To have understanding, knowledge, or comprehension; being easy to understand.

Undocumented workers   Individuals who move from another country illegally, without permission to enter as either immigrants or refugees. Also called illegal aliens.

Uniform system of accounts   A system of accounts used in the hospitality industry whereby all accounts have the same type of coding and all accounting procedures are done the same way.

Upward communication   Upward information flow within the organization from employees to supervisors or managers.

V

Vacation ownership   Offers consumers the opportunity to purchase fully furnished vacation accommodations in a variety of forms, such as weekly intervals or points in point-based systems, for a percentage of the cost of full ownership.

Variable costs   Costs that vary according to the volume of business.

Variable pay plan   A compensation plan that may reduce or increase some portion of an individual employee's pay, depending on whether the company meets its financial goals.

Verbal intonation   The use of voice, such as volume, tone, or pitch, to give emphasis to certain parts of a phrase or word.

Vertical integration   The ownership of or linkage with suppliers of raw materials or airlines owning hotels.

Vintage   Year in which a wine's grapes were harvested.

Voluntary organization   Nongovernmental, nonprofit agencies serving the public.

W

Way of thinking   A personal, usual, or habitual manner of thinking.

Web reservations system (WRS)   Reservations system that allows guests to seek information such as room availability and to make reservations and payments over the Internet.

Weighted average   A method of menu pricing that takes into account the food costs, percentage contribution margin, and sales volume.

Well package   In bar operations, the least expensive pouring brand of drinks that the bar uses when customers do not ask for a specific name brand.

Wheel network   Communication flows between a strong leader and each individual in a group or team.

Whiskey   A liquor distilled from a fermented mash of grain to which malt, in the form of barley, is added.

White spirits   Denomination that classifies spirits such as gin, rum, vodka, and tequila.

Wide-area network (WAN)   Allows high-speed communication among large franchises.

Win   Dollars won by the gaming operation from its customers. The net spending of customers on gaming is called the win, also known as gross gaming revenue (GGR).

Wines   Fermented juice of grapes or other fruits.

Work group information system   Allows groups of associates within a department to share data and information that help manage the department's functions.

Work specialization   The degree to which tasks in an organization are divided into individual separate jobs, also called division of labor.

Workshop   A usually brief intensive educational program, conducted by a facilitator or a trainer, designed for a relatively small group of people that focuses especially on techniques and skills in a particular field.

Wort   In the making of beer, the liquid obtained after the mashing process.

Y

Yacht club   A private club located near a large body of water, whose main purpose is to provide facilities such as marinas to boat owners.

Yield management   Practice of analyzing past reservation patterns, room rates, cancellations, and no-shows in an attempt to maximize profits and occupancy rates and to set the most competitive room rates.

Z

Zero-based budgeting   Managers begin with a budget of zero dollars and justify all the costs of goods sold, controllable costs, and planned capital expenditures in order to ensure an appropriate amount of profit after the deduction of all expenses.

Index